THE HISTORY

OF THE ORIGINS

OF REPRESENTATIVE

GOVERNMENT

IN EUROPE

FRANÇOIS GUIZOT

THE HISTORY
OF THE ORIGINS
OF REPRESENTATIVE
GOVERNMENT
IN EUROPE

FRANÇOIS GUIZOT

TRANSLATED BY ANDREW R. SCOBLE
INTRODUCTION AND NOTES BY AURELIAN CRAIUTU

LIBERTY FUND
INDIANAPOLIS

Printed in the United States of America

02 03 04 05 06 C 5 4 3 2 1
02 03 04 05 06 P 5 4 3 2 1

Library of Congress Cataloging-in-Publication Data

Guizot, (François), 1787–1874.
[Histoire des origines du gouvernement représentatif en
Europe. English]
The history of the origins of representative government in Europe
François Guizot; translated by Andrew R. Scoble.
p.   cm.
Includes bibliographical references and index.
ISBN 0-86597-124-2 (alk. paper)
ISBN 0-86597-125-0 (pbk.: alk. paper)
1. Representative government and representation.
2. Representative government and
representation—Europe—History.
I. Title.
JF1051 .G83713   2002
321.8'094—dc21
2001038083

Liberty Fund, Inc.
8335 Allison Pointe Trail, Suite 300
Indianapolis, Indiana 46250-1684

CONTENTS

INTRODUCTION TO
THE LIBERTY FUND EDITION
～ vii ～

EDITOR'S NOTE
～ xvii ～

PREFACE
～ xviii ～

ORIGINAL TABLE OF CONTENTS
～ xxi ～

PART I

REPRESENTATIVE INSTITUTIONS
IN ENGLAND, FRANCE, AND SPAIN,
FROM THE FIFTH TO THE ELEVENTH CENTURY

LECTURES 1–26
～ I ～

PART 2

ESSAYS OF REPRESENTATIVE GOVERNMENT
IN ENGLAND, FROM THE CONQUEST
TILL THE REIGN OF THE TUDORS

LECTURES 1–25
～ 219 ～

INDEX
～ 437 ～

*The right to power is always
derived from reason, never from will.
The legitimacy of power rests in
the conformity of its laws to
eternal reason.*

GUIZOT

INTRODUCTION TO THE
LIBERTY FUND EDITION

"I do not think I have ever met, in all my life, a Frenchman who was a liberal," the literary critic Émile Faguet once ironically remarked. What seems today to be a paradox was a commonplace in France a century ago; on both the left and the right, liberal society was rejected as inadequate or hypocritical, and liberalism was seen as a mere oxymoron or an exotic eccentricity. Fortunately, much had changed in Paris in the last three decades of the twentieth century when liberalism became the new reigning political ideology. Contemporary French liberals draw upon a rich tradition of nineteenth-century French liberal thinking that has been ignored or systematically distorted by unsympathetic commentators.[1] How can one explain, then, this liberal Renaissance?

To be sure, there has always been an enigmatic and mysterious quality to the liberal phenomenon in France that has puzzled English-speaking scholars over the past century. The complex legacy of the French Revolution and its internal contradictions might explain why nineteenth-century French liberals grappled with a particular set of issues and why their solutions were often found to be unorthodox and unconventional when compared to those advanced by English liberals across the Channel. The particular dilemmas faced by French liberals—how to "end" the French Revolution, and how to reconcile order and liberty in a nation torn by a long civil war—challenged them to rethink their views and made them fully aware of the complexity of their social and political world. These issues also instilled in the French a certain sense of moderation and convinced them that the struggle for new liberties and rights involved an endless series of political settlements in which contingency can be as important as human will. Thus, what emerged from the debate over the nature of post-revolutionary French society was an original type of liberal doctrine that is worth exploring as an alternative to the deontological liberalism of contemporary academic circles.

Not surprisingly, of all the political currents in nineteenth-century France, liberalism has been the least understood by Anglo-American scholars. For a long time, French liberalism was equated with Alexis de Tocqueville, whose *Democracy in America* had gained, almost from the moment of its publication in 1835, the status of a masterpiece in political sociology, and was seen as an

---

1. For a presentation of the new French liberals, see the anthology *New French Thought*, ed. Mark Lilla (Princeton: Princeton University Press, 1994).

inexhaustible source of inspiration for students of liberal democracy. More recently, an English translation of Benjamin Constant's political writings[2] has enriched our understanding of French liberalism. Nonetheless, any picture of French liberalism would be incomplete if we continued to ignore a third towering figure in the history of nineteenth-century French political thought, François Guizot, the most famous representative of the doctrinaires' group.[3]

François-Pierre-Guillaume Guizot was born in Nîmes on October 4, 1787, to a Protestant family; his Girondist father, like many of his innocent fellow countrymen, was sentenced to death by guillotine during the Terror of 1793–94. After that tragic episode, the entire Guizot family moved to Geneva, where the young François received a solid education in history, literature, philosophy, and classical languages. In 1805, Guizot left for Paris to study law. Stimulated by the rich cultural Parisian life, his many talents flourished early; his first article, published in 1807, marked the debut of a long and prodigious intellectual career that spanned more than six decades. The young Guizot was quick to make a name for himself in Parisian circles. The proof of his success was his appointment as a (tenured) professor of history at the Sorbonne in 1812 at the age of twenty-five, a major achievement even by the standards of that romantic age. It was at the Sorbonne that Guizot met Pierre-Paul Royer-Collard, a well-known professor of philosophy and a prominent member of the doctrinaires' group. During the Bourbon Restoration, Royer-Collard became a leading politician and a master of political rhetoric whose parliamentary speeches exerted an important influence on many of his contemporaries, including his

2. Benjamin Constant, *Political Writings*, ed. Biancamaria Fontana (Cambridge: Cambridge University Press, 1988).

3. Initially, the doctrinaires' group included François Guizot (1787–1874), Pierre-Paul Royer-Collard (1763–1845), Prosper de Barante (1782–1866), Victor de Broglie (1792–1867), Hercule de Serre (1776–1824), and Camille Jordan (1771–1821). Other important members such as Charles de Rémusat (1797–1875), Jean-Philibert Damiron (1794–1862), Theodore Jouffroy (1796–1842), and Pellegrino Rossi (1787–1848) joined the doctrinaires' group later on. The very word *doctrinaire* is a misnomer; it was given to Guizot and his colleagues, not for the alleged rigidity of their doctrine, but for their professorial tone in parliamentary debates. For a presentation of Guizot and the French doctrinaires, see C.-H. Pouthas, *Guizot pendant la Restauration* (Paris: Plon, 1923), Luis Diez del Corral, *El liberalismo doctrinario* (Madrid: Instituto de estudios políticos, 1956), Douglas Johnson, *Guizot* (London: Routledge and Kegan Paul, 1963), Pierre Rosanvallon, *Le moment Guizot* (Paris: Gallimard, 1985), and Gabriel de Broglie, *Guizot* (Paris: Perrin, 1990). Also see Larry Siedentop, "Two Liberal Traditions," in *The Idea of Freedom*, ed. Alan Ryan (Oxford: Oxford University Press, 1979), pp. 153–74; Siedentop, *Tocqueville* (Oxford: Oxford University Press, 1994), pp. 20–40; and Siedentop, "Introduction," to Guizot, *History of Civilization in Europe* (London: Penguin, 1997). For a detailed analysis of the doctrinaires' political thought, see Aurelian Craiutu, *The Difficult Apprenticeship of Liberty: Reflections on the Political Thought of the French Doctrinaires* (Lanham, Md.: Rowman & Littlefield, Lexington Books, forthcoming).

younger disciple, Alexis de Tocqueville, with whom Royer-Collard had an important correspondence.

Guizot's political career started in 1814, when he accepted a position in administration as general secretary of the Interior Ministry. After the fall of Napoleon and the return of Louis XVIII, Guizot held other high positions in the Ministry of Justice and the *Conseil d'État* that gave him unique opportunities to follow and participate in some of the most important political debates of his age. Guizot's first major publication, *On Representative Government* (1816), placed him in the ranks of the supporters of constitutional monarchy and limited government. Between 1817 and 1819, Guizot and the other doctrinaires were instrumental in passing important liberal laws—first and foremost, the law of the press and the electoral law—that consolidated the civil liberties enshrined in the Charter of 1814. It was during that period (July 1817 to December 1818) that Guizot edited an important publication, *Philosophical, Political, and Literary Archives*. In his articles, he commented on the political writings of his contemporaries and developed an original political agenda, which was predicated on the assumption that the task of the new generation was to constitutionalize the liberties of 1789 and build new liberal institutions.

The assassination of the heir to the throne, the Duke of Berry, in February 1820 sent the government veering toward the right; the inauguration of the ultra-conservative Villèle government meant that the "doctrinaire moment" was over. Guizot was dismissed from the *Conseil d'État*, and his lectures on the origins of representative government were canceled. Ousted from the political arena, Guizot did not abandon politics. In spite of a hostile political environment, he managed to publish two important books which consolidated his reputation as an original political thinker: *On the Government of France* (1820) and *On the Means of Government and Opposition in the Current State of France* (1821). During these years, he also worked on a treatise, *Political Philosophy: On Sovereignty*, which he never finished, an important and dense twenty-seven-chapter philosophical text that provides a new theory of representative government based on two key concepts: the sovereignty of reason and political capacity. As always, Guizot's tone was affirmative, never purely negative, constantly searching for reasonable solutions and proposals. His interest in studying the origins of representative government and his admiration for the English constitutional monarchy began during that time. To be sure, Guizot collected a prodigious number of documents regarding the history of France and England. In 1823, he commenced the publication of an impressive thirty-volume series of documents regarding the history of France and sent to press another important book, *Essays on the History of France*. Three years later, Guizot published a history of the English Revolution, preceded by another impressive set of twenty-five volumes of documents regarding the events that led to the fall of Charles I in 1649.

Guizot's fame as a historian reached a peak in 1828, when he was finally allowed to resume his teaching. He gave a series of famous lectures on the history of civilization in Europe and France that drew a large audience of enthusiastic students; Tocqueville attended Guizot's lectures, took extensive notes, and shared his admiration for his professor with Gustave de Beaumont, who would accompany him on his American journey three years later. Guizot's *History of Civilization in Europe* soon became one of the most popular books in nineteenth-century France, a true best-seller that brought him well-deserved fame as a first-rate historian and philosopher of history and civilization. A masterpiece of historical writing, this book—according to one commentator "the most intelligent general history of Europe ever written"[4]—introduced a series of topics, such as the class struggle, the idea of civilization, the role of antagonism in society, and the distinction between social order and political order, several of which were subsequently borrowed by other leading figures, such as Tocqueville, Marx, and John Stuart Mill.

Elected into the Chamber of Deputies in early 1830, Guizot hailed the July Revolution and became one of the leading political figures during the July Monarchy. Under the reign of Louis-Philippe (1830–48), he assumed various ministerial positions and proved to be a master of parliamentary management whose skills were acknowledged by close friends and fierce critics alike. As minister of education from 1832 to 1837, Guizot was the author of the Great Schools Law of June 1833, which created the French national primary-school system. In a letter sent to the teachers, he outlined his political vision: "No sectarian or party spirit in your school. The teacher must rise above the fleeting quarrels which agitate society."[5] Appointed ambassador to London in early 1840, Guizot was recalled to Paris in October of the same year to help the king form a new government whose mission was to end a long ministerial crisis. It was the beginning of the new Soult-Guizot cabinet,[6] which lasted (with a few changes) until 1848, thus breaking all records for ministerial longevity in France (there had been fifteen governments between 1830 and 1840).

The Revolution of 1848 marked the end of Guizot's political career. After his fall from power in 1848, he went to England, from where he made a last attempt to return to political life a year later. Defeated at the polls, he decided to abandon parliamentary politics after publishing one last political book, *On*

---

4. Larry Siedentop, "Introduction," in François Guizot, *The History of Civilization in Europe* (London: Penguin, 1997), p. vii.

5. "Biographical Notice of M. Guizot," in François Guizot, *The History of Civilization from the Fall of the Empire to the French Revolution*, vol. 1 (London: Bohn, 1894), p. xvii.

6. During that time, Guizot was minister of foreign affairs and chief spokesman of the government in the Chamber of Deputies.

Democracy in France (1849). Guizot spent the last quarter of his life meditating on religious issues, being active in Protestant circles, writing history, and finishing his memoirs. In 1851, he sent to press *The History of the Origins of Representative Government in Europe*, which contained the lectures on representative government that he had given in the early 1820s. During the last two decades of his life, Guizot remained an indefatigable writer. He published a historical study of George Washington, reflections on the legacy of the French Revolution, and eight volumes of memoirs, along with religious meditations and writings on the English Revolution. When the venerable doctrinaire passed away in 1874 at the age of eighty-seven, France lost a great liberal and a wise statesman, the last representative of a distinguished nineteenth-century liberal tradition.

A cursory look at the particular political situation during the Bourbon Restoration explains why Guizot decided to write about the origin and principles of representative government. "For the first time after 1792," he once claimed, "the French Revolution and the old French society had met face to face, discussed and combated against each other, in full liberty."[7] Under those circumstances, writing about representative government and defending its principles became a powerful means of advancing a particular (reformist) political agenda. Not surprisingly, during the Bourbon Restoration, historical writing underwent a true Renaissance; from a scholarly pursuit, it turned into a political tool that offered an ideal arena for disguised political battles.[8] Those who cherished the noble ideals of 1789 understood that the best way to promote and legitimize the principles of the French Revolution in the face of an avenging aristocracy and zealous radicals on the left was to delve into the history of France and European civilization in order to demonstrate that both the Revolution and representative government had strong roots in the past and were the inevitable outcomes of a long political and social evolution.

Thus, liberal historians such as Guizot resorted to a more or less selective reading of the past, one that insisted on continuities and long-term patterns. To this end, they pointed out that, in France as well as in Europe, liberty was ancient while despotism was modern. Like many of his contemporaries, Guizot, too, believed that knowledge of the past could and should be harnessed to de-

7. François Guizot, *Mélanges d'histoire et de politique* (Paris: Ladvocat, 1869), p. xiii.

8. For a comprehensive discussion of this topic, see Stanley Mellon, *The Political Uses of History: A Study of Historians in the French Restoration* (Stanford: Stanford University Press, 1958). Mellon also edited a substantial selection from Guizot—*Historical Essays and Lectures* (Chicago: University of Chicago Press, 1972)—that included a few chapters from *The History of the Origins of Representative Government in Europe*.

fend present political goals and shape the future. He wrote a history of civilization in Europe which openly praised the virtues of English constitutionalism and the tradition of self-government; at the same time, Guizot described the French Revolution as being the climax of the great European revolution of liberty and as having significant antecedents in the history of Europe. The same vision undergirds Guizot's history of the origins of representative government. In this book, he examined the ancient roots of liberty and the legitimacy of representative government by surveying the long evolution of representative institutions in Europe. "That which is now revealed," Guizot wrote, "has been laboring for more than twelve centuries to manifest itself."[9] More important, he argued that both the spirit of the new age and the new social condition demanded representative government. Hence, the task of the historian was to search for the germs of representative institutions, however crude and imperfect they might be; determine what influences have stifled their progress; and follow their development.

Nonetheless, the importance and originality of *The History of the Origins of Representative Government in Europe* cannot be grasped if we refer only to the historical background in which it was written. It is important to note that, while reflecting on the origins of representative government, Guizot introduced a new political vocabulary and a method of inquiry that were part of an original political philosophy. He emphasized the dependence of political institutions on social conditions and argued that, in order to understand the political institutions of a period or a country, it is necessary to explore different social conditions, the state of persons, and the nature of properties.[10] Guizot's political vision was equally bold and original. He was a proponent of the *juste milieu* theory that defended representative government and constitutional monarchy grounded in the notions of political capacity, publicity, and the doctrine of the sovereignty of reason. As to Guizot's *method* of writing history, he sought to understand and explain the real nature and hidden springs of the institutions of representative government. In following this method, Guizot combined a taste for grand narratives with a particular gift for philosophical generalizations and a tendency toward political instruction. He enjoyed advancing broad philo-

---

9. François Guizot, *History of the Origins of Representative Government in Europe*, p. 221; also see pp. 11–12. All page numbers refer to the present edition.

10. Ibid., pp. 28–29, 90–91. Writes Guizot: "When we are about to speak of the institutions of a country at any given period, we must first understand what was the state of persons in that country at that period. . . . The first question to be solved, then, is that of the state of persons; we must precisely understand which are those classes that really figure in history" (ibid., p. 28). The dependence of political institutions on the social condition is also emphasized in Guizot's *Essays on the History of France* (1823).

sophical views and general ideas on the destiny of the human race; at the same time, his conclusions always retained a strong political import while striving to achieve a sound balance between impartiality and commitment. It is worth noting that his was not a "cold and unprofitable impartiality" which is often the offspring of indifference and lack of vision, but that "energetic and fruitful impartiality which is inspired by the vision and the admiration of truth."[11]

Indeed, a cursory look at the descriptive table of contents of *The History of the Origins of Representative Government in Europe* shows the originality of this unusual book. The *History* combines lengthy narrative chapters full of historical details with theoretical chapters in which Guizot reflects on the principles, goals, and institutions of representative government. The second part of the book analyzes the architecture of the English representative system that was praised and admired by all Restoration liberals from Madame de Staël to Benjamin Constant. Here, Guizot explains the different patterns followed by England and France by tracing the various alliances between the royal power, the nobles, and the commons. Guizot's *History* addresses other equally important topics, such as constitutionalism and limited power, the sovereignty of reason, good government, the relationship between political capacity and political rights, the evolution of Parliament (in England), the prerequisites of a sound electoral system, and the role of religion in the progress of European civilization.

Furthermore, while reflecting on the origin of representative government, Guizot took issue with some of the ideas of his most famous predecessors. He commented on the shortcomings of Montesquieu's theory of the separation of powers, which failed to distinguish between the sovereignty of fact and the sovereignty of right. Guizot also discussed at length Rousseau's most important political ideas, above all his controversial views on political representation and social contract. In a few memorable pages, Guizot refuted the social contract theory and opposed Rousseau's emphasis on individual will by pointing out that the latter could never be the basis of political legitimacy and right.[12] For Guizot, the only legitimate sources of right and sovereignty were reason, truth, and justice, which can be only imperfectly approximated on Earth.

The core of the book is Guizot's analysis of the "true" principles of representative government, which also contains a vigorous defense of political liberty. At the heart of Guizot's theory of representative government are his opposition to arbitrary and absolute power and the idea that no individual (human) will is infallible. It will be recalled that, for Guizot, the debate of the

---

11. Guizot, *History of the Origins of Representative Government in Europe*, p. 9. Also see pp. 4–6, 222–25.

12. *Ibid.*, pp. 47–55.

Restoration was between those who wanted to bring the French Revolution to an end (by constitutionalizing the liberties of 1789 and building a viable representative government) and those who tried to turn back the clock of history or wanted to continue the revolution. Guizot started from the assumption that the doctrine of the sovereignty of reason was the only effective means of preventing tyranny and the usurpation of power by ruthless politicians. In his opinion, the main principle of representative government was precisely the destruction of all sovereignty of permanent right; *de facto* sovereignty is granted only on the condition that it should be continually justified by the conformity of the sovereign's actions to the principles of reason, truth, and justice. On this view, representative government does not recognize the sovereignty of right as an intrinsic attribute of any person or collective body; on the contrary, all powers are expected to strive to discover and fulfill the principles of reason, truth, and justice that ought to govern their actions. In view of the radical imperfection of human nature and because the sovereignty of right belongs only to reason, each appropriation of the sovereignty of fact should be considered temporary and limited.

The *liberal* character of this view must be duly underscored here, since it has often been neglected or even flatly denied. Guizot believed that the goal of the representative system was to provide safeguards against the existence of absolute illegitimate power by making sure that powers would be properly divided and submitted to certain trials, meet with legal obstacles, withstand public opinion, undergo opposition, and be forced to constantly prove their legitimacy in the front of the entire nation.[13] Two fundamental assumptions underlie Guizot's definition of representative government. First, since reason and political capacity are unevenly distributed in any political community, a new doctrine of "true" representation is needed that takes into account and reflects the existence of both civil equality and "legitimate" forms of political inequality. Second, Guizot defined publicity as the cornerstone of representative government and took it to be a new means of government that brings closer together power and society, opinion and government. To be sure, publicity is no substitute for elections, but without publicity there can be no "true" elections. On this view, publicity becomes both the prerequisite of and the necessary outcome of liberty; it has been rendered inevitable by the advent of a new social condition grounded in the equality of conditions.[14]

The originality of Guizot's approach becomes evident once we look at his

13. *Ibid.*, pp. 370–71.

14. *Ibid.*, pp. 69–70, 227, 295–97.

definition of political representation and his views on "true" representation.[15] He opposed the (allegedly) flawed theories of representation advanced by his predecessors and contemporaries, making a strong case for reexamining the "true" meaning of political representation. The fundamental principle of the philosophy that Guizot criticized held that every man is his own absolute master and that the only legitimate law for him is his individual will.[16] Opposing Rousseau, Guizot affirmed the existence of a transcendent law that commands universal obedience regardless of man's explicit consent. From this point of view, political representation can no longer be seen as the delegation of an individual will or as a simple relation based on mandate. It becomes a process in which the elements of reason and knowledge scattered in the bosom of society are collected through elections and publicity, and the most "capable ones" can deliberate on the interests of the nation.[17] Thus, the purpose of representative government is to "constitute the government through the action of society, and society through the action of government."[18] This theme is closely related to another fundamental concern of Guizot, that is, to multiply the contact points between opinion (society) and power, a task that had been rendered possible for the first time by the institutions of representative government, above all publicity and open parliamentary debates.

To conclude, by reading *The History of the Origins of Representative Government in Europe* we stand to discover a powerful defense of liberty and a first-rate political philosopher who speaks to us in strikingly original language about important issues that continue to concern us. Distinguished politician, historian, political philosopher, ambassador, polemicist, and pillar of faith, Guizot has remained after his death a singular character who cannot be understood in terms of black-and-white categories. While Guizot the historian acquired a worldwide reputation a century and a half ago and his words *"Enrichissez-vous"*[19] made him famous as a defender of the middle class, Guizot the political thinker has been neglected in the English-speaking world. The reissue of *The History of the Origins of Representative Government in Europe* should therefore be

15. *Ibid.*, pp. 285–97.

16. *Ibid.*, p. 287.

17. *Ibid.*, pp. 295–97.

18. See Guizot, *Archives Philosophiques, Politiques et Littéraires*, vol. 2 (Paris: Fournier, 1817), p. 184. Although this idea seems to have a strong statist connotation, Guizot's position does not amount to an uncritical defense of state power. Guizot emphasized the importance of publicity as a new means of government and defended limited government (constitutionalism).

19. These words have often been detached from the larger context to which they belong. This is what Guizot in fact said: "Éclairez-vous, enrichissez-vous, améliorez la condition morale et

seen as an act of justice that is supposed to retrieve from oblivion the writings of a great liberal and statesman who remains one of the last great "virgin forests" in modern political thought.

AURELIAN CRAIUTU

Indiana University
Bloomington

---

matérielle de notre France: voilà les vraies innovations." The phrase is taken from *Le Moniteur*, March 2, 1843. For more detail, see J. Allier, "Esquisse du personnage de Guizot," in *Actes du colloque François Guizot* (Paris: Société de l'Histoire du Protestantisme Français), pp. 27–45.

EDITOR'S NOTE

This edition reproduces the original English translation of François Guizot's *History of the Origin of Representative Government in Europe* by Andrew R. Scoble (London: Henry G. Bohn, 1861). Guizot gave these lectures on the history of representative government in Paris in 1820–1822. They were published in French three decades later as *Histoire des origines du gouvernement représentatif en Europe* (Paris, Didier, 1851, 2 vols.). Andrew Scoble's translation is reprinted here without any substantive changes. The only important change is the one operated in the title that was incorrectly printed in the original edition ("History of the Origin of Representative Government in Europe" instead of "History of the Origins of Representative Government in Europe"). In addition to being accurate, Scoble's translation has the unique advantage of being an elegant nineteenth-century English version of a well-written nineteenth-century French text.

As editor, I was responsible for writing the introduction and preparing a set of explanatory notes that shed light on Guizot's theoretical and historical background. The footnotes that appeared in the original English translation are marked with symbols and are reprinted here unchanged. The editor's footnotes (marked with numbers) are the explanatory notes mentioned above, plus translations of the Latin phrases used by Guizot in his text. The translations were made by Christine Clarkson, to whom I would like to extend special thanks. Finally, we have created a new index for this Liberty Fund edition.

Liberty Fund welcomed with enthusiasm my proposal and was extremely supportive of the entire project. Special thanks to the Liberty Fund staff for their dedicated work and genuine commitment to retrieving from oblivion this classic work of Guizot. Liberty Fund also sponsored a colloquium on Guizot's political thought in which we used excerpts of this important book.

We hope that this new edition of Guizot's *History of the Origins of Representative Government in Europe*, that has been out of print for more than a century, will be an opportunity for many readers to rediscover a major thinker and historian whose writings are essential to understanding the evolution of liberal democracy.

PREFACE

In 1820, at the time when the various faculties of the *Académie de Paris* and the *Collège de France* were recommencing their courses of lectures, several persons combined to establish a *Journal des Cours Publiques,* in which they reproduced, from their notes, the lectures which they had attended. The course which I delivered, at this period, on the history of Representative Government, occupies a place in this collection. I did not revise the analyses of my lectures which were published. They were brief and incomplete, and frequently incorrect and confused. I have been requested to authorize a reprint of them. I could not consent to this without bestowing upon these analyses, at the present day, that labour of revision to which they were not subjected at the time of their publication. The two volumes which I now publish are the result of this labour, which has been more protracted, and has involved more considerable alterations than I at first anticipated. In order to accomplish it, I have frequently had recourse to my *Essaies sur l'Histoire de France,* in which I embodied, in 1823, some of my researches on the same subject. This course of lectures on the origin of Representative Government is now as exact and complete as if my lectures in 1820–1822 had been collected and revised with the same care as I bestowed, in 1827–1830, on the publication of my courses on the General History of Civilization in Europe, and on the History of Civilization in France.

When, in the year 1820, I devoted my energies to this course of instruction, I was taking leave of public life, after having, during six years, taken an active part in the work of establishing representative government in our own land. The political ideas and friends with whom I had been associated were, at that period, removed from the head of affairs. I connected myself with their reverses, without abandoning our common hopes and efforts. We had faith in our institutions. Whether they entailed upon us good or evil fortune, we were equally devoted to them. I was unwilling to cease to serve their cause. I endeavoured to explain the origin and principles of representative government, as I had attempted to practise it.[1]

How shall I speak, at the present day, of bad fortune and reverse, in reference to 1820? What shall we say of the fate which has recently overtaken our fa-

---

1. For more details on the historical and political context of the Bourbon Restoration, see C.-H. Pouthas, *Guizot pendant la Restauration* (*Guizot During the Restoration*) (Paris: Plon, 1923); Luis Diez del Corral, *El liberalismo doctrinario* (*The Doctrinaire Liberalism*) (Madrid: Instituto de estudios políticos, 1956); Douglas Johnson, *Guizot* (London: Routledge and Kegan Paul, 1963); Pierre Rosanvallon, *Le moment Guizot* (*The Guizot Moment*) (Paris: Gallimard, 1985); Gabriel de Broglie, *Guizot* (Paris: Perrin, 1990).

therland, and of that which is perhaps in store for us? It is a shame to make use of the same words in respect to evils and dangers so prodigiously unequal. In truth, the trials of 1820 were severe and painful, yet the State was not thrown into confusion by them, and they were followed by ten years of regular and free government. In 1830, a still severer trial, the test of a revolution, was applied to our noble institutions, and they did not succumb; they shook off the revolutionary yoke, and gave us eighteen years more of order and liberty. From 1814 to 1848, notwithstanding so many violent convulsions, constitutional monarchy remained standing, and events justified the obstinacy of our hopes. But now the storm has struck every institution, and still threatens to destroy all that survive. Not merely kings and laws, but the very root of government, of all government—what do I say?—the roots of society itself have been reached, and are left bare and almost torn up. Can we again seek safety at the same source? can we still believe and hope in representative government and monarchy?

I have not escaped, any more than other persons, from the anxiety occasioned by this doubt. Nevertheless, in proportion as the events which have weighed upon us, for the last three years, have received development and elucidation—when I beheld society pausing, by an effort of its own, on the verge of that abyss to which it had been brought by its own weakness—I felt the revival in my soul of that faith and hope which have filled my life, and which, until these last days, have constituted the faith and hope of our time. Among the infinite illusions of human vanity, we must number those of misfortune; whether as peoples or as individuals, in public or in private life, we delight to persuade ourselves that our trials are unprecedented, and that we have to endure evils and to surmount obstacles previously unheard of. How deceitful is this consolation of pride in suffering! God has made the condition of men, of all men, more severe than they are willing to believe; and he causes them, at all times, to purchase, at a dearer price than they had anticipated, the success of their labours and the progress of their destiny. Let us accept this stern law without a murmur; let us courageously pay the price which God puts upon success, instead of basely renouncing the hope of success itself. The leading idea, the national desire of France, in 1789, was the alliance of free institutions with hereditary monarchy. We have been carried far away from our design; we have immensely deceived ourselves and gone astray in our presumptuous hopes; but we should no less deceive ourselves in our sceptical despondency. God, who permits the burden of their faults to fall upon nations, does not make their own life to be to them a continuous falsehood and a fatal snare; our whole history, our entire civilization, all our glories and our greatness urged and led us onward to the union of monarchy and liberty; we have often taken the wrong road in our way towards our object; and in order to reach it, we shall still have to take many new roads and to pass over many difficult spots. But let our object remain the same; for there lies our haven.

If I should apply, at the present day, to these historical studies of 1820, all the lessons which political life has given me since that period, I should perhaps modify some of the ideas which I have expressed in reference to some of the conditions and forms of representative government. This system of government has no unique and solely good type, in conformity to which it must necessarily and universally be instituted. Providence, which allots to nations different origins and destinies, also opens to justice and liberty more than one way of entering into governments: and it would be foolishly to reduce their chances of success if we condemned them to appear always with the same lineaments, and to develope themselves by the same means. One thing only is important, and that is, that the essential principles of order and liberty should subsist beneath the different forms which the interference of the country in its own affairs may assume amongst different peoples and at different epochs. These essential and necessary principles of all representative government are precisely those which, in our days, are ignored and outraged. I venture to believe that they will be found faithfully expounded in these lectures; and that on this account, even at the present day, my work will not be devoid either of utility or of interest.

GUIZOT

CONTENTS

PART I

REPRESENTATIVE INSTITUTIONS IN ENGLAND, FRANCE, AND SPAIN, FROM THE FIFTH TO THE ELEVENTH CENTURY

LECTURE 1

Simultaneous development of history and civilization. ⁓ *Two errors in our method of considering the past; proud disdain, or superstitious admiration.* ⁓ *Historic impartiality the vocation of the present age.* ⁓ *Divisions of the history of the political institutions of Europe into four great epochs.* ⁓ *Representative government was the general and natural aim of these institutions.* ⁓ *Object of the course; inquiry into the origin of representative government in France, Spain, and England.* ⁓ *State of mind appropriate to this inquiry.*

⁓ 3 ⁓

LECTURE 2

General character of political institutions in Europe, from the fourth to the eleventh century. ⁓ *Political sterility of the Roman Empire.* ⁓ *Progress of the Germanic invasions.* ⁓ *Sketch of the history of the Anglo-Saxons.*

⁓ 20 ⁓

CONTENTS

LECTURE 3

Subject of the lecture. ⁓ A knowledge of the state of persons necessary to the proper study of institutions. ⁓ Essential difference between antiquity and modern societies, as regards the classification of social conditions. ⁓ State of persons among the Anglo-Saxons. ⁓ Thanes and Ceorls. ⁓ Central and local institutions. ⁓ Predominance of the latter among the Anglo-Saxons. ⁓ Its cause.

⁓ 28 ⁓

LECTURE 4

Local institutions among the Anglo-Saxons. ⁓ Divisions of territory; their origin and double object. ⁓ Internal police of these local associations. ⁓ Importance of the county-courts; their composition and attributes. ⁓ Complex origin of the Jury. ⁓ Central institutions of the Anglo-Saxons. ⁓ The Wittenagemot; its composition, and the principle on which it was based. ⁓ Increasing preponderance of the large landowners in the Anglo-Saxon monarchy.

⁓ 35 ⁓

LECTURE 5

The Wittenagemot; its business and power. ⁓ Method of its convocation. ⁓ Vicissitudes of its character and importance. ⁓ The kingly office among the Anglo-Saxons. ⁓ Extent and progress of the royal power.

⁓ 41 ⁓

LECTURE 6

The true principle of representative government. ⁓ Error of classifying governments according to their external forms. ⁓ Montesquieu's error with respect to the origin of the representative system. ⁓ Necessary correlation and simultaneous formation of society and government. ⁓ Rousseau's mistaken hypothesis of the social contract. ⁓ The nature of rightful sovereignty. ⁓ Confused and contradictory ideas entertained on this subject. ⁓ Societies, as individuals, possess the right of being placed under laws of justice and reason. ⁓ Governments ought to be continually reminded of their obligation to inquire into and conform to these laws. ⁓ Classification of governments on this principle.

⁓ 47 ⁓

LECTURE 7

Comparison of the principles of different governments with the true principle of representative government. ⁓ Aristocratic governments. ⁓ Origin and history of the word aristocracy. *⁓ Principle of this form of government; its consequences. ⁓ How the principle of representative government enters into aristocratic governments. ⁓ Democratic governments. ⁓ Origin and consequences of the principle of the sovereignty of the people. ⁓ This principle not identical with that of representative government. ⁓ In what sense representative government is the government of the majority.*

⁓ 56 ⁓

LECTURE 8

The forms of a government are related to its principle, but are swayed by circumstances, and vary according to different degrees of civilization. ⁓ What are the forms essential to a representative government? ⁓ 1st. Division of powers; why absolutely essential to the principle of representative government; ⁓ 2nd. Election; ⁓ 3rd. Publicity.

⁓ 66 ⁓

LECTURE 9

Primitive institutions of the Franks. ⁓ Sketch of the history of the Frankish monarchy. ⁓ The Franks in Germany. ⁓ Their settlement in Belgium and in Gaul. ⁓ Character and authority of their chiefs after their establishment in the Roman Empire. ⁓ Early Frankish chieftains. ⁓ Clovis: his expeditions, wars, and conquests. ⁓ Decisive preponderance of the Franks in Gaul.

⁓ 71 ⁓

CONTENTS

LECTURE 10

Division of territory among the sons of the Frankish kings. ⌒ Rapid formation and disappearance of several Frank kingdoms. ⌒ Neustria and Austrasia; their geographical division. ⌒ Early predominance of Neustria. ⌒ Fredegonde and Brunehaut. ⌒ Elevation of the Mayors of the Palace. ⌒ True character of their power. ⌒ The Pepin family. ⌒ Charles Martel. ⌒ Fall of the Merovingians.

⌒ 75 ⌒

LECTURE 11

General character of events under the Carlovingian Empire. ⌒ Reign of Pepin the Short. ⌒ Reign of Charlemagne. ⌒ Epoch of transition. ⌒ Reigns of Louis the Débonnair and Charles the Bald. ⌒ Norman invasions. ⌒ The last Carlovingians. ⌒ Accession of Hugh Capet.

⌒ 82 ⌒

LECTURE 12

Ancient institutions of the Franks. ⌒ They are more difficult of study than those of the Anglo-Saxons. ⌒ Three kinds of landed property; allodial, beneficiary, and tributary lands. ⌒ Origin of allodial lands. ⌒ Meaning of the word allodium. ⌒ Salic land amongst the Franks. ⌒ Essential characteristics of the allods.

⌒ 89 ⌒

LECTURE 13

Origin of military service; its cause and limits. ⌒ It was made a general obligation by Charlemagne. ⌒ Allodial lands were originally exempt from taxation. ⌒ Origin of benefices. ⌒ Change in the position of the German chiefs in consequence of their territorial settlement. ⌒ Their wealth. ⌒ No public treasury. ⌒ The aerarium and fiscus of the old Roman republic. ⌒ Formation of the private domain of the kings of France. ⌒ Character of benefices. ⌒ Error of Montesquieu on this subject.

⌒ 95 ⌒

CONTENTS

LECTURE 14

Proofs of the co-existence of various modes of conferring benefices, from the fifth to the tenth century. ⌒ *Of benefices that were absolutely and arbitrarily revocable.* ⌒ *Of benefices conceded for a limited time; the* pre-caria. ⌒ *Of benefices granted for life.* ⌒ *Of benefices granted hereditarily.* ⌒ *General character of the concession of benefices.* ⌒ *Their tendency to become hereditary.* ⌒ *Its prevalence under Charles the Bald.* ⌒ *Military service.* ⌒ *Judicial and domestic service.* ⌒ *Origin, meaning, and vicissitudes of the fidelity due by the vassal to his lord.*

⌒ IOI ⌒

LECTURE 15

Of benefices conceded by great landowners to men dependent upon them: ⌒ First, *benefices conceded for all kinds of services, and as a mode of paying salary;* Secondly, *larger proprietors usurp the lands adjoining their own, and bestow them as benefices on their subordinates;* Thirdly, *the conversion of a great number of allodial lands into benefices, by the practice of* recommendation. ⌒ *Origin and meaning of this practice.* ⌒ *Permanence of freeholds, especially in certain parts of the Frankish monarchy.* ⌒ *Tributary lands.* ⌒ *Their origin and nature.* ⌒ *Their rapid extension: its causes.* ⌒ *General view of the condition of territorial property, from the sixth to the eleventh century:* First, *different conditions of territorial property;* Secondly, *the individual dependence of territorial property;* Thirdly, *the stationary condition of territorial wealth.* ⌒ *Why the system of beneficiary property, that is to say, the feudal system, was necessary to the formation of modern society and of powerful states.*

⌒ 108 ⌒

LECTURE 16

Of the state of persons, from the fifth to the tenth century. ⌒ *Impossibility of determining this, according to any fixed and general principle.* ⌒ *The condition of lands not always correspondent with that of persons.* ⌒ *Variable and unsettled character of social conditions.* ⌒ *Slavery.*

CONTENTS

~ *Attempt to determine the condition of persons according to the* Wehrgeld. ~ *Table of twenty-one principal cases of* Wehrgeld. ~ *Uncertainty of this principle.* ~ *The true method of ascertaining the condition of persons.*

~ 115 ~

LECTURE 17

Of the Leudes *or* Antrustions. ~ *Men, faithful to the king and to the large proprietors.* ~ *Different means of acquiring and retaining them.* ~ *Obligations of the* Leudes. ~ *The* Leudes *are the origin of the nobility.* ~ *Bishops and heads of monasteries were reckoned among the leudes of the king.* ~ *Moral and material power of the bishops.* ~ *Efforts of the kings to possess themselves of the right of nominating bishops.* ~ *Free men.* ~ *Did they form a distinct and numerous class?* ~ *The* arimanni, *and* rathimburgi. ~ *Mistake of M. de Savigny.* ~ *Rapid and general extension of the feudal hierarchy.* ~ *The freedmen.* ~ *Different modes of enfranchisement:* First, *the* denariales, *enfranchised with respect to the king:* Second, *the* tabularii, *enfranchised with respect to the church:* Third, *the* chartularii, *enfranchised by a charter.* ~ *Different consequences resulting from these different modes of enfranchisement.*

~ 123 ~

LECTURE 18

Simultaneous existence of three systems of institutions, after the settlement of the Franks in Gaul. ~ *Conflict of these three systems.* ~ *Summary of this conflict, its vicissitudes, and results.* ~ *Its recurrence in local and central institutions.* ~ *Of local institutions under the Frankish monarchy.* ~ *Of the assemblies of free men.* ~ *Of the authority and jurisdiction of the great landowners in their estates.* ~ *Of the authority and jurisdiction of the dukes, counts, and other royal officers.*

~ 129 ~

LECTURE 19

Government of Charlemagne. ⁓ *Apparent revival of free institutions.* ⁓ *Individual independence and social liberty.* ⁓ *Organization of monarchical power under Charlemagne.* ⁓ *His active surveillance over his vassals and agents.* ⁓ *Rapid decline of monarchical institutions after his death.* ⁓ *Definitive predominance of the feudal system.* ⁓ *Central institutions during the same epoch: royalty.* ⁓ *Causes of the progress of royalty, and of the principle of hereditary succession among the Franks.* ⁓ *Influence of the clergy.*

⁓ 134 ⁓

LECTURE 20

National assemblies of the Franks; their primitive character, and rapid decline under the Merovingians. ⁓ *They regain importance under the Carlovingians; and are held regularly under Charlemagne.* ⁓ *Letter of Archbishop Hincmar* De ordine Palatii.

⁓ 142 ⁓

LECTURE 21

Decay of national assemblies under Louis the Débonnair and Charles the Bald. ⁓ *Definitive predominance of the feudal system at the end of the tenth century.* ⁓ *Cause of this predominance.* ⁓ *Character of feudalism.* ⁓ *No trace of true representative government in France, from the fifth to the tenth century.*

⁓ 149 ⁓

LECTURE 22

Political institutions of the Visigoths. ⁓ *Peculiar character of Visigothic legislation.* ⁓ *Its authors and its influences.* ⁓ *Destruction and disappearance of the middle class in the Roman empire, at the time of the Barbarian invasion.* ⁓ *History of the Roman municipal system.* ⁓ *Three epochs in that history.*

⁓ 154 ⁓

CONTENTS

LECTURE 23

Of the various social conditions in the Roman Empire, before the final invasion of the Barbarians. ～ The privileged classes, and curials. ～ Their obligations, functions, and immunities. ～ Attributes of the curia as a body. ～ Of the various municipal magistracies and offices. ～ Of the Defender in cities. ～ Comparison of the development of the municipal system, and its relations to the central organization of the State in the Roman Empire and in modern societies.

～ 167 ～

LECTURE 24

Sketch of the history of Spain under the Visigoths. ～ Condition of Spain under the Roman empire. ～ Settlement of the Visigoths in the south-west of Gaul. ～ Euric's collection of the laws of the Visigoths. ～ Alaric's collection of the laws of the Roman subjects. ～ Settlement of the Visigoths in Spain. ～ Conflict between the Catholics and Arians. ～ Political importance of the Councils of Toledo. ～ Principal kings of the Visigoths. ～ Egica collects the Forum judicum. ～ Fall of the Visigothic monarchy in Spain.

～ 178 ～

LECTURE 25

Peculiar character of the legislation of the Visigoths. ～ Different sorts of laws contained in the Forum judicum. ～ It was a doctrine as well as a code. ～ Principles of this doctrine on the origin and nature of power. ～ Absence of practical guarantees. ～ Preponderance of the clergy in the legislation of the Visigoths. ～ True character of the election of the Visigothic kings. ～ The Visigothic legislation characterized by a spirit of mildness and equity towards all classes of men, and especially towards the slaves. ～ Philosophical and moral merits of this legislation.

～ 185 ～

LECTURE 26

Central institutions of the Visigothic monarchy. ⁓ *True character of the Councils of Toledo.* ⁓ *Amount of their political influence.* ⁓ *The* Officium palatinum. ⁓ *Prevalence of Roman maxims and institutions, among the Goths, over Germanic traditions.* ⁓ *Proof of this in the local and central institutions of the Visigoths.* ⁓ *Refutation of the errors of Savigny and the* Edinburgh Review *on this subject.* ⁓ *Conclusion.*

⁓ 196 ⁓

PART 2

ESSAYS OF REPRESENTATIVE GOVERNMENT IN ENGLAND, FROM THE CONQUEST TILL THE REIGN OF THE TUDORS

LECTURE I

Subject of the course: the history of the origin and establishment of representative government in Europe. ⁓ *Different aspects under which history is considered at various epochs.* ⁓ *Poetic history; philosophic history; political history.* ⁓ *Disposition of our time to consider history under these various aspects.* ⁓ *Fundamental principle and essential characteristics of representative government.* ⁓ *Existence of this principle and these characteristics in England at all times.*

⁓ 221 ⁓

CONTENTS

LECTURE 2

Sketch of the History of England, from William the Conqueror to John Lackland (1066–1199). ⁓ *William the Conqueror (1066–1087).* ⁓ *William Rufus (1087–1100).* ⁓ *Henry I. (1100–1135).* ⁓ *Stephen (1135–1154).* ⁓ *Henry II. (1154–1189).* ⁓ *Constitutions of Clarendon.* ⁓ *Richard Coeur de Lion (1189–1199).*

⁓ 231 ⁓

LECTURE 3

Anglo-Saxon institutions. ⁓ *Effects of the Norman Conquest upon Anglo-Saxon institutions.* ⁓ *Effects of the Conquest upon Norman institutions.* ⁓ *Causes which made the Norman Conquest favourable to the establishment of a system of free institutions in England.*

⁓ 240 ⁓

LECTURE 4

The English Parliament in the earliest times of the Anglo-Norman Monarchy. ⁓ *Different names given to the King's Great Council.* ⁓ *Its characteristics.* ⁓ *Its constitution.* ⁓ *Opinions of Whigs and Tories on this subject.*

⁓ 246 ⁓

LECTURE 5

The Anglo-Norman royalty: its wealth and power. ⁓ *Comparison of the relative forces of the Crown and of the feudal aristocracy.* ⁓ *Progress of the royal power.* ⁓ *Spirit of association and resistance among the great barons.* ⁓ *Commencement of the struggle between these two political forces.*

⁓ 252 ⁓

LECTURE 6

History of English Charters. ⁓ Charter of William the Conqueror (1071). ⁓ Charter of Henry I. (1101). ⁓ Charters of Stephen (1135–1136). ⁓ Charter of Henry II. (1154).

⁓ 258 ⁓

LECTURE 7

Charter of John, or the Great Charter (1215). ⁓ Three epochs in John's reign. ⁓ Formation of a coalition among the barons. ⁓ Civil war. ⁓ Conference at Runnymead. ⁓ Concession of the Great Charter. ⁓ Analysis of this Charter. ⁓ Its stipulations refer to national rights as well as to those of the barons. ⁓ John petitions and obtains from Innocent III. a bull to reverse the Great Charter. ⁓ Resistance of the English clergy. ⁓ Recommencement of the civil war (October, 1215). ⁓ Louis of France, son of Philip Augustus, is appealed to by the barons. ⁓ Death of John (October, 1216).

⁓ 263 ⁓

LECTURE 8

Charters of Henry III. ⁓ First Charter of Henry III. (November, 1216). ⁓ Louis of France renounces his title to the Crown, and leaves England. ⁓ Second Charter of Henry III. (1217). ⁓ Forest Charter granted by Henry III. (1217). ⁓ Confirmation of Charters (1225). ⁓ Revocation of Charters (1227). ⁓ New confirmation of Charters (1237). ⁓ Continual violation of Charters. ⁓ Civil war. ⁓ Renewal of Charters (1264). ⁓ New confirmation of Charters (1267). ⁓ Death of Henry III. (November 16, 1272).

⁓ 272 ⁓

CONTENTS

LECTURE 9

Conclusion of the history of Charters under the reign of Edward I. ⁓ Political conflict follows civil war. ⁓ The king frequently violates the Charters, especially in the matter of imposts. ⁓ The barons resist energetically. ⁓ Edward gives a definitive confirmation to the Charters (1298–1301). ⁓ A bull of Clement V., solicited by Edward I., annuls the Charters. ⁓ Its failure. ⁓ Death of Edward I. (July 7, 1307).

⁓ 277 ⁓

LECTURE 10

Necessity of inquiring into the political sense of the word representation *at the time when a representative government began to be formed. ⁓ Mistaken theories on this subject. ⁓ Rousseau's theory, which denies representation and insists on individual sovereignty. ⁓ Theories of writers who attempt to reconcile the principle of representation with that of individual sovereignty. ⁓ Erroneousness of the idea that the sovereignty belongs to the majority. ⁓ True idea of representation.*

⁓ 285 ⁓

LECTURE 11

Formation of a Parliament. ⁓ Introduction of county deputies into the Parliament. ⁓ Relations of the county deputies to the great barons. ⁓ Parliament of Oxford (1258). ⁓ Its regulations, termed the Acts of Oxford. ⁓ Hesitancy of the county deputies between the great barons and the crown.

⁓ 298 ⁓

LECTURE 12

Struggle between Henry III. and his Parliament. ⁓ Arbitration of Saint Louis. ⁓ The Earl of Leicester heads the great barons in their struggle with the king. ⁓ He is defeated and killed at Evesham (1265). ⁓ Admission of deputies from towns and boroughs into Parliament (1264). ⁓ Royalist reaction. ⁓ Leicester's memory remains popular.

⁓ 306 ⁓

CONTENTS

LECTURE 13

Progress of the Parliament under the reign of Edward I. ⁓ Frequent holding of Parliament. ⁓ Different composition of Parliaments. ⁓ Deputies from the counties and towns were not always present. ⁓ Discretionary power of the king in the convocation of barons. ⁓ The varying number of county and borough deputies.

⁓ 313 ⁓

LECTURE 14

Mode of election of the deputies of counties and boroughs. ⁓ Who were the electors? ⁓ No uniform principle to regulate elections in boroughs and towns. ⁓ Voting in public.

⁓ 320 ⁓

LECTURE 15

Philosophical examination of the electoral system in England in the fourteenth century. ⁓ The system was the natural result of facts. ⁓ Who were the electors? ⁓ Four principles which determine the solution of this question.

⁓ 328 ⁓

LECTURE 16

Subject of the lecture. ⁓ Continuation of the philosophical examination of the electoral system in England in the fourteenth century. ⁓ Characteristics of the elections. ⁓ Examination of the principle of direct or indirect election.

⁓ 339 ⁓

LECTURE 17

Origin of the division of the English Parliament into two Houses. ⁓ Its original constitution. ⁓ Reproduction of the classifications of society in the Parliament. ⁓ Causes which led the representatives of counties to separate from the barons, and coalesce with the representatives of boroughs. ⁓ Effects of this coalition. ⁓ Division of the Parliament into two Houses in the fourteenth century.

⁓ 353 ⁓

LECTURE 18

Examination of the division of the legislative power into two Houses. ⁓ Diversity of ideas on this subject. ⁓ Fundamental principle of the philosophic school. ⁓ Source of its errors. ⁓ Characteristics of the historic school. ⁓ Cause of the division of the British Parliament into two Houses. ⁓ Derivation of this division from the fundamental principle of representative government. ⁓ Its practical merit.

⁓ 359 ⁓

LECTURE 19

Power and attributes of the British Parliament in the fourteenth century. ⁓ At its origin, and subsequent to its complete development, the Parliament retained the name of the Great Council of the kingdom. ⁓ Difference between its attributes and its actual power at these two epochs. ⁓ Absorption of almost the entire government by the Crown; gradual resumption of its influence by the Parliament.

⁓ 377 ⁓

LECTURE 20

Condition and attributes of the Parliament during the reign of Edward II. (1307–1327). ⁓ Empire of favourites. ⁓ Struggle of the barons against the favourites. ⁓ Aristocratic factions. ⁓ Petitions to the king. ⁓ Forms of deliberations on this subject. ⁓ Deposition of Edward II.

⁓ 382 ⁓

CONTENTS

LECTURE 21

Of petitions during the early times of representative government. ⁓ Regulations on the subject. ⁓ Transformation of the right of petition possessed by the Houses of Parliament into the right of proposition and initiative. ⁓ Petitions ceased to be addressed to the king, and are presented to Parliament. ⁓ Origin of the right of inquiry. ⁓ Necessity for representative government to be complete. ⁓ Artifices and abuses engendered by the right of petition.

⁓ 389 ⁓

LECTURE 22

Condition of the Parliament under Edward III. ⁓ Progress of the power of the Commons. Their resistance to the king. ⁓ Regularity of the convocation of Parliament. ⁓ Measures taken for the security of its deliberations. ⁓ Division of the Parliament into two Houses. ⁓ Speaker of the House of Commons. ⁓ Firmness of the House of Commons in maintaining its right to grant taxes. ⁓ Accounts given by the government of the collection of the taxes. ⁓ Appropriation of the funds granted by Parliament. ⁓ Parliamentary legislation. ⁓ Difference between statutes and ordinances.

⁓ 399 ⁓

LECTURE 23

Continuation of the history of the progress of the Commons House of Parliament during the reign of Edward III. ⁓ Their interference in questions of peace and war; and in the internal administration of the kingdom. ⁓ Their resistance of the influence of the Pope, and of the national clergy, in temporal affairs. ⁓ First efforts of the Commons to repress abuses at elections. ⁓ First traces of function of Committees of both Houses to investigate certain questions in common.

⁓ 406 ⁓

LECTURE 24

State of the Parliament under Richard II. ⁓ *Struggle between absolute royalty and parliamentary government.* ⁓ *Origin of the Civil List.* ⁓ *Progress of the responsibility of ministers.* ⁓ *Progress of the returns of the employment of the public revenue.* ⁓ *The Commons encroach upon the government.* ⁓ *Reaction against the sway of the Commons.* ⁓ *Violence and fall of Richard II.* ⁓ *Progress of the essential maxims and practices of representative government.*

⁓ 414 ⁓

LECTURE 25

Summary of the history of the Parliament from the death of Richard II. to the accession of the House of Stuart. ⁓ *Progress of the forms of procedure, and of the privileges of Parliament.* ⁓ *Liberty of speech in both Houses.* ⁓ *Inviolability of members of Parliament.* ⁓ *Judicial power of the House of Lords.* ⁓ *Decadence of the Parliament during the wars of the Roses, and under the Tudor dynasty.* ⁓ *Causes of this decadence and of the progress of royal authority, from Henry VII. to Elizabeth.* ⁓ *Conclusion.*

⁓ 425 ⁓

PART I

REPRESENTATIVE

INSTITUTIONS

IN ENGLAND, FRANCE,

AND SPAIN,

FROM THE FIFTH TO

THE ELEVENTH CENTURY

LECTURE I

Simultaneous development of history and civilization. ~ *Two errors in our method of considering the past; proud disdain, or superstitious admiration.* ~ *Historic impartiality the vocation of the present age.* ~ *Divisions of the history of the political institutions of Europe into four great epochs.* ~ *Representative government was the general and natural aim of these institutions.* ~ *Object of the course; inquiry into the origin of representative government in France, Spain, and England.* ~ *State of mind appropriate to this inquiry.*

GENTLEMEN,—Such is the immensity of human affairs, that, so far from exhibiting superannuation and decay with the progress of time, they seem to gain new youth, and to gird themselves afresh at frequent intervals, in order to appear under aspects hitherto unknown. Not only does each age receive a vocation to devote itself especially to a particular region of inquiry; but the same studies are to each age as a mine but little explored, or as an unknown territory where objects for discovery present themselves at every step. In the study of history this truth is especially apparent. The facts about which history concerns itself neither gain nor lose anything by being handed down from age to age; whatever we have seen in these facts, and whatever we can see, has been contained in them ever since they were originally accomplished; but they never allow themselves to be fully apprehended, nor permit all their meaning to be thoroughly investigated; they have, so to speak, innumerable secrets, which slowly utter themselves after man has become prepared to recognise them. And as everything in man and around him changes, as the point of view from which he considers the facts of history, and the state of mind which he brings to the survey, continually vary, we may speak of the past as changing with the present; unperceived facts reveal themselves in ancient facts; other ideas, other feelings, are called up by the same names and the same narratives; and man thus learns that in the infinitude of space opened to his knowledge, everything remains constantly fresh and inexhaustible; in regard to his ever-active and ever-limited intelligence.

This combined view of the greatness of events and the feebleness of the human mind, never appears so startlingly distinct as upon the occurrence of those extraordinary crises, which, so to speak, entirely delocalize man, and transport him to a different sphere. Such revolutions, it is true, do not unfold themselves in an abrupt and sudden manner. They are conceived and nurtured in the womb of society long before they emerge to the light of day. But the moment arrives beyond which their full accomplishment cannot be delayed, and they then take possession of all that exists in society, transform it, and place everything in an entirely new position; so that if, after such a shock, man looks back upon the history of the past, he can scarcely recognise it. That which he sees, he had never seen before; what he saw once, no longer exists as he saw it; facts rise up before him with unknown faces, and speak to him in a strange language. He sets himself to the examination of them under the guidance of other principles of observation and appreciation. Whether he considers their causes, their nature, or their consequences, unknown prospects open before him on all sides. The actual spectacle remains the same; but it is viewed by another spectator occupying a different place—to his eyes all is changed.

What marvel is it, gentlemen, if, in this new state of things and of himself, man adopts, as the special objects of his study, questions and facts which connect themselves more immediately with the revolution which has just been accomplished,—if he directs his gaze precisely towards that quarter where the change has been most profound? The grand crises in the life of humanity are not all of the same nature; although they, sooner or later, influence the whole mass of society, they act upon it and approach it, in some respects, from different sides. Sometimes it is by religious ideas, sometimes by political ideas, sometimes by a simple discovery, or a mechanical invention, that the world is ruled and changed. The apparent metamorphosis which the past then undergoes is effected chiefly in that which corresponds to the essential character of the revolution that is actually going forward in the present. Let us imagine, if we can, the light in which the traditions and religious recollections of Paganism must have appeared to the Christians of the first centuries, and then we shall understand the new aspects under which old facts present themselves in those times of renovation, which Providence has invested with a peculiar importance and significance.

Such is, gentlemen, up to a certain point, the position in which we ourselves are placed with regard to that subject which is to come before us in the present course of lectures. It is from the midst of the new political order which has commenced in Europe in our own days that we are about to consider, I do not say naturally, but necessarily, the history of the political institutions of Europe from the foundation of modern states. To descend from this point of view is not in our power. Against our will, and without our knowledge, the ideas which have occupied the present will follow us wherever we go in the study of the past. Vainly should we attempt to escape from the lights which they cast thereupon; those lights will only diffuse themselves around on all sides with more confusion and less utility. We will then frankly accept a position which, in my opinion, is favourable, and certainly inevitable. We attempt today, and with good reason, to reconnect what we now are with what we formerly were; we feel the necessity of bringing our habits into association with intelligent feeling, to connect our institutions with our recollections, and, in fine, to gather together the links in that chain of time, which never allows itself to be entirely broken, however violent may be the assaults made upon it. In accordance with the same principles, and guided by the same spirit, we shall not refuse the aid which can be derived from modern ideas and institutions, in order to guide our apprehension and judgment while studying ancient institutions, since we neither can, nor would wish to be separated from our proper selves, any more than we would attempt or desire to isolate ourselves from our forefathers.[1]

This study, gentlemen, has been much neglected in our days; and when attempts have been made to revive it, it has been approached with such a strong preoccupation of mind, or with such a determined purpose, that the fruits of our labour have been damaged at the outset. Opinions which are partial and adopted before facts have been fairly examined, not only have the effect of vitiating the rectitude of judgment, but they moreover introduce a deplorable frivolity into researches which we may call material. As soon as the prejudiced mind has collected a few documents and proofs in support of its cherished no-

---

1. A few words about Guizot's historical method are in order here. In Guizot's view, historical investigations must combine respect for the past and the desire to contribute to the progress of society. Not surprisingly, his historical writings had a strong political agenda, as illustrated by the following statement: "Ever since the birth of modern societies, their condition has been such, that in their institution, in their aspirations, and in the course of their history, the representative form of government . . . has constantly loomed more or less distinctly in the distance, as the port at which they must at length arrive, in spite of the storms which scatter them, and the obstacles which confront and oppose their entrance" (*The History of the Origins of Representative Government in Europe*, p. 12; all pages refer to the present edition, henceforth abbreviated as *HORG*). Guizot looked for a *juste milieu*, a middle ground between those who harbored only "proud disdain of the past" (*ibid.*, p. 6) and those who remained mired in the past without being able to understand and adapt to the present (*ibid.*, p. 8). To this effect, he criticized those who wanted to "dissever the present from its connection with former ages and to begin society afresh" (*ibid.*, p. 7). Another important characteristic of Guizot's historical method was the alliance of philosophy and history, the constant passing from the examination of circumstances to that of ideas, from the exposition of facts to the commentary of doctrines. He believed that, in order to apprehend correctly the character and consequences of facts, one must reduce them to general patterns and ideas. For more details, also see *HORG*, pp. 224-25. The same method underlies Guizot's *History of Civilization in Europe*, ed. Larry Siedentop (London: Penguin, 1997), pp. 65-66, 201-202 (henceforth abbreviated as *HCE*).

tion, it is contented, and concludes its inquiry. On the one hand, it beholds in facts that which is not really contained in them; on the other hand, when it believes that the amount of information it already possesses will suffice, it does not seek further knowledge. Now, such has been the force of circumstances and passions among us, that they have disturbed even erudition itself. It has become a party weapon, an instrument of attack or defence; and facts themselves, inflexible and immutable facts, have been by turns invited or repulsed, perverted or mutilated, according to the interest or sentiment in favour of which they were summoned to appear.

In accordance with this prevailing circumstance of our times, two opposite tendencies are observable in those opinions and writings which have passed a verdict on the ancient political institutions of Europe. On the one hand, we see minds so overpowered by the splendour of the new day which has dawned upon mankind, that they see in the generations which preceded, only darkness, disorder, and oppression,—objects either for their indignation or their contempt. Proud disdain of the past has taken possession of these minds,—a disdain which exalts itself into a system. This system has presented all the characteristics of settled impiety. Laws, sentiments, ideas, customs, everything pertaining to our forefathers, it has treated with coldness or scorn. It would seem as if reason, regard for justice, love of liberty, all that makes society dignified and secure, were a discovery of today, made by the generation which has last appeared. In thus renouncing its ancestors, this generation forgets that it will soon join them in the tomb, and that in its turn it will leave its inheritance to its children.

This pride, gentlemen, is not less contrary to the truth of things than fatal to the society which entertains it. Providence does not so unequally deal with the generations of men, as to impoverish some in order that the rest may be lavishly endowed at their expense. It is doubtless true, that virtue and glory are not shared in a uniform degree by different ages; but there is no age which does not possess some legitimate claim upon the respect of its descendants. There is not one which has not borne its part in the grand struggle between good and evil, truth and error, liberty and oppression. And not only has each age maintained this laborious struggle on its own account, but whatever advantage it has been able to gain, it has transmitted to its successors. The superior vantage-ground on which we were born, is a gift to us from our forefathers, who died upon the territory themselves had won by conquest. It is then a blind and culpable ingratitude which affects to despise the days which are gone. We reap the fruits of their labours and sacrifices—is it too much for us to hallow the memory of those labours, and to render a just recompense for those sacrifices?

If those men who affect, or who actually feel, this irreverent disdain or indifference for ancient times, were better acquainted with these times and their history, they would find themselves constrained to entertain a different opinion. When, in fact, we investigate the cause of this unnatural state of mind, only one explanation can be found. At the moment of grand social reforms, during epochs full of ambition and hope, when important changes are on all sides demanded and necessary, the authority of the past is the one obstacle which opposes itself to all tendency to innovation. The present time seems devoted to errors and abuses, and the wisdom of centuries is appealed to by one party in order to resist the future to which the aspirations of the other party are directed. Accordingly, a kind of blind hatred of the past takes possession of a great number of men. They regard it as making common cause with the enemies of present amelioration, and the weapons employed by these latter confirm this idea in their mind. Gentlemen, the notion is full of falsehood and misapprehension. It is not true that injustice and abuses alone can shelter themselves under the authority of antiquity, that they only are capable of appealing to precedent and experience. Truth, justice, and rectitude, are also graced by venerable titles; and at no period has man allowed them to be proscribed. Take in succession all the moral needs, all the legitimate interests of our society, arrange them in systematic order, and then traverse the history of our country;—you will find them constantly asserted and defended,—all epochs will afford you innumerable proofs of struggles endured, of victories won, of concessions obtained in this holy cause. It has been carried on with different issues, but in no time or place has it been abandoned. There is not a truth or a right which cannot bring forward, from any period of history, monuments to consecrate, and facts to vindicate it. Justice has not retired from the world, even when it finds there least support:—it has constantly sought and embraced, both with governments and in the midst of peoples, all opportunities for extending its dominion. It has struggled, protested, waited; and when it has had only glory to bestow upon those who have fought for it, it has bestowed that glory with a liberal hand.

Let us then, gentlemen, reassure ourselves with reference to the study of the past. It contains nothing which ought to alarm the friends of all that is good and true. It is into their hands, on the contrary, and in subservience to interests which are dear to them, that it will ever deposit the authority of antiquity and the lessons of experience.

This unjust contempt for ancient institutions, however, this wild attempt to dissever the present from its connexion with former ages and to begin society afresh, thus delivering it up to all the dangers of a position in which it is deprived of its roots and cast upon the protection of a wisdom which is yet in its infancy, is not an error of which we have been the first to give an example. In one of those ephemeral parliaments which attempted to maintain its existence under the yoke of Cromwell, it was seriously proposed to deliver up to the flames all the archives in the Tower of London, and thus to annihilate the monuments of the existence of England in former ages. These infatuated men wished to abolish the past, flattering themselves that they would then obtain an absolute control over the future. Their design was rejected, and their hope foiled; and very soon England, regaining, with new liberties, respect for all its recollections of the past, entered upon that career of development and prosperity which it has continued up to our times.

Side by side with this infatuation which has induced men, otherwise enlightened, to neglect the study of the ancient institutions of Europe, or only to regard their history with a hasty and supercilious glance, we have seen another infatuation arise, perhaps still more unreasonable and arrogant. Here, as elsewhere, impiety has been the herald of superstition. The past, so despised, so neglected by the one party, has become to the other an object of idolatrous veneration. The former desire that society, mutilating its own being, should disown its former life; the latter would have it return to its cradle, in order to remain there immovable and powerless. And as those lords of the future would in their own wild fancy create out of it, so far as regards government and social order, the most brilliant Utopias, so these, on the other hand, find their Utopia in their dreams of the past. The work might appear more difficult; the field open to the imagination may seem less open, and facts might be expected sometimes to press inconveniently against the conclusions sought. But what will not a preoccupied mind overcome? Plato and Harrington, giving to their thoughts the widest range, had constructed their ideal of a republic; and we, with still more confidence, have constructed our ideal of feudalism, of absolute power, and even of barbarism. Fully organized societies, adorned with freedom and morality, have been conceived and fashioned at leisure, in order thence to be transported into past ages. After having attempted to resolve, according to principles opposed to modern tendencies, the great problem of the harmony between liberty and power, between order and progress, we have required that ancient facts should receive these theories and adapt themselves to them. And since, in the vast number of facts, some are to be found which lend themselves with docility and readiness to the purposes which they are required to serve, the discoverers of this pretended antiquity have not lacked either quotations or proofs which might seem to give it an ascertained and definite existence in the past. Thus, France, after having spent more than five centuries in its struggles to escape from the feudal system, has all at once discovered that it was wrong in liberating itself from this system, for that in this state it possessed true happiness and freedom; and history, which believed itself to be chargeable with so many evils, iniquities, and convulsions, is surprised to learn that it only hands down to us recollections of two or three golden ages.

There is no necessity for me, gentlemen, to offer any very serious opposition to this fantastic and superstitious adoration of the past. It would hardly have merited even a passing allusion, were it not connected with systems and tendencies in which all society is interested. It is one of the collateral circumstances of the grand struggle which has never ceased to agitate the world. The interests and ideas which have successively taken possession of society have always wished to render it stationary in the position which has given it over to their rule; and when it has escaped from them, it has ever, in so doing, had to withstand those seductive images and influences which these interests have called to their aid. There is no fear that the world will allow itself to be thus ensnared—progress is the law of its nature; hope, and not regret, is the spring of its movement—the future alone possesses an attractive virtue. Peoples who have emerged from slavery have always endeavoured by laws to prevent enfranchised man from again falling into servitude. Providence has not been less careful with regard to humanity; and the chains which have not sufficed to confine it, are still less able to resume the grasp which they have lost. But the efforts of a retrograde system have often perverted the study of ancient times. The Emperor Julian saw in the popular fables of Greece a philosophy capable of satisfying those moral necessities which Christianity had come to satisfy, and he demanded that men should see and honour in the history of decayed paganism that which only existed in his dreams. The same demands have been made with as little reason on behalf of the ancient political institutions of Europe. Justice, and justice alone, is due to that which no longer exists, as well as to that which still remains. Respect for the past means neither approbation nor silence for that which is false, culpable, or dangerous. The past deserves no gratitude or consideration from us, except on account of the truth which it has known, and the good which it has aimed at or accomplished. Time has not been endowed with the unhallowed office of consecrating evil or error; on the contrary, it unmasks and consumes them. To spare them because they are ancient, is not to respect the past, but it is to outrage truth, which is older than the world itself.

If I am not mistaken, gentlemen, we are at this time in an especially favourable position for avoiding both of the general errors which I have just described. Perhaps few persons think so; but impartiality, which is the duty of all times, is, in my opinion, the mission of ours—not that cold and unprofitable impartiality which is the offspring of indifference, but that energetic and fruitful impartiality which is inspired by the vision and admiration of truth. That equal and universal justice, which is now the deepest want of society, is also the ruling idea which is ever foremost in position and influence, wherever the spirit of man is found. Blind prejudices, insincere declamation, are no longer any more acceptable in the world of literature, than are iniquity and violence in the world of politics. They may still have some power to agitate society, but they are not permitted either to satisfy or to govern it. The particular state of our own country strengthens this disposition, or, if you please, this general tendency, of the

European mind. We have not lived in that state of repose in which objects appear continually under almost the same aspects, in which the present is so changeless and regular as to present to man's view an horizon that seldom varies, in which old and powerful conventionalisms govern thought as well as life, in which opinions are well nigh habits, and soon become prejudices—we have been cast not only into new tracks, but these are continually interrupted and diversified. All theories, all practices, are displayed in union or in rivalry before our eyes. Facts of all kinds have appeared to us under a multitude of aspects. Human nature has been urged impetuously onwards, and laid bare, so to speak, in all the elements of which it is constituted. Affairs and men have all passed from system to system, from combination to combination; and the observer, while himself continually changing his point of view, has been the witness of a spectacle which changed as often as he. Such times, gentlemen, offer but little tranquillity, and prepare tremendous difficulties for those which shall follow them. But they certainly give to minds capable of sustaining their pressure, an independent disposition, and an extended survey, which do not belong to more serene and fortunate periods. The large number, and the unsettled character of the facts which appear before us, widen the range of our ideas; the diversity of trials which all things undergo within so short an interval, teach us to judge them with impartiality; human nature reveals itself in its simplicity, as well as in its wealth. Experience hastens to fulfil its course, and, in some sort, hoards its treasures; in the short space of one life, man sees, experiences, and attempts that which might have sufficed to fill several centuries. This advantage is sufficiently costly, gentlemen, to act at least as an inducement to our reaping it. It does not become us to entertain narrow views and obstinate prejudices; to petrify the form of our judgments by foregone conclusions; in fine, to ignore that diffusion of truth, which has been attested by so many vissicitudes, and which imposes on us the duty of seeking it everywhere, and rendering it homage wherever we meet it, if we would have its sanction to our thoughts, and its aid to our utterance.

In this spirit, gentlemen, we shall attempt to consider the ancient political institutions of Europe, and to sketch their history. While for this purpose we appropriate such lights as our age can furnish, we shall endeavour to carry with us none of the passions which divide it. We shall not approach past times under the guidance of such impressions belonging to the present, as those whose influence we have just deplored; we shall not address to them those questions which, by their very nature, dictate the answers which they shall receive. I have too much regard for those who listen to me, and for the truth after which I, in common with them, am seeking, to suppose that history can in any sense consent to suppress that which it has asserted, or to utter what is not affirmed by the voice of truth. We must interrogate it freely, and then leave it to full independence.

This study, gentlemen, requires a centre to which it may stand in relation—we must find for so large a number of facts, a bond which may unite and harmonize them. This bond exists in the facts themselves—nothing can be less doubtful. Unity and consecutiveness are not lacking in the moral world, as they are not in the physical. The moral world has, like the system of celestial bodies, its laws and activity; only the secret according to which it acts is more profound, and the human mind has more difficulty in discovering it. We have entered upon this inquiry so late, that events already accomplished may serve us as guides. We have no need to ask of some philosophical hypothesis, itself perhaps uncertain and incomplete, what, in the order of political development, has been the tendency of European civilization. A system which evidently, from a general view of the subject, adheres continually to the same principles, starts from the same necessities, and tends to the same results, manifests or proclaims its presence throughout the whole of Europe. Almost everywhere the representative form of government is demanded, allowed, or established. This fact is, assuredly, neither an accident, nor the symptom of a transient madness. It has certainly its roots in the past political career of the nations, as it has its motives in their present condition. And if, warned by this, we turn our attention to the past, we shall everywhere meet with attempts, more or less successful, either made with a conscious regard to this system so as to produce it naturally, or striving to attain it by the subjugation of contrary forces. England, France, Spain, Portugal, Germany and Sweden, supply us with numerous illustrations of this. If we look to one quarter we shall see these attempts after they have lasted for some time, and assumed an historical consistency; in another, they have hardly commenced before they issue in failure; in a third, they end in a kind of federation of the governments themselves. Their forms are as diverse as their fortunes. England alone continues these struggles without intermission, and enters at last into full enjoyment of their realization. But everywhere they take their place in history, and influence the destinies of nations. And when at last, no longer finding even the shadow of a representative government on the Continent of Europe, and beholding it only in the parliament of Great Britain, a man of genius inquires into its origin, he says that "this noble system was first found in the woods of Germany," from whence the ancestors of the whole of Europe have all equally proceeded.[2]

In this opinion, as will be afterwards seen, I do not agree with Montesquieu; but it is evident, both from ancient facts and from those which we our-

---

2. For more details, see Montesquieu, *The Spirit of the Laws,* Book II; Book XIV, 3; Book XVIII, 23; Book XXX, 19. Unlike Montesquieu, Guizot did not claim that representative institutions could be found "in the woods of Germany." He pointed out that no general political order existed during the first ten centuries because of the incessant conflict between various political powers.

selves have witnessed, that the representative form of government has, so to speak, constantly hovered over Europe, ever since the founding of modern states. Its reappearance at so many times and in so many places, is not to be accounted for by the charm of any theory, or the power of any conspiracy. In the endeavour after it, men have often ignored its principles and mistaken its nature, but it has existed in European society as the basis of all its deepest wants and most enduring tendencies; sovereigns have invoked its aid in their hours of difficulty, and nations have ever returned to it during those intervals of prosperity and repose in which the march of civilization has been accelerated. Its most undeveloped efforts have left behind them indelible mementos. Indeed, ever since the birth of modern societies, their condition has been such, that in their institution, in their aspirations, and in the course of their history, the representative form of government, while hardly realized as such by the mind, has constantly loomed more or less distinctly in the distance, as the port at which they must at length arrive, in spite of the storms which scatter them, and the obstacles which confront and oppose their entrance.

We do not then, gentlemen, make an arbitrary choice, but one perfectly natural and necessary, when we make the representative form of government the central idea and aim of our history of the political institutions of Europe. To regard them from this point of view will not only give to our study of them the highest interest, but will enable us rightly to enter into the facts themselves, and truly to appreciate them. We shall then make this form of government the principal object of our consideration. We shall seek it wherever it has been thought to be discernible, wherever it has attempted to gain for itself a footing, wherever it has fully established itself. We shall inquire if it has in reality existed at times and in places where we have been accustomed to look for its germs. Whenever we find any indications of it, however crude and imperfect they may be, we shall inquire how it has been produced, what has been the extent of its power, and what influences have stifled it and arrested its progress. Arriving at last at the country where it has never ceased to consolidate and extend itself, from the thirteenth century to our own times, we shall remain there in order to follow it in its march, to unravel its vicissitudes, to watch the development of the principles and institutions with which it is associated, penetrating into their nature and observing their action—to study, in a word, the history of the representative system in that country where it really possesses a history which identifies itself with that of the people and their government.

Before undertaking this laborious task, it will be necessary for me, gentlemen, to exhibit before you, in a few words, the chief phases of the political condition of Europe, and the series of the principal systems of institutions through which it has passed. This anticipatory classification,—which is but a general survey of facts which will afterwards reappear before you and bring their own evidence with them,—is necessary, not only in order to clear the way before us in our study, but also to indicate the particular institutions and times which the point of view we have chosen for ourselves especially calls us to consider.

The history of the political institutions of Europe divides itself into four general epochs, during which society has been governed according to modes and forms essentially distinct.

The tribes of Germany, in establishing themselves on the Roman soil, carried thither with them their liberty, but none of those institutions by which its exercise is regulated and its permanence guaranteed. Individuals were free—a free society, however, was not constituted. I will say further, that a society was not then existent. It was only after the conquest, and in consequence of their territorial establishment, that a society really began to be formed either among the conquerors and the conquered, or among the victors themselves. The work was long and difficult. The positions in which they were placed were complicated and precarious, their forces scattered and irregular, the human mind little capable of extensive combinations and foresight. Different systems of institutions, or rather different tendencies, appeared and contended with each other. Individuals, for whom liberty then meant only personal independence and isolation, struggled to preserve it. Those who were strong succeeded in obtaining it, and became powerful; those who were weak lost it and fell under the yoke of the powerful. The kings, at first only the chiefs of warrior bands, and then the first of the great territorial proprietors, attempted to confirm and extend their power; but simultaneously with them an aristocracy was formed, by the local success of scattered forces and the concentration of properties, which did not allow royalty to establish itself with any vigour or to exert any wide-spread influence. The ancient liberty of the forest, the earliest attempts at monarchical system, the nascent elements of the feudal regime,—such were the powers which were then struggling for pre-eminence in society. No general political order could establish itself in the midst of this conflict. It lasted till the eleventh century. Then the feudal system had become predominant. The primitive independence and wild equality of individuals had either become merged into a condition of servitude, or had submitted to the hierarchical subordination of feudalism. All central power, whether of kings or of ancient national assemblies, had well nigh disappeared; liberty existed co-ordinately with power; the sovereignty was scattered. This is the first epoch.*

The second epoch is that of the feudal system. Three essential characteristics belong to it; 1st. The reduction of the mass of the people to slavery or a condition bordering thereon: 2nd. The hierarchical and federative organization of the feudal aristocracy, extending in its application both to persons and lands:

---

* On this see Guizot's History of Civilization in France. Lectures vii and viii.

3rd. The almost entire dissolution of the sovereignty, which then devolved on every feudal proprietor capable of exercising and defending it; from whence resulted the feebleness of the royal power and the destruction of monarchical unity, which disappeared almost as completely as national unity. This system prevailed until the thirteenth century.

Then commenced a new epoch. The feudal lord, already possessed of royal power, aspired after royal dignity. A portion of the inhabitants of the territory, having regained somewhat of the power they had lost, longed to become free. The feudal aristocracy was attacked on the one hand by the enfranchisement of the townsmen and tenants, on the other hand by the extension of the royal power. Sovereignty tended to concentration, liberty to diffusion; national unity began to shape itself at the same time as monarchical unity appeared. This was at once indicated and promoted by attempts after a representative form of government, which were made and renewed during nearly three centuries, wherever the feudal system fell into decay, or the monarchical system prevailed. But soon sovereigns also began almost everywhere to distrust it in their turn. They could not behold with indifference that sovereignty, which after having been long diffused had been regained and concentrated by their efforts, now again divided at its very centre. Besides, the people were deficient alike in such strength and knowledge as would enable them to continue, on the one hand, against the feudal system, a struggle which had not yet ceased, and to sustain, on the other hand, a new struggle against the central power. It was evident that the times were not fully matured; that society, which had not thoroughly emerged from that condition of servitude which had been the successor of social chaos, was neither so firmly consolidated nor so mentally disciplined as to be able to secure at once order by the equitable administration of power, and liberty by the safeguards of large and influential public institutions. The efforts after representative government became more occasional and feeble, and at length disappeared. One country alone guarded and defended it, and advanced from one struggle to another, till it succeeded. In other places, the purely monarchical system prevailed. This result was accomplished in the sixteenth century.

The fourth epoch has lasted from that time to our own days. It is chiefly marked in England by the progress of the representative system; on the Continent, by the development of the purely monarchical system, with which are associated local privileges, judicial institutions which exercise a powerful influence on political order, and some remnants of those assemblies which, in epochs anterior to the present, appeared under a more general form, but which now confine themselves to certain provinces, and are almost exclusively occupied with administrative functions. Under this system, though political liberty is no longer met with, barbarism and feudalism finally disappear before absolute power; interior order, the reconciliation of different classes, civil justice, public resources and information, make rapid progress; nations become enlightened and prosperous, and their prosperity, material as well as moral, excites in them juster apprehensions of, and more earnest longings for, that representative system which they had sought in times when they possessed neither the knowledge nor the power requisite for its exercise and preservation.

This short epitome of facts has already indicated to you, gentlemen, the epochs towards which our studies will be principally directed. The objects of our search are the political institutions of various peoples. The representative system is that around which our researches will centre. Wherever, then, we do not meet with those general institutions, under the empire of which people unite themselves, and which demand the manifestation of general society in its government—wherever we perceive no trace of the representative system, and no direct effort to produce it—there we shall not linger. All forms and conditions of society present rich and curious subjects for observation; but in this inexhaustible series of facts we must choose only those which have a strict relation to one another, and a direct interest for us. The second and the fourth epochs therefore, that is to say, feudalism and absolute power, will occupy us but little. We shall only speak of them so far as a consideration of them is necessary to connect and explain the periods which will more directly claim our attention. I purpose to study with you the first and the third epochs, and the fourth, so far as it relates to England. The first epoch, which shows us the German people establishing themselves on Roman soil—the struggle of their primitive institutions, or rather of their customs and habits, against the natural results of their new position—in fine, the throes attending the earliest formation of modern nations—has especial claims on our notice. I believe that, so far as regards political institutions, this time possessed nothing which deserves the name; but all the elements were there, in existence and commotion, as in the chaos which precedes creation. It is for us to watch this process, under which governments and peoples came into being. It is for us to ascertain whether, as has been asserted, public liberty and the representative system were actually there, whence some symptoms announced that they might one day emerge. When, in the third epoch, we see the feudal system being dissolved—when we watch the first movements towards a representative government appear at the same time with the efforts of a central power which aims at becoming general and organized— we shall recognize here, without difficulty, a subject which immediately belongs to us. We shall seek to learn what societies were then aroused, and by what means they have sought for trustworthy institutions, which might guarantee the continuance at once of order and of liberty. And when we have seen their hopes deceived by the calamities of the times, when we have detected in the vices of the social state, far more than in the influence of any disorderly or perverse desires, the causes of the ill-success of these magnanimous attempts, we shall be brought by our subject into the very midst of that people, then treated more leniently by fortune, which has paid dearly for free institutions, but which has guarded them to the last when they perished everywhere else, and which, while preserving and developing them for itself, has offered to other nations, if not a model, yet certainly an example.[3]

It would be a small matter for us, gentlemen, thus to limit the field of our inquiries so far as epochs are concerned, if we did not also assign some boundaries in respect to place. The inquiry would be too large and protracted were we to follow the course of political institutions throughout the whole of Europe, according to the plan I have just indicated. Moreover, the diversity of events and conditions has been so great in Europe, that, notwithstanding certain general characteristics and certain philosophical results which the facts everywhere present, they very often resist all the attempts we may make to bring them under any uniform guiding principle. In vain do we strive to collect them together under the same horizon, or to force them into the same channel; ever do they release themselves from our grasp in order to assume elsewhere the place assigned to them by truth. We should therefore be compelled either to limit ourselves to generalities yielding but little instruction to those who have not sounded all their depths, or else continually to interrupt the course of our inquiry, in order to rove from one people to another with an attention which would be continually distracted and soon wearied. It will be more profitable for us to take a narrower range. England, France, and Spain, will supply us with abundant materials for our undertaking. In these countries we shall study political institutions under the different phases and in the various epochs which I have just exhibited before you. There we shall find that these epochs are more clearly defined, and that the chief facts which characterize them appear under more complete and simple forms. In France and Spain, moreover, the general attempts after a representative government, made in the thirteenth, fourteenth, and fifteenth centuries, assumed a more definite shape. We are therefore dissuaded by a variety of considerations from carrying our steps beyond these limits. Our researches will thereby gain both in interest and in solidity.

This interest, gentlemen, I must say at the outset, is not that merely which attaches itself to human affairs, which are ever attractive to man, however trivial may be the attention which he bestows upon them. The study of the ancient political institutions of Europe demands serious and assiduous effort. I am here to share this with you, not to undertake it for you. I shall be frequently obliged

---

3. For more details, also see *HORG*, pp. 221–22. In *HCE* Guizot also referred to four epochs: the barbarian epoch; the feudal age; the age in which the first attempts at representative government were made; and, finally, the age marked by the progress of representative system in England and the development of absolute monarchy on the Continent.

to enter into details, which may appear dry at first, but which are important because of the results to which they lead. I shall not content myself with merely presenting before you these results as a general expression of facts; I shall feel called upon to put you in possession of the facts themselves. The truths which they contain must be seen by yourselves to proceed naturally from them, and must not be allowed a final lodgment in your minds except as they are fortified by such evidence as can establish them. Gentlemen, it is to be borne in mind that truth, wheresoever we may seek it, is not easy of access. We must dig deep for it, as for precious metals, before we find it; we must not shrink from the difficulties, nor from the long duration of the enterprise. It only surrenders itself to resolute and patient endeavour. And not only on behalf of our peculiar study do I urge upon you that you should never allow yourselves to be baffled by the fatigue attendant upon some portions of the work;—a more elevated motive, a more comprehensive claim, gives you this advice. Thrasea, when dying, said to his son-in-law, Helvidius Priscus, "Observe, young man: thou art living in times when it is well that the spirit should become fortified by such a scene as this; and learn how a brave man can die." Thankful should we be to Heaven that such lessons as these are not now required by us, and that the future does not demand such hard discipline in order that we may be prepared to meet it. But the free institutions which we are called upon to receive and maintain—these demand of us, from our earliest youth, those habits of laborious and patient application which will constitute our fittest preparation. They require that we should, among our first lessons, learn not to shrink either from the pain, or from the length and arduousness of duty. If our destiny is to be sublime, our studies must be severe. Liberty is not a treasure which can be acquired or defended by those who set a disproportionate value on personal ease and gratification; and if ever man attains it after having toiled for it under the influence merely of luxurious or impatient feelings, it denies to him those honours and advantages which he expected to gain from its possession. It was the error of the preceding age that, while it aimed at urging the minds of men into a wider and more active career, it yet fostered the impression that all was then to become easy, that study would be transformed into amusement, and that obstacles were removed from the first steps of a life that was to issue in something great and impressive. The effeminate weakness of such sentiments were relics of the feebleness of times when liberty did not exist. We who live in the present day, know that freedom requires from the man who would enjoy it a sterner exercise of his powers. We know that it allows neither indolence of soul nor fickleness of mind, and that those generations which devote their youth to laborious study can alone secure liberty for their manhood. You will find, gentlemen, as you watch the development of the political institutions of Europe, that the experience of all ages confirms this of our own. You will not find that those grand designs that have been formed for the promotion of truth, justice, and progress, have ever emanated from the abode of sloth, of frivolity, and antipathy to all that demands labour and patience. As you trace back such enterprises to their source, you will always find there, serious aspect and grave determination, existing, so to speak, in their early life. Only by men formed in this mould have public laws and liberties been defended. They have, according as the wants of their age impelled them, resisted disorder or oppression. In the gravity of their own life and thoughts they have found a true measure of their own dignity, and, in their own, of the dignity of humanity. And, gentlemen, do not doubt, in following their example, of achieving also their success. You will soon become convinced that, in spite of the tests to which it has been exposed, our age is not among the most unrestrained that have existed. You will see that patriotism, a respect for law and order, a reverence for all that is just and sacred, have often been purchased at a far heavier price, and have called for severer self-denial. You will find that there is as much feebleness as ingratitude in the disposition that is intimidated and discouraged by the sight of obstacles which still present themselves, when obstacles of a far more formidable character have not wearied the resolution of noble men of former times. And thus, while early exercising your minds in all those habits which will prepare man for the duties of an exalted destiny, you will meet with nothing that will not continually deepen your attachment to your age and to your country.[4]

So far as I myself am concerned, may I be allowed, gentlemen, in entering with you today upon the study of the ancient political institutions of Europe, to congratulate myself on being able to approach the subject with the liberty that is suitable to it. It was in works of a similar character that I commenced my intellectual life. But at that time the public exposition of such facts and of the ideas related to them, was hardly permitted. Power had arrived at that condition in which it fears equally any representation of the oppression of peoples, and of their efforts to obtain liberty; as if it must necessarily meet in these two series of historical reminiscences at once the condemnation of its past acts, and the prediction of its future perils. We are no longer in this deplorable position; the institutions which France has received from its sovereign have liberated at

---

4. This is an excellent summary of Guizot's political vision. He believed that the mission of his (post-revolutionary) generation was to establish free representative institutions by reconciling freedom and order. This task required a long apprenticeship of liberty, a stern exercise of power, and "habits of laborious and patient application" (*HORG*, p. 17). Worth noting is Guizot's emphasis on the arduousness of duty, self-denial (Kant's influence is obvious in this regard!), laborious study, and determination. In Guizot's view, the just political agenda was dictated by national (as opposed to factional) interests and had to follow both reason and the public interest. For more details, see Guizot, *Mémoires pour servir à l'histoire de mon temps*, Vol. I (Paris: Michel Lévy Frères, 1870), pp. 158–66, 193–205.

once the present and the past. Such is the moral strength possessed by a legitimate and constitutional monarchy, that it trembles neither at the recitals of history nor at the criticisms of reason. It is based upon truth—and truth is consequently neither hostile nor dangerous to it. Wherever all the wants of society are recognised, and all its rights give each other mutual sanction and support, facts present only lessons of utility, and no longer hint at unwelcome allusions. The volume of history can now be spread out before us; and wherever we find the coincidence of legitimacy and constitutional order, we shall behold the prosperity both of governments and of peoples—the dignity of power ennobled and sustained by the dignity of obedience. In all positions, and however great may be the interval which separates them, we shall see man rendering honour to man; we shall see authority and liberty mutually regarding one another with that consideration and respect which can alone unite them in lasting connexion and guarantee their continued harmony. Let us congratulate ourselves, gentlemen, that we are living at a time in which this tutelary alliance has become a necessity—in which force without justice could only be an ephemeral power. The times to which we shall direct our attention experienced a harder lot; they more than once beheld despotism root itself deeply in its position, and at the same time saw injustice assert its claim to a lasting rule. We, gentlemen, who have seen so many and diversified forms of oppression—we have seen them all fall into decay. Neither their most furious violence, nor their most imposing lustre, have sufficed to preserve them from the corruption that is inherent in their nature; and we have at length entered upon an order of things which admits neither the oppression of force which usurps power, nor that of anarchy which destroys it. Let us, gentlemen, reap all the advantages connected with such an order:—let us show our respect for the distinguished author of this Charter by approving ourselves worthy of receiving, and capable of employing, the noble institutions which he has founded. Our gratitude can offer no purer homage.[5]

---

5. Worth noting is the relation between the social and the political order, a theme that looms large in Guizot's writings, most notably in connection with his theory of democracy as social condition. Against those who argued that representative government was a dangerous modern institution, Guizot claimed that it had deep roots in the past and represented the only political regime that was suitable to the new spirit of the age. "Almost everywhere," he wrote, "the representative form of government is demanded, allowed, or established. This fact . . . has certainly its roots in the past political career of the nations, as it has its motives in their present condition" (*HORG*, p. 11). In other words, in France, the establishment of representative government was demanded by the new social condition that was characterized by a new configuration of mores, laws, class structure, property relations, and economic interests. For more details on the doctrinaires' theory of democracy as *état social* (social condition), see Charles de Rémusat, "L'esprit de réaction: Royer-Collard et Tocqueville" ("The Spirit of Reaction: Royer-Collard and Tocqueville"), *Revue des deux mondes*, October 15, 1861, pp. 777–813; Aurelian Craiutu, "Tocqueville and the Political Thought of the French Doctrinaires," *History of Political Thought*, Vol. XX, No. 3, Autumn 1999, pp. 456–93.

LECTURE 2

General character of political institutions in Europe, from the fourth to the eleventh century. ⁓ *Political sterility of the Roman Empire.* ⁓ *Progress of the Germanic invasions.* ⁓ *Sketch of the history of the Anglo-Saxons.*

I HAVE divided the history of the political institutions of modern Europe into four great epochs, the first of which extends from the fourth to the eleventh century. This long interval was required to introduce a little light and fixity into the changeful chaos of those new empires which the successive invasions of the Roman territory by the barbarians had called into being, and whence issued those mighty states whose destiny constitutes the history of modern Europe. The essential characteristics of this epoch are: the conflict and fusion of Germanic customs with Roman institutions, the attempt to establish monarchical government, and the formation of the feudal regime. No general system of political institutions then existed; no great dominant influence can be discerned; all was local, individual, confused, obscure. A multitude of principles and forces, mingling and acting (as it were) by chance, were engaged in conflict to resolve a question of which men were completely ignorant, and the secret of which God alone possessed. This question was: What form of government would issue from all these different elements, brought so violently into contact with each other. Five centuries elapsed before the question was decided, and then feudalism was the social state of Europe.

Before entering, however, upon the history of institutions, let me say a few words upon the progress of the fall of the Roman Empire, and of the invasions of the barbarians.[1]

---

1. For more details on the condition of Europe at the fall of the Roman Empire, see Guizot, *HCE*, Lecture II, pp. 27–46. Of utmost importance is Guizot's emphasis on the coexistence and combat of different principles and systems of political organization (theocratic, monarchic, aristocratic, and popular) that had limited and modified each other over time, thereby contributing to the progress of European civilization. Guizot argued that "in Europe liberty has been the result of the variety of the elements of civilization, and of the state of struggle in which they have constantly existed" (*ibid.*, p. 31).

From the accession of Augustus to the death of Theodosius the Great, the Roman Empire, in spite of its greatness, presents a general character of impotence and sterility. Its institutions, its government, its philosophy, its literature, indeed everything connected with it, bears this sad impress; even the minds of its most illustrious citizens were confined to a circle of antiquated ideas, and wasted in vain regrets for the virtues and glories of the Republic. The fermentation of new ideas produces no decadence; but when, in a great empire, society, feeling itself oppressed and diseased, can conceive no new hopes, no grand ideas,—when, instead of pressing onwards towards the future, it invokes only the recollections and images of the past—then there is a real decline; it matters not how long the state is in falling, its ruin is thenceforward continuous and inevitable. The fall of the Roman Empire occupied fifteen centuries; and for fifteen centuries it continued to decline, until its downfall was consummated by the capture of Constantinople by the Turks. During this long period, no new idea, no regenerative principle, was employed to reinvigorate the life of the government; it was sustained by its own mass. Towards the end of the third century, when the universal servitude seemed to be most firmly established, imperial despotism began to feel the precariousness of its position, and the necessity for organization. Diocletian created a vast system of administration. Throughout this immense machine, he established underworks in harmony with the principle of his government; he regulated the action of the central power in the provinces, and surrounded himself with a brilliant and puissant court: but he did not rekindle the moral life of the Empire; he merely organized more perfectly a material resistance to the principles of destruction which were undermining it; and it was with this organization that, first in the West as well as in the East, and afterwards in the East alone, the Empire was able to struggle on, from the fourth to the fifteenth century. Theodosius the Great, who died in 395, was the last emperor who tightly held and skilfully managed the heterogeneous bundle of the Roman power. He was truly a great man; for great men appear in disgraceful times, as well as in times of success; and Theodosius was still the master of the Roman world. As soon as he was dead, the dissolution broke out, under his sons Honorius and Arcadius.* There was now no real unity or central force in the government; Rome gradually abandoned her provinces—Great Britain, Armorica,† and Narbonnese Gaul.‡ Honorius informed the Britons that he should govern them no longer; and directed the inhabitants of Narbon-

---

* Honorius succeeded peaceably to the sovereignty of the West, which he had received from his father in the preceding year; while his elder brother Arcadius obtained possession of the East.

† The country on the north-west coast of Gaul, from the Loire to the Seine.

‡ The Roman province in the south of Gaul, so called from its chief city, Narbo or Narbonne; Caesar calls it simply *Provincia,* and hence comes the modern name of Provence.

nese Gaul to elect deputies to meet at Arles, and take upon themselves the government of their country. The Empire had become a body destitute of sap and vigour; and in order to prolong the life of the trunk, it was necessary to lop off the branches. But, although despotism was withdrawn from these provinces, servitude remained. It is not easy to return at once to liberty and to political life; and these people, cast upon their own resources, were unable to defend themselves. Great Britain, though more populous than the north of Scotland, was unable to repel a few hordes of Picts and Scots, who, every month, descended from their mountainous abodes, and ravaged the British territory. The Britons besought the Emperor's assistance, and he sent them a legion, which had no difficulty in overcoming enemies who fled before it; but it was soon withdrawn. After its departure, the incursions recommenced, and Britain again implored the Emperor's aid. Honorius sent another legion; but told the suppliants that they must provide for themselves in future, for he would send them no more soldiers. The victorious legion left the country to return no more, and Britain, assailed on all sides by bands of barbarians, exhausted its energies in vain entreaties for deliverance. There still exists a letter, entitled *Gemitus Britannum,* in which the unfortunate inhabitants of that country depict their deplorable condition to Aetius, the Patrician of Gaul. "The barbarians," they wrote, "drive us to the sea, and the sea drives us back to the barbarians; so that, between the two, we must be either slaughtered or drowned." With patriotic susceptibility, some English writers—among others Mr. Sharon Turner, in his *History of the Anglo-Saxons,**—have cast doubts upon the authenticity of this letter, as if the honour of England were at all involved in the weaknesses of the Britons of the fourth century. However this may be, and whether his aid were besought or not, the Emperor had other matters to attend to, and left the Britons to themselves. He abandoned, in like manner, Narbonnese Gaul and Armorica. This last province, which was less corrupted by the influence of Roman civilization, displayed greater energy than the other two. It took measures for its own defence, by forming a kind of federative league against maritime invasions. Spain, which was also deserted, endeavoured to maintain itself in the same manner against attacks of the same nature; but acted with little vigour, and met with small success. In Great Britain, as well as in Gaul, the Roman government had destroyed the energy of their native independence, and had substituted in its stead nothing but its own artificial and despotic organization. When the Romans withdrew, the children of the Gauls, inhabiting Roman cities, were incapable alike of self-government or self-defence, and fell an easy prey to a few bands of foreign marauders, who had come in search of booty and adventures. Let us briefly glance at the progress of their conquests.

* Turner's *History of the Anglo-Saxons,* vol. i., pp. 180–181.

No determinate epoch can be accurately assigned to the first invasions of the Germans. In all ages, their hordes were wont to descend from their forest-fastnesses into countries less wild and more cultivated than their own. Among their early irruptions, the first regarding which we have any precise historical information is that of the Cimbri and Teutones, who, three hundred thousand in number, ravaged Italy during the time of Marius.* From the age of Augustus to the fifth century, these invasions continued, but were very unequal in importance. Bands of men, unable to find means of subsistence in their own country, entered the imperial territory, and pillaged as they went; their fate was decided by the event of a battle; they were dispersed or annihilated by a defeat, or, if victorious, they took possession of some district which pleased them. Frequently, also, they settled in the country by the consent of the emperors. In the third century, Probus received three or four thousand Franks into Auvergne. A band of Alans took up their residence in the neighbourhood of Orleans; there was a colony of Goths in Thrace, and another of Vandals in Lorraine. Those of the barbarian warriors who preferred war and pillage to a fixed habitation, entered the Roman armies. Their chieftains became generals, and even supplied the imperial court with ministers of state. Thus the barbarians were everywhere settled in the country, serving in the armies, surrounding the person of the prince; formidable allies, whose assistance the weakness of the empire was forced to accept, and who were destined to increase in power and influence in proportion as the imperial power decayed.

As soon as the Roman government, by abandoning several of its provinces, proclaimed its inability to maintain its own integrity, the question was decided—the empire passed to the Germans. During the interval which elapsed between the beginning of the fifth and the end of the sixth century, they founded eight great monarchies, some of which were established by force, whilst others received the partial assent of the emperors.

In 409, the Vandals, Alans, and Suevi, after having ravaged Gaul, and crossed the Pyrenees, founded by armed force, in Spain, three monarchies, which were speedily incorporated into one; and this one, in its turn, was, ere long, destroyed by the Visigoths.

In 429, the Vandals passed from Spain into Africa, and founded a monarchy, which was overthrown by Belisarius.

In 414, the Burgundians founded a kingdom in Gaul, with the consent of the emperors.

In 416, the Visigoths penetrated into Southern Gaul, where they founded the kingdom of Aquitaine; and entered by the north-east into Spain, where they settled, after having destroyed the monarchy of the Suevi.

---

* In B.C. 113–101. Marius finally defeated the Teutones at Aix, in the year 102; and the Cimbri, near Vercelli, in the year 101.

In 450, the Saxons, led by Hengist and Horsa, invaded Great Britain, and founded the Saxon Heptarchy.

In 476, the Heruli, under the command of Odoacer, founded a monarchy in Italy.

In 481, the Franks, with Clovis at their head, established themselves in Gaul.

In 568, the Lombards, under the command of Alboin, conquered Italy in their turn, and founded a monarchy.

I do not propose to write the history of these monarchies; but I shall endeavour to delineate their leading institutions and their social condition. In the first place, however, I shall say a few words on the method of their foundation. We must not suppose that there was, in every instance, a cession or complete abandonment of sovereignty by the Roman empire. The residence of a barbarian chieftain in the country was recognised as a fact. He continued to command his own warriors, but no legal authority was granted him over the old inhabitants. The cities long maintained their connexion with Rome; several of them remained municipalities, and continued to appoint their own magistrates. Several towns in Spain, while the country was under the dominion of the Visigoths, received their civic rulers from Constantinople. The emperors, though daily despoiled of some new territory, nevertheless retained, in almost every quarter, an appearance of empire. Thus we find them conferring on the Frankish kings the titles of Patrician of Gaul, and of Consul. This was their protest against the invasion. In scarcely any case was there a transference of sovereign rights. Societies, when abandoned by their government, either received a new one at the hands of the victor, or endeavoured to create one for themselves.

Among these rising states, I shall first refer to the Anglo-Saxons; then I shall pass on to the Franks; and, finally, to the Visigoths in Spain. I have selected these three nations, because, among them, the institutions of this period are most distinctly marked. The Anglo-Saxons, especially, were placed in a position most favourable for this rapid and complete development. Not only were they more isolated than other peoples; they were also less disturbed by continual invasions of a formidable character. They soon became sole masters of the country. The Britons were almost exterminated; some of them retired into Cornwall, Wales, and Armorica; the others were dispersed, or reduced to servitude. The Anglo-Saxons, moreover, were less under the influence of the old Roman institutions. Among modern nations, they are the people who, so to speak, have lived most upon their own resources, and given birth to their own civilization. This character is discernible in their whole history, and even in their literature. The Greek and Latin classics have produced but little effect upon them; primitive and national customs have maintained their sway in England, and received an almost unmixed development. Among the Franks and Visigoths, the old Germanic national assemblies were either suspended for a long period, or entirely transformed; among the Anglo-Saxons, they never ceased; year after year, they occurred to perpetuate ancient recollections, and to exert a direct influence upon the government. It was, then, among the Anglo-Saxons, that, from the fifth to the eleventh century, institutions received the most natural and complete development. This fact has induced me to commence our studies with their history.

Let me briefly refer to the events which occurred during the period of the Anglo-Saxon Heptarchy. From 426 to 450, the Britons, left to themselves, struggled as they could against the inhabitants of the north of Scotland. In 449, some Saxons from the banks of the Elbe disembarked upon the island. This descent was neither novel nor unforeseen. It was a fact so ancient, that the Roman emperors had appointed a magistrate—*comes littoris Saxonici*[2]—whose special duty it was to provide for the defence of the coast. It is affirmed, and Hume has repeated the statement, that this Saxon expedition had been summoned by Vortigern, who was then chief of the Britons, to assist him against the Picts and Scots. This appears to me neither natural nor probable; and I find in the chronicler Nennius, a passage which completely disproves the assertion: "Meanwhile," he says, "there arrived from Germany three vessels full of Saxon exiles."[*] They came therefore spontaneously, according to their custom. The Britons, reduced to extremities by their untiring enemies, the Picts and Scots, endeavoured at first to use the Saxons against them. But the newcomers quickly discovered their strength, attempted the conquest of the country which they had promised to defend, and succeeded in their attempt. The Britons resisted, and even displayed somewhat of the energy of their ancestors, under King Arthur and other leaders. A long time elapsed before they were finally subjugated or expelled. During the period from 455 to 582, the Saxons founded the seven or eight kingdoms which composed the Heptarchy, or the Octarchy, as Mr. Sharon Turner maintains.[†] The kingdom of Kent was the first, founded by Hengist. The others were the kingdoms of Sussex, Wessex, Essex, Northumberland (or Bernicia and Deira), East Anglia, and Mercia. This division continued until the year 800. At that time, Egbert, King of Wessex, attempted to subjugate the other kingdoms, and succeeded in reducing five under his sway; but Northumberland and Mercia continued separate, though subordinate kingdoms, until the end of the ninth century.

It was at this period that the Danes and Normans made their way into En-

---

[*] Nennius, cap. 31.

[†] *History of the Anglo-Saxons*, vol. i. p. 320.

2. Guardian of the Saxon coast.

gland: they long contested the possession of the country with the Saxons; and, at the accession of Alfred, the last newcomers held sway almost all over the land. You are all acquainted with the history of this monarch, the greatest of the kings of England. In the marshes where he had been compelled to seek refuge from the pursuit of his enemies, he formed his plans for the deliverance of his country. Disguised as a harper, he entered the Danish camp for the purpose of learning the amount of their forces; and finally reconquered his kingdom, after a protracted struggle. Restored thus to his throne, Alfred laid the foundation of English institutions, or rather, he reduced them to order, and gave them authority. It is the custom, however, to date their origin from him; and his reign is an era in English legislation. Alfred is a glorious instance of a truth exemplified by Gustavus Vasa and Henry IV. of France in later times, namely, that the greatest princes are those who, though born to the throne, are nevertheless obliged to conquer its possession. To their acknowledged right they thus join ample proof of their merit. They have lived as common individuals in the midst of their people; and have thus become better men and better kings.

After the death of Alfred, the Danes, whose conquests had been suspended only by the victories of that prince, gained possession of England. Canute the Great took possession of the throne; but he reigned with moderation, and did not change the laws of the country. This wisdom on the part of the conqueror mitigated the animosity of the vanquished; and the Danes and Saxons agreed so well together, that, not long after the death of Canute the Great, the old dynasty re-ascended the throne. Edward the Confessor collected together the old Saxon laws; on this account, he is still respected in England as a national legislator. But the collection of laws which now exists under his name was not made by him; that which he composed has unfortunately been lost.

During the reign of Edward the Confessor, a striking exemplification was given of the power of some of the nobles, who were in fact, if not in right, rivals of their monarch. Earl Godwin was so powerful that he, so to speak, allowed Edward to ascend the throne, on condition that he should marry his daughter. At his death, his son Harold succeeded him, and increased his authority. Harold's influence extended all over the kingdom, and he only awaited the king's death to take possession of the crown. When Edward died, Harold naturally succeeded to throne. No one in England contested his usurpation. But William the Bastard, Duke of Normandy, one of his distant relations, alleged that Edward had bequeathed the crown to him by will. He crossed the sea to maintain his pretended rights, and, on the 14th of October, 1066, he gave battle to Harold, at Hastings. Harold was left dead on the field. William the Conqueror introduced into England the feudal institutions which were then in full vigour in Normandy. The reciprocal relations of persons might have conduced, in England, to the establishment of this system, and had prepared the way for it; but the legal and hierarchical subordination of land had not taken firm hold in that country. The conquest of William of Normandy disturbed the natural course of the old Anglo-Saxon institutions, and mingled therewith foreign elements which had already been developed, among the Normans, by their position in Gaul, in the midst of Roman cities, and a Roman population. We shall presently see what decisive influence this circumstance exerted over the political development of England.

LECTURE 3

Subject of the lecture. ⌒ A knowledge of the state of persons necessary to the proper study of institutions. ⌒ Essential difference between antiquity and modern societies, as regards the classification of social conditions. ⌒ State of persons among the Anglo-Saxons. ⌒ Thanes and Ceorls. ⌒ Central and local institutions. ⌒ Predominance of the latter among the Anglo-Saxons. ⌒ Its cause.

IN my preceding lecture, I gave a general outline of the decay of the Roman empire, and of the progress of the barbarian invasions; and I enumerated the principal events in the history of the Anglo-Saxons in England. I now come to their institutions, which form the subject of my present lecture.

When we are about to speak of the institutions of a country at any given period, we must first understand what was the state of persons in that country at that period; for words are very deceptive. History, when speaking of the English nation or the Spanish nation, comprises under that name all the individuals who inhabit the country; but when we examine into the real state of the case, we quickly discover that the facts which history applies to an entire country, actually belong only to a very small section of its inhabitants. It is the work of civilization to raise up, from time to time, a greater number of men to take an active part in the great events which agitate the society of which they are members. As civilization advances, it reaches new classes of individuals, and gives them a place in history. The different conditions of society thus tend, not to confusion, but to arrangement, under different forms and in different degrees, in that superior region of society by which history is made.

The first question to be solved, then, is that of the state of persons; we must precisely understand which are those classes that really figure in history. Then will occur this other question: What are the institutions in accordance with which that political nation acts, which alone furnishes subject-matter for history?[1]

---

1. Guizot's ideas on the relation between the social and the political order had a profound impact on Tocqueville. Guizot emphasized the role of "the habits of the heart"—mores, customs, and

When we address the first question to antiquity, we find, as in Modern Europe, one great classification: freemen and slaves. But there is this difference that, in antiquity, slavery continued stationary and immutable. Its unchangeableness in this particular, was one of the principal characteristics of ancient civilization. Individuals were emancipated; but the great mass of slaves remained in bondage, everlastingly condemned to the same social nonentity. In Modern Europe, social conditions have been in a state of perpetual fluctuation; numerous masses of men have fallen into slavery, while others have emerged therefrom; and this alternation of liberty and servitude is a novel and important fact in the history of civilization.

What was the condition of persons among the Anglo-Saxons? Here, as elsewhere, we at first perceive the two great divisions of freemen and slaves. The freemen, who are the only active elements in history, were divided into two classes, *thanes* and *ceorls*. The thanes were the proprietors of the soil, which was entirely at their disposal: hence the origin of freehold tenure. The ceorls were men personally free, but possessing no landed property. The thanes were subdivided into two classes; king's thanes, and inferior thanes. This distinction is not merely a historical fact; the laws recognize these two divisions. The composition for the life of a king's thane was twelve hundred shillings, while for that of an inferior thane it was only six hundred. Here, as in other states which came into existence at this epoch, punishment was made proportionate, not only to the gravity of the offence, but also to the rank of the person injured. By the substitution of an indemnity for retaliation, a step was taken by these peoples towards social justice. Early ideas of justice inflict evil for evil, injury for injury; but the highest point of its perfection is that decision of society which, embodying supreme reason and power, judges the actions of men accused of crimes, and acquits or condemns them in the name of the Eternal Justice. In the sixth century, society did not inflict punishment; life, like everything else, had its price; and this price was shared between the family of the dead man, the king, and the judge. The penalty of crime was as yet only the price paid for the renunciation of the right of revenge which belonged to every free man. Individuals who were injured, either in the possession of their goods, or in the life of their relatives, received a fixed composition from the guilty person.

I have pointed out the legal distinction which subsisted between the king's

---

laws—as well as their impact on the development of political institutions. The seminal point made by Guizot is that it is necessary to study first society, its composition, mores, and the relations between the different classes and properties in order to understand the nature of political institutions. He also addressed the same topic in his *Essays on the History of France,* originally published in 1823.

thanes and the inferior thanes; but when we seek to discover what constituted the real difference of their condition, we find that this difference was very vague, and belonged to the time when they all led a nomadic life, rather than to their settled agricultural existence. In Germany, or on leaving Germany, bands, more or less numerous, united themselves to the company of some particular chief or king. After the conquest of a country, those chiefs who were nearest the king found themselves in a most favourable position for becoming large landed proprietors. These were called king's thanes, because they belonged to the royal band. But there was nothing to separate them essentially from the other thanes. To be a king's thane, it was necessary to possess about forty or fifty hides of land.* Bishops and abbots were admitted into this class. The inferior thanes were proprietors possessing less land, but able to dispose just as freely of their property as the king's thanes. Some writers have asserted that the king's thanes were the nobles, and that the others were simple freemen. An attentive examination of Anglo-Saxon institutions will prove that there was no such difference of position and rights between the two classes. It is a great error to expect to meet with clearly defined ranks and conditions, at the origin of society. Some writers, however, pretend to discover at the outset what time alone can introduce. We meet with no nobility, constituting a superior social condition, with recognized privileges: we perceive only the causes which will progressively form a nobility, that is, will introduce inequality of power and the empire of the strong. The formation of a class of nobles has been the work of ages. An actual superiority, transmitted from father to son, has gradually assumed the form and characteristics of a right. When societies have not been long in existence, we do not find in them social conditions thus distinctly marked, and the royal family is the only one that can, with any reason, be termed noble. It generally derives its title from some religious filiation; for instance, among nearly all the peoples of the north, in Denmark, in Norway, and in England, the kings descended from Odin; and their divine origin gave high sanction to their power.

Other writers have held that the relations which subsisted between the king's thanes and the inferior thanes were of a different nature, corresponding to the feudal relations of lords and vassals. The king's thanes, they say, were vassals of the king; the inferior thanes were vassals of the king's vassals. We may certainly discover, in the connection of these two classes of men, some of the characteristics of feudalism. But feudalism, such as was established on the Continent as well as in England, after the conquest by William of Normandy, consisted essentially in the simultaneous hierarchy of lands and persons. Such were not the rudiments of feudalism discernible among the Anglo-Saxons. As yet, the only hierarchy existing among them was of persons. All the thanes held

---

* A hide of land was about 120 acres.

their lands in an equally free and independent manner. At a later period, feudalism received a more complete development; from the hierarchy of persons proceeded that of lands, and the latter soon predominated over the former. But this result was not manifested until after the Norman conquest. Before that period, there were no vassals properly so called, although the word *vassus* occurs in a biography of King Alfred. The causes which led to the subordination of persons, independently of their connection with land, are simple and may easily be conceived. When the barbarian chieftains entered the Roman territory, they possessed an influence over their companions which they endeavoured to retain after their settlement. The Saxon laws, with a view to bring this rude and floating state of society into an orderly state, provided for the maintenance of this primitive hierarchy; and compelled every freeman who had attained the age of twelve years, to enrol himself in some corporation of individuals, in a tithing or a hundred, or else to place himself under the patronage of a chieftain. This bond was so strong that the person who made the engagement could not absent himself without the permission of the captain of his corporation, or of his chieftain. A foreigner even might not remain forty days on the English soil without enrolling himself in this manner. This spirit of subordination, this obligation of discipline, is one of the principal characteristics of Anglo-Saxon legislation. All those kings who, after long-continued disorders, were desirous to reorganise society, exerted themselves to restore to vigorous operation these laws of police and classification. They have been attributed to Alfred, but he merely reenacted them.

In my opinion, then, there is no legitimate ground for the doctrine that the relation of the king's thanes to the inferior thanes, was a feudal relation. It was the natural relationship which necessarily arose, at the origin of society, between the various degrees of power and wealth. The poor and the weak lived under the surveillance and protection of those who were richer and more powerful.

As I have already observed, the freemen were divided into two classes—thanes and ceorls. I shall now speak of the second class. The ceorls were freemen who lived on the estates of the thanes, and cultivated them. Their free condition has been called in question, wrongly, as I think, for various reasons: 1st. The composition for the life of a ceorl was two hundred shillings, and the characteristic mark of his liberty is that a portion of this composition was paid to his family, and not to the proprietor of the estate on which he lived; whereas, the composition for the life of a slave was always paid to his owner. 2nd. In the early times of the Saxon monarchy, the ceorls were able to leave the land which they cultivated, whenever they pleased; by degrees, however, they lost this liberty. 3rd. They had the right of bearing arms, and might go to war; whereas, slaves did not possess this right. When Earl Godwin attacked King Edward, he armed all the ceorls on his estates; and, at the time of the Danish invasions, the ceorls fought in defence of their country. 4th. They were also capable of possessing property, and when they owned five hides of land they passed into the class of thanes, as did also merchants who had made three voyages to foreign lands. Hence the origin of the English yeomanry. The yeoman is the freeholder, who, possessing an income of forty shillings from land, votes at county elections, and may sit on juries; *probus et legalis homo.*[2] 5th. The ceorls were admitted to give evidence, only, it is true, in matters which had reference to persons of their own class: whereas slaves did not possess this right. 6th. Nearly all the ceorls were Saxons: we find in a canon of the clergy of Northumberland, that a ceorl accused of a crime, must bring forward as witnesses twelve ceorls and twelve Britons. The ceorls, then, were Saxons, and were distinguished from the ancient inhabitants of the country. It is impossible that so large a proportion of the conquerors should have fallen so quickly into servitude. We may rather feel astonished that they had no landed property in the country, which they had just conquered. But Tacitus, with the accustomed truthfulness and vigour of his pencil, makes us readily understand this circumstance. In the forests of Germany, the barbarian warriors always lived around their chieftains, who had to suggest and command expeditions in times of activity, and to lodge and support their men in times of repose. The same habits were kept up after the conquest of a country; the property acquired was not divided among all the victors. Every chieftain received a larger or smaller division of land, and his followers settled with him upon it. These men, accustomed to a wandering life, did not yet set a high value upon landed property. Being still harassed, moreover, by the ancient possessors of the soil, they found it necessary to keep together, and unite in their own defence. They formed species of camps around the dwelling of their chieftain, whose possessions, according to the ancient Saxon laws, were divided into two parts—*inlands* and *outlands.* And it is clear proof of the great difference then existing between the ceorls and the slaves, that the latter alone cultivated the land adjoining the habitation of the chief, while the ceorls, as a natural consequence of their personal freedom, tilled the outlands. This state of things, however, could not last long. A large number of the ceorls fell into servitude, and assumed the name of *villeins* (villani); while others acquired lands for themselves, and became the *soc-men* of England.

Summing up what we have said, we perceive, in the state of persons under the Anglo-Saxon monarchy, one great division into freemen and slaves: and, among the freemen, another distinction of thanes and ceorls. The thanes themselves are subdivided into king's thanes and inferior thanes. The former are large landed proprietors, the latter hold smaller estates: but both classes possess equal

2. Upright and lawful man.

rights. The ceorls are freemen, without landed property, at least originally. Most of them fall into a state of servitude. With regard to the slaves, we can say nothing except that they were very numerous, and were divided into domestic servants and rural serfs, or serfs of the glebe. The ancient inhabitants of the country did not all fall into servitude; some of them retained their possessions, and a law of King Ina authorized them to appear before courts of justice. They might even pass into the class of thanes if they possessed five hides of land.

The thanes alone, to speak truly, played an active part in history.

Passing now to the institutions which connected and governed these different classes, we find them to be of two kinds; central institutions, entirely in the hands of the thanes, the object of which was to secure the intervention of the nation in its own government; and local institutions, which regulated those local interests and guarantees which applied equally to all classes of the community.

At the origin of Anglo-Saxon society, there existed none but local institutions. In these are contained the most important guarantees for men whose life never goes beyond the boundaries of their fields. At such epochs, men are as yet unacquainted with great social life; and as the scope of institutions always corresponds to the scope of the affairs and relations to which they have reference, it follows that when relations are limited, institutions are equally so. They continue local, because all interests are local; there are very few, if any, general taxes and affairs of public concern; the kings live, like their subjects, on the income derived from their estates. The proprietors care little about what is passing at a distance. The idea of those great public agencies which regulate the affairs of all men, does not belong to the origin of societies. By degrees, in the midst of the chaos of the rising society, small aggregations are formed which feel the want of alliance and union with each other. They establish amongst themselves an administration of justice, a public militia, a system of taxation and police. Soon, inequality of strength is displayed among neighbouring aggregations. The strong tend to subjugate the weak, and usurp, at first, the rights of taxation and military service. Thus, political authority leaves the aggregations which first instituted it, to take a wider range. This system of centralization is not always imposed by force: it sometimes has a more legitimate cause. In times of difficulty, a superior man appears who makes his influence first felt in the society to which he belongs. When attacked, the society intrusts him with its defence. Neighbouring societies follow this example; soon the powers granted in time of war are continued in time of peace, and remain concentrated in a single hand. This victorious power retains the right to levy men and money. These are the rights of which the movement of centralization first deprives small local societies; they retain for a longer period the rights of administering justice, and establishing police regulations; they may even retain them for a very long while, and England offers us many such examples.

The preponderance of local institutions belongs to the infancy of societies.[3] Civilization incessantly tends to carry power still higher; for power, when exercised from a greater distance, is generally more disinterested, and more capable of taking justice and reason for its sole guides. But frequently also, as it ascends, power forgets its origin and final destiny; it forgets that it was founded to maintain all rights, to respect all liberties; and meeting with no further obstacles from the energy of local liberties, it becomes transformed into despotism. This result is not, however, necessary and fatal; society, while labouring for the centralization of authority, may retain, or regain at a later period, certain principles of liberty. When central institutions have obtained too absolute a prevalence, society begins to perceive the defects inherent in an edifice which is detached, as it were, from the soil on which it stands. Society then constructs upon itself the exact opposite of what it built before; looks narrowly into the private and local interests of which it is composed; duly appreciates their necessities and rights; and, sending back to the different localities the authorities which had been withdrawn therefrom, makes an appropriate distribution of power. When we study the institutions of France, we shall be presented with the greatest and clearest example of this double history. We shall perceive the great French society formed from a multitude of little aggregations, and tending incessantly to the concentration of the different powers contained within it. One great revolution almost entirely destroyed every vestige of our ancient local institutions, and led to the centralization of all power. We now suffer from the excesses of this system; and having returned to just sentiments of practical liberty, we are desirous to restore to localities the life of which they have been deprived, and to resuscitate local institutions, with the concurrence and by the action of the central power itself. Great oscillations like these constitute the social life of humanity, and the history of civilization.

---

3. Guizot emphasized the importance of local institutions as safeguards of individual freedom and argued that, without local (municipal) institutions, there can be no liberties. Moreover, he considered the predominance of the municipal form and spirit to be the most important legacy of the ancient Roman civilization and went as far as to praise the barbarians' keen sense of individual independence (for an extensive discussion of this topic, see *HORG*, pp. 156–60). Nonetheless, Guizot argued that, in the infancy of the European civilization, when the principle of individuality reigned supreme, the local assemblies and institutions did not contain the true principle of representative government, because they were based upon the principle of individual right. In Guizot's view, the progress of civilization also implied a trend toward centralization; it is important to note that the tension between centralization and decentralization was a major theme in Guizot's writings.

LECTURE 4

Local institutions among the Anglo-Saxons. ⁓ Divisions of territory; their origin and double object. ⁓ Internal police of these local associations. ⁓ Importance of the county-courts; their composition and attributes. ⁓ Complex origin of the Jury. ⁓ Central institutions of the Anglo-Saxons. ⁓ The Wittenagemot; its composition, and the principle on which it was based. ⁓ Increasing preponderance of the large landowners in the Anglo-Saxon monarchy.

In my preceding lecture I pointed out the causes of the special importance of local institutions, at that epoch in the development of civilization which now occupies our attention. I now proceed to examine into those institutions.

They were of two kinds. One class bound man to a superior, established a certain right of man over man, a personal pre-eminence and subordination, which were the source of mutual duties. On the Continent, this hierarchy of persons became the first principle of feudalism, which would perhaps have received only a very imperfect development in England, had not William the Conqueror transplanted it to that country in its complete state. The other class of local institutions bound men of equal rank to each other, regulated their mutual relations, and defined their reciprocal rights and duties. The first class marked a relationship of protection and dependence; the second summoned all the inhabitants of the same territory, possessing the same rights and the same obligations, to deliberate in common upon affairs of common interest. These were the predominant institutions of the Anglo-Saxons. Norman feudalism could not entirely abolish them.

At this period, England was divided into tithings, hundreds, and counties. This division has been attributed to King Alfred: he seems to be the founder of all the legislation of this epoch, because it all issues in a fixed and precise form from his reign; but he found it already in existence, and did nothing more than arrange it in a written code. He did not, then, originate this division of territory, which appears to be based upon the ecclesiastical partition of the country. After their settlement in Great Britain, the Saxons did not divide it into systematically determined portions, but adopted what they found already established. The portions of territory which were under the direction of the *decanus*,[1] the *decanus ruralis*,[2] and the bishop, formed respectively the tithing, the hundred, and the county. We must not, however, suppose that these names correspond precisely to realities. The tithings and hundreds were not all equal in extent of soil and number of inhabitants. There were sixty-five hundreds in Sussex, twenty-six in Yorkshire, and six in Lancashire. In the north of England, the hundreds bore another name; they were called *Wapentakes.** Here the ecclesiastical division ceases, and a military circumscription prevailed, which still subsists in some counties. An analogous circumscription has continued to the present day in the Grisons, in Switzerland.

These divisions of the soil had a double object. On the one hand, they formed the most certain means of insuring order and discipline; and on the other hand, they supplied the inhabitants with the most convenient method for transacting their public business in common.

By a police regulation which I have already mentioned, every free individual, above twelve years of age, was obliged to enrol himself in a certain association, which he could not abandon without the permission of the chief. A stranger might not remain for more than two days with a friend, unless his host gave surety for him, and at the end of forty days he was compelled to place himself under the surveillance of some association. It is remarkable that the details of these laws of classification and subordination were almost the same in all those parts of the Roman Empire occupied by the barbarians—in Gaul and Spain, as well as in England. When one of the members of a special association had committed a crime, the association was obliged to bring him to trial. This point has given rise to much discussion among learned men. Some have maintained that the association was bail for its members, not only for their appearance before the court of justice, but also for the crime which they might have committed. I think that every Anglo-Saxon association was bound only to bring the culprit to trial. If he had made his escape, the association had to prove, sometimes by twelve and sometimes by thirty witnesses, that it knew nothing of his whereabouts; and it was fined only when it could not produce witnesses to prove that it had not abetted his escape. This obligation of every local corporation to pay for its guilty and absent members, existed also in Gaul at this

---

* From *wapen*, weapons, and *tac*, a touch, *i.e.* a shaking or striking of the arms; or from the same *wapen*, and *tac*, a taking or receiving of the vassal's arms by a new lord in token of subjection; or because the people, in confirmation of union, touch the weapon of their lord. See Blackstone, Introd., sec. 4. and Holinshed, vol. v. p. 37.

1. Chief.

2. Chief of centuriated land.

time. The Gallic corporation was moreover answerable for the execution of the sentence: I do not think this was the case in England, where it was bound only to bring the culprit to trial.

The second object of this division of the land was to appoint centres of union, where the inhabitants might discuss matters of common interest. In every county, and in every subdivision of a county, the landowners held meetings, at which they deliberated upon the affairs of the local association to which they belonged. Originally, therefore, there existed not only county-courts, but also courts of hundred and courts of tithing, which frequently met. By degrees, as the circle of the interests of these little associations continually tended to become larger, the courts of tithing fell into desuetude. The courts of hundred survived for a longer period, and even now retain some shadow of existence. The Saxons, however, dispersed over the country, and busied with their warlike and agricultural labours, gradually lost the habit of attending these meetings. Having scarcely any written rights to defend, and being seldom disturbed in their dwellings, they lived without anxiety for a liberty which was never called in question. The principal guarantee of the liberty of individuals at that time was their isolation: the active surveillance which it requires, when government exercises a direct and frequent influence upon the governed, would have been to them a useless and fatiguing burden. It devolved upon the kings to compel them, as it were, to keep up their old institutions. Athelstane ordained that the county-courts should meet once in every three months. Few persons attended them, and it became necessary to grant further indulgence. The county-courts were allowed to assemble only twice a year. All holders of land were entitled to attend their meetings. The matters discussed were the internal administration of the county, the maintenance of roads and bridges, the keeping in repair of the forts which the Romans had constructed to defend the country against the invasions of the Picts and Scots, and which were still used for the same purpose. All public business was transacted in the county-court, under the presidency of the *alderman*. At its meetings, military forces were levied, justice was administered, and ecclesiastical affairs were treated of. All public acts, sales, manumissions, wills, were conducted before it, and the publicity of the assembly gave an authentic character to these deeds. Every act, however, was authenticated by a certain number of witnesses, and the deeds were afterwards transcribed and intercalated in the parish Bible.

In these meetings, also, we discern the origin of the *Jury*. When there was a trial to be decided, the alderman sent a number of freemen belonging to the same class as the contending parties, to the place where the dispute had occurred, in order to learn the facts of the case. These men were called *assessors*, and when they returned to the county-court, furnished with the necessary information, they naturally became the judges in the case which they had investigated. The contending parties publicly pleaded their own cause, and were obliged to prove their right by witnesses, *compurgatores*. It has been a question much debated whether the institution of the jury arose from these witnesses, or from the assessors. In my opinion, it was the product of neither exclusively, but of both combined. The establishment of a great institution has nearly always something complex about it. The jury came into existence in some measure spontaneously, from the amalgamation of the different classes of persons who combined to investigate and decide the case. Under the Anglo-Saxon monarchy, it was not a very clearly defined institution. It was not universally in practice, its rules were frequently infringed upon: and Alfred, who was the restorer of the ancient institutions of the country, hanged an alderman who had given judgment without the co-operation of his assessors.

The presidents of these different territorial subdivisions, of the county-courts, the hundred-courts, and the tithing-courts, were at first elected by the landowners. I do not suppose the choice was made by individual votes, but rather by a tacit consent given to the personal influence of certain men. Sometimes, however, to repair long disorders, and destroy the injurious consequences of this influence, the central authority interfered in the appointment of these magistrates. When Alfred had vanquished the Danes, he was desirous to reform the abuses which the troubles of war had introduced into the administration of justice; he assumed the right of choosing the *centenarri*[3] and tithing-men, and this novelty was so far from being considered an usurpation of the rights of the nation, that contemporary historians praise the monarch for having given the people such good magistrates. The systematic conflict of the rulers with the ruled had not yet commenced; the limits of their respective rights and duties were neither fixed nor recognised, and as power was not yet extravagant in its exactions, the people did not feel their rights attacked; necessity, or temporary utility, were the tests which decided the value of a measure. We do not find that the kings who succeeded Alfred retained this right of appointment. Under Edward the Confessor, the county-magistrates were chosen by the landowners. The conquest of William the Norman destroyed, in great measure, these free customs. The alderman, the centenarius, and the tithing-man, disappeared before the feudal lords, or became feudal lords themselves. The assemblies of freemen, however, still retained the right of appointing their respective officers. The sheriff was substituted for the alderman, the centenarius merged in the high-constable, and the petty-constable took the place of the tithing-man. These were the officers of the people,—the municipal officers.

Such is a summary of the local institutions which, under the Anglo-Saxon monarchy, maintained the internal order of the state, and constituted the safe-

3. Men in charge of a hundred.

guards of public liberty. Vigorous institutions were they, which feudalism could not overthrow, and which produced, at a later period, representative government in England, although they did not contain, as you will presently see, the true principle of representative government.

Let us now pass to central institutions. Of these, there were two among the Anglo-Saxons: the national assembly, and the royal office.

Tacitus has described to you the general assemblies of the ancient Germans. At those meetings, nothing was decided without the consent of every freeman. Each individual possessed and exercised his own personal rights and influence. The influence of the chiefs was great. The leaders of their men in war, they became, when their conquest was completed, the principal, indeed almost the sole, landed proprietors, and thus they retained among themselves, although the others were not legally excluded, the practice of forming national assemblies. Each kingdom of the Saxon Heptarchy had its own, and it is probable that the thanes, or landowners, enforced the adoption and execution of the resolutions of this assembly, among the ceorls who dwelt on their estates. When the Heptarchy was combined into a single kingdom, one general assembly alone was established; and as its meetings were held in a central locality, at a great distance from many parts of the realm, the large proprietors were the only persons who were able to attend regularly. This assembly was called the *Wittenagemot,* or the assembly of the wise men. From historical documents, we learn that it was composed of bishops, abbots, abbesses, dukes, and earls; but we also find these words, the vagueness of which has given rise to very different explanations: "such a decision was taken *coram proceribus aliorumque fidelium infinita multitudine.*"[4] Some learned men, who are partisans of absolute power, have inferred from this that it existed at the very origin of society; and they assert that the name of the assembly, *Wittenagemot,* was in itself sufficient to prove that it was composed only of the judges and delegates of the sovereign. Other writers, who are zealous advocates of the rights of the people, have held the opinion that this multitude of persons present were the representatives of the various counties and boroughs. I think that both these systems are false. As regards the first, it is evident that there was no distinct class of judges at this period; public functionaries were not then classified as they are now, and the expression *wise men* would apply equally to all those whose condition raised them above the 'vulgar herd.' With reference to the second system, I must say that no idea of representation was entertained at that period. Whoever was entitled to attend the assembly went thither, and went in person. No proxies were allowed. No one was permitted to enter the assembly in any name but his own. When we come to treat of the principles of representative government, we shall see that the for-

4. Before the leading men and the vast multitude of other confidants.

mation of the ancient Germanic assemblies was based upon the principles of individual right, and of the sovereignty of the multitude—principles from which representative government did not take its origin. Besides, the towns at this period were in so miserable a condition, that it was impossible for them to appoint representatives. York, the second city in England, contained fourteen hundred and eighteen families, and Bath sixty-four. A law of King Athelstane declares that no one entered, or could enter, the assembly, except upon his own account; every proprietor possessing five hides of land, it says, and every merchant who has made three voyages to foreign countries, shall be numbered among the thanes, and be admitted as such into the Wittenagemot. The inequality of conditions, however, continued to increase. Those national assemblies, in which, originally, all freemen were entitled to sit, soon became, as you have seen, restricted to landed proprietors. By-and-bye, as power became centralized, and predominant influences gained greater strength, the small proprietors ceased to use a right which had lost all value to them, and the large landowners remained the undisputed masters of the field. The disproportion between the two classes was so great, that a contest was impossible. As each man sat in his own name, each man brought his own personal influence and private interests with him. The general assembly became an arena for individual disputes. This was the necessary consequence of a principle, which, by summoning all persons to exercise the same right, placed inequalities in that position which was most favourable to the development of their power and egotism. It is the work of a widely different principle to seek out among the masses the persons best fitted to represent them, to send these individuals to the central assembly to provide for the safety of all rights in the name of justice, and thus to prevent the evil consequences which must result from the natural or social inequality of mankind, by creating a factitious, but just, equality among their representatives, which leaves them only the legitimate influence of their talents and character. But the foundation of such a government is the work of ages. Nations, in their infancy, cannot possess it. The Anglo-Saxon monarchy was a continual conflict of individual interests, which was carried on in the Wittenagemot, as well as elsewhere, and its general tendency was to the continually increasing preponderance of large landed property.[5]

---

5. This is the first reference to the "true" principles of representative government, a theme to which Guizot frequently returns in this book. For him, representation was not a mechanism to collect individual wills, but a process by which the fragments of reason disseminated in society are collected and brought (through elections and publicity) to form the government of society. This passage also highlights the centrality of political capacity to Guizot's definition of representative government (power must be granted to the "most capable" citizens). For more details on this issue, see *HORG*, pp. 52–54, 226–27, 295–97, 345–47.

LECTURE 5

The Wittenagemot; its business and power. ⁓ *Method of its convocation.* ⁓ *Vicissitudes of its character and importance.* ⁓ *The kingly office among the Anglo-Saxons.* ⁓ *Extent and progress of the royal power.*

WE have already considered the origin and composition of the Wittenagemot, or general assembly of the Anglo-Saxons, it now remains for us to speak of its attributes and method of convocation.

In the infancy of society, everything is confused and uncertain; there is as yet no fixed and precise line of demarcation between the different powers in a state; and thus we find that the attributes of the Wittenagemot were rather indefinite. There was no settled boundary at which its power ceased, and that of the monarchy commenced; both united to transact all the business of the nation, and, if we would ascertain the part actually taken by the Wittenagemot in this business, we must inquire of history what were its real attributes.

The defence of the kingdom was the chief business of the national assemblies. We must not suppose that the obligation of military service is coeval only with feudalism; independently of every feudal bond, it was an obligation imposed on every freeman in the nation, just as at the present day every French citizen is bound to present himself for conscription. The Wittenagemot ordered levies of the landowners, who, in their turn, convoked the freemen resident on their estates.

The Wittenagemot also imposed taxes; at that period, however, there were hardly any public taxes; the first was levied in consequence of the Danish invasion, and the law which imposed it expressly states that it received the consent of all the members present in the Wittenagemot.

The county-courts, as we have seen, provided for the maintenance of the public roads, bridges, and forts. We learn from the deliberations of the Anglo-Saxon national assembly, that such matters fell under its cognizance also.

As the right of coining money did not belong exclusively to the king, but was also possessed by the church and by many powerful subjects, the Wittenagemot had the oversight of this matter, and prevented the debasement of the coinage.

We also find it ratifying or annulling those acts of county-courts which had reference not to private matters, but to affairs of general importance.

The principle of the responsibility of the agents of power was not more clearly and firmly established in the Anglo-Saxon monarchy than the other great principles of free government; but it was, nevertheless, confusedly practised. A vague feeling of justice pervaded these national assemblies; they repressed great abuses, but frequently punished injustice by injustice.

The Wittenagemot in England possessed a power which was not generally exercised by corresponding assemblies on the Continent; it had the oversight of the royal domain. Originally, the kings lived, like other landowners, on the income derived from their own private estates. Their property was a private domain, which they managed as they pleased. As time rolled on, this domain became very largely augmented by confiscations; but the kings, compelled to defend their tottering authority from the frequent attacks to which it was subjected, were incessantly diminishing their estates by gifts to powerful and formidable chiefs. Frequently, also, when they were strong, they resumed the gifts which necessity had extorted from them. The little reliance to be placed upon these purely royal donations, unless they were ratified by the consent of the national assembly; and the knowledge that, if the king were permitted these forced dilapidations of his own domains, the Wittenagemot would one day be obliged to repair them, and compensate the monarch for the loss of his private estates—were the reasons which led to the interference of the national assembly in the administration of the royal domain. In France, this domain did not fall so soon under the influence of the national assemblies, but remained for a much longer period the private property of the kings.

One of the most important attributes of the Wittenagemot was the direction of ecclesiastical affairs. The abbots and bishops, indeed all the high clergy, were members of this assembly. In France, although the clergy formed a part of the national assemblies, they treated of their own affairs as a separate body, and communicated directly with the king. In England, ecclesiastical matters, like all other business, were discussed in the general assembly. For instance, when missionaries from Rome came to invite the kings of the Heptarchy to embrace the Christian religion, the kings replied that they must ask the consent of the Wittenagemot. In Sweden, the king, who had already become a convert himself, proposed to the assembled Diet to adopt Christianity. The Diet sanctioned the new religion, but retained the old creed, and this simultaneous practice of the two religions lasted for a considerable time. The Wittenagemot had not always to discuss such important matters as the conversion of the nation; it appointed bishops, and ordained or sanctioned the foundation of abbeys and monasteries.[1]

The last business of the Anglo-Saxon national assembly was to receive complaints and petitions in denunciation of abuses. It thus became sometimes a judicial court, adjudicating on the appeals of large landowners; but it seldom appears in this character: it was especially a political assembly, whilst, on the Continent, the national assembly frequently acted as a judicial tribunal.

I have now pointed out the various functions of the Wittenagemot, and you have been able, from the acts of that assembly, to form a tolerably accurate idea of it. As regards its convocation, originally its meetings were frequent, but in order not to fatigue its members too much, it became necessary to reduce the meetings to two, held in spring and autumn, as on the Continent. The right of convoking the Wittenagemot became, ere long, one of the prerogatives of the crown. This abandonment of so important a privilege is very characteristic of an age in which political prudence is unknown, and distrust is manifested only at rare intervals, and then by revolt. It seemed natural that the king, the direct centre of all the interests and necessities of the nation, should convoke the as-

---

1. The comparison between England and France is a major theme in *HORG*. In his *Memoirs,* Guizot explained: "Ce fut à cette époque que je m'adonnai sérieusement a l'étude de l'Angleterre, de ses institutions et des longues luttes qui les ont fondées. Passionnément épris de l'avenir politique de ma patrie, je voulais savoir avec précision à travers quelles vérités et quelles erreurs, par quels efforts persévérants et quelles transactions prudentes un grand peuple avait réussi à conquérir et à conserver un gouvernement libre" (*Mémoires,* Vol. I, Paris: Michel Lévy Frères, 1870, p. 318). Like Madame de Staël and Benjamin Constant, Guizot wanted to understand why England and France had followed two different patterns of development and what had made possible the consolidation of moderate constitutional monarchy across the Channel. In Guizot's view, the key point was to look at the relations and alliances between the monarch, the nobles, and the commons in the two countries. In England, the king could not, as in France, make use of the Commons to annihilate the political rights and privileges of the aristocracy, without substituting new liberties in their place. A portion of the feudal class united with the people in order to defend their liberties against the monarch (Tocqueville developed this idea in *Old Regime and the Revolution*). Guizot admired the division of powers in England, the tradition of self-government, the effective limitation of sovereignty, and the absence of absolute power; for more details, see *HORG*, pp. 89, 221–30, 247, 357–58, 377–81, 433–35. In his *History of Civilization in France,* Guizot argued that "English civilization has been especially directed toward social perfection; toward the amelioration of the external and public condition of men; toward the amelioration, not only of their material but also of their moral condition; toward the introduction of more justice, more prosperity into society; toward the development of right as well as of happiness" (I quote from François Guizot, *Historical Essays and Lectures,* ed. Stanley Mellon, Chicago: University of Chicago Press, 1972, p. 271). For a comprehensive discussion of the image of England in nineteenth-century French political thought, see Pierre Réboul, *Le mythe anglais dans la littérature française sous la Restauration* (*The English Myth in the French Literature During the Restoration*) (Lille: Bibliothèque Universitaire, 1962).

sembly for exigencies with which he was better acquainted than any other person; at his death, the large landowners assembled spontaneously, to deliberate on a change of dynasty or the arrangement of the succession.

The inviolability of the members of the Wittenagemot was recognized from the day on which they set out to attend the assembly, till the day on which they returned home again, provided they were not notorious brigands.

Summing up what I have said, the general assembly of the Anglo-Saxons, as of most of the German nations, was, in Germany, composed of every freeman; after the conquest, it consisted only of the landowners; and, towards the end of the monarchy, it was attended by none but the most wealthy proprietors. Each man came in his own right, and on his own behalf; according to a charter of King Athelstane, he might send a proxy in his place. This irrefragable mark of individual right still exists in England. In the House of Peers, every peer may vote by proxy and in his own name. It is from the Wittenagemot, in this last phase of its existence, and from the rights of suzerainty which Norman feudalism conferred on the king over the great barons, who held their titles directly from him, that the English House of Peers, as it now exists, derives its origin. In the Wittenagemot of the last age of the Anglo-Saxon monarchy, we can discern neither of the two elements which composed the House of Commons at a later period. The towns had hardly any existence, and could not, therefore, send deputies: the counties had never sent any. The Wittenagemot was only an assembly of the powerful men of the state, who came on their own account, and in their own personal right. Most other persons neglected rights which were too difficult for them to exercise, and the real impotence of which they felt; by neglecting to exercise them, they eventually lost them; and when the exigencies of liberty occurred to agitate a more advanced and less contented state of society, a new labour was necessary to restore to the citizens, rights which they had allowed to perish, through the want of necessity and capacity.

The second of the central institutions of the Anglo-Saxons, was the kingly office. An important fact has distinguished the formation of all states of Germanic origin, and this is, the speedy establishment of hereditary monarchy—which was the dominant character of this institution at this period, whatever mixture of election may be discerned therein. The causes of this are simple. In warlike tribes, there is, in war at least, a single chieftain; the man of greatest valour and largest experience, says to his comrades, "Come with me—I will lead you where you may obtain rich booty"; his proposition is accepted, and by common consent he becomes the leader of the expedition. Thus, at the origin of society, power is not conferred; he who is able to do so, assumes it by the consent of the others. There is no election properly so called, but only a recognition of authority. The leader who has conducted one or more fortunate expeditions, obtains great importance by success; his influence increases with time, and he hands down to his family the influence and power which he has acquired. This family, thus invested with an actual superiority, gains a natural habit of command, which the others soon grow accustomed to acknowledge. Among the Germans, moreover, the idea of religious filiation contributed powerfully to the establishment of hereditary monarchy. It was almost a national duty to choose kings from the divine race; and all the royal families were descendants of Odin.[2]

Thus hereditary monarchy prevailed among these peoples; but choice among the members of the royal family long existed. It was indispensably necessary that the king should be a capable man, in a state of society in which men were as yet ignorant of the artificial means which supply the deficiencies of royal incapacity. Thus Alfred himself did not simply found his right to the throne on a will of his father, and an agreement with his brother; but he based it especially upon the consent of all the large proprietors of the kingdom of Wessex. Force sometimes gave severe checks to hereditary right; but the usurpation of the throne was always associated with the idea of the violation of a right, and the usurpers invariably strove to atone for this violation, by marriage with one of the legitimate race.

The kings, under the Anglo-Saxon monarchy, were at first called *Heretogs*, leaders of armies; but it is a mistake to explain and limit their prerogatives by the name which they bore. The power of arms was then so great, and all other powers seemed so inferior and subject to it, that they all fell under the generic term which contained within itself nearly every idea of force and empire. The most different powers were embraced under this single denomination, and we must not suppose that the kings limited their functions to those which it seems to indicate; the Anglo-Saxon kings were not merely military leaders; they managed all the internal administration of the realm, in concert with the Wittenagemot. Their attributes were not more determinate than those of that assembly. With it, they directed all the affairs of the nation; and their surveillance, being perpetual, was more close and active. They were addressed as the highest authority, and also as possessing the most information on public affairs. Thus the right of presiding over the general assemblies and proposing the subjects for deliberation, belonged exclusively to them.

The royal authority, however, not being sustained by a strong and regular

2. In Guizot's view, power and excellence (i.e., exquisite talent, qualities, and abilities) were connected; power had always been granted to "the most brave and courageous ones," and had never been based on a social contract among equals. Note that Guizot did not equate superior force with superior virtue; he only claimed that, in virtue of a natural law *sui generis*, the most assertive and brave individuals had always managed to impose their will and extend their domination. Guizot developed this idea in *Des moyens de gouvernment et d'opposition dans l'état actuel de la France* (*On the Means of Government and Opposition in the Actual State of France*) (Paris: Ladvocat, 1821), pp. 163–64.

organization, decreased in power in proportion as the great proprietors increased in influence and became firmly established in their domains. Towards the end of the Anglo-Saxon monarchy, the large landowners, sole masters on their own estates, began to do everything by themselves. They coined money, administered justice, and levied soldiers. And we must not imagine that this assumption of sovereign rights by local chieftains was regarded, by the people, as an act of iniquity and violence: it was a necessity of the social condition of the country. Royalty was no more capable of wielding all the central power, than the nation was of maintaining and exercising all its liberties.

LECTURE 6

The true principle of representative government. ⁓ *Error of classifying governments according to their external forms.* ⁓ *Montesquieu's error with respect to the origin of the representative system.* ⁓ *Necessary correlation and simultaneous formation of society and government.* ⁓ *Rousseau's mistaken hypothesis of the social contract.* ⁓ *The nature of rightful sovereignty.* ⁓ *Confused and contradictory ideas entertained on this subject.* ⁓ *Societies, as individuals, possess the right of being placed under laws of justice and reason.* ⁓ *Governments ought to be continually reminded of their obligation to inquire into and conform to these laws.* ⁓ *Classification of governments on this principle.*

I PROPOSE to examine the political institutions of modern Europe in their early infancy, and to seek what they have in common with the representative system of government. My object will be to learn whether this form of government had then attained to any degree of development, or even existed only in germ; at what times, and in what places it first appeared, where and under what circumstances it prospered or failed. I have just examined the primitive institutions of the Anglo-Saxons. Before leaving our consideration of England, it might be well for me to compare these institutions with the essential type of representative government, in order to see how they agree and in what they differ. But this type is not yet in our possession. In order to find it I shall revert to the essential principle of representative government, to the original ideas out of which it springs; and I shall compare this idea with the fundamental idea that underlies Anglo-Saxon institutions.

The human mind is naturally led to judge of the nature of things, and to classify them according to their exterior forms; accordingly, governments have almost invariably been arranged according to distinctions which do not at all belong to their inherent character. Wherever none of those positive institutions have been immediately recognized which according to our present notions, represent and guarantee political liberty, it has been thought that no liberty could exist, and that power must be absolute. But in human affairs, various elements are mingled: nothing exists in a simple and pure state. As some traces of absolute power are to be found at the basis of free governments, so also some liberty has existed under governments to all appearance founded on absolutism. No form of society is completely devoid of reason and justice—for were all reason and justice to be withdrawn, society would perish. We may sometimes see governments of apparently the most opposite character produce the same effects. During the seventeenth and eighteenth centuries, representative government raised England to the highest elevation of moral and material prosperity; and France, during that same period, increased in splendour, wealth, and enlightenment, under an absolute monarchy. I do not intend by this to insinuate the impression that forms of government are unimportant, and that all produce results of equal quality and value; I merely wish to hint that we should not appreciate them by only a few of their results, or by their exterior indications. In order fully to appreciate a government, we must penetrate into its essential and constituent principles. We shall then perceive that many governments which differ considerably in their forms, are referable to the same principles; and that others which appear to resemble one another in their forms, are in fundamental respects different. Wherever elections and assemblies have presented themselves to view, it has been thought that the elements of a representative system were to be found. Montesquieu, looking at representative government in England, endeavoured to trace it back to the old Germanic institutions. "This noble system," he says, "originated in the woods." Appearances deceived Montesquieu; he merely took into consideration the exterior characteristics of representative government, not its true principles and its true tendencies. That is a superficial and false method which classifies governments according to their exterior characteristics; making monarchy, government by one individual; aristocracy, government by several; democracy, government by the people, the sovereignty of all. This classification, which is based only upon one particular fact, and upon a certain material shape which power assumes, does not go to the heart of those questions, or rather of that question, by the solution of which the nature and tendency of governments is determined. This question is, "What is the source of the sovereign power, and what is its limit? Whence does it come, and where does it stop?" In the answer to this question is involved the real principle of government; for it is this principle whose influence, direct or indirect, latent or obvious, gives to societies their tendency and their fate.[1]

---

1. Guizot's critique of Montesquieu's classification of governments must be understood in relation to his theory of the sovereignty of reason. For Guizot, the key issue was not who exercises power, but the source and limitations of the sovereign power; he also argued that it would be a mistake to concentrate on the exterior characteristics of representative government. The upshot of his view is that no individual or group can ever be granted the possession of an inherent right

Where are we to look for this principle? Is it a mere conventional arrangement by man? Is its existence anterior to that of society?

The two facts—society and government—mutually imply one another; society without government is no more possible than government without society. The very idea of society necessarily implies that of rule, of universal law, that is to say, of government.

What then is the first social law? I hasten to pronounce it: it is justice, reason, a rule of which every man has the germ within his own breast. If man only yields to a superior force, he does not truly submit to the law; there is no society and no government. If in his dealings with his fellows, man obeys not only force, but also a law, then society and government exist. In the abnegation of force, and obedience to law, consists the fundamental principle of society and government. In the absence of these two conditions, neither society nor government can be properly said to exist.

This necessary coexistence of society and government shows the absurdity of the hypothesis of the social contract. Rousseau presents us with the picture of men already united together into a society, but without rule, and exerting themselves to create one; as if society did not itself presuppose the existence of a rule to which it was indebted for its existence. If there is no rule, there is no society; there are only individuals united and kept together by force. This hypothesis then, of a primitive contract, as the only legitimate source of social law, rests upon an assumption that is necessarily false and impossible.

The opposite hypothesis, which places the origin of society in the family and in the right of the father over his children, is less objectionable, but it is incomplete. There is, certainly, a form of society among parents and their rising offspring; but it is a society in some sort unilateral, and of which one of the parties has not any true consciousness. Society, whether in the family or out of the family, is only complete when all its members, those who command as well as those who obey, recognize, more or less vaguely, a certain superior rule, which is neither the arbitrary caprice of will, nor the effect of force alone. The idea of society, therefore, implies necessarily another idea, that of government; and the idea of government contains in it two others, the idea of a collection of individuals, and that of a rule which is applicable to them,—a rule which constitutes

---

to sovereignty. Hence, Guizot proposed a new classification of governments depending on whether they attribute sovereignty as a right to individuals or to reason, truth, and justice. Only those forms of government that recognize the sovereignty of reason, truth, and justice can be said to be legitimate. For more details on the new classification proposed by Guizot, see *HORG*, pp. 52, 64–65. In Guizot's view, representative government was predicated on the assumption that sovereignty does not reside in any person, and that all powers must be directed to the fulfillment of the precepts of reason, truth, and justice.

the right of the government itself; a rule which the individuals who submit to it have not themselves created, and to which they are morally bound to submit. No government ever totally disregarded this supreme rule, none ever proclaimed force or caprice as the only law of society. In seeking the principle of government, we have found the principle of social right to be the primary source of all legitimate sovereignty. In this law of laws, in this rule of all government, resides the principle of government.

Two important questions now present themselves. How is the law formed, and how is it applied? In this lies the distinctive character of the various forms of government; in this they differ.

Even until modern times, the belief has prevailed that the primitive and absolute right of law-making, that is, the right of sovereignty, resides in some portion of society, whether this right be vested in a single man, in several, or in all;—an opinion which has been constantly contradicted by facts, and which cannot bear the test of reason. The right of determining and enforcing a rule, is the right to absolute power; that force which possesses this right inherently, possesses absolute power, that is to say, the right of tyranny. Take the three great forms of government, monarchy, aristocracy, and democracy, and see if a case can be found in which the right of sovereignty was held by one, by several or by all, in which tyranny did not necessarily arise. Facts have been logically correct,—they have inferred from the principle its necessary consequence.

Such, however, is the force of truth, that this error could not reign alone and absolutely. At the very time when men appeared to believe, and did theoretically believe, that the primitive and absolute power of giving law belonged to some one, whether monarch, senate, or people, at the same time they struggled against that principle. At all times men have endeavoured to limit the power which they regarded as perfectly legitimate. Never has a force, although invested with the right of sovereignty, been allowed to develop that right to its full extent. The janissaries in Turkey sometimes served, sometimes abrogated, the absolute power of the Sultan. In democracies, where the right of sovereignty is vested in popular assemblies, efforts have been continually made to oppose conditions, obstacles, and limits to that sovereignty. Always, in all governments which are absolute in principle, some kind of protest has been made against the principle. Whence comes this universal protest? We might, looking merely at the surface of things, be tempted to say that it is only a struggle of powers. This has existed without doubt, but another and a grander element has existed along with it; there is an instinctive sense of justice and reason dwelling in every human spirit. Tyranny has been opposed, whether it were the tyranny of individuals or of multitudes, not only by a consciousness of power, but by a sentiment of right. It is this consciousness of justice and right, that is to say, of a rule independent of human will—a consciousness often obscure but always powerful—which, sooner or later, rouses and assists men to resist all tyranny, whatever may be its name and form. The voice of humanity, then, has proclaimed that the right of sovereignty vested in men, whether in one, in many, or in all, is an iniquitous lie.

If, then, the right of sovereignty cannot be vested in any one man, or collection of men, where does it reside, and what is the principle on which it rests?

In his interior life—in his dealings with himself, if I may be allowed the expression, as well as in his exterior life, and in his dealings with his fellows—the man who feels himself free and capable of action, has ever a glimpse of a natural law by which his action is regulated. He recognises a something which is not his own will, and which must regulate his will. He feels himself bound by reason or morality to do certain things; he sees, or he feels that there are certain things which he ought or ought not to do. This something is the law which is superior to man, and made for him—the divine law. The true law of man is not the work of man; he receives, but does not create it; even when he submits to it, it is not his own—it is beyond and above him.

Man does not always submit; in the exercise of his free will and imperfect nature, he does not invariably obey this law. He is influenced by other principles of action than this, and although he perceives that the motives which impel him are vicious, nevertheless he often yields to them. But whether he obey or not, the supreme law for man is always existent—in his wildest dreams he recognises it, as placed above him.

We see, then, the individual always in presence of a law,—one which he did not create, but which asserts its claim over him, and never abandons him. If he enters into society with his fellows, or finds himself thus associated, what other rule than this will he possess? Should human society involve an abdication of human nature? No; man in society must and does remain essentially the same as in his individual capacity; and as society is nothing but a collection of individuals, the supreme law of society must be the same as that which exercises a rightful control over individuals themselves.

Here, then, have we discovered the true law of society—the law of government—it is the same law as that which binds individuals. And as, for an individual, the true law is often obscure, and as the individual, even when he knows it thoroughly, does not always follow it implicitly; in the same manner with regard to government, whatever it may be, its true law—which must ever reach it through the medium of the human mind, which is ever biassed by passion and limited by frailty—is neither at all times apprehended nor always obeyed. It is then impossible to attribute to one man or to several the possession of an inherent right to sovereignty, since this would be to suppose that their ideas and inclinations were in all cases correspondent to the dictates of justice and of reason—a supposition which the radical imperfection of our nature will not allow us for a moment to admit.

It is, however, owing to the same imperfection that men have accepted, or rather created for themselves, idols and tyrants. A law ready made for them has appeared more convenient than that laborious and unremitting search after reason and justice which they felt themselves obliged to undertake by the imperious voice of that conscience which they could not entirely silence. Nevertheless, men have never been able entirely to deceive their conscience, or to stifle its utterances. Conscience defeats all the arrangements of human ignorance or indifference, and forces men to fight for themselves despite their own unwillingness. Never, in fact, have men fully accepted the sovereignty, the right of which they have admitted; and the impossibility of their thus consenting to it, plainly indicates the superhuman principle which sovereignty involves. In this principle we must seek for the true distinction between governments.

The classification which I am about to present is not, then, one that is merely arbitrary and factitious; it does not concern the exterior forms, but the essential nature of governments. I distinguish two kinds. First, there are those which attribute sovereignty as a right belonging exclusively to individuals, whether one, many, or all those composing a society; and these are, in principle, the founders of despotism, although facts always protest more or less strongly against the principle; and absolute obedience on the one hand, and absolute power on the other, never exist in full vigour. The second class of governments is founded on the truth that sovereignty belongs as a right to no individual whatever, since the perfect and continued apprehension, the fixed and inviolable application of justice and of reason, do not belong to our imperfect nature.

Representative government rests upon this truth. I do not say that it has been founded upon the full reflective acknowledgment of the principle in the form in which I have stated it. Governments do not, any more than great poems, form themselves on an *a priori* model, and in accordance with defined precepts. What I affirm is, that representative government does not attribute sovereignty as inherently residing in any person,—that all its powers are directed to the discovery and faithful fulfilment of that rule which ought ever to govern their action, and that the right of sovereignty is only recognised on the condition that it should be continually justified.

Pascal has said, "Plurality which does not reduce itself to unity, is confusion. Unity which is not the result of plurality, is tyranny." This is the happiest expression and the most exact definition of representative government. The plurality is society; the unity is truth, is the united force of the laws of justice and reason, which ought to govern society. If society remains in the condition of plurality, if isolated wills do not combine under the guidance of common rules, if they do not all equally recognise justice and reason, if they do not reduce themselves to unity, there is no society, there is only confusion. And the unity which does not arise from plurality, which has been violently imposed upon it by one or many, whatever may be their number, in virtue of a prerogative which they appropriate as their exclusive possession, is a false and arbitrary unity; it is tyranny. The aim of representative government is to oppose a barrier at once to tyranny and to confusion, and to bring plurality to unity by presenting itself for its recognition and acceptance.[2]

Let us now see, in the central fact of this method of government, by what means it arrives at its end, and under what forms its principle is developed.

Representative government, wherever it has existed or does exist, is composed of different elements of power, equal among themselves, although one of them, the monarchical or the democratic, ordinarily retains certain peculiar rights. The number and form of these powers are not necessarily determinate or equal; in France, at the present time, there are three, the royal power, the House of Peers, and the Chamber of Deputies. These three powers emanate from different sources, and result from different social necessities. Neither of them, isolated from the rest, possesses a right of sovereignty: it is required of them that they seek the legitimate rule in common, and they are supposed to possess it only when they have found it in a united deliberation, before or after action. Society owes submission to this rule, thus discovered; but as these powers are not all fixed and immutable, so the sovereignty of right does not reside constantly among them. The elective principle, which is by its very nature changeful, can alter its idea and purpose, and exercise upon the other powers an influence that is periodically variable. If the different powers do not agree, they reduce themselves immediately to inaction. The sovereignty which exists in its own right then seems to hesitate to show itself, and government remains in suspense. In order to extricate it from this state, the right has been reserved to royalty of creating peers, and of dissolving the Chamber of Deputies. The powers then proceed afresh to seek for the true law, a work in which they ought not to rest until they have found it. Thus, no power is judged to possess fully the legitimate rule, which is rightfully the principle of sovereignty. The electors themselves are not its absolute interpreters, any more

2. This is another important passage in which Guizot discusses the goal of representative government; in his view, representative institutions must create social unity, preserve liberty, and raise a barrier to tyranny (absolute power) and anarchy. Borrowing a famous aphorism from Pascal, Guizot argues that representative government should be seen as a means of bringing multiplicity to unity and preventing the formation of a fallacious unity (which is not a genuine expression of multiplicity). Moreover, the very principle of representative government is "the destruction of all sovereignty of permanent right" (*HORG*, p. 371). In Guizot's view, publicity plays a key role in helping representative institutions to draw forth from the bosom of society the "veritable and legitimate aristocracy" in order to constitute the government of society. Writes Guizot: "This end is only attained by the triumph of the true majority—the minority being constantly listened to with respect. If the majority is displaced by artifice, there is falsity. If the minority is removed from the struggle beforehand, there is oppression. In either case representative government is corrupted" (*ibid.*, p. 348). For more details, see *ibid.*, pp. 54, 57, 345–48, 371–72.

than are the peers, the deputies, or the king. The electors do not say at the outset to their deputies, "Such is our will: let that be the law." They enjoin upon them nothing precise; they simply confer upon them the mission of examining and deciding according to their reason. They must necessarily trust in the enlightenment of those whom they elect; election is a trial imposed on those who aspire to political power, and a sovereign but limited right exercised by those who confer political power upon such of the claimants as they may select.

From the political powers thus attributed to certain classes, let us now pass to the political rights which are vaguely distributed in the nation. These rights are among the essential conditions of representative government. The publicity of the debates in the deliberative assemblies imposes upon these powers the necessity of commending themselves to that sense of reason and justice which belongs to all, in order that every citizen may be convinced that their inquiries have been made with fidelity and intelligence, and that, knowing wherein they are deficient, he may himself have the opportunity, if he has the capacity, to indicate the remedy. Liberty opens up a career for this inquiry. In this way, every citizen may aid in the discovery of the true law. Thus does a representative government impel the whole body of society—those who exercise power, and those who possess rights—to enter upon a common search after reason and justice; it invites the multitude to reduce itself to unity, and it brings forth unity from the midst of plurality. The public powers—royalty, the deliberative houses, the electors—are bound and incessantly made to return to this work, by the essential nature of their relations, and by the laws of their action. Private citizens even can cooperate, by virtue of the publicity of the debates, and the liberty of the press.[3]

---

3. In Guizot's view, publicity is the cornerstone of representative government because it creates new bonds between society and government. Publicity requires and calls upon all individuals who possess rights to enter upon a common search for reason, truth, and justice. Liberty of the press and the openness of debates in deliberative assemblies are instrumental in limiting political power and preventing the usurpation of the sovereignty of right. It is publicity that places the executive and legislative powers under the control of the citizens, while freedom of the press prompts them to seek reason, truth, and justice in common. Guizot argues that because of publicity and freedom of the press, power is no longer opaque for society, as more transparency and new forms of communication are created between government and society. As to the relation between publicity and elections, Guizot believed that publicity cannot be a substitute for elections and that, without publicity, there can be no true elections. "Où la publicité manque," he wrote, "il peut y avoir des élections, des assemblées, des délibérations; mais les peuples n'y croient pas et ils ont raison. . . . La publicité seule corrige, en grande partie, les fâcheux effets d'une mauvaise machine politique" (Guizot, "Des garanties légales de la liberté de la presse" [On Legal Guarantees for Freedom of the Press], *Archives Philosophiques, Politique, et Littéraires*, Vol. V, Paris: 1818, pp. 186–87). For more details on publicity, see Guizot, *HORG*, pp. 62–63, 69–70, and Aurelian Craiutu, *The Difficult Apprenticeship of Liberty: Reflections on the Political Thought of the French Doctrinaires.* (Lanham, Md.: Rowman & Littlefield, Lexington Books, forthcoming).

I might pursue this idea, and show that all the institutions which are re-garded as inherent in representative government, even those which have not been regarded as assisting in the search for those general rules which ought to preside in the conduct of government, are derived from the same principle, and tend to the same result. The publicity of judicial proceedings, and those who compose the jury, for example, supply a guarantee for the legitimate application of the law to particular cases. But our present concern is especially to determine the principle of those essential combinations by which a representative govern-ment is constituted; they all proceed evidently from this fact, that no individual is fully acquainted with and invariably consents to that reason, truth and justice, which can alone confer the right of sovereignty, and which ought to be the rule of sovereignty as actually exercised. They compel all powers to seek for this rule, and give to all citizens the right of assisting in this research, by taking cog-nizance of the mode in which the powers proceed to it, and in declaring them-selves what they conceive to be the dictates of justice and of truth. In other words, to sum up what I have said, representative government rests in reality upon the following series of ideas. All power which exists as a fact, must, in or-der to become a right, act according to reason, justice, and truth, the sole sources of right. No man, and no body of men, can know and perform fully all that is required by reason, justice, and truth; but they have the faculty to discover it, and can be brought more and more to conform to it in their conduct. All the combinations of the political machine then ought to tend, on the one hand, to extract whatever of reason, justice, or truth, exists in society, in order to apply it to the practical requirements of government; and, on the other hand, to pro-mote the progress of society in reason, justice, and truth, and constantly to em-body this progress of society in the actual structure of the government.

LECTURE 7

Comparison of the principles of different governments with the true principle of representative government. ~ Aristocratic governments. ~ Origin and history of the word aristocracy. ~ Principle of this form of government; its consequences. ~ How the principle of representative government enters into aristocratic governments. ~ Democratic governments. ~ Origin and consequences of the principle of the sovereignty of the people. ~ This principle is not identical with that of representative government. ~ In what sense representative government is the government of the majority.

I HAVE, in my previous lecture, shown the error of those superficial classifications which only distinguish governments according to their exterior characteristics; I have recognised and separated with precision between the two opposite principles, which are, both of them, the basis of all government; I have identified representative government with one of these principles; I have proved that it could not be deduced from the other; I wish now to compare the principle of representative government with the contrary principle, and to show the opposite condition of governments which refer to it as their starting-point. I will begin by an examination of that form of government which is usually termed *aristocratic*.

There is a close connexion between the progressive changes that may be observed in language and those that belong to society. The word *aristocracy* originally signified the empire of the strong; Ἄρης, ἀρείων, ἄριστος, were, at first, terms applied to those who were physically the most powerful; then they were used to designate the most influential, the richest, and finally the best, those possessing the most ability or virtue. This is the history of the successive acceptations of the word in the language from which it is borrowed; the same terms which were first applied to force, the superiority of force, came at length to designate moral and intellectual superiority—virtue.

Nothing can better characterise than this the progress of society, which begins with the predominance of force, and tends to pass under the empire of moral and intellectual superiority. The desire and tendency of society are in fact towards being governed by the best, by those who most thoroughly know and most heartily respond to the teachings of truth and justice; in this sense, all good governments, and pre-eminently the representative form of government, have for their object to draw forth from the bosom of society that veritable and legitimate aristocracy, by which it has a right to be governed, and which has a right to govern it.

But such has not been the historical signification of the word *aristocracy*. If we take the word according as facts have interpreted it, we shall find its meaning to be, a government in which the sovereign power is placed at the disposal of a particular class of citizens, who are hereditarily invested with it, their only qualification being a certain descent, in a manner more or less exclusive, and sometimes almost completely exclusive.

I do not inquire whence this system of government has derived its origin; how, in the infancy of society, it has sprung almost invariably from the moral superiority of its first founders; how force, which was originally due to moral superiority, was afterwards perpetuated by itself, and became a usurper; these questions, which possess the highest interest, would carry me away from my main point. I am seeking for the fundamental principle of aristocratic government, and I believe it can be summed up in the following terms; the right of sovereignty, attributed in a manner if not entirely exclusive, yet especially and chiefly to a certain class of citizens, whose only claim is that of descent in a certain line.

This principle is no other than that of the sovereignty of the people confined to a small number of individuals,—to a minority. In both cases, the right to sovereignty is derived, not from any presumed capacity to fulfil certain conditions, nor from intellectual and moral superiority proved in any particular manner, but from the solitary fact of birth, without any condition. In the aristocratic system, an individual is born to a position of sovereignty merely because he has been born into a privileged class; according to the democratic system, an individual is born to a position of sovereignty by the circumstance that he is born into humanity. The participation in sovereignty is in each case the result of a purely material fact, independent of the worth of him who possesses it, and of the judgment of those over whom it is to be exercised. It follows evidently from this, that aristocratic governments are to be classed among those which rest on the idea that the right of sovereignty exists, full and entire, somewhere on the earth—an idea directly contrary, as we have seen, to the principle of representative government.

If we look at the consequences of this idea—such consequences as have actually manifested themselves in the history of governments of this kind—we shall see that they are not less contrary to the consequences, historical as well as natural, of a representative government.

In order to maintain the right of sovereignty in the class to which it is exclusively attributed, it must necessarily establish a great inequality in fact, as well as in opinion, between this class and the rest of the citizens. Hence arise all those institutions and laws which characterise aristocratic governments, and which have for their object to concentrate, into the hands of the sole possessors of the sovereignty, all wealth and enlightenment, and all the various instruments of power. It is necessary that the sovereign class should not descend, and that others should not be elevated; otherwise actual power ceasing to approximate to rightful power, the legitimacy of the latter would soon be questioned, and, after a short time, its continuance endangered.

In the system of those governments which attribute to no individual upon earth a right of sovereignty, and which impose on the existing government the necessity of seeking continually for truth, reason, and justice, as the rule and source of rightful power, all classes of society are perpetually invited and urged to elevate and perfect themselves. Legitimate forms of supremacy are produced, and assume their position; illegitimate forms are unmasked and deposed. Factitious and violent inequalities are resisted and exhibited in their true colours; social forces are, so to speak, brought into competition, and the forces which struggle to possess them are moral.

A second consequence of the principle of aristocratic governments is their avoidance of publicity. When each one of those who participate in the rightful sovereignty possesses it by the mere accident of birth, and exercises it on his own individual responsibility, he need not recognise any one as claiming a right to call him to account. No one has any right to inquire into the use which he makes of his power, for he acts in virtue of a right which no one can contest, because no one can deprive him of it. It is a right which needs not to justify itself, since it is connected with a fact that is palpable and permanent.

In the other system, on the contrary, publicity follows necessarily from the principle of government; for since the right to power is derived from superiority in the knowledge and practice of reason, truth, and justice, which no one is supposed to possess fully and at all times, it is imperative that this right should justify itself both before it is assumed and all the time that it is exercised.

It would be easy thus, proceeding continually within view of real facts, to compare the different consequences of the principle of purely aristocratic governments and those resulting from the principle of representative government, and to show that they are always opposed to one another. We should thereby demonstrate most completely the opposition of the principles themselves, and bring their true nature into clearer light; but I have already said enough on this point. And if any one asserts that I have too rigorously insisted upon inferences to be drawn from the principle of aristocratic governments, that the consequences which I have depicted do never fulfil themselves in so complete a manner, that, for example, the qualification of birth has never held exclusive possession of a right to sovereignty, that never has publicity been entirely quenched—I freely concede all this. At no time, in no place, has evil been allowed to gain exclusive possession of society and government; struggle between principles of good and evil is the permanent condition of the world. False ideas may achieve a more or less extended, a more or less durable success—they can never extirpate their godlike assailants. Truth is patient—it does not easily surrender its hold on society—it never abandons its purpose—it even exercises some sway over that region where error reigns most despotically. Providence never permits bad governments to become so bad as is logically demanded by the principle upon which they rest. So we have seen institutions of justice and liberty existing and even gaining a powerful existence, in the midst of societies ruled by the principle of hereditary right; these institutions have battled against the principle, and have modified it. When the worse principle has prevailed, then have society and government fallen into impotence and decay; this is the history of the Venetian republic. Elsewhere, the struggle has been attended with happier results: the good principle has possessed sufficient force to be able to introduce into the government elements, which have made it vital, which have protected society against the effects of the evil principle, which have even in some sort saved the evil itself, rendering it tolerable by the good with which it is associated. This is the history of England, that striking example of the mixture and struggle of good and evil principles. But their mixture, however intimate it may be, does not prove that they are confounded in their interior character. Good never springs from evil; and representative government has not sprung in England, any more than elsewhere, from the exclusive principle of aristocratic governments; it has sprung from an entirely different principle; and so far from the distinction which I established at the commencement being compromised by the facts to which I have alluded, it is on the other hand triumphantly confirmed by them.

I have just proved, by a comparison between the principle of the aristocratic and that of the democratic form of government, that they are essentially different; I intend now to show that there is as fundamental a difference between the principle of representative government, and that of democratic government.[1]

1. The difference between the principle of representative government and political democracy is another key idea in Guizot's political thought. It will be recalled that Guizot welcomed democracy as a social condition while also arguing for *limited* franchise. This ambivalent attitude toward democracy was widely shared by nineteenth-century liberals. Haunted by the specter of the darkest episodes of the Revolution, Guizot feared the potentially destructive elements of democracy. Nonetheless, he defended civil equality and civil rights, which he considered to be fundamental principles of the new social order. Furthermore, the distinction between representative govern-

No one has ever understood the sovereignty of the people to mean, that after having consulted all opinions and all wills, the opinion and will of the greatest number constitutes the law, but that the minority would be free to disobey that which had been decided in opposition to its opinion and will. And yet this would be the necessary consequence of the pretended right attributed to each individual of being governed only by such laws as have received his individual assent. The absurdity of this consequence has not always induced its adherents to abandon the principle, but it has always obliged them to violate it. The sovereignty of the people is contradicted at the outset, by its being resolved into the empire of the majority over the minority. It is almost ridiculous to say that the minority may retire from the majority; this would be to keep society continually on the brink of dissolution. On every question the majority and the minority would disagree, and if all the successive minorities should retire, society would very soon exist no longer. The sovereignty of the people then must necessarily be reduced to the sovereignty of the majority only. When thus reduced, what does it amount to?

Its principle is, that the majority possesses right by the mere circumstance of its being the majority. But two very different ideas are included in the one expression—the majority; the idea of an opinion which is accredited, and that of a force which is preponderant. So far as force is concerned, the majority possesses no right different from that possessed by force itself, which cannot be, upon this ground alone, the legitimate sovereignty. As to the expression of opinion, is the majority infallible?—does it always apprehend and respect the claims of reason and justice, which alone constitute true law, and confer legitimate sovereignty? Experience testifies to the contrary. The majority, by mere fact of its being a majority, that is to say, by the mere force of numbers, does not then possess legitimate sovereignty, either by virtue of power, which never does confer it, nor by virtue of infallibility, which it does not possess.

The principle of the sovereignty of the people starts from the supposition that each man possesses as his birthright, not merely an equal right of being governed, but an equal right of governing others. Like aristocratic governments, it connects the right to govern, not with capacity, but with birth. Aris-

---

ment and political democracy must be related to another important dichotomy in Guizot's political philosophy between the sovereignty of reason and popular sovereignty. Unlike political democracy, representative government grants power and political rights only in proportion to the capacity of individuals to act according to reason and justice. Therefore, representative government is not purely and simply the government of the numerical majority, but the "government by the majority of those who are qualified to govern" (*HORG*, p. 62). For another important statement on political democracy, also see Guizot, "De la démocratie dans les sociétés modernes," *Revue française*, Vol. III, 1837, pp. 139–225.

tocratic government is the sovereignty of the people in the minority; the sovereignty of the people is aristocratic despotism and privilege in the hands of the majority. In both cases, the principle is the same; a principle contrary, in the first place, to the fact of the inequality established by nature, between the powers and capacities of different individuals; secondly, to the fact of the inequality in capacity, occasioned by difference of position, a difference which exists everywhere, and which has its source in the natural inequality of men; thirdly, to the experience of the world, which has always seen the timid following the brave, the incompetent obeying the competent,—in one word, those who are naturally inferior recognising and submitting themselves to their natural superiors. The principle of the sovereignty of the people, that is to say, the equal right of all individuals to exercise sovereignty, or merely the right of all individuals to concur in the exercise of sovereignty, is then radically false; for, under the pretext of maintaining legitimate equality, it violently introduces equality where none exists, and pays no regard to legitimate inequality. The consequences of this principle are the despotism of number, the domination of inferiorities over superiorities, that is, a tyranny of all others the most violent and unjust.

At the same time, it is of all others the most transient, for the principle is impossible of application. After its force has spent itself in excesses, number necessarily submits to capacity—the inferior retire to make room for the superior—these enter again into possession of their right, and society is re-established.

Such cannot be the principle of representative government. No one disputes that the true law of government is that of reason, truth, and justice, which no one possesses but which certain men are more capable than others of seeking and discovering. Faithful to this aim, representative government rests upon the disposition of actual power in proportion to the capacity to act according to reason and justice, from whence power derives its right. It is the principle which, by the admission of all, and by virtue of its simple appeal to the common sense of the community, is applicable to ordinary life, and to the interest of individuals themselves. It is the principle which confers the sovereignty over persons, families, property, only to the individual who is presumed to be capable of using it reasonably, and which withdraws it from him who is seen to be positively incapable. Representative government applies to general interests, and to the government of society, the same principle which the good sense of the human race has led it to apply to individual interests and to the control of each man's private life. It distributes sovereignty according to the capacity required for it, that is to say, it only places actual power, or any portion of actual power, where it has discovered the presence of rightful power, presumed to exist by certain symptoms, or tested by certain proofs. It is remembered, that power though legitimate is not to be conceded fully and completely to any one, and not only is it not attributed to the mere fact of birth, but it cannot be allowed to remain by itself in irresponsible isolation, which is the second characteristic of representative government, by which, not less than by the preceding, it is distinguished from the sovereignty of the people.

It has been often said, that representative government is the government of the majority, and there is some truth in the assertion; but it must not be thought that this government of the majority is the same as that involved in the sovereignty of the people. The principle of the sovereignty of the people applies to all individuals, merely because they exist, without demanding of them anything more. Thus, it takes the majority of these individuals, and says—Here is reason, here is law. Representative government proceeds in another way: it considers what is the kind of action to which individuals are called; it examines into the amount of capacity requisite for this action; it then summons those individuals who are supposed to possess this capacity—all such, and such only. Then it seeks for a majority among those who are capable.

It is in this way, in fact, that men have everywhere proceeded, even when they have been supposed to act according to the idea of the sovereignty of the people. Never have they been entirely faithful to it; they have always demanded for political actions certain conditions, that is to say, indications of a certain capacity. They have been mistaken, more or less, and have excluded the capable, or invited the inefficient, and the error is a serious one. But they have followed the principle which measures right by capacity, even when they have professed the principle that right is derived from the simple fact of possessing a human nature. Representative government, then, is not purely and simply the government of the numerical majority, it is government by the majority of those who are qualified to govern; sometimes assuming the existence of the qualification beforehand, sometimes requiring that it should be proved and exemplified. The peerage, the right to elect and to be elected, the royal power itself, are attached to a capacity presumed to exist, not only after certain conditions have been complied with, but by reason of the position occupied by those men in whom the capacity is presumed, in their relations to other powers, and in the limits of the functions assigned to them. No one is recognised as possessing an inherent right to an office or a function. Nor is this all; representative government does not content itself with demanding capacity before it confers power; as soon as the capacity is presumed or proved, it is placed in a position where it is open to a kind of legal suspicion, and where it must necessarily continue to legitimatize itself, in order to retain its power. According to the principle of the sovereignty of the people, absolute right resides with the majority; true sovereignty exists wherever this force is manifested; from this follows necessarily the oppression of the minority, and such has, in fact, generally been the result. The representative form of government, never forgetting that reason and justice, and consequently a right to sovereignty, do not reside fully and constantly in any part of the earth, presumes that they are to be found in the majority, but does not attribute them to it as their certain and abiding qualities. At the very moment when it presumes that the majority is right, it does not forget that it may be wrong, and its concern is to give full opportunity to the minority of proving that it is in fact right, and of becoming in its turn the majority. Electoral precautions, the debates in the deliberative assemblies, the publication of these debates, the liberty of the press, the responsibility of ministers, all these arrangements have for their object to insure that a majority shall be declared only after it has well authenticated itself, to compel it ever to legitimatize itself, in order to its own preservation, and to place the minority in such a position as that it may contest the power and right of the majority.

Thus, the considerations we have suggested show that a representative form of government regards the individuals whom it brings into activity, and the majority which it seeks, from quite another point of view than that involved in the sovereignty of the people. The latter admits that the right of sovereignty resides somewhere upon the earth; the former denies it: this finds the right in question in a purely numerical majority; that seeks it in the majority of those qualified to pronounce on the subject: the one attributes it fully and entirely to number; the other is satisfied with the presumption that it is there, admits at the same time that it may possibly not be there, and invites the minority to substantiate its claims, securing, meanwhile, every facility for its so doing. The sovereignty of the people sees legitimate power in the multitude; representative government sees it only in unity, that is to say, in the reason to which the multitude ought to reduce itself. The sovereignty of the people makes power to come from below; representative government recognises the fact that all power comes from above, and at the same time obliges all who assume to be invested with it to substantiate the legitimacy of their pretensions before men who are capable of appreciating them. The one tends to lower those who are superior, the other to elevate those who are inferior, by bringing them into communication with those who are naturally above them. The sovereignty of the people is full at once of pride and of envy; representative government renders homage to the dignity of our nature, without ignoring its frailty, and recognises its frailty without outrage to its dignity. The principle of the sovereignty of the people is contrary to all the facts which reveal themselves in the actual origin of power, and in the progress of societies; representative government does not blink any one of these facts. Lastly, the sovereignty of the people is no sooner proclaimed, than it is compelled to abdicate its power, and to confess the impracticability of its aims; representative government moves naturally and steadily onward, and develops itself by its very existence.[2]

So far, then, from deriving its existence from the principle of the sovereignty of the people, representative government disowns this principle, and rests upon an entirely different idea, and one which is attended with entirely different consequences. It matters little that this form of government has been often claimed in the name of the sovereignty of the people, and that its principal epochs of development have occurred at times when that idea predominated; the reasons of this fact are easily discovered. The sovereignty of the people is a great force which sometimes interferes to break up an inequality which has become excessive, or a power which has become absolute, when society can no longer accommodate itself to them; as despotism sometimes interferes, in the name of order, violently to restore a society on the brink of dissolution. It is only a weapon of attack and destruction, never an instrument for the foundation of liberty. It is not a principle of government, it is a terrible but transient dictatorship, exercised by the multitude—a dictatorship that ceases, and that ought to cease as soon as the multitude has accomplished its work of destruction.

Briefly, to conclude: as the object of these lectures is to trace the course of representative government in modern Europe wherever it has found any footing, I have looked for the primal type of this government in order to compare it with the government of the Anglo-Saxon monarchy, which we have already examined, and with the other primitive governments which we shall meet with in Europe. In order to distinguish precisely the character of a representative government, I have been obliged to go back to the source of all government. I think I have shown that we must classify all governments according to two different principles. The one class, allied to justice and reason, recognises these alone as their guides; and as it is not in the power of human feebleness, in this world, to follow infallibly these sacred leaders, these governments do not concede to any one the possession of an absolute right to sovereignty, and they call upon the entire body of society to aid in the discovery of the law of justice and reason, which can alone confer it. The other class, on the contrary, admitting a right inherent in man to make a law for himself, thus degrade the rightful sovereignty; which, as it belongs only to justice and reason, ought never to come under the absolute

---

2. This is yet another important passage in which Guizot elaborates on the distinction between the sovereignty of reason and the sovereignty of the people. It will be recalled that for Guizot, the legitimacy of power does not necessarily result from the number of voices that might support a certain course of action, since justice and wisdom are not necessarily present in the will of the majority. Moreover, Guizot argues that it is false to assume that the entire people could ever exercise political power in the proper sense of the word.

control of man, who is ever too ready to usurp sovereignty, in order to exercise it for the promotion of his private interests, or for the gratification of his passions. I have shown that a representative government alone renders homage to true principles, and that all other governments, democratic as well as aristocratic, ought to be arranged according to an entirely different scheme of classification. I have now to enter upon the examination of the exterior forms of representative government, and to compare its principle with the historical principle of the Anglo-Saxon monarchy, as it is exhibited before us in its institutions.

LECTURE 8

The forms of a government are related to its principle, but are swayed by circumstances, and vary according to different degrees of civilization. ⁓ *What are the forms essential to a representative government?* ⁓ *1st. Division of powers; why this is absolutely essential to the principle of representative government;* ⁓ *2nd. Election;* ⁓ *3rd. Publicity.*

THE forms of a government are immediately related to its principle: the principle determines the forms, the forms reveal the principle. It does not therefore follow that the forms correspond exactly to the principle, nor that the principle can only realize itself under a peculiar form. As the principle itself is never alone nor omnipotent in its influence upon the facts, forms are necessarily diverse and mingled. In proportion as the action of any principle extends itself, the form which is truly correspondent to it is developed; but, in the course of this work, the principle embodies itself in the different forms which correspond to the condition of those facts which, in their aggregate, constitute society, and determine the position which it occupies in the scale of civilization.

The same principle can then be contained, and act under different forms. If the forms are the best that can be supplied for the principle, considering the existing state of society, and if, although they do not fully correspond to its nature, they insure the constant and regular progress of its action, there is no blame that can be charged upon them; each epoch, each state of society only allows of a certain development of the principle upon which its government rests. What is the measure of development possible to each epoch, and what is the form which corresponds to it in the present, which will secure for the future a more extended development, and which will bring with it new forms? This is the whole extent of the question—I mean, the question concerning the present, the only one with which political activity has to deal.

Nevertheless there are certain forms of government which are the general conditions of the presence and action of particular principles. Wherever the principle exists, it necessarily produces these forms; where they are wanting the principle does not exist or will soon cease to exist; its action and progress imperatively demand them: so far as they gain consistency at any place, the principle which they suppose is latently present and tends to become predominant.

What are the essential forms of the principle of representative government? By what external indications may we recognize the presence of this principle in a government? What conditions are required in order that it may act and develop itself?

We may, if I mistake not, reduce to three the conditions necessary, and the forms essential, to the representative system; all three are perhaps not equally necessary; their simultaneous existence is not perhaps indispensable in order to indicate the existence and secure the development of the principle from which they are derived. We may, however, justly consider them as fundamental. These forms are: 1st. The division of powers; 2nd. Election; 3rd. Publicity.

We have seen that no really existing power can be a rightful power; except in so far as it acts according to reason and truth, the only legitimate rule of action, the only source of right.

No existing power can fully know and constantly regard the guidance of reason and truth according to which it is bound to regulate its action. No actual power then is, or can be, in itself, a power by inherent right. In other words, as no existing power can be found that is infallible, there is none that may retain its existence on the tenure of absolute right.

Such is, however, the condition of human things that they need, as a last appeal, the intervention of a power which may declare the law to be the rule of government, and which shall impose it and cause it to be respected. In all the relations which the social state admits and to which it gives birth, from domestic order to political order, the presence of a power which may give and maintain the rule of action, is a necessary condition of the very existence of society.[1]

We see then the dilemma in which society is placed. No actual power can vindicate a claim to become an absolute power; hence the necessity, in order to meet particular emergencies, of a power that is definite, that is to say, *actually* absolute.

The problem of government is—how to give society a guarantee that the power, which is in operation absolute, to which all social relations must necessarily be referred, shall be but the image, the expression, the organ of that power which is rightfully absolute and alone legitimate, and which is never to be found

---

1. As in the case of other nineteenth-century liberals, Guizot emphasized constitutionalism, the division of powers, elections, and publicity, which is another way of saying that Guizot's liberalism was fundamentally opposed to any form of absolute power. In his view, the only legitimate sources of right were reason, truth, and justice. The division of powers—i.e., the existence of several powers supplementary to each other in the exercise of actual sovereignty—was a natural consequence of the principle that no power or individual can be granted an inherent right to sovereignty (sovereignty of right). For more details, see *HORG*, pp. 68–69, 328–29.

localized in this world? This is also, as we have seen, the problem which the representative system formally proposes to itself, since all its arrangements assume the existence of this problem and are framed with a purpose to resolve it.

To make actual power, as far as possible, identical with rightful power, by imposing upon it the abiding necessity of seeking for reason, truth, and justice—the sources of right; by investing it with practical power only when it has proved, that is to say, given a presumption of, its success in this search; and by compelling it ever to renew and confirm this presumption under penalty of losing power if it is unable to do so, this is the course of the representative system—this is the end at which it aims and according to which it directs, in their relations and their movement, all the resources which it brings into action.

In order to attain this end, it is indispensable that the existing power should not be simple, that is to say, that it should not be suffered to confine itself to one single instrument. As no force can possess in itself fully the right to authority, if there is one which possesses an absolute power, not only will it abuse this power, but it will very soon claim it as an inherent right. Alone it will become despotic, and in order to sustain its despotism it will call itself legitimately sovereign; and perhaps will end by believing and establishing the fiction. Such is the corrupting effect of despotism, that it destroys sooner or later, both in those who exercise it and in those who submit to it, even the feeling of its illegitimacy. Whoever is solitary in his sovereignty has only one step in order to become accredited as infallible. Alexander was right in wishing that he should be recognized as a god; he deduced a consequence that strictly followed from the fulness of the power which he possessed: and they also are right, who, attributing sovereignty to the multitude, take for their maxim, *Vox populi, vox Dei.* Everywhere where sovereignty rests with a single power, whatever may be the nature of that power, there is a danger that sovereignty will immediately be claimed as a right.

A division of the actual sovereignty is then a natural consequence of the principle, that a right to sovereignty does not belong to any person. It is necessary that there should be several powers, equal in extent and supplementary to each other in the exercise of actual sovereignty, in order that no one of them may be led to arrogate to itself the sovereignty of inherent right. The feeling of their reciprocal interdependence can alone prevent them from regarding themselves as entirely irresponsible.

Further: it is only in this way that the ruling power can be constrained to perpetuate its search for reason, truth, and justice; that is, for the rule which should govern its action, in order that it may become legitimate. The words of Pascal apply not only to the formation of power, they extend also to its exercise. Here are beings, individual or collective, who are called upon to perform the functions of sovereignty in common, each one under the supervision of his fellows. Do they possess among them, or by the fact of their existence, the right to power? No: they must seek it, they must on every opportunity manifest the truth which they proclaim as law. Isolated and distinct, they are only a multitude; when, after having deliberated and laboured, they find a ground of agreement in a common idea, from whence can proceed one will, then alone will the true unity, which resides in reason, be evolved; then there will be a presumption that the ruling power knows accurately and is well disposed to that legitimate rule which alone confers rightful power. If this work were not enforced, if this laborious and common search for the true law were not the necessary result of the reciprocal independence of the several powers, the end of government would not be attained. All the relations of the four great political powers which constitute, with us, the government (that is, the king, the two houses of parliament, and the electors) are intended to compel them to act in harmony, that is to say, to reduce themselves to unity.

The introduction of an elective, that is, a moveable element, into government, is as necessary as a division of forces to prevent the sovereignty from degenerating in the hands of those who exercise it into a full and permanent sovereignty of inherent right. It is therefore the necessary result of a representative government, and one of its principal characteristics. Accordingly we see that actual governments which have aimed at becoming absolute, have always endeavoured to destroy the elective principle. Venice gave a memorable illustration of this tendency, when, in 1319, it conferred an hereditary right on the grand council.* In the first age of governments, at the same time that we see power come from above, that is to say, acquire for itself by its superiority, of whatever kind that may be, either ability, riches, or courage—we see it also obliged to make its title recognised by those who can judge it. Election is the mode of this recognition—it is to be found in the infancy of all governments; but it is generally abolished after a time. It is when it reappears with sufficient energy to influence powerfully the administration of society, that a representative government is rising into being.

Theoretically, publicity is perhaps the most essential characteristic of a representative government. We have seen that it has for its object to call upon all individuals who possess rights, as well as those who exercise powers, to seek reason and justice, the source and rule of legitimate sovereignty. In publicity consists the bond between a society and its government. Looking, however, at facts, we find that of the elements essential to a representative government, this is the last which is introduced and gains a firm footing. Its history is analogous to that of the elective principle. The *Champs de Mars* and *Mai* were held in the

---

* This event is clearly and minutely related by Daru, in his *"Histoire de Venise."* (Vol. i. pp. 449–464.)

open air: many persons were present at them who took no part in the deliberation. The assembly of the Lombards at Pavia took place *circumstante immensa multitudine*.[2] It is probable that the same publicity attended also the *Wittenagemot* of the Saxons. When absolute or aristocratic government prevails, publicity disappears. When representative government begins to be formed by election, publicity does not at first enter into its constitution. In England, the House of Commons was for a long time a secret assembly; the first step towards publicity was to cause its acts, addresses and resolutions, to be printed. This step was taken by the Long Parliament under Charles I. Under Charles II. its proceedings again became secret; some individuals demanded, but in vain, the publication of the acts passed by the House,—the demand was resisted as dangerous. It was not till the eighteenth century that visitors were allowed to be present at the sittings of the English Parliament: this is not now granted as a right, and the demand of a single member who appeals to the ancient law, is sufficient to clear the gallery. Publicity has not then been invariably attached to a representative government; but it flows naturally from its principles—it is accordingly won almost necessarily, and may now be regarded as one of its most essential features. This result is owing to the press, which has rendered publicity easy without resorting to tumultuous meetings.

We have found the fundamental principle and the exterior and essential characteristics of a representative government; we have learnt what it is that constitutes it and distinguishes it from other government: we may now pass to its history. We shall take care to admit its existence only where we recognise the presence or the approach of its true principles; and we shall be convinced that its progress has ever been identical with the development of these principles.

2. With a vast crowd surrounding.

LECTURE 9

Primitive institutions of the Franks. ⁓ *Sketch of the history of the Frankish monarchy.* ⁓ *The Franks in Germany.* ⁓ *Their settlement in Belgium and in Gaul.* ⁓ *Character and authority of their chiefs after their establishment in the Roman Empire.* ⁓ *Early Frankish chieftains.* ⁓ *Clovis: his expeditions, wars, and conquests.* ⁓ *Decisive preponderance of the Franks in Gaul.*

In order to pursue the object of this course, I now proceed to give a sketch of the Franks similar to that which I have already given of the Anglo-Saxons. I shall study with you their primitive institutions, seek out their leading principle, and compare it with that type of representative government which we have just delineated. But before we enter upon the examination of Frankish institutions, I think it advisable briefly to refer to the leading events in the history of France. The institutions of a people cannot be thoroughly understood without a knowledge of their history. I shall devote this lecture to a view of the establishment of the Frankish monarchy; on a future occasion we will trace its progress under the first and second races of its kings.

I shall not now delay to discuss the somewhat uncertain origin of the Franks; there is reason to believe that, in Germany, they did not constitute a separate and homogeneous nation. They were a confederation of tribes settled in the country between the Rhine, the Maine, the Weser, and the Elbe. The Romans seem to have been long ignorant of their existence even after the conquest of Gaul, and history mentions them, for the first time, during the reign of Gordian, about the middle of the third century. A song, composed in celebration of the victories of Aurelian had the following refrain:

Mille Francos, mille Sarmatas,
Semel et semel occidimus.[1]

---

1. A thousand Franks, a thousand Sarmatians, / Once indeed we slew.

After this period, we find the different tribes of Franks advancing from East to West with rather rapid progress. At the beginning of the fourth century, we meet with the Salian Franks settled in Belgium, and the Ripuarian Franks on the two banks of the Rhine. These peoples established themselves on the frontiers of Gaul, sometimes by force, and sometimes with the consent of the emperors, who, after having defeated the barbarians, frequently assigned them lands on which to settle. This was the course pursued by Probus, Constantine, Julian, Constantius, and many others.

The chiefs thus established in the Roman territory retained, over their barbarian comrades, their ancient and independent authority, and received at the same time, from the emperors, certain titles to which were applied certain functions, and a certain amount of authority over the Romans in their district. Thus we find them adorned with the names of *Dux, Magister militae, Comes littoris,* and so forth. Their position was almost identical with that of the leaders of the wandering Tartar tribes in the Russian empire, who are elected by the men of their tribe, but receive their title and a certain jurisdiction from the Emperor of Russia—retaining their independent life, but bound at the same time to render military service, and to pay a tribute of furs.

Childeric, the chief of a Frankish tribe at Tournai, had received the title of *Magister militae* from the empire. When, in consequence of domestic quarrels and treason, he was forced to take refuge in Thuringia, his tribe submitted in 460 to Egidius, master of the Roman militia at Soissons. In 1653, the tomb of Childeric was discovered at Tournai, and several pieces of money were found in it, which are now deposited in the National Library, at Paris.

At the termination of the fifth century, the epoch of the dissolution of the empire, when the provinces were left, according to the expression of Tacitus, *magis sine domino quam cum libertate,*[2] nearly all these local chieftains, Romans as well as barbarians, became independent, and no longer recognised the sovereignty of Rome. Siagrius, the son of Egidius, was appointed King of the Romans at Soissons. He made war with Clovis, in his own name and on his own account.

The Frankish chiefs, who had thus become petty sovereigns, penetrated still farther into the empire. Clodion, who had settled at Cambrai, carried his incursions to the banks of the Somme. Meroveus was present at the battle of Chalons-sur-Marne, at which Attila was conquered. It was, however, under the command of their chieftain Clovis, that these bands of Franks, who originally formed colonies on the frontiers, entered Gaul definitively as conquerors. Clovis was the son of Childeric, who reigned at Tournai; and he succeeded his father in 481. He probably wielded a certain amount of authority in the name of

2. More without a ruler than with liberty.

the empire. Saint Remy, in a letter, gives him the title of *Magister militae*. Other Frankish chiefs were, about this period, almost in the same position as Clovis: Ragnachar ruled at Cambrai, Sigebert at Cologne, and Renomer at Mans. Clovis was the most ambitious, the ablest, and the most fortunate of them all.

His nearest neighbour was Siagrius, who governed at Soissons. In 486, Clovis sent him a defiance; Siagrius accepted it, and appointed the battle-field at Nogent, near Soissons. Siagrius was conquered, and took refuge with Alaric, king of the Visigoths, who gave him up to his conqueror. In 491, Clovis conquered the district of Tongres, now the district of Liege. In 496, he penetrated still further in the same direction; he entered the country of the Alemanni, against whom Sigebert, king of Cologne, had requested his assistance. He defeated them at Tolbiac, and became a Christian in consequence of this victory. A party of the conquered Alemanni took refuge in Rhoetia under the protection of Theodoric, king of the Ostrogoths: there, under the name of Suevi, they became the stem of the Suabians. Another body remained on the banks of the Rhine, and became subject to Sigebert and Clovis. Thus this chieftain extended his dominion in the vicinity of the Rhine. At the same time he overcame most of the Frankish chiefs, his neighbours, and subjected their tribes to his power. In 497, he led an expedition against the Armoricans in the West. In 500, he fell upon the Burgundians in the East, took advantage of their dissensions, and gained a victory between Dijon and Langres. In 507, he advanced into the centre of France, through Anjou and Poitou; near Poitiers, he attacked Alaric II., king of the Visigoths, and killed him. He penetrated as far as Angoulême, Bordeaux, and Toulouse; and boasted of having conquered Aquitaine. In 508, Clovis received the title of *Patrician* from Anastasius, the Emperor of the East. In 509, he returned to the Rhine, defeated his ancient ally, Sigebert, king of Cologne, and subjugated the Ripuarian Franks. In 511, he died, after having led his Frankish warriors, and extended his dominion, over the various parts of Gaul.

The wars and conquests of Clovis had little resemblance to what we understand by the same words at the present day. The principal object of the Frankish expeditions was to make booty, and carry off slaves; this is what was called conquest in those days. The victor sometimes imposed a tribute; but there resulted from his victory hardly any permanent possession, and no civil settlement. Among other proofs of this assertion, I may instance the small number of the warriors who accompanied Clovis, who was never attended, on his expeditions, by more than five or six thousand men. Now, with this number, no civil settlement, not even a military occupation, was possible. When the conqueror had withdrawn, the conquered people gradually resumed their independence—a new chieftain arose. Rarely did the conquerors settle in the lands which they had subjected; thus it was necessary incessantly to make the same conquests over again.

For a detailed narrative of these events, I refer you to the general histories of France, especially to the work of M. Sismondi.[3]

Nowhere do we obtain a better picture of the manners of the Greeks in the heroic age than that supplied by the Iliad. A similar authority, with reference to the expeditions and manners of the Germanic people, exists in the poem of the Nibelungen. There you will best be able to obtain a correct knowledge and thorough comprehension of the state of society, and the nature of the wars at this epoch.

At the death of Clovis, in 571, the Frankish monarchy was definitively established; for he had made the Frankish name and people the most formidable and least contested power in Gaul.

---

3. Guizot refers here to Jean Charles Léonard Sismondi (1773–1842), an influential Swiss historian and economist. Among his most important works were *Nouveaux principes d'économie politique* (*New Principles of Political Economy*), *De la richesse commerciale, ou Principes d'économie politique appliquée à la législation du commerce* (*On Commercial Wealth: Principles of Political Economy Applied to Commercial Legislation*), *Études sur les constitutions des peuples libres* (*Studies on the Constitutions of Free Peoples*).

LECTURE 10

Division of territory among the sons of the Frankish kings. ⁓ Rapid formation and disappearance of several Frank kingdoms. ⁓ Neustria and Austrasia; their geographical division. ⁓ Early predominance of Neustria. ⁓ Fredegonde and Brunehaut. ⁓ Elevation of the May-ors of the Palace. ⁓ True character of their power. ⁓ The Pepin family. ⁓ Charles Martel. ⁓ Fall of the Merovingians.

I HAVE already explained to you how we must understand the historical phrase which attributes to Clovis the foundation of the French monarchy. In the sense and within the limits which I have indicated, Clovis, at his death, was king of the whole of France, excepting the kingdoms of the Burgundians and Visigoths. After his decease, each of his four sons received a portion of his dominions. Theodoric ruled at Metz, Chlodomir at Orleans, Childebert at Paris, and Clotaire at Soissons. The nature of this division has given rise to considerable dissension among learned men; but I think the question may be easily solved. In order to retain his power, it was necessary for the chieftain or king to possess large private domains; in all his warlike expeditions, he acquired for himself large tracts of territory; Clovis had thus obtained immense landed property wherever he had made a conquest. At his death, these estates were divided among his children, as were also his other possessions, flocks, herds, jewels, money, treasures of all kinds: these supplied their owners with the surest means of attaining power. Moreover, it was the custom of the Frankish kings to associate their sons with them in the government, by sending them to reside in that district or province which was afterwards to constitute their kingdom. They thus endeavoured to secure the prevalence of hereditary right over election. The sons of the king became in their turn the natural chieftains of the countries in which they actually possessed the most power. Thus we find that Clotaire II., in 622, associated with himself his son Dagobert, and sent him to Austrasia. Dagobert did the same, in 633, for his son Sigebert.

From this division of private domains and participation in royal power, it was easy to pass to the political partition of the kingdom. It is more difficult to discover whether these partitions were made by the dying king, in his own authority, or by the national assembly. At a later period, under the second race, we find Pepin, Charlemagne and Louis the Débonnair, positively obtaining the consent of the assembly of barons to the division of their states among their children. Facts are not so clear and authentic under the Merovingians. However, as the accession of the second race was a return to old Germanic manners, it is probable that, in the time of Clovis and his successors, every heir, on receiving his portion, was obliged to gain the consent of the chiefs of the country. Five partitions of this kind occurred under the Merovingians; in 511, after the death of Clovis; in 561, after Clotaire I.; in 638, after Dagobert I.; in 656, after Clovis II. From 678 to 752, the whole monarchy was actually united under the authority of the Pepin family, who were originally *Mayors of the Palace* of Austrasia, and nominally under that of titular kings, the first four and the sixth of whom descended from the kings of Neustria, and the fifth and seventh from those of Austrasia. The kingdoms which were constituted by the five partitions which I have just mentioned, were those of Metz, Orleans, Paris, Soissons, Austrasia, Burgundy, Neustria, and Aquitaine.

I shall not here speak of the vicissitudes and perpetual dismemberments of these various kingdoms at various times. I should have only to relate a long series of wars and murders. The ancient kingdom of Burgundy was conquered by the children of Clovis I.; a new kingdom of Burgundy arose, in which the kingdom of Orleans was incorporated. The new kingdom of Burgundy was invaded, sometimes by the kings of Neustria, sometimes by those of Austrasia. The kingdom of Aquitaine appears for a moment only under Childebert II., son of Clotaire II., in 628, and about 716, under Eudes, duke of Aquitaine, who declared himself an independent monarch. At length, these four kingdoms disappeared; the fundamental conflict and division was between the kingdoms of Neustria and Austrasia, the two largest, and last surviving.

The geographical division of the kingdoms of Neustria and Austrasia is uncertain and variable. We find the kings of Austrasia possessing countries far distant from the center of their government—countries, too, which seem to be naturally placed by their position under the sway of the kings of Neustria. Thus, they were the masters of Auvergne, and their dominion extended almost as far as Poitou. These incoherent possessions had their origin in the frequent expeditions of the two countries against each other, or into distant lands which belonged to neither of them. We can, however, obtain some few distinct boundary lines; the forest of Ardennes separated Austrasia from Neustria; Neustria comprised the country between the Meuse and the Loire; Austrasia consisted of that between the Meuse and the Rhine.

This division had a far greater importance than that of a mere geographical division; and there is a deeper cause for the successive disappearance of the other Frankish kingdoms, and the final predominance of these two.

The countries which composed Austrasia were the first which were inhabited by the Franks. They adjoined Germany, and were connected with those portions of the Frankish confederacy which had not crossed the Rhine. They were, therefore, the cradle, the first fatherland, of the Franks. Moreover, after their expeditions, these tribes frequently returned with their booty to their ancient settlement, instead of establishing themselves in their new conquests. Thus Theodoric, son of Clovis, in the fifth century, led a great expedition into Auvergne, and returned afterwards to Austrasia. Roman civilization and manners had been almost completely expelled from that bank of the Rhine; the ancient German manners predominated there. In the countries which composed Neustria, on the other hand, the Franks were less numerous, more scattered, more separated from their ancient fatherland and fellow-countrymen. The ancient inhabitants of the country surrounded them on every side. The Franks were there like colonies of barbarians transported into the midst of Roman civilization and a Roman people. This state of things could not but lead to a far more profound and reasonable distinction between the two kingdoms, than could be occasioned by a purely geographical division. On one side was the kingdom of the Germano-Franks, on the other that of the Romano-Franks.

Historic testimony positively confirms this probable deduction from facts. Austrasia is termed *Francia Teutonica,* and Neustria, *Francia Romana.* The German language prevailed in the former country, and the Roman in the latter. Finally, under the first race of kings, events bear the evident impress of this fundamental distinction, or rather, they are its natural result. When considering them in a general manner, it is impossible to recognize this character. I shall now give a summary of the principal proofs.

I. The original predominance of the kingdom of Neustria. This is an incontestable fact. Four kings, after Clovis, and before the destruction of the royal authority by the Mayors of the Palace, united the whole Frankish monarchy under one head. These were kings of Neustria; Clotaire I., from 558 to 561; Clotaire II., from 613 to 628; Dagobert I., from 631 to 638; and Clovis II., from 655 to 656. This predominance of Neustria was the natural result, 1st, Of the establishment of Clovis in Neustria; 2ndly, Of the central position of that kingdom with reference to the rest of Gaul; 3rd, Of the superior civilization and wealth which accrued to it from its Roman population; 4th, Of the rapid extension which the royal authority obtained in it, in consequence of the prevalence of Roman ideas and customs; 5th, Of the continual fluctuations occasioned in Austrasia, by the proximity of the German barbarians, by wars against the Thuringians and Saxons, and by other causes.

II. The state of the two kingdoms, during the epoch of Fredegonde and Brunehaut, from 598 to 623. The struggle was constant between Neustria and Austrasia, under the name of these two queens. The power of Chilperic and of Fredegonde in Neustria was greater than that of the kings of Austrasia and of Brunehaut. Fredegonde acted upon a country in which the only Roman administration still prevailed; Brunehaut endeavoured in vain to overcome the rude independence of the chiefs of the German bands, who had become large landed proprietors. Her boldness and ability failed in its opposition to the Austrasian and Burgundian aristocracy. The Austrasian aristocracy formed a secret alliance with that of Neustria. The fall and death of Brunehaut were evidently a triumph of the Austrasian aristocracy, which, being stronger and more compact than that of Neustria, imposed upon Clotaire II. the execution of his queen. The remnants of Roman despotism were overcome in Austrasia by the German aristocracy, and the consequences of that event were the enfeeblement of the royal authority and the predominance of Austrasian influence.

III. The elevation of the Mayors of the Palace, and the fall of the Merovingian race, are the third proof of the great fact which I have mentioned. The elevation of the Mayors of the Palace must be ascribed to the same causes in both kingdoms. It is an error to interpret this fact as the conflict of the victorious Franks against the Gauls and Romans. These last, more moulded to despotism, had found a ready access to the court of the barbarian kings, and it has been inferred from this, that it was in order to counteract their influence, that the German aristocracy created the Mayors of the Palace. This is an error; the Mayors of the Palace were the work and instrument of the barbarian aristocracy, whether Roman or Gallic, in opposition to the royal authority.

It has also been said that the kings were desirous of attaching to themselves one of the most powerful members of the territorial aristocracy, in order to control or oppress the others. This might have been the case originally, but the Mayor of the Palace soon found it more advantageous to make himself the leader and instrument of the nobility. He promoted their interests, and assumed the character of a protector to the large proprietors with whom, finally, his appointment rested. From this time forth, the royal authority was almost a dead letter.

The same phenomenon is observable in both kingdoms; but the Austrasian aristocracy was more purely German, and more compact, than that of Neustria. It was consequently more powerful, and its Mayors of the Palace became more deeply rooted in their authority. Thus we behold the family of Pepin gain the royal power by a progressive elevation, from 630 to 752. This family was descended from Carloman, the wealthy proprietor of the domain of Haspengau, situated on the Meuse, between the district of Liege and the duchy of Brabant. It was thoroughly German, and naturally placed itself at the head of the Franco-German aristocracy.

The fall of the Merovingians was, therefore, the work of Austrasia, and, as it were, a second conquest of Roman France, by Germanic France. The kings of Roman France were unable to maintain their position, and the Neustrian Mayors of the Palace, the leaders of a mingled aristocracy of Franks and Gauls, were incompetent to take their place. It was from the banks of the Rhine and from Belgium, that is, from the ancient fatherland of the Franks, that the new conquerors came—and these conquerors were the chiefs of a purely Germanic aristocracy.

This was, undoubtedly, the true character of the fall of the Merovingians, and of the elevation of the Carlovingians, who founded a new Frankish monarchy in that Gaul in which the Neustrian Franks had so greatly degenerated. Thus we shall perceive, at this epoch, and in consequence of this revolution, a marked return towards the primitive institutions and manners of the Franks. This is perceptible, indeed, even in the manner in which the revolution was effected. The details of this event fully confirm what we have first said regarding the general progress of affairs. The Pepin family had laboured for a century to place itself at the head of the Frankish nation. It derived its support not merely from the great landed aristocracy, but also from the patronage of the warriors employed in military expeditions. The development of the power of this family, in the first point of view, was the work of Pepin the Old and of Pepin de Heristal; under the second, it was the work of Charles Martel in particular. His continual wars against the Transrhenane Germans, against the Saracens, and against the petty tyrants of the interior, rendered him a more powerful warrior-chief than any of his ancestors. But Charles Martel employed other means also to attach his companions to his person. He seized the property of the church, and distributed it amongst them. He did not take this property, however, in so absolute a manner as is supposed. The various churches were in the habit of farming out their property for a fixed annual income, and ecclesiastical estates thus farmed out were called *precaria*. Frequently the kings, when desirous of rewarding one of their chiefs, ordered a chapter to farm out an estate to the favourite for a very moderate rent, under the title of a *precarium*. Charles Martel, at first, merely generalised this practice. A very large number of his comrades received from him favours of this kind; in the first instance, they received the ecclesiastical estates only for two or three years; but, when that term had expired, the tenants were unwilling to restore what they had appropriated to themselves by the habit of enjoyment. The conflict of the church against the usurping proprietors long perplexed the kings of the second race. As they often required the help of the clergy, they strove to appease their complaints. Pepin the Short and Charlemagne restored to them a large portion of their property which had formerly been granted to their warriors as *precaria;* or at least, increased the amount paid to the church by the new proprietors, who obstinately refused to consider themselves mere tenants.

The predominance of the Pepin family had commenced before the time of Charles Martel, by their possessing the hereditary office of Mayor of the Palace. During the life of that great chieftain, there were several inter-reigns in Austrasia and Neustria, and he continued to exercise the supreme authority with the simple title of Duke of the Franks. At his death, his children, Pepin and Carloman, divided the kingdom between them, Pepin, still preserving some respect for appearances, made Childeric III. king in Neustria; and soon, by the abdication of his brother Carloman, he found himself Duke of Austrasia, as well as the all-powerful Mayor of the Palace in Neustria. Such was, however, the influence already possessed by the idea of the hereditary legitimacy of the crown, that Pepin did not venture to seize, in the name of force alone, upon the throne which was considered to belong rightfully to the descendants of Clovis. He sought to justify his employment of force by popular election, and an appeal to religion. As the head of an aristocracy, he was obliged frequently to defer to its will, and to give it a share of authority. He revived the ancient assemblies of the large landowners, and restored to them their part in public affairs. Thenceforward he might consider himself certain of his election; but even this did not suffice him. He thought that his usurpation needed a more august and sacred sanction. He gained over to his interests Boniface, bishop of Mayence, and charged him to sound Pope Zachary, who, on his side, was hard pressed by the Lombards, and needed the assistance of the Frankish chieftain. When Pepin was sure of the pontiff's concurrence, he sent Burckhardt, bishop of Wurtzburg, and Fulrad, abbot of St. Denis, to propose to him this question, in the form of a case of conscience. "When there is a king in fact and a king by right, which is the true king?" The pope replied, that he who actually exercised the royal authority ought also to possess the royal title. In 752, Pepin convoked the national assembly at Soissons; he was there elected king, and afterwards consecrated by Bishop Boniface. In 754, Pope Stephen III. made a journey into France, and again consecrated Pepin with his two sons and his wife Bertrade. The pope ordered the Franks, on pain of excommunication, to take none as kings who did not belong to the family of Pepin, and the Franks swore an oath: *Ut nunquam de alterius lumbis regem in aevo praesumant eligere.*[1]

A second dynasty was thus established almost in the same manner as the first had been. The principal warrior-chief, the most powerful of the large landowners, has himself elected by his companions, confines future elections to members of his own family, and obtains the sanction of religion to his election.

---

1. That they never undertake to choose from the loins of another a king for all time.

He holds the actual power from his fathers and from himself; he is desirous of holding the rightful power from God and from the people. German manners and institutions reappear, but in association with Christian ideas. Here is a second conquest of Gaul, accomplished by German warriors, and sanctioned, in the name of the Roman world, no longer by the Emperor, but by the Pope. The church has inherited the moral ascendancy of the empire.

LECTURE II

General character of events under the Carlovingian empire. ⁓ Reign of Pepin the Short. ⁓ Reign of Charlemagne. ⁓ Epoch of transition. Reigns of Louis the Débonnair and Charles the Bald. ⁓ Norman invasions. ⁓ The last Carlovingians. ⁓ Accession of Hugh Capet.

I HAVE sketched the general progress of events in Frankish Gaul, under the Merovingians; I have now to give a similar outline of the reign of the Carlovingians. I shall enter neither into an examination of the institutions, nor a detailed narrative of occurrences; I shall seek to sum up the facts in the general fact which includes them all.

The general tendency of events under the Merovingians was towards centralization; and this tendency was natural. At that period, a society and a state were labouring to form and create themselves; and societies and states can be created only by the centralization of interests and forces. The conquests and authority of Clovis, however fleeting and incomplete they may have been, indicate this need of centralization, which was then pressing upon Roman and barbarian society. After the death of Clovis, his dominions were dismembered, and formed into distinct kingdoms; but these kingdoms could not remain separate; they continually tended to reunite, and soon became reduced in number to two, which finally coalesced. A similar process took place in reference to the authority in the interior of each state. The royal power attempted at first to be the centralizing principle, but did not succeed; the aristocracy of the chiefs, the great landowners, laboured to organize itself, and to produce its own government; it produced it, at length, in the form of the Mayors of the Palace, who eventually became kings. After two hundred and seventy-one years of labour, all the Frankish kingdoms were reunited into one. The supreme power was more entirely concentrated in the hands of the king, aided by the concurrence of the national assemblies, than it had ever been previously.

Under Pepin the Short and Charlemagne, this centralization was maintained, extended and regulated; and it appeared to gain strength. New countries, new peoples, were incorporated into the Frankish state. The relations of the sovereign with his subjects became more numerous and regular. New bonds of union were established between the supreme power, its delegates, and its subjects. A state and a government seemed likely to be formed.

After the death of Charlemagne, affairs presented quite another aspect, and assumed a contrary direction. In proportion as a tendency to the centralization, either of the different states among themselves, or of the internal power of each state, had been visible under the rule of the Merovingian race, in just that proportion did a tendency to the dismemberment, to the dissolution, both of the states themselves and of the power in each state, become evident under the Carlovingians. Under the Merovingians, you have seen that five successive dismemberments took place, none of which was able to last; after the death of Charlemagne, the kingdoms once separated do not reunite. Louis the Débonnair divided the empire among his children, in 838, and made vain efforts to maintain some unity therein. The treaty of Verdun, in 843, definitively separated the three monarchies. Charles the Fat, in 884, made an attempt to unite them again; but this attempt also failed—reunion was impracticable.

In the interior of each state, and particularly in France, the same phenomenon was manifested. The supreme power which, under the Merovingians, had tended to become concentrated in the hands, either of the kings, or of the Mayors of the Palace, and which had seemed to have attained this end under Pepin and Charlemagne, took a contrary direction from the reign of Louis the Débonnair, and tended constantly to dissolution. The great landed proprietors who, under the first race, had been naturally urged to coalesce against the royal authority, now laboured only to elevate themselves, and to become sovereigns in their own domains. The hereditary succession of benefices and offices became prevalent. Royalty was nothing more than a direct lordship, or an indirect and impotent suzerainty. Sovereignty was dispersed; there no longer existed any state, or head of the state. The history of the Carlovingians is nothing but the struggle of declining royalty against that tendency which was continually robbing and contracting it more and more. This was the dominant character, the general progress of events, from Louis the Débonnair to Hugh Capet. I shall now refer to the principal facts of this epoch; in them I shall find proofs of the general fact just stated.

I. Pepin the Short (752–768). As this monarch had risen to power by the aid of the large landowners, the clergy, and the pope, he was obliged, during the whole course of his reign, to treat with consideration those powers which had supported him. He frequently convoked national assemblies, and frequently met with opposition from them. It was not without extreme difficulty that he prevailed upon his chieftains to make war against the Lombards, at the request of Pope Stephen III. In order to retain the support of the clergy, Pepin ordered the holders of ecclesiastical benefices to perform the conditions annexed to their tenure of them; he lavished donations upon the churches, and greatly augmented the importance of the bishops. It is from Zachary's answer to Pepin, that the popes have assumed to deduce their historic right to make and unmake kings. Pepin thus favoured the aggrandizement of the aristocracy, the clergy, and the papacy—three powers which had been very useful, and were still of great service to him, which he knew how to manage and restrain, but which, under other circumstances, would assuredly labour to render themselves independent of the royal power, and would promote the dismemberment, after having assisted in the concentration of the kingdom. The moment most favourable for the development of these powers had arrived. They placed themselves at first at the service of the king, who was useful to them, and knew how to make them serviceable to himself; and thus they became able to free themselves from dependence upon him, and henceforward to act alone and on their own account.

II. Charlemagne (768–814). Epochs of transition, in the history of society, have this singular characteristic, that they are marked sometimes by great agitation, and sometimes by profound repose. It is well worth while to study the causes of this difference between epochs which are fundamentally similar in nature, and which do not constitute a fixed and durable state of society, but only a passage from one state to another. When the transition occurs from a state of things which has long been established and is doomed to destruction, to a new state of things which it will be necessary to create, it is generally full of agitation and violence. When, on the other hand, there exists no previous state of society, which from its long duration is difficult to overthrow, the transition is only a momentary halt of society, fatigued by the disorder of its previous chaotic state, and by the labour of creation. This was the character of the reign of Charlemagne. The whole country of the Franks, wearied by the disorders of the first dynasty, and not having yet originated the social system which was destined to issue naturally from their conquest—I mean the feudal regime—stood still for a time under the government of a great man who procured for it greater order and more regular activity, than it had ever known before. Until then, the two great powers which agitated the country—the great landowners and the clergy—had not been able to take a settled position. The royal authority was hostile to them, and they attacked it. Charlemagne knew how to restrain and satisfy them, and contrived to keep them employed without placing himself in their power. This knowledge constituted his strength, and was the cause of the temporary order which he established throughout his empire. In a future lecture, when studying the institutions of his epoch, we shall see what was the characteristic feature of his government. I am speaking now only of the fact itself—of the singular circumstance of the authority of a very powerful king being interposed between an age in which royalty was held in slight esteem, and an age in which it almost ceased to be of any importance. Charlemagne made of barbarian monarchy all that he possibly could. He possessed within himself, in the necessities of his mind and life, an activity corresponding to the general exigencies of his age, which, indeed, surpassed them. The Franks desired war and booty; Charlemagne desired conquests, in order to extend his renown and dominion; the Franks were unwilling to be without a share in their own government; Charlemagne held frequent national assemblies, and employed the principal members of the territorial aristocracy as dukes, counts, *missi dominici*,[1] and in other offices. The clergy were anxious to possess consideration, authority, and wealth; Charlemagne held them in great respect, employed many bishops in the public service, bestowed on them rich endowments, and attached them firmly to him, by proving himself a munificent friend and patron of those studies of which they were almost the only cultivators. In every direction towards which the active and energetic minds of the time turned their attention, Charlemagne was always the first to look; and he proved himself more warlike than the warriors, more careful of the interests of the church than her most devout adherents, a greater friend of literature than the most learned men, always foremost in every career, and thus bringing everything to a kind of unity, by the single fact that his genius was everywhere in harmony with his age, because he was its most perfect representative, and that he was capable of ruling it because he was superior to it. But the men who are thus before their age, in every respect, are the only men who can gain followers; Charlemagne's personal superiority was the indispensable condition of the transitory order which he established. Order did not at that time spring naturally from society; the victorious aristocracy had not yet attained the organization at which it aimed. Charlemagne, by keeping it employed, diverted it temporarily from its object. When Charlemagne was dead, all the social forces which he had concentrated and absorbed became in want of aliment; they resumed their natural tendencies, their intestine conflicts; they began once more to aspire to the independence of isolation, and to sovereignty in their own neighbourhood.

III. Louis the Débonnair (814–840). As soon as Louis became emperor, he lost the success which had attended him as king of Aquitaine. Facts soon gave proof of that tendency to dissolution which pervaded the empire of Charlemagne, and which dispersed the authority which he had been able to retain entire in his own hands. Louis gave kingdoms to his sons, and they were continually in revolt against him. The great landholders, the clergy, and the pope—those three social forces which Charlemagne had so ably managed and restrained—escaped from the yoke of Louis the Débonnair, and acted some-

1. Inspectors of the state of the kingdom and of the conduct of the nobles.

times in his favour, and sometimes against him. The clergy loaded him with re-proaches, and forced him to do public penance at Worms, in 829. An attempt was made, in 830, to make him a monk, after the assembly at Compiègne, where he had confessed his faults; and he was deposed, in 833, by another assembly at Compiègne, in pursuance of a conspiracy into which Pope Gregory IV. had entered. During the whole course of this reign, nothing held together, everything was disjoined; both the states which constituted the empire, and the great social forces, lay and ecclesiatical, in each state. Each of these forces aspired to render itself independent. Louis the Débonnair presents a singular spectacle, in the midst of this dissolution, attempting to practise as a scholar the maxims of government laid down by Charlemagne, enacting general laws against general abuses, prescribing rules for the guidance of all those forces which had escaped from his hands, and even endeavouring to correct the particular acts of injustice which had been committed under the preceding reign. But the kings, the great landowners, the bishops—all had acquired a feeling of their own importance, and refused to obey an emperor who was no longer Charlemagne.

IV. Charles the Bald (840–877). The dissolution which had commenced under Louis the Débonnair continued under his son Charles the Bald. His three brothers,* relying alternately upon the pretensions of the clergy and of the large landholders, disputed with him for the vast empire of Charlemagne. The bloody battle of Fontenay, fought on the 25th of June, 841, made Charles the Bald king of Neustria and Aquitaine, that is, of France. His reign is nothing but a continual alternation, a scene of futile efforts to prevent the dismemberment of his dominions and of his power. At one time, he robs the clergy in order to satisfy the avidity of the great landholders, whose support he is anxious to gain; at another time, he spoils the landholders in order to appease the clergy, of whose assistance he stands in need. His capitulars contain hardly anything but these impotent alternations. The hereditary succession of benefices and appointments became triumphant, and every chieftain laid the foundation of his own independence.

V. The Normans. This is the generic name of the German and Scandinavian tribes, who inhabited the shores of the Baltic. Their maritime expeditions may be traced back to a very remote period. We meet with them under the first dynasty of Frankish kings; they frequently occur towards the end of the reign of Charlemagne, and under Louis the Débonnair; and they continually appear under Charles the Bald. They constituted a fresh cause of the dismemberment of the empire, and of the royal authority. In the ninth century, the Frankish Gauls present the same appearance which the Roman Gauls had offered four centuries before: that of a government incapable of defending the

---

* Lothaire, Pepin, and Louis the Germanic, the three elder sons of Louis the Débonnair.

country, and expelled or retiring in every direction, and of barbarians pillaging, imposing tribute, withdrawing on payment of large sums of money, and continually reappearing to levy fresh contributions. Nevertheless, a notable difference is to be remarked between these two epochs. In both, the central government was equally incapable and worn out; but, in the ninth century, there existed within the Frankish territory a host of chieftains, who, though lately barbarian invaders themselves, had become independent, and were surrounded by warriors who defended themselves against the new invaders with far greater energy than the Roman magistrates had done, and who took advantage of the disturbed state of society to consolidate firmly their own individual sovereignties. Among these chieftains, we meet with Robert the Strong, the ancestor of the Capetian family, who became Duke of Neustria, in 861, and was killed in 866, while defending Neustria against the Normans. The Normans definitively established themselves in Neustria, in 912, under Charles the Simple, who yielded the province to their chief Rollo, and gave him his daughter Grisella in marriage.

VI. Charles the Fat. In 884, Charles the Fat, son of Louis the Germanic, temporarily collected under his rule nearly all the dominions of Charlemagne. The maintenance of this new concentration of territory and power was impossible, and it was dissolved even before the death of Charles the Fat.

VII. In 888, Eudes, and in 923, Raoul, made themselves kings. The first, a count of Paris, was the son of Robert the Strong, and assumed the title of king, at the national assembly held at Compiègne. The second was Duke of Burgundy, and husband of Emma, the grand-daughter of Robert the Strong, and sister of Hugo the Great, Duke of France. These kings were not, like the Mayors of the Palace at the termination of the first dynasty, the representatives of a powerful aristocracy. The landed aristocracy of the tenth century had no further need of representation; no power could struggle effectively against them. Every great landowner was absolute master in his own estates, and the kings were only great barons, who, having become independent, assumed the title of kings, with the aid of their vassals. A portion of the lords who had thus become independent, remained indifferent to quarrels which did not disturb their rights and their power. They cared little whether there was a king, or who was king. The descendants of Charlemagne retained for some considerable time a party of adherents, for the idea and feeling of the rightfulness of a hereditary succession to the crown, that is, of legitimacy, were already powerful; but in 987, the conflict ceased, and Hugh Capet became king.

The general fact which characterizes this epoch,—a tendency to dismemberment and dissolution,—is frequently met with in the course of the history of the human race. At first, we see the interests, forces, and ideas which exist in society, labouring to become united, to concentrate themselves, and to produce a suitable form of government. When this concentration has been once effected, and this government has been once produced, we find that, at the end of a certain time, it becomes exhausted and incapable of maintaining it entirely; new interests, new forces, and new ideas, which do not harmonize with each other, arise and come into action; then the dissolution begins, the elements of society become separated, and the bonds of government are relaxed. A conflict commences between the forces which tend to separation, and the authority which strives to maintain union. When the dissolution shall be consummated, then will begin a new work of concentration. This occurred after the fall of the second dynasty in France. The prevalence of the feudal system had caused the dissolution of the government and the state; the government and the state laboured to reconstitute themselves, and to regain their unity and consistency. This great work was not definitively accomplished until the reign of Louis XIV.; the social forces had then become once more concentrated in the hands of royalty. Our own times have witnessed a fresh dissolution.[2]

What we observe, then, during the years from 481 to 987, is a general phenomenon, characteristic of the progress of the human race. This phenomenon occurs not only in the political history of societies, but also in every occupation in which the activity of man finds exercise. In intellectual order, for example, we find at first that chaos reigns; the most divergent attempts to resolve the great questions of the nature and destiny of man, are made in the midst of the universal ignorance. By degrees, opinions become assimilated, a school is formed, founded by a superior man; it is joined by almost all men of mind. Ere long, in the midst of this very school, diverse opinions arise, contend, and become separated; dissolution begins once again in intellectual order, and will continue until a new unity is formed, and regains the empire.

Such, also, is the course of nature herself in her great and mysterious operations. This continual alternation of formation and dissolution, of life and death, recurs in all things, and under all forms. Spirit gathers matter together and gives it animation, uses, and then abandons it. It falls a prey to some fermentation, after which it will reappear under a new aspect, to receive once more that spirit which alone can impart to it life, order, and unity.

2. For a comprehensive discussion of this theme, see Guizot, *HCE*, Lectures VII–XI, pp. 119–96.

LECTURE 12

Ancient institutions of the Franks. ⌢ They are more difficult of study than those of the Anglo-Saxons. ⌢ Three kinds of landed property; allodial, beneficiary, and tributary lands. ⌢ Origin of allodial lands. ⌢ Meaning of the word allodium. ⌢ Salic land amongst the Franks. ⌢ Essential characteristics of the allods.

THE primitive institutions of the Franks are much more difficult of study than those of the Anglo-Saxons.

I. In the Frankish monarchy, the old Gallo-Roman people still subsisted; they in part retained their laws and customs; their language even predominated; Gaul was more civilised, more organised, more Romanised than Great Britain, in which nearly all the original inhabitants of the country were either destroyed or dispersed.

II. Gaul was divided among various barbarian peoples, each of whom had its own laws, its own kingdom, its own history; the Franks, the Visigoths, the Burgundians; and the continual alternations of the Frankish monarchy between dislocation and re-union, long destroyed all unity in its history.

III. The conquerors were dispersed over a much larger extent of territory; and central institutions were weaker, more diverse, and more complicated.

IV. Of the two systems of social and political order, contained in the cradle of modern nations—I mean the feudal system and the representative system—the latter has long prevailed in England, while the former long maintained its sway in France. The ancient national institutions of the Franks were absorbed into the feudal system, in whose train came absolute power. Those of the Saxons, on the other hand, were more or less maintained and perpetuated, to end at length in the representative system, which rendered them clear by giving them due development.

Perhaps, also, the difficulty of the study of the ancient Frankish institutions arises in some measure from the fact that we possess more documents respecting the Franks than respecting the Saxons. Because we are acquainted with more facts, we have greater trouble in harmonizing them. We believe we are better informed because we know less.

Such being the case, I wish to state with precision the object of my researches, so as not to lose time in useless digressions. I do not propose that we should study together either the state of Frankish society in all its departments, or the history of all its vicissitudes. I am desirous to investigate and explain to you, first, what constituted in France, from the fifth to the tenth century, the political part of the nation, possessing political rights and liberties; and secondly, by what institutions these rights were exercised, and these liberties guaranteed. We shall frequently be obliged to make excursions beyond these limits in search of the facts necessary to the solution of the questions contained therein; but we shall not dwell long upon such extraneous matter.

In the pursuit of this study, we shall find the works of German authors of incontestable utility. A principal cause of the errors of the leading French writers who have treated of the subject, is that they have attempted to derive all our institutions from Germany, from the condition of the Franks before the invasion, and that, at the same time, they have been unacquainted with the language, the history, and the learned researches of the purely German peoples, that is, of the nations which have most thoroughly retained the primitive elements of Frankish society, and which formed a considerable portion of the Frankish monarchy.

Dr. Hullmann, a professor at the University of Bonn, has written a book on the origin of the various social states or conditions, the object of which is to prove that all modern social order, political as well as civil, derives its origin from the circumstance, that the peoples of modern times have been agriculturists, devoted to the possession and fixed cultivation of land. This view, although incomplete, is of much importance. It is certain that, in the history of Europe, ever since the fall of the Roman Empire, the condition of persons has been closely connected with that of landed property, and that the one throws light upon the other. Though all history would not prove that this has been the case from the beginning, yet the long-continued predominance of the feudal system, which consists precisely in the intimate connection and amalgamation of the relations of lands with those of persons, would alone be sufficient to demonstrate it unquestionably.

At the outset, the condition of persons gave rise to that of lands; according as a man was more or less free, more or less powerful, the land which he possessed or cultivated assumed a corresponding character. The condition of lands afterwards became the symbol of the condition of persons; according as a man possessed or cultivated such and such a domain, he was more or less free and more or less important in the State. Originally, the man gave its character to the estate; in the sequel, the estate gave his character to the man: and as symbols quickly become causes, the condition of persons was at length not only indicated, but determined by, and consequent upon, the condition of lands. Social conditions became in some degree incorporated with the soil: and a man found himself possessed of a certain rank and of a certain degree of liberty and social importance, corresponding to the character of the land which he occupied. In studying modern history, we must not for a moment lose sight of these vicissitudes in the condition of lands, and of the varied influence they exerted upon the condition of persons.

There is some advantage in first studying the condition of lands, in so far as it was a symbol of the condition of persons, because the former is somewhat more determinate than the latter. It is also less complicated; the condition of persons frequently varied upon lands of the same condition; and the same persons have possessed lands of different conditions. Our information, respecting the condition of lands, is also more than exact.

In studying the condition of landed property and its vicissitudes, I do not propose to investigate its civil condition, or to consider property in all its civil relations, such as successions, bequests, and alienations. I intend to consider it only in its relation to the condition of persons, and as a symbol or cause of the various conditions of society. In the period which we are about to study, from the fifth to the tenth century, we have this advantage: that it contains a complete system, both as regards landed property, and also with respect to the condition of persons and the political institutions of the nation.[1]

At this period, we meet with three kinds of landed property: 1st. Allodial lands; 2nd. Beneficiary lands; and 3rd. Tributary lands.

1st. Of allodial lands or *Allods.*—These were lands possessed in absolute right, which the proprietor held from no one, on account of which he owed nothing to any superior, and of which he had full liberty to dispose. The lands taken or received as booty by the Franks, at the time of the conquest of Gaul, or in their subsequent conquests, were originally allodial. At a later period it was said that a man held an allodium, only from God and his sword. Hugh Capet said that he held the crown of France in this manner, because he had received it from no one. Such tenures were mementos of conquest.

---

1. This is an excellent illustration of Guizot's sociological acumen and method. His argument is that, in order to understand political institutions, one must start by studying the condition of persons and landed property that alone can account for the direction of social change. Guizot points to the great diversity in the conditions of property in the Middle Ages (allodial or independent, beneficiary, and tributary) and the ensuing inequality in the amount of wealth. He argues that the condition and the relations of persons did not originally depend on the condition of territorial properties and cannot be deduced from them. He also claims that the destruction of feudal property had led to the atomization of society that contributed to the centralization of government. For more details, see *HORG*, pp. 112–15.

The word, *alode* itself indicates that the first allods were lands, which fell to the conquerors either by lot or division; *loos,* lot; *allotted, allotment;* whence also came the French word, *loterie.* Among the Burgundians, Visigoths, Lombards, and others, we find positive traces of this division of the lands allotted to the conquerors. They took possession of two-thirds of the land, that is, not of the whole extent of the country, but of the land in any locality, where a barbarian of any importance took up his residence. The lands which thus fell to the barbarians, were called *Sortes Burgundionum, Gothorum,* and so on. We do not find among the Franks positive traces of such a division of the land; but we know, nevertheless, that they divided their booty by lot.

The word *alode,* then, was probably applied at first only to the lands taken by the victors in virtue of their conquests. Another proof of this is that allodial property, properly so called, was long distinguished from the lands held also in absolute right, and entailing no acknowledgment of a superior, but which had been acquired by purchase or in any other way. A distinction was also made among allodial lands, of *salio* land, which could be inherited only by males. This was probably the original allod, the land acquired at the time of the conquest, and which thereupon became the primitive and principal establishment of the head of the family. *Terra salica* is the *terra aviatica* of the Ripuarian Franks, the *terra sortis titulo adquisita* of the Burgundians, the *haereditas* of the Saxons, and the *terra paterna* of the formulas of Marculf.[2] Various explanations have been given of the term *salic land.* Montesquieu thinks that it was the land belonging to the house, from the word, *sal,* hall. This explanation is supported by Hullmann. It would thus be the *in-land* of the Anglo-Saxons. It is probable that originally the *terra salica* was in fact the land connected with *the* house, the residence of the chieftain. The two explanations would thus coincide; but the former is more complete and historical than the latter.

The name of *allod* was extended by degrees to all lands possessed in absolute right, and held from no superior, whether they were the original allods or not. The words *proprium, possessio, praedium, haereditas,*[3] were then employed as synonymes of *allodium.* It was probably at this period also that the rigorous interdict which excluded females from succession to salic land, fell into desuetude. It would have been too harsh to exclude them from succession to all allodial property. There were some doubts entertained on this point as early as the time when the salic law was drawn up; and Marculf has transmitted to us a formula which proves that, although it was the common law to deprive females of all succession to primitive allods, a father might, nevertheless, by his will, give

2. Salic land is the maternal land of the Ripuarian Franks, the land acquired by notice of lot of the Burgundians, the inheritance of the Saxons, and the paternal land of the formulas of Marculf.

3. Property, possession, estate, inheritance.

his daughter an equal share with his sons in the division of all his property, of whatever nature.

The essential and primitive characteristic of the *allodium,* consisted in the absoluteness of the property; the right to give it away, to alienate it, to bequeath it by inheritance or will, &c. Its second characteristic was that it depended upon no superior, and involved no service or tribute of any kind to any individual. But although allodial lands were exempt from all private charges towards individuals, does it follow that they were also exempt from all public charges as regarded the state, or the king as head of the State? This question has been differently answered by learned men.

At the period to which we allude, there were no public charges properly so called, no obligations imposed and fulfilled as regarded the State, or its head. All was limited to personal relations between individuals; and from the relations of man with man arose the mutual relations of landed property, which were not carried further than those of persons. We have already seen this; the position of the Franks after the conquest resulted from the combination of their anterior relations with their new position. The freeman, who held his land from no one, had no obligations or charges to fulfil to any one on account of his land. In such a state of civilization, liberty is the appanage of force. The Franks who possessed allodial lands, and were strong enough to be under no obligation of duty to any more powerful individual, would not have comprehended the necessity of owing service to an abstract being like the State, with which, moreover, they had no personal relation.

However, as society cannot exist in such a state of dissolution, arising from the isolation of individuals, new relations were progressively formed between the proprietors of allodial lands, which relations imposed certain charges on them.

1st. The gifts presented to the kings either at the holding of the Champs de Mars or Mai, or when they come to pass any time in any particular province. The kings had no fixed habitation. These gifts, though at first purely voluntary, became gradually converted into a sort of obligation, from which allodial lands were not exempt. That these gifts had become obligatory is proved by a list drawn up at Aix-la-Chapelle in 817, during the reign of Louis the Débonnair, which enumerates the monasteries which had to pay them, and those which had not.

2nd. The supply of provisions and means of transport to the king's ambassadors, and to the foreign envoys, on their passage through the country.

3rd. Of the various barbarian nations which were successively incorporated into the kingdom of the Franks, several paid tribute to the Frankish kings; and of this tribute it is probable that the free or allodial lands, possessed by these nations, contributed their share. It consisted of a certain number of cows, hogs, and horses. The nature of these tributes proves that they were not distributed among the lands, but imposed upon the nation as a whole.

4th. A more important charge, namely, military service, was imposed upon allodial lands. In our next lecture, we shall see how this charge was introduced.

LECTURE 13

Origin of military service; its cause and limits. ⌒ It was made a general obligation by Charlemagne. ⌒ Allodial lands were originally exempt from taxation. ⌒ Origin of benefices. ⌒ Change in the position of the German chiefs, in consequence of their territorial settlement. ⌒ Their wealth. ⌒ No public treasury. ⌒ The aerarium and fiscus of the old Roman republic. ⌒ Formation of the private domain of the kings of France. ⌒ Character of benefices. ⌒ Error of Montesquieu on this subject.

I HAVE indicated some of the new relations which became progressively established between the proprietors of allodial lands and the services that resulted from them. I have to occupy you today with the consideration of military service and benefices.

Originally, military service was imposed on a man by virtue of his quality, his nationality before the conquest, and not by reason of his wealth. After the conquest, there was no legal obligation to it whatever; it was a natural result of the position occupied by the Franks—who were constantly called upon to defend what they had conquered—and of their taste for warlike expeditions, and for pillage. It was, also, a kind of moral obligation which each man owed to the chief whom he had chosen. This connexion continued the same as in Germany; the chief proposed an expedition to his men, and if they approved of it, they set out. Thus, we find Theodoric proposed to the Austrasian Franks an expedition against Thuringia. Often the warriors themselves summoned their chief to conduct them on some particular expedition, threatening to forsake him, and seek another chief, in the event of his refusal. Under the Merovingians, a kind of regularity, some sort of legal obligation, was introduced into the military convocations, and a penalty was inflicted upon those who did not present themselves. The obligation was imposed, and the penalty inflicted, even in cases where no movement was required in defence of the country. The proprietors of allodial lands were not exempted; many, doubtless, went on their own free choice, but the feeble were constrained. This was, however, an obligation attached rather to the quality of a free man, a Frank, or an associate, than to property.

Not until the reign of Charlemagne, do we see the obligation to military service imposed on all free men, proprietors of freeholds, as well as of benefices, and regulated by property qualifications. This service now appeared no longer as a voluntary act; it was no longer the consequence of the simple relation between a chief and his associates, but a truly public service imposed on every individual of the nation, in proportion to the nature and extent of his territorial possessions. Charlemagne was very vigilant in seeing that the system of recruiting which he had established, should be faithfully carried out; we have a proof of this in his capitulary, issued in the form of instructions to the *missi dominici*, in the year 812. This is an exceedingly minute account of the particulars and charges of military service. These charges remained under the same conditions during the reigns of Charlemagne's immediate successors. Under Charles the Bald, they were restricted to the case of an invasion of the country by a foreigner (*landwehr*). The relation of the vassal to his lord, at that time, prevailed completely over that of the citizen to the chief ruler of the state.

Although allodial lands were exempt from imposts, properly so called, more because there were no general imposts whatever than because of any special immunity from them possessed by allodial lands, yet we find the kings used every favourable opportunity to attempt to attach imposts to men and lands, which they believed rightfully exempt from them; complaints were made of these attempts as acts of injustice; they were resisted, and sometimes redress was sought, as under Chilperic, in 578, in Austrasia; under Theodebert, in 547; and under Clovis II., in 615. We find also, that, on the occasion of great and alarming emergencies, the kings imposed certain charges on proprietors, without distinction, requiring them to lend their assistance, either to the poor, or to the state. Thus, Charlemagne, in 779, during a famine, and Charles the Bald, in 877, in order to pay the tribute due to the Normans, made such general claims. In both these cases, the charge was adjusted to the quality of persons and properties.

There is reason to believe that, originally, allodial lands did not exist in large numbers, especially among the Franks.

There is no ground for supposing that the Franks took possession of, and shared the lands, wherever they made expeditions and conquests. They rather cared for the booty which they carried off, and the cattle which they took with them, instead of forming a settlement themselves. For a long time, the greater part of the Franks did not often forsake their first habitations on the banks of the Meuse and the Rhine; thither they returned after their expeditions.

We may conclude that lands were most probably distributed in the following manner. Each chief took a portion for himself and his associates, who lived on the land of their chief. It would be absurd to suppose that each band would dissolve itself, and the separated individuals then retire each to his isolated share of land; there were no individual shares, or, certainly, but few. This is sufficiently proved by the fact that the greater number of Franks appear to have been without landed property, living as cultivators on the lands, and in the *villae* of a chief, or of the king. Often, even, a man would place himself not only under the protection, but at the disposal of another, to serve him during his life, on condition of being fed and clothed, and yet without ceasing to be free. This kind of contract, the formula for which has been preserved, must have been very common, and explains the circumstance that so large a number of free men are found to have lived and served on lands not belonging to themselves. Probably, the number of Franks who became successively proprietors, by means of benefices, was greater than the number of those who were primitively allodial proprietors.

The larger number of small allodial proprietors were gradually robbed of their possessions, or reduced to the condition of tributaries, by the usurpation of their neighbours, or of powerful chiefs. Of this, there are innumerable examples. The laws made, from the seventh to the tenth century, give evidence of the tendency of large allodial estates or benefices to absorb small freeholds. The statute of Louis the Débonnair, referring to the complaints of the Spanish refugees in the south, explains pretty accurately the system according to which properties changed hands.

Donations to churches also tended incessantly to reduce the number of allodial estates. They would probably soon have disappeared altogether, had not a cause of an opposite character tended continually to create new ones. As allodial property was sure and permanent, while benefices were precarious and more dependent, the proprietors of benefices constantly sought to convert their benefices into allodial estates. The capitularies which remain to us prove this at every step. It is probable that large new allodial estates were thus created, but small ones tended to disappear.

Finally, under Charles the Bald, a singular circumstance presents itself. This was the very time when the system of allodial property was preparing, so to speak, to merge itself in the system of beneficiary property, which is synonymous with feudalism; and precisely at that time the name of *Allods* is more frequent than ever. We find it applied to properties which are evidently benefices. This name still designated a property more surely hereditary and independent, and as benefices were ordinarily hereditary and independent, they were called allods, just in order to indicate their new character; and the king himself, whose interest it especially was that his benefices should not become allods, gave them this name, as if it had become their conventional designation. Sixty years previously, Charlemagne had made the greatest efforts to prevent benefices from becoming allods.

Having thus explained the nature and changes of allods, I pass on to the consideration of *benefices.*

Benefices, which constituted the cradle of the feudal system, were a natural result of the relations anciently subsisting in Germany between a chief and his associates. As the power of these chiefs resided only in the strength of their band of associates, all their attention was directed to the means of enlarging the number of these followers. Tacitus relates how, being charged with the maintenance and preservation of their followers, they gained and kept them by means of constant warfare, by dividing to them the spoils of the empire, by gifts of arms and horses. After the conquest, when the territorial establishment took place, the position of the chiefs was altered. Hitherto, in their wandering life, they had lived solely upon rapine; then they possessed two kinds of wealth, moveable booty and lands. They made their companions other presents, which engaged them in another kind of life. These riches, both moveable and fixed, remained for the chiefs, as for all others, as their personal and private property. The Frankish society had not then arrived at any ideas of public property. It consisted only of individuals, powerful by reason of their courage and their talent for war, by the antiquity of their family, and the renown of their name, who collected around them other individuals, who passed their life in the same precarious manner. The republics of antiquity did not commence thus. Rome had soon its public treasure—its *aerarium.* Till nearly the close of the republic, the *aerarium* still remained. Augustus established the *fiscus,* the treasury of the prince, which was destined to absorb the *aerarium.* The *fiscus,* at first, received only private gifts to the prince, but it soon usurped all the public revenues, till it became at length the only repository for public wealth. Thus, despotism transformed a public into a private domain. The states founded on the ruins of the Roman empire have followed an opposite course. At their commencement, all property was private property. It is in consequence of the development of civilization, and free institutions, that in almost all monarchies private domains have gradually become public property.

The private domains of the chiefs of bands, and particularly of the Frankish kings, were at first composed of lands taken from the inhabitants of the countries in which they established themselves. I have already stated that they did not take all the lands, but a large number of them. The share of the chief must have been considerable, as is indicated by the numerous domains of the chiefs of the first two races, in Belgium, in Flanders, and on the banks of the Rhine, where they first formed their settlements. Hullmann has given a list of a hundred and twenty-three domains beyond the Meuse belonging to the Carlovingian family.

The private property of the chiefs of conquered peoples were, to a great extent at least, incorporated into the domain of the conquering chief. Clovis subjected to himself successively several petty monarchs in his neighbour-hood—Ragnachair at Cambray, Chararich in Belgium, and Siegbert at Cologne; and took possession of all their personal property.

The substitution of the royalty of one family for that of another, aug-mented the private domain of the king; the new king would add to his own per-sonal possessions the property of the dethroned king. Thus the large domains possessed by the family of the Pepins, in Belgium, and on the Rhine, became royal domains.

Legal confiscations, as a punishment for crime, cases in which no legal heir was to be found for property, unjust and violent confiscations—were other sources of personal wealth to kings.

In these ways, the private domain of the kings increased rapidly, and it was employed by them especially as a means of attaching their associates to them, and of gaining new ones. Benefices, then, are as ancient as the establishment of the Franks on a fixed territory.

The fundamental question which has divided historians, whether those who are merely scholars or the philosophers, is—were benefices given for a time and revocable at will, or were they for life and yet revertible, or were they hered-itary? Montesquieu has aimed at establishing a historical progression among these different modes; he asserts that benefices were at first revocable, being given for a time, then for life, and then hereditary. I believe he is mistaken, and that his mistake arises from an attempt to systematize history, and bring its facts into regular marching order. In the giving and receiving of benefices, two ten-dencies have always coexisted: on the one hand, those who had received be-nefices wished to retain them, and even to make them hereditary; on the other hand, the kings who granted them wished to resume them, or to grant them for only a limited period. All the disputes that occurred between kings and their powerful subjects, all the treaties which arose out of these disputes, all the promises which were made with a view to appease the dissatisfaction of mal-contents, prove that the kings were in the habit of taking back, by violence, the benefices they had granted, and that the nobles attempted to retain them also by violence. The Mayors of the Palace acquired their power by placing them-selves at the head of the large possessors of benefices, and by seconding their pretensions. Under the administration of Pepin the Short and Charlemagne, the struggle appeared to cease, because the kings had for a time great superior-ity in force; but, in reality, the kings were now the aggressors in their turn, who endeavoured to bring the benefices again into their own hands, and to preserve to themselves the free disposal of them. Under Charles the Bald, the kings again began to get feeble, and, in consequence the treaties and promises became again favourable to the beneficiaries. In fact, the history of benefices, from the time of Clovis till the full establishment of the feudal system, is only a perpetual struggle between these two opposing tendencies. An attentive and accurate examination of the facts will prove that the three modes of conceding benefices did not follow one another in regular chronological succession, but that they are to be found existing and operating simultaneously during the whole course of this period.

LECTURE 14

Proofs of the co-existence of various modes of conferring benefices, from the fifth to the tenth century. ⌇ *Of benefices that were absolutely and arbitrarily revocable.* ⌇ *Of benefices conceded for a limited time, the* precaria. ⌇ *Of benefices granted for life.* ⌇ *Of benefices granted hereditarily.* ⌇ *General character of the concession of benefices.* ⌇ *Their tendency to become hereditary.* ⌇ *Its prevalence under Charles the Bald.* ⌇ *Military service.* ⌇ *Judicial and domestic service.* ⌇ *Origin, meaning, and vicissitudes, of the fidelity due by the vassal to his lord.*

FROM the time of the invasion of the Gauls by the Franks up to the moment when the feudal system was definitely constituted, we find during the whole course of this epoch:

I. That benefices were revoked, not only as a consequence of legal condemnation, but also by the arbitrary will of the donor. The power of absolute and arbitrary transference of benefices was practically in existence under the Merovingian kings. It is however very doubtful whether this has ever been recognised as the right of the donors. Such an act possessed a character of suddenness and violence which gave a shock to ideas of natural justice. Few men would consent to receive a favour of which they might legally have been deprived at the first moment of caprice. Montesquieu affirms that benefices were first held on an entirely uncertain tenure. The proofs which he gives are but of little weight. *First,* the clause contained in the treaty concluded at Andely, in 587, between the two monarchs, Gontran and Childebert, proves the fact but not the right. *Secondly,* the formula of Marculf again does not prove anything more than a common practice. Besides, the giver of the benefice presents a motive in this formula, namely, the necessity of the exchange. *Thirdly,* the law of the Lombards merely characterises the benefice as a precarious property, which it indubitably was. *Fourthly,* the *Book of Fiefs* compiled in the twelfth century, probably converted the fact into a right. *Fifthly,* the letter of the bishops to Louis the Germanic also proves merely the fact. It is evident that the right has always been contested, and that attempts have always been made to prevent the permanency of benefices is a fact also. "Charlemagne," says Eginhard, "did not suffer that every noble should take away from his vassal the benefices which he had granted to him upon any outburst of anger." The capitulary of Louis the Débonnair, which allows a year to the rejected incumbent whose benefice is in a bad condition before it can be finally taken from him, proves likewise that certain forms were observed with this view, and protests against a purely arbitrary disposition. That the patron had a right to take away the benefice, when the occupant had failed to discharge his obligations, is an indisputable fact. Now it would be very easy to abuse this principle of taking away benefices under a pretext of disorderly conduct or infidelity to the trust reposed; accordingly all the protestations that were made, and all the treaties that were enforced, were designed to oppose such a procedure.

Thus we find, from the fifth to the tenth century: *First,* numerous examples of benefices being arbitrarily taken away; this was the practice of the giver, when his power corresponded to his desire. *Secondly,* benefices taken away on account of unfaithfulness, disorder, treachery; this was a right.

II. As to benefices granted for a limited time, Montesquieu affirms, after the *Book of Fiefs,* that they were at first granted for one year. I have not been able to find any positive example of this. It is not however impossible that there may have been such, similar to the *precaria* belonging to churches. *Precarium,* among the Romans, signified a grant of property on the tenure of usufruct for a limited time, which was generally pretty short. Under the monarchy of the Franks, we have seen that the churches often consolidated their wealth in this way, in order to secure a permanent revenue. Charles the Bald decreed that the *precaria* should be held for five years and renewed every five years. The only benefices which appear to me to have been granted for a time, ostensibly so at least, are those which arose out of the ecclesiastical wealth taken by Charles Martel (about A.D. 720), and which were then possessed under the designation *precarious.* Before this period we find kings and mayors interposing their authority in order to obtain, under the title of *precarious,* the enjoyment of certain church wealth for certain persons. It appears that Charles Martel did more at that time than grant or cause the retention of church property, under the title of *precaria*—he also completely stripped the churches, in order to confer their wealth as benefices. But, after him, Pepin and Carloman, his sons, while they also took the wealth of churches in order to confer them on their vassals, only took it on the title of *precaria.* The ecclesiastics protested vigorously against the spoliation of Charles Martel, and it was upon their protestations that Pepin ordained that the wealth which could be restored should be actually returned, and that what could not be so restored, should be held under the title *precaria,* at fixed rentals, till they could again be transferred to the church. Pepin and Charlemagne used rigorous measures to secure that the holders, *in precario,* of church wealth should fulfil their obligations to its primitive proprietors; and we may gather, from the frequency of their orders, that these orders were often treated with contempt. It is nevertheless evident that the practice of taking the goods of the church, and placing them in other hands, whether absolutely, or under the title of precarious, continued under even the most feeble and superstitious kings. The bishops said that Charles the Bald suffered himself to be led astray, being often seduced, partly because of his youth, partly through feebleness of character, by evil counsellors, and often constrained by the threats of the occupants, who told him "that if he did not allow them to possess this consecrated property, they would abandon him immediately." It is probable that but little of this property was restored to the churches, and that the greater part of what was held *sub precario*[1] became, along with the other benefices, the hereditary possession of the occupants.

We see that far from Charles Martel having any claim to be regarded as the first originator of the practice of granting benefices for life, the benefices, on the contrary, which arose either from the act by which he despoiled churches and monasteries, or from acts similar to his, were for a long time more precarious than any others, and even ought legally to have been restored to the churches; certainly at the death of the occupants, and if possible before.

III. We find during the whole of the epoch which we are considering, and at its close as much as at its commencement, benefices conferred for life. It is evident that under Pepin and Charlemagne most benefices were given on this tenure. This was owing to the various precautions taken by the kings to prevent their being transformed into allodial estates. Louis the Débonnair took the same precautions. Mabillon quotes a charter of this king containing the formal concession of a benefice to be held for life. In 889, King Eudes conferred a benefice on Ricabod his vassal, "in beneficiary right, and on a tenure of usufruct"; with this addition, that, if he should have a son, the benefice should pass to his son for his life. We see, under Pepin, a vassal die who had a son, and yet his benefice was given immediately to another vassal.

IV. We find also, during the whole of this epoch, that benefices were given or held hereditarily. In 587, it was stipulated by the treaty of Andely, with regard to the concessions made by queen Clotilda, that they should be perpetual. The law of the Visigoths (of Chindasuinth, about 540) provides that the concessions made by the princes should not be revoked. Marculf gives the formulary for a hereditary concession. In 765, Charlemagne gave to an individual named Jean, who had conquered the Saracens in the province of Barcelona, a domain (says Fontaines) situated near Narbonne; "in order that he and his posterity may possess it without any fee or trouble, so long as they remain faithful to us or to our

---

1. Under loan.

children." The same Jean presented himself to Louis the Débonnair, with the gift of Charlemagne, and demanded his confirmation of it. Louis confirmed it, and added to it new lands. In 884, Jean being dead, his son Teutfred presented himself to Charles the Bald with the two donations just mentioned, and asked him to confirm them to him. The king granted this, as it is expressed, "in order that thou mayest possess them, thou and thy posterity, without any fee." These successive demands of confirmation, either at the death of the original bestower, or at that of the original incumbent, prove that the hereditary character of benefices was not then considered as a right, even when it had been promised, and consequently that it rested on no general law that was recognized by the state.

These three modes of granting benefices, of which I have just given examples, existed therefore at the same time, and I believe that we may assert from them two general facts, which however are not without exceptions: *First,* the usual condition of benefices, during this period, was that they should be given on a tenure of usufruct and for life; *Secondly,* the tendency of the time was to render the benefice a hereditary possession. This result was eventually realized when the feudal or aristocratic system triumphed over the monarchical system. We see under Charlemagne, at which time the monarchical system reached its culminating point, that most benefices were held on a tenure of usufruct for life, and not as personal property. Not only was Charlemagne unwilling that the property in benefices should be usurped, but he was especially vigilant with regard to their right administration. Under Charles the Bald, when the aristocratic system prevailed, benefices came to be held as hereditary possessions. This mode of possession partly arose out of the immense number of hereditary concessions which were made during this reign, and which were commenced under Louis the Débonnair; partly also out of some general arrangements in the capitularies of Charles the Bald, which recognized or conferred upon those who were faithful to the king the right to transmit their benefices hereditarily. We must conclude from this that the hereditary character of benefices at that time prevailed almost universally as a custom, and began to be avowed as a principle, but that it was not yet a general and recognized right. It was demanded and received in individual instances, which would not have been the case had it existed as a common right. In the monarchies consequent on the dismemberment of Charlemagne's empire—in Germany, for example—it was not recognized as a right, and prevailed still less as a custom.

Let us never forget—I repeat it—that all these general facts are subject to exceptional cases, and that different methods of conferring benefices have existed at all times. It would follow, from the nature of things, that the common condition of benefices was, at first, that of possession for life. The relations of the chief to his associates were all personal,—hence his benefactions were personal also. Not less did it follow from the nature of things, that when the Franks were once established and fixed, the associates of the monarch who were able to acquire an independent existence, and to become powerful in their turn, tended to separate themselves from their ancient chief, and to settle themselves in their own possessions, in order that they also might become the centre of groups of men. Hence resulted all the efforts to make benefices hereditary.

After having determined the origin and the mode of conferring and transmitting benefices, it remains that we should learn what conditions were attached to them, and what relations were thereby formed between the giver and the incumbent.

Mably thinks that benefices did not at first impose any particular obligation, and that those of Charles Martel were the first which were formally associated with civil and military services. This opinion is contrary to the nature of things; the origin of benefices testifies to the contrary. They were, as, in Germany, gifts of horses or of arms and banquets had been, a mode of attaching companies to the benefactor. This relation in itself involves an obligation. Mably's idea is equally contradicted by facts. In all the disputes which arose between the incumbents and the Merovingian kings, the benefices are always vindicated in behalf of those who kept faith with their patron. No complaints were made when those were seen to be despoiled who had failed to render the fidelity that was due from them. Siggo we find losing the benefices of Chilperic in 576, because he had forsaken his allegiance and passed over to Childebert II. The law of the Ripuarians pronounced the confiscation of the goods of every man who had been unfaithful to the king. Marculf gives the formula of the act by which a man was received into the number of the faithful. Charles Martel, in giving benefices to his soldiers, only imposed upon them the obligations that had always followed on such appointments. Only these obligations became progressively more formal and explicit, precisely in the measure that the ancient relations of the chief and his associates tended to become weakened and to disappear, in consequence of the dispersion of his men and their settlement on their own properties. Originally, the associates lived with their chief, around him, in his house and at his table, in peace, as well as in war: they were his vassals, according to the original sense of the word, which signified the *guest*, the *companion*, an individual attached to the house.* When most of the

---

* There are different etymologies of the word *vassus*, from *haus*, a house; from *gast*, a guest; from *fest*, fast, established; from *geselle* (vassallus).—The word *Gasinde*, which expresses the *familia*, so far as it comprises the individuals inhabiting the house, the *guests* in opposition to the *mancipia*, induces me to think that *vassus* comes from *gast*. (Anton, *Gesch. der Deuts. Land.*, vol. i. p. 526.)

We read in the Salic law (tit. 43): *Si quis romanum hominem convivam regis occiderit, sol.* 300 *culpabilis judicetur.*[2] The Roman editors of this law would have rendered the word *gast* by *conviva*.

2. If anyone kills a Roman guest of the king, he will be judged liable for 300 *solidi* (a type of gold coin).

vassals had dispersed themselves, in order that each might reside in his own allodial or beneficiary estate, we may easily perceive the necessity that thus arose of determining the obligations that were then imposed upon them; but this was only done imperfectly and by degrees, as is generally the case where matters are at issue which have for a long time had a general and conventional adjustment. As the first race began to disappear and the second to arise in its place, the obligations attached to the conferring of benefices appear to be clearly determined. They range themselves under two principal heads. *First,* the obligation of military service on the requisition of the patron. *Secondly,* the obligation of certain judicial and domestic services of a more personal and household character. It is impossible at the present time to specify what these services were to which the incumbents were held. We see only, among a host of acts, that the kings imposed on the incumbents *servilia,* which obliged them to present themselves at court. These obligations were comprised under the general term *fidelity.* They were at first personal, and attached to the quality of *liege-man,*[3] independently of the possession of any benefice—a connexion identical with that between the ancient German associates and their monarch. When it had become necessary for the king to give lands as a benefice, in order to insure the fidelity of his liege subjects, the obligation attached itself to the quality of beneficiary. We constantly see benefices given under the condition of loyalty. Charlemagne, when he gave a benefice in perpetuity to Jean, annexed to it this condition. There is reason to believe that benefices were also given, conditioned by the payment of certain fees (*census*). I do not find, at this period, the granting of any benefice in which the imposition of a rental is expressly indicated; but the nature of things seems to show that such must have been the case, and I do find mention made of benefices conferred *absque ullo censu.*[4] Anxiety in certain cases to obtain exemption from the fees, proves that in other cases they were imposed. It is probable that rentals were attached to benefices, granted hereditarily, and not to those which were only given for the term of an individual life.

Loyalty was at first due only to that chief to whom it had been expressly promised, and from whom a benefice had been received. Charlemagne attempted to change this into an obligation common to all the freemen in his States. Marculf has preserved to us the formula in which he wrote to his counts, requiring from all individuals the oath of fidelity. Thus did this prince endeavour to break through the feudal hierarchy which was consolidating itself, to bring himself into a direct relation with all freemen, and to make the relation between king and subject predominant over that between lord and vassal. The oath of fidelity was universally exacted by the successors of Charlemagne, Louis

3. A vassal bound to serve his superior; a loyal subject to the king.

4. Without any fee.

the Débonnair and Charles the Bald, but without any effective results; for the tendency to hierarchical and feudal aristocracy had become prevalent. We find besides numerous examples of the maintenance of the relations between incumbent and patron, even under Charlemagne. Under Charles the Bald this relation became more positive and independent of the king. The prince even, for the repression of public crimes, allowed his authority to be exercised through the intervention of the lord; he made each lord responsible for the crimes of his own dependents. It was therefore especially in the empire of the lord over his men, that the means were then sought of sustaining order and repressing crime. This alone will sufficiently indicate the continually growing force of feudal relations and the diminishing authority of royalty.

LECTURE 15

Of benefices conceded by great landowners to men dependent upon them:
~ First, *benefices conceded for all kinds of services, and as a mode of paying salary;* Secondly, *larger proprietors usurp the lands adjoining their own, and bestow them as benefices on their subordinates;* Thirdly, *the conversion of a great number of allodial lands into benefices, by the practice of* recommendation. ~ *Origin and meaning of this practice.* ~ *Permanence of freeholds, especially in certain parts of the Frankish monarchy.* ~ *Tributary lands.* ~ *Their origin and nature.* ~ *Their rapid extension: its causes.* ~ *General view of the condition of territorial property, from the sixth to the eleventh century:* First, *different conditions of territorial property;* Secondly, *the individual dependence of territorial property;* Thirdly, *the stationary condition of territorial wealth.* ~ *Why the system of beneficiary property, that is to say, the feudal system, was necessary to the formation of modern society and of powerful states.*

K INGS were not the sole donors of benefices; all the large proprietors gave them. Many leaders of bands of men were originally united under the conduct of the king; these chiefs became subsequently proprietors of large allodial estates. Portions of these were conceded as benefices to their immediate associates. Afterwards, they became large incumbents, and gave also as benefices portions of the benefice which they held from the king. Hence arose the practice of sub-enfeoffment. In the capitularies, we perpetually meet with the words, *vassalli vassallorum nostrorum.*[1]

We find, during the whole of this period, even under Charlemagne, numerous examples of benefices held otherwise than from the king. Two letters of Eginhard expressly mention the concession, by way of benefice, of certain portions of royal benefices.

1. Vassals of our vassals.

It is the opinion of Mably, that other persons than the king began to give benefices only after the reign of Charles Martel. This mistake arises from his not having apprehended that the relation of the chief to his associate, which afterwards grew into that of lord to his vassal, was at first a purely personal relation, entirely independent of and anterior to any concession of benefices. It is impossible to determine at what particular time the conferring of benefices became connected with the relation of the beneficiary to his patron. This was probably almost immediately after the territorial establishment.

The number of benefices was soon very considerable, and became greater every day.

I. Benefices were given to free men belonging to quite an inferior order, and employed in subordinate services. The *majores villae*, aud the *poledrarii*, that is to say, the stewards of the estates, and the keepers of the horses of Charlemagne, had them. It was the policy of this prince to scatter widely his gifts, and to reward zeal and fidelity wherever he found them.

II. The larger proprietors continually made themselves masters of the lands adjoining their own, whether these were lands belonging to the royal domain, or such as were neglected, and had no very definite owners. They had them cultivated, and often procured subsequently the privilege of adding them to their benefices. The extent of this abuse becomes manifest under Charles the Bald, by the numerous expedients adopted by this prince to remedy it.

III. A large number of allods were converted into benefices by means of a tolerably ancient usage. Marculf has left us the formula by which this conversion was made;—its origin we must seek in the practice of *recommendation.* Recommendation was not primitively anything else than the choice of a chief, or a patron. A law of the Visigoths, called a *lex antiqua,* and which must be referred to king Euric, towards the close of the fifth century, says: "If any one have given arms, or any other thing, to a man whom he has taken under his patronage, these gifts shall remain the property of him by whom they have been received. If this latter choose another patron, he shall be free to *recommend* himself to whomsoever he will: this may not be forbidden to a free man, for he belongeth to himself; but he shall, in this case, return to the patron from whom he separates himself all that he has received from him."

These were, then, the ancient Germanic customs. The relation of the individual *recommended* to his patron was a purely personal one. The presents consisted in arms; his liberty remained unimpaired. The law of the Lombards left to every one the same liberty as the law of the Visigoths. Nevertheless, we see, by the same capitulary, that this liberty began to be restrained. Charlemagne defined the reasons, by which any one might be allowed to quit his lord, when he had received anything from him. We may learn from this; that the ties contracted by recommendation began to be strengthened. This practice became very frequent. By these means order was promoted, so far as the law was concerned, and protection and safety as far as concerned the person recommended. When relations of service and protection bearing a purely personal character were thus established with a patron, other more tangible relations arose in which the property of the parties was considered. The person recommended received benefices from the lord; and became a vassal of his estate; or rather he recommended his lands, as he had previously recommended his person. *Recommendation* thus became a part of the feudal system and it contributed most importantly to the conversion of allodial estates into benefices.

There is, however, no reason to believe that all allods were thus converted into benefices. Originally, such a conversion, or even the mere acceptance of a benefice, was regarded by a free man as, to a certain extent, a surrender of his liberty, being an entrance upon a personal service. The large proprietors, who exercised an almost absolute sovereignty in their own domains, would not readily renounce their proud independence. Etichon, brother to Judith the wife of Louis the Débonnair, was unwilling any longer to receive his son, Henry, who had accepted, without his knowledge, from the king his uncle a benefice of four hundred acres, and thereby entered upon the service of the crown. After the triumph of the feudal system, a considerable number of allods still remained in several provinces, particularly in Languedoc.

After speaking of freeholds and benefices, it remains that I should allude to the tributary lands, whose existence is attested by all the memorials of this period. We do not necessarily understand by this term lands on which a public impost was levied, but lands which paid a fee, a rental, to a superior, and which were not the actual and absolute property of those who cultivated them.

This kind of property existed in Gaul before the invasion of the Franks. The conquest that resulted from this invasion contributed in various ways to augment their number. *First*, wherever a Barbarian possessed of some amount of power established himself, he did not take possession of all the lands, but he most probably exacted certain fees, or services equivalent to them, from almost all whose lands bordered on his own. This is certain from *a priori* considerations, and is proved as a fact by the example of the Lombards, who invariably contended themselves at first with rendering all the lands of the conquered country tributary to themselves. They demanded a third of the revenue, and afterwards took the property itself. This fact shows clearly the mode of procedure that was adopted by the Barbarians. Almost all the lands possessed by Roman or Gallic chiefs, who did not possess sufficient power to rank with the Barbarians, were obliged to submit to a tributary condition.

Secondly, conquest was not the work of a single day; it continued to be carried on after the establishment of the invaders. All the documents of the period indicate that the principal officers and large proprietors continually exerted themselves, either to usurp the possessions of their less powerful neighbours, or to impose upon them rentals or other charges. These usurpations are proved by the multitude of laws that were enacted to prevent it. In the unsettled state of society that then existed, the feeble were entirely placed at the disposal of the strong; public authority had become incompetent for their protection; many lands which were at first free, and belonged either to their ancient owners, or to Barbarians of slender resources, fell into a tributary state; many of the smaller proprietors purchased for themselves the protection of the strong, by voluntarily placing their lands in this condition. The most common method of rendering lands tributary, was to give them either to churches or to powerful proprietors, and then to receive them again, on the tenure of usufruct, to be enjoyed during life, on the payment of fixed fees. This kind of contract is to be met with again and again, during this period. The same causes which tended to destroy allods, or to convert them into benefices, acted with even more energy in augmenting the number of tributary lands.

Thirdly, many large proprietors, whether of allodial lands or of benefices, were unable themselves to cultivate the whole of their lands, and gave them up by small portions to simple cultivators, on the payment of certain fees and services. This alienation took place under a multitude of forms and a variety of circumstances; it certainly occasioned many lands to become tributary. The large number and endless variety of rentals and rights, known in a later time by the name of *feudal,* arose probably either from similar contracts, or from usurpations committed by the powerful proprietors. The constant recurrence in writers and laws of the period of the terms *census* and *tributum;* the multitude of arrangements which relate to them; the general course of events; lastly, the state in which most landed property was found when order began to reappear—all these circumstances render it probable that at the end of the period we are considering, the greater number of lands had fallen into a tributary condition. Property and liberty were alike devoted to be plundered. Individuals were so isolated, and their forces so unequal, that nothing could prevent the results of such a position.

The large number of waste lands, attested by the facility with which any one who was willing to cultivate them might obtain them, bears witness in its turn also to the depopulation of the country, and the deplorable condition in which property existed. The concentration of landed property is a decisive proof of this state of things. When this kind of property is safe and prosperous, it tends to become divided, because every one desires to possess it. When, on the other hand, we see it accumulated more and more in the same hands, we may almost certainly conclude that it is in an unsound condition, that the feeble cannot sustain themselves upon it, and that the strong alone can defend it.

Landed property, like moveable property, is only to be found where it can continue to exist in safety.

There is reason to believe that most tributary lands, even those which were not originally the property of the cultivators who laboured on them, became at length by a right of occupancy in reality their possessions, though burdened by rentals and exactions of service. This is the natural course of things: it is very difficult to remove a cultivator who has with his family for a long time tilled the same soil.

Such were the vicissitudes of landed property, from the sixth to the eleventh century. I will now give a summary view of the general characteristics of this state of things, and endeavour to estimate their influence on the progress of general civilization, and more particularly of political institutions.

I. There was a great diversity in the conditions of property. In our days, the condition of property is uniform and everywhere the same; whoever the proprietor may be, he possesses his property, whatever may be its character, on the same tenure of right, and subject to the same laws as any other. Between properties which are the most distinct in character, there is thus far an identity. This is one of the most unequivocal symptoms and safest guarantees of the progress of legal equality. During the times of which we have been speaking, the diversified conditions under which property was held would necessarily lead to the formation of several classes in society, between which existed great, factitious, and permanent inequality. Men were not merely proprietors to a greater or less extent; besides the inequality in the amount of wealth, there was also an inequality in the nature of the wealth possessed, than which it is impossible to conceive of a more powerful instrument for oppression. Even this, however, was a step in advance out of the slavery existing among the ancients. The slave could possess nothing—was essentially incapable of owning property. In the times of which I am speaking, the mass of the population had not become full and absolute possessors of property, but was attaining to a possession that was more or less imperfect and precarious, by which it had gained the means of yet loftier ascents.

II. Landed property was then submitted to the restraints of dependence on individuals. At present, all property is free, and is at the disposal only of its owner. General society has been formed—the State has been organized—every proprietor is united to his fellow-citizens by a multitude of ties and relations, and to the state by the protection which he receives from it, and the taxes to which he is subject in return: there is, thus, independence without isolation. From the sixth to the eleventh century, independence was necessarily accompanied by isolation: the proprietor of an allod lived upon his lands almost without buying or selling anything. He owed scarcely anything to a State which hardly existed, and which could not assure him of an efficient protection. The condition, therefore, of the allods and their proprietors was at that time a condition that was to a considerable extent anti-social. In more ancient times, in the forests of Germany, men without landed properties lived at least in common. When they became proprietors, if the allodial system had succeeded in becoming prevalent, the chiefs and their associates would have been separated, without ever being summoned to meet and recognize one another as citizens. Society would not have been at all constituted. It exists in those relations which unite men together, and in the ties out of which these relations arise. It necessarily demands a law, a condition of dependence. And when it is not so far advanced as that a sufficient number of these relations and ties have been established between the State and the individual, then individuals become dependent one upon another; and it was to this state of things that the seventh century had arrived. It was the imperfection of society which caused the allodial system in regard to landed property to perish, and the beneficiary or tributary system to prevail. The independence of allods could only exist in connexion with their isolation, and isolation is anti-social. The hierarchical dependence of benefices became the tie to unite properties with one another, and society within itself.[2]

III. Out of this distribution and this character of landed property, a very important fact has resulted; namely, that during several centuries scarcely any means existed by which either the state or individuals could increase their wealth. Most proprietors of any importance did not cultivate the land at all; it was for them merely a capital, the revenues of which they gathered without troubling themselves to augment it, or to render it more productive. On the other side, most of those who cultivated the land were not proprietors, or were only so in a precarious and imperfect manner; they did not seek from the earth more than means of subsistence, and did not look to it as a means of enriching or elevating them. Agricultural labour was almost unknown to the rich, and to

2. The same idea is discussed in *HCE:* "Wherever individuality predominates almost exclusively, wherever man consider no one but himself, and his ideas do not extend beyond himself, and he obeys nothing but his own passions, society (I mean a society somewhat extended and permanent) becomes for him almost impossible. Such, however, was the moral condition of the conquerors of Europe, at the time upon which we are now preoccupied. I remarked in my last lecture that we are indebted to the Germans for an energetic sentiment of individual liberty, of human individuality. But in a state of extreme barbarism and ignorance, this sentiment becomes selfishness in all its brutality, in all its unsociability. From the fifth to the eighth century it was at this point among the Germans. They cared only for their own interests, their own passions, their own will: how could they be reconciled to a condition even approximating to the social? . . . Constantly did society attempt to form itself; constantly was it destroyed by the act of man, by the absence of the moral conditions under which alone it can exist" (*HCE,* p. 56). Also see *HORG,* p. 133.

the poor it yielded nothing beyond the bare necessities of existence. Hence, resulted the continual impoverishment of the larger proprietors, which forced them incessantly to have recourse to violence, in order to preserve their fortune and their rank. Hence, resulted also, at the same time, that stationary condition of the population of the country districts which was prolonged for so long a period. Landed property tended always to become concentrated, from the very circumstance that its products did not increase. Accordingly, it is not in the country districts and in agricultural labour, but in the towns, in their commerce and industry, that we shall find the earliest germs of the accumulation of public wealth, and of the progress of civilization. The indolence of the upper classes, and the misery of the lower classes, in the middle ages, proceeded chiefly from the nature and distribution of territorial property.

IV. Beneficiary property was one of the most influential principles in the formation of large societies. In the absence of public assemblies and of a central despotism, it nevertheless established a bond, and formed relations between men dispersed over a vast tract of country, and thereby rendered possible a federative hierarchy, which should embrace a still wider circle. Among the nations of antiquity, the extension of the State was incompatible with the progress of civilization; either the State must be dislocated, or despotism would prevail. Modern States have presented a different spectacle, and to this result the character of beneficiary property has powerfully contributed.[3]

---

3. Guizot was certainly one of the first authors to perceive the connection between two aspects of political life that account for the paradoxical evolution of liberal societies. First, Guizot grasped that, contrary to the tenets of classical liberalism, the development of representative government inevitably leads to a considerable extension of the power of the state over civil society. Second, he understood that this extension was furthered by social demand and explained that the two tendencies were not contradictory (as many believed), but represented, in fact, the two sides of the same coin.

LECTURE 16

Of the state of persons, from the fifth to the tenth century. ⁓ Impossibility of determining this, according to any fixed and general principle. ⁓ The condition of lands not always correspondent with that of persons. ⁓ Variable and unsettled character of social conditions. ⁓ Slavery. ⁓ Attempt to determine the condition of persons according to the Wehrgeld. ⁓ *Table of twenty-one principal cases of* Wehrgeld. ⁓ *Uncertainty of this principle. ⁓ The true method of ascertaining the condition of persons.*

WE have investigated the condition of territorial properties, from the fifth to the tenth centuries. We have recognized three kinds of territorial property. *First,* allodial or independent; *Secondly,* beneficiary; *Thirdly,* tributary. If from this we should wish to deduce the state of persons, we should find three social conditions corresponding to these: *First,* the free men, or proprietors of allods, bound to, and dependent upon no one, excepting the general laws of the state; *Secondly,* vassals, or proprietors of benefices, dependent in certain respects upon the noble from whom they held their property, either during life or hereditarily; *Thirdly,* the proprietors of tributary lands, who were subject to certain special obligations. To which it is necessary to add a fourth class, namely, the serfs.

We should observe further, that the first of these classes tended to disappear and become absorbed in the second, third, and even the fourth classes. This arose from facts which we have already explained.

This classification of persons is in fact a real one, and is to be met with in history; but we must not regard it as a primitive, general, and perfectly regular classification.

The condition of persons preceded that of lands—there were free men before there were freeholds; there were vassals and associates before benefices. The condition and relations of persons did not therefore originally depend on the condition and relations of territorial properties, and cannot be deduced from them.

Historians have fallen into a double mistake on this point. Some have wished to see in all the Franks, before the conquest, and the establishment of the system of landed estates, which we have already explained, men altogether free and equal, whose liberty and equality for a long time resisted the formation of this system. Others have been unwilling to recognize men as free, except as they are beheld in the condition of land proprietors, whether as allods or as benefices.

The matter is not thus simple and absolute. Social conditions were not thus framed and disposed of by a single process, to suit the convenience of subsequent antiquarians.

What do we find to be the character of liberty in the infancy of societies? Might is its condition, and it has scarcely any other guarantee. So long as society is of small extent and firmly compacted within itself, individual liberty remains, because each individual is important to the society of which he is a member: this was the case with the German tribes in its warrior bands of men. In proportion as society extends and disperses itself, the liberty of individuals is endangered because their personal strength is insufficient for their own protection. This was illustrated by the case of the Germans who established themselves in Gaul. A large number of his associates lived in the house of the chief, without being themselves proprietors or being anxious to become so, for which indifference they were indebted to that want of foresight which is natural to uncivilized men. Property became a prominent instrument for attaining force, yet many free men did not possess any.

The progress of civilization removes the guarantee of individual liberty from the power of the individual himself, and places it in the power of the community. But the very creation of such a public power, and the guarantee thereby of individual liberties, is a gradual and difficult process: it results from a social culture which is of slow growth and must triumph over many obstructions. Wherever there is no power belonging to the community, individual liberties have no guarantee for their continuance.

Hence the error of those who seek for liberty in the infancy of societies. We do in fact find it there, but only when society is quite in its cradle, when each separate individual is sufficiently strong to be able to defend his own liberty in a very limited community. But as soon as society rises and extends itself, we see this liberty perish; the inequality of different forces manifests itself, and individual power becomes incapable of preserving individual liberty. This is the birth-time of oppression and disorder.[1]

---

1. Here Guizot argues that true liberty cannot exist in the infancy of societies when individuals struggle to maintain and assert their independence. In his view, true liberty cannot be secured in the absence of a genuine and stable political society which alone can provide guarantees for the continuance of individual liberties. That is why liberties can only be safeguarded by the institu-

Such was the condition of the Franco-Roman community, at the period which we are considering. It seems somewhat puerile to inquire who was free then; no one was free, whatever his origin might be, if he was not strong. The real inquiry is, who was strong—a point which it is exceedingly difficult to determine.

In a fully settled society which has existed for a long time, it is easy to know who is strong. There is a constant transmission of properties and of ancient influences; power has permanent forms, men are classified. We see where strength resides and who possesses it. But at the time which we are considering, the various elements of social strength were struggling into existence; they scarcely had a being, and they were not familiarly known, nor stably fixed, or in regular possession of power; the violent customs which prevailed rendered property very moveable; individual strength was a poor guarantee for liberty, indeed, it needed itself to be placed in guardianship.

The human mind can hardly believe in disorder, because it cannot picture clearly to itself such a state of things; it does not resign itself to the idea; it desires to introduce an order of its own, in order to discover the light. We must, however, accept facts as they actually are. We may therefore understand how difficult it is to exhibit the condition of men, from the fifth to the tenth centuries; to learn what men were free, and who were not, and especially what a free man really was in his position and influence. We shall understand this difficulty still better when we have attempted to determine the condition of life belonging to certain positions, according to the different principles of classification which we may bring to the task. We shall see that no one principle can be found, by which we can deduce the state belonging to different positions in a manner exactly conformable to known facts, and which is not contradicted at every step by these same facts, or at least shown by them to be utterly insufficient and untrustworthy.

Let us first apply the principle which is inferred from the state of landed property.

The proprietors of allods might seem to be incontestably free men. An allodial proprietor who had extensive estates enjoyed complete independence,

---

tions and principles of representative government; to use Guizot's own words, "liberty cannot exist except by the possession of rights. . . . Where liberties are not rights, and where rights are not powers, neither rights nor liberties exist" (*ibid.*, pp. 177, 331). This idea looms large in Guizot's thought and should be related to his definition of liberty. In Lecture 19, he distinguished between two ways in which we usually conceive of liberty. "First, as the independence of the individual having no law but his own will; and secondly, as the enfranchisement of every individual from every other individual will, which is contrary to reason and justice" (*ibid.*, p. 134).

REPRESENTATIVE INSTITUTIONS IN ENGLAND, FRANCE, AND SPAIN

and wielded an almost absolute sovereignty throughout his territory, and among his associates.

Large allodial proprietors were sometimes able to remain for a considerable time in such a position. But it was not certainly the strongest, nor consequently the most free and fixed condition; for we have seen that allodial property degenerated and declined, until almost all the allodial proprietors became beneficiaries. We have seen how the anger of Etichon was excited. The general fact is a witness against the life of the allodial proprietor. His very independence was a cause of isolation, and therefore of feebleness. The proprietors of allods, wearied with living on their estates, shut out from all society, used to come and live with the king or some large proprietor of greater power than themselves. It was soon a practice to send their children thither, in order that they might become companions of the prince, or of some distinguished noble.

As to the smaller allodial proprietors, they could not keep their standing long; they were not strong enough to defend their independence. The records of the period show that their property was soon alienated, and at the same time many of them became merely cultivators of the lands. The condition of the freeholder thus became merged in that of the tributary. From thence there was but one step to a total loss of liberty. This step was actually taken by a large number of allodial proprietors—wearied out or ruined, they surrendered their liberty into the hands of proprietors more wealthy and powerful than themselves.

We come now to the beneficiaries.

Benefices originated large individual resources—in them we find the source of the feudal aristocracy—large beneficiaries became in time powerful nobles. But we must not from this conclude that the possession of benefices was, during the period we are considering, any security for a permanent social position, to which power and liberty necessarily belonged. *First,* this possession was precarious, moveable, attacked, in the case of the smaller beneficiaries, by the larger ones, and in the case of the latter by the king. Beneficiary property hardly began to possess any fixity at the close of the ninth century. *Secondly,* a number of small benefices were conferred on individuals too weak efficiently to defend their position and their liberty. In order to secure the services of a man who was not a slave, a benefice was given to him—it was therefore a grant for the support of a retainer. The land itself was given for this purpose, as well as its productions. The benefices given to Charlemagne's stewards and the keepers of his horse were actual benefices, and not, as M. de Montlosier thinks, tributary lands. We are not then in a position to say that the rank of a beneficiary was the sign of a definitely marked social position, nor that it could measure the degree of importance and of freedom that belonged to individuals.

When we have mentioned the allodial proprietors and the beneficiaries, it might be thought that the class of freemen is exhausted. Such is not, however, the case. There were different classes of possessors and farmers of tributary lands, known under various names; such as *fiscalini, fiscales, tributarii, coloni, lidi, aldi, aldiones,* &c. These names do not all designate different conditions, but divers shades in conditions substantially the same. There were: *First,* free men, at once allodial proprietors and cultivators; *Secondly,* free men, both proprietors of benefices and cultivators; *Thirdly,* free men, neither properly freeholders nor beneficiaries, and cultivators; *Fourthly,* men not free, to whom the hereditary possession of tributary land had been granted on the payment of certain fees and services; *Fifthly,* men not free, who only enjoyed the permanent occupancy of tributary land. Here again we cannot find any general and fixed social condition which shall determine what were the rank, the rights, and other qualifications of the individuals belonging to it. We are mistaken if we imagine either that every proprietor was free, or that every free man was a proprietor. We find that the cultivators of lands under the king harassed and oppressed the smaller allodial proprietors who resided in their vicinity, and were too feeble to oppose any effectual resistance, although they were Franks.

I need only mention slaves, in order to observe that many free men fell into this state of servitude by means of violence, and through an uncertainty in property which involved a corresponding uncertainty in position. Sometimes one man would surrender himself to his more powerful neighbour, and at the same time completely abandon his liberty. The surrender, however, was sometimes not an entire renouncement of liberty, although it was alienated for life, or a sum was agreed upon to be paid if the engagement should be broken.

It is evident that we cannot derive, from the state and the distribution of territorial properties, any true and fixed table of different social conditions, and of the importance of the rights belonging to each. These conditions were too undefined, too different, while nominally identical, and too fluctuating, to give us a standard to measure the amount of liberty possessed by each man and the place he occupied in society. The state of persons was almost individual; the measure of the importance of any individual was determined by the particular amount of strength which might belong to him, much more than by the general position which he apparently occupied. Individuals constantly passed from one condition into another, neither losing all at once every characteristic of the position which they left, nor assuming at once every characteristic of that upon which they newly entered.

Let us apply another principle.

Attempts have been made to determine the condition of individuals, and to classify men according to the *wehrgeld;* that is to say, according to the sum by which a man might compound for the commission of a murder, which was consequently the measure of the valuation of different lives. Shall we find here any more certain and unvarying principle by which social conditions may be classified?

I have made an abstract of all the cases of *wehrgeld* stipulated in the Barbaric laws. I will not enumerate them all, but will bring before you twenty-one of the principal, ranging from the sum of 1800 *solidi,* the largest value that was legally placed on any man's life, down to 20 *solidi.*

The *wehrgeld* amounted to:

1800 sol. (*solidi*): for the murder of a free barbarian, a companion of the king (*in truste regia*), attacked and killed in his house by an armed band, among the Salian Franks.

960 sol.: 1st. the duke, among the Bavarians; 2nd, the bishop, among the Germans.

900 sol.: 1st. the bishop, among the Ripuarian Franks; 2nd. the Roman, *in truste regia,* attacked and killed in his own house by an armed band, among the Salian Franks.

640 sol.: the relatives of a duke, with the Barbarians.

600 sol.: 1st. every man *in truste regia,* with the Ripuarians; 2nd. the same, with the Salian Franks; 3rd. the count, with the Ripuarians; 4th. the priest, born free, with the Ripuarians; 5th. the priest, with the Germans; 6th. the count, with the Salian Franks; 7th. the *Sagibaro* (a kind of judge) free, *ibid.;* 8th. the priest, *ibid.;* the free man attacked and killed in his own house by an armed band, *ibid.*

500 sol.: the deacon, with the Ripuarians.

400 sol.: 1st. the sub-deacon, with the Ripuarians; 2nd. the deacon, with the Germans; 3rd. the same, among the Salian Franks.

300 sol.: 1st. the Roman living with the king, with the Salian Franks; 2nd. the young man brought up in the service of the king, and those who had been enfranchised by the king, and made counts, with the Ripuarians; 3rd. the priest, among the Bavarians; 4th. the *Sagibaro* who had been brought up in the court of the king, with the Salian Franks; 5th. the Roman killed by an armed band in his house, *ibid.*

200 sol.: the free-born clerk, with the Ripuarians; 2nd. the deacon, with the Bavarians; 3rd. the free Ripuarian Frank; 4th. the German of the middle classes; 5th. the Frank or Barbarian, living under Salic law; 6th. the travelling Frank, with the Ripuarians; 7th. the man who had become enfranchised by purchase, with the Ripuarians.

160 sol.: 1st. the free man in general, among the Germans; 2nd. the same, with the Bavarians; 3rd. the Burgundian, the German, the

Bavarian, the Frison, the Saxon, with the Ripuarians; 4th. the free man cultivating ecclesiastical property, with the Germans.

150 sol.: 1st. the *optimus*, or noble Burgundian, killed by the man whom he had attacked; 2nd. the steward of a royal domain, with the Burgundians; 3rd. the slave who could work well in gold, *ibid.*

100 sol.: any man belonging to the middle classes (*mediocris homo*) with the Burgundians, killed by the person whom he had attacked; 2nd. the Roman possessing personal property, with the Salian Franks; 3rd. the Roman while travelling, with the Ripuarians; 4th. the man in the service of the king, or of a church, *ibid.*; 5th. the planter (*lidus*) by two charters of Charlemagne (an. 803 and 813); 6th. the steward (*actor*) of a domain belonging to any but the king, with the Burgundians; 7th. the slave, a worker in silver, *ibid.*

80 sol.: those enfranchised in presence of the church, or by a special charter, with the Germans.

75 sol.: any man of inferior condition (*minor persona*), with the Burgundians.

55 sol.: the barbarian slave employed in the personal service of a master, or as a bearer of messages, with the Burgundians.

50 sol.: the blacksmith (slave), with the Burgundians.

45 sol.: 1st. the serf of the church and the serf of the king, with the Germans; 2nd. the tributary Roman, with the Salian Franks.

40 sol.: 1st. one merely enfranchised, with the Bavarians; 2nd. the herdsman keeping forty swine, with the Germans; 3rd. the shepherd over eighty sheep, *ibid.*; 4th. the seneschal of the man who has twelve companions (*vassi*) in his house, *ibid.*; 5th. the marshal who kept twelve horses, *ibid.*; 6th. the cook who has an assistant (*junior*), *ibid.*; 7th. the goldsmith, *ibid.*; 8th. the armourer, *ibid.*; 9th. the blacksmith, *ibid.*; 10th. the cartwright, with the Burgundians.

36 sol.: 1st. the slave, with the Ripuarians; 2nd. the slave who had become a tributary planter, *ibid.*

30 sol.: the keeper of swine, with the Burgundians.

20 sol.: the slave, with the Bavarians.

We see by this table that, notwithstanding the common opinion to the contrary, the *wehrgeld* is by no means an exact and certain indication of social conditions. It is not determined uniformly according to the origin, the quality, the position of individuals. The circumstances of the murder, the official character of the criminal, the greater or less usefulness or commonness of the man slain, all these variable elements enter into the determination of the *wehrgeld*.

The simple fact of the murder having been committed at the court of the duke, while the victim is going to or returning from the house of the count, triples the *wehrgeld* of every man, whether he be a slave or a freeman, a Barbarian or a Roman. The elements of the *wehrgeld* are very numerous; it varies according to places and times. The Roman, the tributary, the slave, according to circumstances, may be valued at a greater or a less sum than a barbarian free man. We see many general indications which serve to show that the Roman was commonly less esteemed than a barbarian, the tributary or the slave less than the free man. This is very easily accounted for, and might have been anticipated. But it is not on this account less difficult to draw from such facts a positive indication of the state of individuals—a precise and complete classification of social conditions.

There is no resource left but to renounce the idea of classifying social conditions and of determining the conditions of persons, according to any general principle, resting either on the nature of territorial properties, or in the legal appreciation of the value of different lives. We must simply inquire, by the aid of historical facts, who were the strong and powerful at the time; what common name was given to them; what share of influence and of liberty fell to the lot of those who were simply called free men. We shall thus arrive at clearer and more certain results. We shall often find that landed property is a great and principal source of strength, and that the *wehrgeld* is an indication of the amount of importance or of liberty possessed by individuals; but we shall not attribute to these two principles a general and decisive authority, and we shall not mutilate facts in order that they may harmonize with our hypotheses.

LECTURE 17

Of the Leudes *or* Antrustions. ⁓ *Men, faithful to the king and to the large proprietors.—Different means of acquiring and retaining them.* ⁓ *Obligations of the* Leudes. ⁓ *The* Leudes *are the origin of the nobility.* ⁓ *Bishops and heads of monasteries were reckoned among the* leudes *of the king.* ⁓ *Moral and material power of the bishops.* ⁓ *Efforts of the kings to possess themselves of the right of nominating bishops.* ⁓ *Free men.* ⁓ *Did they form a distinct and numerous class?* ⁓ *The* arimanni, *and* rathimburgi. ⁓ *Mistake of M. de Savigny.* ⁓ *Rapid and general extension of the feudal hierachy.* ⁓ *The freedmen.* ⁓ *Different modes of enfranchisement: First, the* denariales, *enfranchised with respect to the king: Second, the* tabularii, *enfranchised with respect to the church: Third, the* chartularii, *enfranchised by a charter.* ⁓ *Different consequences resulting from these different modes of enfranchisement.*

THE first whom we meet with at this time occupying the highest place in the social scale are the *Leudes,* or *Antrustions.* Their name indicates their quality—*trust* expresses fidelity. They were men who had proved faithful, and they succeeded the associates of the German chiefs. After the conquest, each of the chiefs established himself, together with his own men, on a certain territory. The king had a larger and more considerable number of followers. Many remained with him. He had different means, which he very assiduously employed, of attaching to himself his Leudes, or of acquiring them.

1st. This was evidently the result aimed at in conferring benefices. In 587, Gontran, giving his advice to Childebert II. on his conduct to those who were about him, points out to him "those whom he ought to honour by appointments and by gifts, and those to whom he ought to refuse them."

2nd. The organization of the house, the palace, the court, borrowed in part from the traditions of the Roman empire, the passing amusements and the permanent advantages which were attached to them, induced many men of influence to become Leudes, or gave importance to the original Leudes of the king. The following are names of some of their offices; "count of the palace, referendary, seneschal, mareschal, falconer, butler, chamberlain, porter, headporter, &c."

3rd. Marculf has preserved to us the formula by which a man of importance, *cum arimannia sua,* "with his free men, his band," was accustomed to enroll himself among the king's Leudes. Charlemagne took various precautions in order that persons who came to him in order to become his trusty followers (*de truste facienda*), should meet with no obstacle.

4th. It was to their Leudes that the kings were in the habit of giving important public occupations, such as belonged to dukes, counts, &c. There is reason for believing that these functions originally belonged to the principal chief who established himself in a territory. In the natural course of events these chiefs became themselves Leudes of the king or were supplanted by those who were such.

5th. The number of Leudes was the principal source of strength; accordingly they were multiplied by all kinds of devices. In 587, in the treaty of Andely, between Gontran and Childebert II, "it was agreed that neither of them should attempt to draw over to himself the Leudes of the other, or receive them if they came of their own accord." We continually find Leudes of importance threatening the king to leave his service, and enter into some other.

The general obligation of the Leudes was fidelity, service in the palace, and military service. The price of this obligation was, for the Leudes, power and riches. They had also certain civil advantages, but of a more uncertain nature. Their *wehrgeld* was a larger amount, whatever might otherwise have been their origin. We see that their prerogatives accumulated in proportion as their power was consolidated by the long possession of benefices. Charlemagne desired that his vassals should be honoured, and should hold, after himself, the first place in esteem. There were however among the Leudes of the king some who were less powerful, and some who even were poor.

Every large proprietor had his Leudes; his house was organized after the model of the king's; the same offices existed in each.

It is the opinion of Montesquieu, who is in this opposed by Montlosier, that the origin of the nobility is to be found in the Leudes. Neither of them has formed, in my judgment, a just and clear idea either of the condition of the Leudes or of the character of the nobility. The rank of the Leude and his advantages were purely of a personal character. The rank of a free Barbarian was hereditary, as were also his advantages: but the rank of the Leude, that is to say, the advantages and the superiority which he derived from his position, tended to become hereditary; that of the free man, on the other hand, tended, when he was isolated and left to himself, to become effaced and to lose its advantages. Most free men who did not become beneficiaries, vassals, Leudes of some importance, ceased to be free at all. The aristocracy of the Leudes tended to be constituted, the liberty of the free men tended to be destroyed—the free men were, viewed in contrast with those who were not free, an aristocracy on the decline; the Leudes were, compared with free men, an aristocracy on the increase.

Mannert, in his treatise entitled, *The liberty of the Franks, Freyheit der Franken,* has very clearly explained the formation of the nobility among the Franks. There were many Roman Gauls among the Leudes of the Frankish kings: we find, for example, the names of *Protadius, Claudius, Florentinianus,* among the mayors of the palace towards the close of the sixth, and the commencement of the seventh century. They often changed their names into barbaric names. Thus the brother of Duke Lupus, born a Roman, called himself *Magn-Wulfus* (great wolf), and his son, who was bishop of Rheims, he called *Rom-Wulfus* (Roman wolf). These Romans entered into the company of the Leudes because they needed the protection of the kings; because they were disposed to place what power they had in his service; because they were acquainted with the country, and knew that the king required them; because, lastly, the kings, when they embraced Christianity, became reconciled to many wealthy and influential Gauls.

Bishops, and the principal heads of monasteries, or of large ecclesiastical corporations, were reckoned among the number of the king's Leudes. The power of the bishops among the Gauls, before the arrival of the Germans, is proved directly by facts; their influence, their wealth, is proved indirectly by the eagerness with which the position of a bishop was sought. Their importance was greatly augmented after the establishment of the Barbarians. They protected the ancient inhabitants from the Barbarian kings, and served the latter by their power in governing the ancient inhabitants. They, and scarcely any but they, had preserved some science, some intellectual culture; the influence of religious ideas and practices over the converted barbarians was powerful; the impressions formed were strong and vivid at that stage of civilization: the clergy could excite the imagination, could tranquillize or alarm the conscience. The bishops and heads of monasteries acquired, through a large number of sources, great wealth; they in process of time became large beneficiaries; most of the property given to churches were given as benefices, and consequently involved the obligations belonging to that title; some property was conferred "with the complete right of proprietorship." In 807, Charlemagne charged his son Pepin to prevent the dukes and counts to whom the government of the provinces had been committed, from exacting from churches all the services due in general from free men. In 816, Louis the Débonnair provided that each church should possess a farm absolutely free from all charge. Facts disclose at every step the importance of the bishops; they were employed in important transactions, and assisted in drawing up laws. Counts, dukes, large Barbarian proprietors, became bishops. The temporal consequences attached to ecclesiastical excommunication did not fail to put into their hands a powerful weapon of attack or defence. Churches obtained immunities of all kinds, from military service, rights of custom, &c.; they became asylums of refuge—a popular right which, during these times of brute violence, far more generally protected the innocent than shielded the guilty.

The nomination of bishops was an ancient right of the priests and the faithful. The importance of these functions, and the riches of the churches, induced the king to encroach upon this prerogative. Further, they urged some kind of claim to it, as being lords of the churches on which they had conferred benefices. They used the right of confirmation in order to possess themselves of the right of nomination. At first, bishops were the most sure and devoted Leudes of the king; kings and bishops had need of one another. Very soon afterwards the bishops became so powerful as to be able to act independently of the kings.

At this epoch convents also assumed great importance, although their heads do not seem to have played so prominent a part in France as in England.

Upon the whole, the power of the clergy at this period was as useful as it was great. It awakened and developed moral necessities among the Barbarians—it commanded and inspired a respect for the rights and sufferings of the feeble—it gave an illustration of the reality of moral force, when everything was at the disposal of material force. That is a false notion which assumes that an institution or an influence is to be attacked by reason of the evil effects which it may produce after centuries of existence; we must consider and appreciate it in the times when it was originally formed.

From the Leudes, let us pass to those who were simply free men.

There are words which have, in our time, so simple and absolute a signification, that we apply them without consideration or scruple to times in which their actual significance was not recognized at all. The expression *free man* is an example. If by it we mean the man who is not a slave, the man who is not the property of another man, and can neither be given nor sold as an article of traffic, there were a great number of free men from the fifth to the tenth centuries. But if we attach to this expression the political sense which it possesses in our days, that is to say, the idea of a citizen dependent on no other citizen, who depends for the safety of his person and his property only upon the state, and the laws of the state, the number of free men was very inconsiderable at the period of which we speak, and was continually diminishing. Most of those who were not serfs were engaged or were binding themselves with increasing frequency, either for the security of their persons or of their properties, to the service, and to a certain amount of dependency upon some man more powerful than themselves, who employed them in his house or protected them at a distance. The independence of the citizen as it existed in the republics of antiquity, and as it exists in our public communities, became more and more rare from the fifth to the tenth centuries. Eminent publicists, M. de Savigny among others, in his *Histoire du droit romain dans le moyen âge*, have affirmed that always at this period a numerous class of free men existed, true citizens, exempt from all personal dependence, depending only upon the state and forming the body of the nation. This involves a complete confusion of times and a misapprehension of the natural succession of events. Doubtless at the time of the invasion, and during the period which immediately followed it, there were many free men of this kind; the independence of individuals who live a wandering and barbarian life did not suddenly and completely vanish under the influence of the new circumstances which resulted from their territorial establishment. But, so far as regards the greater number of free men, this independence was rapidly absorbed by new ties, and by the very numerous and various forms of feudal hierarchy. We may think we have found, under certain names which are frequently to be met with in documents and historical works, such as, *Arimanni, Erimanni, Herimanni, Hermanni,* among the Lombards, and *Rachimburgi, Rathimburgi, Regimburgi,* among the Franks, a class of men actually free—citizens in the sense in which we use the words at the present time. But when we investigate more closely, we soon learn that no such class is to be found, and that nearly if not quite all the *Arimanni* or *Rathimburgi,* were bound in the fetters of a feudal organization and depended far more on some superior individual than on the protection of the state.

Many learned men also think that the practice of enfranchisement which prevailed at this period created many free men—as completely so, as if they had inherited their freedom as a birthright. This also is, I think, a mistake. Enfranchisement was frequent, but it conferred complete freedom on very few; it transformed many into cultivators and tributaries, or placed them in other analogous positions, which however did not insure entire liberty. In order to be convinced of this, we have only to examine the acts of enfranchisement themselves. There were several kinds, and each was attended with different consequences. We find, *First,* the *denariales,* or enfranchised with respect to the king; although their life was valued at 200 *solidi,* like the life of a Frank, yet their liberty was incomplete; they could not bequeath property to others than their children; the composition for their lives was paid to the king, not to their relatives, which plainly shows that the king regarded them as *homines regii. Second,* those enfranchised with respect to the church, or *tabularii.* Those thus enfranchised became *homines ecclesiastici;* they could not become *denariales* according to the laws of the Ripuarians, and their property went to the church if they died without issue. *Third,* those enfranchised *per chartam, chartularii.* The expressions of the charter which gave them their liberty seem to be completely unambiguous; but it is doubtful whether the results were similarly unambiguous, since the *denariales* themselves remained, in certain respects, in an inferior condition. The statutes of Charlemagne, which provide that the terms of composition for the *denariales* should be paid to the king, and that they should not possess their liberty as a heritage till after the third generation, apply the same conditions also to the *chartularii,* and even to those who were enfranchised to the church, the *tabularii.*

The act and the consequences of enfranchisement varied in the course of the epoch on which our attention is occupied. This fact has not been observed by M. Montlosier and all those who bring together facts separated from one another by a long interval of time, in order to make a complete system. They apply to the same epoch facts belonging to different times. History presents us with instances of slaves who, after the Germanic invasion, raised themselves to the condition not only of free men, but of Leudes and large proprietors. Individual cases of these are well authenticated, and were very likely to have occurred in these times of disorder; but from these no general rule is to be inferred. In spite of the vast influence of religious ideas—and all formulas of enfranchisement are prefaced by the expression of a religious sentiment and design—the general movement of the epoch which we are considering, so far as regards the condition of persons, was much more towards the extension of servitude, under different forms and in varying degrees, than towards the maintenance or the advancement of liberty.

LECTURE 18

Simultaneous existence of three systems of institutions, after the settlement of the Franks in Gaul. ⁓ *Conflict of these three systems.* ⁓ *Summary of this conflict, its vicissitudes, and results.* ⁓ *Its recurrence in local and central institutions.* ⁓ *Of local institutions under the Frankish monarchy.* ⁓ *Of the assemblies of free men.* ⁓ *Of the authority and jurisdiction of the great landowners in their estates.* ⁓ *Of the authority and jurisdiction of the dukes, counts, and other royal officers.*

Fʀᴏᴍ the ancient condition of the barbarians in Germany, and from their new situation after their establishment in the Roman empire, there issued three systems of institutions, of different principles and results, which, from the fifth to the tenth century, co-existed at first for some time, and afterwards commingled and conflicted with each other with alternate success and defeat.

In their primitive state, in Germany, the Barbarians were all free; every individual was important—nothing of any moment could be undertaken or decided upon without the approbation and concurrence of the majority. Hence arose the common discussion of affairs of common interest, and the influence of election upon the choice of chiefs or judges—or in other words, the institutions of liberty.

The second principle with which we meet is the attachment and subordination of the tribesmen to their chief. Up to a certain point they were dependent upon him, even for their subsistence. This dependence increased after their territorial establishment. The authority of the chiefs over their comrades augmented; and the liberty of the latter diminished with their importance. They became beneficiaries or vassals, colonists, or even serfs; a hierarchy was formed among the landowners. Hence arose those aristocratic and hierarchical institutions which gave birth to the feudal system.

The power of the kings, originally very limited, became extended after conquest by the dispersion of the nation, the concession of benefices, and the predominance of the principle of hereditary succession to the throne. A conflict arose, not between the power of the king and the liberties of the citizens, but between the power of the king and that of the nobles, especially of the king's own Leudes. The kings made attempts to found the entire government upon the monarchical principle, and, with this object, to place themselves in direct connexion with all their subjects. Under Charlemague, this attempt reached its apogee, and seemed likely to succeed. But the monarchical system succumbed beneath the feudal system.

Thus, free institutions, aristocratic institutions, monarchical institutions—local and general assemblies of free men to deliberate on common affairs, military, judicial, or others, in presence of or in concert with the king or his delegates—the subordination of the simple free man to the lord, of the vassal to the chieftain; the nobles administering justice, making war with each other, and imposing certain charges on their vassals; the progressive organization of the royal power; dukes, counts, royal officers, *missi dominici,* transacting public affairs and administering justice, even in opposition to the nobles—these are the three systems of facts, the three tendencies which present themselves to our notice during the period from the fifth to the tenth century. The conflict of these three tendencies constitutes the history of the public institutions of this epoch.

The system of free institutions rapidly declined. It succumbed beneath the system of the predominance of the great landowners, and of the hierarchy of benefices. A conflict arose between the principles of the feudal system, and the endeavours of the monarchical system. In the conflict of these two systems, however, we find remnants of the system of free institutions. These remnants were allied sometimes to the feudal, sometimes to the monarchical system—most frequently to the latter. Charlemagne attempted to render the institutions of liberty auxiliary to the triumph of the monarchical system. We observed something analogous to this in the history of the Anglo-Saxons; but there the system of free institutions never perished; the common deliberation of the free landowners, in the county-courts, always subsisted. Among the Franks, the simultaneity and conflict of the three systems were more distinct and animated; the first was the weakest and perished early.

In treating of the Franks, as of the Anglo-Saxons, we shall first examine their local institutions, and then their general institutions; and we shall everywhere meet with the great fact to which I have just alluded. We shall follow it in its vicissitudes, and we shall see, first, how the system of free institutions perished, in localities and at the centre; secondly, how the monarchical system was for a moment really successful and strongly predominant under Charlemagne alone; and thirdly, how the feudal system, that is to say, the aristocratic and hierarchical organization of territorial properties and sovereignties, could not but prevail, as it really did in the end.

OF LOCAL INSTITUTIONS

In Frankish Gaul, as among the Anglo-Saxons, the territory was divided into counties, hundreds, and tythings.* The counts were called *grafen, judices;* the centeniers, *centgrafen;* and the tything-men, *tungini, thingrafen.* Each of these officers held a court, *placitum, mallum,* at which justice was administered, and the business of the district transacted. This court was at first an assembly of all the free men of the district; they were bound to attend, and a heavy fine was imposed as the penalty for non-attendance. There, as I have said, they distributed justice, and deliberated upon matters of common interest. Civil transactions, sales, wills, enfranchisements, were carried on in public. There, also, military convocations were made. The court or *plaid* of the tything-man, *decanus,* is seldom met with, and was of little importance, as in England. The powers of the courts or assemblies of free men, held by the *centenarii* and *vicarii* were somewhat limited; judgments could not be given upon questions involving property or personal liberty, unless it were in presence of the imperial envoys or the counts.

Such were the free institutions and the meetings for common deliberation, of separate localities. These primitive *plaids* correspond to the ancient assemblies of the Germans in Germany.

Besides the *plaids* of freemen, appears the jurisdiction of the nobles or important landowners over the persons who dwelt on their domains. The chieftain distributed justice to his comrades, or, as they had now become, his colonists. His jurisdiction was not, however, altogether arbitrary; his comrades were his assessors in his court. The *conjuratores,* who attested the truth of the facts stated, almost entirely settled the affair. If we consider these institutions in their origin, we find that the seignorial courts of justice, although obscure and somewhat inactive, existed simultaneously with the assemblies of freemen, exempt from the circumscription and jurisdiction of the officers of the crown. The jurisdiction of the churches was derived from the jurisdiction of the seigneurs, and both were exercised in virtue of the proprietorship of the domain, which rendered the landlord the patron of its inhabitants.

These are the first rudiments of that feudal organization which, by establishing the authority and jurisdiction of the seigneur over his tenants, vassals or colonists, constantly tended to destroy the authority and jurisdiction of the assemblies of free men. A conflict began between the feudal principle of hierarchical subordination, and the principle of the union of equals in common de-

---

* That is, of course, districts analogous to these divisions.

liberation. This conflict commenced as early as the beginning of the epoch which now occupies our attention.

Let us now examine how the royal power was exercised in separate localities during this period. The dukes, counts, centeniers, and others, were probably at the outset, as I have already observed, not mere delegates of the king, but the natural chieftains, the most powerful and extensive landowners. It is quite erroneous to believe that, originally, a county corresponded to what is now called a department, and that the king appointed and sent a count to govern it as he now sends a prefect. The king, the head of the nation, naturally directed the most important man in the district to convoke together the free men of the district for military purposes, and to collect the revenues of the royal domains; and this person thus received a sort of appointment from the king. The increasing importance of the palace and court of the kings—the influence of Roman institutions and ideas, at length made this appointment the source of a title. The counts became Leudes, and *vice versa*, the Leudes became counts.

During a considerable period the hereditariness of these officers was not recognised. Some antiquaries even are of opinion that these employments were given for a fixed time only. There is more reason to believe that this point was not definitely determined, and that, in fact, these offices were long unlimited as to their duration, and always transferable; numerous instances can be brought in support of this theory. The Frankish kings frequently allowed the natural chieftains of the countries which they conquered to retain their former position and ancient rights. Thus the Bavarian dukes were hereditary. When Louis the Débonnair received the Spaniards into the south of France, he permitted their counts to retain their titles and jurisdiction.

The title of count became an object of ambition on account of the advantages connected therewith. The count possessed great power, a share of the fines, *freda,* and immense facilities for acquiring property in the district under his jurisdiction. These offices also supplied the kings with means for enriching their Leudes, or obtaining new ones. Under the Merovingians, perpetual instability prevailed in respect to these offices as well as to benefices; they were obtained by presents or purchased by money. Nevertheless, the office of count was frequently transmitted from father to son; this was natural, and usage could not fail to precede right; the count or duke, being almost always an important personage in his canton or town, independently of his office, his son, who succeeded to his importance, succeeded frequently to his office also.

Some writers have affirmed that there was a great distinction between the dukes and the counts; it has even been asserted that each duke had twelve counts under his orders. No such regularity existed in local administration. We meet with some counts equal in power to dukes; among the Burgundians, for example, some counts ruled over several provinces. We may say, however, that in general the duke was superior to the count. We may even presume that, originally, the office of duke was military, and that of the count, judicial; although the two missions frequently appear confounded. A formula of Marculf assimilates the dukes, counts, and patricians. The margraves were the counts of the marches or frontiers. The men of the court, the delegates of the king, finished by being counts everywhere.

Thus there co-existed the three systems of institutions which I have mentioned: 1. the assemblies of freemen, having authority and jurisdiction; 2. the great landowners, whether beneficiary or allodial, lay or ecclesiastical, proprietors—having authority and jurisdiction; 3. the administrators or delegates of the king, having authority and jurisdiction.

In the midst of the disorders of the Merovingian race, we find that the assemblies of free men rapidly declined. Most of the free men ceased to attend. Some became powerful enough to aim at independence, others became so weak as to lose their freedom. The common deliberation of free men disappeared. The principle of the subordination of the individual to the individual, in virtue of protection, vassalage, patronage, or colonage, prevailed. Seignorial jurisdictions, both lay and ecclesiastical, became extended. Their extension and consolidation were the necessary consequence of the extension and consolidation of benefices. The diminution of the number of allodial estates, the increase of tributary lands, and the corresponding changes which were introduced into the condition of persons, necessarily removed the greater number of justiceables from the jurisdiction of the assemblies of free men and from that of the king. Even the care which was taken by the first Carlovingians to compel the seigneurs to administer justice, and to control their administration of it, proves the progress of this kind of jurisdiction.

The liberty allowed to every man to live under any law he pleased, could not but contribute also to this result; it tended to disperse society, for it placed men under the jurisdiction of those who had their own private code of laws; and thus it opposed union, and common deliberation. It was a kind of liberty, doubtless—a liberty necessary in the state of society which then existed; but this liberty, like almost all other liberties at this period, was a principle of isolation.

LECTURE 19

Government of Charlemagne. ~ *Apparent revival of free institutions.*
~ *Individual independence and social liberty.* ~ *Organization of*
monarchical power under Charlemagne. ~ *His active surveillance*
over his vassals and agents. ~ *Rapid decline of monarchical institu-*
tions after his death. ~ *Definitive predominance of the feudal system.*
~ *Central institutions during the same epoch: royalty.* ~ *Causes of*
the progress of royalty, and of the principle of hereditary succession among
the Franks. ~ *Influence of the clergy.*

AFTER the Merovingian anarchy, at the accession of the Carlovingians and especially during the reign of Charlemagne, two facts, which seem contradictory, present themselves to our notice. Free institutions appear to gain new life, and at the same time the monarchical system evidently prevails. We must closely study this singular coincidence, and endeavour thoroughly to understand its causes.

There are two ways in which we may understand a man's personal liberty; first, as the independence of the individual having no law but his own will; and secondly, as the enfranchisement of every individual from every other individual will, which is contrary to reason and justice.

Liberty, if taken in the first sense, is barbarous and anti-social; it is the infancy, or rather the absence, of society. The word *society* itself indicates the union of individuals in one common idea, feeling, and interest. Society can exist only by the obedience of individuals to one common rule. If the liberty of each man constitutes his only law, if every restriction to the independence of individual will is considered illegitimate, society is impossible. The law which should rule society, according to truth and justice, is exterior to and independent of individual wills. The object of society is to discover this superior law, and to exact obedience to it alone; but to this law obedience must be given; society is possible only by the reign of brute force, or by the government of true law. If the independence of the individual is regarded as the condition of liberty, we may be certain that force will become the dominant power of society, for society there must be; it is an imperious necessity of human nature; and this necessity will receive its gratification from force, if it cannot obtain it from justice and reason.

The object of government, then, is twofold; it proposes, first, to seek out and discover the true law which must decide all the questions to which social relations give rise, and to subject to this law all adverse individual wills; and secondly, to prevent individuals from being subjected to any other laws but the true law, such, for example, as the arbitrary will of other more powerful individuals. Good and true government, then, does not say to every individual: "Thou shalt be subject only to thy own caprice," for on these terms there could be no society, and no government; but it says: "Thou shalt be subject, not to the caprice of any other individual, but only to reason and justice." The progress of civilization consists, on the one hand, in extending the authority of reason over all individuals, and in neglecting no means to convince their individual reason and to render their obedience voluntary; and, on the other hand, in limiting the sway of the arbitrary will of individuals over one another. Where the arbitrary will of one or more individuals prevails, legitimate liberty does not exist; where the isolated independence of every individual is maintained, society is impossible.

The importance of this distinction between moral and natural liberty, between social freedom and individual independence, is immense. It would be easy to demonstrate its intimate connexion with the true theory of liberty, considered in relation to man personally, and independently of society. It is as a reasonable being, capable of recognizing truth, that man is sublime; therein resides the divinity of his nature: liberty is in him nothing but the power of obeying the truth which he recognises, and making his actions conform thereto. On this ground, liberty is very respectable; but liberty is respectable on this ground alone.

In the infancy of society, the liberty which almost all men desire and defend, is natural liberty—liberty to do nothing but what they please. This is caused by the imperfection of the moral development of each individual, and by the imperfection of the same development in the social powers; from which imperfection it results that these powers ill-understand the true law, never apply it, and are themselves directed by individual wills, as arbitrary as they are capricious. On this account, the state of freedom with which we meet at the outset of all societies lasts for so short a time, and is so quickly superseded by the despotism of one or several persons. Society cannot exist if natural liberty, that is, individual independence, exists in all the extent of its desire: and as society is as yet ignorant both how to govern according to the moral law, and how to respect moral liberty, force seizes upon the government.[1]

When, in such a state of society, a man of superior genius and character appears, he is inevitably driven to found a despotism, that is, the empire of his own individual will. He is irritated and offended by the collision of all these barbarous or stupid individual wills; his instinct tells him that society cannot exist in this manner, that such a state of things is not society. He is personally disgusted, moreover, at the sway which all these narrow and ignorant wills claim to exercise over all things, and even over himself. The authority of blind force over enlightened force is nothing but a despotism; and what is greater insolence than the power of a brutal multitude over a lofty individual reason? The superior man becomes indignant and seeks to free himself from this yoke, to impose some rule upon this disorder; and this rule he seeks in his own reason, in his own will. Thus is established, at such epochs, the despotism of a single person; it is not radically illegitimate, and the best proof that it is not, is afforded by the easy reception with which he meets the admiration with which he is regarded, the gratitude even which he inspires, and which lasts as long as the state of things which originated his power. In truth, the loftiest superiority, that which is most naturally called to empire by the disorder and dissolution of society, soon becomes corrupted and rude, by becoming itself a purely individual will, full of egotism and caprice: but that which constituted its force and credit, at the outset, was its better comprehension of the general wants of society; it had obtained a deeper knowledge of the true law which must govern society; and it rescued society from its losing battle with a multitude of ignorant or ferocious individual wills. It is by these means that great men triumph at first. It was thus that Charlemagne triumphed; it was thus that the first three Carlovingians, Pepin of Heristal, Charles Martel, and Pepin the Short, had prepared the way for him. Under the Merovingians, the state was falling into dissolution; every

---

1. This long discussion sheds light on Guizot's distinction between moral and natural liberty, i.e., between social freedom and individual independence. For Guizot, liberty is not the freedom to do what ones pleases, but the freedom to do what the precepts of reason, truth, and justice require us to do. In other words, liberty is respectable only insofar as it is defined as the power of discovering and translating into practice the principles of reason, truth, and justice. Writes Guizot: "Liberty, as existing in the individual man, is the power to conform his will to reason . . . ; accordingly the right to liberty . . . is derived from the right to obey nothing that is not reason" (*HORG*, p. 296). Guizot developed the same idea in his unfinished treatise *Philosophie politique: de la souveraineté* (*Political Philosophy: On Sovereignty*), where he pointed out that liberty cannot be identified with individual sovereignty or will, since no individual will can ever be the source of legitimate power. On the contrary, human beings are (and can remain) free only as long as they obey a transcendent law which does not depend on their will or consent. The upshot of this idea is that only the law of reason, truth, justice can legitimately command universal allegiance. For more details on Guizot's theory of liberty, see *HORG*, pp. 285–97.

strong man was making himself independent, every weak man was falling into subjection to a stronger. Although the Pepins had sprung from the dominant aristocracy, they early struggled against its excesses. Charles Martel put down the petty tyrants who had sprung up in every direction. The tendency of Charlemagne's policy was to establish the monarchical system, that is, to secure the universal prevalence of his will by making it felt everywhere by means of his agents. In order to understand with any exactness what was Charlemagne's pure monarchy, we must see how he managed his own property, and in what manner he administered his palace. The activity of his surveillance was surprising; we shall find details of it in his capitulary *De villis,* and in the first part of one of Hincmar's letters.[2] He governed his empire in the same spirit. This was the only means he possessed for restoring order, and applying the national forces to the accomplishment of his designs. Into the despotism of a superior man, there always enters a powerful instinctive feeling of justice, and of protection to the weak. Charlemagne diligently endeavoured to check the power of the nobles by subjecting them to surveillance, and by bringing his subjects into direct relationship with the royal authority. He paid great attention to the employment and administration of his benefices, even when in the hands of beneficiaries; he was careful not to give more than one county to the same count, and this rule he rarely transgressed; he ordered the nobles to distribute strict justice to their vassals, and took most energetic measures to compel them to do so, and to judge all men according to the law. Charlemagne also kept watch over the conduct of the counts; the assemblies of free men had almost entirely perished; and they requested as a favour to be allowed to absent themselves. To supply the place of the active surveillance exercised by these ancient assemblies, Charlemagne created the *missi dominici.* These were inspectors of the whole state of the kingdom, and particularly of the conduct of the counts and nobles.

The delegates of Charlemagne, the imperial judges, had assessors; and as the free men whose duty it was to fill the office of assessors seldom attended the periodical assemblies, Charlemagne superseded them by the *scabini,*[3] who were appointed by the *missi dominici,* whom he enjoined to select them with the greatest care. This intervention of the delegates of the sovereign himself in judicial affairs, was a powerful means of monarchical centralization.

In his Frankish empire, it was not against the ancient free institutions, but against public anarchy and the disorderly power of the strong, that Charlemagne directed these means of government. In his other dominions, wherever he feared the influence of liberty, his despotism was exerted to crush it rigorously; thus he interdicted all public assemblies of the Saxons.

2. For a detailed discussion of Hincmar's letter (written in 882), see *HORG,* pp. 143–48.

3. Royal judges; also see p. 149.

All this monarchical organization fell with Charlemagne. Its existence is protracted, as if by habit, in the speeches and laws of Louis the Débonnair; but the hand which sustained the edifice is no longer there. The language of Charlemagne in the mouth of Charles the Bald, is nothing but a piece of ridiculous rhodomontade. The feudal system gains the upper hand and organizes itself in every direction. The great vassals either attack the king or isolate themselves from him. The dignity of count became so considerable, that the sons of kings and emperors desire and obtain it. Hereditary succession prevails in the offices of dukes, counts, viscounts, &c. Rhegino cites as a singular fact that the sons of Duke Robert did not succeed to his dukedom, and assigns as the reason, that their tender age rendered them incapable of repulsing the Normans. The sons of two counts of Austria were not put into possession of the counties of their fathers; so their relations took arms, and drove out the usurper. The power of the counts, now they had become hereditary seigneurs, was augmented by the authority they had exercised, under that title, as delegates of the king. The feudal hierarchy, strong by its own intrinsic power, thus gained additional strength from the wreck of royal authority. Hence resulted a new order of local institutions, which I cannot now explain.

The picture of central institutions reproduces, under another aspect, the same facts, and leads to the same results. Central institutions, as you are aware, may be reduced to two—royalty, and the general assemblies of the nation.

To royalty among the Franks you may apply what I have said of royalty among the Anglo-Saxons; only, among the Franks, the royal family does not bear, at the outset, the character of a religious filiation. This is perhaps attributable to the fact that the Franks were a confederation of different tribes; among them, the king appears especially as a military chieftain. Under the first Merovingians, there was always a great mixture of hereditariness and election; hereditariness fluctuated among the members of the same family; election, when it was not an act of violence, was rather a recognition than an election.

It is a grave error to expect to find in facts the basis of a primitive and exclusive law: facts may be made to demonstrate anything. The most opposite parties have fallen into the same error in this respect. Whoever has discovered, at the origin of a state, an act of violence in conformity to his preconceived opinion, takes it as the foundation of what he calls the general law. Some fancy they can discern absolute and well-regulated hereditary succession in the midst of barbarism; others transfer the troubles and violence of a barbarian election into a more advanced stage of civilization; whatever they find existing as *fact* in the infancy of society, they convert into *law* for society in its greatest extension and development. This is neither philosophy nor history. The ruling *law* is that which is conformable to reason and justice. There is always more or less of this law at every epoch in the life of human society; but at no epoch is it pure or complete. We must resign ourselves to the task of freeing it everywhere from all alloy.

Let us then pass by the primitive and exclusive right of royal heredity, which existed neither among the Franks nor in other countries; all that can be said is that the principle of hereditary monarchy tended, early and constantly, to prevail. The heirship of the private domain of the kings, which was of considerable value, powerfully contributed to establish the heirship of the kingdom, just as the partition of the private domain among the sons led to the partition of the royal dominions; but the partition of the kingdom was almost always made with the consent of the nobles, whilst the heirship of the crown, in each state, does not appear to have required their formal assent.

We have already seen what were the causes which occasioned the fall of the Merovingian race, and the accession of Carlovingians. The fall of the latter, in the tenth century presents some features of similarity to that of the Merovingians, but between the two, there was greater diversity than resemblance. The ancient companions of the Frankish kings, the Leudes, the Antrustions, and the beneficiaries, had left the court, established themselves on their lands, and become feudal lords: revolutions were no longer effected at the foot of the throne, and in the interior of the royal palace. The feudal lords were much more isolated, not only from the king, but also from one another, than the Leudes had been under the Merovingians. Pepin the Short was king in fact when Childeric III. was king in name; Pepin assumed the name belonging to his power. At the end of the tenth century, there was no king, and no powerful man in the king's service who wielded the royal power in the name of Louis V. Hugh Capet took possession of an almost vacant place, which, at the moment, added much to his dignity, but little to his authority. After the fall of the Merovingians, Pepin and Charlemagne were able to attempt to establish the monarchical system, and to inaugurate the central authority of the king; Hugh Capet was unable to do this, nor did he attempt it; the feudal lordships had divided the kingdom amongst them. Pepin was the head of an aristocracy which had its centre in the palace of the Merovingian kings. Hugh Capet was one of the principal members of an aristocracy which had no centre; he made himself king because the crown was within his reach. If Louis V. had resided at Rouen, the Duke of Normandy would probably have seized the monarchy.

As regards the nature and extent of the royal authority, what I have already said sufficiently indicates what it was: very limited and precarious before the settlement of the Franks on Roman territory—being nothing but the power of the chief of a warlike band, always restrained by the presence of the free men, his comrades—it became extended and strengthened after the conquest by various causes: 1. By the dispersion of the Franks. They ceased constantly to surround the king; his authority was but slight over those who left him; but those who were habitually near him depended more closely upon him; a court of barbarian servants succeeded to a court of warriors. 2. By the subjugation of neighbouring chiefs or kings. 3. By the increasing inequality of wealth: the royal property greatly augmented, and this was their principal source of power; they devoted all their energies to the amassing of treasure; it was useless to leave their children a kingdom, unless they could at the same time bequeath to them a full exchequer. 4. By the influence of religious and Roman ideas. In the opinion of the Christians, the king was the successor of Saul and of David; in that of the Romans, he was the representative of the emperors. The Frankish kings were fully sensible of the advantages of this two-fold position, and they eagerly accepted the titles of Patrician and Consul. But the royal authority had no definite character; it was proportionate to the ability and energy of those who exercised it.

Nothing can be more different than the idea of royal authority in those times and in our own day. If a village were now to disregard the king's authority, or to refuse to obey him, it would be a serious event, the sign of a great decay of power. Such was not the case then; authority was not universally diffused over the country; remote places and interests were in some sort independent of it. It had no real supremacy, except in case of war; the rays of its influence were short, and wherever it was applied, it was matter of fact rather than of right.

With regard to authority and liberty, right and fact are almost identical in the infancy of society. The idea of right, separate from fact, has but very little power and can scarcely be said to exist. Hence arise the eternal vicissitudes of authority and liberty; whoever ceases to possess them is never permitted to regain them. It is the work and the master-work of civilization to separate right from fact, and to constitute right a power able to maintain, defend, and vindicate itself.

We must not, however, believe that religious ideas exercised no other influence, in regard to the royal authority, than to extend it, and to represent it as absolute and springing from divine right; they contributed powerfully to render it moral. It is true, they rendered it independent of the public liberties, which were frequently mere embodiments of arbitrary power and brute force, and thus they helped to establish absolute power; but at the same time they subordinated it to the divine laws, in which the moral laws are comprised. The limits which Frankish usages imposed on the royal authority were very different from those assigned to it by Christian ideas: "the king," to use the expression of the Councils, "is he who governs with pity, justice, and goodness; he who does not govern thus is not a king, but a tyrant." The restraint which this principle laid upon the royal authority was more efficacious than that which resulted from the influence of Frankish usages. This system, it is true, gave no positive and real guarantee for the observance of the rules which it imposed as duties upon royalty. But the age in which we live has taken too much pains to seek guarantees in physical force, and has neglected to seek for them in the power of moral ideas. In barbarian times, as all powers, both of kings and subjects, are almost equally unregulated, they appear bad guarantees to sensible men, who seek for purer sureties in moral ideas. When, in the epoch of which we are now speaking, the Franks or Leudes repress the abuse of royal authority, they repress it only in virtue of their own powers, and defend their liberties only out of regard to their own interests, and not in obedience to any moral idea of justice and of general right. The ecclesiastics, on the contrary, speak in the name of the general ideas of justice and humanity. They oppose morality rather than force to the abuse of authority. The clergy thus gave utterance to things which answered to the necessities of all the weak, and led them to consider them as their protectors.

The vice of the religious system, doubtless, is that it creates no political institution, and consequently, no effectual guarantee; thus it always ends by being more favourable to power than to liberty: but, in barbarous ages, when power and liberty were almost equally brutal and anarchical, this system has rendered immense services to humanity and to civilization.

LECTURE 20

---

*National assemblies of the Franks; their primitive character, and rapid
decline under the Merovingians. ⁓ They regain importance under the
Carlovingians; and are held regularly under Charlemagne. ⁓ Letter of
Archbishop Hincmar* De ordine Palatii.

Nᴀᴛɪᴏɴᴀʟ assemblies were held among the Franks long previously to their
settlement in the Roman empire, and to the establishment of monarchy
amongst them. In these assemblies were discussed, in Germany, all the affairs
of the confederation, tribe, or band. All the free men, that is to say, all the warriors, were present; but the authority of these assemblies, like the authority of
the kings, was uncertain and precarious. They were formed, not in virtue of the
principle of the sovereignty of the people, but in virtue of the right of every free
man to have the sole disposal of himself. They were convoked especially to determine on military expeditions. Beyond this, every man acted independently,
and was answerable for his conduct to none but the local authorities. The
Champ de Mars, or autumnal assembly, of which we find traces at the beginning
of the monarchy, was habitually held for the purpose of dividing the booty
which had been gained.

The dispersion of the free men, the increasing inequality of social conditions, and the subordination of the comrades to their chief, soon caused the national assemblies of the Franks to lose their character of universality. They
ceased to be attended by any but the large landowners, the Leudes, and the superior clergy. In this state, they appear to have existed under most of the
Merovingian kings. Mention is sometimes made of the people in general; but
evidently the great majority of the free men neither could, nor did attend these
assemblies. Those who possessed power and wealth were almost the only persons who attended; and they regulated the business brought under their notice
solely with a view to their own interest. The increasing disorder, and continual
dislocations of the kingdom, rendered these assemblies less frequent. They
reappear, however, at the establishment of the authority of the Mayors of the
Palace. As leaders of the aristocracy of the great independent landowners, they

had need of their support. The substitution of a new family of kings, instead of the ancient race, was favourable to the importance of the assemblies. They became, under the first Carlovingians, what they had been under the first Merovingians,—a great council of government, in which all great affairs were discussed. Pepin transferred the Champs de Mars to the month of May; and Charlemagne held these assemblies with a regularity heretofore unknown. In order to form a correct idea of what they were under his reign, you must read the text, and the entire text, of the letter written in 882, sixty-eight years after the death of Charlemagne, by the celebrated Hincmar, archbishop of Rheims, in compliance with the request of some of the nobles of the kingdom who had asked his advice with regard to the government of Carloman, one of the sons of Louis the Stammerer. In this letter, Hincmar, as he himself informs us, does nothing but copy a treatise *On the Order of the Palace, De ordine Palatii,* written before 826 by the celebrated Adalhard, abbot of Corbia, and one of the principal advisers of Charlemagne. It is, therefore, a contemporary document, and its authority is great.

"It was the usage at that time," says Hincmar,

> to hold in each year two assemblies, (*placita,*) and no more. The first took place in the spring; at it were regulated the general affairs of the whole kingdom; no occurrence, unless it were an imperious and universal necessity, could alter what had been decreed thereat. In this assembly, met together all the great men (*majores*), both lay and ecclesiastic; the more influential (*seniores*), to discuss business and agree on decisions; the less influential (*minores*), to receive these decisions, and sometimes also to deliberate upon them and confirm them, not by a formal consent, but by the exercise of their opinion and the assent of their understanding.
>
> The other assembly, in which the general gifts of the realm were received, was composed only of the more influential members (*seniores*) of the first assembly, and of the principal councillors. Here the affairs of the following year were treated of, if there were any which it was necessary to deliberate upon beforehand; as also those which might have occurred during the course of the year which was about to expire, and which required provisional attention without delay. For example, if, in any part of the kingdom, the governors of the frontiers (*marchisi*) had concluded a truce for any time, the course to be pursued on the expiration of these truces was discussed, and it was determined whether they should be renewed or not. If, in any other quarter of the kingdom, war seemed imminent, or peace appeared likely to be established, it was examined whether the exigencies of the moment required, in the first case, that incursions should be commenced or endured, and, in the second, how tran-

quillity might be insured. These lords thus deliberated long before-hand on what the affairs of the future might require; and when suitable measures had been agreed upon, they were kept so secret, that before the next general assembly they were no more known than if no one had paid any attention to the matter, and no decision had been arrived at regarding it. The object of this was, that if it were necessary to take, either within or without the kingdom, any measures which certain persons, when informed thereof, might wish to prevent, or frustrate, or render difficult, by any artifice, those persons might never have the power to do so.

In the same assembly, if any measure were necessary either to satisfy absent nobles, or to calm or excite the spirit of the people, and such measure had not previously been taken, it was discussed and adopted by the consent of those present, and it was executed in concert with them by the orders of the king. The year being thus terminated, the assembly of the following year was arranged as I have said.

With regard to the councillors, both lay and ecclesiastic, care was taken, as far as possible, to select such persons as, from their condition and duties, were filled with the fear of God, and animated, moreover, by unalterable fidelity, so as to consider nothing superior to the interests of the king and kingdom, except eternal life. Men were sought who could be turned aside from the path of duty neither by friends, nor enemies, nor relatives, nor gifts, nor flatteries, nor reproaches; men were sought who were wise and skilful, not with that sophistical skill and worldly wisdom which are so opposed to God's will, but with a just and true wisdom that might enable them not only to repress, but also fully to confound the men who place all their reliance in the tricks and stratagems of human policy. The maxim of the councillors thus elected, and of the king himself, was, never to confide, without their mutual consent, to their domestics or any other person, what they might have said familiarly to one another, either upon the affairs of the kingdom, or about any particular individuals. It made no difference whether the secret ought to be kept for a day or two, or more, or for a year, or even for ever.

It invariably happens that, if the conversation held in such meetings, with regard to any individual, either by way of precaution, or in reference to any other public interest, come afterwards to the knowledge of that individual, he cannot but feel great anxiety, or be driven to despair thereby, or, which is a much more serious matter, be stimulated to infidelity; and thus a man who might perhaps still have done service to the State, is rendered useless,—which never would have happened if he had not known what was said about him. That which is true of one man may be true of two, of a hundred, or of a greater number, or of a whole family, or of an entire province, unless the greatest caution be observed.

The *apocrisiary,* that is, the chaplain or keeper of the palace, and the *chamberlain,* were always present at these councils; they were therefore chosen with the greatest care; or else, after having been chosen, they were furnished with such instructions as should render them worthy of being present. As to the other officers of the palace (*ministeriales*), if there were any one who, first by gaining instruction, and afterwards by giving advice, proved himself capable of honourably occupying the place of one of these councillors, or fit to become one, he received orders to attend the meetings, giving the greatest attention to the matters discussed thereat, correcting his erroneous ideas, learning that of which he was ignorant, and retaining in his memory that which had been ordained and determined. The object of this was, that, if any unforeseen accident occurred, either within or without the kingdom; if any unexpected news arrived, in reference to which previous provision had not been made (it rarely happened, however, that in such cases, profound deliberation was necessary, or that there was not time to convoke the councillors already mentioned); the object of this, I say, was that, under such circumstances, the officers of the palace, with the grace of God, and by their constant habit of both attending at the public councils and deliberating upon the domestic affairs of the realm, might be capable, as need was, either to advise what had best be done, or to point out how matters might be arranged without inconvenience, until the next meeting of the council. So much with regard to the principal officers of the palace.

In reference to the inferior officers, properly called *palatines,* who had not to do with the general affairs of the kingdom, but only with those in which the persons specially connected with the palace were concerned, the sovereign regulated their duties with great care; in order that, not only might no evil arise therefrom, but also that if any disorder were manifested, it might at once be repressed and extirpated. If the affair were urgent, but might nevertheless without injustice or wrong to any person be deferred for decision until the meeting of the general assembly, the emperor expected the *palatines* to indicate the best means of delay, and to imitate the wisdom of their superiors in a manner pleasing to God and useful to the kingdom. As to the councillors whom I first mentioned, they were careful, when summoned to the palace, not to occupy themselves with private affairs, or with the disputes which might have arisen with regard to the possession of property or the application of the law, until they had arranged, with the help of God, everything that concerned the king and kingdom in general. This being done, if, in obedience to the orders of the king, there remained any affair which could not be settled either by the Count of the palace, or by the officer under whose cognizance it fell, without the assistance of the councillors, they proceeded to investigate it.

At one or other of the two assemblies, and in order that they might not appear to be convoked without reason, there were submitted to the examination and deliberation of the great personages whom I have mentioned, as well as of the chief senators of the realm, and in virtue of the orders of the king, those articles of law named *capitula*, which the king himself had drawn up under the inspiration of God, or the necessity of which had been manifested to him in the interval between the meetings. After having received these communications, they deliberated upon them for one, two, or three days, or more, according to the importance of the matter. Messengers from the palace, going and coming, received their questions and brought back answers; and no stranger approached the place of their meeting, until the result of their deliberations was placed before the eyes of the great prince, who then, with the wisdom which he had received from God, adopted a resolution which all obeyed. This course was pursued for one, two, or more capitularies, until, by the help of God, all the necessities of the time had been duly regulated.

Whilst these affairs were thus arranged out of the presence of the king, the prince himself, in the midst of the multitude who had come to the general assembly, was busied in receiving presents, greeting the most important individuals, conversing with those whom he saw but seldom, exhibiting an affectionate interest in the old, laughing and joking with the young, and doing these and similar things to ecclesiastics as well as laymen. However, if those who were deliberating upon the matters submitted to their judgment desired it, the king went to them, and remained with them as long as they wished; and there they reported to him, with entire familiarity, what they thought of various matters, and what were the friendly discussions which had arisen amongst them.

I must not forget to mention that, if the weather were fine, all this went on in the open air; but if not, in several distinct buildings, by which those who had to deliberate upon the king's propositions were separated from the multitude of persons who had come to the assembly; and then the less important men could not enter. The building intended for the meeting of the nobles was divided into two parts, so that the bishops, abbots, and superior clergy could meet together without any mixture of laymen. In the same way, the counts and other distinguished personages of the State separated themselves, in the morning, from the rest of the multitude, until the time came, when, whether the king were present or absent, they all met together; and then the nobles above-mentioned, the clergy on their side, and the laymen on theirs, proceeded to the hall which was assigned to them, and where seats had been honourably prepared for them. When the lay and ecclesiastical lords were thus separated from the multitude, it was in their power to sit either together or separately, according to the nature of the affairs which they had to discuss, whether ecclesiastical, secular, or mixed. In the same way, if they wished to send for any one, either to bring them food, or to answer any question, and to dismiss him after having obtained what they desired, it was in their power to do so. Thus proceeded the examination of the affairs which the king proposed for their deliberation.

The second occupation of the king was to demand of each what he had to report or relate to him regarding that part of the kingdom from which he had come; not only was this permitted to all, but they were specially enjoined to make inquiries, during the interval between the assemblies, about what was going on both within and without the kingdom; and they were to seek information from foreigners as well as natives, from enemies as well as friends, sometimes by employing envoys, and without being very scrupulous as to the way in which the information was obtained. The king desired to know whether in any district or corner of his kingdom the people were murmuring or disaffected, and what was the cause of their disaffection, and whether any disorder had occurred which required the attention of the general council, and other similar details. He also sought to know whether any of the conquered nations were likely to revolt, or whether any that had revolted seemed disposed to submit, or whether those that still remained independent threatened the kingdom with any attack, and so forth. Upon all these matters, wherever disorder or danger appeared, his chief care was to learn what was the motive or occasion thereof.

It is evident that these assemblies were considered by Charlemagne as an instrument of authority, order, and administration, much rather than as a national institution rendered necessary by the rights and free spirit of his people. The employment of this means of government, however, does not do the less honour to the genius of Charlemagne. He had perceived that the principal vice of the social system of his time, and the principal cause of the weakness of his own authority, were the absence of concentration, the isolation of individuals, and the independence of his agents. Periodical convocations gave a centre to all. The efforts of a great man in a barbarous age have as their especial object the creation of a nation, for therein lies his power; Charlemagne sought to find his nation lower than among the great land-owners and the great beneficiaries. He wished to rally together the entire mass of the people, in order to increase his own power, and to have at his disposal everywhere potent means of action. His was a skilful despotism. Despotism, in barbarous times, sometimes announces the presence of a man who is before his age, and who has necessities and views in relation to the future. Despotism, in the midst of an advanced state of civilization, indicates the presence of a man who may be great and even necessary to society, but who cares only for himself, and for the times in which he lives.

LECTURE 21

Decay of national assemblies under Louis the Débonnair and Charles the Bald. ⁓ Definitive predominance of the feudal system at the end of the tenth century. ⁓ Cause of this predominance. ⁓ Character of feudalism. ⁓ No trace of true representative government in France, from the fifth to the tenth century.

AFTER the death of Charlemagne, and under Louis the Débonnair, national assemblies were still frequently held. The movement which Charlemagne had begun, had not yet entirely ceased. Unable to create, Louis the Débonnair sought to imitate; at the spring or autumn assemblies, he passed several useful rules, amongst others the capitulary which summoned the *scabini,* or royal judges, to the Champs de Mai. But the government, even with this sanction, was lifeless and inefficient. The assemblies had been nothing but an instrument of the monarch, and the monarch was now no longer able to make use of them. Their decay was complete under Charles the Bald. They began again to be nothing more than meetings of the bishops and the great lay landowners. There were forty-six assemblies held under Charles the Bald; but they were almost all confined to the negotiations of the great nobles with the king, respecting their private interests. Such was the progress made by feudalism that the central aristocracy of the great landowners, beneficiaries, and others, dissolved of itself. They isolated themselves from one another in order to exercise, each in his own domains, the almost absolute sovereignty which they had acquired. The fall of the Carlovingians was the work of Hugh Capet alone, and not of an aristocratic coalition. An assembly did not meet, as at the fall of the Merovingians, to elect a new king. Hugh Capet made himself king, and was acknowledged as such, first by the vassals whom he possessed as Duke of France, and afterwards, successively, by the great lords of the kingdom, who remained, nevertheless, almost his equals in power. Then the assemblies almost entirely disappeared, together with every national and central institution; and nearly three centuries elapsed before anything analogous to them was established.

Thus, at the end of the tenth century, of the three systems of institutions which we characterized at the outset, viz.: free institutions, monarchical institutions, and feudal institutions, the last had completely prevailed; the first had perished early, and Charlemagne had vainly attempted to establish the second. The hierarchical organization of the proprietors of estates, and the dislocation of France into as many petty sovereignties as there were proprietors sufficiently strong to be almost independent and absolute masters in their own domains—such was the natural result of the settlement of the Franks in Gaul.

During the five centuries which we have now briefly examined, institutions, customs, and powers appear to be in a constant state of disorder and conflict. The ancient liberties of the Franks, the primitive independence of the warriors, royal authority, the first rudiments of the feudal system—all these different elements present themselves to our view as obscure, incoherent, and in opposition. We pass incessantly from one system to another, from one tendency to another. At the end of the tenth century, the struggle has almost ceased; the mass of the population have fallen into a state of serfage, or become tributary colonists; the possession of fiefs confers a real sovereignty, more or less complete according to the power of the possessor; these petty sovereigns are hierarchically united and constituted by the bonds of suzerainty and vassalage. Nowhere is this bond weaker than between the king and his vassals; for there the pretensions to authority on the one hand, and to independence on the other, are most earnestly contested.

The fundamental characteristics of this state of things are the destruction of all centrality, both national and monarchic; the hierarchical constitution of landed property; the distribution of sovereignty according to the various degrees of this hierarchy; and the servitude or quasi-servitude of the mass of the inhabitants of the country.

I have said that this system was the natural result of the condition of the Franks in Gaul after the conquest; its definitive success is proof of this. Another circumstance, also, may be adduced in evidence. Before the tenth century, we witness the constant struggle and alternating success of free, monarchical, and feudal institutions. The efforts made in favour of the first two systems, although some were supported by the ancient independence of the Franks, and others by the ability of great kings, were unsuccessful,—a more powerful tendency frustrated and overcame them. When the struggle ceased, when the feudal system had fully prevailed, a new conflict almost immediately commenced; the victorious system was attacked: in the inferior classes of society, by the mass of the inhabitants, citizens, colonists, or serfs, who strove to regain some rights, some property, and some liberty; in the superior class, by royalty, which laboured to resume some general sway, and to become once more the centre of the nation. These new efforts were made, not, as during the period from the fifth to the tenth century, in the midst of the confusion arising from the conflict of opposing systems, but in the very interior of a single system, of the system which had prevailed over, and taken possession of, the whole of society. The combatants are no longer free men, uncertain of their position and their rights, who feebly defend the wreck of their ancient existence against the overpowering invasion of the feudal system; they are citizens, colonists, serfs, whose condition is clear and determined, who become in their turn aggressors, and labour to free themselves from the yoke of feudalism. We no longer behold the king uncertain of his authority, and subject to have it unceasingly attacked, not knowing whether he is king or lord, and defending his power against the Leudes, or great landowners, who attempt sometimes to infringe it, and sometimes to set it aside altogether; now it is the chief of the nobles labouring to make himself the king of all, and to convert suzerainty into sovereignty. From the fifth to the tenth century, the feudal system had been in progress, in development, and in aggression. From the eleventh century onwards, this system had to defend itself against the people and the king. The struggle was long, difficult, and terrible; but the results altered with the position of the combatants. In spite of the servitude into which the people fell in the tenth century, from that time forth the enfranchisement of the people made progress. Notwithstanding the impotence of the royal power at the same period, thenceforward the royal power gained ground. No effort was vain, no step was retrograde. That monarchical system which the genius of Charlemagne had been unable to establish, was gradually founded by kings far inferior to Charlemagne. Those ancient liberties, which neither Franks nor Gauls had been able to preserve, were regained piecemeal by the commons and the third estate. During the first period, monarchy and liberty had failed to establish their position; it was destined that monarchy should issue out of feudalism itself, and that emancipation should spring from the bosom of servitude.

With regard to feudalism itself, it is not my intention to sketch its history. I hasten to arrive at that period at which I shall again meet with a nation and a king, and at which endeavours after a free government and a monarchical system will recommence. I will only state here what were the dominant character and general influence of the feudal system, in relation to power and liberty—those two constituent elements of social order.

The feudal system brought the master into close connection with the subject, and the sovereign with those who depended upon him; in this sense it was a cause of oppression and servitude. It is difficult to escape from a power that is ever near, and almost present. The human will is subject to strange caprices, and never is this more frequently exemplified than when the objects on which it acts are in its power. You may breathe a little under an arbitrary power, if it be very lofty and very distant; but if it be at your elbow, you are truly a slave. Local tyranny is the worst of all; though difficult to avoid, it can easily defend itself.

A handful of men have often kept the population of a large town in servitude for ages. The citizens, colonists, and serfs felt themselves so grievously oppressed by the feudal lords that they preferred to their absolute power the absolute power of the kings, even with more extensive and irresistible rights than those possessed by the lords. A certain and general despotism has neither the same interest in being tyrannical, nor the same means of oppression. This will explain the intensity of feudal oppression, and the profound hatred which it inspired.

The feudal system placed the inferior near his superior; and, in this sense, it was a principle of dignity and liberty. Many vassals were equal in rank to each other, and on terms of familiarity; frequently the inequality between the superior and inferior was not great, so that the latter was neither humiliated thereby, nor obliged to play the courtier. Protection was a right; the suzerain had absolute need of his vassals. There was no room, in their relations to one another, for servility and baseness of soul. Moreover, the vassals had reasons and means for banding together to defend themselves against oppression; they possessed common rights and interests. The intimacy in which they lived with their lord prevented the feeling of their mutual rights from becoming effaced within them; thus feudal relations are generally full of dignity and high-spiritedness; a noble sentiment, fidelity instead of submission, guides their conduct. Now, wherever a profound moral sentiment exists, it must necessarily call others into action; hence the many splendid and honourable developments of human nature under the feudal system: these developments were concentrated, it is true, within the circle of the lords and vassals; but even that is better than the equal abasement of all under an universal despotism.

Thus, whilst feudalism disregarded and insulted both justice and the dignity of man among the masses whom it claimed as subjects, it respected and developed both among its own hierarchy. In this hierarchy, liberty existed, with all its accompaniments. Below were servitude and its attendant evils, with all the shames that follow in their train.

I may now fearlessly affirm that, in the institutions of the period from the fifth to the tenth century, there is no trace of the representative system. We pass from the independence of individuals, sometimes to the power of the king, sometimes to the predominance of the great landowners. But there is no political organization founded upon ideas of general law and public interest; all institutions have reference to private rights and interests. Two opposite forces are in conflict; there is nothing to reveal the division of powers, and their tendency towards one common object. There are no representatives of the rights of all; none elected in the name of the interests of all; those who have rights exercise them personally; those who do not exercise them personally do not possess them. The ecclesiastics alone preserve the idea of the general right of all men to justice and to good government; but this idea is not transfused into any institutions. Neither the philosophic principle, nor any of the true external characteristics of representative government, can anywhere be met with.[1]

1. This is the conclusion of a long discussion that started from the assumption that true liberty cannot exist in the infancy of society. Guizot is keen on pointing out that there is no trace of the principle of representative government in the general assemblies of the Germanic tribes, since they were based on the principle of individual right (might), not upon any ideas of general law and public interest.

LECTURE 22

Political institutions of the Visigoths. ⁓ Peculiar character of Visigothic legislation. ⁓ Its authors and its influences. ⁓ Destruction and disappearance of the middle class in the Roman empire, at the time of the Barbarian invasion. ⁓ History of the Roman municipal system. ⁓ Three epochs in that history.

In conformity to the plan which I sketched out for our guidance at the commencement of these lectures, I have studied with you the political institutions of the Anglo-Saxons and Franks, from the fifth to the tenth century. I now come to those of the Visigoths, the third of the Barbarian peoples established in the Roman empire, about whom I propose to give you some information.

On opening the collection of the laws of the Visigoths, it is impossible not to be struck with the compactness which distinguishes them. The Franks and Burgundians have laws partially anterior to their establishment upon the Roman territory; customs handed down and gathered together from age to age. The Visigoths have a code which was systematically drawn up, and promulgated on an appointed day.

This fact alone indicates that the laws of the Visigoths were not the work of the Barbarians themselves. The influence of the clergy, indeed, was more potent among the Visigoths than among the other Barbarian conquerors; not only did the clergy take part in their government, but they acted as their civil and political legislators. The Visigothic code was their work. How did this happen?

Before the foundation of the Barbarian States, under the dominion even of the last Roman emperors, the power of the new religion gradually placed the Christian clergy at the head of the peoples; the bishop was the defender and chief of the towns. After the conquest, the Barbarians embraced the religion of the vanquished; and as the Christian clergy were powerful in the towns, by virtue of the municipal institutions, they used every effort to preserve to the municipal system its form and efficacy. In this they succeeded to a great extent. It is therefore of essential importance to have some precise knowledge of the Roman municipal system and its vicissitudes until the period of the great Barbarian invasions, in order properly to understand the condition of the urban populations at that epoch, and the part which their clergy played in their new position, especially in the kingdom of the Visigoths.

As I have already observed, the fall of the Roman empire in the West is a strange phenomenon. Not only did the population not support the government in its struggles against the Barbarians, but the population, when left to itself, did not attempt any resistance on its own behalf. More than this—nothing, during this protracted conflict, revealed the existence of a nation; scarce any allusion is made to what it suffered; it endured all the scourges of war, pillage, and famine, and suffered an entire change in its destiny and condition, without acting, speaking, or even appearing.

This phenomenon is not merely strange, it is unexampled. Despotism has reigned elsewhere than in the Roman empire; more than once, foreign invasion and conquest have devastated countries that had long groaned beneath a tyrannical government. Even where the nation has not resisted, its existence has been manifested in some manner in history. It suffers, it complains, and, notwithstanding its humiliation, it struggles against its evil fate; narratives and monuments attest what it experienced, what it became, and if not what it did, at least what was done with it.

In the fifth century, the remnants of the Roman legions disputed with hordes of Barbarians the possession of the immense territory of the empire, but it seemed as if this territory were a desert. When the soldiers of the empire had departed or been defeated, mention is made of no other person or thing. The Barbarian tribes seize upon the provinces in succession; beside them, facts exhibit to us only one other real and living existence, that of the bishops and the clergy. If the laws did not remain to inform us that a Roman population still covered the soil, history would give us good reason to doubt its existence.

It was especially in the provinces which had long been subject to Rome, and wherein civilization was more advanced, that the people thus disappeared. We look upon the letter of the Britons, tearfully imploring the assistance of Aetius and the despatch of a legion, as a singular monument of the cowardice of the subjects of the empire. This astonishment is unjust: the Britons, being less civilized and less Romanized than the other subjects of the empire, resisted the Saxons, and their resistance has a history. At the same period, under similar circumstances, the Italians, the Gauls, and the Spaniards have no history; the empire withdrew itself from their country, and the Barbarians took possession of it, without the mass of the inhabitants taking the least part in the transaction, or giving the slightest indication of the place they occupied in the events which gave them over to so many scourges.

Nevertheless Gaul, Italy, and Spain were covered with towns, which had lately been wealthy and populous; civilization had there received a splendid development; roads, aqueducts, circuses, and schools, were abundant. Everything that can attest wealth, or procure for a nation an animated and brilliant existence, they possessed. The invasions of the Barbarians occurred to pillage them of all their wealth, to disperse all their friendly meetings, to destroy all their pleasures. Never had the existence of a nation been more completely overthrown; never had individuals had more evils to endure and more dangers to apprehend. Whence came it that the populations were dumb and dead? How is it that so many sacked towns, so many ruined positions, so many blasted careers, so many ejected proprietors, have left so few traces, I do not say of their active resistance, but only of their sufferings?

The despotism of the imperial government, the degraded condition of the people, the profound apathy which had seized upon both masters and subjects, have been alleged to account for this—and justly so: therein consisted the great cause of this strange phenomenon. But it is easy thus to enunciate in a general manner a cause which, though apparently in existence elsewhere, did not elsewhere produce the same results. We must penetrate more deeply into the state of Roman society, in the condition to which it had been reduced by despotism. We must inquire by what means it had been so utterly deprived of all consistency and life. Despotism can clothe itself in very different forms, and exhibit itself in proceedings which impart to its action a far higher energy, and give a far wider scope to its consequences.

The great fact which had resulted from the system of imperial despotism, and which alone can explain the phenomenon of which I speak, is the destruction and disappearance of the middle class from the Roman world: at the arrival of the Barbarians, this class no longer existed; and for this reason also, the nation had ceased to exist. This annihilation of the middle class in the Roman empire was especially the result of a municipal system, which had rendered it completely the instrument and the victim of the imperial despotism. All the batteries of that despotism were directed against this class; and it was imprisoned within the municipal system that it might be turned to account, and made to supply the necessities of the existence of the power that crushed it.

Such a fact renders it worth while to study, in all its parts, the machine by which it was produced. Those who are unacquainted with the organization of the municipal system at this period, and its effects upon Roman society, cannot properly understand the history of these times.

In the constitution and existence of cities, within the Roman world, we may discern three epochs, very distinct from each other, and clearly marked out by actual revolutions. It is well known that the Romans, adopting, in their conquests, a system widely different from that of most ancient nations, were careful not to exterminate or reduce to servitude the nations which they had conquered. This difference of procedure was, I think, occasioned by the condition of most of the neighbouring nations, against which Rome first waged war. They were collected together in towns, and not dispersed throughout the country; they formed civic bodies, cultivating and governing a territory of greater or less extent. These cities were numerous and independent. A nation scattered over the land which it cultivates, may easily be destroyed or enslaved; but the task is more difficult and less profitable when that nation dwells within walls and has already assumed the consistency of a petty State. Moreover, the nations which, in ancient times, were enslaved or exterminated, received this treatment almost invariably from conquerors who were in search of a home, and who had settled in the territory they had won. When the war was ended, the Romans returned to Rome. Enslavement and extermination cannot be effected either all at once or from a distance. The victors who intend to do this must be ever present among the vanquished, ceaselessly depriving them of their wealth, their liberty, and their lands. The primitive condition of the Romans, at the commencement of their conquests, exercised a decisive influence upon the fate of nations.

Originally, it does not appear that the Romans ventured to leave their former inhabitants in the conquered towns. It is said that violence supplied Rome with women; the same proceeding furnished her with new citizens. The vanquished, when transferred to Rome, became Romans like their victors. The conquered town was occupied, either by soldiers, or by inhabitants of Rome, belonging to the lowest class of the people, and sent thither to form a kind of colony. The town of Coere was the first which, on being united to Rome, was allowed to retain its own laws and magistrates after receiving, at least in part, the right of Roman citizenship. According to Livy, in the year of Rome 365, a decree of the Senate ordained *ut cum Coeretibus publice hospitium fieret.*[1]

This system prevailed and received continual development. The conquered towns were united to Rome by receiving the right of citizenship. Some of them, like Coere, only received the title of Roman citizens for their inhabitants, and still retained their own Senate and laws; others were admitted into the Roman city, but without obtaining the right of suffrage in the *comitia*[2] of Rome. With regard to others, again, their political incorporation was complete; their inhabitants enjoyed the right of suffrage at Rome like the Romans themselves. These last alone had a tribe in Rome.

The right of suffrage was granted successively to several towns which had not received it at first. Finally, all Italy after the war of the allies, and ere long a portion of Southern Gaul received the right of Roman citizenship in all its plenitude.

The towns thus admitted to all the rights of Roman citizenship were

1. That there be public hospitality with the inhabitants of Coere.

2. Assembly.

called *municipia*. When the whole of Italy was invested with these rights, those towns which had not at first fully possessed them retained for a considerable period the names of *coloniae, praefecturae,* and so forth, which they had originally borne; but, in fact, their condition was completely assimilated to that of the ancient *municipia*.

Out of Italy, the condition of the conquered towns and districts was still very various. History tells us of *coloniae,* some of which were Roman, and others Latin, of *populi liberi, civitates faederatae, reges amici, provinciae.*[3] These different denominations indicated different modes of existence under the domination of Rome, and different degrees of dependence—but these differences successively disappeared. I am referring merely to the *municipia*.

Before conferring on a town the full rights of Roman citizenship, inquiry was made whether it would accept them or not. On consent being given, and, to use the legal phrase, *ubi fundus ei legi factus erat,*[4] the concession took place. Its principal consequences were these: municipal rights, interests and offices, in that town, were then separated from political rights, interest and offices. The former remained in possession of the town, and were exercised on the spot by the inhabitants, with entire independence: the latter were transferred to Rome, and could be exercised only within its walls. Thus, the right of making peace or war, of passing laws, levying taxes, and administering justice, ceased to belong to the *municipium* individually; but the citizens shared these rights, and exercised them at Rome in common with the citizens who inhabited Rome; they repaired thither to vote at the *comitia,* both upon the laws and upon appointments to magisterial functions: they sought and might obtain all the offices of the State. The city of Rome possessed the privilege that these political rights could be exercised only within its walls. Its inhabitants possessed no privilege above those of the *municipia*.

The rights, interests, and offices, which we now call municipal, and the entire disposal of which was secured to each locality, are nowhere regularly distinguished and enumerated. At this degree of civilization, neither the rulers nor the ruled feel the necessity of foreseeing, defining, and regulating everything; they trust to the good sense of mankind, and to the nature of things. History, however, indicates the principal prerogatives which continued local. 1. Worship, religious festivals, and ceremonies. Not only did each town retain its ancient usages and independent authority in this respect, but the Roman laws watched over the preservation of these rights, and even made it a duty. Each *municipium,* therefore, had its own priests and flamens, as well as the right of choosing them, and of regulating all matters in relation thereto. 2. Every *municipium* also pos-

3. Free peoples, allied cities, allied kings, provinces.
4. When property had been established by the law.

sessed the administration of its own private property and revenues. In ceasing to be a political personage, it became a civil personage. Public edifices, whether devoted to purposes of utility or of pleasure, festivals, local and general amusements, all expenses of this kind, and all the revenues by which they were defrayed, continued to be absolutely local matters. The inhabitants appointed the magistrates who were charged with these functions. 3. The police also remained, to a certain extent at least, in the hands of the local magistrates; they had to watch over the internal security of their town, and provisionally to arrest those who disturbed its peace. 4. Although the judicial power had been withdrawn from the localities, we nevertheless meet with some traces of a jurisdiction somewhat similar to that which we call municipal police, giving judgment upon offences against the laws, with regard to public health, weights and measures, markets, and so forth.

All these local affairs were managed either by magistrates appointed by the inhabitants, or by the *curia* of the town or *college of decurions,* that is, of all the inhabitants who possessed a fixed landed income. In general, the *curia* appointed the magistrates; we meet with some instances, however, of their being appointed by the general body of the inhabitants. But at this period, and by a necessary consequence of the existence of slavery, there were few free men who did not belong to the *curia.*

The origin of the word *decurio* is uncertain. Some writers are of opinion that he was an officer placed at the head of ten families, like the *tything-man,* or *tunginus* of the German peoples. Others think that *decurio* simply means member of a *curia.* The last interpretation seems to me the more probable of the two. At a later period, the decurions were called *curiales.*

Such was the constitution of the *municipia* at the end of the Roman republic. It presents, as results, the following general facts:—1. All political rights and interests, all political life, in short, was centralized at Rome, not merely morally and by law, but materially and in fact. Within the walls of Rome alone could be consummated all the acts of a Roman citizen. 2. No centralization of this kind had taken place in reference to what we now call administrative interests. Each town had remained isolated and distinct in this respect, regulating its own affairs, just as a private individual would do. 3. The appointment and surveillance of the magistrates who administered the local affairs of the town took place on the spot, without any intervention of the central power, and by the assembly of the principal inhabitants. 4. Into this assembly were admitted all the inhabitants who possessed a certain income. There is reason to believe that a few free men only were excluded therefrom.

Here begins a second epoch in the history of the Roman municipal system.

The absolute separation of political from local existence, and the impossibility of exercising political rights elsewhere than in Rome, could not fail to deprive the towns of their principal citizens, and also of a great part of their importance. Thus, during the epoch which we have just surveyed, purely local interests occupied only a small place. Rome absorbed everything. The independence left to other towns, as regarded matters that were not treated of at Rome, or did not emanate from Rome, arose from the slight importance of those matters.

When liberty began to totter at Rome, the decadence of the political activity of the citizens necessarily diminished its concentration. The chief men of the *municipia* repaired to Rome to take their part in the government of the world, either by voting in the *comitia,* or discharging great public functions. When the *comitia* and the high magistracies ceased to have any perceptible influence in the government, when political life became extinct in Rome, together with the movement of liberty, this affluence of all the important men towards Rome decreased. Such a decrease was advantageous to the rising despotism, and met with no opposition. Here, as in every instance, the necessary consequences of general facts are revealed in particular and positive facts. Up to that time, no political act could be performed, and no suffrage be exercised, elsewhere than within the walls of Rome. Suetonius informs us that Augustus conferred upon the citizens of a large number of Italian *municipia* the right of giving their votes without leaving their town, and sending them to Rome in a sealed packet, that they might be properly scrutinized in the *comitia.* Thus was exhibited, at once, the progress of public indifference, and the growth of absolute power.

This progress continued rapidly. Ere long, the *comitia* met with the fate of all shams, and were abolished; all free intervention of the citizens in the government disappeared, and no political acts remained to be performed, either at Rome, or at a distance therefrom; and as it is always a trick of nascent despotism to offer to all men the deceptive advantages of a shameful equality, the right of Roman citizenship was, almost at the same period, bestowed indiscriminately upon the whole Roman world. This right no longer possessed any political significance, nor did it confer any real importance upon those who received it; and yet this concession deprived those whom it levelled to the condition of the multitude, of any importance they might still have retained. There is reason to believe that this measure was rather the consequence of a financial speculation than of a clever despotic combination. But despotism, even when its conduct is least guided by scientific principles, is never deceived by its instincts. Such was, moreover, the natural course of things; and degraded peoples must inevitably suffer their fate. All the blame must not be laid on the master of the flock; and the hatred which tyranny merits cannot save from our contempt nations that are incapable of liberty.

However, as the degradation and ruin of an empire cannot be effected in a moment, or by a single blow; as there still existed in the Roman world some habits of liberty which despotism had not had time or need to destroy, it was necessary to make some sort of compensation for this complete disappearance of political rights and life; and this compensation naturally resulted from the change which had occurred. A portion of the importance which Rome had lost, had returned to the *municipia*. A large number of wealthy citizens no longer left their homes. Having been excluded from the government of the State, their attention spontaneously turned to the affairs of their own city. Nothing had yet stimulated the central power to interfere in their administration. The treasures of Rome, and the ordinary contributions of the provinces, were sufficient for the imperial wants, and even for its follies. Tyranny then felt but slightly the necessity of penetrating into every quarter, and of possessing a detailed organization; and did not even know how to set about it. The municipal system, therefore, retained considerable importance; it even constituted itself with greater regularity, and according to more positive, perhaps more extensive rights, than those which it had previously possessed.

It is during the period from the reign of Nerva to that of Diocletian, that the state of the *municipia* appears under this new aspect. A great many laws were passed to increase and secure the property and revenues of towns. Trajan permitted them to receive inheritances by way of *fidei commissus;*[5] and, ere long, they were authorized to receive them directly. Hadrian granted them the right of receiving legacies, and ordained that any administrator who should misappropriate the property of a town should be considered guilty, not of simple theft, but of embezzlement. The ordinary income usually sufficed to meet the expenditure, and it was not necessary to lay fresh taxes upon the citizens. The State did not cast upon the cities any burdens which did not directly concern them; and there were but very few citizens exempt from that which was onerous in municipal duties. The common people bore their part, by hard labour, in the public works which interested each town; the dignity of the decurions was recognised and sanctioned. Hadrian freed them from the punishment of death, except in cases of parricide. The decurionate was still sought after as an honour; and lastly, the best proof of the importance and extension of the municipal system, during this period, will be found in the number of laws passed in relation to it, and the particular attention paid to it by jurisconsults. Evidently, in the absence of political rights and guarantees, the municipal system was the depository in which all the rights and securities of citizens were contained.

But the attempt to preserve this system could not long succeed. We must,

5. Given over on assurance.

indeed, date revolutions from the day on which they break out; this is the only precise epoch which we can assign to them, but it is not that in which they originate. The convulsions which we call revolutions, are far less symptomatic of what is commencing than declaratory of what has passed away. The crisis of the municipal system under Constantine is one of many proofs of this truth.

Ever since the reign of Septimius Severus, the central power in the Roman empire had been falling into ruin; its strength decreased in proportion as its burdens and dangers augmented. It became indispensable to cast upon others the burdens which it could no longer bear, and to seek new strength in order to confront new dangers. At the same time, there arose, in the midst of the old Roman society, a society both young and ardent, united in a firm and fruitful faith, gifted from within with principles admirably adapted to fortify its internal constitution, and also with an immense power of external expansion; I refer to Christian society. It was by the action of these two causes, at first divided and afterwards united, that the municipal system of the Roman empire was dissolved, and ended by deteriorating into a principle of ruin, and an instrument of oppression.

It is one of the thousand vices of despotism that its exigencies increase in proportion as its means diminish; the weaker it becomes, the greater is its need of exaggeration; the more it is impoverished, the more it desires to spend. In point of strength, as of wealth, sterility and prodigality are equally imposed upon it; society, both men and things, in its hands, is but a lifeless and limited material which it expends for its own support, and into which it is compelled to penetrate more deeply as it becomes more exhausted, and as it is itself more nearly losing all.

The despotism of the Roman emperors existed in presence of three dangers: the Barbarians, who were continually advancing, and whom it was necessary to conquer or to bribe; the populace, which was continually increasing, and which it was necessary to feed, amuse, and restrain; the soldiers, the force to be opposed to this twofold peril,—a force all the more dangerous in itself, as it was necessary to increase it, and grant it daily fresh concessions. This position imposed immense burdens on despotism. In order to obtain resources, it was compelled to create an administrative machine capable of carrying its action into every quarter, and which became itself a new burden. This system of government, which commenced under Diocletian and ended under Honorius, had no other object but to extend over society a network of functionaries, who were incessantly occupied in extracting from it wealth and strength, which they afterwards deposited in the hands of the emperors.

The revenues of the towns, like those of private individuals, were laid under contribution by the exigencies of power, and were speedily invaded in a still more direct manner. On various occasions, amongst others under Constantine, the emperor took possession of a large number of municipal properties; but the local charges which these properties were intended to meet were, nevertheless, left undiminished. Nay, more, they were increased; as the populace everywhere became more numerous and more disposed to sedition, it became more expensive to feed and amuse them, and greater force was required to keep them in check. The central power, itself overburdened, cast a portion of its load upon the towns. Now, whenever the regular revenues of a town did not suffice to meet its expenditure, the *curia*, that is, the body of wealthy citizens, the decurions, were bound to supply the deficiency from their own private purse. They were, moreover, in almost every place, the collectors of the public taxes, and were responsible for this collection; their private property had to make up for the insolvency of the tax-payers, as well as to supply the deficiency of the communal revenues. The dignity of decurion thus became a cause of ruin; this condition was the most onerous of all social conditions; it was, nevertheless, that of all the well-to-do inhabitants of all the *municipia* in the empire.

Nor was this all; as soon as the position of the decurions became burdensome, there was a tendency to leave it, as well as an advantage in doing so. Exemption from curial functions became a privilege; and this privilege received an ever-increasing extension. The emperors, who disposed of all public dignities and employments, conferred them upon the men and the classes whom they felt it necessary to gain. Thus arose within the State, as a necessary result of despotism, an immense class of privileged persons. In proportion as the revenues of the towns diminished, their burdens augmented, and fell upon the decurions, now fewer in number in consequence of the concession of privilege. It was, however, needful to leave enough to bear the burdens imposed on the *curiae*. Hence the origin of that long series of laws which make of each *curia* a prison-house in which the decurions were hereditarily confined; which deprived them, in a multitude of cases, of the free disposal of their property, or even disposed of it without their consent for the benefit of the *curia;* which pursued them into the country, into the army, wherever they attempted to take refuge, in order to restore them to the *curiae*, from whence they desired to escape: laws, in fine, which bound an immense class of citizens, in property as well as in person, to the most onerous and ungrateful of public services, just as you would compel animals to perform this or that species of domestic labour.

Such was the place which despotism finally assigned to the municipal system; such was the condition to which municipal proprietors were reduced by the laws. And whilst despotism was straining every nerve to tighten the bonds of the municipal system, and to compel the inhabitants to perform, as charges, functions which had formerly been considered as rights, the second cause to which I have alluded, Christianity, was labouring to dissolve or dismantle municipal society, in order to substitute another in its place.[6]

During nearly three centuries, Christian society had been silently forming in the midst, and, so to speak, beneath the surface of the civil society of the Romans. It was at a very early period a regularly-constituted society, with its chiefs, its laws, its expenditure, and its income. Its organization, originally entirely free and founded upon purely moral ties, was by no means deficient in strength. It was at that time the only association which could procure for its members the joys of the inner life—which possessed, in the ideas and sentiments that formed its basis, matter to occupy lofty minds, to exercise active imaginations, and to satisfy the requirements of that moral and intellectual existence which neither oppression nor misfortune can completely extinguish throughout a nation. The inhabitant of a *municipium,* when he became a Christian, ceased to belong to his town, and entered into the Christian society, of which the bishop was chief. There alone, henceforward, was the centre of his thoughts and affections, and the abode of his masters and brethren. To the necessities of this new association were devoted, if needful, his fortune and his activity; thither, in fine, his entire moral existence was in some measure transported.

When such a displacement has occurred in the moral order of things, it speedily becomes consummated in the material order also. The conversion of Constantine, in fact, declared the triumph of Christian society, and accelerated its progress. Thenceforward, power, jurisdiction, and wealth poured in upon the churches and bishops, as upon the only centres around which men were spontaneously disposed to group themselves, and which could exercise the virtue of attraction upon all the forces of society. It was no longer to his town, but to his church that the citizen desired to bequeath his property. It was no longer by the construction of circuses and aqueducts, but by the erection of Christian temples, that the rich man endeavoured to rest his claim to public affection. The

6. For a comprehensive discussion of the role of Christianity in the progress of the European civilization, see *HCE,* Lectures V and VI (pp. 82–118). Guizot concludes: "Upon the whole, the influence [of the Church] has been salutary; not only has it sustained and fertilized the intellectual movement in Europe, but the system of doctrines and precepts . . . was far superior to anything with which the ancient world was acquainted. There was at the same time movement and progress" (*HCE,* p. 109). Guizot's reevaluation of the role of the attitude of the Church toward the modern world was a response to the anti-clericalism of many eighteenth-century writers. To this effect, he argued that some of the principles upon which the doctrines of the Church were founded, such as the equality of all creatures in the face of God, played a key role in the political development of Western Europe. In other words, Guizot claimed that, far from being a rejection of the ideals of Christianity as ultra-conservative writers (Joseph de Maistre, Louis de Bonald) argued, the movement to democracy as social condition (equality of conditions) reflected and followed Christian ideas and principles.

parish took the place of the *municipium;* the central power itself, hurried on by the course of the events with which it had become associated, used all its efforts to swell the stream. The emperors deprived the communes of a portion of their property, and gave it to the churches; they deprived the municipal magistrates of a portion of their authority, and gave it to the bishops. When the victory had been thus avowed, interest combined with faith to increase the society of the conquerors. The clergy were exempted from the burden of municipal functions; and it became necessary to pass laws to prevent all the decurions from making themselves clerks. Without these laws, municipal society would have been entirely dissolved; its existence was protracted that it might continue to bear the burden to which it was condemned; and, strange to say, the emperors most favourable to the ecclesiastical order, and most liberal in augmenting its advantages, were compelled at the same time to struggle against the tendency which induced men to leave every other association, in order to enter into the only one in which they could find honour and protection.

Such then, was, in truth, the state of things. Despotism, urged by its own necessities, incessantly aggravated the condition of the *curia*. That of the church flourished and improved as incessantly, either by the aid of the peoples, or by the action of despotism itself, which had need of the support of the clergy. It was therefore necessary continually to relegate to the *curia* the decurions who were ever anxious to leave it. In proportion as their number decreased, and as those who remained became ruined and unable to bear the burden, their condition became less and less endurable. Thus, evil sprang from evil; oppression rendered ruin certain by its efforts to delay it; and the municipal system which, as I have said, had become an actual gaol to one class of citizens, daily hastened onwards to its own destruction, and to that of the class which was chained to its destiny.

Such was, with regard to the *municipia,* the course of events and laws from the reign of Constantine until the fall of the Western Empire. In vain did some emperors strive to raise the communes; in vain did Julian restore to them a portion of the property which they had previously lost. These changes in legislation were ineffectual; a fatal necessity weighed upon the *municipia;* and whenever the municipal system bordered closely upon dissolution, and it was felt necessary to support it, no other aid was given than by redoubling the energy of the causes which urged it to destruction. Thus violent is the course of decaying despotism. The municipalities were daily sacrificed in greater measure to the empire, and the decurions to the municipalities; the external forms of liberty still existed within the *curiae,* as regarded the election of magistrates and the administration of the affairs of the city; but these forms were vain, for the citizens who were called upon to give them life by their actions, were stricken to death in their personal independence and in their fortune. It was in this state of material ruin and moral annihilation that the Barbarians, when they established themselves in the Roman territory, found the towns, their magistrates, and their inhabitants.

In the East, the agony of the *municipia* was prolonged with the duration of the empire. Here also some emperors made unsuccessful attempts to restore them to prosperity. At length, the progress of the central despotism became so great, and the forms of municipal liberty so evidently a dead letter, that, towards the end of the ninth century, the Emperor Leo, called the Philosopher, abolished the whole municipal system at once, by the following decree:—

> As, in things which serve for use in common life, we esteem those which are convenient and useful, and despise those which are of no utility, so we ought to act in reference to laws; those which are of some advantage, and which confer some benefit on the commonwealth, should be maintained and honoured; but as for those whose maintenance is troublesome and unimportant, not only should we pay no attention to them, but we should reject them from the body of the laws. Now, we say, that among the ancient laws passed in reference to *curiae* and *decuriones,* there are some which impose intolerable burdens on the decurions, and confer on the *curiae* the right of appointing certain magistrates, and of governing cities by their own authority. Now that civil affairs have assumed another form, and that all things depend solely upon the care and administration of the imperial majesty, these laws wander, in some sort, vainly and without object around the legal territory; we therefore abolish them by the present decree.*

Such were, during the period of twelve centuries which elapsed between the treaty of Rome with Coere and the reign of Leo the Philosopher, the great revolutions of the municipal system in the Roman world. We may characterize them by saying that, during the first period, the municipal system was a liberty granted, in fact, to the inhabitants of the towns; during the second, it was a right legally constituted, as an indemnity for the loss of political privileges; and, during the third, it was a burden imposed upon a certain class of citizens.

I now terminate its history. In our next lecture, we shall investigate the real state of the municipal system during the third period, and its influence upon the condition of the citizens.

* Novell. Leo. 46.

LECTURE 23

Of the various social conditions in the Roman Empire, before the final invasion of the Barbarians. ⁓ *The privileged classes; and the curials.* ⁓ *Their obligations, functions, and immunities.* ⁓ *Attributes of the* curia *as a body.* ⁓ *Of the various municipal magistracies and offices.* ⁓ *Of the* Defender *in cities.* ⁓ *Comparison of the development of the municipal system, and its relations to the central organization of the State, in the Roman Empire and in modern societies.*

AT the commencement of the fifth century the subjects of the Empire were divided into three classes, forming three very distinct social conditions: 1. The privileged classes; 2. The curials; 3. The common people. I speak only of free men.

The privileged class included: 1. The members of the Senate, and all those who were entitled to bear the name of *clarissimi;* 2. The officers of the palace; 3. The clergy; 4. The cohortal militia, a sort of *gendarmerie* employed in the maintenance of the internal order of the State, and the execution of the laws; 5. The soldiers in general, whether included in the legions, or in the troops attached to the palace, or in the corps of barbarian auxiliaries. The class of curials comprehended all the citizens inhabiting towns, whether natives or settlers therein, who possessed a certain landed income, and did not belong, by any title, to the privileged class. The common people were the mass of the inhabitants of the towns, whose almost absolute want of property excluded them from a place among the curials.

The privileged members of the first class were numerous, of various rank, and unequally distributed among the five orders of which it was composed; but that which was, in fact, the most important and most sought after of their privileges, that which alone was more valuable than all the rest, was common to the five orders which constituted this class—I mean, exemption from municipal functions and offices.

When we come to treat of the curials, you will learn what was the extent of these duties; but you must first understand clearly who were exempt from them. 1. The whole army, from the lowest *cohortalis* to the *magister equitum peditumve;*[1] 2. The entire body of the clergy, from the simple clerk to the archbishop; 3. It is an easy matter to define the two foregoing classes; but it is not so clear who were the members of the class of senators and *clarissimi.* The number of the senators was unlimited; the emperor appointed and dismissed them at his will, and could even raise the sons of freedmen to this rank. All those who had filled the principal magisterial offices in the Empire, or who had merely received from the prince the honorary title belonging to those magistratures, were called *clarissimi,* and had the right, when occasion required, of sitting in the Senate. Thus the class of *clarissimi* included all the functionaries of any importance: and they were all appointed and might be dismissed by the emperor.

The body of privileged individuals, then, was composed: 1. Of the army; 2. Of the clergy; 3. Of all the public functionaries, whether employed at the Court and in the palace, or in the provinces. Thus despotism and privilege had made a close alliance; and, in this alliance, privilege, which depended almost absolutely on despotism, possessed neither liberty nor dignity, except perhaps in the body of the clergy.

This privilege, and especially exemption from curial functions, was not purely personal, but also hereditary. It was so, in the case of military men, on condition that the children also should embrace the profession of arms; and in the case of civilians, it was continued to those children who were born since their fathers had belonged to the class of *clarissimi,* or had occupied posts in the palace. Among the classes exempt from curial functions was the cohortal militia, a subaltern service to which those who entered it were hereditarily bound, and from which there was no means of passing into a superior class.

The class of curials comprehended all the inhabitants of the towns, whether natives thereof, *municipes,* or settlers therein, *incolae,* who possessed a landed property of more than twenty-five acres, *jugera,* and did not belong to any privileged class. Members of the curial class became so either by origin, or by appointment. Every child of a curial was a curial also, and liable to all the charges attached to that quality. Every inhabitant who, by trade or otherwise, acquired a landed property of more than twenty-five acres, might be summoned to enter the *curia,* and could not refuse to do so. No curial could, by a voluntary act, pass into another condition. They were interdicted from dwelling in the country, entering the army, or engaging in employments which would have liberated them from municipal functions, until they had passed through every curial gradation, from that of a simple member of a *curia* to the highest civic magistracies. Then alone they might become military men, public functionaries, and senators. The children born to them before their elevation remained curi-

---

1. Chief of horsemen or foot-soldiers.

als. They were not allowed to enter the clergy except by granting the enjoyment of their property to any one who agreed to be a curial in their place, or by making a present of their possessions to the *curia* itself. As the curials were incessantly striving to escape from their bondage, a multitude of laws were passed directing the prosecution of those who had escaped from their original condition, and succeeded in effecting their entrance furtively into the army, the clergy, public offices, or the Senate; and ordaining their restoration to the *curia* from which they had fled.

The following were the functions and charges of the curials thus confined, voluntarily or perforce, in the *curia*. 1. The administration of the affairs of the *municipium*, with its expenditure and revenues, either by deliberating thereon in the *curia*, or by discharging the magisterial offices of the town. In this double position, the curials were responsible not only for their individual management, but also for the necessities of the town, for which they were bound to provide out of their own resources, in case the municipal revenues were insufficient. 2. The collection of the public taxes, also under the responsibility of their private property in case of defaulters. Lands which were subject to the land-tax and had been abandoned by their possessors, were allotted to the *curia*, which was bound to pay the tax thereon until it had found some one willing to take them off its hands. If it could find no one, the tax on the abandoned land was divided amongst the other estates. 3. No curial could sell the property from which he derived his qualification, without the permission of the governor of the province. 4. The heirs of curials, when not members of the *curia*, and the widows or daughters of curials, who married men belonging to other classes, were bound to give a fourth part of their goods to the *curia*. 5. The curials who had no children could not dispose, by will, of more than a fourth of their property: the other three-fourths went, by right, to the *curia*. 6. They were not allowed to absent themselves from their *municipium*, even for a limited time, without permission from the judge of the province. 7. When they had withdrawn from their *curia*, and could not be brought back, their property was confiscated to the benefit of their *curia*. 8. The tax known by the name of *aurum coronarium*, and which consisted in a sum to be paid to the prince, on the occasion of certain events, was levied on the curials alone.

The only advantages granted to the curials in compensation for these burdens were: 1. Exemption from torture, except in very serious cases. 2. Exemption from certain afflictive and dishonouring punishments which were reserved for the populace; such as being condemned to work in the mines, to be burned alive, and so forth. 3. Decurions who had fallen into indigence were supported at the expense of the *municipium*. These were the only advantages possessed by the curials over the common people, who, on the other hand, enjoyed the benefit that every career was open to them, and that, by entering the army, or engaging in public employments, they might raise themselves at once into the privileged class.

The condition of the curials, then, both as citizens and in relation to the State, was onerous and devoid of liberty. Municipal administration was a burdensome service, to which the curials were doomed, and not a right with which they were invested. Let us now see what was the condition of the curials, not in relation to the State, and to the other classes of citizens, but in the *curia* and amongst themselves. Here still existed the forms, and even the principles, of liberty. All the curials were members of the *curia,* and sat therein. The ability to bear the burdens of the office entailed that of exercising its rights, and taking part in its affairs; the names of all the curials of each *municipium* were inscribed, in an order which was determined according to their dignity, age, and other circumstances, in a book called the *album curiae.* When there was occasion to deliberate upon any matter, they were all convoked together by the superior magistrate of the town, the *duumvir, aedilis* or *praetor,* and they all gave their opinions and their votes; everything was decided by the majority of votes: and no deliberation of the *curia* was valid unless two-thirds of the curials were present.

The attributes of the curia as a body were: 1. The examination and decision of certain affairs; 2. The appointment of magistrates and municipal officers. Nowhere can I find an enumeration of the affairs which fell under the cognizance of the *curia* as a body. Everything, however, indicates that most of those municipal interests which required more than the simple execution of the laws or of orders already given, were discussed in the *curia.* The proper and independent authority of the municipal magistrates appears to have been very limited. For example, there is reason to believe that no expense could be incurred without the authorization of the *curia.* It fixed the time and place for holding fairs; it alone granted recompenses; and so forth.

There were even occasions on which the authorization of the *curia* was not sufficient, and when it was necessary to have the sanction of all the inhabitants, whether curials or not; for example, for the sale of any property belonging to the commune, or for the despatch of deputies to wait on the emperor in reference to any grievance or request. On the other hand, it is evident that, by the general progress of despotism, the imperial power continued daily to interfere more and more in the affairs of the *municipia,* and to limit the independence of the *curiae.* Thus they might not erect new buildings without the permission of the governor of the province; the reparation of the walls around the towns was subject to the same formality; and it was also necessary for the emancipation of slaves, and for all acts which tended to diminish the patrimony of the city. By degrees, also, even those affairs the final decision of which had previously belonged to the *curiae* fell, by way of objection or appeal, under the authority of the emperor and his delegates in the provinces. This occurred in consequence of the absolute concentration of judicial and fiscal power in the hands of the imperial functionaries. The *curia* and the curials were then reduced to be nothing more than the lowest agents of the sovereign authority. There was left to them hardly anything beyond the right of consultation and the right of complaint.

With regard to the appointment to municipal magistracies, it remained for a long time, in reality, in the hands of the *curia*, without any necessity for its confirmation by the governor of the province, except in exceptional cases of towns which it was specially intended to ill-use or punish. But even this right soon became illusory by reason of the power given to provincial governors to annul the appointment on the demand of the person elected. When municipal functions had become merely burdensome, all the curials elected to discharge these offices, who had any influence with the governor, were able, under some pretext or another, to get their election annulled, and thus to escape from the load.

There were two kinds of municipal offices: the first, called *magistratus,* which conferred certain honours and a certain jurisdiction; the second, called *munera,* simple employments without jurisdiction and without any particular dignity. The *curia* appointed to both kind of offices; only the magistrates proposed the men whom they thought competent to fulfil the *munera;* but even these were not really appointed until they had obtained the suffrages of the *curia.*

The *magistratus* were: 1. *Duumvir;* this was the most usual name of the chief municipal magistrate. He was also called, in certain localities, *quatuorvir, dictator, aedilis, praetor.* His tenure of office was for a year; it corresponded pretty nearly with that of our mayors; the *duumvir* presided over the *curia,* and directed the general administration of the affairs of the city. He had a jurisdiction confined to matters of small importance; he also exercised a police authority which gave him the right of inflicting certain punishments upon slaves, and of provisionally arresting freemen. 2. *Aedilis;* this was a magistrate generally inferior to the *duumvir;* he had the inspection of public edifices, of the streets, of corn, and of weights and measures. These two magistrates, the *duumvir* and *aedilis,* were expected to give public festivals and games. 3. *Curator reipublicae;* this officer, like the aedile, exercised a certain oversight over public edifices; but his principal business was the administration of the finances; he farmed out the lands of the *municipium,* received the accounts of the public works, lent and borrowed money in the name of the city, and so forth.

The *munera* were: 1. *Susceptor,* the collector of taxes, under the responsibility of the curials who appointed him. 2. *Irenarchae,* commissaries of police, whose duty it was to seek out and prosecute offences, in the first instance. 3. *Curatores,* officers charged with various particular municipal services; *curator fru-*

menti, curator calendarii, the lender out on good sureties of the money of the city, at his own risk and peril. 4. *Scribae,* subaltern clerks in the two offices. To this class belonged the *tabelliones,* who performed almost the same functions as our notaries.

In later times, when the decay of the municipal system became evident, when the ruin of the curials and the impotence of all the municipal magistrates to protect the inhabitants of the cities against the vexations of the imperial administration, became evident to despotism itself; and when despotism, suffering at length the punishment of its own deeds, felt society abandoning it on every side, it attempted, by the creation of a new magistracy, to procure for the *municipia* some security and some independence. A *defensor* was given to every city; his primitive mission was to defend the people, especially the poor, against the oppression and injustice of the imperial officers and their agents. He soon surpassed all the other municipal magistrates in importance and influence. Justinian gave the *defenders* the right to exercise, in reference to each city, the functions of the governor of the province during the absence of that officer; he also granted them jurisdiction in all cases which did not involve a larger sum than 300 *aurei.* They had even a certain amount of authority in criminal matters, and two apparitors were attached to their person; and in order to give some guarantees of their power and independence, two means were employed; on the one hand, they had the right of passing over the various degrees in the public administration, and of carrying their complaints at once before the praetorian prefect; this was done with the intention of elevating their dignity by freeing them from the jurisdiction of the provincial authorities. On the other hand, they were elected, not by the *curia* merely, but by the general body of the inhabitants of the *municipium,* including the bishop and all the clergy; and as the clergy then alone possessed any energy and influence, this new institution, and consequently all that still remained of the municipal system, fell into its hands almost universally. This was insufficient to restore the vigour of the *municipia,* under the dominion of the empire; but it was enough to procure for the clergy great legal influence in the towns after the settlement of the Barbarians. The most important result of the institution of *defenders* was to place the bishops at the head of the municipal system, which otherwise would have dissolved of itself, through the ruin of its citizens and the nullity of its institutions.

Such are the facts: they demonstrate the phenomenon which I indicated at the outset, namely, the destruction of the middle class in the empire; it was destroyed materially by the ruin and dispersion of the curials, and morally by the denial of all influence to the respectable population in the affairs of the State, and eventually in those of the city. Hence it arose that, in the fifth century, there was so much uncultivated land and so many towns almost deserted, or inhabited only by a famished and spiritless population. The system which I have just explained contributed, much more powerfully than the devastations of the Barbarians, to produce this result.

In order rightly to apprehend the true character and consequences of these facts, we must reduce them to general ideas, and deduce therefrom all that they contain in regard to one of the greatest problems of social order. Let us first examine them on the relations of the municipal system with political order, of the city with the State. In this respect, the general fact which results from those which I have stated, is the absolute separation of political rights and interests from municipal rights and interests; a separation equally fatal to the political rights and interests, and to the municipal rights and interests of citizens. So long as the principal citizens possessed, at the centre of the State, real rights and an actual influence, the municipal system was not wanting in guarantees of security, and continued to develop itself. As soon as the principal citizens lost their influence at head quarters these guarantees disappeared, and the decay of the municipal system was not long in manifesting itself.

Let us now compare the course of things in the Roman world, with what has occurred in the modern states. In the Roman world, centralization was prompt and uninterrupted. In proportion as she conquered the world, Rome absorbed and retained within her walls the entire political existence of both victors and vanquished. There was nothing in common between the rights and liberties of the citizen, and the rights and liberties of the inhabitant; political life and municipal life were not confounded one in the other, and were not exhibited in the same localities. In regard to politics, the Roman people had, in truth, only one head; when that was stricken, political life ceased to exist; local liberties then found themselves unconnected by any bond, and without any common guarantee for their general protection.

Among modern nations, no such centralization has ever existed. On the contrary, it has been in the towns, and by the operation of municipal liberties, that the mass of the inhabitants, the middle class, has been formed, and has acquired importance in the State. But when once in possession of this point of support, this class soon felt itself to be in straits, and without security. The force of circumstances made it understand that, so long as it was not raised to the centre of the State, and constitutionally established there; so long as it did not possess, in political matters, sights which should prove the development and pledge of those which it exercised in municipal affairs—these last would be insufficient to protect it in all its interests, and even to protect themselves. Here is the origin of all the efforts which, from the thirteenth century onwards, either by States General or Parliaments, or by more indirect means, were made for the purpose of raising the burghers to political life, and associating with the rights and liberties of the inhabitant, the rights and liberties of the citizen. After three centuries of endeavour, these efforts were unsuccessful. The municipal system was unable to give birth to a political system which should correspond with it and become its guarantee. The centralization of power was effected without any centralization of rights. Thenceforward the municipal system proved weak and incapable of defending itself; it had been formed in spite of feudal domination; it was unable to exist in presence of a central authority, and in the midst of administrative monarchy. The towns gradually lost, obscurely and almost unresistingly, their ancient liberties. No one is ignorant that, at the moment when the French revolution broke out, the municipal system in France was nothing more than a vain shadow, without consistency or energy.

Thus although, in the Roman world and amongst ourselves, matters have progressed in inverse proportion, although Rome began by the centralization of public liberties, and modern States by municipal freedom, in both cases facts alike reveal to us the double truth that the two orders of liberties and rights are indispensable to one another, that they cannot be separated without mutual injury, and that the ruin of one necessarily entails the ruin of that which at first survives.

A second result of no less importance is revealed to us by the same facts. The separation of the municipal from the political system led, in the Roman empire, to the legal classification of society and to the introduction of privilege. In modern States, an analogous classification and the presence of aristocratic privileges prevented the municipal system from raising itself to political influence, and from producing the rights of the citizen from the local rights of the inhabitant. Where, then, municipal and political life are strangers to one another, where they are not united in the same system and bound together in such a manner as reciprocally to guarantee each other's security, we may be certain that society either is or soon will be divided into distinct and unchangeable classes, and that privilege either already exists or is about to make its appearance. If the burgesses have no share in the central power, if the citizens who exercise or share in the central power do not at the same time participate in the rights and interest of the burgesses, if political and municipal existence proceed thus collaterally, instead of being, as it were, included in each other, it is impossible for privilege not to gain a footing, even beneath the iron hand of despotism and in the midst of servitude.

If from all this we desire to deduce a still more general consequence, and to express it in a purely philosophical form, we shall acknowledge that, in order that right may certainly exist in any place, it must exist everywhere, that its presence at the centre is vain unless it be present also in localities; that, without political liberty, there can be no solid municipal liberties, and *vice versa*. If, however, we consider the facts already stated in reference to the municipal system taken in itself and in its internal constitution; if in these facts we look for principles—we shall meet with the most singular amalgamation of the principles of liberty with those of despotism; an amalgamation, perhaps unexampled, and certainly inexplicable to those who have not well understood the course of circumstances, both in the formation and in the decline of the Roman world.

The presence of principles of liberty is evident. They were these. 1. Every inhabitant possessing a fortune which guaranteed his independence and intelligence, was a curial; and, as such, called upon to take part in the administration of the affairs of the city. Thus, the right was attached to presumed capacity, without any privilege of birth, or any limit as to number;[2] and this right was not a simple right of election, but the right of full deliberation, of immediate participation in affairs, as far as they related to what occurred in the interior of a town, and to interests which might be understood and discussed by all those who were capable of raising themselves above the cares of individual existence. The *curia* was not a restricted and select council, it was an assembly of all the inhabitants who possessed the conditions of curial capacity. 2. An assembly cannot administrate—magistrates are necessary. These were all elected by the *curia,* for a very short time; and they answered for their administration by their private fortune. 3. In circumstances of importance, such as changing the condition of a city, or electing a magistrate invested with vague and more arbitrary authority, the *curia* itself was not sufficient; the whole body of the inhabitants was called in to take part in these solemn acts.

Who, on beholding such rights, would not think that he saw a small republic, in which municipal and political life were merged in one another, and in which the most democratic rule prevailed? Who would think that a municipality thus regulated formed a part of a great empire, and depended, by narrow and

---

2. The notion of capacity (*capacité*) plays a central role in Guizot's political philosophy and his conception of representative government. In his view, political capacity requires a certain degree of wealth, education, independence, intellectual maturity, reason, and liberty and is defined as "the capacity to act according to reason and justice" (*HORG*, p. 61). This principle of distinction was predicated on a twofold assumption: (1) electors must have certain qualities in order to be allowed to vote; (2) elected representatives should be highly distinguished citizens who have a stake in the preservation of the social order. On this view, only those who possess a certain amount of wealth and education could be free from dependence on the will of others. They alone were considered capable of developing a sound, enlightened, and free political judgment, since they were free to dispose of their person and wealth and were in a position to rise to some ideas of social interest. Finally, it is important to note that Guizot and the other doctrinaires did not conceive of political capacity as a form of aristocratic inheritance. They insisted that limited suffrage was not supposed to create an oligarchy of wealth, "the most absurd of all types of oligarchies" according to Royer-Collard. For more details, see *La vie politique de M. Royer-Collard: ses discours et ses écrits* (*Royer-Collard's Political Life: His Discourses and Writings*), ed. Prosper de Barante, Vol. I, Paris: Didier, pp. 409-10). As Guizot pointed out, "no one is recognized as possessing an inherent right to an office or a function . . . as soon as the capacity is presumed or proved, it is placed in a position where it is open to a kind of legal suspicion" (*HORG*, p. 62).

necessary bonds, on a remote and sovereign central power? Who would not, on the contrary, expect to meet with all the outbreaks of liberty, all the agitations and cabals, and frequently all the disorder and violence which, at all periods, characterize small societies thus shut up and governed within their own walls?

Nothing of the kind was the case, and all these principles of liberty were lifeless. Other principles existed which struck them to death. 1. Such were the effects and exactions of the central despotism that the quality of curial ceased to be a right confessedly belonging to all who were capable of exercising it, and became a burden imposed upon all who were able to bear it. On the one hand, the government discharged itself from the care of providing for those public services which did not affect its own interests, and so cast the obligation on this class of citizens; and, on the other hand, it employed them to collect the taxes destined for its use, and made them responsible for the payment thereof. It ruined the curials in order to pay its own functionaries and soldiers; and it granted to its own functionaries and soldiers all the advantages of privilege, in order to obtain their assistance forcibly to prevent the curials from escaping from their impending ruin. Complete nullities as citizens, the curials lived only to be fleeced. 2. All the elective magistrates were, in fact, merely the gratuitous agents of despotism, for whose benefit they robbed their fellow-citizens, until they should be able, in some way or another, to free themselves from this unpleasant obligation. 3. Their election even was valueless, for the imperial delegate in the province could annul it, and they had the greatest personal interest in obtaining this favour from him; in this way also, they were at his mercy. 4. Lastly, their authority was not real, for it had no sanction. No effective jurisdiction was allowed them; they could do nothing that might not be annulled. Nay, more: as despotism daily perceived more clearly their impotence or ill-will, it daily encroached further upon the domain of their attributes, either by its own personal action, or by its direct delegates. The business of the *curia* vanished successively with its powers; and a day was not far distant when the municipal system would be abolished at a single stroke in the rapidly decaying empire, "because," the legislator would say, "all these laws wander, in some sort, vaguely and objectless about the legal territory."

Thus, the municipal power, having become completely estranged from political and civil power, ceased to be a power itself. Thus, the principles and forms of liberty, isolated remains of the independent existence of that multitude of towns which were successively added to the Roman empire, were impotent to defend themselves against the coalition of despotism and privilege. Thus, here also, we may learn what so many examples teach us; namely, that all the appearances of liberty, all the external acts which seem to attest its presence, may exist where liberty is not, and that it does not really exist unless those who possess it exercise a real power—a power, the exercise of which is connected with that of all powers. In the social state, liberty is participation in power; this participation is its true, or rather its only, guarantee. Where liberties are not rights, and where rights are not powers, neither rights nor liberties exist.

We must not, therefore, be surprised either at that complete disappearance of the nation which characterized the fall of the Roman empire, or at the influence which the clergy soon obtained in the new order of things. Both phenomena are explained by the state of society at that period, and particularly by that state of the municipal system which I have just described. The bishop had become, in every town, the natural chief of the inhabitants, the true mayor. His election, and the part which the citizens took in it, became the important business of the city. It is to the clergy that we owe the partial preservation, in the towns, of the Roman laws and customs, which were incorporated at a later period into the legislation of the State. Between the old municipal system of the Romans, and the civil-municipal system of the communes of the Middle Ages, the ecclesiastical municipal system occurred as a transition. This transition state lasted for several centuries. This important fact was nowhere so clearly and strongly developed as in the monarchy of the Visigoths in Spain.

LECTURE 24

Sketch of the history of Spain under the Visigoths. ⁓ Condition of Spain under the Roman empire. ⁓ Settlement of the Visigoths in the south-west of Gaul. ⁓ Euric's collection of the laws of the Visigoths. ⁓ Alaric's collection of the laws of the Roman subjects. ⁓ Settlement of the Visigoths in Spain. ⁓ Conflict between the Catholics and Arians. ⁓ Political importance of the Councils of Toledo. ⁓ Principal kings of the Visigoths. ⁓ Egica collects the Forum judicum. *⁓ Fall of the Visigothic monarchy in Spain.*

Under the Roman empire, before the Barbarian invasions, Spain enjoyed considerable prosperity. The country was covered with roads, aqueducts, and public works of every description. The municipal government was almost independent; the principle of a landed census was applied to the formation of the *curiae;* and various inscriptions prove that the mass of the people frequently took part with the Senate of the town, in the acts done in its name. There were *conventus juridici,* or sessions held by the presidents of the provinces and their assessors in fourteen towns of Spain; and *conventus provinciales,* or ordinary annual assemblies of the deputies of the towns, for the purpose of treating of the affairs of the province, and sending deputies to the emperor with their complaints and petitions.

All these institutions fell into decay at the end of the fourth century. The imperial despotism, by devolving all its exactions upon the municipal magistrates, had rendered these offices onerous to those who filled them, and odious to the people. On the other hand, since the emperor had made himself the centre of all, the provincial assemblies were useless except as intermediaries between the cities and the emperor; when the municipal organization had become enervated, and the emperor had almost entirely disappeared, these assemblies were found to be inconsistent and powerless in themselves. The sources whence they emanated, and the centre at which they terminated, were devoid of strength, and perished.

Such was the condition of Spain when, in 409, the Vandals, Alans, and

Suevi crossed the Pyrenees. The Vandals remained in Galicia and Andalusia until 429, at which period they passed into Africa; the Alans, after having dwelt for a time in Lusitania and the province of Carthagena, emigrated into Africa with the Vandals. The Suevi founded a kingdom in Galicia, which existed as a distinct State until 585, when Leovigild, king of the Visigoths, reduced it under his sway. Finally Ataulphus, at the head of the Visigoths, entered Southern Gaul, acting sometimes as an ally, and sometimes as an enemy of the empire. He was assassinated at Barcelona, in the year 415.

I shall now pass in rapid review the principal events which mark the history of the Visigoths in Spain, subsequently to the death of Ataulphus.

1. Wallia, king of the Visigoths, from 415 to 419, made peace with the Emperor Honorius, on condition of making war against the other Barbarians in Spain. He was furnished with supplies, and authorized to establish himself in Aquitaine. He fixed his residence at Toulouse, and waged war against the Alans and Vandals. The Romans regained possession of a part of Spain; Wallia's Goths, mingled with the Alans, settled in the province of Tarragona. Catalonia (*Cataulania, Goth-Alani*) derives its name from this commingling of the two nations. The settlement of the Goths in Gaul lay between the Loire, the Ocean, and the Garonne, and comprehended the districts of Bordeaux, Agen, Perigueux, Saintes, Poitiers, and Toulouse.

2. Theodoric I. (419–451). Under this monarch, the Visigoths extended their dominion in the south-east of Gaul. Their principal wars were with the Roman empire, which, after having made use of the Goths against the Vandals and Suevi, was now using the Huns against the Goths. In 425, occurred the siege of Arles by Theodoric; in 436, the siege of Narbonne. There was a disposition among the inhabitants of the country to range themselves under the dominion of the Goths, who were able to defend them against the other Barbarians, and to renounce their allegiance to Rome, which was bringing other Barbarians to subdue the Goths. About 449, the kingdom of the Visigoths extended as far as the Rhone. Theodoric made several expeditions into Spain; generally as the price of peace with the Romans. In 451, Theodoric was killed at a battle fought against Attila, either at Chalons-sur-Marne, or Mery-sur-Seine.

3. Thorismund (451–453). A victory was gained over Attila, who had attacked the Alans settled on the Loire and in the neighbourhood of Orleans. It was evidently the Visigoths who drove the Huns out of Gaul. Thorismund was assassinated.

4. Theodoric II. (453–466). Avitus, *Magister militiae* in the south of Roman Gaul, travelled to Toulouse to treat of peace with Theodoric, and was made emperor by the aid of the Visigoths. In concert with the Romans, Theodoric II. made an expedition into Spain against the Suevi. Rechiar, king

of the Suevi, was defeated on the 5th of October, 450, near Astorga. This was rather an expedition than a conquest on the part of the Visigoths. Theodoric II., a curious portrait of whom has been left us by Sidonius Apollinarius, was assassinated in 462; he had acquired the district of Narbonne.

5. Euric (466–484). This reign was the culminating point of the Visigothic monarchy in Gaul. Euric led expeditions beyond the Loire against the Armoricans; in 474, he conquered Auvergne, which was then ceded to him by treaty; he had already conquered Arles and Marseilles, so that the monarchy of the Visigoths then extended from the Pyrenees to the Loire, and from the Ocean to the Alps, thus adjoining the monarchies of the Burgundians and Ostrogoths. Euric had also extended his dominions into Spain, where he possessed the Tarragonese district and Boetica, which he had conquered from the Suevi. Euric had the laws and customs of the Goths written in a book. A passage of Sidonius Apollinarius which speaks of *Theodoricianae leges,* has led to the belief that Theodoric commenced this collection; but Euric is also called Theodoric.

6. Alaric II. (484–507). This reign was the epoch of the decay of the Visigothic monarchy in Gaul. Alaric, less warlike than his predecessors, gave himself up to the pursuit of pleasure. He was defeated by Clovis, at Vouillé near Poitiers, and left dead on the field. The Franks in the east, and the Burgundians in the west, dismembered the Visigothic monarchy, which thus became reduced to Languedoc, properly so called, and a few districts adjacent to the Pyrenees.

Alaric did for his Roman subjects what Euric had done for the Goths. He collected and revised the Roman laws, and formed them into a code called the *Codex Alaricianus.* This code was based upon the *Codex Theodosianus* published in 438 by Theodosius the Younger, and upon the *Codex Gregorianus,* the *Codex Hermogenianus,* the *Pauli Sententiae,* and the *Constitutiones Imperiales,* published subsequently to the reign of Theodosius. This code was also called the *Breviarium Aniani.* It has been thought that Anianus, the referendary of Alaric, was its principal editor; but Père Sirmond has proved that Anianus only published it by order of the king, and sent authentic copies of it into the provinces. By an act of Alaric, the Roman legislation was, so to speak, revived, rearranged, and adapted to the monarchy of the Goths. It thenceforth emanated from the Gothic king himself. In the north of Gaul, whilst the Barbarian laws ceased to be customs and became written laws, the Roman laws lost their force as a whole, and became customs; in the south, on the other hand, they remained written laws, and retained much greater power, exercising an important influence upon the laws of the Barbarians. It would appear that this twofold written legislation must tend necessarily to maintain the separation of the two nations; but it contributed on the contrary to bring it to an end.

7. After the death of Alaric II., his legitimate son Amalaric, still a child,

was taken into Spain. His natural son, Gesalic, became a king in Gaul. At this period, the monarchy of the Visigoths was transferred from Gaul into Spain. The Franks, Burgundians, and Ostrogoths, seized the Gallic possessions of the Visigoths. Gesalic was defeated, and Amalaric reigned under the protection of his grandfather Theodoric, and the tutelage of Theudes.

8. On the death of Amalaric, Theudes was elected king, and reigned from 531 to 548. He fixed the seat of the Visigothic monarchy in Spain. He waged long wars against the Franks, and, though an Arian, behaved with tolerance towards the Catholics. He authorized the bishops to meet annually in council at Toledo. Until the reign of Theudes, the principle of hereditary succession to the throne appears to have prevailed among the Visigoths; after Theudes, the principle of election prevailed in fact and in law.

9. From 548 to 567, reigned Theudegisil, Agila, Athanagild. There were continual wars between the Franks, the Suevi, and the Romans. To obtain the assistance of the Romans in his rebellion against Agila, Athanagild gave up to the Emperor Justinian several places between Valentia and Cadiz. Roman garrisons were accordingly sent into those towns. The Romans had also retained possession of other towns in Spain. Athanagild took up his residence at Toledo. He was the father of Queen Brunehault. At his death, the grandees remained five months without electing his successor. At length they elected Liuva, the governor of Narbonne, who associated his brother Leovigild with him on the throne. Leovigild governed Spain, and Liuva, Visigothic Gaul. Liuva died in 570, and Leovigild became sole king. With him commences, to speak truly, the complete and regular monarchy of the Visigoths in Spain.

10. Leovigild, from 570 to 586, consolidated and extended the monarchy. He gained great victories over the Greco-Romans who had recovered a part of Spain, and won from them Medina-Sidonia, Cordova, and other towns. He also defeated the Vascons* who had maintained their independent occupation of the country on both sides of the Pyrenees. In 586, he completely subdued the Suevi; he greatly extended the royal power, made large confiscations of the property of the church and the nobles, persecuted the Catholics, and convoked a council of Arian bishops at Toledo, in 582, to endeavour to explain Arianism in such a manner as to satisfy the people, and to insure its general reception in his dominions. A civil war broke out between Leovigild and his son Hermenegild, who was a Catholic. After various vicissitudes, Hermenegild was taken, confined at Seville in a tower which bears his name, and put to death in 584. Before his insurrection, he was associated with his father in the crown, as was also his brother Recared, who governed the provinces in Gaul. Leovigild corrected and completed the laws of Euric.

---

* Probably the Basques of the present day.

Up to this period, there was no unity in the Visigothic monarchy. General institutions were wanting. The national assemblies were more irregular than in other countries. Neither the principle of hereditary succession, nor that of election, prevailed as regarded the kingly office. Out of fourteen kings, six had been assassinated. There was no coherence among the provinces of the kingdom. The clergy were deeply divided amongst themselves. The king gave a factitious preponderance to the Arian minority.

11. In 586, Recared I. succeeded Leovigild, declared himself a Catholic, and convoked the third general council of Toledo, in 587. A union was effected between the royal and ecclesiastical authority. Recared found himself in a position somewhat analogous to that of Constantine the Great, after his conversion to Christianity. He was energetically supported by the Catholic clergy, whom he, in his turn, as zealously maintained. At the third council of Toledo, the two powers made in common the laws of which they both had need. An important fact should be noticed in the tenure of this council. During the first three days the ecclesiastics sat alone, and regulated religious affairs exclusively. On the fourth day, laymen were admitted; and affairs both civil and religious were then treated of.

Recared made war against the Franks of Gothic Gaul, and against the Romans in Spain. This last war was terminated by the intervention of Pope Gregory the Great, who negociated a treaty between the Emperor Maurice and Recared, the latter of whom, since 590, had sent ambassadors to the Pope. The Arian clergy excited several rebellions against Recared.

12. In 601, Recared was succeeded by his son Liuva II., who was assassinated in 603. Withemar, his successor, was assassinated in 610. Gundemar was then elected, but he died in 612. Sisebut acceded to the throne in 613, and made war against the remnant of the Roman Empire in Spain. He reduced to a mere nullity the possessions which the emperor had until then retained. He imposed upon the Jews the necessity of being baptized. Heraclius had commenced this persecution in the Eastern Empire; and it entered as a condition into the treaty which he made with Sisebut. The Jews, when driven from Spain, took refuge in Gaul, where they were equally persecuted by Dagobert: so that they knew not whither to flee for refuge. The laws of Sisebut were issued in virtue of the king's authority alone, without the concurrence of the councils.

13. Recared, the second son of Sisebut, reigned for a few months. He was succeeded, in 621, by Suinthila, son of Recared I., who was elected king. Suinthila had served as a general under Sisebut. We frequently meet with similar cases in the history of the Visigoths; and they prove that the idea of hereditary succession was still not firmly established. Suinthila made a great expedition against the Basques. He drove them to the other side of the Pyrenees, and built a fortress which is believed to have been Fontarabia. He completely ex-

pelled the Romans from Spain, by sowing dissension between the two patricians who still governed the two Roman provinces, and by granting the Roman troops who remained in the country permission to return home.

14. In 631, occurred the usurpation of Sisenand by the aid of King Dagobert, who sent an army of Franks, which penetrated as far as Saragossa. Suinthila abdicated the throne. Sisenand succeeded him, and reigned from 631 to 636. In 634, Sisenand's usurpation was confirmed by the fourth council of Toledo. The crown was declared elective by the bishops and nobles, and ecclesiastical privileges received great extension. From 636 to 640, Chintila reigned. During his reign, the fifth and sixth councils of Toledo passed laws regarding the elections of kings and the condition of their families after their death, against the Jews, and on other subjects. Chintila was succeeded by his son Tulga, who was deposed in 642.

15. Chindasuinth reigned tyrannically from 642 to 652. Two hundred of the principal Goths were put to death, and their property confiscated; many of the inhabitants emigrated; Chindasuinth convoked the seventh council of Toledo, the canons of which against the emigrants were very rigorous. In all the measures of his government, we may discern the influence of the Catholic clergy, intimately connected with the king against the Arian faction. One canon ordained that every bishop residing near Toledo, should spend one month in every year at the court of the king. Chindasuinth revised and completed the collection of the laws relating to different classes of his subjects, and entirely abolished the special employment of the Roman law in his dominions. In 649, he associated his son Recesuinth with him in the crown, and obtained his recognition as his successor.

On opening the eighth council of Toledo, Recesuinth said; "The Creator raised me to the throne by associating me in the dignity of my father, and by his death the Almighty has transmitted to me the authority which I have inherited." These words are the expression of the theory of divine right. Recesuinth directed the council to revise and complete the collection of laws; imposed a fine of thirty pounds of gold on any one who should appeal to any other than the national law; permitted marriages between the Romans and Goths, which had been until then interdicted; revoked the laws of his father against the emigrants; and restored a portion of the confiscated property. A law was also passed, separating the private domain of the king from the public domain. The preponderance of the bishops in the council is evident. The canons are signed by seventy-three ecclesiastics, and by only sixteen counts, dukes, or *proceres*.[1] Recesuinth died on the 1st September, 672.

16. Wamba, elected on the 19th September, 672, manifested great repug-

1. Grandees.

nance to accept the crown. He repressed the rebels in Gothic Gaul, and besieged Narbonne and Nismes. He also vigorously opposed the descents of the Saracens, who were beginning to infest the coasts of Spain, as the Normans were infesting those of Gaul. He fortified Toledo and many other towns. During his reign the division of the kingdom into dioceses took place; six archbishoprics and seventy bishoprics were established. Wamba made several laws for organizing military service, and repressing the excesses of the clergy.

17. In 680, Wamba was deposed by the intrigues of Erwig, who was supported by the clergy. Wamba abdicated, and withdrew to a convent. Erwig convoked the twelfth council of Toledo, at which Wamba's voluntary abdication was announced, and Erwig appointed his successor. The new monarch directed the council to revise and modify the laws of Wamba regarding military service, and the penalties to be imposed upon delinquents. A less severe legislation was the work of the twelfth and thirteenth councils of Toledo.

18. Erwig had given his daughter Cixilone in marriage to Egica, a near relation of Wamba. In 687, Egica succeeded Erwig. He charged the sixteenth council of Toledo to make a complete collection of the laws of the Visigoths; and this collection, under the name of the *Forum judicum*, or *Fuero juzgo,* long ruled the Spanish monarchy.

19. Egica had associated with himself his son Witiza, who succeeded him in 701. Witiza was tyrannical and dissolute. He allowed the priests to marry, recalled the Jews, entered into conflict with the Spanish clergy and the Pope; violently persecuted the principal lay lords, among others Theutfred and Favila, dukes of Cordova and Biscay, and sons of king Chindasuinth; and fell a victim, in 710, to a conspiracy formed against him by Roderic, son of Theutfred. Roderic, or Rodrigo, became king of the Visigoths, and his reign was the last of this monarchy. I shall not relate to you his wars with the Saracens, or the celebrated adventure of Count Julian and his daughter La Cava, who was violated by Roderic, or any of the last scenes of this history which have now become popular poetry.* Political institutions are now the sole subject of our study. In my next lectures, I shall tell you of the *Forum judicum,* a very remarkable legislative work, which deserves our serious examination and attention.

* For the legend of Count Julian, and other information regarding this most interesting period of Spanish history, see Washington Irving's "Legends of the Conquest of Granada and Spain," in Bohn's edition of his works.

LECTURE 25

Peculiar character of the legislation of the Visigoths. ⁓ *Different sorts of laws contained in the* Forum judicum. ⁓ *It was a doctrine as well as a code.* ⁓ *Principles of this doctrine on the origin and nature of power.* ⁓ *Absence of practical guarantees.* ⁓ *Preponderance of the clergy in the legislation of the Visigoths.* ⁓ *True character of the election of the Visigothic kings.* ⁓ *The Visigothic legislation characterized by a spirit of mildness and equity towards all classes of men, and especially towards the slaves.* ⁓ *Philosophical and moral merits of this legislation.*

OF all the Barbarian codes of law, that of the Visigoths is the only one which remained in force, or nearly so, until modern times. We must not expect to find in this code itself the only, or even the principal, cause of this circumstance. And yet the peculiar character of this code contributed powerfully to determine its particular destiny; and more than one phase in Spanish history is explained, or at least elucidated, by the special and distinctive character of its primitive legislation. This character I wish to make you thoroughly understand. I cannot now deduce therefrom all the consequences which it contains; but I think they will readily be perceived by the careful observer.

The legislation of the Visigoths was not, like that of the Franks, Lombards, and others, the law of the Barbarian conquerors. It was the general law of the kingdom, the code which ruled the vanquished as well as the victors, the Spanish Romans as well as the Goths. King Euric, who reigned from 466 to 484, had the customs of the Goths written out. Alaric II., who ruled from 484 to 507, collected and published in the *Breviarium Aniani,* the Roman laws which were applicable to his Roman subjects. Chindasuinth, who reigned from 642 to 652, ordered a revision and completion of the Gothic laws, which had already been frequently revised and augmented since the time of Euric; and completely abolished the Roman law. Recesuinth, who reigned from 652 to 672, by allowing marriages between the Goths and Romans, endeavoured completely to assimilate the two nations: thenceforward, there existed, or at least there ought to have existed, on the soil of Spain, one single nation formed by the union of the two nations, and ruled by one single code of laws, comprising the essential parts of the two codes. Thus, whilst the system of personal laws, or laws based on the origin of individuals, prevailed in most of the Barbarian monarchies, the system of real laws, or laws based upon land, held sway in Spain. The causes and consequences of this fact are of great importance.

Four different kinds of laws may be distinguished in the *Forum judicum*. 1. Laws made by the kings alone, in virtue of their own authority, or merely with the concurrence of their privy council, *officium palatinum*. 2. Laws made in the national councils held at Toledo, in concert with the bishops and grandees of the realm, and with the assent, more frequently presumed than expressed, of the people. At the opening of the council, the king proposed, in a book called *tomus regius*, the adoption of new laws or the revision of old ones; the council deliberated thereupon; and the king sanctioned and published its decisions. The influence of the bishops was predominant. 3. Laws without either date or author's name, which seem to have been literally copied from the various collections of laws successively compiled by Euric, Leovigild, Recared, Chindasuinth, and other kings. 4. Lastly, laws entitled *antiqua noviter emendata*,[1] which were mostly borrowed from the Roman laws, as is formally indicated by their title in some manuscripts.

The *Forum judicum*, as we possess it at the present day, is a code formed of the collection of all these laws, as finally collected, revised, and arranged at the sixteenth council of Toledo, by order of King Egica. The most ancient Castilian version of the *Forum judicum* appears to have been made during the reign of Ferdinand the Saint (1230–1252).

Legislation is almost always imperative; it prescribes or interdicts; each legal provision usually corresponds to some fact which it either ordains or prohibits. Rarely does it happen that a law, or code of laws, are preceded by a theory on the origin and nature of power, the object and philosophic character of law, and the right and duty of the legislator. All legislations suppose some solution or other to these primary questions, and conform thereto; but it is by a secret bond, frequently unknown to the legislator himself. The law of the Visigoths has this singular characteristic, that its theory precedes it, and is incessantly recurrent in it—a theory formally expressed, and arranged in articles. Its authors wished to do more than ordain and prohibit; they decreed principles, and converted into law philosophical truths, or what appeared to them to be such.

This fact alone indicates that the *Forum judicum* was the work of the philosophers of that period; I mean, the clergy. Never did such a proceeding occur to the mind of a new people, still less to a horde of Barbarian conquerors.

---

1. Ancient matters newly corrected.

Assuredly a doctrine which thus serves as preface and commentary to a code, merits our best attention. "The law," says the *Forum judicum*,

> is the emulator of divinity, the messenger of justice, the mistress of life. It regulates all conditions in the State, all ages of human life; it is imposed on women as well as on men, on the young as well as on the old, on the learned as well as on the ignorant, on the inhabitants of towns as well as on those of the country; it comes to the aid of no particular interest; but it protects and defends the common interest of all citizens. It must be according to the nature of things and the customs of the State, adapted to the time and place, prescribing none but just and equitable rules, clear and public, so as to act as a snare to no citizen.

In these ideas on the nature and object of written law, the fundamental idea of the theory is revealed. There is an unwritten, eternal, universal law, fully known to God alone, and which the human legislator seeks after. Human law is good only in so far as it is the *emulator* and *messenger* of the divine law. The source of the legitimacy of laws is, then, not to be found on earth; and this legitimacy originates, not in the will of him or them who make the laws, whoever they may be, but in the conformity of the laws themselves to truth, reason, and justice—which constitute the true law.[2]

All the consequences of this principle were certainly not present to the mind of the Spanish bishops, and many of the consequences which they deduced were very false; but the principle was there. They deduced from it this other principle, then unknown to Europe, that the character of law is to be universal, the same for all men, foreign to all private interests, given solely for the common interest. On the other hand, it was the character of the other Barbarian codes that they were conceived for the furtherance of the private interests, either of individuals or of classes. Thus the whole system of laws, whether good or bad, which issued therefrom, bore this imprint; it was a system of privileges,

---

2. This passage that explains the relation between human and divine law is essential for understanding the theological background of Guizot's political thought and his doctrine of the sovereignty of reason (on this issue, also see *HCE*, pp. 50–51). In Guizot's view, man-made laws are legitimate only insofar as they are in conformity with the dictates of reason, truth, and justice "which constitute the true law." Two corollaries of this idea are worth pointing out. First, no human will can confer legitimacy to power since the principle of legitimacy has a transcendent origin. Legitimate power does not come from below; only that power which acts according to the "true" law of reason, justice, and truth is legitimate and comes "from above" (*ibid.*, p. 189). Second, force can never be the foundation of political legitimacy. As Guizot himself explains in *HCE*, one of the most important characteristics of political legitimacy "is to reject physical force as a source of power, and to connect it with a moral idea, with a moral force, with the idea of right, of justice, and of reason" (*HCE*, p. 50).

privatae leges. The councils of Toledo alone attempted to introduce into politics the principle of equality in the sight of the law, which they derived from the Christian idea of equality in the sight of God. Thus, the law of the Visigoths was, at this period, the only one that could be called *lex publica.*

From this theory on the nature of law, resulted the following theory on the nature of power. 1. No power is legitimate except in so far as it is just, as it governs and is itself governed by the true law, the law of justice and truth. No human will, no terrestrial force can confer on power an external and borrowed legitimacy; the principle of its legitimacy resides in itself and in itself alone, in its morality and its reason. 2. All legitimate power comes from above. He who possesses and exercises it, holds it solely by reason of his own intellectual and moral superiority. This superiority is given to him by God himself. He does not, therefore, receive power from the will of those over whom he exercises it; he exercises it legitimately, not because he has received it, but because he possesses it in himself. He is not a delegate or a servant, but a superior, a chief.

This two-fold consequence of the definition of law frequently occurs in the legislation of the Visigoths. "The king is called king (*rex*) in that he governs justly (*recte*). If he acts with justice, he legitimately possesses the name of king; if he acts with injustice, he miserably loses it. Our fathers, therefore, said with reason: *Rex ejus eris si recta facis; si autem non facis, non eris.*[3] The two chief virtues of royalty are justice and truth." "The royal power, like the whole of the people, is bound to respect the laws. Obeying the will of heaven, we give, to ourselves as well as to our subjects, wise laws, which our own greatness and that of our successors is bound to obey, as are also the whole population of our realm."

"God, the Creator of all things, in arranging the structure of the human body, raised the head above, and willed that thencefrom should issue the nerves of all the members. And he placed in the head the torch of the eyes, that thence might be detected all things that might be injurious. And he established therein the power of intellect, charging it to govern all the members, and wisely to regulate their action. We must therefore first regulate that which concerns princes, watch over their safety, protect their life; and then ordain that which has relation to peoples, in such sort that while suitably guaranteeing the safety of kings, we may at the same time better guarantee that of the peoples."

After having established that that power is alone legitimate which acts according to justice and truth, which obeys and prescribes the true law, and that all legitimate power comes from above, and derives its legitimacy from itself, and not from any terrestrial will, the theory of the councils of Toledo comes to a stop. It does not regard that which is actually occurring in the world: it forgets

---

3. You will be the king of this if you do just things; if, however, you do not do [just things], you will not be [king].

that, with such a definition, no one here below possesses legitimate power or can fully possess it, and that, nevertheless, society has a right to exact that actual power should be legitimate. This theory knows and lays down the true principles of power; but it neglects its guarantees.

Here we come to the junction-point of the two doctrines which have ever contested, and still contest, the possession of the world. One maintains that power comes from below; that, in its origin as well as in right, it belongs to the people, to numbers; and that those who exercise it, exercise it only as delegates, as servants. This theory misunderstands the true principles and the true nature of power; but it tends to constitute those guarantees which rightfully belong to society. Considered as a theory, it maintains, and assumes to render legitimate, the despotism of numbers. But as, in practice, this despotism is impossible, it soon violates its own principle, and limits its operation to the organization of a system of guarantees, the object and result of which is to constrain actual power to become, in its conduct, rightful and legitimate power. The opposite theory, which is more profound and true at its starting-point, assigns absolute power and sovereignty to that Being alone, in whom resides all truth and justice: it refuses it, at the outset, to chiefs, as well as to peoples; it subordinates both alike to eternal laws which they did not make, and which they are equally bound to observe. It reasonably affirms that all legitimate power comes from above, that it is derived from superior reason, not from number, and that number should submit to reason; but soon, forgetting that it has placed sovereignty beyond the earth, and that no one here below is God, it becomes dazzled by its own lustre; it persuades itself, or tries to do so, that the power which comes from above, descends upon earth as full and absolute as it is at its source; it is indignant that limits should be affixed to its exercise, and if there is nothing to stop its progress, it establishes, in fact, a permanent despotism, after having denied, in principle, its legitimacy; whereas, the opposite theory, which assumes to found despotism in principle, almost invariably ends by destroying it in fact, and by establishing only a limited power.

Such, then, are the consequences of the theory regarding power and law, conceived by the Visigothic legislators. I do not say the consequences which logically flow from it, when the theory is held in all its bearings and faithfully followed out; but the actual consequences which it almost always entails, by the natural tendency of things, and by the deviation into which they are forced by the passions of mankind. 1. The best depositaries of legitimate power, those who most probably possess a knowledge of the true law, are the ecclesiastics. Ministers of the divine law in the relations of man with God, they naturally hold the same office in the relations of man with man. It may then be presumed that, wherever this theory prevails, the political predominance of the clergy is already established, and will continue to increase. The theory is at first its symptom, and becomes afterwards its cause. 2. The political predominance of the clergy does not well accord with the principle of hereditary monarchy. The history of the Jews furnishes an example of this. The transmission of actual power taking place altogether independently of the men who are thought to possess rightful power in a higher degree than all others, is an inconsistency. The theory will, therefore, tend to make monarchy elective, or at least to place every monarch, at his accession, under the necessity of obtaining the recognition and sanction of the clergy. 3. The election of the monarch, or the necessity for his recognition, must be the only political guarantee, the only limit affixed to the exercise of actual power. This power, once constituted in this manner, is sovereign; for the depositaries of true sovereignty, which emanates from God, have conferred it upon its possessor by election. It would be absurd and impious to seek for guarantees against its excess in powers of an inferior order, less enlightened and less pure. Therefore, every institution the object of which is either to divide power, or to limit it in its exercise by opposing to it other powers emanating from other sources, is proscribed by this theory. Elective monarchical power is absolute. All the inferior powers necessary for the government of society are derived from it, and are instituted by it in its own name.

These consequences are met with in the legislation of the Visigoths to as great an extent as the necessary incoherence of human affairs will allow.

I. The political predominance of the bishops in the Visigothic monarchy, is a fact evident throughout its history. The councils of Toledo made both the kings and the laws. The principal Gothic laymen who attended and deliberated thereat were few in number, as is proved by the signatures to the canons of the councils. The phrases with which we sometimes meet, *cum toto populo, populo assentiente*,[4] are mere formulas which pay a kind of homage to ancient facts rather than to present and real facts. Excommunication is the legal punishment decreed against bad kings, against attempts at usurpation, insurrection, and other crimes. The predominance of the bishops was not confined to the councils. The oversight of local functionaries and judges was also intrusted to them, and they had the power of provisionally overruling any judgments of which they disapproved. The bishops and the king were the only persons who could not personally defend their own cause, and who were bound to appear by proxy in such cases, lest their personal presence should influence the decision of the judge. The personal and real privileges granted to the clergy, the facility and perpetuity accorded to donations made to churches, everything in fact in the laws as well as in history, testifies that, in political matters, the bishops occupied the foremost rank, and that their predominance daily increased.

4. With the entire people, with the people giving assent.

It must not however be supposed that this predominance was unlimited, or that it was established without efforts; it was a difficult task to subjugate a Barbarian king and people to an almost exclusively moral power, and the code of the Visigoths contains several enactments tending to restrain the independence of the clergy, and to keep them under obedience to the civil power. Ecclesiastics of every rank were bound, under the same penalties as laymen, to appear and defend their causes before the civil judges. These same judges were competent to punish licentious priests, deacons, and sub-deacons. The eleventh council of Toledo ordained that bishops guilty of certain crimes should be judged by the ordinary laws, and punished in the same cases as laymen, by the *lex talionis*.[5] The laws of Wamba compelled ecclesiastics as well as laymen to do military service, and other duties of a corresponding kind. In a word, that clergy which we behold at the head of society and constituting the national assembly almost by themselves, was at the same time less isolated from the civil order, and less constituted as a distinct body by jurisdiction and privilege, than it was elsewhere at the same period. However, the coincidence of these two facts is natural. We feel less need of separation from a society, as we become nearer subduing it.

II. As to the election of kings, which may be regarded as the natural consequence of the system, or simply of the theocratic tendency, it is formally laid down as a principle in the *Forum judicum,* and was the common law of the Visigothic monarchy: but we must not mistake as to the origin and character of this institution; in Spain, it was much less an institution of liberty than an institution of order, a means of preventing civil wars and the disorders attendant upon usurpations.

From causes difficult to discover, the principle of the regular hereditariness of royalty did not prevail among the Visigoths as among the other Barbarian peoples. The throne at the death of the kings, and even during their lifetime, was the object aimed at by a host of ambitious individuals, who contested for it *vi et armis,*[6] and seized or lost it according to the powers of the claimants and their factions. It was against this state of things, much more than with a view to establish or maintain the right of the nation to choose its own sovereign, that the election of the monarch by the bishops and grandees assembled in council at Toledo, was instituted. The text of the law clearly lays this down. "Henceforth the sovereigns shall be chosen for the glory of the kingdom, in such sort that, in the royal town, or in the place in which the prince shall have died, his successor shall be chosen by the consent of the bishops, the grandees of the palace, and the people: and not at a distance by the conspiracy of a few perverse

5. The law of retaliation.

6. By force and arms.

persons, or by a seditious tumult of an ignorant multitude." Various canons of the fifth, sixth, seventh and thirteenth councils of Toledo, inserted as laws in the *Forum judicum,* have as their only object the repression of attempts at usurpation, and interdict all seizure of the throne by force, determine what classes of men can never be eligible to the kingly office, and also guarantee the lives and property of the families of the dead kings, against the violence and avidity of their elected successors. In a word, all tends to prove that this election was intended to counteract violent usurpation much more than to prevent regular hereditary succession.

Historical facts lead us to the same result. The succession of the Visigothic kings was a series of violent usurpations. Scarcely do we meet with one or two examples of veritable elections, made freely and without any anterior constraint, in consequence of the throne falling vacant. Almost always the election by the council only sanctioned the usurpation; and at the same time that we may doubt of its liberty, we see that its special object is to prevent the return of a great disorder. Neither is there anything to indicate that when, by reason of the preponderance of a more powerful or more popular king, the principle of hereditary succession was on the point of introducing itself, the councils either attempted to oppose its entrance, or considered the act as an infraction of their fundamental law. In every circumstance, at this period, in this state of society, and particularly in great monarchies, the want of order, of rule, of some check to restrain the irregular operation of force, was the dominant want felt by men who, like the bishops, were much more enlightened and much more civilized than the Barbarian conquerors; and political institutions, as well as civil laws, were framed rather with this object than with a view to the assurance of liberty.

Such being its true nature, the election of the kings by the councils of Toledo could evidently not have rested entirely in the hands of the clergy. Armed and ambitious Barbarians would not have endured patiently to receive the crown at the will of bishops, nearly all of whom were Romans. Originally, the bishops exercised, in fact, no other right than that of sanctioning present usurpation, by anathematizing similar conduct in the future. In proportion as their moral influence and real power became consolidated and extended, they attempted higher things, and appeared to aspire to the famous right of giving and taking away the crown. The *Forum judicum* furnishes two remarkable proofs of this progress. The fourth council of Toledo, held during the reign of Sisenand, in 671, decreed by its seventy-fifth canon, "that when the king had died in peace, the grandees of the realm and the bishops should elect his successor, by common consent." At a later period, when this canon was transported as a law into the national code, it was amplified in these terms: "Let no one, therefore, in his pride, seize upon the throne; let no pretender excite civil war among the people; let no one conspire the death of the prince; but, when the king is dead in peace, let the principal men of the whole kingdom, together with the bishops, *who have received power to bind and to loose, and whose blessing and unction confirm princes in their authority,* appoint his successor by common consent and with the approval of God." A similar interpolation occurs in the insertion of a canon of the eighth council, which began: "We, the bishops, priests, and other inferior clerks, in concert with the officers of the palace, and the general assembly, decree," &c. In the *Forum judicum,* after the word *priests,* these words are added: "*Who have been established by our Lord Jesus Christ, to be the directors and heralds of the people.*" Such phrases as these clearly indicate the progress of ecclesiastical pretensions, and their success. It is, however, certain as a fact, that the councils of Toledo never really disposed of the crown, but that it was almost always taken by force; and that the election of the kings by the grandees and bishops, though established as a principle by the laws, must not be considered as a proof either of the complete predominance of the theocratic system, or of the extent of the national liberty.

III. But if, after having ascertained who possessed the right of appointment to the highest political office, and the mode in which this office was conferred, we endeavour to discover, from the laws of the Visigoths, what duties were imposed on their kings, and what guarantees they gave their subjects for the performance of those duties, the consequences which we have already indicated, as likely to result from the theory that presided over this code, become clearly revealed. Good precepts abound, but real guarantees are wanting.

To those who read these laws, the legislator appears much better aware of the duties of the sovereign, and of the rights and necessities of the people, than were the other Barbarian legislators; and, in fact, he was so. But if they next inquire where were the independent forces capable of procuring or insuring the maintenance of these principles, and how the citizens exercised their rights or defended their liberties, they find absolutely nothing. The code of the Visigoths, though more enlightened, more just, more humane, and more complete than the laws of the Franks or Lombards, left despotism at greater liberty, and almost entirely disarmed freedom. Texts in abundance might be quoted in support of this assertion.

If, from these general principles, we descend to the details of legislation, we shall find that the code of the Visigoths was, in this respect also, much more provident, more complete, more wise, and more just, than any other Barbarian code. The various social relations were much better defined therein; and their nature and effects more carefully analyzed. In civil matters, we meet with repetitions of the Roman law at almost every step; in criminal matters, the proportion of punishments to crimes was determined according to moral and philosophical notions of considerable justice. We discern therein the efforts of an enlightened legislator struggling against the violence and inconsiderateness of

Barbarian manners. The title, *De caede et morte hominum,*[7] compared with the corresponding laws of other peoples, is a very remarkable example of this. In other codes the injury done seems almost alone to constitute the crime, and the punishment is fixed in that material reparation which results from a pecuniary composition. In this code, crime is measured by its moral and true element—intention. The various shades of criminality, absolutely involuntary homicide, homicide by inadvertence, homicide by provocation, homicide with or without premeditation, are all distinguished and defined almost as accurately as in our codes, and the punishments vary in an equitable proportion. The justice of the legislator went further than this. He attempted, if not to abolish, at least to diminish that diversity of legal value established among men by the other Barbarian codes. The only distinction which it maintained was that between the freeman and the slave. In regard to freemen, the punishment does not vary, either according to the origin or rank of the dead man, but simply according to the different degrees of the moral culpability of the murderer. With regard to slaves, though not daring completely to deprive masters of the right of life and death, the *Forum judicum* at least attempted to subject them to a public and regular course of procedure:

> If no one who is guilty or accomplice of a crime should remain unpunished, how much more should those be punished who have committed homicide wickedly and with levity. Thus, as cruel masters, in their pride, frequently put to death their slaves without any fault on their part, it is fitting altogether to extirpate this license, and to ordain that the present law shall be eternally observed by all. No master or mistress may, without a public trial, put to death any of their male or female slaves, or any person dependent upon them. If a slave, or any other servant, commit a crime which may lead to his capital condemnation, his master or accuser shall immediately give information thereof to the judge of the place where the action was committed, or to the count, or to the duke. After the discussion of the affair, if the crime be proved, let the culprit suffer, either by sentence of the judge, or of his master, the punishment of death which he has deserved; in such sort, however, that if the judge will not put the culprit to death, he shall draw up a capital sentence against him, in writing, and then it shall be in the power of the master to kill him or to keep him in life. In truth, if the slave, by a fatal boldness, while resisting his master, has struck him or attempted to strike him with a weapon, or a stone, or by any other blow, and if the master in self-defence has killed the slave in his anger, the master shall in no wise suffer the punishment of homicide. But he must prove that this was

7. On the slaughter and death of men.

the case; and he must prove it by the testimony or oath of the slaves, both male and female, who were present at the time, and by the oath of himself, the author of the deed. Whosoever, from pure wickedness, and by his own hand or that of another, shall have killed his slave without bringing him to public trial, shall be branded with infamy, declared incapable of giving evidence, and doomed to pass the rest of his life in exile and penitence; and his property shall be given to his nearest relatives, to whom the law grants it as an inheritance.

This law alone, and the efforts which its passage reveals, do great honour to the Visigothic legislators; for nothing honours the laws and their authors so much as a courageous moral conflict against the bad customs and evil prejudices of their age and country. We are often forced to believe that the love of power has a great share in the construction of laws which aim at the maintenance of order and the repression of violent passions; the excess of passion borders closely on the rights of liberty, and order is the hackneyed pretext of despotism. But here, power has nothing to gain; the law is disinterested; it seeks after justice only; it seeks after it laboriously, in opposition to the strong who reject it, and for the benefit of the weak who are unable to call in its aid—perhaps, even, in opposition to the public opinion of the time, which, after having had great difficulty in looking on a Roman as a Goth, had still more in regarding a slave as a man. This respect for man, whatever may be his origin or social condition, is a phenomenon unknown to Barbarian legislation; and nearly fourteen centuries elapsed before the doctrine passed from religion into politics, from the Gospel into the codes. It is therefore no slight honour to the Visigothic bishops that they did their best to guard and transfer into the laws this noble sentiment, which it is so difficult to disentangle from the meshes of fact, and which is continually in danger of being crushed beneath the pressure of circumstance. It continually recurs in their legislation, both in general precepts and in special regulations; and when it yields, either before the inconsiderate brutality of Barbarian customs, or before the despotic traditions of Roman jurisprudence—traditions with which the minds of the Spanish bishops themselves were imbued—we still discern, even in these bad laws, the obscure presence of a good principle labouring to surmount the obstacles beneath which it has succumbed.

LECTURE 26

Central institutions of the Visigothic monarchy. ⁓ *True character of the Councils of Toledo.* ⁓ *Amount of their political influence.* ⁓ *The Officium palatinum.* ⁓ *Prevalence of Roman maxims and institutions, among the Goths, over Germanic traditions.* ⁓ *Proof of this in the local and central institutions of the Visigoths.* ⁓ *Refutation of the errors of Savigny and the* Edinburgh Review *on this subject.* ⁓ *Conclusion.*

MY last lecture, I think, convinced you, gentlemen, that the code of the Visigoths, taken in itself, and in its intentions as expressed by written laws, gives the idea of a better social state, a juster and more enlightened government, a better regulated country, and, altogether, a more advanced and milder state of civilization, than that which is revealed to us by the laws of the other Barbarian peoples. But to this more humane and wise legislation, to the general principles dictated by superior reason, there is wanting, as I have already observed, an actual sanction, an effective guarantee. The laws are good; but the people, for whose benefit they were enacted, have hardly any share in their execution, and the business resulting therefrom. Up to a certain point, the code bears testimony to the wisdom and good intentions of the legislature; but it presents no evidence of the liberty and political life of the subjects.

Let us first look at the centre of the State. The single fact of the political predominance of the bishops, the sole name of the councils of Toledo, indicate the decay of the old Germanic customs, and the disappearance of national assemblies. The Anglo-Saxons had their *Wittenagemot;* the Lombards their assembly at Pavia, *circumstante immensa multitudine;*[1] the Franks their *Champs de Mars* and *Champs de Mai,* and their *placita generalia.*[2] Doubtless, the existence of these assemblies entailed scarcely any of the consequences which we attach at the present day to the idea of such institutions; and they certainly constituted

1. With a vast crowd surrounding.

2. General assemblies.

a very slight guarantee of liberty, which it was then impossible to guarantee. In reality, also, they took a very small part in the government. Nevertheless, the simple fact of their existence attests the prevalence of Germanic customs; arbitrary power, though exercised in fact, was not established in principle; the independence of powerful individuals struggled against the despotism of the kings; and in order to dispose of these isolated independencies, to form them into a national body, it was necessary occasionally to convoke them together in assemblies. These assemblies live in the laws as well as in history; the clergy were received therein, because of their importance and superior knowledge,— but they were merely received. Far from being their sole constituents, they did not even form their centre.

In Spain, instead of entering into the national assembly, the clergy opened the assembly to the nation. Is it likely that the name only was changed, and that Gothic warriors came to the council, as formerly to their Germanic assemblies? We have beheld the same name applied to very different things: for example, judicial parliaments have superseded political parliaments; but we have never seen the same thing represented under different names, especially during the infancy of nations. When existence consists almost solely of traditions and customs, words are the last things to change and perish.

The councils of Toledo, then, were actually councils, and not *Champs de Mai* or *placita*. Morally, this fact is probable; historically, it is certain. Their acts have come down to us, and they are acts of an entirely ecclesiastical assembly, specially occupied with the affairs of the clergy; and into which laymen entered only occasionally, and in small numbers. The signatures of laymen, affixed to the canons of the thirteenth council, only amount to twenty-six; and in no other are they so numerous.

These councils were not held, like the *Champs de Mars* or *de Mai* and the *placita generalia* of the Carlovingians, at fixed, or at least, frequent periods. Between the third and fourth councils, forty-four years elapsed; between the tenth and eleventh, eighteen years . The king convoked them at his pleasure, or as necessity required. The Visigothic code ordains absolutely nothing in this respect, either on the kings, or on the members of the assembly. None of its enactments have reference, even indirectly, to a national assembly.

The nature of these councils of Toledo being thus clearly determined, it remains for us to inquire what influence they exerted in the government. What were they as guarantees of the public liberties, and of the execution of the laws?

Before consulting special facts, the very nature of these assemblies may furnish us with some general indications with regard to their political influence. The clergy, taking a direct and active part in the government, were never in a natural and simple position. I do not speak either of the ecclesiastical law, or of the special mission of the clergy, or of the separation of the spiritual from the temporal order, which are questions still involved in obscurity. I examine facts alone. In fact, in the States of modern Europe, and at their origin, as well as in later times, the clergy did not govern, they neither commanded armies, nor administered justice, nor collected the taxes, nor held sway over the provinces. They penetrated to a greater or less distance, by more or less regular means, along the various paths of political life; but they never traversed them fully, freely, and thoroughly; politics never were their special and avowed career. In a word, the social powers, from the lowest to the highest degree, never were, either in law, or in fact, naturally lodged in their hands. When the bishops, therefore, in council assembled, interfered in the civil government, they were called to regulate affairs which did not concern them, and to occupy themselves about matters which did not constitute the habitual and recognised business of their position and life. This intervention, therefore, necessarily bore an equivocal and uncertain character. Great influence might have been attached thereto; but it could not possess any power of energetic and effectual resistance. If warrior chiefs meet together in assembly around their monarch, they can rely on their comrades and their soldiers to support their resolutions; if elected deputies assemble to vote taxes and ratify the laws of the country, they are sustained by the number, credit, and opinion of those who chose and deputed them. If bodies charged with the administration of justice are, at the same time, called to deliberate upon certain acts of the sovereign, they may, by suspending the exercise of their functions, place the government in an almost untenable position. In these various combinations, a positive force, more or less regular in its character, stands at the back of the men appointed to control the supreme power. On the part of the clergy, any decisive resistance, in political matters, is almost impracticable, for not one of the effective forces of society is naturally at their disposal; and, in order to gain possession of such a force, they must abandon their position, abjure their character, and thus compromise the moral force whence they derive their true point of support. Thus, by the nature of things, the clergy are but ill-adapted to be constituted into a political power, with the mission of exercising control, and offering resistance. If they desire to remain within the limits of their position, they find themselves, at the decisive moment, unprovided with effective and trusty weapons. If they seek after such weapons, they throw the whole of society into disturbance, and incur the legitimate reproach of usurpation. Modern history, at every step, demonstrates this two-fold truth. When the clergy have believed themselves strong enough to resist in the same way as civil powers would have done, they have compromised themselves as clergy, and have increased disorder rather than obtained reform. When they have not made such attempts, their resistance has almost invariably been ineffectual at the moment when it was most necessary; and as, in such cases, ecclesiastics generally feel conscious of their weakness, they have not opposed any solid barrier to the encroachments of power; and, when they have not consented to be the instruments of its will, they have yielded after an impotent admonition.

Such was the position of the Visigothic bishops. They had not yet acquired, in temporal matters, sufficient force to struggle openly against the crown. They felt that a great part of their importance was due to their close alliance with the royal power, and that they would be great losers by breaking off the connection. They could not, therefore, carry their resistance very far, or establish in reality an independent political assembly. They went as far as to sanction the royal power, and to associate themselves with it by becoming its advisers; but they attempted nothing beyond. Facts prove this. These councils of Toledo, whither usurpers came to be elected, and which gave an entire code to the Visigoths, exercised in fact, over the great events of this period in Spain, less influence than was exerted in France by the *Champs de Mars* and *de Mai*. They occupied, but did not supply, the place of the old Germanic assemblies, for they did not possess their brute force, and were not in a position to substitute for it any sufficient regular force. Spain was indebted to them for a much better legislation than that possessed by other Barbarian nations, and probably also, in their daily practice, for a more enlightened and humane administration of justice; but in vain do we seek to find therein the principle of a great institution of liberty, and the characteristics of a veritable resistance of absolute power. During the period which now occupies our attention, the reigning power in the other States founded by the Barbarians was force—disorderly, capricious, and unsettled force, sometimes distributed amongst a multitude of almost independent chieftains; sometimes concentrated, for a brief space, and according to circumstances, in the hands of one man, or of a brutal and transitory aristocracy. No principle was acknowledged; no right was legal; all was matter of fact, liberty as well as power; and the germs of free institutions existed in the disorderly relations of these independent or ill-united forces, although, to speak the truth, liberty was nowhere visible. In Spain, and through the influence of the clergy, the government undoubtedly assumed greater generality and a more regular form; the laws afforded greater protection to the weak; the administration paid more attention to their condition; and there was less disorder and violence in society at large. Broader and more elevated moral ideas frequently governed the exercise of power. But, on the other hand, power was constituted under a more absolute form; Roman maxims prevailed over Germanic traditions; theocratic doctrines lent their aid to the arbitrary power of the Barbarians. The councils of Toledo modified and enlightened despotism, but did not limit the exercise of power.

Some writers have thought they perceived, in another institution which existed at the centre of the Visigothic monarchy, the principle and instrument of a limitation of the sovereign authority. I refer to the *officium palatinum*, a species of council formed around the king, by the grandees of his Court, and the principal functionaries of the government. The importance of this council, and its participation in public business, are attested by a large number of laws passed either independently of the councils of Toledo, or in virtue of their deliberation. The words, *cum omni palatino officio, cum assensu sacerdotum majorumque palatii, ex palatino officio*,[3] and the like, frequently occur in the code of the Visigoths. These texts and the voice of history do not admit of a doubt that the *officium palatinum* frequently interfered in the legislation, in the government, and even in the elevation of kings.

It would be a mistake, however, to regard it as a political institution, a guarantee of liberty, a means of exercising control and offering resistance. Power could not, in any case, subsist alone, by itself and in the air; it must, of sheer necessity, conciliate interests, appropriate forces, in a word, surround itself with auxiliaries, and maintain its position by their aid. In the Roman Empire, this necessity had given birth to the creation of the Court and of the *officium palatinum*, instituted by Diocletian and Constantine. In the Barbarian States, it led the kings to surround themselves with *Antrustions, Leudes*, sworn vassals, and all those natural or factitious grandees, who, becoming dispersed at a later period, and settling in their own domains, became the principal members of the feudal aristocracy. From these two sources arose the *officium palatinum* of the Visigothic kings, with this difference, that, in this point as in others, Roman institutions prevailed over Barbarian customs, to the great advantage of absolute power.

The *officium palatinum* of the Visigoths was composed of the grandees of the realm (*proceres*), whom the kings attached to themselves by donations of lands and offices, and of the principal functionaries, dukes, counts, vicars, and others, who held their functions from the kings. This court undoubtedly formed a sort of aristocracy which was frequently consulted on public affairs, which sate in the councils, and which furnished the king with assessors whenever he delivered judgments. The necessity of things required that it should be so; and as necessity always entails consequences which far exceed the wishes of those who are constrained to yield to its sway, there is also no doubt that this aristocracy, on many occasions, thwarted the kings who could not dispense with its assistance, and thus limited their empire.

But human nature is the same amongst barbarian nations as amongst civilized peoples; and the coarseness of forms, the brutality of passions, and the limited range of ideas, do not prevent similar positions from leading to the same

---

3. With the entire palace council, with the assent of the priests and the majority of the palace, from the palace council.

results. Now, it is in the nature of an aristocracy that is closely pent up around the prince, of a Court aristocracy, to use power for their own advantage rather than to limit it for the benefit of the State. It almost inevitably becomes a focus of faction and intrigue, around which individual interests are set in motion, and not a centre of controlment and resistance in which the public interest finds a place. If the times are barbarous and manners violent, individual interests assume the forms of barbarism and use the means of violence; if satisfied, they obey with the same servility as before; if discontented, they poison, assassinate, or dethrone. Such was the case in the monarchy of the Visigoths. All usurpations and revolutions in power originated in the *officium palatinum;* and when a king attempted to subject the nobles to the performance of public services, to limit or even to examine into the concessions which they demanded, that king lost the empire. Such was the fate of Wamba.

The Visigothic sovereigns had, moreover, in the bishops, a powerful counterpoise, which they set in opposition to the nobles of their Court, in order to prevent them from aspiring to entire independence. The influence of the clergy, too weak to act as an effectual check on the power of the prince, was strong enough, in the hands of the prince, to prevent the check from coming from any other quarter. The reign of Chindasuinth affords an example of this.

Finally, as I have already said, the predominance of Roman maxims and institutions in Spain was so great, that the central aristocracy bore more resemblance to the *officium palatinum* of the emperors than to the *Antrustions* or *Leudes* of Germanic origin. Elsewhere, these last were not slow to obtain sufficient strength to assert their independence, to isolate themselves from the prince, and finally to become petty sovereigns in their own domains. In Spain, things did not occur precisely thus. It appears that the *proceres* received from the king dignities and offices in greater abundance than lands, and thus acquired less individual and personal strength. Perhaps the equality granted to the Roman population, and the fusion of the two peoples, did not permit so great a dilapidation of property and distribution of domains as that which took place in France. What would have occurred if the monarchy of the Visigoths had not been interrupted in its course by the conquest of the Arabs? Would the dismemberment of the royal power and the dispersion of the Court have led to the dispersion and independence of the landed aristocracy? We cannot say. This much is certain, that the phenomenon which was exhibited in France, at the fall of the Carlovingians, did not occur among the Visigoths, in the eight century: the *officium palatinum* had neither destroyed nor divided the royal power, and made but feeble attempts to limit it.

One fact must be added, which, though universally attested, is not explained in a satisfactory manner. Of the various German peoples, the Goths preserved in the smallest degree their primitive institutions and manners. The

Ostrogoths in Italy, under Theodoric, like the Visigoths in Spain, allowed Roman habits to prevail amongst them, and permitted their kings to arrogate to themselves the plenitude of imperial power. We even find, among the Goths of Italy, still fewer traces of the existence of the old national assemblies, and of the participation of the people in the affairs of the State.

It would therefore be vain to seek, in the Visigothic monarchy, for the principles, or even the remnants, of any great institution of liberty, or of any effectual limitation of power. Neither the councils of Toledo, nor the *officium palatinum* present this character; but there resulted from them something that did not result from the *Champs de Mars* and *de Mai*, or from the Saxon Wittenagemot—a code of laws, which, for that period, are very remarkable for their large philosophical views, their foresight, and their wisdom; but this code, though it indicates the handiwork of enlightened legislators, nowhere reveals the existence of a free people. It contains even fewer germs or monuments of liberty than the rudest of Barbarian laws; and the royal power, thus considered as in itself the centre of the State, appears as much more absolute in right, and much less limited in fact, than it was anywhere else. An examination of the local institutions of the Visigoths will lead us to the same result.

Local institutions are the most real, perhaps the only real, institutions of Barbarian peoples. They do not possess sufficient vitality or enlargement of mind to originate or preserve general institutions. The material contiguity of individuals is an almost indispensable condition of the existence of society amongst them; it is therefore in the local institutions of the German peoples that we must seek the history of their political life. The forms of these institutions, and the modifications which they underwent, exercised far greater influence over their destiny, than the revolutions which occurred in central institutions, such as the Wittenagemot, the *placita generalia,* and the royal power.

As you have already seen, the laws of most of the German peoples present three co-existent and conflicting systems: institutions of liberty; institutions of territorial patronage, which gave birth to feudalism; and monarchical institutions. The assembly of free men transacting the general business, and administering justice in every district; the landowners, exercising authority and jurisdiction throughout their domains; the king's delegates, whether dukes, counts, or others, also possessing authority and jurisdiction: such are the three powers which have reciprocally contested the government of localities, and whose existence and vicissitudes are proved by the laws as well as by facts.

The code of the Visigoths presents no trace whatever of the first of these systems, and scarcely any of the second; the third immensely predominates. There was no *mallum,* no *placitum,*[4] no assemblies of free men in the provinces;

---

4. *Mallum:* assembly in which important debates were held; *placitum:* agreement.

no enactment ordains, or even refers to them. Scarcely does there exist any indication of the power of the patron over his client, of the landowner over the inhabitants of his domains. The law which I quoted in my last lecture, with reference to slaves, proves that, even in their case, the jurisdiction belonged to the royal judge of the district.

The *Forum judicum* mentions a large number of local magistrates who were invested with the power of administering affairs and distributing justice.

> As there is a great variety in the means of remedying evils and terminating affairs, let the duke, count, vicar, conservator of the peace (*pacis assertor*), *tinfadus*,[5] *millenarius, quingentenarius, centenarius, decanus, defensor, numerarius*,[6] and those who are sent to any place by order of the king, and those who are accepted as judges by the agreement of the litigant parties,—let all persons, in fine, of whatever order they may be, who are regularly invested with power to judge, and each person in such proportion as he has received power to judge, equally obtain from the law the name of judges, in order that, having received the right to judge, the duties as well as the advantages connected with that right may devolve upon them.

It is difficult to determine with precision the different functions of all these magistrates, the hierarchy which existed among them, and the manner in which each of them received and exercised his power. Those who belonged to towns, as the *defensor* and the *numerarius*, were certainly elected by the clergy and inhabitants. Several others, as the *millenarius* and *centenarius*, seem to have been appointed by the dukes and counts of the provinces; but however this may be, nothing indicates that they received their authority in a popular and independent way; the opposite principle is formally laid down in these terms:

> No one shall be permitted to judge suits, except those who have received power from the prince to do so, or those who have been chosen as judges, by agreement of the litigants; the choice of these last shall be made in presence of three witnesses, and shall be attested by their mark or signature. If those who have received from the king power to judge, or those who exercise judicial power by commission from the counts or other royal judges, have charged, by writing, and according to the prescribed rules, other persons to fill their places, these last shall exercise, in the regulation and decision of affairs, a power similar to that of those by whom they were appointed.

5. Seneschal.

6. Commander of a thousand, commander of five hundred, commander of a hundred, commander of ten, defender, keeper of accounts.

Thus, all the judges, all the local officers, received their power from the king or his delegates. Of the three systems of institutions, whose co-existence and conflict are manifested amongst most of the German peoples, the monarchical system is the only one with which we meet in the code of the Visigoths.

In addition to the permanent judges, established in various localities, the kings had power to send special commissioners, either to restore order in disaffected provinces, or to give judgment in cases of particular importance. Criminal as well as civil affairs were submitted to the decision of the royal judges. All these judges received salaries from the king; but they also levied such enormous fees on the litigants, that the fees frequently amounted to one-third of the value of the object in litigation. A law was passed, limiting them to one-twentieth. Any who thought they had reason to complain of the decision of the judge might appeal, either to the duke or count of the province, or to the king himself. If the appeal was deemed well-founded, in addition to gaining the cause, the judge had to pay the appellant a sum equal to the value of the object in litigation. If the judgment was confirmed, the appellant had to pay the same amount to the judge, and if he could not do so, he was condemned publicly to receive a hundred lashes.

Up to this point, nothing in the constitution of judicial authority exhibits any of those guarantees of liberty contained in the laws of the other Barbarian peoples. Nothing discloses any remnant or even remembrance of the old forms of judgment by the assembly of free men, *per Rachimburgos, bonos homines*, &c. Some passages of the *Forum judicum*, however, prove that the judges, at least, had assessors. The fourth council of Toledo formally prohibits the kings from administering justice alone; and several texts allude to *auditores*.[7] Most learned men, and amongst others Heineccius, are of opinion that the assessors were not mere councillors; and that the judge was bound to take the opinions of a majority of them. I am inclined to think so too. Several texts, however, formally indicate that the judge was at liberty to take assessors or not, as he pleased.

In the absence of those real guarantees of liberty, which originated elsewhere in the more or less effectual intervention of the freemen in the judgment of cases, the *Forum judicum* contains a multitude of precautions or laws against bad judges. In case of appeal to the count or king, if it were proved that the wrong decision of the judge was occasioned by malice, corruption, or prevarication of any kind, and if he were unable to pay the appellant the requisite sum, he was given to him as a slave, and condemned to receive besides fifty lashes in public. He was absolved from all penalty, however, if he proved, under oath, that his decision was pronounced in error or ignorance. The judges who ne-

7. Hearers, assessors.

glected to prosecute the licentious were punished with a hundred lashes, and fined 300 *solidi*. The priests and bishops everywhere were enjoined to exercise a strict surveillance over the judges; and as the former then derived their chief strength from their superior knowledge and their protection of the weak, it is not unlikely that this guarantee was effective.

But all this was defective, as you perceive, by the radical defect of the system of pure monarchy, which gives, as the only guarantee for the good conduct of the depositaries of power, the surveillance and authority of superior depositaries placed in the same position, and invested with the same functions.

> . . . Sed quis custodiet ipsos
> Custodes? . . .[8]

The true guarantees of liberty can only reside in the concurrence of collateral and independent powers, none of which is absolute, and which mutually control and limit each other. Of this the *Forum judicum* affords us no trace, at any stage in the long hierarchy of the government.

The local government of the Visigoths, then, presents still fewer institutions containing any active principle of liberty, any real force of control or resistance, than are found in their political *regime,* and at the centre of the State. Such is, at least, the unavoidable result to which we are led by an examination of the general and definitive code of this nation.

This result has appeared so singular, so opposed to German customs, and to the state of things among other peoples of the same origin, that hardly any man of erudition has been willing to read it in the *Forum judicum;* and that those even who have failed to find in this code any proof of the existence of free institutions, and almost any trace of old Barbarian institutions, have striven to discover them elsewhere in Spain at this period. I shall say nothing of Abbé Mariana,[9] who, in his *Teoria de las Cortes,* is determined to discover, in the councils of Toledo, not only the Spanish Cortes of the thirteenth and fourteenth centuries, but also all the principles and guarantees of liberty—all, in fine, that con-

---

8. But who will guard the guardians themselves?

9. Juan de Mariana (1536–1624) was educated at the University of Acala, taught in Paris, and then moved to Toledo, where he remained until his death. He was the author of *Historiae de rebus Hispaniae* and *De Rege et regis institutione,* an important philosophical treatise on the origin and nature of the state. Karl Friedrich von Savigny (1779–1861) was a distinguished German historian whose most famous work was *Geschichte des Römischen Rechts im Mittelalter,* translated into English by William Holloway as *The History of the Roman Law During the Middle Ages* (Westport, Conn.: Hyperion Press, 1979). The article quoted by Guizot and published in *Edinburgh Review* (vol. 31, pp. 94–132), a review of M. Sempere's *Histoire des Cortés d'Espagne* (Bordeaux, 1815), was written by John Allen.

stitutes a national assembly and a representative government. I have already demonstrated the moral improbability and the historic unreality of the fact. Two more learned men than Abbé Mariana, and less inclined than he to find what they seek, have thought that they perceive, in the *Forum judicum,* proofs that the purely monarchical system, associated with the theocratic system, did not prevail so completely among the Visigoths; and that they can discover among them evidences of effective and extended public liberties: I refer to M. de Savigny, in his *History of Roman Law in the Middle Ages,* and to a writer in the *Edinburgh Review,** in an article on *The Gothic Laws of Spain.* I do not think that the researches of these two learned critics destroy the general results which I have just laid before you. They nevertheless contain many curious facts hitherto little noticed, and which throw much light on the study of the political institutions of the Visigothic monarchy. I shall, therefore, make you acquainted with them, and examine the consequences to which they lead.

M. de Savigny, when investigating the traces of the perpetuation of the Roman law after the fall of the Empire, expresses himself in these terms, in reference to the Visigoths: "Upon the constitution of this monarchy," he says,

> we possess sufficiently complete information in the *Breviarium Aniani,* who, about the year 506, that is, nearly a century after the foundation of the State, drew up the Roman law into a sort of code for the ancient inhabitants of the country. This code consists, as is well known, of two parts: one contains texts quoted word for word from the Roman law; the other an interpretation specially prepared on this occasion. With regard to the texts quoted from the Roman law, we cannot attach great importance to them, when we speak of the real state of things at the period of this publication; as they were drawn from sources much more ancient, expressions and even entire phrases were necessarily retained which had reference to various circumstances of a social state that had already passed away and fallen into desuetude; the interpretation was intended to explain this disagreement. But this interpretation, drawn up *ad hoc,* is, on the other hand, very trustworthy, especially when it does not implicitly follow either the words or the sense of the text, for then we can no longer regard it as a servile and thoughtless copy, especially in what relates to matters of public law. It is impossible to believe that real establishments, institutions set before the eyes of all, and with which all might be acquainted, could have been mentioned unintentionally and described without an object. Now, in this interpretation, the Roman *praeses* has entirely disappeared; but the municipal community, with its particular jurisdiction and its decurions taking part in

* Edinburgh Review, vol. xxxi., pp. 94–132.

the administration of justice, subsists in all its integrity: it even appears to possess more individual consistency and independence than it had enjoyed under the emperors.

The general principle of the *defensores,* of their duties and the mode of choosing them, is explained in the interpretation, as well as in the text of the Theodosian code. According to the text, the governor of the province was not to be burdened with the judgment of petty offences; but it does not mention who was to judge them, whereas the interpretation expressly names the *defensor.* According to the text, the introduction of a civil suit might take place either before the governor, or before those who had the right to draw up the necessary acts; the interpretation adds the defensor. . . .

M. de Savigny then quotes a number of other examples to prove the maintenance, and even extension, of the functions of the defenders of the cities. "Other passages," he continues,

have reference to the *curia,* the decurions, and even to the citizens in general. The system of decurions, in general, is received in the *Breviarium,* with very few modifications, but merely great abridgement. To one passage of the text which casually mentions *adoption,* the interpretation adds, as a commentary, that it is the choice of an individual as a child, made in presence of the *curia.* The Visigothic jurisconsult, Gaius, says, that *emancipation,* which formerly took place before the president, was, at the period at which he wrote, performed before the *curia.* The text determines by whom tutors were appointed at Constantinople, namely, by the prefect of the city, ten senators, and the praetor, whose duty it was to watch over the interests of the pupils: the interpretation substitutes in their place the judge, with the chief men of the town. The text speaks of the necessity of a decree to authorize the alienation of the property of a minor: the interpretation adds, that this decree must be obtained from the judge or the *curia.* The text ordains that, at Constantinople, wills should be opened by the same office that received them: the interpretation substitutes the *curia* in its place. According to the text, donations should be registered either before the judge (the governor of the province), or before the municipal magistrate (the *duumvir*): the interpretation substitutes the *curia* for the municipal magistrate—which does not, in reality, alter the sense of the law, but which proves what is demonstrated by many other passages, that the general point of view was completely changed; anciently the chief municipal authority, and especially jurisdiction, was considered, according to Roman maxims, to be a personal right of the magistrate: according to the interpretation, it belonged less to the *defensor* himself, than to the *curia* taken collectively. . . . Under the emperors, the *honorati*, that is, those who had occupied high municipal dignities, had a seat of honour near the governor of the province when he administered justice; they were only expected to abstain from being present when their own causes were under consideration. The interpretation applies this to the curials; an application which is remarkable in two respects, first, because it proves that the curials were held in great consideration, and secondly, because this does not merely refer to the possession of a seat of honour by them, but to an actual participation in the jurisdiction of the municipal judge, that is, of the *duumvir* or *defensor*. . . . The text of the code ordains that, out of Rome, in order to pronounce sentence on a criminal accusation brought against a senator, five senators shall be chosen by lot: the interpretation makes this rule general, and requires five men to be chosen from the leading members of the same rank as the accused person, that is, decurions or plebeians, according to the condition of the accused person himself. Finally, the text ordained that every judge should receive his *domesticus* or *cancellarius* from the choice of the principal persons employed in his chancery: the interpretation retains the rule, merely substituting the burgesses of the city for the persons employed in the chancery.

Such are the traces of municipal liberties which M. de Savigny discovers in the *Breviarium Aniani,* and which he considers as the common and permanent law of the Visigothic monarchy. They prove, in fact, not merely the maintenance, but also the extension and enfranchisment, of the rights and guarantees possessed by the inhabitants of the towns before the settlement of the Barbarians. But strong objections may be raised against the importance which the author attaches to these texts, and the extent of the conclusions which he deduces therefrom.

I. The *Breviarium Aniani* does not contain the common and permanent law of the Spanish monarchy of the Visigoths. It only gives the special legislation of the Roman subjects of the Visigothic kings, when the kings resided at Toulouse, and had as yet only uncertain possessions in Spain; when the South of Gaul constituted the bulk, and almost the whole, of the kingdom. There is nothing to prove that all that is contained in the *Breviarium Aniani,* towards the end of the fifth century, for the benefit of the Romans of Southern Gaul, subsisted in Spain until the eighth century, for the benefit of the Goths and Romans, when merged into a single nation. The silence of the *Forum judicum,* which is the true code of the Spanish Visigoths, upon most of these arrangements, proves more against their maintenance than is demonstrated in their favour by the text of the *Breviarium,* which was drawn up in another place, at an earlier period, and for a portion only of the people.

II. About a hundred and fifty years after the publication of the *Breviarium,* the Goths and Romans were united into a single nation. The collection of laws, successively augmented under the different reigns, and completed by Chindasuinth, became the sole code of the kingdom; all other laws were abolished, and the *Breviarium* was necessarily included in this abolition. The text of the law of Recesuinth is formal:

> That absolutely none of the men of our realm be permitted to lay before the judge, for the decision of any affair, any other collection of laws than that which has just been published, and according to the order in which the laws are unscribed therein; and this, under penalty of a fine of thirty pounds of gold to our treasury. Any judge who should hesitate to decline any other book that might be presented to him as suited to regulate his decision, will be punished by the same fine.

M. de Savigny foresaw this objection; and without absolutely dissembling it he has tried to weaken it by not quoting the text of the law of Recesuinth, and by speaking only of the attempts made by the Visigothic kings, that Spain should contain only a single nation, and be governed by a single code. These evasions are in striking contrast with his usual candour. He then makes use of the existence of the *defensores,* proof of which is found in the *Forum judicum,* to assume the maintenance of all the prerogatives and liberties attributed to them by the *Breviarium.* This conclusion is evidently hasty and excessive.

I do not dispute that the towns of Spain were able to retain, or indeed that they did necessarily retain, some institutions, some guarantees of municipal liberty. I should not infer their absolute disappearance from the silence of the *Forum judicum.* The despotism of the Barbarian kings, however careful it may have been to gather the heritage of Roman maxims, was neither as wise nor as circumstantial as that of the emperors. It allowed the *curiae* and their magistrates to continue in existence, and these petty local powers assuredly had more reality and independence under its rule than they had possessed under the Empire. The clergy, principally dwelling in the towns, and bound by strong ties to the Roman race, was itself interested in protecting them, and the more so, because it naturally placed itself at the head of the municipalities. Thus much is certain, that the remnants of institutions of surety and liberty which existed there, occupy no place in the written laws, although these laws are much more detailed than those of other Barbarian peoples, and embrace the whole civil order. They could not, therefore, be considered as forming a part of the general constitution of the kingdom; they neither modified its political character, nor changed the results of the principles that prevailed therein.

If M. de Savigny has looked for the institutions of the Visigoths in an epoch anterior to the definitive establishment of their true monarchy, and in a collection of laws abolished by the *Forum judicum,* the author of the dissertation contained in the Edinburgh Review has addressed his inquiries to times and documents posterior by four or five centuries to the destruction of the kingdom of the Visigoths by the Arabs; and by transporting the consequences which he has obtained therefrom into the epoch which occupies our attention, he has fallen into an error still less supported by facts than was that of M. de Savigny. His researches and inferences are the following:

> It must not be supposed that the whole body of the law of the Visigoths appears in the twelve books of their code. They had their common or traditionary law, still existing in unwritten usages and customs, as well as their written law; and we are supported by analogy in asserting that this common law often spoke, when the statute law was silent. It outlived the monarchy; and we now collect it from the *Fueros* or ancient customs of Castile and Leon. The customs in question are preserved in the charters of the towns, which gave bye-laws to the inhabitants, confirming the unwritten common law of the country, sometimes with greater or lesser modifications in the detail, but agreeing in general principles. We equally discover them in the acts of Cortes, which, to borrow the expression of Sir Edward Coke, are often "affirmances of the common law." The traditionary Fueros of Castile also formed the basis of the *Fuero Viejo de Castilla,* which received its last revision under Peter the Third. And even Alonso the Wise, though he planned the subversion of the ancient jurisprudence of his kingdom, admitted into the Partidas such of those *Fueros de España* as relate to the tenures of land, and to military service. Consisting of ancient usages, neither refined by the learning of the councils nor restrained by the power of the kings, the Fueros of Castile and Leon bear a nearer affinity to the jurisprudence of the Teutonic nations than the written code. The water ordeal is noticed only once, in a law newly amended by Flavius Egica. But ordeal by compurgation, the most ancient form of trial by jury, and the battle ordeal, do not appear at all. Neither do we find any notice of the custom of returning military leaders by the *verdict of a jury.* All these customs, however, were Fueros of Spain in the Middle Ages.

Nor could they possibly have then existed, had they not been pre-served by immemorial usage and tradition.

The author then passes these ancient usages in review. The first to which he refers is the appointment of military leaders by a jury. He traces this cus-tom back to the forests of Germany: and then shows how it could not fail to succumb universally beneath the establishment of the feudal system, and in consequence of the hierarchical subordination of persons and lands. He dis-covers traces of this in the nomination, by the people, of the Anglo-Saxon *heretochs*[10] and *constables*,[11] who were at first military officers; and also in the election of the kings of Norway by the verdicts of twelve of the principal men of each province. He then returns to Spain, "where," he says,

> we shall find our old Gothic juries employed in electing the chief officers of the army and navy of the Castilians, the Adalid, the Almocaden, the Alfaqueque, and the Comitre. Who was to be the Adalid? The question must be answered in the words of the wise king Alonso. It is said by the ancients that "the Adalid should be endowed with four gifts—the first is wisdom, the second is heart, the third is good common sense, and the fourth is loyalty; and when a king or any other great lord wishes to make an Adalid, he must call unto himself *twelve of the wisest* Adalides that can be found, and these must *swear* that they will *truly say*, if he whom they wish to choose to be an Adalid hath the four gifts of which we have spoken, and if they answer *yea*, then they are to make him an Adalid."

Here we have clearly an inquest by twelve men giving their verdict upon oath. If it happened that twelve Adalides could not be found, then a kind of *tales de circumstantibus*[12] was added to this special jury of Adalides. The king or lord was to make up the full number of twelve with other men well approved in war and deeds of arms, and their verdict was as good as if they had been all Adalides. And he who dared act as an Adalid without being fully elected, was to suffer death. "It was advised in ancient times," says Alonso, "that they were to have the qualities before mentioned, because it was necessary that they should possess them, in order to be able to guide the troops and armies in time

10. The leader of an army, the commander of a militia of a shire or district (also *heretogas*).

11. The chief officer of the household, court, administration, or military force of a ruler. It derives from *comes stabuli*, count or officer of the stable, marshal (in the Theodosian Code, A.D. 438).

12. Such men from those surrounding.

of war, and therefore they were called *Adalides,* which is equivalent to *guides* (*que quiere tanto decir como guiadores*)."

The author is, therefore, of opinion that this word comes from *adal, adel,* noble, and *leid, lead, leiten,* to guide or conduct. The Adalid was the guide or chief of the *Almogavars,* or cavalry soldiers. The *Adalid mayor* was commander-in-chief of all the Almogavars, or Castilian cavalry.

After his election by this species of jury, the Adalid was thus solemnly admitted to his office.

> The king gave him rich garments, and a sword and a horse, and arms of *wood and iron,* according to the customs of the country. By a *rico hombre,* a lord of knights, the sword was to be girt, and then a shield was placed upon the ground, the future Adalid stepped upon it, and the king drew the sword out of its scabbard, and put it naked in his hand. And now as many of the twelve Adalids as can assemble round the shield, grasp its edge, and lift him up as high as they may: they turn his face towards the east.—"In the name of God," exclaims the Adalid, "I defy all the enemies of the faith, and of my lord the king, and of his land." And, thus speaking, he lifted up his arm, and struck a stroke downward, and he then struck another stroke across, thus describing in the air the sweet and holy sign of redemption, and he repeated this challenge four times towards each of the quarters of the world. Then the Adalid sheathed his sword, and the king placed a pennon in his hand, saying, "*I grant unto thee that henceforward thou art to be an Adalid.*" An Adalid might have risen to command from the lowest rank in the Castilian army. He might have been a *peon* or foot-soldier, but he became the fellow and companion of the hereditary nobles, the lords of vassals, and the *ricos hombres.*

In this ceremony, the author perceives a repetition of the forms used at the election of kings among the Germans, or at least at the choice of military leaders; *duces ex virtute sumunt.*[13]

I would by no means affirm that there does not exist, in this mode of choosing captains, in the concurrence of these twelve jurymen, and even in the number twelve itself, any remnant of old Germanic customs. This much is evident, that what has just been described was much rather a sort of chivalric ceremony in connection with the elevation of a man to a superior rank, than the election of a barbaric chief; all the forms, all the details of the elevation of an Adalid, remind us much more of chivalric usage than of Germanic custom; and it is a strange anachronism to suppose that all this took place, five hun-

---

13. Kings are chosen based on virtue.

dred years before, among the Visigoths, notwithstanding that no mention is made of it in any historic monument, and, what is still more conclusive, notwithstanding that the general state of manners at that time gives no hint of anything of the kind. It is much more probable that these customs originated among the Goths during their struggle against the Arabs, in the mountains of Northern Spain, and in consequence of the new direction of mingled feudalism and liberty, which was imparted to their manners by this new position.

The *Almocadene* or captain of foot soldiers, the *Alfaqueque* or officer employed to treat for the ransom of captives from the Moors, and the *Comitre* or captain of a ship, were appointed in a similar manner, and by the recommendation of a jury composed, not of members of the class to which the candidate belonged, but to members of the class to which he aspired. This circumstance alone settles the question; for it is a result of chivalric, and not of Barbarian manners; it reminds us of the squire who was dubbed knight by knights, and not of the warrior who was chosen or judged by his peers.

I shall not follow the author in his researches on ordeal by boiling water and by fire, or upon trial by combat. Although we meet with traces of these customs in the old monuments of some Barbarian legislations, they were not the common law of modern peoples, during the first epoch of their establishment on the Roman territory. It was at a later period, and by the influence either of the corruption of religious ideas by superstition, or of the military organization of the feudal system, that they became developed, recognized, and formed into a veritable jurisprudence. The general facts of Europe do not, therefore, authorize us to conclude that, because they existed among the Spaniards in the fourteenth century, they also existed among the Visigoths in the seventh century. The almost absolute silence of the historic monuments of the first epoch, here retains all its authority.

The facts relative to compurgation,[14] by the oath of a certain number of witnesses, are more important and more curious. "Compurgation," says our author, "is directed in express terms in all the Teutonic laws; but it does not appear to have been admissible in trials conducted according to the forms prescribed by the *Fuero juzgo*. Yet afterwards, this ordeal was widely spread as a *fuero*, both in civil and criminal trials. Though discountenanced by the legislature, it was retained in practice; and a forcible illustration is thus given of the stubbornness with which the Goths adhered to their usages and customs. *Trial by jury*, through it, in its germ was felt to be a benefit."

---

14. Compurgation is the action of clearing a man from a charge or accusation by the oaths of a number of other citizens. This mode of trial prevalent among the old Teutonic peoples began to lose its importance as trial by jury imposed itself in the twelfth century.

As an ancient and general usage of Castile, the trial is sanctioned in the *Fuero Viejo*. As a local custom or bye-law of the cities of Castile and Leon and their dependencies, it was very frequently established, or rather *declared,* by the charters granted by their founders.

Three thousand *sueldos,* according to the *Fuero Viejo,* were paid for dishonouring the palace of the king, or spoiling his castle; and five hundred *sueldos* was the price of the head of the *merino,* or the composition for scandalizing him; and every man who wished to save himself from the payment of these mulcts, was to defend himself by the oath of *twelve men, for such was the usage of Castile in the old time.* When accused of the death of another *fijo d'algo,* the suspected noble defended himself by the oath of eleven other *fijos d'algo,* himself *the twelfth,* and, as true knights, they were all *sworn,* upon the Gospel Book, with their spurs upon their heels. There were two insults only which gave a Dueña, or a squire, the right of complaining that a *fijo d'algo,* had scandalized them, viz., a blow or a wound, or the robbery of their mules or garments. Within three days, the party so injured by a caitiff knight was obliged to complain of the offence, and to disclose the injury to the *fijos d'algo* of the town, the *labradores,* and to the inmates of the *fijos d'algo,* if there were any, and to cause the town-bell to be rung, saying, "such a one hath thus dishonoured me." These formalities having been observed, the *fijo d'algo* was bound to answer the complaint; reparation was made if he confessed it, by forfeiting five hundred *sueldos,* the price of his own head; but if he denied it, he was to clear himself by the oath of eleven other *fijos d'algo,* himself the *twelfth.* But a *labrador* accused of injuring a *fijo d'algo* was not to be admitted to defend himself by his peers; and he was unfairly compelled to swear with eleven *fijos d'algo,* himself the twelfth.

These customs are taken from the general code. In peculiar districts, compurgation was so much in vogue, that compurgatrixes were allowed to female culprits. At Anguas, as well as in other towns, a woman charged with theft could defend herself by the oaths of a jury of other women. More whimsical was the Fuero of Cuenca, which is passing strange, both for the spirit of the law and the terms in which it is expressed. If perchance any husband suspected that his wife had planted horns upon his head, although he was not able to prove the fact by evidence, the wife was to justify herself by swearing to her chastity, with twelve good wives of the neighbourhood; and if they pronounced her to be pure, her husband was obliged to be persuaded that she was so.

The customs of St. Sebastien in Guipuscoa, allowed an odd

kind of proceeding, resembling the assessment of damages by the verdict of a jury. The ravisher was to pay the price of virginity, or he was to marry the object of his ungovernable passion; which punishment, as the charter wisely observes, "is fully equal to a fine." But if she, who had been a maid, was unworthy of becoming his wife, he was to provide her with such a husband as she might have reasonably expected to have obtained previous to her mishap, "according to the estimation of the alcalde, and of twelve good men of St. Sebastien."

The fullest directions concerning the use of the ordeal are contained in the charter of Molina. Don Molrique de Lara incorporated the town of Molina, the seigniory of the noble house of Lara, in the year 1152. His charter may be quoted as the most valuable record concerning the ancient municipal jurisprudence of Castile which has yet been published, as it displays the entire constitution and government of a Castilian town. * * * * Fines, according to the old Gothic law, were enacted at Molina for wounds and maims. The accuser was to support his charge by three "*vecinos*" or burghers of the town, if the offence was committed within its walls. Two *vecinos* sufficed if without. And, in default of full proof, the culprit either swore with twelve *vecinos*, or fought with the accuser; but the latter had the choice of the ordeal. * * * * When a murder had been committed, if one of those engaged in the fray took the guilt on his own head, saying, "*I killed him*," the others were "to save themselves with twelve true burghers,"—*los otros salvense con doce vecinos derecheros.* It might happen, that none would confess the crime; and as all were then equally liable to suspicion, the relations of the dead man were at liberty to select any one as the murderer, "just as they thought fit"; after which the supposed murderer named eleven relations of the slain, and these, together with the accuser, swore to his being guilty or not guilty. Unanimity was required; and if one or two would not swear, that is to say, if they could not agree with the majority, each one who was so dissentient swore with twelve, that neither he, nor any one for his use, had received any bribe; then he was discharged. But if the defendant did not "fall" by the withdrawing of his juror, he was at liberty to name another. This proceeding is remarkable; a new aspect is given to the ordeal by calling in the compurgators to swear with the accuser instead of the accused; and in this form it is, perhaps, more closely assimilated to a jury-trial. It may be observed, that a practice once prevailed in England of withdrawing the dissentient jurors, and replacing them by others, till an unanimous verdict was obtained.

Such are the facts which the author of these researches has collected on the existence of ancient Germanic customs, or analogous usages, in the towns of Castile and Leon, dating from the twelfth century. He unhesitatingly concludes therefrom that these same customs existed in the sixth and seventh centuries among the Spanish Visigoths, and formed a part of their institutions.

It is inconvenient to prove that facts are not true, for it devolves on him who affirms them to prove that they are so; and, in such a case as this, when we speak of epochs separated by five or six centuries, and by such a revolution as the dispossession of a people and a foreign conquest, inductions are not sufficient. The *Forum judicum* is absolutely silent upon the appointment of military leaders, and upon compurgation by juries; nay, more, this latter institution is incompatible with the arrangements of this code in reference to judges and the administration of justice. No other contemporary authority contradicts the *Forum judicum.* Must we, upon the authority of facts of much more recent date, and which refer to an entirely different state of civilization, refuse to believe proofs so direct, and testimonies so positive?

I am aware of all that may be said about the disorders of these times, the continual gaps in the laws, and the disposition of legislators to omit precisely those usages which were most simple and universal, as though they had no need to be consecrated or even indicated by formal enactment. It is, in fact, very possible that the practice of compurgation by juries was not completely unknown to the Visigoths; it recurs in all Germanic customs, and it may not have disappeared either entirely or all at once, even after the introduction of a code derived principally from the Roman laws. But it is impossible to believe, in spite of this code, that it continued to be the common law, the fundamental institution, the veritable judicial system of the nation.

It is more easy to explain, with likelihood, the existence of these practices among the Spanish Goths of the twelfth century, than to justify, without proofs, or rather in opposition to all evidence, the arbitrary supposition of their prevalence among the Visigoths of the seventh. Such institutions have in themselves something of spontaneity; they correspond to a certain degree of civilization, to a certain state of social institutions; we meet with them under forms more or less similar, but fundamentally analogous, not only among all the Germanic peoples, but also among nearly all those barbaric peoples which, scarcely issued from a nomadic life, begin to establish themselves on a new territory, after they have conquered it. Now, the destruction of the monarchy of the Visigoths by the Arabs suspended the course of the institutions which it had received two centuries before, broke off the councils of Toledo, crushed or greatly diminished the predominance of the clergy, and, in fine, put a stop to the civilization which had commenced, and gave to affairs an entirely new direction. Scattered among the mountains, frequently wandering, separated into various bands, those of the Goths who did not submit to the conquerors, returned, so to speak, toward the life which their ancestors led in the forests of Germany. Roman institutions, Roman maxims, all that collection of laws and ideas which they had received from the clergy, and which had prevailed over their own habits, disappeared almost necessarily in this shock, or at least were retained only by those Goths who remained under the dominion of the Mussulmans. The companions of Pelagius, up to a certain point, became Germans once more, from sheer necessity. It was after this involuntary return to their primitive condition, and, by consequence, to their ancient institutions, that they resumed the offensive against the Arabs, and reconquered Spain by degrees, bringing back with them those political and judicial customs, usages, and practices, which they had partially regained. Free institutions, moreover, could not fail to regain vitality at this period; for they alone can supply strength in times of danger or misfortune. It was not in the power of the customs of the *officium palatinum,* and of the maxims of the councils of Toledo, to restore the Goths to their subjugated country, and reinstate the descendants of Chindasuinth upon the throne of their fathers. The participation of the people in public affairs, the sternness of Barbarian manners, and the energy of irregular liberty, could alone produce such effects. There is every reason to believe that the institutions of Spain, after the re-establishment of the kingdoms of Castile, Leon, Arragon, &c, were new institutions, and the result of the new position of the Goths, much more than the legacy of the ancient Visigoths. We find proofs of this in the general Cortes of the kingdom, in the constitutions and liberties of the towns, in the whole political order of the State, which has no connection whatever with the old monarchy, and follows much more naturally as a result of the condition and necessities of new monarchies. The political system established by the councils of Toledo and the *Forum judicum* could not have taken deep root; it fell before necessities which it was unable to meet. The *Forum judicum* itself would perhaps have completely succumbed, had it not continued to be the law of those Goths who had submitted to the yoke of the Moors; it moreover regulated civil order, which is always more firmly fixed, and less influenced by revolutions. It therefore continued, in this respect, to be the general law of Spain; whilst political order assumed a new form and was regulated by other institutions.

The *Forum judicum* and contemporary authorities are the only true source at which we can study the political institutions of the ancient Visigoths; a source which is doubtless incomplete, and which does not inform us of all that existed; a source which, probably even, especially neglected to gather up what still remained of Germanic manners and habits, but which it is impossible to repudiate in order to admit facts and general institutions which are directly contrary to it. The consequences which I have deduced from these original and contemporary authorities, therefore, still subsist, and determine the true political system of the monarchy of the Visigoths. The imperial government, and ecclesiastical theories, were its constituent elements. These elements prevailed over Germanic customs. They were doubtless modified in order that they might be adapted to a Barbarian people; but, by modification, they gained dominion, and became the general form, the fundamental law, of the State. If the Spanish Goths afterwards entered upon a course more analogous to that pursued by other modern nations of the same origin, it is in the invasion of the Arabs, in the second conquest of Spain by the re-Germanized Goths, and in the effects of this great revolution, but not in the institutions of the monarchy of the Visigoths, that we may discern the causes of this procedure.

END OF PART I

PART 2

ESSAYS OF

REPRESENTATIVE

GOVERNMENT IN ENGLAND,

FROM THE CONQUEST

TILL THE REIGN

OF THE TUDORS

LECTURE I

Subject of the course: the history of the origin and establishment of representative government in Europe. ⁓ *Different aspects under which history is considered at various epochs.* ⁓ *Poetic history; philosophic history; political history.* ⁓ *Disposition of our time to consider history under these various aspects.* ⁓ *Fundamental principle and essential characteristics of representative government.* ⁓ *Existence of this principle and these characteristics in England at all times.*

I THINK it necessary to remind you, gentlemen, of the plan which I adopted last year with regard to our study of the political institutions of Europe. The essential object of that plan was to give some unity and compactness to this vast history. And this is not an arbitrary and self-chosen object. In the development of our continent, all its peoples and all its governments are connected together; in spite of all struggles and separations, there is really some unity and compactness in European civilization. This unity, which has been revealing itself from day to day, is now evident; never have geographical limits possessed less sway than in our times; never has such a community of ideas, feelings, aspirations, and efforts united, in spite of territorial demarcations, so great a mass of men. That which is now revealed has been labouring for more than twelve centuries to manifest itself; this external and apparent community has not always existed; but such has always been, at bottom, the unity of European civilization, that it is impossible thoroughly to understand the history of any of the great modern peoples without considering the history of Europe as a whole, and contemplating the course pursued by humanity in general. It is a vast drama in which every people has its part to perform, and with the general events of which we must be acquainted in order to understand the particular scenes connected therewith.

I have divided the history of the political institutions of Europe into four great epochs, which are distinguished from each other by essentially different characteristics. The first is the barbarian epoch; a time of conflict and confusion, in which no society could be established, no institution be founded and become regularly prevalent in any part of Europe; this epoch extends from the fifth to the tenth century. The second is the feudal epoch, and extends from the tenth to the fourteenth century. The third is the epoch of efforts towards constitutional monarchy; feudalism declines, the populations become free, and royalty employs them to extend and augment its power; this epoch embraces the period from the fourteenth to the sixteenth century. In the fourth period, on the Continent, all efforts towards a representative system have failed or almost entirely disappeared; pure monarchy prevails. England alone decidedly obtains a constitutional government. This epoch lasts from the sixteenth century to the French Revolution.

These epochs were not determined by an arbitrary choice,—their division results from the general facts which characterize them. They will not all form the subject of this course of lectures. I wish to study the political institutions of Europe with you, and representative government is the centre towards which all our studies tend. Where I perceive no trace of the representative system, and no direct effort to produce it, I turn aside, and transfer my attention to some other quarter. Nor shall I merely limit our studies in reference to epochs only; I shall limit them also in respect to places. Last year, in my lectures on the first epoch, I did not follow the progress of political institutions in the whole of Europe, but confined my observations to France, Spain, and England. We have now to study the third epoch; but the States-General of France and the Cortes of Spain were only unfruitful attempts at representative government. I shall therefore postpone our study of them, and devote this year's course to the attentive examination of the origin of representative government in England, the only country in which it received uninterrupted and successful development. This study is particularly necessary to us at the present day, and we are ourselves well-disposed to enter upon it with an earnest desire to reap advantage from it.

According to their political state, and in the degree of their civilization, do the peoples consider history under various aspects, and look to it for various kinds of interest. In the early ages of society, whilst all is new and attractive to the youthful imagination of man, he demands poetical interest; the memories of the past form the groundwork of brilliant and simple narratives, fitted to charm an eager and easily satisfied curiosity. If, in such a community, where social existence is in full vigour, and the human mind is in a state of excitement, Herodotus reads to the Greeks assembled at Olympia his patriotic narratives, and the discoveries of his voyages, the Greeks delight in them as in songs of Homer. If civilization is but little advanced—if men live more isolated—if "country," in the concrete, at least, exists but slightly for them—we find simple chronicles intermingled with fables and legends, but always marked with that *naïf* and poetical character which, in such a condition of existence, the human mind requires in all things. Such are the European chronicles from the tenth to the fifteenth century. If, at a later period, civilization becomes developed in a country without the coeval establishment of liberty, without an energetic and extensive political existence, when the period of enlightenment, of wealth, and of leisure, does arrive, men look for philosophical interest in history; it no longer belongs to the field of poetry; it loses its simplicity; it no longer wears its former real and living physiognomy; individual characters take up less space, and no longer appear under living forms; the mention of names becomes more rare; the narrative of events, and the description of men, are more its pretext than its subject; all becomes generalized; readers demand a summary of the development of civilization, a sort of theory of the peoples and of events; history becomes a series of dissertations on the progress of the human race, and the historian seems only to call up the skeleton of the past, in order to hang upon it general ideas and philosophic reflections. This occurred in the last century; the English historians of that period, Robertson, Gibbon, and Hume, have represented history under that aspect; and most of the German writers still follow the same system. The philosophy of history predominates; history, properly so called, is not to be found in them.

But if advanced civilization and a great development of the human intellect coincide, in a nation, with an animated and keen political existence; if the struggle for liberty, by exciting the mind, provoke energy of character; if the activity of public life be added to the general claims of thought, history appears in another light; it becomes, so to speak, practical. No longer is it required to charm easily excited imaginations by its narratives, nor to satisfy by its meditations active intellects debarred from exercising themselves upon aught but generalities. But men expect from it experience analogous to the wants they feel, to the life they live; they desire to understand the real nature and hidden springs of institutions; to enter into the movements of parties, to follow them in their combinations, to study the secret of the influence of the masses, and of the action of individuals; men and things must resuscitate before them, no longer merely as an interest or diversion, but as a revelation of how rights, liberties, and power are to be acquired, exercised, and defended; how to combine opinions, interests, passions, the necessities of circumstances, all the elements of active political life. That is what history becomes for free nations; it is from that point of view that Thucydides wrote the history of the Peloponnesian war, Lord Clarendon and Bishop Burnet that of the English Revolution.

Generally, and by the very nature of things, it is in regular order, and at distant intervals, that history assumes one or other of these various kinds of interest in the eyes of the people. A taste for simple narratives, a liking for philosophic generalizations, and a craving for political instruction, almost always belong to very different times and degrees of civilization.

By a rare concurrence of circumstances, all these tastes and acquirements seem to unite at the present day; and history is now susceptible amongst us of all these kinds of interest. If it narrate to us with truth and simplicity the first attempts at social life, the manners of infant nations; that singular state of society in which ideas are few in number but keen, and wants are energetic although unvaried, in which all the pretensions of barbarian force struggle against all the habits of wild liberty, it will find us capable of understanding such a recital, and somewhat disposed to be charmed therewith. Fifty years ago, a faithful picture of this age in the life of peoples would have appeared only coarse and revolving; its interesting and poetical character would have been neither relished nor understood; conventionalisms were then turned into habits, and factitious manners held sway over the whole of society; Homer himself, in an age so destitute of simplicity and naturalness, was admired on hearsay only; and if no one dared to call in question his title to glory, he was pitied for having been obliged to shed the lustre of his genius upon an epoch of barbarism and ignorance. Prodigious events have since renewed the state of society, broken up old forms, conventional habits, and factitious manners; simple ideas and natural feelings have resumed their empire; a kind of rejuvenescence has taken place in the minds of men, and they have become capable of understanding man at every degree of civilization, and of taking pleasure in the simple and poetic narratives of infant society. In our days it has been felt that barbarian times also deserved, in some respects, to be called heroic times; in our days, mankind has discovered the faculty, as well as the necessity, of obtaining a true knowledge of the institutions, ideas, and manners of peoples, on their entrance into social life. Thus this section of history has regained an interest which it had ceased to possess; it is no longer regarded as the patrimony of the erudite; it has been seized upon by novelists themselves, and the public have taken delight in following their footsteps.

At the same time, the need of broad philosophical views of the course of human affairs and the progress of society, has gained strength instead of becoming extinguished; we have not ceased to look to facts for something more than mere narratives; we still expect them to be summed up in general ideas, and to furnish us with those great results which throw light on the sciences of legislation and political economy, and on the vast study of the destiny of the human race. Far, then, from being less inclined to consider history under a philosophic point of view, it seems to have acquired a wider interest in this respect. More than ever, we feel the necessity of tracing events back to their primitive causes, of reducing them to their simplest expression, of penetrating into their remotest effects; and if old chronicles have regained their charm in our eyes, the great combinations of historic philosophy still constitute a pressing necessity of our minds.

Finally, our birth into public life, the institutions that we possess and that we will not lose, that aurora of liberty which, though it arose in the midst of tempests, is not destined to perish therein, the past which we leave behind us, the present with which we are busied, the future which awaits us, in fine, our entire position—all impart to history, considered under the political point of view, the most imperious interest. Before our time, the movement of public life, the game of parties, the war of factions, the struggles of assemblies, all the agitations and developments of power and liberty, were things which men had heard of but had not seen, which they had read of in books but which were not actually existing around the reader. These things have occurred, and are now occurring under our very eyes; every consideration leads us to study them, every circumstance aids us to comprehend them. And not to us alone has political life been restored: it has returned into history, hitherto cold and vague to the minds of those who had not been struck by the real visions of the scenes which it relates. And while regaining our comprehension of history, we have also become aware of the counsels and the lessons which it can furnish us; its utility no longer consists, as formerly, in a general idea, a sort of moral and literary dogma professed by writers rather than adopted and practised by the public. Now, a more or less thorough acquaintance with history, and especially with that of free peoples, is not merely an accomplishment of cultivated minds; it is a necessity to every citizen who feels desirous to take part in the affairs of his country, or merely to appreciate them correctly. And thus this great study now presents itself to us with all the kinds of interest that it is able to offer, because we have in us ability to consider it under all its aspects, and to seek and to find all that it contains.[1]

Such are the motives which induce me to select the history of the political institutions of England as the subject of this course of lectures. Here, in effect, history considered under its three different aspects, presents itself with the greatest simplicity and richness. Nowhere have the primitive manners of modern peoples been preserved for a longer period, or exercised so decisive an influence upon the institutions of a country. Nowhere do great philosophical considerations spring with greater abundance from the contemplation of events and men. Here, in fine, representative government, the special object of our study, developed itself without interruption, received into its bosom and fertilized by its alliance the religious movement imparted to Europe in the sixteenth century, and thus became the starting point of the political reformation which is now beginning on the Continent.

---

1. These passages are important for understanding the relation between history and politics in Guizot's writings. Guizot's method combines broad philosophical views with historical narratives; he writes a political history that seeks to offer political instruction by explaining how rights and liberties were acquired and how various opinions and interests could be combined in political life. In Guizot's view, a thorough acquaintance with the history of free peoples is necessary to every citizen who wants to get involved in politics.

It is by no means my intention to relate to you the history of England. I intend merely to consider it under its political point of view; and even under this point of view, we shall not study all the institutions of the kingdom. Representative government is our theme; and we shall therefore follow the history of the Parliament step by step. We shall only refer to judicial, administrative, and municipal institutions in so far as they are connected with representative government, and have contributed either to form it, or to determine its character.

Last year, before entering upon our examination of facts, I attempted to define with precision what we ought to understand by representative government. Before seeking for its existence, I desired to know by what signs we might discern its presence. Now that we are about to study the history of the only representative government which, until our days, has existed with full vitality in Europe, I think it well to recapitulate some of these ideas.

I have said that I had no very high opinion of the division of governments by publicists, into monarchical, aristocratic, and democratic; and that, in my opinion, it was by their essential principle, by their general and internal idea, that governments were characterized and distinguished. The most general idea that we can seek out in a government is its theory of sovereignty, that is, the manner in which it conceives, places, and attributes the right of giving law and carrying it into execution in society.

There are two great theories of sovereignty. One seeks for it and places it in some one of the real forces which exist upon the earth, no matter whether it be the people, the monarch, or the chief men of the people. The other maintains that sovereignty as a right can exist nowhere upon earth, and ought to be attributed to no power, for no earthly power can fully know and constantly desire truth, reason, and justice—the only sources of sovereignty as a right, and which ought also to be the rule of sovereignty in fact. The first theory of sovereignty founds absolute power, whatever may be the form of the government. The second combats absolute power in all its forms, and recognises its legitimacy in no case. It is not true to say that of these two theories, one or the other reigns exclusively in the various governments of the world. These two theories commingle in a certain measure; for nothing is completely destitute of truth or perfectly free from error. Nevertheless, one or the other always dominates in every form of government, and may be considered as its principle.

The true theory of sovereignty, that is, the radical illegitimacy of all absolute power, whatever may be its name and place, is the principle of representative government.

In fact, in representative government, absolute power, sovereignty as a right, inhere in none of the powers which concur to form the government: they must agree to make the law; and even when they have agreed, instead of accepting for ever the absolute power which actually results from their agreement, the representative system subjects this power to the variableness of election. And the electoral power itself is not absolute, for it is confined to the choice of the men who shall have a share in the government.

It is, moreover, the character of that system, which nowhere admits the legitimacy of absolute power, to compel the whole body of citizens incessantly, and on every occasion, to seek after reason, justice, and truth, which should ever regulate actual power. The representative system does this, 1. by discussion, which compels existing powers to seek after truth in common; 2. by publicity, which places these powers when occupied in this search, under the eyes of the citizens; and 3. by the liberty of the press, which stimulates the citizens themselves to seek after truth, and to tell it to power.

Finally, the necessary consequence of the true theory of sovereignty is, that all actual power is responsible. If, in fact, no actual power possesses sovereignty as a right, they are all obliged to prove that they have sought after truth, and have taken it for their rule; and they must legitimize their title by their acts, under penalty of being taxed with illegitimacy. The responsibility of power is, in fact, inherent in the representative system; it is the only system which makes it one of its fundamental conditions.

After having recognised the principle of representative government, we investigated its external characteristics, that is to say, the forms which necessarily accompany the principle, and by which alone it can manifest its existence. These forms we reduced to three: 1. division of powers; 2. election; and 3. publicity. It is not difficult to convince ourselves that these characteristics necessarily flow from the principle of representative government. Indeed, 1. all sole power in fact soon becomes absolute in right. It is therefore necessary that all power in fact should be conscious of dependence. "All unity," says Pascal, "that is not multitude, is tyranny." Hence results the necessity for two Houses of Parliament. If there be only one, the executive power either suppresses it, or falls into so subaltern a condition that there would soon remain only the absolute power of the single House of Parliament. 2. Unless election occurred frequently to place power in new hands, that power which derived its right from itself would soon become absolute in right; this is the tendency of all aristocracies. 3. Publicity, which connects power with society, is the best guarantee against the usurpation of sovereignty as a right by the actual power.

Representative government can neither be established nor developed without assuming, sooner or later, these three characteristics; they are the natural consequences of its principle; but they do not necessarily co-exist, and representative government may exist without their union.

This was the case in England. It is impossible not to enquire why representative government prevailed in that country, and not in the other States of the Continent. For, indeed, the Barbarians who settled in Great Britain had the same origin and the same primitive manners as those who, after the fall of the Roman Empire, overran Europe; and it was not in the midst of very different circumstances that they consolidated their dominion in that country.

From the fifth to the twelfth century, we find no more traces of true representative government in England than upon the Continent; its institutions were analogous to those of the other European nations; and we behold in every land the conflict of the three systems of free, feudal, and monarchical institutions.

We cannot fully resolve this question beforehand, and in a general manner. We shall answer it gradually, as we advance in the examination of facts. We shall see by what successive and varied causes political institutions took a different course in England to that which they pursued on the Continent. We may, however, indicate at once the great fact which, from a very early period, determined the character and direction of British institutions.

The first of the great external characteristics of representative government, division of power, is met with in every age, in the government of England. Never was the government concentrated in the hands of the king alone; under the name of the *Wittenagemot,* of the *Council* or *Assembly of the Barons,* and after the reign of Henry III., of the *Parliament,* a more or less numerous and influential assembly, composed in a particular manner, was always associated with the sovereignty. For a long period, this assembly somewhat subserved despotism, and sometimes substituted civil war and anarchy in the place of despotism; but it always interfered in the central government. An independent council, which derived its strength from the individual power of its members, was always adjoined to the royal authority. The English monarchy has always been the government of the king in council, and the king's council was frequently his adversary. The great council of the king became the Parliament.

This is the only one of the essential characteristics of the system of representative government, which the government of England presents, until the fourteenth century. During the course of this epoch, the division of power, far from efficiently repressing despotism, served only to render it more changeful and more dangerous. The council of barons was no more capable than the king himself, of comprehending and establishing a stable political order and true liberty; these two forces were incessantly in conflict, and their conflict was war, that is to say, the devastation of the country, and the oppression of the mass of the inhabitants. But from this there resulted, in process of time, two decisive facts, from which liberty took its origin; they were these:

1. From the very fact that power was divided, it followed that absolute power, sovereignty as a right, was never attributed to the king, nor supposed to be in itself legitimate. Now, this is the very principle of representative government; but this principle was far from being understood, or even suspected, philosophi-

cally speaking. It was incessantly stifled by force, or else it was lost in the confusion of the ideas of the time regarding divine right, the origin of power, and so forth; but it existed in the depths of the public mind, and became by slow degrees a fundamental maxim. We find this principle formally expressed in the writings of Bracton, Lord Chief Justice under Henry III., and of Fortescue, who held the same office under Henry VI. "The king," says Bracton, "should be subject to no man, but only to God and to the law, for the law makes him king; he can do nothing upon earth but that which, by law, he may do; and that which is said in the Pandects, that that which pleases the king becomes law, is no objection; for we see by the context, that these words do not mean the pure and simple will of the prince, but that which has been determined by the advice of his councils, the king giving the sanction of his authority to their deliberations upon the subject."

"The English monarchy," says Fortescue, "*non solum est regalis, sed legalis et politica potestas,*"[2] and he frequently develops this idea. The limitation of powers was, thus, at a very early period, a matter of public right in England; and the legitimacy of sole and absolute power was never recognized. Thus was established and preserved, for better times, the generative principle of all legitimate power as well as of all liberty; and by the virtue of this principle alone was maintained, in the souls of the people, that noble sentiment of right which becomes extinguished and succumbs wherever man finds himself in presence of an unlimited sovereignty, whatever may be its form and name.

2. The division of the supreme power produced yet another result. When the towns had acquired greater wealth and importance, when there had been formed, beyond the circle of the king's immediate vassals, a nation capable of taking part in political life, and which the government found it necessary to treat with consideration, this nation naturally adjoined itself to the great council of the king, which had never ceased to exist. In order to gain itself a place in the central government, it had no need abruptly to create new institutions; a place was already prepared to receive it, and although its entrance into the national council ere long changed its nature and forms, it at least was not under the necessity of asserting and re-animating its existence. There was a fact capable of receiving extension, and of admitting into its bosom new facts, together with new rights. The British Parliament, to say truth, dates only from the formation of the House of Commons; but without the presence and importance of the council of Barons, the House of Commons would, perhaps, never have been formed.

Thus, on the one hand, the permanence of the idea that the sovereignty ought to be limited, and, on the other, the actual division of the central power,

2. Not only is a kingly, but a lawful and civil power.

were the germs of representative government in England. Until the end of the thirteenth century we met with no other of its characteristics; and the English nation, until that period, was not perhaps actually more free and happy than any of the peoples of the Continent. But the principle of the right of resistance to oppression was already a legal principle in England; and the idea of the supremacy which holds dominion over all others, of the supremacy of the law, was already connected, in the mind of the people and of the jurisconsults themselves, not with any particular person, or with any particular actual power, but with the name of the law itself. Already the law was said to be superior to all other powers; sovereignty had thus, in principle at least, left that material world in which it could not fix itself without engendering tyranny, to place itself in that moral world, in which actual powers ought constantly to seek it. Many favourable circumstances were doubtless necessary to fecundate these principles of liberty in England. But when the sentiment of right lives in the souls of men, when the citizen meets with no power in his country which he is bound to consider as infallible and absolutely sovereign, liberty can never fail to spring up. It has developed itself in England less universally, less equally, and less reasonably, we venture to believe, than we are permitted to hope will be the case at the present day in our own country; but, in fine, it was born, and increased in growth in that country more than in any other; and the history of its progress, the study of the institutions which served as its guarantees, and of the system of government to which its destinies seem henceforward to link themselves, is at once a great sight and a necessary work for us. We shall enter upon it with impartiality, for we can do so without envy.[3]

3. The emphasis on the division and limitation of power and sovereignty is central to Guizot's liberalism. He pointed out that the limitation of powers and the affirmation of the right of resistance to oppression were matters of public right in England. Guizot also mentioned that, in England, local powers subsisted and successfully defined and regulated their own action *vis-à-vis* the central power, while on the Continent, centralization resulted from the vanishing of local powers and the rise of absolute power (*HORG*, p. 240-47). Not surprisingly, Guizot believed that, if France were to build a true representative government, the country ought to reinvent local autonomy and local institutions. Madame de Staël's book *Considerations on the French Revolution* is essential reading for understanding how England became an object of praise and admiration during the Bourbon Restoration in France. For more details on Guizot's understanding of English constitutionalism, see *HORG*, pp. 300-305, 353-58, 377-81, as well as the note on p. 43.

LECTURE 2

*Sketch of the History of England, from William the Conqueror to John
Lackland (1066–1199). ⁓ William the Conqueror (1066–1087). ⁓
William Rufus (1087–1100). ⁓ Henry I. (1100–1135). ⁓ Stephen
(1135–1154). ⁓ Henry II. (1154–1189). ⁓ Constitutions of Clarendon. ⁓ Richard Coeur de Lion (1189–1199).*

BEFORE entering upon the history of representative government in England,
I think it necessary, in the first place, to remind you of the facts which served,
as it were, as its cradle—of the movements of the different nations which successively occupied England—the conquest of the Normans—the state of the
country at the period of this conquest, about the middle of the eleventh century—and the principal events which succeeded it. A knowledge of facts must
always precede the study of institutions.

The Britons—Gauls or Celts in origin—were the first inhabitants of
Great Britain. Julius Caesar subjugated them, and the Roman dominion substituted a false and enervating civilization in the place of their barbarian energy.
On being abandoned by Rome, when that city abdicated piecemeal the empire
of the world, the Britons were unable to defend themselves, and summoned the
Saxons to their assistance. The latter, finding them already conquered, from
their allies became ere long their masters, and exterminated or drove back into
the mountains of Wales, the people whom the Romans had subdued. After a
long series of incursions, the Danes established themselves in the north of England, during the ninth century, and in the latter part of the eleventh century,
the Normans conquered the whole country.

Towards the middle of the eleventh century, and before the Norman conquest, great enmity still subsisted between the Saxons and the Danes, whereas
between the Danes and Normans the recollections of a common origin were
still fresh and vivid. Edward the Confessor had been brought up at the Court
of Normandy, and the Normans were held in great favour by him. He had appointed several of them to great offices in his realm. The primate, the Archbishop of Canterbury, was a Norman; and Norman was spoken at the Court of

Edward. All these circumstances seemed to prepare the way for the invasion of England by the Normans.

The internal state of England was equally favourable to it. The Saxon aristocracy had risen in proportion as the royal power had declined; but the power of the great land-holders was a divided power, and their dissensions opened a door for foreign interference. Harold, the brother-in-law of king Edward, who had died without issue, had just usurped the crown; so that William had not even to oppose a legitimate monarch. "Whether the English make Harold or another their duke or king, I grant it," said William on the death of Edward; but he, nevertheless, assumed to be heir of the kingdom, by virtue of a will of the deceased monarch, and came to assert his right at the head of an army of 40,000 men. On the 14th of October, 1065, Harold lost both the crown and his life at the battle of Hastings. The primate then offered the crown of England to William, who accepted it after some show of hesitation, and was crowned on the 6th of December. He at first treated his Saxon subjects with mildness, but ordered the construction of a number of fortresses, and gave large grants of lands to his Norman comrades. During a journey which he made into Normandy, in the month of March, 1067, the Saxons revolted against the tyranny of the Normans. William suppressed the revolt, and continued for some time still faithful to his policy of conciliation. But rebellions continued to arise, and William now had recourse to rigorous measures. By repeated confiscations he ensured the sovereign establishment of the Normans, and of the feudal system. The Saxons were excluded from all great public employments, and particularly from the bishoprics. William covered England with forts, substituted the Norman language for the Anglo-Saxon, and made it the language of law—a privilege which subsisted until the reign of Edward III. He enacted very severe laws of police, among others the law of curfew, so greatly detested by the Saxons, but which already existed in Normandy; and finally, he laid waste the county of Yorkshire, the stronghold of the Saxon insurgents.

The Pope had given his approval to William's enterprise, and had excommunicated Harold. Nevertheless, William boldly repulsed the pretensions of Gregory VII, and forbade his subjects to recognize any one as Pope, until he had done so himself. The canons of every council were to be submitted to him for his sanction or rejection. No bull or letter of the Pope might be published without the permission of the king. He protected his ministers and barons against excommunication. He subjected the clergy to feudal military service. And finally, during his reign, the ecclesiastical and civil courts, which had previously been commingled in the county courts, were separated.

After the death of William, in 1087, his States were divided among his three sons, Robert, William, and Henry. William Rufus succeeded to the throne of England, and Robert to the dukedom of Normandy. William's reign is remarkable only for acts of tyranny, for the extension of the royal forests, and for odious exactions; he would not appoint bishops to any of the vacant episcopal sees, but appropriated their revenues to his own use, considering them as fiefs whose possessors were dead.

William Rufus was almost constantly at war with his brother Robert. He ended by buying Normandy of him, or, to speak more correctly, he received it in pledge for thirteen thousand silver marks which he lent to Robert when about to join the Crusaders. In the year 1100, he made a similar bargain with William, Count of Poitou and Duke of Guienne. The Norman barons bitterly regretted that Robert was not King of England, as well as Duke of Normandy. They rebelled several times against William; and various facts indicate that the Saxon nation gained something by these revolts, and was rather better treated, in consequence, by its Norman monarch. But the relations of the two peoples were still extremely hostile when William Rufus was killed while hunting, on the 2nd of August, 1100.

Henry I. usurped the crown of England from his brother Robert, to whom it rightfully belonged; and the Norman barons, who preferred Robert, offered only a feeble resistance to Henry; he was crowned in London. His first act was a charter, in which, to gain forgiveness for his usurpation, he promised not to seize upon the revenues of the church during the vacancy of benefices; to admit the heirs of the crown vassals to the possession of their estates, without exposing them to such violent exactions as had been usual during the preceding reigns; to moderate the taxes, to pardon the past, and finally to confirm the authority of the laws of St. Edward, which were so dear to the nation. A short time after the concession of this charter, Henry married Matilda, the daughter of the King of Scotland, and niece of Edgar Atheling, the last heir of the Saxon dynasty; by this marriage he hoped to conciliate the attachment of the Saxon people. In order to marry him, Matilda was liberated from her vows, for she had taken the veil, not with the intention of becoming a nun, says Eadmer, but in order to escape from the brutal violence of the Normans.

In 1101, Robert returned from the Crusades, and invaded England, but a treaty soon put a stop to his progress, and he renounced his pretensions on receiving a pension of 3000 marks, and the promise of succeeding to Henry's inheritance. The bad government of Robert in Normandy occasioned continual disturbances in that country, and maintained the ever-increasing tendency towards the union of Normandy with England. Henry, taking advantage of this state of things, invaded Normandy, where he had many powerful adherents, and after three years of war, in 1106, the battle of Tenchebray decided the fate of Robert, who was taken prisoner and confined in Cardiff Castle, where he languished twenty-eight years. Normandy was then united to England.

The reign of Henry I. was disturbed by continual quarrels with the clergy;

he was obliged to renounce the right of investiture, which was held to confer spiritual dignity, but the bishops continued to swear to him fidelity and homage, by reason of their temporal possessions. In the midst of the obstacles which lay in his path, Henry governed with vigour and prudence; he humbled the great barons, restored order, and restrained the clergy; and these were the qualities which then constituted a great king. The pretended code which is ascribed to Henry I. is a later compilation; but he effected several important reforms, among others, by repressing the abuses of the right of purveyance, by which the socage tenants of the king were bound gratuitously to supply the court, while journeying, with provisions and carriages. It is also said that he substituted, for tenants of this class, the payment of a money rent instead of the rent in kind which they had formerly paid; but it is not probable that this was a general rule.

Henry I. died in 1135. His reign promoted, to some extent, the fusion of the two peoples: but the separation was still wide. His son William being dead, Henry had appointed as his successor his daughter Matilda, the wife of Geoffrey Plantagenet, Count of Anjou; and an assembly of barons had ratified his choice. But, during the absence of Matilda, Stephen, Count of Boulogne, the grandson of William the Conqueror by his mother Adela, the wife of Stephen, Count of Blois, usurped the crown of England; but only a few barons attended at his coronation, on the 22nd of December, 1135. Stephen was anxious, by making large concessions, to obtain pardon for his usurpation; and he published two charters, which promised all that those issued by Henry had promised, including the maintenance of the laws of Edward the Confessor. The clergy and barons, however, swore to him only a conditional oath; and wishing to make him pay dearly for their support, the church exacted from him the sanction of all its privileges, and the barons obtained permission to build fortresses upon their estates. The kingdom soon bristled with castles and ramparts. Eleven hundred and fifteen were erected during the reign of Stephen, and assured, far more effectually than his charters, the power and independence of the barons.

In 1139, an insurrection broke out in favour of Matilda. King Stephen was defeated and made prisoner at the battle of Lincoln, on the 26th of February, 1141. A synod of ecclesiastics, without the co-operation of any laymen, gave the crown to Matilda; the deputies of the city of London were the only laymen present, and they demanded the liberation of King Stephen, but in vain; they were admitted into the synod merely to receive orders. A conspiracy against Matilda overthrew, ere long, the bold work of the clergy; Stephen regained his liberty in 1142, and the civil war recommenced. But a new enemy had now arisen against him. Prince Henry, the son of Matilda, though still young, had already rendered himself remarkable for his bravery and prudence. His mother promised him the dukedom of Normandy; the death of his father, Geoffrey Plantagenet, had given him Maine and Poitou; and his marriage with Eleanor of Guienne had gained him two other vast provinces of France. In 1154, he appeared in England with an army, but a negotiation speedily terminated the conflict, and Henry was acknowledged as the successor of Stephen, who died a year afterwards, on the 25th of October, 1154.

A variety of circumstances were favourable to the power of Henry II. at his accession. He united in his own person the rights of both the Saxon and Norman dynasties. He possessed immense dominions on the Continent; he was Count of Anjou, Duke of Normandy, Duke of Guienne Maine, Saintonge, Poitou, Auvergne, Périgord, Augoumois and Limousin. He married his third son, Geoffrey, while still a child, to the infant heiress of the duchy of Brittany. He soon became engaged in war with the nobility and the clergy. He revoked all the gifts of the royal domains which had been granted by Stephen and Matilda, and regained by arms all that was not restored to him peaceably. He demolished a large number of the feudal fortresses. No coalition of the barons had as yet been formed, and their individual power was utterly unable to compete with that of Henry; they therefore submitted. The king also rallied around him a great number of interests by the maintenance of strict order, and by the appointment of itinerant justices to secure a more equitable administration of the laws. His struggle with the clergy was more stormy, and its success less complete; for the clergy, who were already constituted into a most powerful corporation, and were sustained from without by the Holy See, had found within their own body a chieftain capable of resisting even the greatest monarch. Thomas Becket, born in London in 1119, had advanced so far in the favour of Henry as to be appointed his Lord High Chancellor. His services, his devotedness, the magnificence of his mode of life, all combined to persuade Henry that, by elevating Becket to the highest ecclesiastical dignities, he would gain a powerful supporter in the church; he, therefore, had him appointed Archbishop of Canterbury and Primate of the kingdom. But no sooner was Becket appointed to this office than he devoted himself to the interests of his order, and boldly undertook to exercise, and even to extend the rights of his position. A clerk had committed a murder; Becket punished him according to the laws of the clergy: Henry desired to have him judged by the civil law; Becket resisted; and Henry seized this opportunity for attacking openly and systematically the ecclesiastical power. He assembled the bishops, and inquired of them whether they would submit to the ancient laws of the realm, or not; and they were forced to consent to do so. The famous Council of Clarendon was convoked in 1164 to define these laws, and fix the limits of the two powers. The king had conciliated the support of the lay barons. Sixteen articles resulted from the deliberations of this assembly; they are to the following effect:

1. All suits concerning the advowson and presentation of churches shall be determined in the civil courts. 2. Ecclesiastics, when accused of any crime, shall appear before the king's justices, who shall determine whether the case ought to be tried in the secular or episcopal courts. The king's justices shall inquire into the manner in which causes of this kind are judged by the ecclesiastical courts; and if the clerk is convicted or confesses his crime, he shall lose his benefit of clergy. 3. No archbishop, bishop, or ecclesiastic of high rank shall leave the kingdom without the king's permission. If he should go abroad, he must give surety to the king for his return, and for his good conduct in all matters affecting the interests of the king. 4. Excommunicated persons shall not be bound to give security for continuing in their present place of abode, but merely for presenting themselves to suffer the judgment of the church and to receive absolution. 5. No tenant in chief of the king, no officer of his household, or of his demesnes, shall be excommunicated, or his lands put under an interdict, until application has been made to the king, or, in his absence, to the grand justiciary, in order to obtain justice at his hands. 6. All appeals in spiritual causes shall be carried from the archdeacon to the bishop, from the bishop to the primate, and from him to the king, and shall be carried no further without the king's consent. 7. If any law-suit arise between a layman and an ecclesiastic concerning the nature of a fief, the question shall be decided by the king's chief justice, by the verdict of twelve *probi homines;*[1] and according as the nature of the fief may be determined, further proceedings shall be carried on before the civil or ecclesiastical courts. 8. Any inhabitant of a city, town, borough or manor in the king's demesnes, who has been cited before an ecclesiastical court to answer for some offence, and who has refused to appear, may be placed under an interdict; but no one may be excommunicated till the chief officer of the place where he resides be consulted, that he may compel him by the civil authority to give satisfaction to the church. 9. The judgment of all causes, for debts contracted by oath or otherwise, is referred to the civil courts. 10. When any archbishopric, or bishopric, or abbey, or priory of royal foundation is vacant, the king shall enjoy its revenues; and when it becomes necessary to fill up a see, the king shall summon a chapter to proceed, in the royal chapel, to the election, which must obtain the sanction of the king, according to the advice of the prelates whom he may have thought proper to consult; and the bishop-elect shall swear fealty and homage to the king as to his lord, for all his temporal possessions, with the exception of the rights of his order. 11. Churches belonging to the king's fee shall not be granted in perpetuity without his consent. 12. No layman shall be accused before a bishop, except by legal and reputable promoters and witnesses; and if the culprit be of such high rank that no one dares to accuse him, the sheriff, upon the demand of the

1. Upright men.

bishop, shall appoint twelve lawful men of the neighbourhood, who, in presence of the bishop, shall pronounce upon the facts of the case, according to their conscience. 13. Archbishops, bishops, and other spiritual dignitaries who are immediate vassals of the king, shall be regarded as barons of the realm, and shall possess the privileges and be subjected to the burdens belonging to that rank, except in the case of condemnation to death or to the loss of a limb. 14. That if any person resist a sentence legally pronounced upon him by an ecclesiastical court, the king shall employ his authority in obliging him to make submission. In like manner, if any one throw off his allegiance to the king, the prelates shall assist the king with their censures in reducing him. 15. Goods forfeited to the king shall not be protected in churches or churchyards. 16. No villein shall be ordained a clerk without the consent of the lord on whose estate he was born.

When the constitutions of Clarendon had once been adopted, the king required that the bishops should affix their seals thereto; all consented with the exception of Becket, who resisted for a long while, but yielded at length, and promised "legally, with good faith, and without fraud or reserve," to observe the constitutions. The king sent a copy of them to Pope Alexander, who approved only the last six articles, and annulled all the rest. Strong in the support of the Pope, Becket did penance for his submission, and renewed the conflict. It soon became desperate. The king harassed Becket with persecutions of all kinds, requiring him to give an account of his administration while Chancellor, and charging him with embezzlement; the bishops became alarmed and deserted the cause of the primate. Becket resisted with indomitable courage; but he was finally compelled to fly to the Continent. Henry confiscated all his property, and banished all his relatives and servants, to the number of four hundred. Becket excommunicated the servants of the king, and, from his retirement in a French monastery, made Henry totter on his throne. At length, the Pope with his legates, and the King of France, interfered to put an end to this conflict. Henry, who was embarrassed by a multitude of other affairs, yielded, and Becket returned to his see. But his conscience united with his pride to rekindle the war. He censured the prelates who had failed to support him, and excommunicated some of the king's servants who had been active in their persecution of the clergy. "What!" cried Henry, in a transport of passion, "of the cowards who eat my bread, is there not one who will free me from this turbulent priest?" He was then at Bayeux; four of his gentlemen set out at once for Canterbury, and assassinated Becket on the steps of the altar of his cathedral, on the 29th of December, 1170. The king dispatched a courier in pursuit of them, but he arrived too late to prevent the consummation of the deed. Henry manifested the utmost grief at the death of Becket; we may, however, suppose his sorrow to have been feigned. In order to avert the consequences, he at once sent envoys to Rome to attest his innocence, and the Pope contented himself with fulminating a general excommunication against the authors, fautors, or instigators of the assassination.

Other events, wars with Scotland and France, and an expedition into Ireland, diverted the public attention from Becket's death. In 1172, Henry resumed his negotiations with Rome, and concluded a treaty which, on the whole, ratified the enactments of the Council of Clarendon. When he had thus become reconciled with the Pope, he made his peace with his subjects, whose enmity he feared, by a public penance on the tomb of Becket, who was honoured by all England as a martyr.

In 1172, some English adventurers conquered without difficulty, and almost without a battle, a part of Ireland. Henry led an expedition into that country, and his authority was recognized. The remainder of his life was agitated by continual wars in defence of his possessions on the Continent, and by the rebellions of his children, who were anxious to divide his power and dominions before his death. He died of grief at their conduct on the 6th of July, 1189, at Chinon, near Saumur; and the corpse of one of the greatest kings of England and of his age was left for some time, deserted and stripped, upon the steps of an altar. His eldest son, Richard Coeur-de-Lion, succeeded him without difficulty.

In every age, and at every great epoch of history, we almost invariably witness the appearance of some individuals who seem to be the types of the general spirit and dominant dispositions of their time. Richard, the adventurer-king, is an exact representation of the chivalrous spirit of the feudal system and of the twelfth century. Immediately upon his accession, his only thought was the accumulation of money for the Crusades; he alienated his domains; he publicly sold offices, honours, and even the loftiest dignities, to the highest bidder; he even sold permissions not to go on the Crusade; and he was ready to sell London, he said, if he could find a purchaser. And while he was sacrificing everything to his passion for pious adventures, his people massacred the Jews because some of them had appeared at the coronation of the king, notwithstanding the prohibition.

Richard set out at length for the Crusades, leaving as Regent during his absence his mother Eleanor, who had excited the princes her sons to rebellion against the king their father; and he associated the Bishops of Durham and Ely with her in the regency. The tyranny of the Bishop of Ely spread confusion throughout England; he placed his colleague under arrest, and governed alone with boundless arrogance, until at last Prince John had him deposed by a council of barons and prelates. Richard, on his return from the Crusades, was, as is well known, detained prisoner in Austria, from the 20th of December, 1193, to the 4th of February, 1194, when he recovered his liberty by the devotedness of one of his vassals. The power of feudal feelings and ties was also manifested in the eagerness of his subjects to pay his ransom. Richard, when restored to his kingdom, spent the remainder of his life in continual wars in France, and died, on the 6th of April, 1199, of a wound received at the siege of the castle of Chalus, near Limoges, while endeavouring to gain possession of a treasure which, it was said, the Count of Limoges had found.

During the reign of Richard, the liberties of the towns and boroughs, which had commenced under William Rufus, made considerable progress, and prepared the way for that decisive advance of national liberties and representative government in England—the Great Charter of King John.

LECTURE 3

Anglo-Saxon institutions. ⁓ *Effects of the Norman Conquest upon Anglo-Saxon institutions.* ⁓ *Effects of the Conquest upon Norman institutions.* ⁓ *Causes which made the Norman Conquest favourable to the establishment of a system of free institutions in England.*

AFTER having given a summary, in the preceding lecture, of the principal historical facts, we are now about to survey Anglo-Norman institutions during the period to which we have just turned our attention, namely, from the middle of the eleventh century until the end of the twelfth.

How came it that free institutions were established from this time forth among this people, and not in other countries? The answer to this question may be found in the general facts of English history, for institutions are much more the work of circumstances than of the texts of laws.

The States which were founded in Europe, from the fifth to the seventh century, were established by hordes of wandering Barbarians, the conquerors of the degraded Roman population. On the side of the victors, there existed no fixed and determinate form of social life; on the side of the vanquished, forms and institutions crumbled into dust; social life died of inanition. Hence arose long disorders, ignorance and impossibility of a general system of organization, the reign of force, and the dismemberment of sovereignty.

Nothing of the kind occurred in England in the eleventh century, in consequence of the Norman Conquest. A Barbarian people which had already been established in a country for two hundred years conquered another Barbarian people which had been territorially established for six hundred years. For this reason, many decisive differences may be observed between this conquest and those which took place on the Continent.

1. There was much more resemblance, and consequently much more equality, between the two peoples; their origin was the same, their manners and language were analogous, their civilization was almost identical, and the warlike spirit was as powerful among the vanquished as among the victors. Thus, two nations under almost similar conditions, found themselves in presence of

one another, and the conquered nation was able, as well as disposed, to defend its liberties. Hence arose many individual evils, but no general and permanent abasement of one race before the other. Oppressed at first, but retaining its warlike character, the Saxon race offered an energetic resistance, and gradually raised itself from its inferior position.

2. The two peoples also possessed political institutions of a singularly analogous nature, whereas elsewhere, in France and in Italy, the Roman populations, to speak the truth, possessed no institutions at all. The communes and the clergy were required to maintain, even obscurely, the Roman law among societies on the Continent; whereas in England, Saxon institutions were never stifled by Norman institutions, but associated with them, and finally even changed their character. On the Continent, we behold the successful sway of barbarism, feudalism, and absolute power, derived either from Roman or ecclesiastical ideas. In England, absolute power was never able to obtain a footing; oppression was frequently practised in fact, but it was never established by law.

3. The two peoples professed the same religion; one had not to convert the other. On the Continent, the more Barbarian victor adopted the religion of the vanquished, and the clergy were almost entirely Romans; in England, they were both Saxons and Normans. Hence resulted an important fact. The English clergy, instead of enrolling themselves in the retinue of the kings, naturally assumed a place among the landed aristocracy, and in the nation. Thus the political order has almost constantly predominated in England over the religious order; and ever since the Norman Conquest, the political power of the clergy, always called in question, has always been on the decline.

This is the decisive circumstance in the history of England—the circumstance which has caused its civilization to take an altogether different course to that taken by the civilization of the Continent. Of necessity, and at an early period, a compromise and amalgamation took place between the victors and the vanquished, both of whom had institutions to bring into common use; institutions more analogous than existed anywhere else—stronger and more fully developed, because they belonged to peoples which had already been territorially established for a considerable time.

Thus, Saxon institutions and Norman institutions are the two sources of the English government. The English commonly refer their political liberties to the former source; they see that, on the Continent, feudalism did not produce liberty; and they attribute their feudalism to the Normans, and their liberty to the Saxons. This distinction has even become a symbol of modern political parties; the Tories, in general, affect a neglect of Saxon institutions, whilst the Whigs attach to them the greatest importance. This view of events appears to me to be neither exact nor complete. Saxon institutions were not, by themselves, the principle of English liberties. The forced assimilation of the two peoples and of the two systems of institutions, was their true cause. There is even room for doubt whether, without the Conquest, liberty would have resulted from Saxon institutions; and we may believe that they would have produced in England results analogous to those which occurred on the Continent. The Conquest inspired them with new virtue, and caused them to produce results which, if they had been left to themselves, they would not have produced. Political liberty issued from them, but was begotten by the influence of the Conquest, and in consequence of the position in which the Conquest placed the two peoples and their laws.

I will now recall to your recollection Anglo-Saxon institutions as they existed before the Conquest; and you will soon see that it was the forced approximation of the two peoples which gave them vitality, and brought forth the liberties of England.

Among local institutions, some were based upon common deliberation, and others upon hierarchical subordination; that is to say, some upon a principle of liberty, and others upon a principle of dependence. On one side, were the courts of hundred and the county-courts; on the other, the great landowners and their vassals: every man of fourteen years old and upwards was obliged to belong either to a hundred or to a lord, that is, to be free or vassal. These two hostile systems, then, placed in presence of one another, conflicted as upon the Continent. There is some doubt about the question whether, before the Conquest, feudalism existed with regard to lands: that it existed with regard to persons there can be no doubt, for their hierarchical classification was real and progressive. In localities, although the system of free institutions subsisted, the system of feudal institutions was gaining ground; seignorial jurisdictions were encroaching upon free jurisdictions; and almost the same process, in fact, was going on as upon the Continent.

If we look at central institutions, we observe the same phenomenon. On the Continent, feudalism was produced by the aggrandizement of the king's vassals, and by the dislocation of the sovereignty. The national unity, which resided in the assembly of the nation, became dissolved; the monarchical unity was unable to resist; and monarchy and liberty perished together. Events had taken the same course among the Anglo-Saxons. Under Edward the Confessor, the decay of the royal authority is evident. Earl Godwin, Siward, Duke of Northumberland, Leofric, Duke of Mercia, and many other great vassals, are rivals rather than subjects of the king; and Harold usurping the crown from Edgar Atheling, the legitimate heir, bears a strong resemblance to Hugh Capet. The sovereignty tends to dismemberment. Monarchical unity is in danger; national unity is in the same declining state, as is proved by the history of the Wittenagemot. This general assembly of the nation was at first the assembly of the warriors; afterwards the general assembly of the land-owners, both great and small; and at a later period, the assembly of the great land-owners alone, or of the king's thanes. Even these at last neglect to attend its meetings; and isolate themselves upon their estates, in which each of them exercises his share of the dismembered sovereignty. This is almost identical with the course of affairs on the Continent. Only, the system of free institutions still subsists in England with some energy in local institutions, and especially in the county-courts. The feudal system is in a less advanced state than on the Continent.

What would have happened if the Conquest had not occurred? It is impossible to say with certainty, but probably just what happened on the Continent. The same symptoms are manifested, the decay of the royal authority and of the national assembly; and the formation of a hierarchical landed aristocracy, almost entirely independent of the central power, and exercising almost undisputed sovereignty in its domains, excepting only feudal liberties.

While Anglo-Saxon institutions were in this state, the Normans conquered England. What new elements did they introduce, and what effect did the Conquest produce upon the Saxons?

The feudal system was completely established in Normandy; the relations of the duke with his vassals, the general council of the barons, the seignorial administration of justice, the superior courts of the duke, were all organized already. This system is impracticable in a large State, especially when manners have made but little progress; it leads to the dislocation of the State and of the sovereignty, and to a federation of powerful individuals, who dismember the royal power. But in a State of limited extent, like Normandy, the feudal system may subsist without destroying unity; and notwithstanding William's continual wars with some of his vassals, he was in very reality the powerful chieftain of his feudal aristocracy. The proof of this is contained in the very enterprize upon which he led them. He had, say the chronicles, from forty to sixty thousand men, of whom twenty-five thousand were hired adventurers or men who joined his standard in the hope of obtaining booty. He was not a leader of Barbarians, but a sovereign undertaking an invasion at the head of his barons.

After the Conquest and their territorial establishment, the bonds which united the Norman aristocracy were necessarily drawn still closer together. Encamped in the midst of a people who regarded them with hostility and were capable of vigorous resistance, the conquerors felt the need of unity; so they linked themselves together, and fortified the central power. On the Continent, after the Barbarian invasions, we hear of hardly any insurrections of the original inhabitants: the wars and conflicts are between the conquerors themselves; but in England they are between the conquerors and the conquered people. We indeed meet, from time to time, with revolts of the Norman barons against the king; but these two powers generally acted in concert, for their interest was their bond of union. Moreover, William had found a royal domain of large extent, already in existence: and it received immense increase from confiscations of the lands of Anglo-Saxon rebels. Although the spoliation was not universal, it was carried out with unexampled promptitude and regularity. William soon had 600 direct vassals, nearly all of whom were Normans, and his landed property was divided into 60,215 knight's fees, a large quantity of which frequently belonged to the same master; for example, Robert de Mortaigne alone possessed 973 manors, the Earl of Warrenne 278, and Roger Bigod 123; but they were all scattered through different counties, for though the prudent William was willing to make his vassals rich, he was not desirous of making them too powerful.

Another proof of the cohesion of the Norman aristocracy is supplied by the Doomsday Book; a statistical account of the royal fiefs, and register of the demesne lands and direct vassals of the king, which was begun in 1081 and terminated in 1086: it was compiled by royal commissioners. King Alfred had also directed the compilation of a similar register, but it has been lost. Nothing of the kind was ever done in any other country.

The same cause which rendered Norman feudalism in England more compact and regular than on the Continent, produced a corresponding effect upon the Saxons. Oppressed by a powerful and thoroughly united enemy, they formed in serried ranks, constituted themselves into a national body, and clung resolutely to their ancient laws. And in the first instance, the establishment of William did not appear to have been entirely the work of force; there were even some forms of election; after the battle of Hastings, the crown was offered to him by the Saxons, and at his coronation at Westminster, he swore to govern the Saxons and Normans by equal laws. After this period, we incessantly find the Saxons claiming to be ruled by the laws of Edward the Confessor, that is to say, by the Saxon laws, and they obtained this right from all the Norman kings in succession. These laws thus became their rallying point, their primitive and permanent code. The county-courts, which continued to exist, also served to maintain the Saxon liberties. Feudal jurisdiction had made but little progress among the Saxons; it received extension on the arrival of the Normans; but it had no time to strike deep root, for it found itself limited on the one hand by the county-courts, and on the other by the royal jurisdiction. On the Continent, the royal authority conquered judicial power from feudalism; in England, the royal authority was superimposed upon the county-courts. Hence arises the immense difference between the two judicial systems.

Lastly, the Saxons still possessed landed property, which they defended or claimed in reliance upon titles anterior to the Conquest, and the validity of these titles was recognised.

To sum up the whole matter, the Norman Conquest did not destroy right among the Saxons, either in political or civil order. It opposed in both nations that tendency to isolation, to the dissolution of society and of power, which was the general course of things in Europe. It bound the Normans to one another, and united the Saxons among themselves; it brought them into presence of each other with mutual powers and rights, and thus effected, in a certain measure, an amalgamation of the two nations and of the two systems of institutions, under the sway of a strong central power. The Saxons retained their manners as well as their laws; their interests were for a long time interests of liberty, and they were able to defend them. This position, far more than the intrinsic character of Saxon institutions, led to the predominance of a system of free government in England.

LECTURE 4

The English Parliament in the earliest times of the Anglo-Norman Monarchy. ～ *Different names given to the King's Great Council.* ～ *Its characteristics.* ～ *Its constitution.* ～ *Opinions of Whigs and Tories on this subject.*

You have already seen what was the influence of the Norman Conquest on the political destinies of England; and what was the position in which the two peoples were placed by it. They did not unite, nor did they mutually destroy one another. They lived in a state of national and political conflict, the one people being invested with a large power of government, while the other was far from being destitute of the means of resistance. We have now to enquire what were those institutions upon which this struggle was founded. We shall not concern ourselves with all the institutions which then existed in society: we are now looking for the sources of representative government, and are therefore at present only interested in those in which the germs of a representative system existed.

In order to determine with some precision the object of our study, it will be necessary to form some idea of the different functions of the power which is applied to the government of society. In the foremost rank is presented the legislative power, which imposes rules and obligations on the entire mass of society and on the executive power itself. Next appears the executive power, which takes the daily oversight of the general business of society—war, peace, raising of men and of taxes. Then the judicial power, which adjusts matters of private interest according to laws previously established. Lastly, the administrative power, charged, under its own responsibility, with the duty of regulating matters which cannot be anticipated and provided for by any general laws.

During three centuries these powers have tended to centralization in France; so much so, that if we would study the government of the country we must attend to them all, for they were all united and limited to the same individuals. Richelieu, Louis XIV, the Revolution, Napoleon, though in different positions, seem to have inherited the same projects and moved in the same direction. Such has not been the case in England. The administrative power there, for example, is to the present time divided and subdivided; it belongs either to those who are themselves interested in its movements, or to local magistrates, independent of the central power of the State, and forming no corporation among themselves. The judicial power itself is divided. It was so to some extent, through another and stronger cause, in the earlier times of England's social life, as in all societies which have made but small advancement. Different powers are then not only distributed but commingled. The legislative power is no more central than others: its functions are continually usurped by local powers. Judicial power is almost entirely local. Centralization commences with the executive power properly so called, and this for a long time remains the only one in which any centralizing tendency is found. The proof of this is furnished by the feudal system, when almost all powers—those connected with justice, militia, taxes, &c.—were local, although the feudal hierarchy had at its head the king, and the assembly of the most important possessors of fiefs.

In this distribution and confusion of powers at the period we are considering, the institutions which we have especially to study in order to find the origin of representative government, are those which were central, that is to say, the Parliament and the king. On the Continent, centralization has resulted from an absolute power which has broken up and absorbed all local powers. In England, on the other hand, local powers have subsisted after a thousand vicissitudes, while they have increasingly regulated and defined their own action. A central government has emanated from them by degrees—it has progressively formed and extended itself. We shall trace this formation step by step, and shall only study local institutions as they relate to this one fact; and we shall see that this circumstance has been the principal cause of the establishment of a free government in England.

It is easily presumed that, in such a state of society, no other central institution, properly so called, existed for a long time, except royalty. There are certain maxims, certain habits of central political action, but no constant rule: the facts are varied and contradictory. Men of considerable influence, almost sovereigns in their own domains, are much less desirous of any participation in the central power; they rather attempt to defend themselves from it as often as it infringes upon their interests, than endeavour at all to control it beforehand, and to act upon it in a general manner. As in France, at the end of the Carlovingian dynasty, a king can hardly be met with, so in England, under the first Norman kings, a Parliament can hardly be found. That which existed bearing any resemblance to one differs but little from the Saxon Wittenagemot in the form which belonged to it immediately before the Conquest, or from the Council of Barons in Normandy. We find in the works of historians, and in charters, the following names: *Curia de more, Curia regis, Concilium, Magnum Concilium,*

Commune Concilium, Concilium regni. But these are to be regarded only as vague expressions which designate assemblies, without giving any clue by which to determine their constitution and their power. Hale sees in them "a Parliament as complete and as real as has ever been held in England." Carte and Brady see in them only tribunals, privy councils dependent upon the king, or pompous gatherings for the celebration of certain solemnities. It will be better for us to examine each of these words, and seek for the actual facts which correspond to them in the period to which our attention is directed.

According to the Tories in general, the words *Curia de more,* or *Concilium, Curia regis, Magnum* or *Commune Concilium,* represent different assemblies. *Concilium* is a privy council composed of men chosen by the king to serve him in the government. This *Concilium* was at the same time *Curia regis,* a tribunal to judge of matters brought before the king, and presided over by him, or, in his absence, by the chief justice. It was called also *Curia de more,* because its assemblies were held, according to ancient usage, three times in the course of the year, at Easter, Whitsuntide, and Christmas, and was even adjourned regularly from one period to another, as is done to the present day by the Courts at Westminster.

According to the Whigs, all these words originally designated, and continued to the reign of Henry II. (1154–1189) to designate the general assembly of the nobles of the kingdom, who necessarily assembled before the king in order to try cases, to make laws, and to give their concurrence to the government.

The first of these opinions puts too great a restraint upon the meaning of the words; the second generalizes too much on isolated facts, and assigns to them an importance which does not belong to them.

Curia de more, Curia regis, signified originally neither the merely privy council of the king nor his tribunal; it was evidently a grand assembly at which all the nobles of the kingdom were present, either to treat of the affairs of State, or to assist the king in the administration of justice. "The king," says the Saxon Chronicle, "was wont to wear his crown three times a year—at Easter in Winchester; at Whitsuntide in Westminster; at Christmas in Gloucester; and then there were present with him all the great men of all England, archbishops and bishops, abbots and counts, thanes and knights."—"A royal edict," says William of Malmesbury, "called to the *Curia de more* all the nobles of every grade, in order that those sent from foreign countries might be struck with the magnificence of the company, and with the splendour of the festivities."—"Under William Rufus," says Eadmer, "all the nobles of the kingdom came, according to usage, to the king's court, on the day of our Saviour's nativity." Anselm, Archbishop of Canterbury, having presented himself *ad Curiam pro more,* "was received with joy by the king and all the nobility of the kingdom." In

1109, at Christmas, "the kingdom of England assembled at London, at the court of the king, according to custom."

Curia regis designates generally the place of the king's residence, and by an extension of meaning the assembly held in that place; this assembly was general, and not a mere gathering of permanent judges. William I., summoning the Dukes of Norfolk and Hereford to attend and receive judgment *in Curia regis,* "convoked," says Ordericus Vitalis, "all the nobility to his court." Several judicial assemblies held under William Rufus, are called *ferme totius regni nobilitas, totius regni adunatio.*[1] Facts and expressions of the same kind are to be found in documents of the time of Stephen. Even under Henry II., when the Court of King's Bench had already become a distinct tribunal, the expression *Curia regis* is applied to the general assembly collected for the transaction of public business. Henry convoked his *Curia* at Bermondsey, *cum principibus suis de statu regni et pace reformanda tractans.*[2] The second of the Constitutions of Clarendon orders all the immediate vassals of the crown *interesse judiciis curiae regis.*[3] The great Council of Northampton, which passed judgment in the complaints of the crown against Becket, is called *Curia regis;* it comprised not only the bishops, counts and barons, but besides these, the sheriffs and the barons *secundae dignitatis.*[4] Lastly, under Richard I., the general assembly of the nobles of the kingdom is still called *Curia regis* in the trial of the Archbishop of York: "On this occasion there were present the Earl of Morton and almost all the bishops, earls and barons of the kingdom."

A little consideration will show us the inferences to be drawn from all these facts. At this period the legislative and judicial powers were not separated; both of them belonged to the assembly of the nobles, as they had previously belonged to the Wittenagemot of the Saxons. When deliberations with reference to a subject or personage of importance were required, this was the assembly that judged, as it interposed on all great occasions in the government. Thus all these different expressions denote originally the same assembly, composed of the nobles of the kingdom who were called to bear their share in the government.

How did they interpose? What power, what functions belonged to them?—these are questions which were futile at that time: for no one then had determinate functions, but everything was decided according to fact and necessity. The facts are these: "It was the ancient usage that the nobles of England

---

1. The nobility of almost the entire kingdom, the union of the entire kingdom.

2. With his princes discussing the state of the kingdom and restoring peace.

3. To be among the judges of the king's court.

4. Of second rank.

should at Christmas time meet at the king's court, either to celebrate the festival, or to pay their respects to the king, or to deliberate concerning the affairs of the kingdom." We find that these assemblies were occupied in legislation, in ecclesiastical affairs, in questions of peace and war, in extraordinary taxes, in the succession of the crown, in the domestic affairs of the king, his marriage, the nuptials of his children, dissensions in the royal family, in one word, in all matters of government, says Florence of Worcester, whenever the king did not feel himself strong enough to settle them without the assistance of the general assembly, or when the mode in which he had settled them had excited complaints in sufficient number to admonish him of the necessity of taking the advice of others.

As to the holding of these assemblies, they were not regular: the Whigs have attached too much importance to the three periods mentioned as the times of their annual convocation: these gatherings were rather of the nature of solemnities, or festivals, than public assemblies. The king at that time considered it very important that he should exhibit himself surrounded by numerous and wealthy vassals, *species multitudinis;*[5] his force and dignity were thereby displayed, just as that of every baron was exhibited in his own dominions. Besides, under Henry II. and Stephen, these three epochs ceased to be regularly observed. The Tories, on the other hand, not considering the gatherings called *Curiae de more* and *Curiae regis* as political assemblies, have represented them as extremely infrequent, which they were not; there is not a single reign, from the Conquest to the times of King John, in which several instances of them are not to be found; only there was nothing settled and fixed in this respect.

The question of the constitution of these assemblies remains. Historians and charters say nothing definite on this point: they speak of their members as *magnates, proceres, barones,* sometimes as *milites, servientes, liberi homines.* There is every reason to suppose that the feudal principle was here applied, and that, as a matter of right, all the immediate vassals of the king owed to him service at court as well as in war. On the other hand, the number of the vassals attached to the crown under William I. exceeded 600; and there is no reason for believing that all these would present themselves at the assembly, nor are there any facts to indicate that they did so. It had already become, for the most part, rather an onerous service than a right; accordingly they only presented themselves in small numbers.

The word most frequently employed is *barones:* it would appear to have been originally applied to all the direct vassals of the crown, *per servitium militare,* by knightly service; we find that the use of the word was limited more and more till it was applied almost exclusively to those vassals of the crown who were

---

5. The spectacle of a multitude.

sufficiently wealthy and large proprietors to have a court of justice established in the seat of their barony. It is even difficult to admit that this last principle was generally followed. The name of *barones* was finally applied only to those immediate vassals who were so powerful that the king felt himself obliged to convoke them. There was no primitive and constant rule to distinguish the barons from other vassals; but a class of vassals was gradually formed who were more rich, more important, more habitually occupied with the king in affairs of state, and who came at last to arrogate to themselves exclusively the title of *barons*.

The bishops and abbots also formed part of these assemblies, both as being heads of the clergy, and as immediate vassals of the king or of the barons.

No trace of election or of representation is to be found, either on the part of the king's vassals who did not present themselves at the assembly, or on the part of the towns. These last had in general suffered very greatly by the Norman Conquest. In York the number of houses was reduced from 1607 to 967; in Oxford from 721 to 243: in Derby from 243 to 140; in Chester from 487 to 282.

These, then, are the essential facts which we may gather with reference to the constitution and power of the King's Court, or general assembly of the nobles of the nation. We see how little influence must have been exerted by an assembly of so irregular a character; and we shall see this still more strikingly illustrated when we have brought it into comparison with the rights, the revenues, and all the powers which were at that time enjoyed by royalty.

LECTURE 5

The Anglo-Norman royalty: its wealth and power. ⁓ *Comparison of the relative forces of the Crown and of the feudal aristocracy.* ⁓ *Progress of the royal power.* ⁓ *Spirit of association and resistance among the great barons.* ⁓ *Commencement of the struggle between these two political forces.*

IN order to judge accurately of the power and importance of royalty at the period we are considering, we must first ascertain its actual position and resources; and we shall see by the extent of these resources, and by the advantages of this position, how feeble in its action on the royal power must have been the influence of the assembly of barons.

The riches of the Norman king were independent of his subjects; he possessed an immense quantity of domains, 1,462 manors, and the principal towns of the kingdom. These domains were continually being augmented, either by confiscations, causes for which were of frequent occurrence, or by the failure of lawful heirs. The king gave lands on a free tenure to those cultivators who would pay for them a determinate rent (*free socage tenure*). This was the origin of most of the freeholders, whether in the king's domains or in those of his barons. The king, in his domains, imposed taxes at will; he also arbitrarily imposed customhouse regulations on the importation and exportation of merchandize; and he fixed the amount of fines and of the redemption money for crimes. He sold public offices, among others that of sheriff, which was a lucrative one on account of the share in fines which belonged to it. The county sometimes would pay for the right to nominate its sheriff, or to avoid a nomination already made. Lastly, the sale of royal protection and justice was a source of considerable revenue.

As to the immediate vassals of the king, they owed him, *First,* a military service of forty days whenever it was required; *Secondly,* pecuniary aid under three circumstances—to ransom the king when made prisoner, to arm his eldest son as a knight, or to marry his eldest daughter. The amount of this aid was undetermined up to the reign of Edward I.; it was then fixed at twenty shillings for the fief of a knight, and as much for every twenty pounds sterling value in land held in socage tenure. *Thirdly,* the king had a right to receive from his vassals a relief or fine on the death of the possessor of a fief; he was guardian if the heir were a minor, and enjoyed all the revenues of the fief till the majority of the heir; he also had a control over their marriages, that is to say, the vassal of a king could not marry without his consent. All these rights were indeterminate, and negotiations were substituted for them in which the greater force always had the advantage. *Fourthly,* the dispensation from feudal military service gave rise to an impost termed *escuage,* a kind of ransom-money fixed arbitrarily by the king, as representative of a service to which he had a claim; and he even imposed it in many cases on his vassals when they would have preferred to serve in person. Henry II., by his purely arbitrary will, levied five *escuages* in the course of his reign.

In addition to these taxes levied by the king, another must be mentioned called the *danegeld,* or tax paid for defence against the Danes; this tax was raised several times during this period on all lands throughout the kingdom. The last example of it is to be found in the twentieth year of the reign of Henry II.

By means of these independent revenues and arbitrary taxes, the Norman kings constantly kept up bodies of paid troops, who could enable them to exercise their power without restraint, which did not take place till a considerably later period on the Continent.

Lastly, from William the Conqueror till Henry II. the judicial power tended always to concentrate itself in the hands of the king. In this last reign the work was very nearly accomplished: how this came to pass, I will endeavour to show.

Originally the jurisdictions that co-existed were as follows: 1. The courts of hundred and the county-courts, or meetings of the freeholders of these territorial subdivisions, under the presidency of the sheriff: 2. The courts-baron, or feudal jurisdictions: 3. The grand court of the king, where the king and the assembled barons administered justice to the barons in cases between any of themselves, or in cases of appeal, which could only take place when justice had been refused in the court of the manor or county.

The Court of Exchequer, instituted by William the Conqueror, was, at first, only a simple court for receiving the accounts of the administration of the king's revenues, and those of the sheriffs, bailiffs, &c., and for judging the suits that arose on this subject. It was composed of barons, chosen by the king to form his council, and to aid him in his government. In proportion as the larger assembly, the *Curia regis,* came to be held less frequently, so did the Court of Exchequer gain in importance. The barons who composed it began to judge on their own responsibility, and alone, in the absence and before the convocation of the assembly; this change was introduced by necessity, confirmed by custom, and finally sanctioned and established by law. About the year 1164, another royal court of justice, distinct from the Court of Exchequer, arose out of it, the members of which, however, were the same as those composing the Court of Exchequer. The kings lent their assistance to this change, because it benefited their revenues. At this period were established *writs of chancery*, which gave to purchasers the right to apply at once to the royal justice, without previously passing the subordinate courts of justice. Soon the ignorance of the freeholders, who composed the county-courts, necessitated the same extension of the royal justice there also, and, in the reign of Henry I., *itinerant justices* were sent into the counties, in order to administer there in the same way as was done by the Court of Exchequer. This institution was in full vigour only during the reign of Henry II.

In this way the predominant influence of the king, in judicial order, was established; this was a powerful instrument in producing centralization and unity, and yet, as the royal judges only interposed their services as supplementary to the institution of the jury, and did not substitute them for it—for questions of fact and questions of right remained distinct—the germ of free institutions, that existed in the judicial order, was not entirely destroyed.

A king invested with such powerful resources could with difficulty be restrained by an irregular assembly; accordingly the government of the Norman kings was almost always arbitrary and despotic. Persons and property were never in security; the laws, taxes, and judicial sentences were almost always merely an expression of the royal will.

When we consider these facts collectively, we may be led to two very opposite results, according to the point of view from which we regard them: on the one hand, we see the general assembly of the nation interfering pretty frequently in public affairs, not by virtue of any particular official character it possessed, nor for the purpose of exercising any one special right, such as that of making general laws, or of voting supplies, but on occasions widely differing from one another, and for the purpose of acquiescing in the entire course of government. Laws, external relations, peace, war, ecclesiastical affairs, the judgment of important cases, the administration of the royal domains, nominations to great public offices, even the interior economy and proceedings of the royal family, all seem to belong to the province of this national assembly. No matter is foreign to it, no function forbidden to it, no kind of investigation or of action refused to it. All distinction of provinces, all lines of demarcation between the prerogatives of the crown and those of the assembly, appear to be unknown; we might say that the entire government belonged to the assembly, and that it exercised in a direct way that activity, that general supervision, which belongs indirectly to the mature and perfected representative system, by virtue of its influence on the choice of those who are to be the depositaries of power, and by means of the principle of responsibility.

On the other hand, if we forget the assembly and examine the royal power, as isolated, we shall see it exercising itself in a multitude of cases, in as absolute and arbitrary a manner as if no assembly had existed to share in the government. The king, on his own responsibility, made laws, levied taxes, dispossessed proprietors, condemned and banished important persons, and exercised, in a word, all the rights of unlimited sovereignty. This sovereignty appears entire, sometimes in the hands of the assembly, sometimes in those of the king; when the assembly proceeds to interfere in all the details of government, we do not find any complaint from the king, as if an encroachment had been made on his prerogatives; and when, on the other hand, the king governs despotically, we do not find the assembly bestirring itself to protest against the extension of royal power, as a blow aimed at their rights.

Thus we are met by two classes of facts, simultaneously existing in this infancy of society—facts which seem to belong to a fully developed system of free institutions, and facts which are characteristic of absolute power. On the one hand, the aim of free governments, which is, that the nation should interfere, directly or indirectly, in all public affairs, seems to be attained; on the other hand, the independent and arbitrary domination of the royal power appears to be recognized.

This is a result that must necessarily arise in the disorder of a nascent and troubled stage of civilization. Society is then a prey to chaos—all the rights and all the powers of a community co-exist, but they are confounded, unregulated, unmarked by limits, and without any legal guarantee—freemen have not yet abdicated any of their liberties, nor has force yet renounced any of its pretensions. If any one had said to the barons of William, or of Henry I., that they had nothing to do with affairs of State, except to comply when the king demanded an impost, they would have been indignant. All the affairs of the State were theirs, because they were interested in them; and when they were called upon to deliberate concerning peace or war, they believed that they were exercising a right belonging to them, and not making a conquest over royal authority. No freeman, who was strong enough to defend his freedom, recognized any right in another person to dispose of him without his consent, and found it a very simple matter to give his advice on questions that were interesting to him. The king, in his turn, measuring his right by his force, did not recognize in any person, nor, consequently, in any assembly, the legal right to prevent him from doing that which he was able to do. There were then, properly speaking, no public rights or powers at all; they were almost entirely individual and dependent on circumstances; they are to be found, but in a state of isolation, unconscious of their own nature, and, indeed, of their very existence.

In this disorderly state of things, the able and energetic government of William I., Henry I. and Henry II. caused the royal power gradually to assume a much more general and consistent character. Accordingly, national assemblies became by degrees more rare and less influential; under Stephen, they almost entirely disappeared. The barons no longer had a common meeting-point, and were more occupied with the rule of their own domains than with any association with the royal power for the purpose of controlling or restraining it. Each devoted himself more exclusively to his own affairs, and the king, following this example, made himself almost the sole master of those of the State. He availed himself of the need of order and regularity that made itself felt every day, in order to constitute himself, in some sort, the dispenser of them. By these means he soon became the first in name, as well as the most powerful in fact. Through him, the roads became more secure; he protected the feeble, and repressed robbers. The maintenance of public order devolved upon the royal power, and became the means of extending and strengthening it more and more. Whatever the king had possessed himself of by conquest, he vindicated as his own by right. Thus was formed the royal prerogative.

But at the same time different circumstances concurred to draw the barons forth from their isolation, to unite them among themselves, and to form them into an aristocracy. The Anglo-Norman throne was successively occupied by three usurpers, William II., Henry I., and Stephen. Invested with a power whose title was doubtful, they felt the necessity of bringing the barons to recognize their claims; hence the first charters were conceded. No one of the barons was powerful enough, in himself, to restrain the threatened extension of royal power, but they formed the habit of making coalitions; and as each of the barons entering into such coalitions, felt the necessity of attaching his vassals to himself, concessions were made to them also. The absence of large fiefs, in England, served the cause both of power and of liberty; it allowed power to form itself into unity with greater facility, and it obliged liberty to seek for guarantees in the spirit of association. That which finally contributed in the most decided way to form and consolidate this aristocratic coalition, was the irregular and usurping conduct of John during the long absence of Richard Coeur-de-Lion, and the disorders and civil wars which were naturally the results of this absence. In the midst of these disorders the government fell into the hands of a council of barons, that is to say, of a portion of the aristocracy. Those who had no share whatever in the central power did not cease to control it, and to regard it as rightfully theirs; in this way, the one party formed a habit of governing, the other that of resisting a government which was in the hands of their equals, and not of the king himself. John, by his cowardice and ill-judged familiarity, had brought the throne into disrespect before he himself ascended it, and his barons much more easily conceived the idea of resisting as a king, one whom they had despised as a prince.

Thus, in the space of a hundred and thirty years, two elements in the

State, which were at first confounded and had almost acted in common, were separated and formed into distinct powers—the royal power on the one hand, and on the other, the company of barons. The struggle between these two forces then commenced, and we shall see royalty continually occupied in defending its privileges, and the aristocracy as unweariedly busying itself in the endeavour to extort new concessions. The history of the English charters, from the reign of William I. to that of Edward I., who granted them a general confirmation, is the history of this struggle, to which England is indebted for the earliest appearance of the germs of a free government, that is to say, of public rights and political guarantees.

LECTURE 6

History of English Charters. ⁓ *Charter of William the Conqueror (1071).* ⁓ *Charter of Henry I. (1101).* ⁓ *Charters of Stephen (1135–1136).* ⁓ *Charter of Henry II. (1154).*

Lɪʙᴇʀᴛɪᴇs are nothing until they have become rights—positive rights formally recognized and consecrated. Rights, even when recognized, are nothing so long as they are not entrenched within guarantees. And lastly, guarantees are nothing so long as they are not maintained by forces independent of them, in the limit of their rights. Convert liberties into rights, surround rights by guarantees, entrust the keeping of these guarantees to forces capable of maintaining them—such are the successive steps in the progress towards a free government.[1]

This progress was exactly realized in England in the struggle, the history of which we are about to trace. Liberties first converted themselves into rights; when rights were nearly recognized, guarantees were sought for them; and lastly, these guarantees were placed in the hands of regular powers. In this way a representative system of government was formed.

We may date from the reign of King John as the period when the efforts of the English aristocracy to procure a recognition and establishment of their rights became conspicuous; they then demanded and extorted charters. During the reign of Edward I., the charters were fully recognized and confirmed; they became real public rights. And it was at the same epoch that a Parliament began to be definitely formed, that is to say, the organization of political guarantees commenced, and with it the creation of the regular power to which they are entrusted.

---

1. This passage is important for understanding the relation between rights and liberties in Guizot's political thought. The key idea is that liberties must be duly protected by rights if they are to be effective; free government requires not only liberties and rights (as guarantees), but also forces capable of maintaining them in practice. Not surprisingly, Guizot was a great admirer of *Magna Charta*, "the most complete and important [charter] that had yet appeared" (*HORG*, pp. 266–67), by virtue of which the rights of all three orders of the English nation were equally respected and promoted.

I have shown how the two great public forces—royalty and the council of barons, were formed, cemented, and brought into juxtaposition. We must now follow these forces into the combats in which they engaged their energies in order to have their reciprocal rights recognized and regulated; and to do this we must trace the history of English charters. I shall then enquire how the guarantees were organized, that is to say, how the Parliament was formed.

When William the Conqueror arrived in England, his position with respect to the Norman barons and knights had been already regulated on the Continent by the feudal law; their respective rights were fixed and recognized. After the Conquest, fear of the Anglo-Saxons kept the king and the Normans so far united, that neither of them cared much to extort concessions from the other. Very different, however, were the relations between William and his English subjects. He had to adjust these relations—here was a legislation to be created, and rights to be recognized or contested. The English made the most strenuous efforts to preserve their Saxon laws, and it appears to have been in the fourth year of William's reign (the year 1071) that they succeeded in gaining an assurance that these laws should be maintained. There is reason to believe that on this occasion he granted the charter intituled, "*Charta regis de quibusdam statutis per totam Angliam firmiter observandis.*"[2] Some have asserted that this charter was not granted till nearly the end of William's reign, but I see no reason for assigning any other period to it than that which I have mentioned.

This charter, the authenticity of which* has been sometimes questioned, I think on insufficient grounds, is a kind of vague declaration containing the general principles of feudal political law. William, in it, recognizes rights which he often allowed himself to violate; for his power rendered the violation of his promises easy. The Norman barons did not form themselves into any body, unless perhaps against the English; they were all too much occupied in the work of establishing themselves in their new domains. If they sometimes roused themselves to oppose the tyranny of William, their revolts were only partial, and the king adroitly used the English in order to put them down. His son, William Rufus, by adopting the same policy, obtained similar success. But Henry I. had to pay for his usurpation; the charter which he granted was the inevitable consequence of his possession of the throne.

This charter of Henry's contains a solemn promise to respect all ancient rights. In it the king promises no more to follow *all the evil practices* by which the kingdom of England was oppressed under the king his brother, that is to say, not to appropriate the revenues of vacant abbacies and bishoprics, nor again to

---

* The original is lost, but a copy of it exists in the Red Book of the Exchequer, which gives a strong presumption for its authenticity. Besides, the charter of Henry I. makes a distinct allusion to it.

2. Charter of the king concerning certain laws to be observed steadfastly throughout all England.

sell or farm ecclesiastical benefices, and to permit the heirs of his vassals to inherit their possessions on paying a just and legitimate fine. He assures to his barons their right to give their daughters or sisters in marriage to whomsoever they will, provided it be not to one of the king's enemies; he grants to widows who are left without children the possession of their dowry and jointure, and liberty to marry again according to their free choice; and he renounces the right of guardianship, placing it in the hands either of the wife or some relative. He gives to all his vassals the right to dispose of their property either by gift or by will, renounces the right arbitrarily to levy taxes on the farms of his vassals, abandons the forests which William Rufus had usurped, and abolished feudal aids, even in the three cases which we have already specified. Lastly, he withdraws the right of coining from the towns and counties, pardons all the offences and crimes committed before his reign, and recommends his vassals to allow their vassals to enjoy all the advantages which he accords to them.

These concessions were merely recognitions of rights, without guarantees. Henry, accordingly, despite his oaths, violated these magnificent promises; and the abuses which they ought to have removed were not diminished in any degree, during the whole extent of his reign.

Another charter was granted by Henry I. to the city of London, by which it was authorized, among other things, to elect its own sheriff and chief magistrate, to hold its accustomed assemblies, not to pay either the *danegeld* or any other *scot*, or imposts for works along rivers, and not to give lodging to the retinue of the king.

Lastly, we find new promises and new concessions made by Henry I. in 1101, when his brother Robert laid claim to his rights. Wishing to assure himself of the fidelity of his barons, Henry assembled them at London, and delivered to them a speech, in which, after having given a hideous representation of Robert's person, he added:—"As for me, I am truly a mild king, modest and pacific; I will preserve to you, and diligently guard your ancient liberties, which I have before sworn to maintain; I will listen with patience to your wise suggestions, and will govern you justly after the example of the best princes. If you desire it, I will confirm this promise by a written charter, and I will swear afresh to observe inviolably all the laws of the holy king Edward," &c. &c.

These promises, made in a moment of danger, were always forgotten as soon as ever the danger had disappeared. During his entire reign, Henry continually violated the charter to which he had bound himself by oath, both as regards matters relating to feudal dependence, and in the levying of imposts. According to the historians, he levied each year a tax of twelve pence on every hide of land, a tax which was probably identical with the *danegeld*.

Stephen, Henry's successor, granted charters to his subjects as Henry had done, and these charters were also the result of usurpation. He published two;

the first only confirmed the liberties granted by Henry I., and the laws of Edward the Confessor. The second is remarkable as containing a promise made by Stephen to reform the abuses and exactions of his sheriffs. At this period public offices were farmed, and those who filled them, seeking to gain all the advantages possible from them, were far more oppressive on their own account than on account of the king. Accordingly it was no difficult matter to appeal to the king against his own officers. Such a mode of appeal, however, indicates that legal and regular guarantees were unrecognized and but little thought of. The barons however began to procure them, by force. They obtained from the king permission to fortify their castles and put themselves in a state of defence. And the clergy on their part, while taking the oath of fidelity, attached to it a condition that they should be released from its obligation as soon as the king should trespass on ecclesiastical liberties.

The charter granted by Henry II., about the year 1154, still expresses nothing more than a recognition of rights; it does not contain any new promise, or any concession of guarantees. The reign of this prince, I need hardly remind you, was entirely occupied with his disputes with the clergy, with the revolts of his sons, and with his conquests, both on the Continent and in Ireland. No important differences were brought into discussion between him and his barons; no progress in existing institutions is visible, and we may say that the reign of Henry II., considered from this point of view, was orderly and stationary.

If, however, the king, so far as his relations to his barons were concerned, obtained an almost uninterrupted submission, and caused the demolition of most of those fortified castles which had been constructed during the preceding reign, the towns on the other hand, and especially the city of London, increased in strength and importance, and the aristocracy became every day more compact by means of the fusion of the Normans and the English, a fusion which was almost completed during this reign, at least among the upper classes.

The fact of this period which bears most importantly upon the subject which we have under consideration, is the substitution of the *escuage* for the personal service of the vassals. It is under the reign of Henry II. that we find this impost collected for the first time, at least in the form of a general measure. The establishment and limitations of the *escuage* became soon the principal object of contention between the king and his barons. The use which the kings came to make of the resources derived from this impost was fatal to them, for they employed it in order to keep up armies of foreign mercenaries, especially Brabanters; and by these measures, they gave a new motive to the English barons to coalesce. The expulsion of foreign soldiers became at length one of the continually recurring demands of the barons.

Henry II. towards the close of his reign, imposed by his own authority a tax of one sixth on all moveable property. He abandoned the *danegeld*.

The reign of Richard, which was entirely occupied with his brilliant but unfortunate expeditions, offers nothing especially illustrative of the history of institutions. The absence of the king and the weakness of the royal power supplied the feudal aristocracy with opportunities for extending their importance; but they did not at that time take advantage of their superiority to procure a recognition of their rights—not until the reign of John did the struggle become violent and the victory decisive.

LECTURE 7

Charter of John, or the Great Charter (1215). ⁓ Three epochs in John's reign. ⁓ Formation of a coalition among the barons. ⁓ Civil war. ⁓ Conference at Runnymead. ⁓ Concession of the Great Charter. ⁓ Analysis of this Charter. ⁓ Its stipulations refer to national rights as well as to those of the barons. ⁓ John petitions and obtains from Innocent III. a bull to reverse the Great Charter. ⁓ Resistance of the English clergy. ⁓ Recommencement of the civil war. (October 1215). ⁓ Louis of France, son of Philip Augustus, is appealed to by the barons. ⁓ Death of John. (October 1216).

Dᴜʀɪɴɢ King Richard's absence, the administration of the kingdom had fallen into the hands of the barons: the feudal aristocracy had begun again to interfere directly in the government, both by way of encroachment and of resistance. Still, the acts of the barons had no longer the same character which they possessed under the preceding reigns; they no longer offered an open resistance; they did not demand any new charters; they did not petition for the observance of former ones: but they silently collected their forces in anticipation of a struggle which was to be decisive. We find them submitting to the exactions which Richard imposed on all classes of society, both for his crusade and for his ransom. Nevertheless, the old maxims as to the necessity of obtaining the consent of the barons to every extraordinary imposition, had revived with new vigour. This right of giving consent to tributes was vindicated with an increasingly determined firmness; and in the first assembly, which Richard held at Nottingham after his return from the East, he was unable to establish an impost of two shillings on every hide of land until he had obtained the consent of his barons. Already every tribute that was levied on the sole authority of the king had begun to stir up a spirit of resistance. This resistance declared itself as soon as John ascended the throne, and the opposition which had been preparing during the reign of Richard then started into prominence.

The reign of John may be divided into three epochs: from 1199 till 1206, he was occupied with his quarrels with the king of France, and with the struggle which arose from the refusal of the barons to second him in his continental enterprises. From 1206 to 1213, John was occupied by his disputes with the Pope and the clergy. Lastly, from the year 1213 to the close of his reign, his position with reference to the barons and the clergy became more and more hostile; it revealed to him their power and his own feebleness; and constantly succumbing before them, we see him yielding one point after another to the clergy and barons, who were always united in their attacks upon him, until at length he granted that celebrated charta usually called Magna Charta, which is a lasting monument of John's defeat and the abiding basis of the English constitution.

John was not the lawful heir to the crown; it belonged to his nephew, Arthur, Duke of Bretagne, whose rights were further confirmed by a testament of Richard. Nevertheless, by his largesses and his yielding disposition, John found no difficulty in usurping the throne of England. The opposition was stronger in his continental possessions; the feudal ideas there prevailing favoured the system of representation, and the people were more disposed to recognize the claims of a son than those of a brother. Anjou, Poitou, Maine and Touraine declared for Arthur. In 1201 (others say in 1204) John demanded of the barons, whom he had assembled at Oxford, that they should assist him in the war which he purposed carrying on in France. They required, as the price of their assistance, that the king should promise to restore to them their liberties and privileges. John, without having granted anything to them, succeeded in winning over one after another, until he had obtained from each individually what had been refused to him by all when assembled. Nevertheless, this opposition showed that the coalition among the barons had taken shape and consistence.

John, who had as yet done nothing to deserve that his usurpation should be overlooked, rendered himself odious by an imprudent divorce, and by vexatious indignities. He introduced into his retinue, bullies, whom he called champions of royalty; and he obliged the discontented barons to enter into the lists with them, and to settle, by these pretended judicial combats, their disputes with the crown. At length, his exactions, his tyrannical proceedings, and above all, the murder of Arthur, whom he is said to have assassinated with his own hand, excited against him an almost general rising. Abandoned by his barons, driven from Normandy, Anjou, Maine, Touraine, and a part of Poitou, John, instead of conciliating the minds of his people, only acted in such a manner as to alienate them more and more, and only defended himself by rendering himself more odious. A new *escuage* of two marks and a half for every knight's fief was extorted from the barons. John had, therefore, to endure a new refusal when he asked them a second time to follow him to the Continent. In vain was it that he employed those means which had before succeeded; he was obliged to yield, and to allow Philip Augustus to take possession of Normandy, and reunite it to the crown of France.

It was not enough for John that he had entered into hostilities with the lay aristocracy; he still further made himself inimical to the clergy. On the death of the Archbishop of Canterbury, the Augustin monks had arrogated to themselves the right of appointing his successor without the consent of the king. John, nettled by this invasion of his prerogatives, united with the bishops, who also protested against an election in which they had taken no part, and in concert with them, nominated the Bishop of Norwich to the vacant see. Upon this, Innocent III. interfered in the dispute; but without confirming either of the two elections, he ordered the English clergy to choose Cardinal Stephen Langton. The king, enraged against the Court of Rome, drove all the monks from Canterbury, and made himself master of their revenues. Accordingly, the Pope excommunicated the monarch, placed the whole kingdom under his ban, and released his subjects from the oath of fidelity which they had sworn to John. Moreover, he charged Philip Augustus to execute his decrees, and offered to him the crown of England. Philip eagerly accepted the present, while John, frightened by the double danger which pressed upon him, demanded, but in vain, assistance from his barons; he had acted unjustly towards them, and now he found them indifferent to his misfortunes. At last, stripped of all resources and left without hope, he sought safety in submission, and saved himself by means of base servility: he declared himself a vassal of the pope, and engaged to pay him annually a tribute of a thousand marks.

After John had thus ransomed his crown, he soon endangered it again by renewed acts of imprudence; his base tyranny, and his criminal attempts on the wife of Eustace de Vesci, roused the barons against him, and their opposition was directed and stimulated by the primate Langton.

It is not to be wondered at that the feudal aristocracy should act under the guidance of an ecclesiastic; the two orders made common cause, and this coalition, which preceding kings had always endeavoured to prevent, was one of the effects of John's odious and absurd conduct. He forgot that the royal power could only maintain itself so long as the power of the clergy and that of the barons balanced one another; when they united, he was obliged to succumb. Their union was the result of John's base submission to the Holy See; the English clergy, tired of the despotism of Rome, and regretting the loss of their privileges, openly embraced the cause of national liberty.

Such was the pervading feeling, when (August 25, 1213) an assembly of the barons was convened at London. In one of their meetings, Cardinal Langton informed them that he had found a copy of the charter of Henry I., which was then entirely forgotten; this charter was read to the assembly, and received with enthusiasm. Another meeting was held at Saint Edmundsbury (November 20, 1214), and there each baron, laying his hand upon the altar, took an oath that he would use his efforts to force the king to restore in full vigour the charter of

Henry I. They soon presented themselves at London in arms, and on January 5, 1215, they demanded from John, in a formal and positive way, the renewal of this charter, as well as of the laws of Edward the Confessor. John, terrified by their firmness, requested that some leisure might be granted to him in order to think over these demands, and accordingly his answer was deferred till Easter. During this interval, he endeavoured to introduce division among his enemies, and in the first place, wishing to conciliate the clergy, he granted them by a charter the liberty of electing their own bishops and abbots, and sent William de Mauclerc to Rome to complain of the audacity of the barons. They too despatched Eustace de Vesci to Rome, to represent to the pontiff the justice and sacredness of their cause. This embassy, however, failed in its object; the Pope condemned the barons: but they were not to be intimidated from their purposes, and John, determining to make another effort in order to secure the support of the church, took the cross on the 2nd of February, 1215, and made a vow to lead an army into Palestine.

The respite, however, which the barons had granted to the king came to an end, and they met again at Stamford in Lincolnshire, on the 19th of April, 1215, being followed by nearly two thousand knights in arms. The king asked them what their claims were; they made at Stamford the same answer as they had made in London, and presented the charter which they had sworn to establish. "And why do they not demand my crown also?" exclaimed John in his fury; "by God's teeth, I will not grant them liberties which will make me a slave." This answer was taken as a declaration of war, and on the 5th of May following, the barons met at Wallingford, solemnly renounced their oath of allegiance, and at the same time named Robert Fitz-Walter general of the "army of God and of Holy Church."

War was declared: in vain did the Pope address letters to the barons, in which he commanded them to desist from their enterprise; the hostilities which had been commenced only continued with greater vigour, and on the 24th of May, the triumphant barons took possession of London with the consent of the citizens. John left the city and retired to Odiham, in the county of Hampshire, with no other escort than seven knights. From his retreat he attempted, without success, to enter into negociations; he proposed the intervention of the Pope, but this was also refused: baffled in all his attempts, he was at length necessitated to acquiesce in the law which had been forcibly imposed on him.

On the 13th of June, a conference was opened in the plain called Runnymead, between Windsor and Staines. The two parties had separate encampments, as declared enemies; after some trifling debates, the king at first adopted the preliminary articles, and four days after, on the 19th of June, 1215, he made the grant of the famous act known by the name of the Great Charter—Magna Charta.

This charter, the most complete and important that had yet appeared, may be divided into three distinct parts; one referring to the interests of the clergy, another regulating those of the nobility, and the third, those belonging to the people. This methodical division is not taken from the order in which the articles of the actual charter are distributed, but I have here adopted it in order to render my account of it more natural and distinct.

The Great Charter refers but little to ecclesiastical interests, since they had been settled by the charter already granted to the clergy. All that was therefore required was that this should be confirmed. This accordingly is done in the first article, which grants a general confirmation to all ecclesiastical immunities and privileges.

The privileges of the laity, on the other hand, were more uncertain, and more strongly contested; it was therefore necessary that they should be minutely investigated and separately conceded. The Great Charter is almost entirely devoted to the settlement of the rights, and the confirmation of the privileges, claimed by the laity.

In the first place, it determines with precision what had been obscure and ambiguous in the feudal laws; and it fixes the amount of relief which the immediate or indirect inheritors of fiefs should pay. Hitherto this relief had been indeterminate. (Arts. 2 to 3.)

Then follow the precautions prescribed respecting the marriage of feudal wards, and those which regard the widows and children of vassals. (Arts. 6 to 8.)

The right and mode of collecting aids and escuages, are regulated by the two following articles:

> Art. 12. That no escuage or extraordinary aid shall be imposed in our kingdom, except by the national council of our kingdom, unless it be to ransom our person, to equip our eldest son as a knight, and to marry our eldest daughter: and for these last cases only a reasonable amount of aid shall be demanded, &c.

> Art. 14. In order to hold the national council of the kingdom, for the purpose of imposing any other aid than for the three cases heretofore mentioned, or to impose an escuage, we will call together the archbishops, bishops, abbots, earls and great barons, individually and by letters from ourself; and we will assemble together by means of our viscounts and bailiffs, all those who are directly dependent upon us. The great convocation shall be made on a fixed day, namely, at intervals not greater than forty days, and in an appointed place; and in the letters of convocation we will expound the reason of such convocation; and the convocation thus made, the business shall be transacted on the day appointed, by the council consisting of those who are present, although all those who have been summoned may not have arrived.

This charter is the first document in which we find a distinction established between the greater and lesser barons, and the higher and lower clergy; an important fact, since it may perhaps be regarded as the original source of the separation between the two Houses of Parliament.

Lastly, several articles have for their object to limit the rights of the king on the lands of his tenants, to fix the amount of fine imposed on beneficiaries according to the gravity of their offence, to determine the length of time during which lands should remain sequestrated on account of felony; in one word, to give to the barons greater independence and security than they had ever before enjoyed.

These are the principal enactments of the Great Charter in favour of the nobility; up to this point, we find only sanctions given to particular privileges, we have only met with that which favours the interests of certain classes in society. But it contains also clauses of wider and more general application; it has for its object also the interests of the nation as a whole.

First of all, almost all the immunities granted to the barons with respect to the king, the vassals obtained with respect to their lords. These were not allowed from this time to collect aids and escuages on their lands, except in the same cases and in the same manner as the king. (Art. 15.)

Justice was for the future to be administered in a fixed and uniform manner; the following are the articles in which this important provision is expressed:

> Art. 17. The court of common pleas shall not follow our court (*curia*), but shall be held in a fixed place.
>
> Art. 18. We, or if we are absent from the kingdom, our chief justiciary, shall send four times a year into each county two judges, who, with four knights, chosen by each county, shall hold the assizes at the time and place appointed in the said county.
>
> Art. 39. No freeman shall be arrested or imprisoned, or dispossessed of his tenement, or outlawed, or exiled, or in anywise proceeded against; we will not place or cause to be placed hands upon him, unless by the *legal judgment of his peers or by the law of the land.*
>
> Art. 40. *Justice shall not be sold, refused, or delayed to any one.*

Moreover, the king promises to appoint only capable and upright judges (Art. 41); to forbid their condemning any person whatever, without having previously heard the witnesses (Art. 38); to reinstate every man who had been dispossessed without legal judgment (Art. 32); to repair the injuries committed under Henry II., and Richard I. (Art. 53); to put a stop to the imposts for the construction of bridges (Art. 23); and to interdict annoyances of all kinds inflicted either on townsmen, merchants, or villeins (Arts. 20, 26, 28, 30, 31).

He grants and assures to the city of London, as well as to all other cities, boroughs, towns, and harbours, the possession of their ancient customs and liberties (Art. 13).

Lastly, the 41st Article provides that all merchants shall have full and free liberty of entering England, of leaving it, of remaining there, and of travelling there by land and by water, to buy and to sell without being subject to any oppression (*male tolta*) according to the ancient and common usages, &c.

These, then, are the concessions made to promote the interests of all.

It is not, however, enough that rights should be recognized and promises made; it is further necessary that these rights should be respected, and that these promises should be fulfilled. The 61st and last article of the Great Charter is intended to provide this guarantee. It is there said that the barons shall elect twenty-five barons by their own free choice, charged to exercise all vigilance that the provisions of the Charter may be carried into effect; the powers of these twenty-five barons is unlimited: if the king or his agents allow themselves to violate the enactments of the Charter in the smallest particular, the barons will denounce this abuse before the king, and demand that it be instantly checked. If the king do not accede to their demand, the barons shall have the right, forty days after the summons has been issued by them, to prosecute the king, to deprive him of his lands and castles (the safety of his person, of the queen, and of their children, being respected), until the abuse has been reformed to the satisfaction of the barons.

Though such a right was granted, no guarantee was thereby given; it only authorized civil war; it was to perpetuate the struggle indefinitely, and formally to leave the ultimate decision of the question to force. It was still far from being a regularly constituted political guarantee; but the spirit of that age was not capable either of discovering or of comprehending such a guarantee—it could only understand the recognition of its rights. However, the forcible guarantee which the Great Charter established was so far valuable, inasmuch as it centralized the feudal aristocracy by organizing the council of barons.

It has been often said that the Great Charter would not have been supported by the barons had not it not been for its influence on their special interests. This opinion is untenable: how is it possible that at least a third of the articles should have related to promises and guarantees made on behalf of the people, if the aristocracy had only aimed at obtaining that which should benefit themselves? We have only to read the Great Charter in order to be convinced that the rights of all three orders of the nation are equally respected and promoted.

Another question has been raised, as to whether John did or did not grant a special charter relating to forests at the time when he granted the Great Charter. Mathew Paris is the only author who speaks of this charter of forests, and there are several reasons why his authority should in this matter be rejected.

First of all, the preliminary articles of the Great Charter contain nothing on this point; in the second place, Articles 44, 47, and 48 in the Great Charter itself settle whatever relates to forests; and lastly, the king and the Pope, in their correspondence prior to these events, make no allusion to this twofold concession.

When the king had distinctly adopted each article of the Great Charter, the agreement between him and his barons, which had been concluded on the 15th of June, was executed in order to ensure the fulfilment of his engagements. The guarding of the city of London was entrusted to the barons till the 15th of August following, and that of the Tower to the Archbishop of Canterbury.

John dissembled at first, and appeared to submit without any reserve to all the sacrifices which were imposed upon him; but such a mask soon became intolerable to him. After a short time he broke out into complaints and threatenings, and retired in fury to the Isle of Wight. While there, he procured the enrolment of an army of Brabanters in order to regain his power by battle, and despatched a messenger to Rome beseeching for aid against the violence that had been done him. Innocent III., hearing what had occurred, and irritated by the audacity of the barons, whom he called his vassals, annulled the Great Charter, and excommunicated all the barons who had joined in the rebellion.

The king, trusting to this powerful support, threw aside the mask, and retracted all his engagements. But he speedily perceived that those spiritual weapons, which had recently been so potent when opposed to him, were now without value when placed in his own hands. Archbishop Langton refused to pronounce the sentence of excommunication. He was summoned to Rome and suspended, but in vain; the clergy sustained him in his disgrace, and confirmed his refusal. John attempted ineffectually to divide the two orders—whenever he made any preparations for fighting, they became inseparable allies.

John had now no other hope except in the support of his foreign mercenaries; he made one last effort, and in the month of October 1215, war was again enkindled between him and the barons. The attack was unforeseen; the barons being suddenly surprised retreated before the king, who advanced in triumph as far as Rochester Castle, of which he made himself master after an obstinately resisted siege. He made prisoner its governor, William d'Albiney, one of the twenty-five barons appointed to guard the maintenance of the charter, and the most distinguished captain among them: this was an irreparable loss to their party; and from this moment the king met with no regular resistance. His tyranny might now glut itself with vengeance; he let loose his satellites, and the entire kingdom was soon filled with the devastating effects of his rage.

Nevertheless, some barons in the north still resisted him manfully; and the remnants of the coalition combined with them; but feeling themselves too weak, they sought in their turn safety from a foreign ally. The crown of England was offered in their name to Prince Louis, son of Philip Augustus, who there-upon sent an army to attempt the conquest of England.

Louis had scarcely landed when the aspect of affairs entirely changed. John, abandoned by his friends and by his soldiers, lost in a short time all that he had recovered. The entire kingdom fell into the hands of his young rival, and Dover was the only town which remained faithful to John. Prince Louis, how-ever, though he had so far succeeded, did not establish himself on his newly ac-quired throne. The predilection which he invariably manifested for the French nobles could not but be distasteful to the English barons, and the avowals of the Count of Melun, made on his deathbed, had the effect of detaching almost all the nobility of the kingdom from the side of Louis. This noble induced the barons to distrust the king, who, he affirmed, fully intended to dispossess all of them, and to distribute their lands among his favourites and natural subjects. This disclosure, whether it was true or false, had a powerful effect on the minds of the barons, and most of them renewed their allegiance to their former king.

John had now set his army on foot, and fortune seemed to promise him new successes, when death surprised him on the 17th of October, 1216. This event was more fatal to Louis than a lost battle could have been. The hatred of the English to their king died with him—they hastened to rally round his young son—a general defection quickly ruined the already tottering cause of the French prince, and after he had continued this useless struggle for a short time, he abandoned a throne for the offer of which he was indebted merely to the accidental distress of the English barons, and which he would never have been able to secure by the mere force of his arms.

LECTURE 8

Charters of Henry III. ⁓ *First Charter of Henry III. (November 1216).* ⁓ *Louis of France renounces his title to the Crown, and leaves England.* ⁓ *Second Charter of Henry III. (1217).* ⁓ *Forest Charter granted by Henry III. (1217).* ⁓ *Confirmation of Charters (1225).* ⁓ *Revocation of Charters (1227).* ⁓ *New confirmation of Charters (1237).* ⁓ *Continual violation of Charters.* ⁓ *Civil war.* ⁓ *Renewal of Charters (1264).* ⁓ *New confirmation of Charters (1267).* ⁓ *Death of Henry III. (November 16, 1272).*

HITHERTO we have only seen, in the charters, recognitions of rights more or less open and complete; they are transactions between two rival powers, one of whom gives promises while the other establishes rights; but there is no power to guarantee that these promises shall be faithfully kept and these rights duly regarded. The only curb placed on royalty is the prospect of a civil war that is always threatening to break out—a remedy which is incompatible with order and stability, two elements which are indispensable to a free government.

Under the reign of Henry III., the feeling began to be entertained that civil war is an evil guarantee; and other means of preventing the violation of oaths were sought and dimly apprehended. The charters which were obtained in this reign have still as their chief aim the obtaining of new concessions and promises; but efforts towards the formation of guarantees are also apparent, and we may now trace the first attempts after a legal and efficient constitution.

This reign must be regarded under the two aspects which have been indicated. Our object at present being only to follow the history of English Charters, we shall examine the facts of this period only under the first point of view: when we come to treat of the formation of the Parliament, we shall search there for the first attempts after an organized constitution.

Henry, who was but a child when his father died, found an able protector in William, Earl of Pembroke, Marshal of England, who was then commander of the royal armies. Pembroke had been a faithful servant to King John, and transferred to the son that friendship which he had given to the father. His only thought was that Henry should succeed to the throne, and accordingly the ceremony of coronation was performed at Gloucester, on the 28th of October, 1216. Afterwards, in a council of barons assembled at Bristol, on the 11th of November, he assumed the title of Regent, and in order to render the cause of the young king popular he granted a new charter in his—the king's—name. This charter corresponded, with the exception of a few modifications, to that given by King John. All the articles are omitted which refer to the establishment of *escuages,* to the liberty of entering and leaving the kingdom, to the preservation of forests and dykes, and to the customs of the counties; moreover, the article was suppressed which granted the right of resistance by armed force in case the king should violate his promises. These suppressions were not, however, definitely concluded; it is stated in the charter that "the prelates and lords have determined that these things shall remain open, until they have more fully deliberated concerning them."*[1]

We see by this that the barons at that time showed themselves less exacting than they had been during John's reign, or rather that they no longer stipulated for any other interests than those which personally affected themselves, neglecting those belonging to other classes in the nation.

However this may be, this new charter produced the effect which Pembroke had desired; it finally broke up the party which had been formed in favour of Prince Louis of France, and strengthened that of King Henry. The French, however, had still some adherents left; the city of London especially persisted, with an obstinate determination, in remaining faithful to them. But after numerous reverses, they could hold out no longer; a treaty was concluded between the two monarchs on the 11th of September, 1217; Louis abandoned all pretensions to the crown, left England with the remnant of his party, and Henry remained in quiet possession of the sovereignty.

The retreat of the French re-established harmony in the kingdom, but in order to render the concord more certain and immediate two more charters

---

* The original of this charter still exists in the archives of Durham Cathedral.

1. These passages explain Guizot's opposition to Rousseau's ideas on liberty, representation, sovereignty, and social contract. It is worth noting that Guizot's critique of Rousseau differed, for example, from Constant's. If the latter criticized the author of the *Social Contract* for advocating a flawed theory of (absolute) sovereignty that threatened individual freedom, Guizot loathed Rousseau's "individualism," which he believed to be "destructive not only of all government, but also of all society" (*HORG*, p. 288). Unlike Rousseau, Guizot believed that popular sovereignty might lead to despotism and anarchy instead of liberty. Reason, he argued, is superior to individual will; that is why, for Guizot, Rousseau's famous definition of liberty as obedience to the laws we have prescribed to ourselves was mistaken. For a comprehensive discussion of the legacy of Rousseau, see Jean Roussel, *Jean-Jacques Rousseau en France après la Révolution* (*Jean-Jacques Rousseau in Post-revolutionary France*) (Paris: Armand Collin, 1972).

were granted. One was similar to the preceding; only one remarkable modification is to be found, namely the decision that the escuage should be levied as in the time of Henry II. The other is known under the name of the Charta de Foresta, being the same that has been erroneously attributed to King John: it has only one special aim, and contains nothing but a series of regulations as to the extent and limits of the forests belonging either to the nobility or to the crown.

These charters were perpetually violated by the agents of power. For several years these infractions did not occasion more than partial complaints, but at length, in the year 1223, the protestation became general and urgent. The council of barons was summoned to London, where they demanded a new confirmation of the charters. One of the councillors of the regency, William de Briwere, ventured to oppose, saying that "all these liberties had been extorted from the king;" but the Archbishop of Canterbury smartly reproved him, telling him that if he loved the king, he at all events would not venture to trouble the kingdom. The young king promised that the charters should be henceforth observed, and twelve knights were appointed in each county, who should enquire what were, according to ancient usages, the rights of the king and the liberties of his subjects.

Still, new anxieties soon excited new protestations. Since the preceding reign the barons had held in trust most of the royal castles and domains, and this was the principal guarantee they had that their treaties should be observed. Suddenly their possession of this guarantee was threatened: a bull of Pope Honorius III., which declared Henry to be of age when he was seventeen years old, ordered at the same time that all those who had royal domains in their hands should restore them to the king. This bull occasioned many suspicions as to Henry's intentions; fears began to be entertained lest, having obtained his majority, he should revoke the two charters to which he had sworn during his minority. The king and his advisers perceived the necessity of meeting this disturbed state of feeling, and on the 11th of February, 1225, the king granted of his own accord a new confirmation of the charters. As an acknowledgment of this they granted him a fifteenth part of all the moveable property of the kingdom as a subsidy.

But this mutual accommodation did not last long. At the end of two years, Henry, having obtained his true majority, revoked all the charters, under the pretext that they had been granted when he was not in the free possession of his body and of his seal; "*cum nec sui corporis nec sigilli aliquam potestatem habuerit.*"

This revocation excited the most active discontent. The indignant barons turned their rage against the man whom the public voice accused as the author of these proceedings. This was Hubert de Burgh, the grand justiciary and intimate counsellor of Henry. This minister was from that time exposed to the most violent attacks, and did not cease to be persecuted by the rage of his opponents till at length, in 1232, the king yielded to the storm, withdrew his favour from the obnoxious minister, and exiled him from the court.

The murmurs of the barons were hardly appeased when Henry seemed as if desirous of exciting them afresh, by again surrounding himself with men who were hated by his subjects. This was a foreigner, a Poitevin, Peter des Roches, Bishop of Winchester, who became the king's favourite on the disgrace of Hubert de Burgh. From that time, only foreigners were trusted with places and favours by the prince. Not content with draining the coffers of the State, they burdened the people with exactions—their insolence was perfectly unbridled. When the laws of England were appealed to against them, "we are not English," they said, "we do not know what is the purport of these laws." The indignant barons urgently demanded justice, and in the year 1234, two years after the disgrace of Hubert de Burgh, the king found himself compelled to abandon Peter des Roches and to dismiss the foreigners from his court. But shortly after, on his marriage with Eleanor, daughter of the Count of Provence, the Provençals took the place of the Poitevins, and in their turn drew on themselves the hatred of the English barons.

The irritation was general, when the king, who was in want of money, assembled the barons at Westminster, in the month of January, 1237, in order to demand of them a subsidy. The barons answered him with a refusal and with menaces. Henry, alarmed at this, had recourse to a remedy which had not yet lost its efficiency, namely, a new confirmation of the charters. Hardly was it granted before he obtained a subsidy of a thirtieth part of all moveable property.

But his prodigality soon dissipated these feeble resources; again was he obliged to resort to arbitrary and tyrannical means in order to provide himself with money—to exactions, to forced loans, a new kind of impost which is then for the first time to be met with in English history. It is remarkable, however, that Henry never dared to levy any general tribute on the nation on his own personal responsibility. Imposts that were really public were never collected except under the professed sanction of a council of the barons, and after the king had purchased their good will by a new confirmation of the charters.

On the 13th of May, 1253, a sentence of excommunication was solemnly pronounced against any person who should infringe the royal charters; and at the close of the ceremony the prelates threw down their extinguished but smoking tapers, exclaiming, "May the soul of every one who incurs this sentence so stink and be extinguished in hell!" And the king added, "So help me God! I will keep these charters inviolate, as I am a man, as I am a Christian, as I am a knight, and as I am a king crowned and anointed!"

Again were the charters violated, and at length it was seen that their repeated renewals were vain—civil war was therefore declared. The Earl of Leicester, at the head of a party of barons, took up arms, at first with the intention of effectually limiting, but afterwards of entirely usurping the royal authority. This rebellion had now no longer for its aim to obtain the renewal of charters, it tended also to found practical guarantees of recognized rights. Of these I shall speak more in detail when I come to consider the formation of the Parliament. At present I will content myself with observing that the result of the insurrection headed by the Earl of Leicester was a general renewal of the charters, granted on the 14th of March, 1264—a kind of treaty of peace between the king and the barons, the king's object being to obtain from them the enlargement of Prince Edward, whom they retained as a hostage.

At length, three years after, on the 18th of November, 1267, some time before the departure of Prince Edward for Palestine, the king once more confirmed the charters in the Parliament assembled at Marlborough. This confirmation was the last granted by Henry III.; he died five years afterwards, on the 16th of November, 1272, having passed a long reign in making promises to be afterwards violated, renewed, retracted, and then renewed again.

LECTURE 9

Conclusion of the history of Charters under the reign of Edward I. ⌒
Political conflict follows civil war. ⌒ *The king frequently violates the
charters, especially in the matter of imposts.* ⌒ *The barons resist energetically.* ⌒ *Edward gives a definitive confirmation to the charters
(1298–1301).* ⌒ *A bull of Clement V., solicited by Edward I., annuls the
charters.* ⌒ *Its failure.* ⌒ *Death of Edward I. (July 7, 1307).*

DURING the two preceding reigns the struggle between the feudal aristocracy
and the royal power has been really a civil war. Under Edward I. the struggle
continued, but the civil war ceased. The barons did not protest in favour of their
liberty with any less resolute determination than they had hitherto manifested,
nor did the king defend his prerogatives less vigorously, but neither party appealed to arms. This is the general history of important struggles; they are begun by a trial of strength between the two contending parties, and when the
problem of material forces has been resolved, the struggle changes its direction
and its theatre; it becomes concentrated into an assembly, and the victorious
party has no longer any other aim than to legalize the victory already gained,
and thus add a constitutional validity to a material victory. Parliamentary debates follow civil war. When the parliamentary debates have lasted through a
certain number of years, and have received the sanction of time, the struggle
may be regarded as terminated. To this stage had matters arrived in the reign of
Edward I.; the resistance which was shewn during his reign only displayed itself in Parliament; and, when it had lasted for thirty years, the rights which it
had tended to consecrate were for ever recognized and tolerably respected.

At the time of Henry's death, his son Edward was in Palestine; notwithstanding his absence, however, he was proclaimed king without any opposition.
The capacity which he had displayed in the troubles of the kingdom, and the
moderation which he had often shewn, had gained for him general favour.
Upon his return to England, he justified the expectations which had been
formed concerning him; many abuses were reformed, and a better order was introduced into the administration of justice.

I shall pass rapidly over the first twenty-four years of this reign. They were occupied with the conquest of Wales, and with Edward's wars in Scotland, which were incessantly renewed by the insurrections of the Scotch. During all this time, although we hear of very frequent assemblies of Parliament, we scarcely hear anything even of the charters. The administration of the kingdom, which was vigorous and fair, excited few complaints, and public attention was absorbed by the expeditions and victories of the monarch.

Nevertheless the necessity of frequently raising subsidies, in order to keep up his numerous armies, soon obliged Edward to adopt violent and arbitrary measures. He limited the quantity of wool which might be exported, and placed on every sack of wool, that was exported, a duty of forty shillings, that is to say, more than a third of its value; all the rest of the wool and hides, that were ready for shipping, were confiscated to the service of the king. He demanded of each sheriff two thousand quarters of wheat, and as many of oats, authorising them to take the required wheat or oats wherever they could lay their hands upon them; besides which he caused a large quantity of cattle to be seized. Lastly, showing no regard for feudal right, he imposed on every landed proprietor, having a larger revenue than twenty pounds sterling, whatever might be the nature of his domains, the obligation to attend him in the war which he was about to prosecute in France.

The dissatisfaction among the people and barons was general, and it was soon redoubled, in consequence of a fraud to which Edward did not hesitate to resort in raising a subsidy, which had been granted to him by the Parliament, held at Saint Edmundsbury in the preceding year (1296). Instead of contenting himself with the eighth* of the moveable property, which had been granted to him, he assumed that the impost was much larger, and obliged his subjects to pay it.

In the midst of the excitement caused by these measures, Edward convoked his barons at Salisbury to arrange with them for the departure and march of his armies. He had intended to send one of his armies to Gascony, and to lead the other into Flanders, himself taking the command of the latter in person, while the former was to march under the direction of Humphrey Bohun, Earl of Hereford, and of Roger Bigod, Earl of Norfolk, the one the Constable, the other the Lord Marshal of England. These two men, who were vigorous champions of the national cause, refused to accept the mission which was offered to them. The object of their refusal was to compel the king to purchase their com-

---

* An eighth, a tenth, &c. was a money tax levied on counties, cities, boroughs, or other towns, and so called because it was the eighth, tenth, &c. of the sum at which these counties, towns, &c. had been anciently valued under the reign of William I. Thus each town knew what it had to contribute. The valuations were contained in the Doomsday Book. (*Parliam. Hist.*, vol. i. p. 83.)

pliance by a renewed promise to confirm the charters, a promise which he had already made, but which he seemed in no haste to carry out. When Edward gave them the order to repair to Gascony, they answered that they were ready to follow him to Flanders, but that the character of their offices would not allow them to separate themselves from his person. "You shall go," said the king, "whether I go with you or not." Hereford replied that he would not go; upon which Edward exclaimed, "By the everlasting God, sir earl, you shall either go or hang." "By the everlasting God, sir king," replied Hereford, coolly, "I will neither go nor hang." Edward did not feel himself sufficiently powerful to punish this haughty reply; and, fearing lest he should find the same spirit of resistance in all the barons, he abandoned his intention of sending an army into Gascony. The two earls quitted Salisbury with their retinue, and the king, after he had placed their offices in the hands of two other lords, prepared to embark for Flanders.

But before his departure, on the 12th of August, 1297, he addressed to all the sheriffs of the kingdom a singular kind of manifesto, one which was, perhaps, unique at that period, which he intended should be read before the assembled people. In it the king explained the causes of his quarrel with the two earls, excused the exactions he had made by pleading the necessities of war, and desired his subjects to maintain peace and order. This proclamation, or, perhaps, rather this appeal to the public, shews how greatly power already felt itself dependent upon the support of opinion, and constrained in some way to acknowledge a responsibility to it.

To this apology for his conduct, which the king put forth, the Earls of Norfolk and Hereford replied by another manifesto, which was presented to the king at Winchelsea, in which they recounted all the public wrongs and demanded redress. Edward answered that his council was dispersed, and that he could not attend to these protests till his return, and he accordingly went on his expedition, leaving his son regent of the kingdom.

Upon this the two earls, after having published their manifesto and the king's reply to it, presented themselves before the treasurers and barons of the exchequer, and forbade them, as they would dread to excite a civil war, to collect, for the king, the tribute of one-eighth, which had been granted by the Parliament at Saint Edmundsbury, affirming that the granting of it had been illegal.

In order to bring these differences to a close, the prince-regent assembled a Parliament in London, on the 10th of October, 1297. The two earls were invited to take their place in the assembly, and came escorted by five hundred horse and a body of infantry, and would not consent to enter London until they had obtained permission to place a guard at each gate. They demanded a general confirmation of the charters, and, moreover, asked that several additions should be made to them. The prince-regent subscribed to all their demands, and the act of confirmation signed by him was immediately sent to the king, who was at Ghent. Edward, after he had taken three days to consider the matter, sanctioned the confirmation,* and granted an amnesty to the two earls, who, satisfied with this exhibition of generosity on the part of the king, went, subsequently, to Scotland to assist him in the war which he was carrying on there.

When Edward returned again to England, the barons demanded that he, in his own person, should confirm the charters which had been granted to them. The king evaded these demands, and retired to Windsor. Thither the barons followed him to renew their importunities and their complaints. The king excused himself on the ground of ill-health, and told them to return to London, where he would send them an answer. This answer was a new confirmation of the charters, but contained one restrictive clause: *salvo jure coronae nostrae.*[1] At the public reading of the charter, which was made at St. Paul's Cathedral, the assembly hearing how all their rights were definitely confirmed in it, made the most lively manifestations of joy; but hardly had the reserve clause been pronounced, when violent murmurs were raised on all sides; the people immediately left the church, and the angry barons retired to their domains, resolved once more to appeal to force.

Edward perceived that he had raised a storm of opinion against him, and, after innumerable delays and evasions, and complaining haughtily that he was too closely pressed, he, at length, decided upon convoking a Parliament on the 6th of March, 1300, and confirmed without any restriction all the concessions which he had already made; he even added new guarantees, which were contained in articles called *articuli super chartas.* The chief provisions contained in these additions consist in a regulation that the charters should be publicly read in the county courts four times every year, and that there should be elected in each county court, from among the knights of the court, three justices, sworn to receive all complaints of infractions of the charters, and to pronounce penalties against the offenders.

Lastly, in the following year, 1301, at a Parliament held at Lincoln, Edward, after having received its approval to a new limitation of the forests, which had been for a long time demanded and at length concluded, yet once more confirmed the charters.

From the time when this charter of confirmation was granted, the rights which it proclaimed were definitively recognized. The open and exterior struggle ceased at this period, but the secret and concealed did not. Edward en-

---

* A copy of this charter will be found, in a note, at the end of this lecture. It is of all others the most explicit in favour of public liberties. It was given at Ghent, Nov. 5, 1297; the original is preserved in the British Museum.

1. With the law of our crown preserved.

dured impatiently the yoke which he had taken upon himself, and endeavoured to release himself from it. He did not, however, dare to raise the mask, but concealed all his efforts. Towards the close of the year 1304, he petitioned Pope Clement V. to release him from his oaths. The pontiff complied with his wishes, and by a bull, dated January 5, 1305, declared that all the promises and concessions made by Edward were *abrogated, null and void.*[*]

This prince did not dare, as John had formerly done, to take advantage of this bull, and he therefore kept it quite secret; but he still had recourse to secret manoeuvres. He began by a series of vile persecutions of those who had headed the confederation of the barons, and especially of the Earl of Norfolk and the Archbishop of Canterbury. These two men, though they were in former years so boldly courageous, now yielded with a feebleness that can only be excused by their great age. But it was too late; the authority of the king could no longer effect anything against the charters, and the feebleness even of their former defenders could not add to the power of royalty. Death soon after put a stop to all Edward's efforts to carry out the designs he had formed: it surprised him suddenly while he was in Scotland, on the 7th of July, 1307. From that period the charters, notwithstanding all attacks made upon them, have remained as the immoveable basis of public right in England.

STATUTE ISSUED BY EDWARD I., IN CONFIRMATION OF THE CHARTERS. NOVEMBER 5, 1297

Edward, by the grace of God, King of England, Lord of Ireland, and Duke of Guyan, to all those that these present letters shall hear or see, greeting. Know ye that we, to the honour of God and of Holy Church, and to the profit of our realm, have granted that, for us and for our heirs, the charter of liberties and the charter of the forest, which were made by common consent of all the realm, in the time of King Henry our father, shall be kept in every point without breach. And we will that the same charters shall be sent under our seal, as well to our justices of the forest as to others, and to all sheriffs of shires, and to all our other officers, and to all our cities throughout the realm, together with our writs in the which it shall be contained; that they cause the aforesaid charters to be published, and declare to the people that we have confirmed them in all points; and that our justices, sheriffs, and mayors, and other ministers, which, under us,

[*] A copy of this bull will be found in a note at the end of this lecture.

have the laws of our land to guide, shall allow the said charters, pleaded before them in judgment, in all their points, that is to wit, the Great Charter as the common law, and the charter of the forest for the wealth of our realm.

And we will that if any judgment be given from henceforth contrary to the points or the charters aforesaid by the justices, or by any other our ministers, that hold pleas before them against the points of the charters, it shall be undone and holden for nought.

And we will that the same charters shall be sent, under our seal, to cathedral churches throughout our realm, there to remain, and shall be read before the people two times by the year.

And all archbishops and bishops shall pronounce the sentence of excommunication against all those that by word, deed, or counsel do contrary to the foresaid charters, or that in any point break, or undo them. And that the said curses be twice a year denounced and published, by the prelates aforesaid. And if the same prelates, or any of them, be remiss in the denunciation of the said sentences, the Archbishops of Canterbury and York, for the time being, shall compel and distrain them to the execution of their duties in form aforesaid:

And foresomuch as divers people of our realm are in fear that the aids and tasks which they have given us beforetime towards our wars, and other business, of their own grant and goodwill, howsoever they were made, might turn to a bondage to them and their heirs, because they might be at another time found in the Rolls, and likewise for the prises taken throughout the realm by our ministers, we have granted for us and for our heirs, that we will not draw such aids, tasks, nor prises into a custom, for any thing that hath been done heretofore, be it by Roll or any other precedent that may be found.

Moreover we have granted for us and for our heirs, as well to archbishops, bishops, abbots, priors, and other folk of Holy Church, as also to earls, barons, and all the commonality of the land, that for no business for henceforth we shall take such manner of aids, tasks, or prises, but by the common assent of the realm, and for the common profit thereof, saving the ancient aids and prises due and accustomed.

And foresomuch as the more part of the commonality of this realm find themselves sore grieved with the maletent of wool, that is to wit, a toll of forty shillings for every sack of wool, and have made petition for us to release the same; we at their requests, have clearly released it, and have granted, for us and our heirs, that we shall not take such things without their common consent and goodwill; saving to us and our heirs the custom of wools, skins, and leather, granted before by the commonality aforesaid. In witness of which things we have caused these our letters to be made patents. Witness,

Edward, our son, at London, the 10th day of October, the five and twentieth year of our reign.

And be it remembered that this same charter, in the same terms, word for word, was sealed in Flanders, under the king's great seal, that is to say, at Ghent, the 5th day of November, in the twenty-fifth year of the reign of our aforesaid lord the king, and sent into England.

LETTER OF CLEMENT V. TO EDWARD I

Clement, bishop, servant of God's servants, to our well-beloved son in Jesus Christ, Edward, illustrious king of England, health and apostolic benediction:

The purity of thy loyal devotion, which is and has been uniform and conspicuous in thy unwearied attention to the desires of the Holy See, well deserves that the Holy See itself should remove all that is hostile to thy welfare, should suppress whatever displeases thee, and should ever secure for thee the enjoyment of all good.

We have learnt recently, by an account worthy of credit, that lately, when thou wert in Flanders, and even before thy arrival there, when thy efforts were being used to maintain thy prerogatives against thy enemies and rivals, that then certain magnates and nobles of thy kingdom, and other persons who are hostile to thy authority, taking advantage of the opportunity when thou wert occupied in fighting against those in another kingdom, who were opposed to thy rule, threatened that, unless thou wouldst make certain concessions of a diverse and unjust character, both relating to forest and other rights, which have, from time immemorial, belonged to the crown, and the dignity of thy rank, (which also, previously, they had importunately sought before thy departure from the said kingdom,) they would conspire against thee, would excite the people, and disseminate various scandals:

And that thou, prudently treating their conspiracy, and wishing then to avoid the dangers that were pressing upon thee, didst grant these concessions, more by constraint than with thy free consent:

And that, finally, on thy return to thy kingdom, the wars not having then terminated, the said magnates, and others, through their importunate and presumptuous suggestions, did obtain from thee the renewal of these concessions; and that they have, moreover, extorted royal orders to the effect that in every cathedral church in the kingdom there should be pronounced, twice every year, a sentence of excommunication against those who should violate the said concessions, as is expounded formally and in detail in the said commands, under the authority of the royal seal:

As, therefore, the Holy Apostolic See regards thy kingdom favourably, even above all other kingdoms, and entertains for thee, personally, the most friendly feelings, and recognizes that all these concessions have been made and extorted at the expense of thine honour, and to the detriment of thy royal sovereignty:

So by the apostolic authority, and by our full power, we revoke, annul, and dissolve the said concessions and all their effects, and all that can result from them, as also the sentences of excommunication which have or may be pronounced in order to their observance, either in the said churches or elsewhere, we declare them abolished, null, and without authority; annulling also the orders and letters to which they have given occusion; we decree for thee and for thy successors on the throne of England, that ye neither are nor ever shall be bound to observe them, even although ye may have engaged yourselves so by oath; besides that, as thou hast assured us, at the time when thy coronation was solemnized, thou didst swear to maintain the honours and the prerogatives of thy crown; so that, if even thou hast bound thyself to any penalty on this account, we absolve thee therefrom, as well as from the accusation of perjury if it should be made against thee.

To ensure the execution of our desires, we expressly forbid our venerable brethren, the archbishops, bishops, and others, ecclesiastical as well as secular, who are settled in thy kingdom, to do or attempt anything against the tenor of the present annulment, abrogation, revocation, and abolition, under penalty, as regards the archbishops and bishops, of suspension from their offices and benefices; and, if they persist for one month, under penalty of excommunication, which shall be, for this sole reason, pronounced against them, and all who are accessory to their designs.

We declare beforehand that every attempt against our present decree is null and void.

If, however, there is any right belonging to the inhabitants of the said kingdom, which they possess by virtue of previous letters and concessions so made by thee, we mean not to withdraw these from them.

It shall not be allowed to any one absolutely to violate in any particular, or only to contradict the present act of abrogation, revocation, annulment, and abolition.

If any one dare to allow this in himself let him know that he incurs the indignation of the Almighty, and of the blessed apostles Peter and Paul.—(Rymer, *Acta Publica*, vol. ii., p. 372.)

LECTURE 10

Necessity of inquiring into the political sense of the word representation *at the time when a representative government began to be formed.* ᔔ *Mistaken theories on this subject.* ᔔ *Rousseau's theory, which denies representation and insists on individual sovereignty.* ᔔ *Theories of writers who attempt to reconcile the principle of representation with that of individual sovereignty.* ᔔ *Erroneousness of the idea that the sovereignty belongs to the majority.* ᔔ *True idea of representation.*

WE have studied the primitive institutions of the Anglo-Norman government; we have traced the successive steps in the history of the charters, and of the struggle which was carried on by the barons to secure their confirmation by the royal power; but up to this point we have not seen anything of a representative government. We have, however, now arrived at the point when this government began to appear. Our attention is now to be called to the creation of a Parliament, that is to say, to the birth of a representative system.

As we approach this great historical question, a question in political philosophy presents itself before us:—what is the true and legitimate sense of this word *representation* as applied to the government of a community? It is not for us to pass over this question without noticing it: the history of political institutions is now no longer a bare recital of facts—it must rest on principles; it neither deserves the name nor possesses the authority of science, till it has sounded and placed in clear light the primary foundation in reason, from which the facts which it collects trace their origin. Political history cannot now be otherwise than philosophical; this is demanded by the stage of human culture which the mind of society has reached.

Let us now suppose a representative government, aristocratic or democratic, monarchical or republican, completely established and in action: if any one were to ask a citizen of such a State—supposing him to be a man of good sense but unversed in political speculations—"Why do you elect such a deputy?" he would answer, "Because in the consideration of public affairs, I believe him to be more capable than any other of sustaining the cause to which my opinions, my feelings, my interests, are allied."

Now bring this man before the political theorists who have treated of representation; let his good sense be brought into contact with their systems—truth would soon be perplexed and obscured by the falsities of science.

One learned gentleman would thus address him:—"What have you done? You have supplied yourself with a representative—you are no longer free—you are no longer in truth a citizen of a free State. Liberty means a man's sovereignty over himself, the right to be governed only by his individual will. And sovereignty cannot be represented, just because the will cannot be represented—it is either the same or something entirely different, there is no medium. Who has certified you that your representative will always and on all occasions have the same will as yourself? He will certainly not be so accommodating. So far then from your being represented, you have surrendered to him your will, your sovereignty, your liberty. You have given yourself up not to a representative, but to a master. And why? Because you are an indolent, grasping, cowardly individual, who pay far more regard to your own personal concerns than to public matters, who will rather pay for soldiers than go to war, who will rather appoint deputies and stay at home than go yourself and share in the deliberations of a national council."

This is the way in which Rousseau conceives of representation: he considers that it is delusive and impossible, and that every representative government is in its own nature illegitimate.*

Let the same citizen be addressed by other doctors who, entertaining the same ideas of sovereignty and liberty as those held by Rousseau, and nevertheless believing in representation, endeavour to harmonize these different conceptions. They might say to him: "Most true; sovereignty resides in yourself and in yourself alone; but you may delegate without abandoning it;—you do so every day; to your steward you commit the management of your lands, to your physician the care of your health, and you place your legal affairs into the hands of your solicitor. Life is vast and complicated, your personal control is insufficient for all its activity and demands; everywhere you avail yourself of others in the exercise of your own power—you employ servants. This is only a new application of the same principle—you employ one servant more. If he swerve from your directions, if he fail in giving expression to your will, we grant that he abuses his trust. When you give him your suffrage, you do not surrender to him your liberty—he on the other hand in receiving them has renounced his own. The mandate which he holds from you makes him a slave while it makes you

* *Du Contrat Social*, b. iii. c. xv.

free. On this condition representation becomes legitimate, for the person represented does not cease to be sovereign."

What will the citizen say to this? He must make his choice: such, he is told, is the nature of representation that, in one way or another, whenever he appoints a deputy he makes some one a slave, either his representative or himself. This was far from his intention; wishing to live at once in freedom and in security, he connected himself, acting in concert with his fellow citizens, with a man whom he regarded free as well as himself, and whom he judged capable of defending his liberty and ensuring his tranquillity; when he gave this man his suffrage he did not believe he was either enslaving himself or the object of his choice—he thought to enter into a relation of alliance with him, not of sovereignty or of servitude—he only did what is virtually done every day by men, who, having interests which are identical and not being able to manage them individually and directly, entrust them to that individual among their number who appears to be most capable of efficiently conducting them, thus shewing by their confidence their respect for his superiority, and preserving at the same time the right to judge, by his conduct, if the superiority is real and the confidence deserved. Regarded in itself, this is the fact of election—neither more nor less. What then is to be said of the theory which comes to denaturalize the fact, and to give it an import and significance which it never had in its origin either in the intention or the reason of the parties interested.

The source of all this confusion is to be found in a wrong apprehension of the word *representation;* and the word has been misunderstood, because false ideas have been entertained regarding sovereignty and liberty. We must therefore revert to earlier stages of the enquiry.

The fundamental principle of the philosophies which we oppose is, that every man is his own absolute master, that the only legitimate law for him is his individual will; at no time had any one, be his credentials what they may, any right over him, if he does not give his consent to it. Starting from this principle, Rousseau saw, and saw truly, that as the will is a purely individual fact, so all representation of the will is impossible. Assuming that the will is the sole source of the legitimate power which a man exercises over himself, it follows that no man can transmit this power to another, for he cannot determine that his will shall be conveyed to another man and cease to reside in himself. He cannot confer a power which would certainly involve the risk of his being obliged to obey another will than his own; for on this very account, if on no other, that power would be illegitimate. All thought of representation, therefore, is a delusion, and all power founded on representation is tyrannical, for a man only remains free so long as he obeys no law but that of his own will.

The conclusion is inevitable—Rousseau's only fault was that he did not push it far enough. Going as far as this would lead him, he would have entirely abstained from seeking after the best government, he would have condemned all constitutions—he would have affirmed the illegitimacy of all law and all power. In fact, how does it concern me that a law emanated yesterday from my will, if today my will has changed? Yesterday my will was the only source of legitimacy for the law; why then should the law remain legitimate when it is no longer sanctioned by my will? Can I not will more than once? Does my will exhaust its rights by a single act? And because it is my only master, must I, therefore, submit slavishly to laws from which this master who has made them bids me to enfranchise myself? This was not overlooked by Rousseau: "It is absurd," he says, "to suppose that the will should fetter itself with chains for the future."*

This then is the consequence of the principle when fairly carried out. Rousseau did not see this, or did not dare to see it; it is destructive not only of all government, but also of all society. It imposes upon man an absolute and continued isolation, does not allow him to contract any obligations, or to bind himself by any law, and brings an element of dissolution even into the bosom of the individual himself, who can no more bind himself to his own nature than to any other person: for his past will, that is to say, what he no longer wills, has no more right over him than the will of a stranger.

Rousseau was at least sometimes doubtful as to the application of his principle, and he only lost sight of it when, if he had remained faithful to it, he would have been obliged to sacrifice all else to it. Minds less powerful than his, and therefore less able to cast off the yoke of social necessities, have believed that they could preserve the principle without admitting all its consequences. Like Rousseau, they have admitted that, every man being the sole master of himself, no law can be binding upon him which is not conformed to his will—an axiom which has become popular under this form: *No one is bound to obey laws to which he has not given his consent.* Reasoning with strict logical rigour, Rousseau would have perceived that this axiom did not leave any standing place for organized power. He had, at all events, clearly shown that all representation of power was condemned by it as illegitimate and delusive. Other political theorists have undertaken to deduce from it representation itself, and all the powers of which it is the basis. They have proceeded in some such manner as the following:—

They have placed themselves fearlessly in presence of existing facts, determined to regulate them according to their convenience by imposing alternately upon the facts a principle which they reject, and upon this principle consequences which it will not naturally admit. Given—society to maintain and government to construct, without ceasing to affirm that the will of man is the source of legitimacy for power. It is required that this work should follow from this principle—they determine that it shall.

* *Du Contrat Social,* b. ii. c. i.

But an impossibility confronts them at the outset; how to avoid imposing upon men any law without their consent. How shall all individual wills be consulted regarding each particular law? Rousseau did not hesitate; he pronounced great States to be illegitimate, and that it was necessary to divide society into small republics in order that, once at least, the will of each citizen might give its consent to the law. Even if that could be done, the problem would be far from being solved, so that the principle should appear fully exemplified, whatever tests might be applied to it. But still an impossibility had at length disappeared, and logical consistency was preserved. The political theorists of whom we are speaking, far more timid than Rousseau, have not dared to protest against the existence of large communities, but they have not feared to get over the impossibility by the aid of a new inconsistency. While they do not allow to individuals the right only to obey laws conformed to their will, they substitute for it the right only to obey laws which emanate from a power which has been constituted by their will; they have thought to pay respect to the principle, by basing the legitimacy of the law on the election of the legislative power. Thus the theory of representation, that is, of the representation of wills, has re-appeared, in spite of Rousseau's logical reasonings: for, so long as the will of man is recognized as the only legitimate sovereign for him, if the creation of a power be attempted by means of representation, the kind of representation that will really be attempted will be the representation of wills.

But this theory must be carried out, and reduced to practice. Now, after having annulled, so far as the creation of the law is concerned, so many individual wills, the least that could be expected is that all should be called upon to give their voice in the nomination of those who shall be commissioned to make laws. Universal suffrage was therefore the inevitable consequence of the principle already so violently perverted; it has been sometimes professed, but never actually adopted. Here then once more a new impossibility has occasioned a new inconsistency. Nowhere has the right of voting for the legislative power belonged to more than a fragment of society; women, at least, have always been excluded from it. Thus then, while the will has been recognized as the sole legitimate sovereign in every individual, a large number of individuals have not even taken any part in the creation of that factitious sovereignty which representation has given to all.

We might pursue these investigations, and we should find at every step some new deviation from the principle which, it is pretended, is always to be respected as forming the abiding basis on which the formation of governments depends. The most remarkable of these deviations is certainly the supremacy which is everywhere attributed to the majority over the minority. Who does not see that, when the principle of the absolute sovereignty of the individual over himself has been once admitted, this supremacy is entirely false? And if false, how is society possible?

I have said enough, I think, to shew that this alleged principle is powerless for the legitimate creation of the government of society, and that it must incessantly yield to necessity, and finally vanish altogether. I will now consider it from another point of view. I will suppose that the work has been accomplished, that a government has been constructed; and I inquire what will be the influence of this principle upon the government which, it is affirmed, is derived from it, and which has only been created by the suffrance of numerous inconsistencies. What right will the government have over individuals, by whose will alone, it is said, it possesses any legitimacy? Here, as elsewhere, it is necessary that the principle should again be referred to; it must determine the right of the government when it has been established, just as it must have guided its formation.

Two systems present themselves. According to the one, the individual wills which have created a legislative power have not thereby lost their inherent sovereignty; they have provided themselves with servants and not with masters; it is true they have created this power in order that it may command, but on condition that it shall obey. In itself, and in relation to those from whom it holds its commission, it is nothing but a kind of executive power, appointed to put in form the laws which it has received, and constantly subordinated to that other power which remains diffused among the individuals with whom it originally resided, and which, although without form and without voice, is nevertheless the only absolute and permanently legitimate authority. In fact, there is a sovereign, which not only does not govern, but which obeys, while there is a government which commands, but is not sovereign.

According to the other system, those individual wills which have created the legislative and central power are, so to speak, absorbed into it; they have abdicated in favour of the power which represents them; and it represents them in the whole extent of their inherent sovereignty. This is, obviously, pure and unmixed despotism, rigorously deduced from the principle that wills are to be represented in government, and which has in fact been assumed by all governments which have emanated from this source. *"The elect of the sovereign is itself sovereign"*: such was the declaration both of the Convention and of Napoleon; hence the destruction of all responsibility in power, and of all the rights belonging to citizens. This certainly was not the consummation which the friends of liberty demanded of representation.

The first of these systems is the most plausible, and still possesses many conscientious advocates. This system is so far good, inasmuch as it ignores an inherent right to sovereignty as the possession of any government; its error is, that this right is allowed to exist elsewhere. I do not here examine it in relation to any other principle than that from which it professes to be derived; and if the individual wills which have created the legislative power are bound to obey its laws, what becomes of this principle? Every man, you say is free only in so far as he is left master of his own will. Those then alone will be free in your government, who, by a happy coincidence of sentiment with their legislators, approve the laws as thoroughly as if they had made them themselves; for whoever is bound to obey laws, whether he approve them or not, immediately loses his sovereignty over himself—his liberty. And if he has a right to disobey, if the will of the legislative power is not authoritative over the wills which have created it, what becomes of this power? What becomes of government? What becomes of society?

It must seem a somewhat superfluous expenditure of logical force to appeal so often to a principle while power is being gradually constructed, when the same principle, if once more appealed to when the business is apparently completed, is found to give a death-blow to this very power. Such, however, must be the result: for the principle has disavowed, from the outset, the power which was to be deduced from it.

If, then, we find that this principle, consistently pursued, can only result in the dissolution of society or the formation of a tyranny—if it can issue in no legitimate power whatever—if it finally lands us, after our inquiries after a free and reasonable political order, in the alternative of impossibility or inconsistency—must we not most evidently seek for the evil in the principle itself from which we started?

It is not true, then, that man is the absolute master of himself—that his will is the only legitimate law—that no one, at any time, under any circumstances, has any right over him unless he has consented thereto. When philosophers have considered man in himself, apart from all connection with his fellows, only regarding his active life in its relation to his own understanding, they have never thought of declaring that his will is for him the only legitimate law, or, which amounts to the same thing, that every action is just and reasonable merely because it is voluntary. All have recognized that a certain law which is distinct from the individual will encircles him—a law which is called either reason, morality, or truth, and from which he cannot separate his conduct without making the exercise of his liberty either absurd or criminal. All systems, on whatever principles they may found the laws of morality and reason—whether they speak of interest, feeling, general consent, or duty—whether they are spiritualistic or materialistic in their origin—whether they emanate from sceptics or from dogmatists—all admit that some acts are reasonable and others unreasonable, some just and others unjust, and that if the individual does in fact remain free to act either according to or in violation of reason, this liberty does not constitute any right, or cause any act which is in itself absurd or criminal to cease to be so because it has been performed voluntarily.

More than this: as soon as an individual prepared to act demands from his understanding some enlightenment for his liberty, he perceives the law which enjoins upon him that which is in itself true, and at the same time he recognizes that this law is not the product of his own individual nature, and that, by the volitions of his will, he can neither disown nor change it. His will remains free to obey or to disobey his reason: but his reason, in its turn, remains independent of his will, and necessarily judges, according to the law which it has recognized, the will which revolts against it.

Thus, speaking philosophically and rightfully, the individual considered in himself, may not dispose of himself arbitrarily and according to his solitary will. Laws which are obligatory are not created or imposed upon him by his will. He receives them from a higher source; they come to him from a sphere that is above the region of his liberty—from a sphere where liberty is not—where the question to be considered is not whether a thing is willed or not willed, but whether it is true or false, just or unjust, conformable or contrary to reason. When these laws descend from this sublime sphere in order to enter into that of the material world, they are constrained to pass through the region where liberty, which exists on the confines of these two worlds, has its sway; and here it is that the question arises whether the free will of the individual will or will not conform to the laws of this sovereign reason. But in whatever way this question is decided, sovereignty does not forsake reason and attach itself to will. In no possible case can will of itself confer upon the acts which it produces the character of legitimacy; they have, or they have not this characteristic, according as they are or are not conformed to reason, justice, and truth, from which alone legitimate power can spring.

To express the same thought in a different way—man has not an absolute power over himself in virtue of his will: as a moral and reasonable being he is a subject—subject to laws which he did not himself make, but which have a rightful authority over him, although, as a free agent, he has the power to refuse them, not his consent but his obedience.

If we look at all philosophical systems in their basis—if we rise above the differences that may exist in their forms—we shall be convinced that no one is to be found which has not admitted the principle which I have now expressed. How then does it arise that philosophers, when they leave man regarded as an isolated being, and look at him in his relations with other men, have started from a principle which they would not have dared to adopt as the foundation of their moral doctrines, but which has served as a basis to their political theories? How comes it that the will which, in the solitary individual, has never been raised to the position of an absolute and solely legitimate sovereign, does yet suddenly find itself invested with this title and its corresponding rights, as soon as the individual is brought into the presence of other individuals of like nature with himself?

The fact may be thus represented: In that commingling and collision of individuals which we call society, the philosophers of whom we speak have pertinaciously adhered to that which does in fact first present itself, namely, the commingling and collision of individual wills. A true instinct, unrecognized perhaps by them, has suddenly reminded them that the will is not, in itself, and by its essential constitution, the legitimate sovereign of man. If it does not occupy this position in the individual and so far as he is himself concerned, how should it be elevated to such a rank when another individual is concerned? How should that which, in its own acts, has nothing that is legitimate in the view of reason, when it says *I will*—how should it have any right to impose its will as the law for another person? No will, merely because it is a will, has any authority over another will:—this is evident; any opposite assumption is revolting; it is brute force, sheer despotism.

How shall these perplexities be removed? How shall individual wills be made to co-operate without conflicting, to shelter without overpowering one another? Philosophers have only seen one method of accomplishing this, and that is to attribute to each will an absolute sovereignty, an entire independence; they have declared that every individual is the absolute master of his own person; that is to say, they have elevated all individual wills to the rank and position of sovereignty. Accordingly the will which, in man considered apart and by himself, possesses no sovereign and legitimate power, has been invested with it as soon as man is viewed in his relations with other men. Thus the reply, *my will does not consent*, which, within the individual himself, cannot establish any right if it be contrary to the laws of the reason, has become, outside of the individual, the foundation of right, the ever-sufficient and finally authoritative reason.

Is it necessary that we should prove that a principle, which, in its application to man considered as an individual, is evidently false and destructive of all morality and of all law, is equally so in the relations between man and man; and that in the one case as in the other, the legitimacy of law and of power, that is to say, of obedience or of resistance, is derived from quite another source than the will?—Two facts shall serve us in the stead of arguments:

Who has ever denied the legitimacy of parental authority? it has its limits, and may be carried to excess like every other human power; but has it ever been alleged that it is illegitimate so often as the obedience of the child, whom it seeks to control, is not voluntary? An instinctive sense of the truth has in this case prevented any one from even maintaining such an absurdity. Nevertheless the will of the child, considered in itself, does not at all differ from that of the fully-grown man; it is of the same nature, and it is equally precious to the individual. Here then is an illustration of legitimate power in cases in which obedience to it is not voluntary. And from whence does this power borrow its legitimacy? evidently from the superiority of the father's reason to that of the child, a superiority which indicates the position which the father is called to occupy by a law above him, and which establishes his right to assume that position. The rightful sway here does not belong to the will of the child, who wants the reason that is necessary for such sway, nor even does it belong to the mere will of the father, for will can never vindicate right from itself; it belongs to reason, and to him who possesses it. The mission which is given by God to the father to fulfil, is that he should teach his child what reason teaches him, and should bend his will to the claims of reason, until he shall be able to control his will for himself. The legitimacy of parental power is derived from the fact of this mission: this establishes its right and also determines its limits, for the father has no right to impose upon the child any laws except such as are just and reasonable. Hence the rules and processes of a judicious education, that is to say, of the legitimate exercise of parental power; but the principle of right is in the mission and the reason of the parent, and not in either of the wills which are here brought into relation one to the other.

Let me remind you of another fact. When any man is well known to be mad or idiotic, it is customary to deprive him of his full liberty. On what grounds? has his will perished? if it is the principle of legitimate power, is it not always there to exercise it? The will is still there; but the true sovereign of the man, the lord of the will itself, reasoning intelligence, has departed from the individual. It must therefore be supplied to him from another source—a reason external to himself must govern him, since his own has become incapable of controlling his will.

What is true concerning the child and the imbecile is true of man in general: the right to power is always derived from reason, never from will. No one has a right to impose a law because he wills it; no one has a right to refuse submission to it because his will is opposed to it; the legitimacy of power rests in the conformity of its laws to the eternal reason—not in the will of the man who exercises, nor of him who submits to power.

If therefore philosophers desired to give a principle of legitimacy to power, and to restrain it within the limits of right, instead of raising all individual wills to the position of sovereigns and of rivals in sovereignty, they should have brought them all into the condition of subjects, and appointed over them one sovereign. Instead of saying that every man is his own absolute master, and that no other man has a right over him against his will, they should proclaim that no man is the absolute master either of himself or of any other person, and that no action, no power exercised by man over man, is legitimate if it wants the sanction of reason, justice, and truth, which are the law of God. In one word, they should everywhere proscribe absolute power, instead of affording it an asylum in each individual will, and allow to every man the right, which he does in fact possess, of refusing obedience to any law that is not a divine law, instead of attributing to him the right, which he does not actually possess, of obeying nothing but his own will.

I may now return to the particular question which I proposed in starting, and determine what *representation* truly is—thus justifying in its principle as in its results, the system of government to which this name is applied.

We are no longer concerned to represent individual wills, which is really an impossibility, as Rousseau has fully demonstrated, though he was mistaken in thinking that this is the aim of representation. We are not, therefore, careful to evade this impossibility, and so fall into inconsistency, as has been done by other political theorists. These attempts, illegitimate in principle and vain in their issues, are, besides, chargeable with the immense mischief of deceiving men; for they profess to establish themselves on a principle which they constantly violate; and by a culpable falsehood, they promise to every individual a respect for his individual will—whether enlightened or ignorant, reasonable or unreasonable, just or unjust—such as, in fact, they cannot give to it, and which they are of necessity obliged to deny.

The true doctrine of representation is more philosophical and more sincere. Starting from the principle that truth, reason, and justice—in one word, the divine law—alone possess rightful power, its reasoning is somewhat as follows:—Every society, according to its interior organization, its antecedents, and the aggregate of influences which have or do still modify it, is placed to a certain extent in a position to apprehend truth and justice as the divine law, and is in a measure disposed to conform itself to this law. Employing less general terms:—there exists in every society a certain number of just ideas and wills in harmony with those ideas, which respect the reciprocal rights of men and social relations with their results. This sum of just ideas and loyal wills is dispersed among the individuals who compose society, and unequally diffused among them on account of the infinitely varied causes which influence the moral and intellectual development of men. The grand concern, therefore, of society is—that, so far as either abiding infirmity or the existing condition of human affairs will allow, this power of reason, justice, and truth, which alone has an inherent legitimacy, and alone has the right to demand obedience, may become prevalent in the community. The problem evidently is to collect from all sides the scattered and incomplete fragments of this power that exist in society, to concentrate them, and from them, to constitute a government. In other words, it is required to discover all the elements of legitimate power that are disseminated throughout society, and to organize them into an actual power; that is to say, to collect into one focus, and to realize, public reason and public morality, and to call them to the occupation of power.

What we call *representation* is nothing else than a means to arrive at this result:—it is not an arithmetical machine employed to collect and count individual wills, but a natural process by which public reason, which alone has a right to govern society, may be extracted from the bosom of society itself. No reason has in fact a right to say beforehand for itself that it is the reason of the community. If it claims to be such, it must prove that it is so, that is to say, it must accredit itself to other individual reasons which are capable of judging it. If we look at facts, we shall find that all institutions, all conditions of the representative system, flow from and return to this point. Election, publicity, and responsibility, are so many tests applied to individual reasons, which in the search for, or the exercise of, power, assume to be interpreters of the reason of the community; so many means of bringing to light the elements of legitimate power, and preventing usurpation.

In this system, it is true—and the fact arises from the necessity of liberty as actual in the world—that truth and error, perverse and loyal wills, in one word, the good and evil which co-exist and contend in society as in the individual, will most probably express themselves; this is the condition of the world; it is the necessary result of liberty. But against the evil of this there are two guarantees: one is found in the publicity of the struggle, which always gives the right the best chance of success, for it has been recognized in all ages of the world that good is in friendship with the light, while evil ever shelters itself in darkness; this idea, which is common to all the religions of the world, symbolizes and indicates the first of all truths. The second guarantee consists in the determination of a certain amount of capacity to be possessed by those who aspire to exercise any branch of power. In the system of representing wills, nothing could justify such a limitation, for the will exists full and entire in all men, and confers on all an equal right; but the limitation flows necessarily from the principle which attributes power to reason, and not to will.

So then, to review the course we have taken, the power of man over himself is neither arbitrary nor absolute; as a reasonable being, he is bound to obey reason. The same principle subsists in the relations between man and man; in this case also, power is only legitimate in so far as it is conformed to reason.

Liberty, as existing in the individual man, is the power to conform his will to reason. On this account it is sacred; accordingly the right to liberty, in the relations of man with man, is derived from the right to obey nothing that is not reason.

The guarantees due to liberty in the social state have, therefore, for their aim, to procure indirectly the legitimacy of actual power, that is to say, the conformity of its wills to that reason which ought to govern all wills, those which command as well as those which obey.

Therefore no actual power ought to be absolute, and liberty is guaranteed only in so far as power is bound to prove its legitimacy.

Power proves its legitimacy, that is to say, its conformity to the eternal reason, by making itself recognized and accepted by the free reason of the men over whom it is exercised. This is the object of the representative system.

So far then from representation founding itself on a right, inherent in all individual wills, to concur in the exercise of power, it on the other hand rests on the principle that no will has in itself any right to power, and that whoever exercises, or claims to exercise power, is bound to prove that he exercises, or will exercise it, not according to his own will, but according to reason. If we examine the representative system in all its forms—for it admits of different forms according to the state of society to which it is applied—we shall see that such are everywhere the necessary results and the true foundations of that which we call representation.[1]

1. This lecture, a true *tour de force,* is one of the most important theoretical chapters of the book and could be seen as an excellent outline of Guizot's political vision. Here Guizot elaborates on "true" representation, the distinction between reason and will, the object of representative system, Rousseau's "mistake," the role of publicity, and political capacity. For another statement of Guizot's political philosophy, see his *Philosophie politique: de la souveraineté* (*Political Philosophy: On Sovereignty*). For more details on Guizot's reading of Rousseau's *Social Contract,* see n. 1 on p. 273.

LECTURE II

Formation of a Parliament. ⁓ Introduction of county deputies into the Parliament. ⁓ Relations of the county deputies to the great barons. ⁓ Parliament of Oxford (1258). ⁓ Its regulations, termed the Acts of Oxford. ⁓ Hesitancy of the county deputies between the great barons and the crown.

Before we commenced the history of the charters, and after we had for some time fixed our attention on the Anglo-Norman government, we saw that this government was composed of but two great forces, royalty and the council of barons, a unique and central assembly, which alone shared with the king the exercise of power. Such was the state in which we found the government of England under William the Conqueror and his sons. But from their reigns to that of Edward I., a great change was being gradually evolved; after a laborious struggle, the charters were finally conceded, and the rights which they proclaim were definitively recognised. If, after this complete revolution, we cast a glance over the institutions of the country, we find them all changed; we perceive that the government has taken another form, that new elements have been introduced into it, that the Parliament—composed in one of its divisions of the lords spiritual and temporal, in the other of deputies from the counties and boroughs—has taken the place of the great council of barons.

This transformation is a fact; how was it produced? what were its causes and its mode of advance? what was the new Parliament after its formation? how far and in what respects did the introduction of these deputies change the character of the government? These are the questions that we have now to consider; and in order to answer them we must analyze and examine the principal individual facts which here combine to produce the common result.

The first of these facts is the introduction of county deputies into the national assembly. I shall first enquire how this event was brought about; and I shall then propose similar enquiries with respect to the introduction of town and borough representatives into the same assembly.

Two causes effected the introduction of county deputies into Parliament:

---

first, the privileges belonging to knights as immediate vassals of the king; secondly, their interference in county affairs by means of the county-courts.

The immediate vassals of the king had in that capacity two fundamental rights; that no extraordinary charge should be imposed without their consent, and that they should have a place in the king's court, either to give judgments, or to treat of public affairs. They were from both these circumstances, members of the general assembly by inheritance. They formed the political nation. They took a part in the government, and in the determination of public charges, as a personal right.

Although they were not elected and had received neither appointment nor mandate, we may nevertheless say that they were regarded as representing their own vassals, and that it was only in virtue of the power which was attributed to them in this fictitious representation that they exercised the right of levying imposts on all the proprietors in the kingdom.*

Perhaps they never could have fully organized themselves into a united body, and soon this became impossible. On the one hand, there rose up among the direct vassals of the king, some influential barons, who united a considerable number of knights' fiefs into one, and became by this cause much more powerful; and on the other hand, the number of knights with smaller wealth became much more considerable by the division of fiefs, which was itself the result of a vast variety of causes. However, the right of appearing at the general assembly and of giving their personal sanction to all extraordinary imposts, always remained to them. This is formally recognized in Magna Charta, Article 14.

This same article proves at the same time that there existed an evident inequality between different immediate vassals, for it ordains that the great barons should be summoned individually, while the others should be convoked *en masse* by means of the sheriffs. This is not the first time that such a difference in the mode of convocation is to be observed; it had already existed for some time, and was exemplified whenever the king required from his vassals the military service which they were bound to give him.

Thus, at the commencement of the thirteenth century, the right to take a seat in the national assembly belonged to all the immediate vassals of the king, but it was scarcely ever exercised on account of obstacles which increased every day. The assembly was almost entirely composed of the great barons.

But the other vassals, on the other hand, did not renounce their political existence; if their influence daily became more and more limited to their own county, there at least they exercised their rights and interfered actively in affairs. We often find that knights were nominated, sometimes by the sheriff, some-

---

* This is expressly indicated by two writs, one in the reign of John, dated Feb. 17, 1208; the other issued by Henry III., July 12, 1237.

times by the court itself, to give their decision on matters connected with the county. Thus William the Conqueror charged two free men in each county with the business of collecting and publishing the ancient laws and local customs. The Great Charter provides that twelve knights shall be elected in each county to enquire into abuses. These examples are frequent in the reigns of Henry III. and Edward I. Two writs of Henry III.* prove that subsidies were at that time assessed, not, as previously, by the judges in their circuits, but by knights elected in the county-court. The knights in this way brought their influence to bear upon government by the offices they discharged in their provinces, while at the same time they preserved, though without exercising it, the right to appear at the general assemblies.

But, on the other hand, in proportion as they thus became separated from the great barons, the knights who were direct vassals of the king united themselves more closely to another class of men, with whose interests they after a time completely identified themselves. They did not alone occupy a position in the county courts; many freeholders, subordinate vassals of the king, also constantly presented themselves at these courts, and performed the same administrative or judicial functions. Service in the county court was an obligation imposed in common, by their tenure, on all freeholders, whether vassals of the king or of any other feudal lord. Many of the latter were more wealthy and influential than certain direct vassals of the king. The practice of sub-enfiefment augmented their number continually. Many who were simply *socagers* gradually became considerable freeholders by receiving free lands from different nobles. Thus, a body of freeholders was formed in every county, the county court being its centre. There they all discharged the same functions, and exercised the same rights; whatever, in other respects, might be their feudal relations with the crown. We thus see that the dissolution, on the one hand, of the ancient general assembly of immediate vassals of the king, and the localisation, on the other hand, of a great number of them in the county courts, while at the same time their interests were united with those of the freeholders, prepared the elements of a new nation, and consequently of a new political order.

Let us now see how this new nation manifested its existence, and was brought to a central position in the State by means of representation.

In 1214, while the discontented barons were preparing for revolution, John convoked a general assembly at Oxford. The writs of the king ordered the sheriffs to demand for that assembly the assistance of a certain number of armed knights; while other writs† ordered that the followers of the barons should present themselves at Oxford *without arms,* and enjoined besides that the sheriffs

---

* One in 1220, the other in 1225.

† Dated November 15, 1214.

should send to Oxford four approved knights from each county "in order to consider, with us, the affairs of our kingdom."

This is the first indication of knights being represented in Parliament, that is to say, of the admission of certain individuals, who should appear and act in the name of all.

Was then this idea at that time present to their minds? Probably not. How were these four knights nominated? Were they chosen by the sheriff, or elected by the county court? Were these writs actually executed? All this is uncertain. But that which admits of no doubt is the aim and tendency of this innovation. The contents of the writs themselves, and the circumstances in the midst of which they were issued, clearly indicate its object. It is evident that John wished to find in the knights of the shires a means of defence against the barons, and that consequently the former already formed a class so far distinct from the latter that the attempt to separate them entirely from it was not altogether unreasonable, while they were sufficiently important to be appealed to as powerful auxiliaries.

John's attempt did not succeed. Facts prove that, in the struggle between the royal power and the barons, the knights and other freeholders espoused the cause of the latter, who, as they protested in favour of public rights, were acting no less for the interest of the knights than for their own.

The struggle continued during the whole of Henry the Third's reign, and throughout this period we find the king constantly endeavouring to alienate the knights from the party of the barons and win them over to his own, while the barons exerted themselves to keep the knights attached to themselves.

The following is an illustration of the attempts made by the royal power. In 1225, one of the periods when the charters were confirmed by Henry III., we find that writs were addressed to the sheriffs of eight counties, requiring them to cause to be elected in each of these counties four knights who should present themselves at Lincoln, where the council of barons was then assembled, in order to set forth the grievances of their counties against the said sheriffs, who also should be present to explain or defend themselves. In this case, there is no reference except to merely local affairs of particular counties, and the four knights are not called upon to take any part in the general assembly, but they are elected and sent in order to treat of the affairs of their counties before the central council. Here the election is a positive fact in the case, and the nature of their commission—to protest against local grievances—is one of the principles of representation.

In 1240, we find a general assembly of barons meeting in London, in which, however, there is nothing remarkable except the name given to it by the chroniclers. In speaking of it, Matthew Paris employs for the first time, the word *Parliament* (*parliamentum*).

Lastly, in 1254, when Henry III. was in Gascony and wanted money, he ordered the convocation of an extraordinary Parliament in London in order to demand of it an extraordinary subsidy. At the same time, he addressed a writ to the sheriffs, enjoining them to cause two knights to be elected in the county courts, "in the stead of each and all of them" (*vice omnium et singulorum eorumdem*), to deliberate on the aid to be granted to the king. Here then is a real and positive instance of representation; deputies are elected, they are introduced into the assembly, and a deliberative voice is there given to them. Certain historians have maintained that these writs were not executed, but on this point no satisfactory information is to be had. However, as it is proved that a subsidy was granted to the king, there is reason to believe that it was consented to by this assembly, composed of barons and knights.

Up to this time, the great feudal aristocracy had retained the knights and other freeholders on their side; we have now to see how they became alienated from them, and how, after having been for a long time the allies of the barons, they became afterwards allies of the throne.

During the year 1254, a general irritation broke out in the kingdom on the occasion of the demand for an extraordinary subsidy. Henry III., who was misled by the artifices and promises of Pope Innocent IV., had engaged in an adventurous war against Manfred, the usurper of the throne of Naples—a war in which Henry must have borne all the expense, and of which the Pope would doubtless have reaped all the advantages, if it had succeeded. But there was no occasion that his good faith should be put to such a test, for the war was an entire failure. Henry, however, had contracted an enormous debt; his prodigality and extravagance had drained his resources; and he was obliged to appeal to his subjects in order to relieve himself of this burden. These demands for money, which indicate what progress the principle that the king cannot levy imposts on his sole responsibility had made, served as a pretext for the discontented barons to take arms against their king. Simon de Montfort, Earl of Leicester, placed himself at their head, and civil war was declared.

But the aristocracy were weary of these incessant combats, which only yielded momentary advantages. The insurgents formed the project of no longer contenting themselves with conquering the king—they determined so far to fetter him as that henceforth he should be fully dependent upon them. The barons who had wrested Magna Charta from King John had attempted, in order to provide themselves with guarantees, to give beforehand a legal organization to civil war, in case the charter should be violated. The barons who dictated the law to Henry III., went farther: they attempted to organize, not a resistance but a power, and to secure for themselves guarantees, not in civil war but in the very constitution of the government. Not being able to restrain the authority of the king within just limits, they undertook to deprive him of it altogether, and to assume it themselves—in one word, to substitute the government of an aristocracy for that of the king.

They had already made a similar attempt in 1244, when their design had been that four prominent members of their body should be admitted to the council of the king, who would have followed him constantly and governed under his name. At that time the attempt had been unsuccessful, but at the time which we are now considering, their endeavours were followed by better results. In the Parliaments convoked successively in 1255, 1257, and 1258, the most violent reproaches were heaped upon Henry III. as to his prodigality, his faults, his infatuated enterprises, and above all the violation of his oaths of fidelity to the Great Charter. Henry was intimidated, and, as he desired to appease his barons in order to obtain from them a subsidy, he promised to repair his errors and reform his government. It was determined that this reform should be regulated by a Parliament convoked at Oxford, June 11, 1258.

This is the first assembly that has received the official designation of Parliament. The barons attended it, armed and followed by a large retinue; Henry, on the contrary, not having taken any precautions against them, found himself their prisoner. Nevertheless they performed what had been agreed upon, that is to say, that they should commit the care of deciding on the projected reforms to twenty-four barons, of whom twelve were chosen by them, and twelve nominated by the king.[1]

An unlimited authority was conferred upon these twenty-four mediators. They began by making a complete change in the form of government. Their first concern was to form the king's council, and four barons chosen by the confederation were commissioned to organize it. They composed it of fifteen members, and of these fifteen, nine at least were taken from the party of the barons, so that the chief power was placed entirely in the hands of these nine persons, and consequently, in the hands of the barons.

A large number of regulations, known under the name of the *Acts of Oxford,* were determined upon by this assembly, that is to say, by the council of twenty-four barons. No complete collection of them is to be found in any authentic document. The following may be gathered from different historians; among other things the barons demanded:

1. That the charters should be confirmed;
2. That they themselves should annually nominate the judges, the chancellor, the treasurer, and other officers of the king;
3. That they should have the keeping of the royal castles;

---

1. These pages contain important insights on the formation of Parliament as a fundamental institution of representative government. Also see *HORG,* pp. 311–19, 399–435.

4. That three Parliaments should be convoked every year, in the months of February, June, and October;

5. That a permanent commission of twelve barons should be appointed, who should be present at these Parliaments, and assist the royal council in the transaction of all business;

6. That four knights should be appointed in each county, to receive all complaints against the sheriffs or other officers of the king, and to give an account of these to the next Parliament;

7. That, for the future, the sheriffs should be nominated by the county courts;

8. Lastly, that the king, his son Edward, his brothers, the archbishops, bishops, &c., should be obliged on oath to promise fidelity to the Acts of Oxford.

It was further agreed that the committee of twenty-four barons should reform all the abuses that had been committed in the kingdom, and administer, in the name of the king, the laws that were necessary for this purpose; and then allow the government thus regulated to proceed in an orderly way.

But after the separation of the Parliament, the barons, under the pretext that they had yet abuses to reform and laws to administer, refused to resign their power; and not content with retaining it illegally, they employed it to their own advantage. Their acts and laws had no other object than their own personal interest. Without knowing it, they were acting ruinously to themselves, for they detached from their party that part of the population which clearly apprehended their designs. Two laws especially alienated the minds of the people from them; one of these laws took away from the sheriffs the right to fine those barons who should refuse to present themselves at the county courts, or at the assizes held by the judges in circuit. The second decided that the judges' circuits should only take place every seven years.

These measures opened the eyes of the people, and they speedily abandoned the authors of them. One fact may prove how far their tyranny had been already exercised at the expense of the country. A deputation was sent to Prince Edward in the name of the English bachelors (*communitatis bachelariae Angliae*), praying him to compel the barons to finish their work and fulfil their promises, as the king had fulfilled his. The prince replied that he had sworn fidelity to the Acts of Oxford, and that he was resolved to keep his oath. Nevertheless, he demanded of the barons that they should resign their power, threatening if they refused, to compel them to do so, and to take into his hands the interests of the community.

What was this *communitas bachelariae Angliae*? There is reason to believe that by this name, the body of knights of shires represented themselves. We see by this that the great barons had alienated from themselves this class of men, and that the king had begun to attach them to his party.

From these facts we see that besides the two great powers anciently established—the nobility and royalty—a third power had been formed at this period, which alternately inclined to one or other of these rival powers, and which already exercised a strong influence, since it ensured victory to the party in whose favour it might pronounce.

LECTURE 12

Struggle between Henry III. and his Parliament. ⁓ *Arbitration of Saint Louis.* ⁓ *The Earl of Leicester heads the great barons in their struggle with the king.* ⁓ *He is defeated and killed at Evesham (1265).* ⁓ *Admission of deputies from towns and boroughs into Parliament (1264).* ⁓ *Royalist reaction.* ⁓ *Leicester's memory remains popular.*

WE have seen how, in the midst of the struggles between royalty and the feudal aristocracy, an intermediate class arose—a new but already imposing power—and how the two contending powers each felt the necessity of securing an alliance with this third power; we have now to follow, by the examination of authentic documents, that is to say, of the writs and laws of the period, the progress of this new class, which we shall find taking an increasingly active part in the government of the country.

We have seen how the twenty-four barons, who were commissioned to reform the constitution of the kingdom, abusing the power which they thus held in trust, had refused, in spite of the king and the country, to resign their dictatorship. This refusal soon excited violent dissensions between them and the king, and civil war was on the point of being again enkindled. In 1261, Henry sent writs to several sheriffs, enjoining them to send to him, at Windsor, the three knights of each shire who had been summoned to St. Albans by the Earl of Leicester and his party. These writs plainly show that the king and the barons endeavoured more than ever to conciliate the body of knights, and that the king had then succeeded in attaching them to his party.

Henry sought yet another assistance. On his entreaty, the Pope released him from his oath of fidelity to the Acts of Oxford. Delivered from his scruples, Henry now openly broke off his agreements with the barons, and again possessed himself of the reins of government. In 1262, he convoked a Parliament at Westminster, that his authority might be sustained by its sanction. He met with but little opposition: wishing, however, to deprive the barons of every motive for revolt, he agreed to leave the adjustment of their claims to the judgment of an arbitrator. The great renown for wisdom and equity which Saint Louis possessed pointed him out as the best judge in this important dispute. Accordingly Henry and his barons agreed to abide by his decision.

Saint Louis assembled his great council at Amiens, and after careful deliberations, he recorded a judgment by which the Acts of Oxford were to be annulled, and the king to be placed again in possession of his castles, as well as of the right to nominate his own counsellors. But as he was equally careful to preserve the lawful prerogatives of the English people and those of the crown, Saint Louis gave his formal approval to all the ancient privileges, charters, and liberties of England, and proclaimed an absolute and reciprocal amnesty for both parties.

Scarcely had this decision been made known than Leicester and his party refused to submit to it, and took up arms for the purpose of seizing by force that which had been refused to them by justice. Civil war was recommenced with much animosity, but it was not of long duration. Leicester surprised the royalist army at Lewes, in the county of Sussex, on the 14th of May, 1264. Henry and his son Edward, being vanquished and taken prisoners, were constrained to receive the terms offered them by the conqueror. The conditions which he imposed were severe, but he did not assume to himself the right of settling the reforms that were to be made in the government; he only retained as hostages the brother and son of the king, and left to Parliament the care of settling political questions. Ideas respecting the legal authority of Parliaments, and the illegitimacy of force in matters relating to government, must have made considerable progress, when we find that the victorious Earl of Leicester did not venture to regulate on his own sole responsibility the plan of administration for the kingdom.

He did not, however, scruple to exercise other rights which did not belong to him any more than these. Under the king's name, who, though to all appearance set at liberty, did in fact remain his prisoner, Leicester governed the kingdom. In each county he created extraordinary magistrates, called preservers of the peace. Their duties were almost identical with those of the sheriffs, but their power was of much wider range. Leicester enjoined them to cause four knights to be elected in each county, and to send them to the Parliament which was to meet at London in June 1264.

This Parliament assembled and passed a decree which was designed to organize the government. This decree constrained the king to follow in everything the advice of a council composed of nine members, nominated by three principal electors, the Earls of Leicester and Gloucester, and the Bishop of Winchester.

Leicester still remained the real head of the State. In the midst of his power he was troubled by alarming disturbances; powerful preparations to oppose him were being made in France. These attempts were unsuccessful, and

Leicester, in order to anticipate any fresh opposition, undisguisedly sought protection from that part of the population, which was every day becoming more numerous and powerful—the middle classes. On the 14th of December 1264, he summoned a Parliament, and gave to it all the extent which it has since preserved, that is to say, he called to it the peers, county deputies, and also borough deputies. This innovation was intended to conciliate popular favour, and Leicester did not relax in his endeavours to preserve it. Relieved from royal authority, he wished also to free himself from the aristocracy by whose assistance he had conquered the king. He turned his tyranny against the great barons who were not pliant to his caprices. He confiscated their lands, no longer summoned them to Parliament, and annoyed them in a thousand ways in their persons and their rights. But this was the infatuated course of a conqueror intoxicated by success. As soon as the royal power and the aristocracy combined against him, Leicester was obliged to yield. On the 28th of May, 1266, Prince Edward escaped from his confinement, raised an army against Leicester, and offered him battle on the 4th of August at Evesham. Leicester was defeated and killed in the combat. His conduct was, though factious, yet great and bold, so that he may be called the founder of representative government in England, for, while he struggled at one time against the king, at another time against the barons who were rivals to himself, he hastened the progress of the middle classes, and definitely established for them a place in the national assembly.

Henry, delivered from slavery by the death of Leicester, recovered his power and used it with moderation. Several Parliaments were convoked during the last years of his reign, but it is not proved that any deputies from the counties and boroughs sat in them. There is even reason for thinking that, in the midst of the disorder that then prevailed in the kingdom, the trouble of convoking them, which was always tedious and difficult, was dispensed with. The Parliament held at Winchester on the 8th of September 1265, in which the confiscation of the goods of the rebels was granted to the king, was composed entirely of prelates and barons. This also was the case with regard to that which was convened by the king at Kenilworth, the 22nd of August, 1266, in which, after the rigour of the confiscations had been somewhat moderated, the Acts of Oxford were annulled, but the charters were solemnly confirmed. Nor do we find that deputies were present at the Parliament held at St. Edmundsbury in 1267; but they were admitted to that held at Marlborough, convened in 1269, to which were called "the wisest in the kingdom, as well those belonging to a lower as to a higher rank." Two years afterwards the deputies from counties and boroughs were summoned to a grand ceremony, in order to transfer the remains of Edward the Confessor to a tomb which the king had caused to be prepared in Westminster Abbey. After the ceremony a Parliament assembled; but it is uncertain whether or not the deputies had a place in it. This fact, however, does not the less prove the great importance which had at this time been acquired by the towns, and the habit which had been gradually established of summoning their deputies on all great occasions.

Such are the facts of the reign of Henry III. which relate to the introduction of county deputies into Parliament. No general act, no constitutional statute, called them thither. Indeed the idea of such political proceedings hardly existed at that period. Neither the government nor the people felt the need of regulating facts in a general manner, and fixing them on an absolute basis. The human mind had not arrived at that state of progress in which the conception of such a design is possible. Facts spontaneously developed themselves, in isolation and confusion, and according to the influence of existing circumstances. We may present a summary exhibiting the nature of their progress, and the causes by which the representation of counties was accomplished, in the following manner:—

All the king's vassals originally formed one body, and were entitled to a seat in the general assembly.

This class of proprietors became divided; some became great barons, and continued to sit in the central assembly. Others continued to possess only a local influence. By this cause they were separated from the great barons, and became united by common interests to other free proprietors. The county courts became the point of convergence for this new class.

A struggle arose between the king and the great barons. Both of these sought support from the class of freeholders which existed in the counties. A part of these preserved, as direct vassals of the king, the right to take their seat in the central assembly. The great barons certainly alone exercised this right; but as their tendency was to possess themselves of authority, and to identify the great council of barons with the government, they felt the necessity of conciliating the body of freeholders who were vassals of the king or of themselves; and the idea of causing them to be represented by means of election was so much the more natural, inasmuch as elections had often taken place in the county courts, when there was any occasion to commit local affairs into the hands of certain proprietors. Thus the centralization of the higher aristocracy to resist the royal authority did of necessity involve and cause the centralization of the inferior proprietors, who could only exert their influence in the way of election.

Lastly, the principle that consent was necessary before any impost could be levied had prevailed; the charters established it to the advantage of the barons with regard to the king, and of the inferior vassals in reference to their lords. The more that power became centralized either in the hands of the king or of the assembly of barons, the more did the consent of the other proprietors to imposts also necessarily centralize itself. That which had previously been local became general, and the centralization of the aristocracy of great barons involved the centralization of the aristocracy of free proprietors.

Another question now presents itself for examination: namely, the admission of town and borough deputies to parliament.

In general the towns possessed, before the Norman Conquest, considerable wealth and importance. We have seen them take a part in political events, and interfere actively in state affairs. The citizens of London concurred in the election of several Saxon kings; and those of Canterbury attended, under Ethelred II., at the county court. It is, however, nearly certain that the towns never sent deputies to the Wittenagemot. Their rights were limited within the circle of their own walls, and when they took part in politics, it was in an accidental and irregular manner.

After the Norman Conquest, the towns fell into decay, and lost not only their influence on general affairs, but even their local and individual rights. Their riches vanished with the commerce whence they had been derived, and the oppression of the conquerors completed their ruin.

They progressively recovered, especially after the reign of Henry II. At that time, considerable rights began to be granted or rather to be restored to them. The lord of the domain in which they were situated was at first the proprietor of them, and received tribute from their inhabitants; but they were allowed to ransom themselves from this burden by taking the town in *fee-farm*, a kind of tenure analogous to that of *socage*. Lastly, several towns obtained charters of incorporation, which gave them a more or less free municipal system.

The lord, whether king or baron, retained the right of imposing taxes upon them at will. This right, called the right of *tallage*, was at first exercised in an entirely arbitrary way, in virtue of the very superior force possessed by the lords; but in proportion as this superiority became enfeebled, and the towns, on the other hand, became strong enough to defend their independence, it was found necessary to make terms with them. In order to obtain money from them, privileges had to be granted to them; and if they did not exact concessions of this kind, they at least contended with their lord on behalf of their interests. Those towns especially which lay in the domain of the king, and were the most important of all, vindicated their rights with the greatest degree of vehemence. The royal judges had now no other occupation in their circuits than to obtain tribute from the towns and boroughs, leaving those which could resist pretty nearly to dictate their own terms, and making arbitrary charges on those which were not in a condition to defend themselves.

By these causes the admission of town deputies into the national assembly was delayed, while, on the other hand, the admission of county deputies was hastened. In the counties there was not that unity which is the natural characteristic of towns; there was hardly any possibility of treating separately and successively with proprietors scattered over their domains; and in order to obtain money from them, they had to be united. It was not so in the towns; the king dealt with them separately, made his advances upon them as they became isolated from one another, and always obliged them either to yield or to make him presents, to all appearance voluntarily.

However, some towns early acquired sufficient importance not only to gain and defend their liberties, but also to take part in general politics. Among these towns, London and the *Cinque ports** must especially be mentioned. The importance which these possessed is established by a great number of facts, and we often find their inhabitants called *nobiles* and even *barones*. Indeed, their deputies appeared sometimes at the general assembly even before the Parliament of 1264, but in this there was no general principle, no public right recognized. There was this difference between the introduction into Parliament of county deputies, and that of town deputies—that the former is associated with a right, the right of the immediate vassals of the king, and therefore possessed from the first a character of generality; while the second, the introduction of town deputies, was dissevered from every idea of right, and resulted simply from isolated facts bearing no relation to one another. Representatives were granted to a particular town, but this did not involve any similar concession to all towns. Hence the arbitrariness that of necessity prevailed in the division of representation among towns and boroughs. Hence the vices which still actually exist in the electoral system of England.[†] There remain to the present day towns of considerable importance which send no deputies to the House of Commons; and these abuses arise from the fact that the elections of towns and boroughs have never been regulated in a general manner, and as public rights. In the first instance, all was decided by a solitary fact, and the right to representation has still continued as a right in the case of many boroughs and towns, although the primitive fact which originally suggested the right has disappeared—the fact, namely, of the importance of the town or borough. Through these causes the evil of rotten boroughs was introduced into the representative system of England.

However this may be, not till the parliament of 1264 do we see deputies from towns and boroughs appear in any large numbers in the Parliament. We do not know how many towns were then called upon to exercise this right; but the writs were addressed to them directly, and not by the intervention of the sheriffs. This innovation was doubtless a result of the policy of the Earl of Leicester. He had sought for protection against the king in the knights of the

---

* The five towns of Dover, Sandwich, Romney, Hastings and Hythe, were called the *Cinque ports*.

[†] It must not be forgotten that this course of lectures was delivered in 1821, ten years before the passing of the Reform Bill.

shires, and through these auxiliaries the king and the royal authority had fallen into his hands; but soon finding the want of another support against the barons, who had become his rivals, he found it in the towns, and called upon them to take a share in the exercise of power. This it was that rendered his memory so popular that the king was obliged especially to forbid his being spoken of as a saint.

We must then refer the complete formation of the English Parliament to the year 1264. Its existence was still very precarious; it rested on no law, on no public right; it was the creation of a time of faction. The first Parliament, in which Leicester had principally ruled (the Parliament of Oxford) was soon called the Mad Parliament—*Parliamentum insanum.* It might have been expected that the new form of Parliament, the presence of county and borough deputies, would have shared the same fate as that suffered by the other institutions which were introduced by Leicester for the purpose of organizing a purely aristocratic government, and which disappeared with him. But these rudiments of parliamentary organization were of a different character; they were veritably public institutions, which, instead of attaching themselves merely to particular interests, had for their basis the interests of the entire population. They survived Leicester, and his attempts against the royal power, which was itself obliged to adopt them. Under the reign of Edward I. they became definitely established, and acquired a consistency and stability which would no longer allow of their being attacked with success.

LECTURE 13

---

*Progress of the Parliament under the reign of Edward I. ⌒ Frequent
holding of Parliament. ⌒ Different composition of Parliaments. ⌒
Deputies from the counties and towns were not always present. ⌒ Discretionary power of the king in the convocation of barons. ⌒ The varying number of county and borough deputies.*

Great political institutions generally originate under feeble and incapable
princes; in the midst of the troubles which arise in their reign, they are extorted
from them. They are consolidated under more able princes, who know how to
recognize the necessity for them, and to understand the advantages which they
may derive from them.

This was the case in England under Henry III. and Edward I. Henry, who
was entirely deficient in firmness, allowed, although quite against his inclina-
tion, all the concessions which were demanded of him to escape from his hands;
his son, who was able and energetic, instead of setting himself to destroy the institutions which his father had permitted to come into being, made himself
master of them, and turned them to his own advantage. Edward I. would not
perhaps have allowed them to begin in his reign; but finding them in vigorous
existence, he accepted them as they were, and instead of dreading or dispersing
the new Parliament, he availed himself of it as an instrument to serve and
strengthen a power which he exercised with intelligence. It was by the aid of the
Parliament that Edward I. conferred, so to speak, a national character upon his
wars and conquests—enterprises which might perhaps have excited his people
against him, if he had reigned alone, and acted at once without public support
and public control.

Two kinds of Parliament appeared under Edward I. The one kind was
composed only of the higher barons, and seemed to form the grand council of
the king; in the other, deputies from counties and boroughs had a seat.

No legal and fixed distinction existed between these assemblies; their attributes were almost identical, and they often exercised the same powers. However, the meetings of those Parliaments which were composed only of the

higher barons were very frequent; they took place regularly four times a year. The other Parliaments, on the contrary, were only convened on extraordinary occasions, and when it was necessary to obtain from the freeholders, either of the counties or of the towns and boroughs, some general impost.

This, however, was not the only motive which could lead to the convocation of this last mentioned assembly, which, in truth, alone deserves the name of Parliament. Whenever business arose of so great importance that the concurrence of a great number of interests was judged necessary, the great Parliament was assembled, and by this cause its range of deliberation became more extended, and it assumed a greater consistency.

We may infer the moral force which the Parliament had already acquired at this period, by the political maxims which were generally admitted. Robert of Winchelsea, Archbishop of Canterbury, speaking to the Pope on behalf of the king and his barons, addressed to him this remarkable sentiment: "*It is the custom of the kingdom of England that, in matters which regard the state of that kingdom, the advice of all those interested in the matter should be consulted.*"* There is no need that we should take this principle in its most rigorous application; it is not the fact that all those who were interested in these matters were consulted about them; but the sentiment is still a witness of the progress which had already been made by the ideas of a free and public government. This progress is still further attested by the answer which Edward himself made to the clergy, who demanded of him the repeal of a statute designed to restrain the accumulation of property in mortmain: "*This statute,*" said he, "*had been made by the advice of his barons, and consequently it could not be recalled without their advice.*"† In this case, also, the principle was very far from being strictly observed, and Edward himself, in 1281, on his own authority, altered several of the statutes which had been passed in 1278 by the Parliament at Gloucester. Nothing therefore was more irregular and uncertain than the rights of the public and the forms of government at this period. Principles were professed which were only very partially carried into practice, and which were often entirely neglected. But in the midst of this apparent disorder, great institutions were gradually being formed; the innovations of the preceding reign became habits, and these habits, sanctioned by time, became necessities. Thus rights were established.

As to the distinction which I have just made between the different assemblies which met at this period, as they are all equally called Parliaments, and exercised at various times the most different powers, it is difficult to fix precisely upon those which ought to be regarded as positive Parliaments. The boundaries

---

* "Consuetudo est regni Angliae quod in negotiis contingentibus statum ejusdem regni, requiritur consilium omnium quos res tangit."

† "Consilio magnatum suorum factum crat, et ideo absque eorum consilio non crat revocandum."

which separate them are contracted and often imperceptible; it would be great temerity to pretend accurately to determine what was the real character of any particular assembly, and consequently whether it ought or ought not to be regarded as a Parliament. Whenever Tory writers have not found the presence of county and borough deputies attested by positive and official proof, such as the writs of convocation, they have denied the fact of their presence. But this is an excessive and partial exactness: very often the chronicles of the period supply the lack of writs, and indicate that these deputies were present. I will now point out the principal facts which have been omitted by these writers, which prove that complete Parliaments were frequently holden.

While Edward was still in Palestine, a Parliament was assembled in Westminster to take an oath of fidelity to the new king from the hands of the Archbishop of York, and, according to several chroniclers, four knights from each shire and four deputies from each city were summoned thither.

Edward, on his return to England, convened a new Parliament at Westminster, on the 25th of April, 1275. The preamble to the statutes which were on that occasion decreed has been preserved: it declares that "these statutes have been made by king Edward by the advice of his council, and with the consent of the archbishops, bishops, abbots, priors, barons, and *of the commonalty of the kingdom.*"

In the following year another Parliament was assembled in the same place; it was constituted in the same manner, and, to all appearance, consisted of the same members.

The year 1283 offers many proofs of the admission of deputies from the Commons into Parliament. In the month of January two extraordinary assemblies were convened, one at Northampton, the other at York, to raise the forces and obtain the subsidies that were necessary for the conquest of Wales. The writs of convocation have been preserved: in the one case, the sheriffs were ordered to send to Northampton all the freeholders who possessed a revenue of more than twenty pounds sterling; in the other case, they are enjoined to cause to be elected in each county, city, borough, and mercantile town (*villa mercatoria*), four knights and townsmen having full power "for the whole of the commonalty." Lastly, in the month of June of this same year, a Parliament met at Shrewsbury, in order to decide on the fate of David, prince of Wales, who had been made prisoner, after the conquest of that country. The writs of convocation are of four kinds: the first are addressed individually to one hundred and eleven earls or barons; the second to the magistrates of twenty-one towns or boroughs; the third enjoin the sheriffs to cause two knights to be elected for each county; the fourth are addressed to seventeen members of the king's privy council, among whom are the judges. From 1283 to 1290 we meet with several Parliaments, some of which are even celebrated by the statutes which emanated from them; however, there is no proof that any deputies from counties and boroughs were present at them.

But, in 1290, Edward on his return from France convened a Parliament at Westminster, in which it is certain that some county deputies sat. A writ has been preserved dated June 14th, 1290, addressed to the sheriff of Northumberland, and ordering him to cause *two* or *three* knights to be elected. There is every reason to believe that this county was not the only one thus privileged, and that there were others which also sent deputies to this Parliament. This convocation was probably intended to enable the county deputies to pronounce concerning the statute *Quia emptores terrarum,* which authorised the proprietors of fiefs to sell them at their discretion, and rendered the subsequent possessors direct vassals of the lord of the fief, while the sellers ceased to be such; this removed the necessity of sub-enfeofment, and must have considerably increased the number of the direct vassals of the king. Boroughs were not represented in this Parliament: probably because the matters of which it treated did not immediately concern them.

From 1290 to 1294 we find several Parliaments in which there is no indication that county and borough deputies had a seat. In these Parliaments the affairs of Scotland were considered. The magnates of the kingdom alone took part in them. In the Parliament held at Westminster in the month of October, 1294, only borough representatives are wanting; county deputies were admitted to it; they granted to the king a tenth of the moveable wealth of the kingdom.

In the following year we find that not only the boroughs and counties, but even the inferior clergy, exercised the right to be represented in the great assembly held at Westminster in the month of September, 1295. We possess the writs of convocation addressed to the bishops and archbishops, ordering them to cause a certain number of deputies for the chapters and for the clergy to be nominated; we have also those which summon forty-nine earls or barons individually, and those which enjoin the sheriffs to cause two knights to be elected for each county, and two deputies for each borough in the county. These boroughs were about a hundred and twenty in number. This assembly was more general in its character than any other that had as yet met; all classes of society had access to it, and we may truly say that the entire nation was represented. Accordingly the regular and complete establishment of the British Parliament is generally dated from this year, 1295.

This great assembly did not act as one single body; it was divided into two houses, the one containing lay representatives, the other ecclesiastical; and not only was the place of their meeting distinct, but their votes were distinct also. The barons and knights granted to the king an eleventh of their moveable wealth; the townsmen gave a seventh, and the clergy, after long disputes with the king, ended by only granting him a tenth, which was the offer originally made.

The Parliament which was held in the month of August, 1296, was constituted in the same way as its predecessor, and the votes in it were similarly divided. The barons and knights granted only a twelfth part of their moveable property, and the burgesses an eighth.

In 1297, a Parliament met at Salisbury, but the writs by which it was convened are lost; we do not therefore posess any direct proof of the presence of deputies from counties and boroughs in this assembly; however, there is extant a writ of the 30th of July, in the same year, in which Edward states that the towns and counties have granted him subsidies, and this indirect proof may supply the want of the writs of convocation.

During this same year (1297), the quarrel broke out between the aristocracy and the crown on the subject of the confirmation of the charters, and the Earls of Norfolk and Hereford, by their bold steadfastness, secured victory for the national cause, and extorted from the king a complete and definite sanction to the rights and institutions whose maintenance they vindicated. We find at this time that two deputies were summoned from each county to receive from the hands of the prince-regent those charters which had been confirmed by the king.

From the time when these charters were definitely confirmed, the convocation of deputies from the counties and boroughs was no longer an irregular and arbitrary transaction—it became a necessity. Accordingly, their presence in the Parliaments is constantly attested by authentic proofs.

Thus they were admitted to the Parliament convened at York, on the 15th of April, 1298; the writs of convocation of which are preserved. They were also present in the Parliament held at Lincoln on the 29th of December, 1299. The writs of convocation for this Parliament are similar to those which convened the preceding one. They summon the same deputies who had been present at the last Parliament, enjoining further that substitutes should be chosen in the place of any who had died since that time. We find, moreover, that writs were addressed to the chancellors of the Universities of Oxford and Cambridge, requiring them to send to the Parliament four or five deputies in the case of Oxford, and two or three from Cambridge; and directing them to select such deputies from among those who were most discreet and most learned in the law—*de discretioribus et in jure scripto magis expertis praedictae Universitatis.*

Lastly, the writs of convocation for the Parliament held at Westminster on the 24th of July, 1302, are in all respects similar to the preceding.

I will not further trace this series of facts, which henceforth ceases to be remarkable because of its unvarying uniformity. Suffice it to say that all the Parliaments which were held during the last five years of the reign of Edward I. were of the same nature and composed of the same members. Two of these, however, deserve special attention. The first is that held at Westminster in 1305.

The particulars of its dissolution are preserved to us, as well as those which relate to the mode in which the petitions which already flowed into it were received. The second is that which met at Carlisle in 1307. We have the lists of the bishops, abbots, priors, earls, barons, &c., who sat in it. The number of earls or barons amounts to eighty-six, that of the bishops and abbots to sixty-eight. There were besides a great number of deputies from the inferior clergy, forming the lower house of the ecclesiastical convocation; and there were, moreover, two knights from each county, two citizens from each city, and two burgesses from each borough.

From all these facts it follows that, if at the commencement of the fourteenth century the Parliament was not yet constituted in an actual and definite form, yet it already rested on a fixed basis: moreover, as to its composition, we may deduce from the facts to which I have already referred, the following results:

I. The Parliament was composed, in the *first* place, of earls or lay barons convened individually by the king; *secondly,* of archbishops, bishops, abbots, and priors, also summoned individually; *thirdly,* of deputies from the knights or freeholders of the counties; *fourthly,* of deputies from cities, towns, and boroughs.

II. No law or statute, no ancient or recognized right, determined who were the earls, barons, abbots, &c., whom the king was bound to convoke individually. He acted somewhat arbitrarily in this respect, often omitting to summon those whom he had summoned on previous occasions.* These omissions were sometimes, though rarely, resisted by protests. The importance of a noble and of his family was the only guarantee of his convocation to the Parliament. Disorder, civil wars, and confiscations, prevented this convocation from being an incontestable and hereditary right, except in the case of a permanent feudal tenure.

---

* Thus Edward summoned to the Parliament of Shrewsbury (1283) a hundred and eleven earls or barons; to the Parliament of Westminster (1295), he only summoned fifty-three; and out of the hundred and eleven who were present in 1283, sixty were absent in 1295. The latter Parliaments of his reign furnish several instances of similar irregularities. Thus we find at this time ninety-eight lay *proceres* who were only once summoned to the Parliament, and fifty who were summoned once, twice, or three times. There was a distinction among the barons who were summoned individually: some were summoned by virtue of their feudal tenure, others, only in virtue of the writ of convocation, whether they were or were not immediate vassals of the king. These last exercised in the Parliament the same rights as the former, only it does not appear that the sole fact of a writ of convocation conferred upon them a hereditary right. There are even several examples of ecclesiastical peers who were convened by special writs, and who obtained a discharge from the obligation to attend the Parliament by proving that they held no fief of the king. The practice of creating barons or peers was of later introduction: *first,* by a statute of the Parliament (under Edward III.); *secondly,* by letters patent from the king (under Richard II.).

III. The principal functionaries of the king, such as the judges and members of the privy council, were almost always convened to the Parliament by virtue of their official position; indeed, they were uniformly either earls or barons.

IV. The convocation of county and borough deputies was not a legal or public necessity; but it became an actual necessity by the predominance of the principle that consent in all matters of impost was a right.

V. The convocation of county deputies was more certain and regular than that of borough deputies; more certain, because it originated partly in a right which had not then been questioned, and which it was necessary to respect— the right, namely, of every immediate vassal to a seat in the general assembly; more regular, because the county courts, which were all composed of the same elements and possessed of the same interests, constituted a uniform and identical whole throughout England, so that some could not be admitted to the privilege of representation without all the rest being admitted also. As the towns and boroughs, on the other hand, only owed their admission into Parliament to varying causes without unity or connexion with each other, and were only called to assist in matters which concerned themselves individually; so the admission of a representative from one town did not at all involve the admission of representatives from other towns, nor even the continuance of this privilege in any one case.

VI. The number of town and borough deputies was not fixed. The king determined this arbitrarily. Nevertheless the convocation of two deputies for each county, and as many for each borough, passed into a rule.

VII. However irregular the convocation of borough deputies might be, there is no reason to think that the number of boroughs which were then represented in the assembly was as limited as has been assumed; there is no reason to think, as has been maintained by Tory historians, that only towns in the domains of the king originally sent deputies to Parliament. The assumption is, on the contrary, contradicted by facts which prove that, besides the towns belonging to the royal domain, those which had received a charter of incorporation, either from the king or from some great baron, were represented; as were also those which, without having received any such charter, were rich enough to pay the expenses of their deputies. However, the importance of particular towns, and the necessity that was felt for their concurrence in public business, was in this respect the only rule; and most frequently, the choice of the towns which should be represented was left to the arbitrary decision of the sheriffs.

LECTURE 14

Mode of election of the deputies of counties and boroughs. ⁓ Who were the electors. ⁓ No uniform principle to regulate elections in boroughs and towns. ⁓ Voting in public.

WE have seen how county and borough deputies were introduced into Parliament; but we are still far from having obtained a complete and correct idea of representative government as it existed in England at the period at which we have now arrived. We have yet to learn by whom and in what manner these members were nominated—in a word, what was then the electoral system, if we may be allowed to give this name to a collection of isolated customs and institutions unconnected with each other, and almost entirely destitute of any generality or unity of character.

The two political parties, whose opposition and debates are met with at every step in the study of English institutions, have not failed to resolve this question, each in a different manner. The Tories, always disposed to limit the boundaries of public liberty, maintain that the introduction of county members into Parliament arose primarily from the impossibility of uniting in the general assembly all the direct vassals of the king, the whole body of whom alone had the right to be present; and that landowners of this class were originally the sole electors of these representatives. The Whigs assert, on the other hand, that all the freeholders in the county, whether direct or indirect vassals of the king, have always taken part in this election.

I shall seek the solution of this question exclusively in the facts which have special reference to the introduction of county members into Parliament; and as this change has been the result not of secondary or unforeseen circumstances, but of the natural course of time and of events, it is needful first to call to mind the general facts which preceded it and gave it birth.

We have seen that, a large number of the direct vassals of the king having very early renounced, on account of their small wealth or influence, their attendance at the general assembly, their political existence became localized and restricted to county affairs, and to attendance at the county court, at which those affairs were transacted. The direct vassals of the king, however, were not the only persons interested in the affairs of the county. Many other freeholders, whether vassals of the great barons or originally simple socagers, possessed considerable wealth and influence;* and as actual possession at this period was almost the only arbiter of right, there is little doubt, *a priori,* that all the freeholders of any importance in the county were then admitted to the county-court, to direct the administration of justice and to discuss their common interests.

These probabilities are changed into absolute facts by the testimony of history. It is proved that the knights, who were direct vassals of the king, did not alone compose the county-courts. From the time of William the Conqueror to the end of the reign of Edward I. a multitude of deeds, laws, writs, and historic records prove that all the freeholders, or nearly all, sat in these courts; and that if there were some exceptions to this rule, they did not in the least proceed from any general distinction between the direct or indirect vassals of the king, but merely from particular conditions imposed on individual tenures. For it does not appear that all freemen-landholders were equally compelled to make their appearance at the county-courts, as this service was esteemed a burden rather than a privilege.

It may then be regarded as certain, that either by the fall of many of the direct vassals of the king, or by the elevation of a great number of the simple vassals of the nobles, there had arisen in every county a body of freeholders, all of whom, in reference to the affairs of the county, and independently of the nature of their feudal relations, possessed the same importance and equal rights.

The county-courts, thus composed, exercised the right of election long before the regular and definitive introduction of their representatives into Parliament. Here officers invested with the powers necessary for the transaction of the county business were sometimes elected; and sometimes knights were appointed to execute the measures of the central government, or sent thither as bearers of complaints or representations. Instances of such elections are numerous. The charters have frequently prescribed them, and they are continually spoken of in the chronicles.

It cannot be affirmed that this appointment of particular knights for the transaction of specific local business was always conducted in a regular manner and by a distinct election. It was sometimes done by the sheriffs alone: but it is certain that most generally it took place "by the community of the county, with the consent and by the advice of the county, *per communitatem comitatus, de assensu et consilio comitatus.*"

---

* It may be seen in the Black Book of the Exchequer that Godfrey Fitzwilliam, in Buckinghamshire, held twenty-seven knights' fiefs of Earl Walter Gifford, whilst Guilbon Bolbech, in the same county, held of the king only one knight's fief.

We gather from all these facts, first, that before the introduction of county-members into Parliament, the direct vassals of the king, who, on account of their inferior importance, had ceased to attend at the general assembly, did not form a distinct body in the county-courts, or a particular class of landowners invested with peculiar rights; but that, on the contrary, they were merged in the general class of freeholders, nearly all of whom also attended the county-court, and there exercised the same rights; and, secondly, it is unquestionable that this assembly of freeholders was in the habit, in certain cases, of appointing some one of its members either for the management of the county business, or for any other purpose.

Are we to believe that when the object in view was sending representatives of the county to Parliament, there was substituted, in place of the existing order of things, a new order by which to elect them? or, in other words, that those freeholders, who, though direct vassals of the king, were on the same footing with the other freeholders as regarded all the operations of the county-court, were distinguished from them by being alone called upon to elect members of Parliament? Nothing is less probable in itself, and in fact nothing is less true than that there was such a disorganization of the county-courts at election times.

It is not at all probable, because, in the state of society at this period, the *status quo* almost always ruled. We are greatly deceived if we expect to find the institutions of the time under the sway of some general rule, and issuing in the inevitable consequences of a principle. There was no such dominant general rule or principle. When a new law appears, it is the product of facts, not of a theory. When any new demand is made upon society, it is society in its actual condition, and not a systematically constituted society, which replies to the demand.

The freeholders in general formed the county-court on every occasion, and took part in all its acts. What reason could there be for suddenly setting aside an established custom in order to create a privilege in favour of certain landowners whose position, although special in some respects, was but little distinguished from that of others? Was there any occasion for an act so unusual that it could not be put in force without subverting the customs then in vogue? There was none: on the contrary, this act appeared to the county landowners as only another circumstance allied to the many existing facts of the same description: they neither foresaw all the importance which this fact could not fail to acquire, nor all the consequences to which it would necessarily lead. This election of knights summoned to Parliament, although somewhat more important than other elections, resembled all those which were frequently made in the county-court, and in which every freeholder took part. Why should the right of voting on such occasions have belonged exclusively to particular individuals among them? Were they not all equally interested, as the majority of the taxes were levied on their personal property; and the principal duty of the deputies was the settlement of the taxes? How is it possible to believe otherwise than that this, like every other election, was made by all the members of the county-court without distinction?

Facts, I repeat, confirm these probabilities. The writs addressed to the sheriffs by the king for the election of county members, are conceived in the same terms as those issued for elections relating exclusively to the administration of local affairs. They equally set forth that these knights shall be elected with the assent of the community of the county, *de assensu communitatis comitatus*. Further, the returns of the sheriffs declare that the election has been made "in full county, by the whole of the community of the county," *in pleno comitatu, per totam communitatem comitatus*. Under the succeeding reigns, terms yet more formal were employed; thus, about the middle of the reign of Edward III. the writs contain, that the election ought to be made "according to the will, and with the consent, of the men of the county," *de arbitrio et consensu hominum comitatus*. Finally, facts which have come down to us from later times prove that all freeholders possessed an equal right of participation in these elections. In 1405, a statute of Henry IV., intended to prevent certain abuses committed on these occasions by sheriffs under the preceding reign, orders among other things, that "all those who should be present at the county-court, even when they had not been duly summoned thither by the sheriff, should take part in the election." Lastly, under Henry VI., the great number of the freeholders having given rise to many disturbances during the elections, two statutes (the first issued in 1429, and the second in 1432) limited the right of suffrage to freeholders possessing an annual income of forty shillings: this was the first and last limitation of the kind, and it still continues to subsist in England.

Thus, moral probabilities and historical facts alike indicate, that since the origin of the Parliament in its actual form, the representatives of counties have been elected not only by the direct vassals of the king, but by all the freeholders, whether mediate or immediate vassals, who composed the county court. In order definitively to establish this opinion, nothing remains but to examine the proofs that are alleged in favour of the opposite opinion. These may be reduced to two: first, it is said, that as the direct vassals of the king alone possessed originally the right of sitting in the general assembly, and as the election of knights of the shire arose entirely from the impossibility of assembling in Parliament all the direct vassals of the king, the latter alone must have been the electors of the representatives who were sent in their place. Secondly, the vassals of the barons long demanded exemption from the obligation of contributing to the payment of the fees allotted to the county members, which proves that they could not have shared in the election; for had they done so their claim would have been absurd. Both these proofs have the fault of being indirect, and of resting upon consequences deduced from general facts, and not upon special and positive facts, such as those I have just adduced in support of the contrary opinion. Moreover, the first argument supposes the existence of a general and absolute principle which was invariably followed; and that the county members were summoned to Parliament only to represent the direct vassals of the king. This supposition is neither probable nor conformable to facts. We again repeat, that there was at this period no general principle, no fixed and invariable rule. General principles and their consequences exist only in a calm and settled state of society; they are incompatible with a rude population and long-continued disorder. How, then, could social classifications and their corresponding rights have remained fixed and distinct in the midst of such chaotic confusion? Besides, the feudal system never exercised such complete sway in England as to insure anything like a strict observance of its principles. It is true that the right possessed by all the direct vassals of the king to appear in the central assembly, was one of the sources of county representation; but when this right, after having fallen into desuetude, began to revive in the persons of representatives, it was outweighed by an actual and more powerful circumstance, the formation of the general class of freeholders, meeting at the county-court, and there exercising the same functions and equal rights. This fact is incontestible; so the Tories are compelled to acknowledge that the deputies were elected by all present at the county-court. But how do they attempt to escape from the consequences of this confession? They maintain that the direct vassals alone sat in the county-court: an opinion too much opposed to the nature of things and to all the facts which I have brought forward, to require refutation.

There is another difficulty which perplexes Tory writers, and which they are equally unsuccessful in their attempts to surmount. It is impossible for them to deny that under the reigns subsequent to that of Edward I., and especially under Henry IV., all the freeholders in the county took part in the election: now, to avoid this embarrassment, it is pretended, that taking advantage of the disorder of the times they had usurped the right of suffrage, and that the statute of Henry IV. (in 1405) for the first time legalized this abuse, and lawfully summoned the freeholders to the election of deputies. There is no probability in this supposition, which is not supported by a single fact. Between the reigns of Edward I. and Henry IV., nothing can be discovered which indicates the usurpation of the electoral right by a portion of the freeholders who had remained till then strangers to the election. No trace of change in the composition of the county-courts is to be found, nor any alteration in the form or language of the writs of convocation. Everything indicates, on the contrary, that the elections continued to be conducted as in former times; and that the statute of Henry IV. has evidently no other object than to prevent the illegal practices of the sheriffs, which had become scandalous under the reign of Richard II. Thus, in whatever light it is viewed, this first argument is utterly valueless.

The second is of no greater worth. It is founded upon the supposition that those only who have a voice in the election of representatives ought to contribute to the payment of their salary. Now this supposition is explicitly contradicted by a writ of Edward III., which proves that even the *villani*, the simple husbandmen, who certainly took no part in the election, were required to contribute to the payment of the fees. If it appear, then, that the freeholders demanded release from this impost, it cannot thence be concluded that they had no share in the election.

In these demands there is nothing extraordinary. The office of member of Parliament was originally more an onerous burden than an advantage. The person elected was compelled to give security to guarantee his attendance at the assembly. A curious instance is mentioned of an elected knight who could not find the required bail; the sheriffs, therefore, seized his oxen and farm-horses to compel him to fulfil the duties of his office. In a short time, to render the charge less onerous it was made lucrative: fees being awarded to the representatives. These fees were levied on the entire county, with the exception of certain particular immunities. A writ of Edward III. proves this distinctly. It is true that the vassals of the barons, chiefly under the reign of Edward III., made frequent claims of exemption from payment of the salaries due to the members: but these were not founded upon the circumstance that they had had no share in the election; they rested on a pretext derived from feudal law, maintaining that, as their lords sat in Parliament in their own right, that is to say, in their quality of peers, they were represented by them, and ought not to pay the salaries of the county representatives. It is evident that these claims proceeded from confusing ideas of the ancient feudal representation (a fiction which rendered the noble in some sort the proxy of his vassals) with ideas of the new system of representation. These facts in no way prove that the vassals of the barons took no part in the election of the county members; all that they indicate is that the collection of the members' salaries was very arbitrary, and was regulated by different customs in each county; no conclusion can, however, be drawn from them relative to electoral rights.

Now that I have reduced to their just value these two arguments, the sole support of the opinion which I oppose, it appears very nearly certain that all the freeholders who attended the county-court united in the election of the representatives, whatever might be the nature of their feudal relation to the crown.

Having completed our researches into the election of county members, let us next examine how the election of the representatives of boroughs was conducted.

Although in the county-courts no fixed rule nor systematic distinction regulated the distribution of electoral rights, there was at least something general and identical in them throughout England. The counties were territorial districts of the same nature; the county-courts, wherever situated, were the same institution, and the freeholders formed one class of men. Out of circumstances nearly everywhere alike, there naturally arose an electoral system in all places the same.

It was not, nor could it be thus with respect to the boroughs. They had acquired their liberties successively to a greater or less extent, and under a thousand different forms. The political state of one town gives no clue to that of other towns, as they were not at all correspondent to one another. Sometimes the municipal rights belonged to the more or less numerous corporation which held the town in *fee-farm;* sometimes to the general body of freeholders who held their houses in *burgage-tenure,* a kind of tenure analogous to the tenure in *socage;* sometimes to the entire body of householders; occasionally, but more rarely, to the whole of the inhabitants. When any particular borough was summoned to send deputies to Parliament, it occurred to no one to consider this new right as distinct from their municipal rights, and to regulate the electoral system on a separate basis. This summons had reference to the borough in its existing condition, and did not introduce the slightest innovation into the exercise of the civic authority. The citizens who, in virtue of their charter, enjoyed the right of managing the affairs of the borough, also exercised that of naming its representatives. There was then nothing general or uniform in the foundation of this new right, and it would be impossible to reduce the elections in towns and boroughs to any common principle. We can only examine a number of particular facts, and derive from them the following results:

I. The political right of electing members of Parliament was not distinct from the municipal rights of the borough, and was exercised in the same manner and by the same citizens.

II. From this it follows that the election was commonly made by the council, who directed the local interests of the borough: the number of electors, therefore, was very limited at the outset.

III. Where a corporation held a town in *fee-farm,* it also possessed the right of appointing the members of Parliament. These corporations were generally composed of a few individuals.

IV. As the freeholders of many boroughs sat in the county-courts, not a few of the elections of borough members took place originally in these very county-courts, and by the borough freeholders who repaired thither, and who exercised this power either on their own account, or as authorized by their fellow-citizens.

V. The writs or orders for the election of deputies were at first addressed directly to the borough magistrates themselves. This, at least, was the case in 1264, the period of the first convocation with which we are acquainted of the representatives of boroughs under Henry III. In 1283, the same procedure was followed by

Edward I. for the convocation of the Shrewsbury Parliament, to which the representatives of twenty-one boroughs were summoned. In 1295, the writs were addressed to the sheriffs of the counties in which the boroughs were situated, and from that period, this has been the habitual and legal form of convening the boroughs. In 1352 and 1353, however, Edward III. addressed his writs directly to the municipal magistrates, on the first occasion for ten boroughs, and on the second for thirty-eight. These are the last examples of similar convocations. The Cinque-ports remained the only boroughs which received the writs directly.

These facts explain how borough-representation has been so easily corrupted in England, and remains so disgraceful to this day.* In every town political rights have remained restricted to the municipal bodies, who, originally, were usually comprised in a very narrow circle. The general tendency has been ever since, and especially at the period of the revolution of 1640, to extend electoral rights in boroughs, and thus to render the election more popular; but, on the whole, the choice is invariably made by the municipal powers, organized according to their ancient charters of incorporation. In the counties, electoral rights have adapted themselves to all the vicissitudes of property, and have become proportionably extended: in the boroughs, they have remained unaltered. Every unchangeable institution is vicious, because ultimately it will be sure to establish privileges in opposition to the actual state of society.

I should wish to be able to add to these researches into the electoral system of England in the thirteenth century some particular and circumstantial details concerning the forms of elections; but nothing can be discovered on this subject, either in history or in the laws. The laws did not mention the matter, because at this stage of civilization it is not thought that such things require to be either regulated or expressed. It is probable that the electors, who were generally very few in number, agreed among themselves, in presence of the sheriff, on the representatives they wished to appoint; and that the sheriff, by a writ, informed the Court of Chancery of the nomination. The only important circumstance in this mode of election was the open voting, which has been perpetuated to this day. Nobody then attached sufficient importance to his choice to think concealment necessary.

Until the reign of Henry IV., we do not find any law respecting the forms of election. In proportion as the elections became important, the sheriffs, profiting by the absence of all forms, took the matter into their own hands, and managed it agreeably to their own will. The law to which I refer was passed in order to prevent these abuses. Here, as everywhere, the organization of sureties took place long after the recognition and exercise of rights.

* Before the reform of Parliament in 1832.

LECTURE 15

Philosophical examination of the electoral system in England in the four-
teenth century. ~ *The system was the natural result of facts.* ~ *Who*
were the electors? ~ *Four principles which determine the solution of*
this question.

THE facts adduced in my previous lecture, prove that the electoral system of England in the fourteenth century was determined by no philosophical combination, by no general intention. This system arose naturally and spontaneously, out of facts. Its study is therefore more curious and interesting: modern times are full of science and artifice; institutions do not now become developed with simplicity and freedom; under the pretext of giving them regularity, things are distorted, to suit some particular interest, or to accommodate a theory. Nothing of this nature occurred in the formation of the British Parliament; science did not then exist, and cunning was unnecessary. The House of Commons was not of sufficient importance for the executive to be much disturbed about its origin; the office of member for a county or borough was not enough sought after to induce different interests and parties to direct all their instruments of warfare and stratagems of policy to this end. Representatives of the country were required, who were to be chosen by the method of election—but this election had no occasion to adapt itself to a theory, or to be false in any way. In such a state of society, the electoral system might be vicious and incomplete in a thousand ways; its forms might be irregular and destitute of all needful guarantees, but its general principles would be natural and sound. These principles are what I propose to seek after, and to bring to light, in the present Lectures. They were neither known or thought of in the fourteenth century, but they exist in facts; for there is a reason for every fact, and all are subject to certain laws. Before entering upon the ancient English electoral system, singly and in itself, we should first consider it in its relations to society in general, to the powers by which it was ruled, and to the liberties which it enjoyed.

In the present day, political science has rarely considered questions in this point of view, though it is the first and most important of all; it has operated on society and its government by a process of dissection; it has taken all powers and rights one by one, and has endeavoured to define each separately, and with regard to itself alone; seeking first completely to disjoin them from one another, and then to make them to proceed together, confining each strictly to its own sphere. In this manner have we seen enumerated the legislative power, the executive power, the electoral power, the judicial power, and the administrative power, and every effort of science has been exerted to make these different powers co-exist, while maintaining among them a rigorous distinction, and enjoining upon them never to fall into confusion, nor even to assimilate their offices and action. The same system has been applied to the rights and liberties of citizens. It is easy here to discern the triumph of the fondness for analysis which characterized the last century. But analysis is a method of study, not of creation. The spirit of analysis is scientific, but never political. In politics, whether dealing with rights or powers, the object is to create real vital forces, capable either of enforcing obedience or resisting oppression. This can never be attained by analysis; for, in reality, actual life is a very complicated matter, requiring the union and amalgamation of a multitude of different elements, each modified and sustained by the others. Analysis elucidates and separates into parts, but never constructs. This truth is demonstrated by the political history of our own time. All these powers and rights, so carefully enumerated and distinguished by science, so narrowly enclosed within specified limits, were found in the time of action to be destitute of consistency, energy, and reality. It was decreed that the legislative power should be absolutely separated from the executive power, the judicial power from the administrative, the municipal from the electoral power: liberties and rights have been isolated and dissected just in the same way as powers; and ere long all these rights and powers, incapable of existence and action in their isolated condition, have become centralized or lost in the hand of an individual or collective despotism, which alone was powerful and real, because it alone was other than a theoretic design or a scientific conception.[1]

It may be fearlessly affirmed that rights, like public powers, will never regain reality and energy until they escape from this pretended science, which, under the pretext of classifying, enervates and nullifies them; until, united by positive ties, they mutually rest on one another, and coalesce to bring about the same results. Doubtless, the great analytical labour performed in our own time will not prove fruitless; many well grounded distinctions and necessary limitations will be maintained; all powers will not again fall into general confusion, nor will all rights become concentrated. There is some truth and usefulness in

1. This is a good illustration of Guizot's views on the division (separation) of powers. He believed that the art of politics requires the harmonious co-existence of various powers and principles that would limit and control each other.

the results of the social dissection which has been performed; but if it were to be perpetuated, if rights and powers were to remain in the state of isolation and dissolution in which science has placed them at the present day, we should never possess either government or freedom.

It is very evident that nothing of this kind occurred at the period of the formation of the British Parliament. Politics did not wear so scientific a character, nor lay claim to such consideration, as at present. It was necessary to summon together the principal men in the kingdom—merchants, landowners, and others—that they might assist in particular public business. But this was never imagined to be the creation of a new right, or of a new power. Established rights and existing powers were called upon to exercise this new function, and to appear under this new form. The freeholders, that is to say, every free and varitable landowner, used to assemble in the county-courts, to administer justice and to treat together of common interests; and these county-courts were charged with the nomination of representatives. In towns of any importance, the citizens, under forms more or less liberal, regulated their own affairs, chose their own magistrates, and exercised in common certain rights and powers; and these municipal corporations were required to send members to Parliament. Thus, the assemblies which we now designate electoral colleges were never at that period, as they now are, special and isolated assemblies, invested with a temporary duty, and in all other respects unconnected with the administration of the country. County courts and municipal corporations, which were already firmly planted and established, and possessed inherent strength, were constituted into electoral colleges. Thus the electoral system from its origin was united with every right and institution, and with almost every local and real power. It was the extension and development of existing liberties, a powerful force added to other forces previously in action and exercising government over other interests. It was not that in one place there were merely electors, in another administrators, and elsewhere judges; but there was a body of citizens who participated in the administration of local affairs, and in rendering justice; and who elected deputies for the transaction of general business. It is easily understood that—being thus deeply rooted in the community at large, and closely united to all other powers—the electoral power (to employ the language of the present day) was defended from every vicissitude through which we have seen it pass, when attempts have been made to establish it, by itself, in some particular aspect or combination.[2]

2. Guizot's views on what a "sound" electoral system should look like are worth examining in detail. He admired the English electoral system because it was linked to local liberties, rights, and strong habits of self-government. Those who had the right to vote, claimed Guizot, were not merely electors, but also citizens who participated in the direction of local affairs; in other words,

This then is the first characteristic of the electoral system which occupies our attention. We need not hesitate to elevate this characteristic into a principle, and to assert that where it is not met with, election, that is to say, representative government itself, will be either powerless or harassed by continual storms.

It is an error in modern politics immoderately to fear power, whatever may be its form or situation. It is divided and subdivided infinitesimally, until it no longer exists, so to speak, except as powder. This is not the way to establish liberty.[3] Liberty cannot exist except by the possession of rights, and rights are worthless if they are not themselves powers—vital and strongly constituted powers. Placing right on one side and power on the other is not constituting a free government, but establishing a permanent tyranny, sometimes under the name of despotism, and sometimes under that of revolution; the problem is to place power everywhere in the hands of right, which can only be done by organizing or accepting at once, in the very centre of the government, and in every stage of its action, authority and resistance. Now resistance is only real and effectual when capable on all occasions of opposition to

---

the right to vote must be rooted in the mores and practices of society. That is why Guizot argued that it is not sufficient to summon the electors together and ask them to choose their representatives; instead, they must know each other well, understand thoroughly what they are supposed to do, and be entirely familiar with those who compete for office. The key idea is that electors must not listen to their transient passions and impulses that might distort their judgment, but must be united by common interests and ties. On this topic, also see *HORG*, pp. 340–52.

3. The originality of Guizot's theory of power must be underscored here. He criticized those classical liberals who wanted government to be a humble servant and its tasks to be strictly limited. In Guizot's opinion, to ask the state to be nothing but a passive and powerless umpire would amount to subverting authority and society alike. Believing in the virtues of wise political crafting, Guizot defended a more nuanced theory of power that was supposed to replace the negative view of state power held by classical liberals. He believed that it would be mistaken to claim that power is *a priori* (intrinsically) bad, for this would amount to misunderstanding the dignity of power properly exercised. What we should fear, he concluded, is not power *tout court,* but unaccountable, absolute power; this explains the need to prevent actual power-holders from using their influence in order to transform their *de facto* power into an inherent right. For a clear statement of Guizot's constitutionalism, see *HORG,* pp. 371–76, where he speaks about individual rights, the separation of powers, and the need to divide the legislative power into two houses. "There is not then," writes Guizot, "and there cannot be, any omnipotence by right, that is to say, any power which should be allowed to say: 'that is good and just because I have so decided it'; and every effort of political science, every institution, ought to tend to the prevention of such a power being anywhere formed; and should provide that the actual omnipotence which exists under so many names in society, should everywhere meet with restraints and obstacles enough to prevent its conversion into an omnipotence by right" (*ibid.,* p. 371). An excellent summary of Guizot's theory of power can also be found in his *Des moyens de gouvernement et d'opposition* (1821) and *HCE,* pp. 228–45.

authority, when authority is compelled to treat with it at all times, to conquer or to yield. What then is the electoral right or power, if so it is called, when isolated from every other power? Its exercise is transient and infrequent; it is the crisis of a day imposed upon actual authority, which may, it is true, be defeated, but which, if it escapes, is afterwards perfectly free, and continues its course without the least obstruction, or sleeps in blind security. If, on the other hand, the electoral right is supported by other rights of more direct and frequent occurrence, if the electoral system is closely interwoven with the whole government, if the same citizens who have nominated the members, interfere in the affairs of the country under other forms but by the same title, if the central authority needs on other occasions their assent and support, if it finds them elsewhere also grouped and united for the exercise of other functions of power, then all rights serve as guarantees to one another; the electoral system is no longer suspended in air, and it becomes difficult to violate it in principle, or to elude it in its consequences.

It is impossible to doubt that to this close union of electoral rights, with a multitude of other public and local rights, the electoral system is indebted in England for its strength and permanence. One fact among a thousand others will prove this. When the central power, finding itself threatened by the elections, has endeavoured to rid itself of their influence, it has been compelled to withdraw from the towns and corporations, their charters and liberties. Without this nothing could have been done. But by this also, everything was attacked, and liberty and right being everywhere emperilled, the nation put forth its efforts not only to re-establish a House of Commons, but also to regain a multitude of other rights which had no reference to the election of representatives. It is the secret of good constitutional legislation, thus to unite all rights with each other in such a manner that it is impossible to weaken any one of them without endangering all.

This characteristic of the British electoral system has also produced, in regard to the elections themselves, other consequences no less felicitous, which I shall presently indicate. I shall now consider this system in itself, in its interior organization.

All the elements and laws of every electoral system resolve themselves into these two questions: I. In whom are the electoral rights vested? that is to say, who are the electors? II. How are these rights exercised? that is to say, what are the modes of procedure and the forms of election?

I wish to bring together in succession under these two questions, all the facts which relate thereto in the electoral system in England, in the fourteenth century, and to examine what general principles are contained in these facts.

And first, who were the electors? There were two classes of electors, in the same manner as there were two kinds of elections—those for counties and those for boroughs. This classification was not the result of a systematic combination nor of any previous intention: it was the expression of a fact.

Originally the knights, and a little later, the freeholders, alone formed the political nation, and alone possessed political rights. All enjoyed the same right of assisting at the court or council of their lord; politically, therefore, they were equal. When the towns had acquired sufficient importance to assist the central power when needful, and strength enough to resist it if occasion required, then inhabitants became citizens. A new nation truly then entered the state. But in entering there, it remained distinct from that by which it was preceded. The representatives of boroughs never deliberated with those of counties. Each of these two classes treated with the government of those affairs which interested itself, and consented on its own account to the taxes which weighed on itself alone. Originally there was no more coalition between the representatives than between the electors: the distinction was complete. It cannot be said that there was inequality, for there was no room for comparison. They were simply two different societies represented by their deputies to the same government; and the difference of the representation arose from no other principle than the real and primitive difference between the two societies.

Now if each of these societies is considered singly and in itself, an equality of political rights will be found among the citizens called to enjoy them. As, in the counties, all the freeholders had the same right to participate in the election, so, in the towns, every member of the corporation to which a charter had been granted shared in the election of their representatives.

Thus the variety of classes existing in society was reproduced in the representation. But, on the one hand, the different classes were completely independent of one another: the knights of the shire did not tax the citizens, nor the citizens the knights of the shire; much less did either take part in the other's elections. On the other hand, the principle of the equality of right prevailed in each class, among the citizens summoned to share in the election.

There is nothing, then, that can be deduced from this in favour of an inequality among men called by virtue of the same principle to take part in a like action. Such an inequality never existed in the electoral administration of England in the fourteenth century. The difference that existed was derived from society itself, and was continued even to the very centre of representation, which did not present a more uniform whole than society itself.

The true, the sole general principle which is manifested in the distribution of electoral rights as it then existed in England, is this, that right is derived from, and belongs to, capacity. This requires some explanation.

It is beyond doubt that, at this period, setting aside the chief barons whose personal importance was such that it was necessary to treat with each of them individually, the freeholders, the clergy, and the burgesses of certain towns, could alone act as citizens. Those not comprised in one or other of these classes were chiefly poor husbandmen, labouring on subordinate and precarious property. They included all men invested with real independence, free to dispose of their person and wealth, and in a position to rise to some ideas of social interest. This it is which constitutes political capacity. This capacity varies according to time and place; the same degree of fortune and enlightenment is not everywhere and always sufficient to confer it, but its elements are constantly the same. It exists wherever we meet with the conditions, whether material or moral, of that degree of independence and intellectual development which enables a man freely and reasonably to accomplish the political act he is required to perform. Assuredly, considering the masses, as they should be considered in such a matter, these conditions are not met with in England in the fourteenth century, elsewhere than among the freeholders, the clergy, and the burgesses of the chief towns. Beyond these classes nothing is found but almost servile dependence and brutal ignorance. In summoning these classes, then, to join in the election, the electoral system summoned every capable citizen. It was derived, therefore, from the principle that capacity confers right; and among citizens whose capacity was recognized, no inequality was established.

Thus neither the sovereignty of the majority nor universal suffrage, were originally the basis of the British electoral system. Where capacity ceased, limitation of right was established. Within this limit the right was equal in all.

It is easy to prove that this is the sole principle on which it is possible to found a national and true electoral system. Let us for the moment forget facts, and consider the question from a purely philosophical point of view.

What motive has assigned in all times and countries a fixed age at which a man is declared to have attained his majority, that is to say, is considered free to manage his own affairs according to his own will? This appointment is nothing more than the declaration of the general fact, that, at a certain age, man is capable of acting, freely and reasonably, in the sphere of his individual interests. Is this declaration arbitrary? No, for if the period of his majority were fixed at ten years or at forty, the law would evidently be absurd; it would assume the presence of capacity where it did not exist, or else would not recognize it where it did exist—that is to say, it would confer or withhold the right wrongfully.

It is capacity, then, that confers right; and capacity is a fact independent of law, which law cannot create or destroy at will, but which it ought to endeavour to recognize with precision, that it may at the same time recognize the right which flows from it. And why does capacity confer right? because in reason, and reason alone, is right inherent. Capacity is nothing else than the faculty of acting in accordance with reason.

What is true of the individual considered in relation to his personal interests, is true also of the citizen in relation to social interests. Here, also, capacity confers right. Here, also, right cannot be refused to capacity without injustice. Here, also, capacity is a fact which the law, if it be just, asserts and distinguishes, to attach thereto the right.

This is the only principle in virtue of which the limitation of electoral rights can be reasonably assigned, and it was this which, without general intention or philosophic views, the nature of things and good sense caused to prevail in England at the end of the thirteenth century.

This principle equally repels the admission of the incapable, which would give dominion to the majority, that is, to material force; and would lead to the exclusion of some portion of the capable citizens, which would be an injustice; and to inequality between capacities, of which the least is declared sufficient, which would institute privilege.

This principle once laid down, whether by the enlightened intention of the legislator, or by the simple force of things, it becomes necessary to put it in practice, that is, to seek and recognize in society those capacities which confer rights. By what exterior signs, susceptible of determination by law, can this capacity be recognized? this is the second enquiry which presents itself when the question is to fix the limit of electoral rights.

Evidently, we can only proceed here upon assumptions, and those of a general character. The capacity of acting freely and reasonably for the promotion of social interests, is revealed by no more distinct signs than any other internal disposition. Besides, the law operates on the masses; its decisions will necessarily be inexact, and yet must be rigorous. In their application to individuals they will often assume capacity where it is not, and will not in all instances discern it where it is. This is the imperfection of human science; the endeavour of the wise is to restrict this imperfection within its narrowest limits.

The electoral system of England was less faulty, in this respect, at its commencement, than it has since become. It is very probable that, in the fourteenth century, all political capacity was almost entirely contained in the classes of the freeholders, the clergy, and the burgesses of the important towns. This kind of qualification corresponded, then, very nearly with the true external signs of capacity. It may even be said that if the representative system had then possessed all its energy, if the assembly of representatives had had power and importance to become the principal spring of government, and the object of individual ambition, it would very soon have been discovered that the legal conditions of capacity included a multitude of individuals in whom capacity did not truly exist. It was because many of those who possessed the right of sharing in elections took no part in them that the inconvenience of so much latitude was not at first experienced. The principle remained intact because it did not bear all its fruits. When the House of Commons occupied a higher place in the State, it became necessary to restrict the electoral right by requiring the freeholders themselves to possess an annual income of forty shillings. The action of Parliament in the government, and by consequence the importance of electoral rights, far surpassed the intelligence and independence of many of the men to whom ancient custom had accorded them. Thence arose the limitation established by the Parliament under Henry IV. Since that period, the progress of society and the changes which have occurred in the condition of property and industry, have altered in this respect the exactness, and therefore the excellence, of the electoral system. The legal signs of electoral capacity remain the same as to right, but, in fact, they have changed. Formerly, the freeholders were the only landowners who were truly free and capable of exercising political rights; the copyholders were then little better than *villani:* this has long ceased to be the case; although the legal distinction still subsists, it is merely nominal: copyholds are properties as free, as secured, and as fully hereditary as freeholds. The title of freeholder is now no longer, as formerly, the only one which designates a landowner capable of exercising political rights. The law, in its description of the external characters of electoral capacity, no longer corresponds really and truly with social facts. This inconvenience is not very great in practice, because there are few copyholders of any importance who do not possess a freehold of forty shillings rent. It is however real, for it maintains a distinction between properties as to electoral rights, which is not founded upon any real difference between the nature of the properties, and the capacity of their possessors. The system has become much more vicious as regards electoral rights in boroughs. Here the external signs by which the law pretends to recognize capacity, are become, in many instances, utterly false. The importance of particular towns, and the material or intellectual development of their inhabitants, was originally the cause of their investiture with electoral rights. The capacity was there; the right followed. Now the principle has disappeared; there are some boroughs destitute of importance, the inhabitants of which possess neither wealth nor independence; capacity is no longer there, but nevertheless the right continues still. It might be supposed that the name of the borough, its site, or its walls, are the signs of an electoral capacity which ought to reside there for ever—that the privilege appertained to the stones. On the other hand there are other towns, which in the fourteenth century would not have failed to obtain their electoral rights, because in effect the capacities of their citizens would have been recognized, that do not yet possess them.

Thus a principle, equitable at first, has ceased to be so, because attempts have been made to arrest the progress of its effects; or rather the principle itself has perished, and a great part of the electoral system of England is nothing more than a violation of it.

By this it may be seen that, if the principle which attaches right to capacity in the matter of election, is universal in its nature, and susceptible of constant application, the conditions of this capacity and the external signs by which it is to be recognized are essentially variable, and can never be restricted to the terms of a law without endangering the existence of the principle itself. The vicissitudes of electoral rights, even in the earliest time of the existence of Parliament, demonstrate this. Political rights belonged at first to the freeholders alone. Who could reasonably have sought deputies and electors in those devastated boroughs, abandoned for the most part by their ancient inhabitants, peopled only by a few poor families, whose condition and ideas were not elevated above those of the most miserable peasants?

Some towns rose again and became repeopled; commerce brought with it wealth, and wealth procured social importance, and the development of mind. Representatives should emanate from these bodies; for there were certainly electors. New capacities form and declare themselves by new symptoms. At the same time, or soon after, the number of freeholders increases by the division of fiefs, many among them fall to a much lower condition than that of the ancient freeholders, and no longer possess the same independence. Will they preserve the same rights when their capacity is no longer the same? no, necessity makes each to know his value; the mere title of freeholder is no longer a correct sign of electoral capacity. Another is sought, and the condition of forty shillings rent enters into the laws. Thus, without any violation, and even by the authority of the principle, the conditions and signs of electoral capacity vary according to the real state of society. It is only when this portion of the electoral system becomes invariable that the principle will be violated.

It would then be vain and dangerous to pretend to regulate, beforehand and for ever, this part of the electoral system of a free people. The determination of the conditions of capacity and that of the external characteristics which reveal it, possess, by the very nature of things, no universal or permanent character. And not only is it unnecessary to endeavour to fix them, but the laws should oppose any unchangeable prescription regarding them. The more numerous and flexible the legal characteristics of electoral capacity, the less need this danger be dreaded. If, for example, the land-tax was regulated and fixed once for all, as it is to be desired that it may be, this tax alone would be an incorrect sign of electoral capacity; for it would not follow the vicissitudes of property: it would enfeoff the land itself with the right of election; the rent would be a better indication, because it would be more pliable. If, instead of attributing electoral rights by name and for ever to a particular borough, the English laws had conferred them upon every town whose population reached a certain limit, or the revenue from which attained a certain amount, the representation of boroughs, instead of becoming corrupt, would have followed the changes and progress of true political capacity. We could multiply these examples, and prove in a thousand ways that it is better neither to adopt any one legal sign of electoral capacity, nor to place this sign beyond the reach of the vicissitudes of society.

In summing up, we may deduce, from our examination of the electoral system of England in the fourteenth century, these three conclusions: I. The right ought to be co-extensive with the capability of judicious election, for it is its source. II. The conditions of electoral capacity should vary according to time, place, the internal state of society, public intelligence, &c. III. The external characteristics prescribed by the laws, as declaring the accomplishment of the conditions of electoral capacity, should neither be utterly immutable nor derived entirely from purely material facts.[4]

4. This lecture and the next one (16) are particularly important for understanding Guizot's views on the relation between political capacity and representative government. He was keen on pointing out that it would be dangerous and futile to try to regulate once and forever the conditions and signs of electoral capacity, because these qualifications change as new capacities arise and impose themselves. The key point is that capacity confers right, since capacity is a fact which is independent of law and which law cannot destroy or ignore. It is also worth noting that, in Guizot's opinion, the individual superiorities who will seek a place in government ought *not* to obtain it for their personal interest, but must always follow what the public interest and the common good dictate (*HORG*, p. 369–71). In Guizot's view, representatives ought to be those who are most capable to discover, by means of their common deliberations, and translate into practice the dictates of reason, truth, and justice (also see *ibid.*, pp. 346–48). Their capacity must, however, be constantly legitimated and proved in front of the entire nation.

LECTURE 16

Subject of the Lecture. ⁓ *Continuation of the philosophical examination of the electoral system in England in the fourteenth century.* ⁓ *Characteristics of the elections.* ⁓ *Examination of the principle of direct or indirect election.*

I NOW pass to the second of the great questions to which every electoral system gives rise. What are the proceedings and forms of the election? In this question many others are comprised. These may be divided into two classes: the one class relating to the manner of assembling the electors; the other, to their mode of operation when assembled.

The close union of the electoral system with the exercise of other rights and political powers, has been productive in England of extensive and very beneficial consequences with regard to the mode of collecting the electors together.

Originally the election of county representatives required no special and extraordinary convocation of the electors. At appointed times, they repaired to the county-court to fulfil the functions with which they were charged, and on these occasions they elected their representatives. The first writs addressed to the sheriffs set forth: *Quod eligi facias in proximo comitatu,* "you will elect in the next county-court."

When the importance of the House of Commons had imparted a corresponding importance to the election of its members, and the necessity of preventing the abuses arising from elections made, so to speak, by chance, and without any one receiving special notice thereof, had become felt, the election was announced throughout the country by a proclamation summoning the attendance of all the electors and indicating the time and place of the convocation of Parliament. The election thus became a special and solemn act; but was always conducted in the county-court, and at one of its periodic meetings.

Ultimately, by the lapse of time, the changes of the judicial system, and the development of every institution, the county-courts ceased to retain in England that position which they anciently occupied. Their jurisdiction is now rare and very limited; the greater part of the freeholders never attend them; nor are they of any considerable political importance. At the present day the sole important object of any assembly of freeholders in these courts is the election of representatives, but the circumscriptions remain the same: frequent relations still exist among the freeholders of the county; the county-court is still their centre: it is now the electoral college, and that is its sole important character; but the electoral college is still the ancient county-court.

The great political result of all these facts is this, that the election of representatives has always been, and still is, not the work of an assembly of men extraordinarily and arbitrarily convened for that purpose, among whom no other tie subsists, and who possess no regular and habitual common interests, but the fruit of ancient relations, of constant and tried influences among men otherwise united in the transaction and possession of common affairs, functions, rights, and interests. In examining the question in itself, we shall very soon become convinced that this is the only way to insure veracity in elections, and suitableness and authority in the elected representatives.

The object of election is evidently to obtain the most capable and best accredited men in the country. It is a plan for discovering and bringing to light the true, the legitimate aristocracy, which is freely accepted by the masses over whom its power is to be exercised. To attain this end it is not sufficient to summon the electors together and to say to them, "Choose whom you will"; but they should have the opportunity of understanding thoroughly what they are about, and of concerting together how to do it. If they do not know each other, and are equally unacquainted with the men who solicit their suffrages, the object is evidently defeated. You will have elections which will result neither from the free choice nor the actual wishes of the electors.

Election in its nature is a sudden act which does not leave much room for deliberation. If this act is not linked with the habits and previous doings of the electors, if it is not in some sort the result of long anterior deliberation, and the expression of their habitual opinion, it will be too easy to take the real wish of the electors by surprise, or to induce them to listen only to the passion of the moment; and the election will thus be deficient either in sincerity or in nationality. If, on the contrary, the men who have met to elect a representative have long been united by common interests; if they are accustomed to conduct their affairs among themselves; if the election, instead of taking them out of the habitual sphere in which their lives are passed, their activity displayed, and their thoughts exchanged, only assembles them at the centre of that sphere, to obtain the manifestation, the summary of their opinions, their wishes and the natural influence which they exercise over each other; then the election can, and generally will be, both rational and sincere.

The whole of that part of the electoral system which relates to the assembling of the electors ought, then, to be founded upon respect for natural influences and relations. The election should assemble the electors together at that centre towards which they are habitually attracted by their other interests. Well-tried and freely accepted influences constitute true and legitimate society among men. Far from dreading them, in them alone should the real desire of society be sought. Every method of uniting electors which annuls or destroys these influences, falsifies the elections, and makes them run counter to their intended object: the less the electoral assembly is extraordinary, the more will it be adapted to the regular and constant existence of those who compose it, and the better will it attain its legitimate end. On these terms only can there be electoral colleges that do what they wish, and know what they are doing; on these terms only can there be representatives who exercise over the electors a solid and salutary influence.

The maintenance of natural influences, and thereby the sincerity of elections, has not been the only good effect of the primitive identity of the electoral assemblies and the county-courts.

These courts being the centre of a multitude of administrative, judicial, or other interests, presided over by the interested persons themselves, it was impossible that the boundaries of the district to which they related could be very extensive; as much inconvenience would thereby have resulted to the men who frequently repaired thither. The division of England into counties was not a systematic performance, and it presents some striking irregularities. But the force of events prevented most of the counties from including a very extended territory. This advantage is retained in the electoral system. The connections and ideas of the great majority of citizens do not stretch beyond a certain material sphere: and it is only within the limits of this sphere that they are really conversant with affairs and act upon their own knowledge. If the election is at too great a distance from them, they cease to be enlightened and free agents, and become tools. Now, since it is of the will and judgment of the citizens that the choice is required, it is absurd to withhold from them, at the same time the necessary conditions of reason and liberty. There is always, then, a limit beyond which the extent of an electoral convocation should not be carried, and this limit is itself a fact, which results from the manner in which men and interests are grouped together, in the divisions and subdivisions of the country. It ought to be large enough for the election to produce representatives capable of fulfilling their public mission, and contracted enough to insure that the greater number of the citizens who take part in the election may act with discernment and freedom. If the elections were conducted in England according to hundreds they would yield, perhaps, obscure and ignorant representatives; if by episcopal dioceses, they would in fact annul a great part of the electoral body. The material circumstance of the necessity of a distant removal is of least consequence. The moral disorder which would result from too widely extended boundaries is much more serious.

Further; the extension of political rights is no less interested in this than the excellence of the results of the election. It is desirable to enlarge the sphere of their rights, as far as it is admitted by the imperious condition of capacity. Now, capacity depends upon a multitude of causes. A man perfectly capable of prudent choice within a radius of five miles from his dwelling, becomes absolutely incapable of doing so if the radius be extended to twenty miles: in the first case, he had the full use of his reason and freedom; in the second, he loses it. If, then, you would judiciously multiply the number of the electors, do not place the electoral centre too far from the points of circumference from whence some will have to repair thither. In all this we must proceed to some extent upon supposition, and general results alone are sought; but the principle is invariably the same. The election must be made by electors capable of choosing wisely, and must supply in those who are elected, men capable of thoroughly comprehending the interests upon which they will have to administrate. These are the two requirements, between which the limits of electoral boundaries should be sought, subject always to the condition of never determining these boundaries in an arbitrary way, so as to break through the habits, and destroy the natural and permanent state of society. Generally speaking, the division into counties formerly attained this twofold object in England.

The boundaries being defined, in accordance with the natural grouping of the citizens, and the electors being assembled, what is required of them?

Custom, and no standard derived from population, wealth, or any other cause, has ordained in England, that two members only should be returned from each district, with the exception of a very few places. This custom probably derives its origin from the impossibility which formerly existed of finding in the boroughs, and even in the counties, a greater number of men able and willing to undertake a mission then very little sought after. It has been seen that on several occasions three or four knights were required from the county-courts. The number was very soon reduced to two, and this fact has become the general law. Whatever may be its historic principle, this fact contains a rational principle, viz., that the election is neither sound nor good, except when the number required to be elected is very small.

No one has ever denied that the fundamental law of all election is this, that the electors should do what they desire, and understand what they are doing. In practice, however, this is often forgotten. It is forgotten when electors, meeting together but for a short space of time, are required to make choice of more than one or two. The great merit of election is, that it should proceed from the elector, that on his part it is a true choice, an act both of judgment and will. Beyond doubt, no extraneous will or judgment may in any case be rightfully imposed upon him; though he may always accept or reject that which is proposed to him: but this is not sufficient; the elector must be placed in such a position that his personal judgment, his own will, shall be not only free, but stimulated to display themselves in their actual character. Their exercise must be not only possible, but must not be too difficult. Now, this error is fallen into when, instead of one or two names, a whole list of names is demanded. The elector, almost always incapable of completing this list of himself and by the help of his own discernment, falls under the dominion of combinations which he suffers rather than accepts; for he does not possess the knowledge necessary for judging correctly of their whole aim and effect. Who does not know that almost every elector in such a case cannot include in his list more than one or two names that are truly known to him, and which he really desires? The choice of the remainder is made for him, and he writes them in confidence or out of complaisance. And who makes this choice? The party to which the elector belongs. Now, party influence, like every other influence, is good only so far as it is exercised upon those who can form a just opinion of it, and not submit to it blindly. The despotism of party spirit is no better than any other despotism, and all good legislation should tend to preserve citizens from its sway. Into elections, as into every other act, levity, inconsiderateness, or passion may enter: but to these dispositions the law is not bound to show respect and afford facility. It should, on the contrary, strive to prevent their having any effect; and by the process of the election itself, it should, as far as possible, secure to the citizen the exercise of his judgment as well as the independence of his will. It is not requisite to repel all influences, or to declare them illegitimate beforehand. Every election is the result of influences, and it would be folly to pretend to isolate the elector under the pretext of obtaining his unbiassed opinion and desire. This would be to forget that man is a reasonable and free being; and that reason is called to debate, and liberty to choose. The soundness of election arises precisely from the conflict of influences. The law must allow them to reach the elector, and grant them all natural means of acting upon his judgment; but it ought not to deliver him up to them defenceless. It should take certain precautions against human weakness, and the most efficacious of these precautions will be, to require nothing of the elector that he cannot perform with true spontaneity of action. The citizen being thus left to himself, all influences may act upon him: they may perhaps induce him to abandon the name that he loved for one with which he was previously unacquainted; but they will need at least to exert greater efforts to conquer his reason or to subdue his will. Now, it is right that they should be condemned to make such efforts, and that they should not be able to obtain from levity, precipitation, or ignorance alone, an assent, the effect of which is to give to the whole country an exponent whom the elector himself would not have desired had he been able, in nominating him, to make a full use of his reason.

When we investigate the causes which have introduced into certain countries, in the matter of election, a custom so opposed to the true interests of liberty, and which is never met with where liberty has really been introduced into the practice of political life, we perceive that it is derived, in part at least, from the evil principle on which the whole electoral system has been founded. Electoral rights have been isolated from other rights, and separately constituted; electoral assemblies have been in no way connected with other public affairs, with local administration, or with common and permanent interests. They have been made extraordinary and solemn assemblies of very brief duration. The electoral boundaries have in general been too widely extended: hence has arisen the necessity of suddenly assembling together the whole body of electors, of dismissing them almost immediately, and at the same time, of requiring from them the choice of too many representatives. In England, the poll remains open at least fifteen days for the election of one or two members. Every one gives his vote when it bests suits him. In America, the other forms are yet more mild and free. In the system which has prevailed with us, on the contrary, all is sudden and precipitate: everything is done *en masse,* and by masses of people whose reason and liberty are in a great measure disabled from acting, by the haste and extent of the operation. Hence also is derived the scheme of the ballot, and of an absolute majority, consequences inevitably flowing from a rapid and numerous election; whilst elsewhere, the system of a relative and long-contested plurality affords public opinion leisure to select, and freedom to manifest its choice. And hence, finally, arises the necessity of an elected bureau, which entrusts beforehand to the majority the inspection of all the electoral operations, thus casting suspicion upon the authenticity of the results. When liberty is everywhere to be found, when all rights are bound together and mutually sustained, when publicity is real and universally present, there will always be independent magistrates to whom the direction and superintendence of elections may be confided; and there is then no necessity for placing them under the influence of party spirit, in order to withdraw them from the always-suspected influence of superior authority.

These details relate to the forms of electoral operations; but as their vices flow from the general principles which regulate them, it was necessary to point out this connection.

Direct election has been the constant practice of England; and America has adopted the same system. It has been otherwise in most of the European States in which representative government has been established in our own times. This is one of the most important facts presented to our view by the British electoral system. In this system, direct election has been the natural consequence of the idea that was then entertained regarding political rights. Not only were these rights unshared by all, but they were not even distributed systematically, or upon one general plan. They were recognized wherever the capacity of exercising them was actually to be met with. The importance of freeholders and citizens had entailed upon them the right of interference in public affairs. This intervention was their right when these affairs related to themselves. Being unable to exercise this right personally, they elected representatives. In the spirit of the time, this right of election corresponded exactly to the right that the powerful barons exercised of being represented in Parliament by delegated agents. The individual importance of a powerful baron being very great, his proxy was individual. The freeholders and citizens also possessed an individual right, but not the same importance, and they therefore had one proxy to represent many of them. But, fundamentally, the representation was founded on the same principle—the individual rights of the electors to debate on and consent to such matters as interested them.

In this point of view, it is easy of comprehension that direct election prevailed, and that no other idea presented itself to the public mind. All indirect election, every new medium placed between Parliament and the elector, would have appeared, and would in fact have been, a diminution of the right, a weakening of the importance and political intervention of the electors.

Direct election, then, is the simple idea, the primitive and natural electoral system of representative government, when representative government is itself the spontaneous produce of its true principle—that is to say, when political rights are derived from capacity.

In considering this mode of election under a purely philosophical point of view, and as it respects not merely the electors alone, but society in general, does it remain equally preferable to every other more artificial combination?

It is necessary to examine it first in its relation to the rational principle of representative government; and, in the second place, in its practical results.

We have in a previous lecture laid down the rational principle of representative government. In right, this principle asserts, that true sovereignty is that of justice; and that no law is legitimate if it is not conformable to justice and to truth, that is to say, to the divine law. In fact, this principle recognizes, that no man or assembly of men, in a word, no terrestrial force, is fully conscious and constantly desirous of reason, justice, and truth—the true law. Connecting this right and fact together, the inference is, that the public powers which actually exercise sovereignty ought to be constantly required and constrained on every occasion to seek after the true law, the sole source of legitimate authority.

The object of the representative system, in its general elements as well as in all the details of its organization, is, then, to collect and concentrate all the scattered elements of reason which exist in society, and to apply it to its government.

From thence it necessarily follows that representatives ought to be the men most capable: 1. To discover, by means of their united deliberation, the law of reason, the truth which, on all occasions, the least as well as the greatest, exists, and ought to be the ground of decision; and 2. To enforce the recognition and observance, by the citizens in general, of this law when once discovered and expressed.

In order to discover and secure the men most capable of fulfilling this mission, that is to say, good representatives, it is necessary to compel those who think or profess themselves to be such, to prove their capacity, and to obtain its recognition and assertion from the men who, in their turn, are capable of forming a judgment upon it, that is to say, upon the individual capacity of any man who aspires to become a representative. Thus does legitimate power evidence itself, and it is thus that, in the fact of election, philosophically considered, this power is exercised by those who possess it, and accepted by those who recognize it.

Now, there is a certain relation, a certain tie, between the capacity of being [a good representative or otherwise], and the capacity of recognizing the man who possesses the capacity of being. This is a fact which is continually illustrated in the world. The brave man excites those to follow him who can associate themselves with his bravery. The skilful man obtains obedience from those who are capable of comprehending his skill. The wise man engages the belief of those who are capable of appreciating his knowledge. Every superiority has a certain sphere of attraction in which it acts, and gathers around itself real inferiorities, which are, however, in a condition to feel and to accept its action.

This sphere is by no means boundless. This also is a simple, self-evident fact. The relation which connects a superiority with the inferiorities by which it is recognized, being a purely intellectual relation, cannot exist where there does not also exist a sufficient degree of knowledge and intelligence to form the connection. A man, though very fit to recognize the superiority capable of deliberating on the affairs of his commune, may be quite unfit to distinguish and point out by his vote a person who shall be capable of deliberating on the affairs of the State. There are, then, some inferiorities, destitute of all true relation with certain superiorities, and which, if they were called upon to distinguish between them, would be either unable to do so, or would arrive at a most incorrect conclusion.

The limit at which the faculty ceases of recognizing and accepting the superiority which constitutes the capacity of being a good deputy, is that at which the right of election ought to cease; for it is here that the capacity ceases of being a good elector.

Above this limit, the right of election exists only because of the actual existence of the capacity of recognizing the superior capacity that is sought. Below it, there is no right.

From thence, the necessity of direct election philosophically results. Evidently it is desired to obtain that which is sought. Now, that which is sought, is a good representative. Superior capacity, that of the representative, is necessarily, therefore, the dominant condition, the starting-point of the whole operation. You will obtain this superior capacity by requiring its recognition by all those capacities which, although inferior, stand in natural relation with it. If, on the contrary, you begin by electing the electors, what will be the result? you have to accomplish an operation analogous to the preceding, but the point of departure is altered, and the general condition is lowered. You take as your foundation the capacity of the elector, that is to say, a capacity inferior to that which you wish definitively to obtain; and you necessarily address yourself to capacities still more inferior and quite unfit to conduct you, even under this form, to the more elevated result at which you aim; for the capacity of the elector being only the ability to select a good representative, it would be necessary to be in a position to comprehend the latter condition in order to comprehend the former, which can never happen.

Indirect election, therefore, considered in itself, derogates from the primitive principle as well as from the ultimate object of representative government, and debases its nature. Considered in its practical results, in facts, and independently of every general principle, this system appears equally unsatisfactory.

In the first place, we regard it as admitted, that it is desirable that the election of representatives should not be in general the work of a very small number of electors. When electoral assemblies are very limited, not only is the election deficient in that action and energy which sustain political life in society, and afterwards contribute in great measure to the power of the representative himself, but general interests, expansive ideas, and public opinions cease to be the motive and regulating power. Coteries form themselves—in the place of political parties, personal intrigues spring up; and a struggle is established between interests, opinions, and relations, which are almost individual in their nature. The election is no less disputed, but it is less national, and its results possess the same fault.

Starting, then, from this point, that electoral assemblies ought to be sufficiently numerous to prevent individualities from obtaining such easy dominion, I seek to discover how, by indirect election, this end can reasonably be attained.

Two hypotheses alone are possible: either the territorial boundaries, within which the assembly will be formed, charged with the nomination of the electors, will be very narrow, or will be of considerable extent. In England, for example, the electors would be required from the tithings or the hundreds, which correspond very nearly to our *communes* and *cantons*. If these boundaries are very narrow, and only a very small number are required to be selected from each—two electors for example—very probably some of these electors will be of a very inferior order.

True electoral capacities are by no means equally divided among communes; one commune may possess twenty or thirty, while another contains only a few, or perhaps none at all; and this is the case with the majority. If each district is required to furnish the same, or nearly the same number of electors, great violence will be done to realities. Many of the incapable will be summoned; many who are capable will be excluded; and, finally, an electoral assembly will be constituted, but little adapted for the wise choice of representatives. If, on the contrary, each district is required to designate a number of electors proportioned to its importance, its population, and the wealth and intelligence that are concentrated in it, then, wherever the number to be chosen is considerable, there will no longer be any true choice.

It has already been shown, that elections, when they are numerous and simultaneous, lose their character. There will be lists of electors prepared by the external influence either of parties or of power, which will be adopted or rejected without discernment or freedom. In this respect experience has everywhere confirmed the previsions of reason.

If the districts summoned to name the electors possess any great extent, another alternative presents itself. Either each will be required to choose only a small number, and then the object will be defeated, for the assembly whose duty it will be to elect the representatives will be very innumerous: or a large number of electors will be required from each district, and then the inconvenience which has been already pointed out will be incurred.

Let all the possible combinations of indirect election be exhausted, and there will not be found one which can finally supply, for the election of representatives, an assembly sufficiently numerous, and formed at the same time with discernment and liberty. In this system these two results mutually exclude each other.

I proceed now to another vicious practice connected with this system, which is no less serious than those just indicated.

The end of representative government is to bring publicly into proximity and contact the chief interests and various opinions which divide society, and dispute for supremacy, in the just confidence that from their debates will result the recognition and adoption of the laws and measures which are most suitable for the country in general. This end is only attained by the triumph of the true majority—the minority being constantly listened to with respect.

If the majority is displaced by artifice, there is falsity. If the minority is removed from the struggle beforehand, there is oppression. In either case representative government is corrupted.

All the constituent laws of this form of government have, then, two fundamental conditions to fulfil: first, to secure the manifestation and triumph of the true majority; and, secondly, to insure the intervention and unshackled endeavour of the minority.

These two conditions are as essential to the laws which regulate the mode of the election of representatives, as to those which preside over the debates of deliberative assemblies. In neither case ought there to be falsehood or tyranny.

An electoral system which would annul beforehand—with regard to the final result of the elections, that is to say, with regard to the formation of the deliberative assembly—the influence and participation of the minority, would destroy representative government, and would be as fatal to the majority itself as any law which, in the deliberative assembly, should condemn the minority to silence.

This, to a certain extent, is the result of indirect election.

By direct election, and supposing that the limit of electoral capacity has been reasonably fixed by law, that is to say, at the point at which true capacity actually ceases, all the citizens whose social position, fortune, or intelligence place them above this limit, are equally summoned to unite in the choice of representatives. No inquiry is made of them concerning the opinions or interests which they advocate. The result of the election will make known the true majority; but whatever that may be they will have no cause to complain: the trial will have been complete, and they will have taken their rightful part in it.

Indirect election, on the contrary, effects beforehand a thorough purgation of the electoral capacities, and eliminates a certain number, solely on account of the opinions or interests which they may hold. It intrudes into the sphere of these capacities in order to exclude a part of the minority, so as to give to the majority a factitious force, and thus to destroy the true expression of the general opinion. We should exclaim loudly against a law which should say, *a priori:* "All the men, or only the third or fourth part of the men, attached to such an interest or such an opinion, shall be excluded from all participation in the election of representatives, whatever may otherwise be their importance and social position." This is precisely what is done, *a posteriori,* by indirect election; and thereby it introduces into representative government positive disorder, for it creates a means of tyranny for the benefit of the majority. It may even happen, and examples of this are not wanting, that indirect election, when thus employed to eliminate a portion of the natural electoral capacities, may result in turning against the majority itself, and putting it in the minority. A supposition will clearly explain this idea. If, in the fourteenth century, it had been decreed in England, that "the copyholders and villeins should unite in nominating the electors of the members of Parliament," is it not evident that their choice would have fallen on the lords whose lands they rented or cultivated by any particular title; and that the inhabitants of the towns, the citizens, would have been almost absolutely excluded from the House of Commons? Thus, this part of the nation, which had already attained so much importance, would have seen themselves deprived of the exercise of political rights by a system which urged, as its sole specious pretext, the extension of these rights to a greater number of individuals.

This is, in fact, the true source of indirect election; it is derived from the sovereignty of numbers, and from universal suffrage: and as it is impossible to reduce these two principles to practice, it is attempted to retain some shadow of their existence. The principle of representative government is violated, its nature debased, and the right of election weakened, in order that consistent adherence to an erroneous doctrine may, to all appearance, be maintained. Who can fail to see that such a system must necessarily enervate election, and that reality and energy can be preserved by the system of direct election alone? Every action, the result of which is distant and uncertain, inspires little interest; and the same men who will unitedly display great discernment and animation in the choice of their municipal officers, would give their suffrage blindly and coldly to subsequent electors whom their thoughts never follow into the future in which they interfere so little. This pretended homage to wills not sufficiently enlightened to be trusted with a greater share of influence in the choice of representatives, is at the bottom nothing but miserable quackery and lying adulation; and under a simulated extension of political rights there is concealed the restriction, mutilation, and enfeebling of these rights in the sphere in which they really exist, and in which they might be exercised in all their fulness and with complete effect.

The true way to diffuse political life in all directions, and to interest as great a number of citizens as possible in the concerns of the State, is not to make them all combine in the same acts, although they may not all be equally capable of performing them; but to confer upon them all those rights which they are capable of exercising. Rights are worth nothing unless they are full, direct, and efficacious. In place of perverting political rights by weakening them, under the pretext of giving them diffusion, let local liberties everywhere exist, guaranteed by real rights. The electoral system itself will thus become much more powerful than it could possibly be under a pretended system of universal suffrage.

The last important fact to be noticed in the electoral system of England in the fourteenth century, is open voting. Some have attempted to regard this as an absolute principle capable of constant application; but we think it ought not so to be considered. The only absolute principle in this matter is, that election should be free, and should truly display the true thoughts and real wishes of the electors. If open voting puts a serious restraint on liberty of elections and perverts their results, it ought to be abolished. Doubtless such a condition argues infirmity of liberty and timidity of morals, and proves that a portion of society is in conflict with influences which it is afraid to shake off, though it ardently desires to be rid of them. This is a melancholy fact, but it is one which liberty, rendered fruitful by time, can alone destroy. It is very true that open voting in elections, as well as in the debates of deliberative assemblies, is the natural consequence of representative government. It is quite true that there is a degree of shame attached to liberty if it claim secrecy for itself while imposing publicity on power. That liberty which can only attack is still very feeble; for the true power of freedom consists in its bold defence and avowal of its rights. Certainly there is an ill grace in the complaints of the niggardliness and delay with which power grants rights, when concealment is necessary for the exercise of rights already possessed. But when reason is applied to practice, it regards, for some time at least, nothing besides facts; and the most imperious of all principles is necessity. To impose open voting when it would injure freedom of election would be to compromise general liberty itself, which, ere long, must necessarily establish open voting.

To sum up what I have said. Nearly all the fundamental principles of a free and reasonable electoral system may be discovered in the electoral system of England in the fourteenth century. Bestowal of electoral rights upon capacity; close union of electoral rights with all other rights; regard to natural influences and relations; absence of all arbitrary and factitious combinations in the formation and proceedings of electoral assemblies; prudent limitation in the number to be chosen by each assembly; direct election, and open voting; all are to be met with. These are entirely due to the decisive circumstance that the electoral system and representative government itself were in England the simple and natural result of facts, the consequence and development of real and powerful anterior liberties, which served as their basis, and guarded and nourished in their bosom the roots of the tree which is indebted to them for its growth.[1]

By another equally decisive circumstance, this system, though so national and spontaneous in its origin, became corrupted, at least in part, and appears at

---

1. This is a clear statement of Guizot's views on what good government requires: union of electoral right with all other rights; inclusion of "natural superiorities" in the direction of political affairs; political prudence in promoting reforms; direct elections; bestowal of electoral rights according to political capacity. This was, in fact, Guizot's *juste milieu* theory, a cautious middle ground between the ideal of Revolution and Reaction. As he wrote in his *Mémoirs:* "Ce fut à ce mélange d'élévation philosophique et de modération politique, à ce respect rationnel des droits et des faits divers, à ces doctrines à la fois nouvelles et conservatrices, antirévolutionnaires sans être rétrogrades et modestes au fond, quoique souvent hautaines dans leur langage, que les doctrinaires dûrent leur importance comme leur nom. . . . Les doctrinaires répondaient à un besoin réel et profond quoique obscurément senti des esprits en France, ils avaient à coeur l'honneur intellectuel comme le bon ordre de la société, leurs idées se présentaient comme propres à régénerer en même temps qu'à clore la Révolution. (Guizot, *Mémoires*, Vol. 1, pp. 157–58).

the present day to require correction. Perhaps it is owing to its very power that it remains inflexible: it has only followed at a distance the vicissitudes and progress of social conditions. It now protects the remnants of those abuses against which, at first, and for a long time, it was directed; and yet the reform of these abuses, by whatever means and at whatever period it may be effected, will be the fruit of the institutions, habits, principles, and sentiments which this system has established.

LECTURE 17

Origin of the division of the English Parliament into two Houses. ~
Its original constitution. ~ *Reproduction of the classifications of society
in the Parliament.* ~ *Causes which led the representatives of counties
to separate from the barons, and coalesce with the representatives of boroughs.* ~ *Effects of this coalition.* ~ *Division of the Parliament into
two houses in the 14th century.*

Our attention has hitherto been directed only to the elements of which the
Parliament was composed, and to the proceedings that took place at its formation, that is to say, to the process of election: we have now to consider another
question; we must enquire what were the internal and external constitution and
organisation of the Parliament thus composed.

The Parliament at the beginning of the fourteenth century was not divided, as at present, into the House of Lords and the House of Commons; nor
did it, on the other hand, consist of a single body. Accounts vary regarding the
date at which it assumed its present form. Carte fixes it in the seventeenth year
of the reign of Edward III. (1344); the authors of the Parliamentary History, in
the sixth year of the same reign (1333); Mr. Hallam in the first year of the reign
of Edward III. (1327), or, perhaps, even in the eighth year of the reign of Edward II. (1315).

The principal cause of this diversity of opinion is the different circumstance with which each author connects the fact of the union of county and borough members into one single assembly. This fact is deduced by some from the
date of their assembling together in the same place; by others from the period
of their common deliberation; and by others again, from the union of their votes
upon the same question. And as each of these circumstances occurred in one
particular Parliament independently of the others, the period which Parliament
first existed in its present form is carried back or forward according to the circumstance which is regarded as decisive in this respect. However this may be, it
may be affirmed that the division of Parliament into two Houses—one comprising the lords or great barons individually summoned, and the other all the

elected representatives of counties and boroughs; and both these houses deliberating and voting together in all matters of business—was not completely and
definitively effected, until towards the middle of the fourteenth century. It is
necessary to trace the steps by which this fact was gradually accomplished. This
is the only way thoroughly to comprehend its nature and its causes.

Originally, as we have seen, all the immediate vassals of the king had the
same right of repairing to Parliament and taking part in its deliberations. Mere
knights, therefore, when they repaired thither, sat, deliberated, and voted, with
the great barons.

When election was substituted for this individual right in the case of the
knights of shires, and only those elected by the county-courts were entitled to
attend the Parliament, they still continued to be members of the class to which
they had previously belonged. Although elected and deputed not only by those
knights who were immediate vassals of the king, but also by all the freeholders
of their county, they continued to sit, deliberate, and vote, together with the
great barons who were individually summoned.

The representatives of the boroughs, on the contrary, whose presence in
Parliament was a novel circumstance (which was not connected with any anterior right exercised merely under a new shape), formed a distinct assembly from
their first appearance in Parliament, sitting apart, deliberating and voting on
their own account, and as thoroughly separated from the knights of the shire as
from the great barons.

This separation is evident from the votes of Parliament at this period. At
the Parliament held at Westminster under Edward I., in 1295, the earls, barons,
and knights of the shire granted the king an eleventh part of their personal
property, the clergy a tenth part, and the citizens and burgesses a seventh. In
1296, the former granted a twelfth part, and the latter an eighth. In 1305, the former gave a thirtieth part, and the clergy, the citizens, and burgesses a twentieth.
Under Edward II., in 1308, the barons and knights granted one twentieth, the
clergy a fifteenth, the citizens and burgesses a fifteenth. Under Edward III., in
1333, the knights of the shire granted a fifteenth, the same as the prelates and the
nobles, and the citizens and burgesses a tenth; and yet the records of this Parliament expressly declare that the knights of the shire and the burgesses deliberated in common. In 1341, the prelates, earls and barons, on the one hand, and
the knights of the shire on the other, granted a ninth of their sheep, lambs, and
fleeces; and the burgesses, a ninth of all their personal property. In 1345, the
knights of the shire granted two-fifteenths, the burgesses a fifth: the lords
granted nothing but promised to follow the king in person. Thus, at this latter
period, the knights of the shire no longer voted in common with the lords, but
they still voted apart from the burgesses.

In 1347, the commons without distinction granted two-fifteenths, to be levied in two years in the cities, the boroughs, the ancient domains of the crown, and the counties. At this period, then, the fusion of the two elements of the Commons House was complete: and it continued so ever afterwards, although a few examples are still found of special taxes, voted by the representatives of the towns and boroughs alone in the case of customs, especially in 1373.

The original separation, then, was between the representatives of the counties and those of the boroughs. The recollections of feudal law allied the former to the great barons during more than fifty years. This separation was not confined solely to voting the supplies. Everything indicates, although it is nowhere proved by written evidence, that the knights of the shire and the representatives of the boroughs did not deliberate together any more on other affairs, either legislative or otherwise, which interested only one of the two classes. When mercantile interests were in question, the king and his council discussed them solely with the representatives of the towns and boroughs. Thus, there is reason to believe that the statute entitled *The Statute of Acton-Burnel,* passed in 1283, was enacted in this manner on the advice of the borough representatives alone, who met for this purpose at Acton-Burnel, whilst the knights of the shire sat with the great barons at Shrewsbury, to assist at the trial of David, Prince of Wales, then a prisoner. The separation of the two classes of representatives could therefore be carried thus far, that each class may have sat in different, though neighbouring towns.

When they sat in the same town, and especially at Westminster, the whole Parliament met together, most probably in the same chamber; but the great barons and knights of the shire occupied the upper end, and the borough representatives the lower part, of the chamber.

A distinction existed even among the borough members. Until the reign of Edward III., the representatives of those boroughs which formed part of the ancient domain of the crown constituted a separate class, and voted distinct supplies.

The division of Parliament, then, far from having originated in the forms which prevailed fifty years later, arose from principles altogether different. No idea then existed of truly general interests and a national representation. The particular interests which were of sufficient importance to take part in the government, intervened in it solely on their own account, and treated separately of their own affairs. Did the matter in hand relate exclusively to things in which the great barons appeared to be interested, and where the king required their assistance alone—they alone assembled and deliberated. Was the question one of modifications in the nature or mode of the transmission of feudal territorial property—the knights of the shire were summoned; and in this way the statute *Quia emptores* was enacted under Edward I. Were commercial interests concerned—the king treated of them with the borough representatives only. In these various cases, as in the matter of supplies, the deliberation and vote of the different classes of members of Parliament were distinct. These classes were formed in reference to their common interests, and took no part in each other's affairs: and very rarely, probably never, at this period, was there any matter of sufficiently general and common importance to all, for all to have been summoned to deliberate and vote in common.

Thus the classification of society was perpetuated in the Parliament, and was the true principle of the division between the members of Parliament.

This state of things did not long continue, because the classification of society itself, in which it originated, also tended to its own effacement. The county members could not fail to separate themselves altogether from the great barons, and completely to combine with the borough representatives; and for the following reasons.

If the knights of the shire continued for some time to sit and vote with the great barons, this was merely the effect of old association, a relic of the ancient parity of their feudal position. This equality had already received a severe check by the substitution of election for individual right of presence. The cause which had led to this change continued at work; the disparity of importance and wealth between the great barons and plain knights of the shire went on increasing; the remembrance of feudal political right became weakened; and the social position of the knights of the shire daily became more different from that of the great barons. Their parliamentary position could not fail to follow the same course. All things combined to separate them more and more.

At the same time every circumstance tended to associate the representatives of the counties with those of the boroughs. They had the same origin, and appeared in Parliament by virtue of the same title—election. The tie which had attached the county elections to feudal right became progressively enfeebled. Furthermore, these two classes of deputies were alike correspondent to certain local interests. These interests were often identical or of the same nature. The inhabitants of the towns situated in a county, and the rural landowners of the county, were often engaged in the same affairs, and frequently entertained the same claims and desires. Besides, the county-courts were a common centre at which they habitually assembled together. Both the county and borough elections frequently took place in these courts. Thus, while certain causes increasingly separated the knights of the shire from the great barons, other causes approximated them more closely to the borough representatives. The analogy of social positions naturally hastened the fusion of parliamentary positions.

Lastly, the great barons constituted the chief council of the king. They often assembled around him in this capacity, and independently of any convocation of the elected deputies. By reason of their personal importance, they engaged in public affairs, and took part in the government in an habitual and permanent manner. The representatives of the counties and boroughs, on the contrary, interfered in the administration of public affairs only from time to time, in certain particular cases. They possessed rights and liberties, but they neither governed, nor contested with each other for the government, nor were they constantly associated in it. Their political position was in this respect the same, and was therefore very different from that of the great barons. All things tended, then, broadly to distinguish them from the latter class, and to connect them together.

The constitution of Parliament in its present form is the result of all the above causes. It was accomplished in the middle of the fourteenth century, although some instances of separation between the two elements of the House of Commons may subsequently be met with. These cases very soon disappeared and the union became complete. One fact alone remained, and that was the superiority in importance and influence of the county representatives over the representatives of boroughs, notwithstanding the habitual inferiority of their numbers. This fact, with the exception of only a few intervals, is met with throughout the whole course of the history of Parliament.

Thus was effected, on the one side, the separation of the Houses of Peers and Commons, and on the other, the union of the different elements of the House of Commons into a single assembly, composed of members exercising the same rights and voting on all occasions in common.

This is the great fact which has decided the political destiny of England. By themselves alone, the borough deputies would never have possessed sufficient power and importance to form a House of Commons capable of resisting sometimes the king, and sometimes the great barons, and of gaining an ever-increasing influence in public affairs. But the aristocracy, or rather, the feudal nation, being divided into two parts, and the new nation which was forming in the towns becoming combined with the county freeholders there, arose from the combination a competent and imposing House of Commons. There was a large body of the nation independent both of the king and of the great nobles. It happened also that the king could not, as in France, make use of the Commons to annihilate the political rights and privileges of the ancient feudal system, without substituting new liberties in their places. On the Continent, the enfranchisment of the Commons definitively led to absolute power. In England, a portion of the feudal class having united with the Commons, they combined to defend their liberties. On the other hand, the crown, supported by the great barons, who could not hope to set up as petty independent sovereigns in their own domains, possessed sufficient power to defend itself in its turn. The great barons consequently were obliged to rally round the throne. It is not true, though it is constantly reiterated, that the aristocracy and people have made common cause in England against the regal power, and that English liberty has arisen out of that circumstance. But it is true that the division of the feudal aristocracy having prodigiously augmented the power of the Commons, popular liberties at an early date possessed sufficient means of resistance, and the royal power received at the same time sufficient support.

Thus, considering the division of Parliament into two houses under the historic point of view, we see both how it was effected, and how favourable it has been to the establishment of popular liberty. Is this, then, all? Are this fact and its results mere accidents arising out of circumstances peculiar to England, and to the state in which society happened to be in the fourteenth century? Or is this division of legislative power into two houses a constitutional form intrinsically good, and everywhere as well founded in reason as it was, in England, in the necessities of the times? This question must be examined in order properly to appreciate the influence which this form has exercised on the development of the constitutional system in England, and rightly to understand its causes.

LECTURE 18

Examination of the division of the legislative power into two Houses. ⁓ Diversity of ideas on this subject. ⁓ Fundamental principle of the philosophic school. ⁓ Source of its errors. ⁓ Characteristics of the historic school. ⁓ Cause of the division of the British Parliament into two Houses. ⁓ Derivation of this division from the fundamental principle of representative government. ⁓ Its practical merit.

In ORDER to judge in itself of the division of the legislative power into two Chambers, and to estimate its merit, we must first detach it from certain particular and purely local characteristics, which are not essentially inherent in it; and which have associated it in England with causes which are not in all times and places to be met with. Not a few writers have fallen into grave errors, on this and many other questions, by neglecting to take this step at the outset. Some have formed their judgment of this institution entirely from a few of the causes which led to its establishment in England in the fourteenth century; and as, generally speaking, they did not approve either of these causes or their effects, and had a bad opinion of the social condition of which they formed part, they have condemned the institution itself, appearing to believe that it was derived solely from that social condition, and could not possibly be detached from it. Others, on the contrary, struck either with the general reasons which may be urged in favour of the institution, or with the good effects which it has produced in England and elsewhere, have adopted it exactly in that particular form in which it was introduced among our neighbours by their ancient social condition, asserting that all the characteristics which it there presents are essential to it, and even constitute it. Thus, the institution has sometimes been censured on account of particular facts which accompanied its establishment and combined to produce it, and sometimes these facts and their special consequences have been adopted as principles, simply because they were associated with an institution deemed intrinsically good. These two modes of judgment, both of which are equally erroneous, characterize the two schools, which may be called distinctively the philosophic school and the historic school. As this twofold method of considering political questions has warped them, sometimes in one sense and sometimes in another, it appears to me that it would be useful to offer some general observations on this subject, which may afterwards be applied to the particular question with which we are now occupied.

One idea reigns in the philosophic school—that of Right. Right is constantly taken both as its starting-point, and as its goal. But right itself requires to be investigated; before adopting it as a principle or pursuing it as an object, we must know what it is. To discover right, the philosophic school commonly confines itself to the individual. It takes hold of man, considers him isolatedly and in himself, as a rational and free being, and deduces from an examination of his nature that which it denominates his rights. Once in possession of these rights, they are advanced as a requirement of justice and reason, which ought to be applied to social facts as the sole rational and moral rule by which these facts should be judged, if judgment only be required—or instituted, if the object be to institute government.

The historic school is held in bondage by another idea—that of Fact. It does not, if possessed of any good sense, deny right: it even proposes right as its goal, but it never adopts it as its starting-point. Fact is the ground to which everything is brought; and as facts cannot be considered isolatedly, as they are all bound up together; and as the past itself is a fact with which the facts of the present are connected, it professes great respect for the past and admits right only so far as it is founded on anterior facts; or at least this school seeks to establish right, only by uniting it closely with these facts, and striving to deduce it from them. Such are the points of view, not exclusively, for that cannot be, but dominantly, of the two schools. How much is true, and how much erroneous in each? That is to say, what is there incomplete in both?

The philosophic school is correct in adopting Right not only as its end but also as its starting-point. It is right in maintaining that an institution is not good, simply because it exists or has existed, and that there are rational principles by which all institutions should be judged, and rights superior to all facts—rights which cannot be violated unless the facts which violate them are illegitimate, although real, and even powerful.

But though right in standing upon this foundation, which is its principal characteristic, the philosophic school is often mistaken when it attempts to go farther. We say that it is mistaken, philosophically speaking, and independently of all ideas of application and practical danger.

Its two chief errors, in my opinion, are these: I. Its researches after right are misdirected; and, II. It mistakes the conditions under which right can be realised.

It is not by considering man in isolation, in his single nature, and individually, that his rights may be discovered. The idea of right implies that of rela-

tion. Right can be declared only when relation is established. The fact of a connexion, of an approximation, in a word, of society, is implied in the very word
right. Right originates with society. Not that society, at its origin, created right
by an arbitrary convention. Just as truth exists before man becomes acquainted
with it, so does right exist before it is realised in society. It is the legitimate and
rational rule of society in every step of its development, and at every moment of
its existence. Rules exist before their application; they would still exist even if
they were never applied. Man does not make them. As a reasonable being, he is
capable of discovering and understanding them. As a free being, he can either
obey or violate them; but whether he be ignorant of them or knowingly violate
them, their reality, so far as they are rules, that is to say, their rational and moral
reality, is independent of him, superior and antecedent to his ignorance or his
knowledge, to the respect or neglect with which he treats them. Laying down
this principle then on the one side, that rule virtually exists before the relation
or society to which it corresponds, and on the other side, that it is not manifested and declared until society is established, that is to say, that it can only be
applied when society really exists, we inquire, What is this right and how can it
be discovered?

Right, considered in itself, is the rule that each individual is morally bound
to observe and respect in his relations with another individual; that is to say, the
moral limit at which his lawful liberty is arrested and ceases in his action on that
individual; or, in other words, the right of a man is the limit beyond which the
will of another man cannot morally be exercised over him in the relation which
unites them.

Nothing can be more certain than that every man in society has a right to
expect that this limit will be maintained and respected as regards himself by
other men and by society itself. This is the primitive and unalterable right
which he possesses in virtue of the dignity of his nature. If the philosophic
school had confined itself to laying down this principle, it would have been perfectly correct, and would have reminded society of the true moral rule. But it
has attempted to go further: it has pretended to determine, beforehand and in
a general way, the exact limit in every instance in which the will of individuals
over each other, or of society over individuals, ceases to be legitimate. It has not
contented itself with establishing right in principle, but has considered itself capable of enumerating all social rights *a priori*, and of reducing them to certain
general formulae which should comprise them all, and might thus be applied to
every relation to which society gives birth. By this it has been led to overlook
many very positive rights, and to create many pretended rights which have no
reality. If it be true, as we have laid it down, that right is the legitimate rule of a
relation, it is plain that the relation must be known before the right which ought
to govern it can be understood. Now social relations, whether between one man

and another, or between one and several, are neither simple nor identical. They are infinitely multiplied, varied, and interwoven; and right changes with relation. An example will best explain our meaning. We will select the most simple and natural of social relations, that of the father to the child. Nobody will presume to assert that here no right exists, that is to say, that neither the father nor the child have any respective rights to be mutually observed, and that their will alone should arbitrarily regulate their reciprocal relations. In the outset, whilst the child is devoid of reason, his will has little or no right: the right belongs entirely to the will of the father, which even then is, doubtless, legitimate only so far as it is conformable to reason, but which is not and cannot be subordinate to that of the child, on which it is exercised and which it directs. In proportion as reason becomes developed in the child, the right of the father's will becomes restricted; this right is always derived from the same principle, and ought to be exercised according to the same law; but it no longer extends to the same limit, but becomes changed and narrowed day by day with the progress of the intellectual and moral development of the child, up to the age when at length the child, having become a man, finds himself in a totally different relationship to his father—a relationship in which another right holds sway, that is to say, in which the paternal right is enclosed within entirely different limits, and is no longer exercised in the same way.

If, in the most simple of social relations, the right, though immutable in its principle, suffers so many vicissitudes in its application—if the limit at which it stops is so continually altered, according as this relation changes in nature and character—to a far greater extent will this be the case in all other social relations, which are infinitely more changeful and complicated. Every day old rights will perish; every day new ones will arise; that is to say, different applications will daily be made of the principle of right; and each occasion will vary at the limits at which the right ceases, either on one side or the other, in the innumerable relations which constitute society.

It is not, then, a simple matter to determine right, nor can it be done once for all, and according to certain general formulae. Either these formulae must be reduced to this dominant truth, that no will, whether that of man over man, of society over the individual, or of the individual over society, ought to be exercised contrary to justice and reason—or else these formulae are vain; that is to say, they confine themselves to expressing the principle of right, or try unsuccessfully to enumerate and regulate beforehand all its applications.

In this there consists the first error of the philosophic school, that, proud of having re-established the principle of right (a matter, certainly, of immense importance), it has thenceforth esteemed itself, by continuing the same process, in a condition to recognise and define all rights; that is to say, all applications of the principle to social relations; an attempt which is most dangerous because it is impossible. It is not granted to man thus to discern, beforehand and at a glance, the whole extent of the rational laws which ought to regulate the relations of men both among themselves and with society in general. Doubtless, in each of these relations and in all the vicissitudes which they undergo, there is a principle which is their legitimate rule, and which determines rights; and it is this principle which must be discovered. But it is in the relation itself, over which this principle should hold sway, that it is contained and may be discovered; it is intimately connected with the nature and object of this relation, and these are the first data that must be studied in order to arrive at a knowledge of the principle. The philosophic school almost constantly neglects this labour. Instead of applying itself to the discovery of the true rights which correspond to the various social relations, it arbitrarily constructs rights while pretending to deduce them from the general and primitive principle of right; an attempt the reverse of philosophical, for special rights are applications, not consequences logically deduced from this principle; which is perfectly exhibited in each particular case, but which does not contain within itself all the elements or all the data required for the discovery of the right in every case.

The second error of the philosophic school is that of mistaking the conditions under which right may be realised, that is to say, under which it may become associated with facts, so as to regulate them.

It has long been said that two powers, right and might, truth and error, good and evil, dispute the mastery of the world. What is not so often said, though it is no less true, is this—they dispute for it because they simultaneously possess it, because they co-exist in it everywhere at the same time. These two powers, so opposite in their nature, are never separated; in fact, they meet and mingle everywhere, forming by their co-existence and conflict that sort of impure and troubled unity which is the condition of man on earth; and which is reproduced in society as well as in individuals. All mundane facts bear this character: there are none that are completely devoid of truth, justice, and goodness; none that are wholly and purely right, good, or true. The simultaneous presence, and at the same time the struggle, of might and right, forms the primitive and dominant fact which is reproduced in all other facts.

The philosophical school habitually loses sight of this intimate and inevitable amalgamation of might and right in all that exists and takes place upon the earth. Because these two powers are hostile, it thinks them separate. When it recognises some great violation of right in an institution, a power, or a social relation, it concludes that right is utterly absent from it; and imagines, at the same time, that if it can succeed in laying hold of this fact, and shaping and regulating it according to its own will, it will secure the undisputed sway of right in that fact. Hence the contempt, one might almost say the hatred, with which it judges and treats facts. Hence also, the violence with which it pretends to impose upon them those rules and forms which constitute right in its eyes: what regard is due to that which is only the work of might? what sacrifices are not due to that which will be the triumph of right and reason? and the firmer the minds and the more energetic the characters of these reasoners, the more will they be ruled and the further misguided by this method of viewing human things. Facts past and present do not deserve so much disdain, nor do future ones merit so much confidence. We do not here adopt the views of the sceptics, nor would we regard all facts as equally good or bad, and equally invested with or destitute of reason and right. Nothing can be more contrary to our opinion. We firmly believe in the reality and legitimacy of right, in its struggle against might, and in the utility as well as the moral obligation of sustaining right in this eternal but progressive combat. We only ask that, in this struggle, nothing may be forgotten, and nothing confounded; and that indiscriminate attacks may not be made. We ask that because a fact may contain many illegitimate elements, it is not therefore to be supposed *a priori* to contain nothing besides, for such is not the case. Right exists everywhere more or less, and everywhere right ought to be respected. There is also more or less falsity and incompleteness in the speculative idea which we form to ourselves of right, and there will be unjust force and violence employed in the strife in which this idea is made to prevail, and in the new facts which will result from its triumph. This is not saying that the combat ought to be suspended, or that the triumph ought not to be pursued. It is only necessary truthfully to recognise the condition of human things, and never to lose sight of it, whether the question be one of judgment or of action.

This is what the philosophic school can rarely consent to do. Taking right for the point at which it sets out, and also that at which it aims, it forgets that facts subsist between these two extremes—actual and existing facts, independent data; a condition which of imperative necessity must be submitted to, when the extension of right is sought after, since these facts are the very matters to which right must be applied. This school begins by neglecting one of the fundamental elements of the problem which it has to solve; it falls into reverie, and constructs imaginary facts, whilst it ought to be operating on real facts. And when compelled to quit hypotheses, and deal with realities, it becomes irritated at the obstacles which it meets, and unreasonably condemns the facts which throw them in its way. Thus, through having desired impossibilities, it is led to forget a part of that which is actually true. Society at every period swerves more or less from the general type of right; that is to say, the facts which constitute its material and moral condition are more or less regulated according to right, and also become in a greater or less degree susceptible of receiving a more absolute form, a more perfect rule, and of continually assimilating more closely to reason and truth; and this it is which must be absolutely studied and understood before passing a judgment on these facts, or endeavouring to effect their change and improvement. Perfection is the aim of human nature and of human society; perfection is the law of their existence, but imperfection is its condition. The philosophic school does not accept this condition; and is thus misled in its endeavours towards attaining perfection, and even in its own idea of the perfection to which it aspires.

The historic school possesses other characteristics, and falls into different errors. With the utmost respect for facts, it easily allows itself to be induced to attribute to them merits to which they are not entitled; to see more reason and justice, that is to say, more *right*, in them than they really contain, and to resist even the slightest bold attempt to judge and regulate them according to principles more conformable to general reason. It is even inclined to deny these principles, to maintain that there is no rational and invariable type of right that man can take for a guide in his efforts or his opinions: an error of great magnitude, and sufficient to place this school, philosophically considered, in a subordinate rank. What then is perfection, if there is no ideal perfection to be aimed at? What is the progress of real rights, if there is no rational right to comprehend them all? What is the human mind, if it is incapable of penetrating far beyond actual realities in its knowledge of this rational right? and how can it judge of them except by comparing them with this sublime type, which it never holds in full possession, but which it cannot deny without abnegating itself, and losing every fixed rule and guiding thread? Doubtless, facts command respect, because they are a condition, a necessity; and they deserve it, because they always contain a certain measure of right. But the judgment ought never to be enslaved by them, nor should it attribute absolute legitimacy to reality. Is it so difficult, then, to perceive that evil is evil even when it is powerful and inevitable? The historic school constantly endeavours to evade this confession. It tries to explain every institution, and to abstain from giving judgment upon them, as if explanation and judgment were not two distinct acts, which possess no right over one another. It never suffers the institution of a comparison between the real state of any society and the rational state of society in general; as if the real, or even the possible, were the limit of reason; as if, when judging, reason should be deposed, because when applied it is compelled to undergo conditions and to yield to obstacles which it cannot conquer. The historic school would be perfectly right if it confined itself to the careful study of facts, bringing to light that portion of right which they contain, and searching out the degree of perfection which they are capable of receiving, and if it restricted itself to maintaining that it is not easy to distinguish real rights, unjust to condemn facts *en masse*, and impossible and dangerous to neglect them altogether. But when it undertakes to legitimise facts by facts; when it refuses to apply the invariable law of justice and rational right to all, it abandons every principle, falls into a sort of absurd and shameful fatalism, and disinherits man and society of that which is most pure in their nature, most legitimate in their pretensions, and most noble in their aspirations.

To sum up, the philosophic school possesses the merit of everywhere acknowledging the principle of right, and adopting it as the unchangeable rule of its judgment on facts. Its errors consist in its knowledge of facts being slight, imperfect, and precipitate; and in not allowing to facts the power which is inseparable from them, and the degree of legitimacy which they always contain. The historic school is better acquainted with facts, appreciates their causes and consequences more equitably, effects a more faithful analysis of their elements, and arrives at a more exact knowledge of particular rights as well as at a more just estimate of practicable reforms. But it is deficient in general and fixed principles: its judgments fluctuate according to chance; and accordingly it almost always hesitates to come to a conclusion, and never succeeds in satisfying the mind, which the philosophic school, on the contrary, always impresses strongly, at the risk of leading it astray.

We have insisted on the distinctive characters and opposite errors of these two schools, because we meet with them unceasingly when investigating how institutions and social facts have been appreciated and understood. Of this we have given an example by indicating the two points of view under which the division of the legislative power into two Chambers has been commonly considered. The historic school approves and recommends it; but it often founds its reasons on illegitimate facts, and adheres too absolutely to the forms which this institution has assumed in the past, while it refrains from attaching itself to any rigorous and rational principle. The philosophic school has long maintained, and many of its disciples still believe, that this is an accidental and arbitrary institution, which is not founded on reason and the very nature of things.

Let us now consider this institution in itself, after having disentangled it from that which, in England, has related merely to its actual origin, and to the local circumstances in the midst of which it took its rise.

It is beyond doubt that the immense inequality of wealth and credit—in a word, of power and social importance, which existed between the great barons and the other political classes of the nation, whether freeholders or burgesses, was in England the sole cause of the institution of the House of Peers. No political combination or idea of public right had anything to do with its formation. The personal importance of a certain number of individuals, in this case, created their right. Political order is necessarily the expression, the reflection, of social order. In this stage of civilisation especially, power is indisputably conveyed from society into the government. There was a House of Peers because there were men who, bearing no comparison with others, could not remain confounded with them, exercising only the same rights, and possessing no greater amount of authority.

To the same cause must be ascribed several of the leading characteristics of the House of Peers; the hereditary transmission of social importance, wealth, and power (the result of the feudal system as regards property), carried with it the inheritance of political importance. This is proved by the fact, that originally the sole hereditary peers were the barons by feudal tenure. Hereditary right did not originally belong to the *barons by writ*; although individually summoned to the Upper House, they exercised, when sitting there, the same rights. The judicial functions of the House of Peers also had the same source. At first they belonged to the general assembly of the direct vassals of the king. When the greater number of these vassals ceased to attend that assembly, the great barons who alone attended, continued to exercise nearly all its functions, and especially its judicial authority. Of this they continued to hold possession when the knights re-entered Parliament by means of election. Thus, a right, which originally devolved upon the general assembly of the political nation, became concentrated in the new House of Peers, at least in every case unaffected by the new jurisdictions instituted by the king. On examining in all its details the political part now performed in England by the House of Peers, it will be found that a great number of its attributes are only the results of ancient facts, that they are not inherent in the institution itself, but solely derived from the social position of the great barons; and at the same time it will be perceived that all these facts are connected with the general and primitive fact of the great inequality then subsisting between the great barons and the citizens.

As this inequality really existed, and could not fail to re-appear in the government, it was very fortunate for England that it assumed the form of the House of Peers. Inequality is never more oppressive and fatal than when displayed solely for its own advantage, and in an individual interest. This is the invariable result when the upper ranks are dispersed over the country, and are brought into contact with, and into the presence of, their inferiors alone. If, instead of uniting in the House of Peers to exercise, as members of that assembly, the power they possessed over society, the great barons had each remained on his own estates, their superiority and power would have weighed heavily on all their vassals and farmers, and social emancipation would have been very much retarded. Every baron would then have had to do with his inferiors alone. In the House of Peers, on the contrary, he had to deal with his equals; and to obtain influence in that assembly, and effect his will, he was obliged to have recourse to discussion, to the advancement of public reasons, and to constitute himself the exponent of some interest superior to his own personal interest, and of opinions around which it would be possible for men to unite together. Thus men, who, had they remained isolated on their domains, would have acted only upon inferiors and for their own interest, were constrained, when they had met together, to act upon their equals, and for the interests of the masses, whose support alone could increase their power in the frequent struggles which this new situation imposed upon them. Thus by the single fact of its concentration, the high feudal aristocracy insensibly changed its character. Each of its members possessed rights originally derived entirely from his own power, which he came to the House of Peers to exercise solely for his own interest; but when once brought together into each other's presence, all these individual interests experienced the necessity of seeking new means of obtaining credit and authority elsewhere than in themselves. Personal powers were constrained to sink themselves into a public power. An assembly composed of individual superiorities, jealous only to preserve and increase their power, became gradually converted into a national institution, compelled to adapt itself, in many points, to the interest of all. As I have elsewhere had occasion to say, one of the greatest vices of the feudal system was to localise sovereignty, and to bring it everywhere, so to speak, to the door of those over whom it was exercised. The formation of the House of Peers weakened this evil in England, and thus, at least in a political point of view, struck a deadly blow at feudalism.

Further, the great barons thus formed into a body, had the power and duty of defending in common their rights and liberties against the royal power; and their resistance, instead of consisting in a series of isolated wars, as was the case in France, immediately assumed the character of a collective and truly political resistance, founded on certain general principles of right and liberty. Now there is something contagious in these principles and their language, which very soon extends them beyond the limits within which they are at first enclosed. Right calls forth right, liberty engenders liberty. The demands and resistance of the great barons provoked similar demands and resistance in other classes of the nation. Without the concentration of the high aristocracy in the House of Peers, the House of Commons would probably have never been formed. From all these facts flows this consequence, that when great inequality actually exists in society between different classes of citizens, it is not only natural but useful to the progress of justice and liberty, that the superior class should be collected and concentrated into a great public power, in which individual superiorities become placed on a more elevated level than that of personal interest; they learn to treat with their equals, to meet with opposition, and to furnish an example of the defence of liberties and rights; while by exposing themselves in some sort to the view of the whole nation, they experience by this fact alone the necessity of adapting themselves, to a certain extent, to its opinions, sentiments, and interests.

But, it may be said, a social inequality of sufficient magnitude to occasion the formation of such a power, is neither a universal fact, nor one in itself good and desirable; and under this point of view the House of Peers, as it is constituted in England, was simply a remedy for an evil. There can be no doubt that the accumulation of land, wealth, and positive power which belonged to the great barons, and the securing of all these social advantages, were the result of violence, and as contrary to the internal tendency as to the rational principles of society in general. If then the division of the legislative power into two Chambers is derived only from such causes, it might in certain cases be inevitable and even beneficial; but where these causes are not met with, nothing would recommend it, or ought to make its necessity a matter of regret. The equitable and natural distribution of social advantages, their rapid circulation, the free competition of rights and powers—this is the object, as it is the rational law of the social condition. An institution which, in itself and by its nature, is opposed to this object and derogates from this law, contains nothing which ought to lead to its adoption when not imposed by necessity.

Is this the case with regard to the division of the legislative power into two Chambers, setting aside those particular characteristics which, in the English House of Peers, are derived solely from local and accidental facts, and cannot be referred to rational causes of universal validity?

Before considering this question in its relation to the fundamental principle of representative government, some observations are necessary.

It is by no means true, that similar inequalities to those which produced the preponderance of the great barons in England, and a permanent classification of society in conformity to these facts, are natural conditions of the social state. Providence does not always sell her benefits at so high a price to the human race, and has not rested the very existence of society on this denomination, this immovable constitution of privilege. Reason must believe, and facts prove, that society can not only subsist, but is even better off in another condition; in a condition in which the principle of free competition exercises more dominion, and where the different social classes are more nearly allied. It is certain, however, that there exist in society two tendencies, equally legitimate in their principle, and equally salutary in their effects, although in permanent opposition to each other. The one is the tendency to the production of inequality, the other, the tendency to maintain or restore equality between individuals. Both are natural and indestructible: this is a fact which requires no proof, the aspect of the world displays it everywhere; and if we look within, we shall perceive it in ourselves. Who does not desire, in some respect or another, to raise himself above his equals? and who would not also wish, in some particular, to bring down his superiors to an equality with himself? These two tendencies, considered in their principle, are equally legitimate: the one is attached to the right of the natural superiorities which exist in the moral as well as in the physical order of the universe; the other, to the right of every man to that justice which desires that no arbitrary force should deprive him of any of the social advantages which he possesses, or might acquire, unaided and without injury to his fellows. To prevent natural superiorities from displaying themselves, and exercising the power that belongs to them, is to create a violent inequality, and to mutilate the human race in its noblest parts. To enslave men in regard to those rights which are common to all, by reason of the similitude of their nature, to unequal laws imposed or maintained by force, is to insult human nature and to forget its imperishable dignity. In fine, these two tendencies are equally salutary in their effects: without the one, society would be inert and lifeless; without the other, might alone would dominate, and right would for ever be suppressed. In considering them as respects that which is legitimate and moral in each, let us ask what is this tendency to inequality but the desire to elevate ourselves, to extend our influence, and to bring to light and effect the triumph of that portion of moral power which is naturally placed by the will of God the Creator, in each particular individual? and is it not this impulse which constitutes the life and determines the progress of the human race? On the other hand, what is this tendency to equality except resistance to force, to capricious arbitrary wills, and the desire to yield obedience only to justice and true law? Doubtless, in both these tendencies, the bad as well as the the good parts of our nature display themselves: there is a taint of insolence in the desire of self-elevation, and of envy in the passion for equality. Injustice and violence may be employed either to abase superiors or to surpass equals; but in that conflict of good and evil, which is everywhere the condition of man, it is not the less true that the two tendencies of which I am speaking constitute the very principle of social life, the twofold cause which makes the human race advance in the career of improvement, which leads it back when it wanders astray, and urges it forward when perverse powers or wills seek to arrest its course.

The tendency to inequality is then a fact inevitable in itself, legitimate in its principle, and salutary in its effects, if it is restrained by the law of competition, that is to say, beneath the condition of a permanent and free struggle with the tendency to equality, which, in the order of Providence, appears to be the fact by which it is destined to be balanced. In every country there will always arise and exist a certain number of great individual superiorities, who will seek an analogous place in government to that which they occupy in society. They ought not to obtain it for their personal interest, nor to extend it beyond what comports with the public interest, nor should they retain it longer than they possess the title in virtue of which they assumed it, that is to say, their actual importance, nor should they preserve this title by means violative of the principle of free competition, and the maintenance of the rights which are common to all. All this is indubitable, but, this being allowed, there will still remain the necessity of introducing and concentrating among the superior powers all the great superiorities of the country, in order to engage them in the transaction of public affairs, and in the defence of the general interests.

This, as we have seen, is the sole object of the representative system: its precise purpose is to discover and concentrate the natural and real superiorities of the country, in order to apply them to its government. Now, is it good in itself, and in conformity with the fundamental principle of this system, to apply only one method of seeking out these superiorities, and to gather them all into a single voting urn? that is to say, must they be united in one single assembly, formed upon the same conditions, after the same tests, and by the same mode? We now reach the pith of the question.

The principle of the representative system is the destruction of all sovereignty of permanent right, that is to say, of all absolute power upon earth. The question of what is now called *omnipotence* has at all times been agitated. If by this is understood an actually definitive power, in the terms of established laws, such a power always exists in society, under a multitude of names and forms: for wherever there is a matter to be decided and completed, there must be a power to decide and complete it. Thus, in the family, the father exercises the power of definitively determining, in certain particulars, the conduct and destiny of his children; in a well regulated municipality, the municipal council definitively enacts the local budget; in civil trials, certain tribunals give final judgment upon cases submitted to their decision; and in the political system, electoral omnipotence belongs to the electors. Definitive power is thus disseminated through the social state, and is necessarily met with everywhere. Does this imply that a power ought somewhere to exist, which possesses omnipotence by right, that is to say, which has the right to do anything it pleases? That would be absolute power; and it is the formal design of the representative system, as well as the object of all its institutions, to provide against the existence of such a power, and to take care that every power shall be submitted to certain trials, meet with obstacles, undergo opposition, and, in fine, be deprived of sway until it has either proved its legitimacy, or given reason for presuming it.

There is not, then, and there cannot be, any omnipotence by right, that is to say, any power which should be allowed to say: "that is good and just because I have so decided it"; and every effort of political science, every institution, ought to tend to the prevention of such a power being anywhere formed; and should provide that the actual omnipotence which exists under so many names in society, should everywhere meet with restraints and obstacles enough to prevent its conversion into an omnipotence by right.

Until the summit of society is reached, and while those powers only are constituted, above which other permanent powers will be placed for the purpose of controlling them, and with power to enforce their authority, this end appears easy to attain.

Judicial power, municipal power, and every second class power may be definitive without much danger, because if they are abused in a manner likely to become fatal, the legislative or executive power will be there to repress them. But we must necessarily come at last to the supreme power, to that power which superintends all others, and is not itself ruled or restrained by any visible and constituted power. Shall the right of omnipotence appertain to this? Certainly not, whatever may be its form or name. It will, however, be always prone to aspire to it, and able to usurp it, for in the political system it possesses omnipotence, and of this it cannot be deprived; for in reference to general interests, as well as to local and private interests, a definitive power is a necessity.

Here then, all the foresight of the politician ought to be displayed: he will need all his art and all his efforts, to prevent actual omnipotence from asserting its inherent rightfulness, and general definitive power from becoming absolute power.

This result is endeavoured to be secured by a variety of means: I. by recognising the individual rights of citizens—the effect of which is to superintend, control, and limit this central supreme power, and constantly to subject it to the law of reason and justice to which it ought to be subordinated; this is the object of the jury, of the liberty of the press, and of publicity of all kinds: II. by constituting, in a distinct and independent way, the principal powers of the second class, such as the judicial and municipal powers; on such a plan that these being themselves repressed and restrained when necessary by the central power, may restrain and repress it in their turn if it should attempt to become absolute: III. by organising the central power itself in such a manner as to make it very difficult for it to usurp rightful omnipotence, and to provide that it shall meet with such oppositions and obstacles within itself as will not admit of its attaining actual omnipotence except under laborious conditions, the accomplishment of which gives ground to presume that it does in effect act in accordance with reason and justice; that is to say, that it possesses legitimacy.

This last description of means is the only one connected with the question that now occupies our attention. The division of the legislative power into two Chambers has precisely this object. It is directed against the easy acquisition of actual omnipotence at the summit of the social system, and consequently against the transformation of actual omnipotence into rightful omnipotence. It is therefore conformable to the fundamental principle of the representative system, and is a necessary consequence of it.

Why is it undesirable that the legislative and executive powers, that is to say, the entire supreme power, should reside either in one man or in a single assembly? why does tyranny always spring from these two forms of government? Because it is in the nature of things, that a power which has no equal should think itself rightfully sovereign, and should very soon become absolute. It has happened thus in democracies, aristocracies, and monarchies; wherever actually sovereign power has been conferred upon a single man, or a single body of men, that man, or that body, has assumed to be rightfully sovereign; and more or less frequently, and with greater or less violence, it has exercised despotism.

The art of politics, the secret of liberty is, then, to provide equals for every power for which it cannot provide superiors. This is the principle which ought to preside in the organisation of the central government: for on these terms only can the establishment of despotism at the centre of the State be prevented.

Now if the legislative power is entrusted to a single assembly, and the executive power to one man, or if the legislative power is divided between one assembly and the executive power, is it possible for each of these powers to possess sufficient force and consistence to admit of the necessary equality between them, that is to say, to secure that neither shall become the sole and undisputed sovereign power? Such an example has never been witnessed: where-ever the central power has been thus constituted, a struggle has arisen, which has resulted, according to the times, either in the annihilation of the executive power by the legislative assembly, or of the legislative assembly by the executive power. Some countries have been governed by a single assembly, others by several assemblies, of which some have been aristocratic and others democratic; while all have contested with each other for the sovereignty. These various forms of government have given rise either to tyranny or to continued commotions, and have nevertheless endured. But a government in which the legislative assembly and the executive power have remained distinct, preserving their personality and their independence, and reciprocally limiting each other, is a phenomenon without example, either in antiquity or in modern times. One of these powers has always speedily succumbed, or been soon reduced to a state of subordination and dependence equivalent to nonentity, at least as regarded the essential purposes for which it was instituted.

This could not fail to be the case. Equality is impossible between powers which are completely dissimilar, either in their nature, or in their means of obtaining power or credit. The dominion of one person, that is to say, the pure monarchical form of government, derives its springs and means of action from certain dispositions of human nature, and certain conditions of society. The full and exclusive rule of a single assembly derives the same from other dispositions and other social circumstances; according as one or other class of these circumstances predominate, kings have abolished assemblies, and assemblies have overthrown kings. But the co-existence of these two systems of government, when confronted with each other and acting in direct opposition, is impossible. They do not then act as a restraint upon each other, but they wage a war of extermination: such an event has accordingly never been met with except in revolutionary times: it may possibly have been an unavoidable condition of such epochs; but then it has always involved one or other of these forms of despotism: it has never become the basis of a free and regular government.

When it is once admitted that the division of the central power is indispensable, in order to prevent all usurpation of rightful omnipotence, or, at least, to render such usurpation infrequent and difficult, it necessarily follows that this division ought to be effected in such a way that the resulting powers shall be capable of regular co-existence, that is to say, of mutually restraining, limiting, and compelling each other to seek in common for that reason, truth, and justice, which ought to regulate their will and preside over their actions. It is essential that neither of these powers should elevate itself so much above the others as to be able to throw off their yoke; for the excellence of the system consists precisely in their mutual dependence, and in the efforts which it imposes on them to secure unanimity. Now there can be no mutual dependence, except between powers which are invested with a certain degree of independence, and with strength enough to maintain it.

The division of the central power, or of the actual sovereignty, between the executive power and two legislative assemblies is, therefore, strictly derived from the fundamental principle of the representative system; or rather it is the sole constitutional form which fully corresponds to this principle, and guarantees its maintenance, since this is the only form which, by providing equals for powers which admit of no superiors, prevents them all from claiming and usurping rightful sovereignty, that is to say, absolute power.

Why has this truth been so frequently forgotten? why has this constitutional form been so often repudiated by men who, nevertheless, desired to establish representative government?—Because they have forgotten the principle of this form of government. At the very moment when they were directing their efforts against absolute power, they have imagined that it legitimately existed somewhere; and they have attributed it to society itself—to the entire people. They have thus proved wanting in consistency and courage in their opposition to absolute power; and either have not known, or have not dared, to pursue it wherever it might be found; to leave it no refuge; to denounce and banish it under every possible name and form. Thus, admitting the existence of one sole sovereign, naturally and eternally legitimate, they have also been obliged to admit an undivided representation of this undivided sovereign. The sovereignty of the people, thus understood, necessarily carries with it the unity of the legislative power: and when tyranny has sprung from it, when the lessons of experience have led men to seek other combinations, when it has been considered right to divide the legislative assembly, it has been done with the assertion, that such a step was contrary to the principle of representative government, but necessary: that principles cannot rigorously be followed, and that it is necessary to believe in the theory, but not to practise it. Such language is an insult to truth, for truth never contains evil; and when evil does appear anywhere, it arises not from truth but from error. If the consequences of a principle are fatal, it is not because the principle, though in itself true, is not applicable, but because it really is not true. It has been said by the advocates of divine right: There is only one God; there ought therefore to be only one king; and all power belongs to him because he is the representative of God. The advocates of the sovereignty of the people say: There is only one people; there ought therefore to be only one legislative assembly, for that represents the people. The error is the same in both cases, and in each instance it leads equally to despotism. There is only one God, that is certain: but God exists nowhere upon the earth, for neither is any man nor is the entire people God, nor do any perfectly know his law, or constantly desire it. No actual power, then, ought to be undivided, for the unity of actual power supposes a plenitude of rightful power which nobody possesses or can possess.

Far, then, from the division of legislative power being a derogation from the principles of political liberty, it is, on the contrary, in perfect harmony with these principles, and is specially directed against the establishment of absolute power.

Having thus established the principle, it would be easy to consider it in practice, and to demonstrate its good effects. It would be easy to prove that it is indispensible for realising the responsibility of the executive power; for curbing inordinate ambition, and turning every kind of superiority to the profit of the State; for preventing fundamental institutions, the public rights of citizens, and all the higher branches of legislation, from being treated as simple measures of government, and made subject to the instability of political experience: but these considerations would lead me too far; I wished to establish this constitutional form in principle, because it is owing to the want of such foundations that it has long been regarded with mistrust and doubt by many enlightened men. Its utility is never disputed; its good results are acknowledged; but men are generally ignorant how it can be made to agree with the general principles of a free government; and it has been found, not without reason, that these principles would be weakened by any derogation from them. In times when the human race is subject to regenerative influences, empiricism is never the ruling spirit: man then requires some rational and rigorous principles which may furnish a solution to every difficulty; and he mistrusts experience when he finds her counsels at variance with those primitive axioms which his reason has firmly adopted. This is our natural disposition: let us not lament it, it characterises all great epochs; it is then only necessary rigidly to examine principles themselves, and to grant dominion to those ideas only which truly deserve it.

A second question remains for consideration: it is, to ascertain how the division of the legislative power into two houses ought to be effected, and what should be the mode of formation, what the attributes and the relations of the two assemblies. This, at least to a great degree, is a question of circumstance, the solution of which is almost entirely dependent upon the state of society, its internal constitution, and the manner in which wealth, influence, and intelligence, are distributed; this is sufficiently indicated by what I have said about the causes that led to the formation of the House of Peers in England. It is evident, for example, that those countries in which there was no such inequality as then existed between the different classes of society, would be ill adapted for a division of the legislative power based upon the same ideas, presenting the same characteristics, and entailing the same consequences. Perhaps the only general idea which can be laid down beforehand upon this subject is, that the two assemblies should not proceed from the same source, and be constituted in the same manner; in a word, that they should not be exactly alike. The object of their separation would then be defeated, for their similitude would destroy the mutual independence which is the condition of their utility.

LECTURE 19

---

*Power and attributes of the British Parliament in the fourteenth century.
⁓ At its origin, and subsequently to its complete development, the Parliament retained the name of the Great Council of the kingdom. ⁓ Difference between its attributes and its actual power at these two epochs.
⁓ Absorption of almost the entire government by the Crown; gradual resumption of its influence by the Parliament.*

THE first name borne in England by the assembly which was succeeded by the Parliament, was, as you have seen, that of the great council, the common council of the kingdom,—*magnum commune consilium regni.* The same name has also been given to the Parliament in England for the last two centuries, when it is desired to indicate completely the nature of its interference in the government, and the part which it there performs. It is called the great national council: the king governs in Parliament, that is to say, with the advice and consent of the great council of the nation.

Thus, both at the origin of the British government, and since it has attained its complete development, the same idea has been attached to the assembly, or union of the great public assemblies; and they have both been designated by the same word.

At both these periods, the Parliament or the corresponding assembly which preceded it, has never actually been, and, indeed, could not be considered as a special power, distinct from the government properly so called—an accessory limited in its action to a certain number of affairs or emergencies. The government itself has resided in it. All superior powers have there been concentrated and called into exercise.

At the origin of modern States, and especially of England, it was very far from being thought that the whole and sole right of the body of capable citizens, of the political nation, consisted in consenting to the imposition of taxes; that they were otherwise subjected to an independent authority, and were not authorized in any way to interfere, either directly or indirectly, in the general affairs of the State. Whatever these affairs might be, they were their affairs, and they always occupied themselves with them, when their importance naturally called for their intervention. This is testified by the history of the Saxon *Wittenagemot*, of the Anglo-Norman *Magnum Consilium* and of all the national assemblies of the German peoples, in the earliest period of their existence. These assemblies were truly the great national council, deliberating and deciding on the affairs of the nation in concert with the king.

When the representative system has achieved all its mighty conquests, and borne its essential fruits, it has invariably resorted to this; and returned in fact to the point from which it set out. In spite of all distinctious and apparent limitations, the power of Parliament has extended to everything, and has exercised a more or less immediate, but in reality a decisive influence on all the affairs of the State. Parliament has again become the great national council in which all the national interests are debated and regulated, sometimes by means of anterior deliberation, at other times by those of responsibility.

When this first and last condition of free governments has been recognized, it will be perceived that a very different intermediate condition is to be met with, in which Parliament, although sometimes styled the great national council, exercises none of its functions, does not in a permanent manner interfere in political affairs, and is not, in a word, the seat and habitual instrument of government. During the whole of this period, the government is separate from the Parliament, and resides altogether in the royal power, around which are grouped the principal members of the great aristocracy. The Parliament is necessary in certain cases, but it is not the centre, the focus, of political action. It exercises rights, defends its liberties, and labours for their extension; but influences the government in no decisive way: and principles which belong only to absolute monarchy co-exist with the more or less frequent convocation of the representatives of the nation.

Such was the state of the British Parliament, from its formation in the thirteenth century until nearly the end of the seventeenth. It was only at the end of the seventeenth century that it resumed all the characteristics of a great national council, and became once more the seat of the entire government.

The British Parliament was not, then, in the fourteenth century either what the public assemblies of the German peoples had originally been, nor what it is in the present day. In order properly to comprehend what, at that period, was the nature of its power and the scope of its influence, we must follow the progress of events.

Common deliberation on common affairs is the principle, as well as the most simple form, of political liberty. This principle fully obtained at the infancy of modern nations. The national assembly was the great council in which public affairs of every kind were transacted. The king, the natural head of this council, was required to convoke it, and to follow its advice.

By the dispersion of the nation over an extended territory, the great national council became dispersed, and could not be assembled: for some time, however, it retained its ancient form, and the full extent of its ancient rights; but power is attached to continual presence, and the great council became of rare occurrence. Its numbers rapidly thinned; and it was very soon composed of great landowners alone, whom wealth, political importance, and that ambition which increases with the growth of power, frequently assembled round the king. The government, which formerly resided in the great national council, now resided only in this new council, formed of the king and the great barons, who became daily further separated from the body of the nation. The same words continued to be employed: the king always governed with his great council; but this was no longer the same assembly; the government and the body of the nation had become disjoined.

The king endeavoured to free himself from the great barons, and to govern alone; they resisted; and in the struggle in which they engaged for the defence of their liberties or the preservation of their influence in the central government, they were compelled to seek support from the body of the nation, the freeholders and the burgesses. The issue of this struggle was favourable to liberty; the freeholders and the burgesses, who were become almost strangers to the central government, renewed their connection with it by the formation of Parliament; and this great council of the king, which for two centuries had been continually contracting, once more began to extend.

But at their return, the new citizens were very far from taking the same place which their ancestors had occupied. The development of inequality is always the first result of the progress of the social state. Royalty had extended and fortified its power; it now existed by itself, powerful and independent, and claiming distinct rights proportionate to its own strength. It was the same with the great barons, who also were strong and independent in themselves. If it had been possible to congregate in a single assembly all the descendants of those ancient Saxons or Normans who had originally formed the great common council, a very different spectacle would have been presented. Instead of finding an assembly of warriors, not enjoying perfect equality, certainly, but sufficiently equal for each to preserve his personal importance, and to consider himself in a condition to defend it; instead of seeing a chief at their head, too little distinguished from the principal men among them to be powerful without their adherence—there would have been a king invested with great wealth and power, mighty barons followed by a multitude of retainers almost entirely dependent upon them, and a body of citizens obliged to unite and act collectively for the recovery of some influence over those measures which interested them most directly. In this new composition of society and of the national assembly, the deputies of the counties and boroughs were very far from pretending to associate themselves with the government properly so called, or from thinking to control or direct the central power in all public affairs; several centuries necessarily elapsed before their ideas could acquire so much generality, and their interference in Parliament became so comprehensive. They assembled there for the sole purpose of defending themselves, and those whom they represented, against the most crying abuses of power, against the violent and arbitrary invasion of their persons and their possessions. Discussing the demands for supplies that were addressed to them, and presenting their complaints to the government against the most perilous acts of injustice of the agents of the king or of the great nobles, constituted the whole of their mission, and, in their own opinion, the full extent of their rights. Their personal importance was too trivial, and their intellectual activity too limited, for them to imagine themselves called to discuss and regulate the general affairs of the State. They resisted power when it directly attacked them, or required great sacrifices from them; but royalty and its prerogatives, the ordinary council of the king, and his measures in regard to legislation, peace and war, or general politics, in a word, the government properly so called, were entirely beyond their interference. They had not the power, or even the wish, to meddle with such matters; it was all discussed and decided between the king, his ministers, and the great nobles who were naturally called to take part therein by the elevation and importance of their social position.

Both the ancient assembly of the Saxon or Norman warriors, then, and the existing Parliament, would be vainly sought for in the Parliament of the fourteenth century. No violence is done to facts: a new society had been formed which could only engender a political order in accordance with its own character. Great inequality prevailed, and this inequality would naturally reappear between the powers to which it gave birth. The primitive and simple unity which exists in an uncivilized community had disappeared; the wise unity to which a state of civilised society can elevate itself by the diffusion of wealth and intelligence, was still far distant. There was a king, a House of Lords, and a House of Commons: but there was not a Parliament in the political sense which is now attached to that word.

The permanent co-existence of royalty and a great public council, through all these vicissitudes of government and liberty, is an important fact. This council, formed at first by the general assembly of the nation, afterwards restricted to the great barons, and speedily admitting within its circle the representatives of other social conditions, has always been in England the principal organ of the central government. The English monarchy has never succeeded in isolating and enfranchising itself therefrom. It has been narrowed or extended by reason of changes occurring in society: but it has always constituted the condition and form of the monarchy. Popular liberty, so to speak, has always maintained a footing in the central power; the nation has never been completely excluded from participation in its own affairs. The progress of Parliament has been the progress of the government itself. In vain was the House of Commons feeble and inactive at its origin: it did exist, and it formed part of the king's council; it was always present to embrace, in some measure, every opportunity of extending its influence, and aggrandising its position and the part it had to perform. In the fourteenth century, its power was very limited, its attributes very restricted, and its intervention in public affairs very infrequent; but it was impossible that it should not daily increase. In effect it did greatly increase from the time of Edward I. to that of Henry VI. During the wars of the Red and White Roses, the great feudal aristocracy destroyed itself by its contentions. When Henry VII. ascended the throne, there no longer existed a body of great barons capable of offering armed resistance to the royal power. The House of Commons, though strengthened, had not yet emerged from its condition of inferiority, and was incapable of taking the place of the great barons in resistance to royalty. Hence the Tudor despotism in the sixteenth century, the only period at which the maxims of absolute power have prevailed in England; but even in that very century, the House of Commons daily penetrated further into the government, until its power was fully revealed by the great Revolution of the seventeenth century.

I have now given you a glimpse of the space between the period of the definitive formation of the British Parliament, and that at which it sought to obtain its entire dominion. In our subsequent lectures we shall examine the principal phases in the development of this great government during those three centuries.

LECTURE 20

Condition and attributes of the Parliament during the reign of Edward II. (1307–1327). ⁓ *Empire of favourites.* ⁓ *Struggle of the barons against the favourites.* ⁓ *Aristocratic factions.* ⁓ *Petitions to the king.* ⁓ *Forms of deliberations on this subject.* ⁓ *Deposition of Edward II.*

In order to explain the manner in which the British Parliament was formed, I have found it necessary, up to this point, to follow history step by step—to enter into all the details, and to collect all the facts, that might serve as proofs either of its existence, or of its participation in public affairs. I have now another object to attain, and I must therefore pursue another course. The Parliament is now definitively formed; and if I were to continue to narrate all the facts which relate to it, and to keep a register, as it were, of all its acts, I should write the history of the country, and not that of its institutions. What I am seeking to describe, is the development of representative government; and I shall avoid all questions unconnected with this object. The extension which the Parliament received, the revolutions which it underwent—in a word, its personal and internal life, will constitute the subject to which our attention must be directed.

On considering the reign of Edward I. from a political point of view, it is evident that, notwithstanding the agitations by which it was disturbed, there was, during that reign, some wholeness and unity in the exercise of power. Edward was a firm and capable prince, who well knew how to concentrate and direct the various forces of society; in him, the State possessed a centre and a chief. Under Edward II., the English government lost all solidity and unity: no intelligent and determined will presided over it; the nation had no rallying-point; the string of the bundle was broken; all forces and all passions were displayed at hap-hazard, and came into conflict upon the interests of individuals or factions.

In such a state of things, what could the Parliament be? Nothing, or next to nothing, unless it were an instrument of factions. The body of barons was then, and long continued to be, the preponderant portion of the assembly: the Commons, though strong enough sometimes to defend themselves when their own interests were at stake, were not sufficiently powerful to interfere, in a decisive manner, in public affairs, and to become the centre of the government. All matters were, therefore, arranged between the court and the barons, or rather between the different factions into which the body of barons was divided. The Commons appeared in the train of one or other party, to give their alternate triumphs the appearance of a national adhesion, but without ever determining the course of events, or even modifying them in any effectual manner. The supreme power and the country were a prey to the conflicts and schisms of the high aristocracy.

In order clearly to demonstrate that such was the state of institutions and of the central government at this period, it will be sufficient to refer to the three principal events of this reign.

The first is the conflict which the English barons maintained against the king, with regard to a favourite, Piers Gaveston, whom, in spite of his father's advice, Edward II. had persisted in retaining in his confidence. The favourite and his creatures absorbed all the power and advantages of the court; and in 1311, the barons, desiring their share of riches and favours, after having attempted all other means for his overthrow, demanded his dismissal with arms in their hands. Their enterprise was evidently intended neither to promote the interests of the people nor those of the king; it was a revolt of courtiers. They fought, not to assert the inviolability of charters or rights, but to obtain the employments and treasures of a favourite. Nevertheless, they attempted to give a national colour to their rebellion. The plans and measures of the great rebel Parliament held at Oxford during the reign of Henry III. were revived; Lords Ordainers were appointed to reform the State; they bid for public favour by the abolition of a few abuses; they enacted that the possessors of landed property alone should be appointed sheriffs; they limited the right of purveyance, which was held by the crown; and they prohibited all grants of royal letters-patent ordering the suspension of the regular course of justice. But these were merely outward appearances intended to conceal the selfish egotism of the great barons; their only object was to make themselves masters of the royal authority, of the right of appointing to the chief offices of state, and of the revenues of the crown. They put Gaveston to death, and seized upon the whole power. The representatives of counties and boroughs, who were present in the Parliament by which these designs were executed, gave their consent; but they were mere followers of the rebellion, and had no influence upon the government. The great barons, who came to Parliament in arms and accompanied by their troops, had the entire management of everything in their own hands.

Edward escaped from the tutelage imposed upon him by the coalition of the barons, only to fall under the sway of two new favourites, Hugh le Despencer, or Spencer, and his son. The elevation of these two courtiers raised up against them a storm similar to that which had overthrown Gaveston. The new rebellion which broke out in 1321 is the second remarkable event of this reign. It was first manifested by a sentence passed against the two Spencers by the great barons of the realm. They passed it by their own authority alone, without the concurrence either of the Commons or of the king, and at the same time compelled the king to grant them an amnesty for themselves and their adherents; shortly afterwards, the civil war began, and the confederated barons were overcome. Edward convoked a Parliament at York, in 1322, at which the Commons attended, and which repealed first the sentence against the two Spencers, and afterwards all the ordinances passed by the Lords Ordainers in 1311 and 1312, as being contrary to the rights of the king, and to the laws and usages of the country. Thus, whether the court or the rebels prevailed, a Parliament always sanctioned their triumph, saving only the ever-ready recourse to civil war, the only true means of decision.

Moreover, it is evident that the riches which were amassed by court favours and the exercise of royal power were a constant subject of jealousy and faction. The petition presented to the king in 1322 by Hugh Spencer the elder against the barons who had condemned him, sets forth that they had devastated sixty-three of his manors or domains in fifteen different counties—that they had carried off 28,000 sheep, 22,000 head of cattle, two harvests, one from his barns and granaries, and one of standing corn, 600 horses, a great quantity of provisions of all kinds, and complete suits of armour to equip 200 men—and that they had moreover done damage, in his castles and lands, to the amount of more than 30,000l. sterling. Such was then the wealth of a great English baron; and herein resided an inexhaustible source of rebellions.

A third event, the deposition of Edward II., presents a spectacle of the same character as the two preceding occurrences. This was the result of a new confederation of the barons, at whose head the queen, Isabella, had placed herself. A Parliament, convoked at Westminster, on the 7th of January, 1327, declared the incapacity of the king, then a prisoner in Kenilworth Castle. A deputation, composed of four bishops, two earls, four barons, three deputies from each county, and several burgesses of London, of the Cinque Ports, and of other cities, was sent to acquaint him with the resolution of the Parliament, and formally to renounce the oath of fidelity. This deputation received from Edward II. his abdication in favour of his son Edward III., then fourteen years of age, under whose name the dominant faction expected to wield the supreme power to its own advantage.

Notwithstanding the interference of the Commons in this and the preceding acts, it is clear that the whole affair was managed between aristocratic factions influenced by personal interests, and profiting by the king's incapacity to appropriate to themselves the government and all its advantages. There is nothing to indicate any progress of political institutions and triumph of national liberties. The government of the barons, after such scenes, was even more arbitrary and oppressive than that of the king.

It is, nevertheless, a remarkable fact that, in all these occurrences, the sanction of the Parliament was always regarded as necessary, and as the only means of terminating and legalizing the works of violence. The Parliament, or at least the House of Commons, was merely a passive instrument in the matter; but it was already thought impossible to dispense with its concurrence. Now, as it is part of the nature of this instrument to serve the cause of public liberties and to lead, sooner or later, to their extension, every circumstance that augmented its importance and established its necessity may be considered as a progress of the representative system.

I will now bring under your notice the principal parliamentary facts of this period, and inquire in what respects the principles of a free government were manifested or introduced in them.

It was at this time that the Parliament decidedly became the centre towards which all demands for the reform of abuses, the redressing of grievances, the modification of laws, in a word, all petitions, were directed; it had possessed this character from its origin, but in a less extended measure. When the Parliament, or rather the body of barons in Parliament assembled, had begun once more to act as the great council of the king, a host of applications which had previously never been made, or had been addressed to the king alone, were addressed to the king in Parliament, and became a subject for deliberation at its meetings. Thus, in the Parliament held at Westminster, in 1315, we find that 268 petitions were presented.

These petitions were of two kinds. Some were presented by the Commons to the king in council, and had reference to demands or complaints of general interest. Others were presented by individuals, corporations, or towns, and had reference to private or local interests. The former class gave birth to the right of initiative; the latter to the right of petition. Both classes were addressed to the king, in whom the actual power resided; and upon whom, on this account, it devolved not only to provide for the general necessities of the State, but also to do justice to special interests.

On the opening of each Parliament, a certain number of days were fixed for the reception of petitions. A certain number of persons, chiefly judges or councillors of the king, were appointed to receive them, to investigate their nature, to classify them according to their objects, to set aside those which were to form the subject of discussion in the Parliament itself, and finally to present them to Parliament. This discussion was almost confined to the House of

Barons, who were supposed to form a great intermediary council between the privy council of the king and the entire Parliament. The barons, when assembled in the privy council, deliberated and decided upon the demands of the Commons relative to matters of general interest. If these demands referred to certain complaints against abuses of the exercise of the royal power, or against the conduct of the sheriffs, for example, the king answered them in his own name alone, after having taking the advice of his privy council, of the judges, or of the barons, according to circumstances. If the petitions prayed for some interpretation or declaration of the existing law, the answer was given in the same manner. If they suggested the enactment of a new law, the king, when he judged it convenient, proposed this law to the Parliament; but in early times, this was very rarely the case; and when the petition had once been presented, the Commons ordinarily had nothing further to do with the matter than to receive the answer of the king.

As to those petitions which originated from individuals or from bodies unconnected with the Parliament, and which related only to matters of private interest, the meeting of Parliament was merely chosen as the occasion of their presentation, because it was more favourable than any other period for obtaining a reply. The royal council decided upon all those petitions which did not require the intervention of the barons or of the entire Parliament.

The presentation of petitions at this period is, therefore, a very complex fact with which are connected not only the right of petition to the Houses of Parliament, but also the right of petition to the government generally, the right of initiative, the jurisdiction of the Houses of Parliament, in short, a host of institutions essential to the representative system, and each of which it is necessary to consider separately. They all existed, but in a confused and embryo state, in this affluence of petitions of all kinds, which called into action very different powers, then exercised indiscriminately. This original confusion was, undoubtedly, one of the principal causes of the universality of the power of the British Parliament. We cannot now examine into all the institutions which sprang from this source, and progressively disentangled themselves, assuming a distinct form. The question of the right of petition, in the sense which is attached to it at the present day, is in itself deserving of our careful examination, and will form the subject of our next lecture.

One particular fact attests the progress which the Commons were beginning to make in the comprehension of their power and rights. It is beyond doubt that, originally, the voting of supplies always furnished them with an opportunity of obtaining some concessions or the redress of their grievances; this is proved by the history of English charters. But, in 1309, when granting Edward II. a twentieth part of their moveable goods, they expressly attached the condition that "the king should take into consideration, and should grant them the redress of certain grievances of which they had to complain."* These grievances had existed for a long while, and were perpetuated for a considerable period afterwards; but the Commons had begun to look them full in the face, and to insist year after year upon their redress, as the only condition upon which they would grant the supplies.

A statute passed in 1322, by the Parliament at York, which revoked the sentence against the two Spencers, declared that "thenceforward all laws respecting the estate of the crown, or of the realm and people, must be treated, accorded, and established in Parliament by the king, by and with the assent of the prelates, earls, barons, and commonalty of the realm." This is a formal recognition of the right of the Commons to interfere in the legislation of the country, and in all great public affairs.

Many English publicists attach great importance to this statute, and regard it as the first act which officially sanctioned the fundamental principle of the British government. This importance appears to me to be exaggerated. The principle enunciated by this statute had been put into practice on many previous occasions, and a sufficiently clear knowledge was not then possessed of that which constituted matter of legislation and general interest to obtain conformity to it in practice. It is, therefore, far from being the case that the Commons, from this time forth, always exercised the power allotted to them by this statute. Nevertheless, the official exposition of the principle indicates progress in the ideas of the times.

Such are the principal facts of the reign of Edward II., with regard to the condition and action of the Parliament. They contained no very important innovation, but they announce the consolidation and natural progress of the institutions definitively established under Edward I. Tory writers, taking their stand upon the preponderant influence exercised by the great barons during the reign of Edward II., have attempted to cast doubts even upon the presence of the Commons at several of the Parliaments of this period. Whig writers, on

---

* These grievances were eleven in number, viz: 1. That the king's purveyors took all kinds of provisions without giving any security for the payment; 2. That additional duties had been imposed on wine, on cloth, and on other foreign imports; 3. That by the debasement of the coin, the value of all commodities had been advanced; 4. That the stewards and marshals of the king's household held pleas, which did not fall under their cognizance; 5. And exercised their authority beyond the verge, that is, a circuit of twelve leagues round the king's person; 6. That no clerks were appointed, as they had been under the last monarch, to receive the petitions of the Commons in Parliament; 7. That the officers appointed to take articles for the king's use in fairs and markets, took more than they ought, and made a profit of the surplus; 8. That in civil suits, men were prevented from obtaining their right by writs under the privy seal; 9. That felons eluded the punishment of their crimes by the ease with which charters of pardon were obtained; 10. That the constables of the castles held common pleas at their gates without any authority; and 11. That the escheators ousted men of their inheritances, though they had appealed to the king's courts.—*Rot. Parl.* i. 441.

their side, endeavour to deduce, from the proofs which are extant of the presence of the Commons, an argument for their great importance and decisive participation in events. The former are mistaken when they deny the presence of the Commons in Parliament, from their having been unable to find any writs of convocation addressed to the sheriffs; for the writs which order the payment of the salaries of the representatives are extant for nearly all the Parliaments of this period. The latter deduce too extensive results from the presence of the Commons in the Parliament: it is beyond all doubt that the high aristocracy, who sat in the House of Lords, then managed and directed affairs almost entirely alone. The progress of liberty is not so rapid; the most important point is, that it be certain. Thenceforward it was certain, and it received great development during the two following reigns.

LECTURE 21

Of petitions during the early times of representative government. ⁓ Regulations on the subject. ⁓ Transformation of the right of petition possessed by the Houses of Parliament into the right of proposition and initiative. ⁓ Petitions cease to be addressed to the king, and are presented to Parliament. ⁓ Origin of the right of inquiry. ⁓ Necessity for representative government to be complete. ⁓ Artifices and abuses engendered by the right of petition.

THE circumstances which occur at the origin of an institution are well calculated to make us acquainted with its nature. At such periods, events are simple, and produce themselves spontaneously. No effort has yet been made either to evade them or to change their nature, and the state of society is not sufficiently complicated to render it impossible to attain the object aimed at by any but subtle and indirect means.

To say truth, in what does the right of petition consist? It is the right to demand the reparation of an injury, or to give expression to a desire. Such a demand must naturally be addressed to the power which is capable of satisfying the desire or repairing the injury—which has authority, and power enough to grant the prayer of the petition.

Accordingly, in the fourteenth century, all petitions, whether they emanated from the two Houses of Parliament, or from individuals unconnected with those Houses, whether they had reference to general or private interests, were addressed to the king. No one had any idea of petitioning the Houses themselves; the king governed; in him resided both the right and the power to redress public or private grievances, and to satisfy the requirements of the nation. To him the barons, commons, corporations, and citizens applied whenever they had need.

The king governed in his council: and of all his councils, the Parliament was the most eminent and the most extensive. In certain cases, the advice and acquiescence of the Parliament, as a whole or in part, were necessary to the exercise of the royal authority. The meeting of Parliament was, therefore, the natural opportunity for the presentation of all petitions. It was, as it were, the moment at which the nation and the government met face to face, either to transact in common those affairs which required their concurrence, or to make those reciprocal demands of which they mutually stood in need. Private citizens naturally availed themselves of this opportunity for presenting their own petitions, either because the co-operation of the great powers of the State was necessary to grant their prayers, or because they referred to demands upon which the king was competent to decide alone, but to which his attention would then be more effectually directed, as they might receive support from the patronage of the barons or deputies met in council with the king.

In all cases, it was to the king in his council, that is to say, to the government itself, that petitions were addressed; and far from the Houses of Parliament, after having received and examined them, referring them to the government for decision, it was the king who, by officers specially appointed for the purpose, received and examined them, and afterwards called the attention of both Houses to those with whose prayers he could not comply without their sanction. All complaints and demands were thus forwarded directly to the power entrusted with the duty of coming to a definitive decision regarding them; and the Houses of Parliament interfered subsequently only in certain cases, and then as a necessary council.

Such was the primitive and natural fact. The progress of the representative system, however, completely changed its course and character.

We have seen that, in the fourteenth century, petitions were of two kinds; first, those drawn up or presented to the king, by one or both Houses, and relating to grievances of a more or less general character; secondly, those addressed to the king by corporations or citizens, and relating to collective or private interests. We have now nothing further to do with the first class of these petitions. As far as the Houses of Parliament are concerned, they have become transformed into a right of initiative, more or less efficacious and more or less direct. This right, its importance and its forms, give rise to questions of an entirely distinct character. At the present day, the complaints or demands addressed by private citizens to the legislative authorities, are alone called by the name of petitions.

There is now no further question about the right of addressing such demands to the executive power itself—to the government properly so called. No one thinks of contesting the right of citizens to seek in this manner the redress of their grievances, or the satisfaction of their desires. Nor that this right, in itself so simple and incontestable, has not sometimes assumed great political importance, and thereby occasioned animated discussions. In 1680, Charles II., having ceased for several years to convoke a Parliament, a great number of petitions were addressed to him demanding its convocation. The king, by proclamation, declared them seditious, and refused to receive them; but the Parliament having met at last, the House of Commons enacted, on the 27th of October, 1680; "1. That it is, and ever hath been, the undoubted right of the subjects of England to petition the king for the calling and sitting of Parliaments, and redressing of grievances. 2. That to traduce such petitioning as a violation of duty, and to represent it to his Majesty as tumultuous or seditious, is to betray the liberty of the subject, and contribute to the design of subverting the ancient legal constitution of this kingdom, and introducing arbitrary power. 3. That a committee be appointed to enquire after all such persons, that have offended against the right of the subject."*

A state of crisis could alone lead to such an attempt to destroy the most natural of the right of citizens—the right of addressing the government itself in order to make known to it their desires—and the Charter, reasonably, neither sanctioned nor limited it. The right to which it gave sanction, and which alone now bears the name of the *right of petition,* is the right of applying to the two Houses of Parliament to urge their interference, either in some matter of general legislation, or for the redress of private grievances. To this right the question which we have now under consideration is restricted. We must enquire how it became introduced into the representative system of government and in what respects the various forms which it has successively assumed correspond to the various stages of the development of that system.

In fact, this right did not exist in the fourteenth century; that is to say, nobody thought either of exercising or of demanding it. The Houses of Parliament, and particularly the House of Commons, were themselves the great public petitioner. They had quite enough to do to present and obtain the reception of their own demands, without incurring the labour of interfering on behalf of private interests, which at that time were treated generally with much less consideration. They were, moreover, too slightly connected with the government thus to meddle with the details of its action. They were neither the seat nor the centre of power. Their assembly lasted only for a short period. The king's answers to their own demands were ordinarily given only during the next session. In such a state of things, it was natural that all private petitions should go directly to the king in council, for from that source alone could redress be expected.

When the Houses had acquired greater importance, sat for a longer period, and interfered in all great public affairs—when, in full and secure possession of their fundamental rights, they began to apply them to practice instead of limiting their efforts to defend their existence—when, in a word, they had acquired, in public opinion and in reality the consistency of public powers associated in the government of the State, it became natural that petitions should

---

* Parliamentary History, vol. iv. p. 1174.

be presented to them against the abuses or errors of the government which they were appointed to control. The right of petition to the Houses of Parliament was then regarded as a natural consequence of the right of petition to the king. The Parliament was always considered and called the great council of the king. This council, it is true, was habitually in opposition and conflict with the government of the king, which still remained exterior to it, and endeavoured to free itself from its control: but ancient traditions retained their sway; complaint was made to one part of the government against the injuries committed by the other part. The new mode of petitioning did not, therefore, appear extraordinary, and no attempt was made either to authorize or prohibit it. It was brought into use without opposition.*

But when this practice was introduced, the Houses of Parliament themselves had undergone great change of form, and received considerable development, as regarded their internal constitution, their proceedings, and their privileges. Instead of those petitions which, at the outset, they had been accustomed to present to the king, the right of initiative had been substituted, and this right belonged to every member of either of the two Houses of Parliament who might exercise it by bringing forward, with such formalities and delays as were required by usage, any motion with which he thought it fitting to occupy the assembly. With the right of initiative was connected the right of enquiry into all

---

* Mr. Hallam is of opinion that the interference of the Commons in regard to petitions relating to matters of private interest originated solely in this desire to repress the encroachments of the Privy Council. "From the first years of Henry V.," he says, "though not, I think, earlier, the Commons began to concern themselves with the petitions of individuals to the Lords or Council. . . . Many of the requests preferred to them were such as could not be granted without transcending the boundaries of law. A just inquietude as to the encroachments of the king's council had long been manifested by the Commons: and finding remonstrances ineffectual, they took measures for preventing such usurpations of legislative power, by introducing their own consent to private petitions. These were now presented by the hands of the Commons, and in very many instances passed in the form of statutes with the express assent of all parts of the legislature. Such was the origin of private bills, which occupy the greater part of the rolls in Henry V. and VI.'s Parliament." (Hallam's Middle Ages, vol. ii. p. 224.)

Beginning from the reign of Edward III. (1322), or, as Mr. Hallam thinks, from that of Edward II. (1310), we find both Houses, at the opening of the session, each appoint a committee for the purpose, not only of receiving, but of examining petitions, in order to enquire into the truth of the facts stated, before the petitions became the subject of deliberation in Parliament. (Parliamentary History, vol. i. p. 230.) It is doubtful whether the committees received directly the petitions addressed to the king in council, or whether those which fell under the cognizance of the Parliament were referred to them by the officers of the king. In 1410, we meet with an instance of a private petition, addressed to the Commons, and transmitted by them to the king, with their recommendation. (Report of the Lords Commissioners, p. 362.) For the mode of the presentation of petitions, both to the Privy Council, and to the House of Lords, see Hallam's dissertation on the Privy Council, in the second volume of his History of the Middle Ages.

such facts or acts as appeared to the House of sufficient importance to induce it to desire a thorough knowledge of them and afterwards to adopt a resolution regarding them, either of prosecution or of censure, or simply to declare its opinion. On coming before Houses invested with such rights, petition necessarily took another course than would have been the case had those rights been wanting. And in the first place it passed into a custom that they must be presented by a member; this custom was not, originally, a precaution against the abuse of the right of petition, but the natural form of its exercise. As every member enjoyed the right to call the attention of the House, by motion, to any particular subject it was natural that he should make use of this right when ever he became the exponent, to the House, of the demand of his constituents or his friends. By this means, they acquired an authority which they could not otherwise have obtained; the House was thus made to deliberate, not upon the petition, but upon the motion of the member who has presented it, and who had based upon it a proposition either for an enquiry, or for an address, or for a prosecution, or for a law, or for any other act which the House was entitled to accomplish. And whatever this motion might be, it was subjected to all the formalities and all the delays which, on every occasion, regulated the debates and deliberations of the assembly.

Thus invested with all the rights necessary for exercising over the government, by one mode or another, the influence which properly belonged to them, the English Houses of Parliament regarded the petitions which were presented to them merely as an opportunity for exercising this influence in virtue of these rights. They did not act as a sort of patron placed between the petitioners and the government from which the redress of the grievance was definitively demanded; nor did they refer the petition to the government, with a postscript of their own to request the passing of any act of which they were unable to superintend or compel the execution. After its presentation, they no longer had anything whatever to do with the petition; if the motion to which it had given rise were adopted, then began an act of the House itself, accomplished with all the usual formalities and terminated by a resolution which specially belonged to it, and which placed the government in presence of the thoroughly-discussed and clearly-expressed opinion or will of the assembly which shared with it in the exercise of the supreme power in the nation.

When, by a further progress, the government found itself at last obliged to fix its seat within the Houses of Parliament, when they had become once more the great national council, discussing and deciding public affairs in public, petitions also were restored to their natural state, to their primary condition— that is to say, being addressed to the Houses of Parliament, they were addressed to the king in council, to the government itself, which consisted in the royal power, surrounded by the parliamentary majority, and compelled to justify its wishes and acts against the attacks of the opposition, which sat in the same council, by virtue of the same title, and with the same rights. What has been the consequence of this? Every petition, when converted into a motion by a member of the House, gives rise to a regular combat, conducted according to the usual formalities, between the ministry and the opposition. The issue of this conflict fully decides the fate of the petition, that is to say, the result at which it aims; it has not to go elsewhere in search of a solution; the House has neither compromised itself frivolously, nor given its verdict inconsiderately; and, with the exception of the case of appeal to a new House after a dissolution, all its acts, after having been accomplished in obedience to those formalities which give pledge of their maturity, directly attain their object.

Such has been the course of the right of petition in England. Closely connected with the whole system of representative government, it has kept pace with the progress of that system, adapting itself to its various successive stages, and holding the same rank with the other rights of deliberative assemblies. It has thus been brought back to its true nature, which is incessantly to proclaim and assert, in the centre of the government itself, the grievances and the requirements of citizens, so as to ensure, after mature deliberation, the redress of the former and the satisfaction of the latter.

I do not say that this result is always attained in England; other causes have, in certain respects, neutralized the natural virtue of representative government, and prevented it from producing all its legitimate results. I merely say that the right of petition has there assumed its reasonable form, and that, but for the action of causes which effect a general change of the system, it would by that form attain the object which its advocates should propose to themselves.

Let us now enquire what must happen in a different state of things, when representative government, though perhaps less changed in certain particulars, is nevertheless much more incomplete. It will be seen how the right of petition may introduce disorder among the public powers of a State and yet remain almost illusory.

This is the hypothesis upon which I stand. I suppose the Houses of Parliament invested, by right, with great power, associated in the legislation of the country, voting taxes, receiving accounts of the administration of the revenue of the State, carrying on their discussions in public, and enjoying a large amount of liberty in these debates. It is beyond a doubt that, in the public opinion, they will be held to possess the mission and the power to obtain the redress of all grievances, and the satisfaction of all legitimate requirements, and to compel the executive power to act, on all occasions, in accordance with justice, the laws, and the general interests of the country. It is from the action of the Houses of Parliament that the public and the citizen will expect all that they desire or hope; and towards them they will turn their eyes to obtain it.

Such being the disposition of the public mind, if these same Houses do not possess the right of initiative, or the right of enquiry, or any positive external jurisdiction—if it is not in their power to set themselves in motion and to pursue their own objects—in a word, if their means of direct action are far below their written mission and the public expectation, what will be the consequence?

Evidently both the Houses and the public will seek for indirect means of exercising that influence which rightfully belongs to them, and which is actually imputed to them. And if the right of petition had been solemnly sanctioned, to it will resort be made to supply the place of deficient rights, and by it will members of the Houses strive to obtain that control over the whole government, of which it has been tempted to deprive them.

Who cannot perceive, for example, that the right of petition is a real right of initiative, since its effect is to introduce, into the Houses of Parliament, questions which the government has not brought forward, and to give rise to discussions which the government has not originated? Thus, the right of initiative, though denied to members of the Houses, belongs to all citizens, to the first comer, even to a fictitious name. The elect of a large number of citizens may not provoke his colleagues to discuss with him a solemnly propounded question: but if he leave the House, if he cast aside his character of representative and assume that of petitioner, he has the power to do so, and the humblest citizen possesses it finally with himself. Thus, instead of an initiative, the utility and propriety of which would be guaranteed by the character and position of the members of the Houses, an initiative is substituted which is guarded by no guarantee, and which imposes no moral obligation upon the man who exercises it, since he is not a part of the public power which he sets in motion.

And as this power holds a very lofty position in the public opinion, as it is supposed to possess the mission and the power to remedy every evil, its interference will be solicited in matters of all kinds; it will be called upon to deliberate upon affairs most foreign to its attributes; and its petitioners will afterwards be astonished to find its actual power so limited in comparison with the immensity of the rights which it is supposed to enjoy.

It will soon be felt that there is disorder in such a state of things, and attempts will be made to remedy it. Restrictions will be imposed, if possible, upon this universal initiative. The remedy would present itself spontaneously, if every member of the legislative assemblies had the right to propose such motions as he judged fitting. It would then come to pass, as it did in England, that every petition must be presented by a member, and must become, on his part, the subject of a motion. Thus the members themselves would exercise over petitions that kind of censorship from which it is impossible to liberate them. In the absence of this censorship, another kind is invented; the petitions are referred to a committee *ad hoc,* appointed to examine them beforehand, and to call the attention of the House to those which appear to deserve its notice; but to whom does this censorship belong? to the parliamentary majority which names the committee. This is the reverse of the natural order of things. Petitions almost always belong to the minority. The minority presents and supports them. The minority is, consequently, placed, in this respect, at the discretion of the majority, whose censorship may become a means of tyranny; whereas, if the right of initiative belonged to all the members, a legitimate censorship would be established, which would refuse to bring forward a multitude of unsuitable petitions, and would neither reject nor postpone any of those which were possessed of real importance.

After the first step in the exercise of the right, that is to say, after the presentation of petitions, comes their discussion. If they could be introduced by a member only, this discussion would be subject to all the delays and formalities required for the due regulation of legislative debates. A first motion, for instance, would suggest that the petition should be read; a second, that it be printed; a third, that it form the subject of an enquiry, or of an address to the crown, or of a law. During this process, facts would be cleared up, and opinions would be formed; and a conflict would occur between the minority and the majority, only if the latter should formally refuse to grant the justice demanded, or to comply with the wish expressed. In the other system, on the contrary, the debate must be precipitate and confused; the House and the government must adopt their resolution in a few moments, often without thoroughly understanding what they demand of, or refuse to, one another. Petitions succeed and fall upon one another with a rapidity that produces sometimes violence, and sometimes indifference; and the right of petition itself thus becomes an occasion of disorder, or is treated with a sort of levity and disdain which compromises it in the legislative chambers, and also compromises the Chambers in the opinion of the public.

The manner in which petitions are introduced into the Chambers is not the only cause of so vicious a mode of deliberation, but the absence of the right of enquiry also contributes greatly towards it. Every petition received by one of the Chambers calls for a resolution on its part; there is therefore something more than mere singularity in depriving it of the means of adopting that resolution with a full knowledge of the cause. It is a great defect of representative government that, leading as it necessarily does to the systematic organization and permanent conflict of parties, it habitually divides the truth into two parts, and induces men never to consider questions on more than one side, and to see only half the ideas or facts in reliance upon which their decision must be made. It is, without doubt, a system of exaggeration and partiality; and this evil is, to a certain point, inevitable. All means of diminishing it are, therefore, of great importance. Now, the most effectual, indisputably, is to compel opposing opinions to unite, on certain occasions, in a common search after truth. This is the effect of the right of enquiry. When these opinions reach the moment of decision, without having been brought into contact or made acquainted with each other, without having been constrained mutually to communicate motives and facts, their resolution will chiefly be dictated by party spirit, and by anterior engagements which have experienced no necessity to modify it. Everything, on the other hand, that brings the minority and the majority into presence, before the moment when they must appear in public and pronounce their decision, draws them for a time out of their habitual sphere, and leads them to extend or to correct their ideas. This is especially the case in reference to facts. It is immensely inconvenient if all communications of this kind can only be made at the rostrum, and in the midst of the decisive combat; for they are then rejected, and scarcely ever influence the decision. Thus, as the absence of the right of enquiry leaves parties in their natural ignorance and primitive crudity, it is injurious not only to the goodness of the special resolutions of deliberative assemblies, but also to the wisdom of their general arrangements.

Besides, when the right of enquiry is wanting, its absence is supplied in the same way as that of the right of initiative by the right of petition. As it is impossible to undertake a serious and complete investigation of any particular kind of abuse which appears to have introduced itself into the government, special complaints are suggested and multiplied. Now, the right of petition is no more competent to supply the place of the right of enquiry than that of the right of initiative. The revelation of abuses or grievances which it occasions is, by the very nature of things, full of confusion and error; matters are seldom presented without prejudice and with generality. And yet, from the very fact that there are no means of going into the details, and examining them in all their bearings, men are involuntarily led to put confidence in these complaints. Never were the demands presented by the House of Commons itself for the redress of grievances so numerous and violent as in those times when it was allowed to address them to the king only, and was permitted neither to have them thoroughly investigated by its own members, nor to sum them up in a body of facts accompanied by satisfactory proofs.

Finally, when the representative system of government is complete, and provided with all the rights and all the means of action which it needs in order to accomplish its ends, the right of petition is nothing but the right of calling the attention of the Houses of Parliament, by means of one of their members, to any particular question, or act of the governing power. When once this first provocation has taken place by way of petition, the petition has attained its object; nothing more is necessary but a discussion and resolution of the House itself, which takes place according to the ordinary formalities, as if it had originated within the assembly itself, and independently of all relations with the external world. Thus the exercise of a right which should belong to all citizens is reconciled with the dignity of the public power of the nation, and with the maturity befitting their acts. Thus all grievances may solicit redress, all desires may be expressed, without giving rise to any disorder, any precipitation, or any subversion of the procedure of the great deliberative bodies. When, on the contrary, these deliberative bodies themselves are deprived of the rights and means of action which are necessary to them for the fulfilment of their destination, the right of petition becomes an irregular and often violent means by which the public and the legislative chambers endeavour to supply their deficiencies. And then this right, by all the practices to which it lends itself, and by the vicious mode of deliberation which it entails, creates, in its turn, new disorders which men undertake to remedy by imposing upon the right itself restrictions or trammels which would be completely useless if the legislative chambers were invested with all the means of action which are their due. Political liberty has this in common with science generally; it is most dangerous when it is incomplete. The history of the British Parliament proves this at every step.

LECTURE 22

Condition of the Parliament under Edward III. ⁓ *Progress of the power of the Commons.* ⁓ *Their resistance of the King.* ⁓ *Regularity of the convocation of Parliament.* ⁓ *Measures taken for the security of its deliberations.* ⁓ *Division of the Parliament into two Houses.* ⁓ *Speaker of the House of Commons.* ⁓ *Firmness of the House of Commons in maintaining its right to grant taxes.* ⁓ *Accounts given by the government of the collection of the taxes.* ⁓ *Appropriation of the funds granted by Parliament.* ⁓ *Parliamentary legislation.* ⁓ *Difference between statutes and ordinances.*

Hitherto we have only met with political struggles between the king and his barons, or between opposite aristocratic factions; the Commons have hitherto appeared only in a second rank; they exercised as yet hardly any direct influence over general affairs, over the government properly so called; or if they occasionally interfered in the administration of the country, it was merely as the auxiliary or the instrument of some particular faction.

The reign of Edward III. presents a different aspect; the conflict between the king and his barons has ceased, and all the great aristocracy seems to be grouped around the throne; but at the same time, the Commons have formed themselves into a body, distinct and powerful in itself. They do not aspire to snatch the supreme power from the hands of the king and the barons; they would not have strength enough to do so, nor do they entertain any thought of it; but they resist every encroachment upon those rights which they are beginning to know and to appreciate; they have acquired a consciousness of their own importance, and know that all public affairs properly fall under their cognizance. Finally, either by their petitions, or by their debates in reference to taxation, they are daily obtaining a larger share in the government, exercise control over affairs which, fifty years before, they never heard mentioned, and become, in a word, an integral and almost indispensable part of the great national council, and of the entire political machine.

Thus, whereas hitherto the political aspect of England has been the conflict of the great barons with the king; from the reign of Edward III., the resistance of the Commons to the king's government, generally formed and sustained by the barons, becomes the great fact of the history. It is not unintentionally that I here employ the words *conflict* and *resistance*. In the first period, in fact, the barons struggled, not only to defend their rights, but to invade the supreme power, and to impose their own government upon the king. This conflict was consequently nothing but a permanent civil war. But during the second period, this was no longer the case; we hear of no revolts, and of no civil wars: under Edward III., at least, the Commons do not arm to attack the government with force; but they oppose to it a political resistance, they constantly protest against the abuses and arbitrariness of the central power. Instead of directing their attacks against the king himself, they lay all blame upon his ministers, and begin to assert and popularize the principles of parliamentary responsibility. Finally, they separate completely from the great barons, act on their own account, and become the true depositaries of the pledges of public liberties.

This was a great revolution, and it prepared the way for all others. The more minutely we examine into the events of the reign of Edward III., the more proofs shall we discover of this important change. I shall content myself with giving a rapid summary of these proofs by recapitulating the general facts which characterize this reign.

The first of these facts is the regularity, previously unexampled, with which the Parliament was convoked. A measure was adopted for this purpose in 1312, during the reign of Edward II., by the Lords Ordainers. Subsequently we meet with two statutes relative to the convocation of this assembly, one of which was passed in 1331, and the other in 1362. Finally, in 1377, the last year of the reign of Edward III., the Commons themselves demanded by petition that the sessions of Parliament should take place regularly every year. It is curious to compare this petition with the requests addressed to the king, under previous reigns, by the members of the House of Commons, to be exempted from serving in Parliament: they had now begun to feel that their mission was not a burden, but a right.

During the reign of Edward III., we may enumerate forty-eight sessions of Parliament, which makes nearly one session in each year.

Nor did the Parliament merely provide for the regularity of its convocation; it took measures, at the same time, to ensure the security of its deliberations. In 1332, a royal proclamation forbade all persons to wear coats of mail, or to carry any other offensive or defensive arms, in those towns in which the Parliament was sitting: it also prohibited all games and diversions which might disturb the deliberations of the assembly. The frequent recurrence of proclamations of this kind announces the formation of a regular assembly.

It is also during the reign of Edward III., in 1313, that we hear for the first time of the Parliament being divided into two Houses. According to historical documents of that year, the prelates, counts and barons, on the one hand, and the representatives of the counties and boroughs, on the other, sat at Westminster, the former in the White Chamber, and the latter in the Painted Chamber; and deliberated thus upon the question of peace with France.

Finally, it is also at the end of this reign, in 1377, that the rolls of Parliament first make mention of the Speaker of the House of Commons; Sir Thomas Hungerford is the first person upon whom this title was conferred. Previously, the House used to select one of its members whenever it was necessary to speak in its name, either to the king, or in the full Parliament: and it was probably in 1377, that it began to appoint its Speaker for the whole session, and at its commencement.

It has been asserted that, during this reign and in earlier times, every session of Parliament involved a fresh election; and that the right of proroguing the existing Parliament to a new session did not appertain to the king. This is an error. It was necessary that a session of Parliament should take place in each year, but not an election. The following fact proves this. The Parliament held under Edward I. in 1300, resumed its session in 1301. The writs summon the deputies of the previous year, except in cases in which a new election was necessary on account of death or absolute inability to serve. In 1305, the king prorogued Parliament on the 21st of March, and allowed the deputies to return home, "*Issint qu'ils reveignent prestement et sanz délai, quele houre qu'ils soient autrefois remandez.*"—"On condition that they should return readily and without delay, at such time as they might be previously recalled." In 1312, during the reign of Edward II., the Parliament separated after having sat two months, and on the same day the king addressed writs to the sheriffs, ordering them to send "the same knights and burgesses—*eosdem milites et cives,*" to Westminster on the 2nd of November following, "to the same Parliament which we have thought should be continued there—*ad idem Parliamentum quod ibidem duximus continuandum.*" This Parliament thus prorogued actually met, and sat from the 2nd of November to the 18th of December, after which it was dissolved. In 1329, during the reign of Edward III., the Parliament which sat at Salisbury, from the 15th to the 31st of October, was adjourned to Westminster, where it held a second session, from the 10th to the 22nd of February, 1330. We meet with similar instances in 1333 and 1372. The Parliaments were, therefore, not elected annually, and the right of prorogation was in full vigour.

Thus was developed and regulated the internal constitution of the Parliament: thus, instead of being merely an accidental meeting, limited to the accomplishment of a single object, it gradually assumed the consistency of a political assembly of periodical obligation.

A second general fact, which serves to support the views which I have advanced, is the voting of taxes. There is, perhaps no reign which presents so many instances of arbitrary and illegal imposts as that of Edward III., and yet there is not one which contributed more powerfully to secure the triumph of the principle that taxes are legitimate only when they are freely granted. This principle was incessantly lost sight of practically by the king, who was pressed by necessities, created partly by his wars, and partly by the bad administration of his revenues. His whole reign was spent in efforts to regain, under forms more or less indirect, the right of taxing his subjects at his pleasure; but the Commons, on their side, never ceased to protest against these efforts, sometimes attaching the revocation of an arbitrary tax to the concession of a legal subsidy, and sometimes by endeavouring to introduce the principle of the necessity of consent into all those ways by which the king attempted to elude it. Thanks to their perseverance, the schemes of power were, if not always frustrated, at least always unmasked, and thereby rendered impotent for the future.

Instances of this conflict abound in the Parliaments held in the years 1333, 1340, 1347, 1348, and 1349, which are in general filled only with complaints of the Commons, demanding either the abolition or the diminution of unjust and illegal taxes, which had been imposed without their consent. To all these demands the king replied, sometimes by a formal refusal, sometimes by reference to the consent which had been granted him by the Lords, and sometimes by an assurance that the tax should not be levied for any length of time; but if the Commons threatened to refuse him new subsidies, he felt himself compelled to meet these demands by some new concessions.

Nor was it merely by keeping a firm hand upon the voting of taxes that the House of Commons maintained its rights; it also extended them beyond the concession of subsidies on two important occasions. In 1340, the Parliament, suspecting that a portion of the subsidies voted by it had not found its way into the royal exchequer, appointed certain persons to receive the accounts of the tax-collectors, and required them to give security for the payment of all that they received. This is the first instance of any account whatever being given to Parliament with regard to taxes; it began by desiring to make sure of the fidelity of the receipts, and thus took a first step towards asserting its rights to receive an account of the employment of the funds, that is to say, of their expenditure. In 1354, we perceive the dawn of another parliamentary right, that of the appropriation of the public funds. The Parliament, when granting a tax upon wool, added to its vote the condition that the money derived from this subsidy should be devoted to the expenses of the war then waging, and not to any other purpose.

After all, it is not to be wondered at that the king and his Parliament were incessantly at variance with regard to subsidies, and mutually occasioned each other continual miscounts. There was then no means of estimating receipts and expenditure beforehand. The king involved himself in an expense without knowing to what sum it would amount; and the Parliament voted a subsidy without knowing what it would produce. In 1371, the Parliament granted a subsidy of £50,000, to be levied at the rate of 22s. 3d. on every parish, which supposed the existence of 45,000 parishes in England. It turned out, however, that there were only 9,000. The king convoked a great council, to which he summoned only half the deputies of the last Parliament, one from each county and borough, "to save expense—ad parcendum sumptibus." The matter was laid before this council, which ordained the assessment of every parish at 116s. instead of at 22s. 3d., in order to raise the sum of £50,000. Great disorder must necessarily have accompanied such ignorance.

The third general fact which proves the great increase of importance which the Parliament had obtained at this period, is its participation in the legislation. When we open a collection of the statutes of this reign, we find at the head of each statute one of the two following formulas: "*A la requeste de la commune de son roïalme par lor pétitions mises devant lui et son conseil, par assent des prélats, comtes, barons, et autres grantz, au dit Parlement assemblés,*" &c.* Or: "*Par assent des prélats, comtes, et barons, et de tote la commune du roïalme, au dit Parlement assemblés,*" &c.† Sometimes the statute begins with these words: "*Ce sont les choses que notre seigneur le roi, les prélats, seignours, et la commune ont ordiné en ce présent Parlement.*"‡

All these formulas express the participation of the House of Commons in the legislation of the country; and prove, as I have already observed, that this participation was generally exercised by the presentation of petitions to the king; the lords deliberated upon these petitions, which were afterwards converted into statutes by the king, without being returned to the House of Commons to receive its express assent under the form of statutes. Accordingly, as the Commons did not interfere in the enactment of statutes by any direct vote, their petitions were frequently mutilated and altered; and the statutes, which were drawn up either by the judges or by the members of the privy council, did not always faithfully convey their meaning. It was probably with a view to remedy this inconvenience that, in the Parliament of 1341, a certain number of prelates,

---

* "At the request of the commons of his realm, by their petitions laid before him and his council, and by the assent of the prelates, earls, barons, and other nobles, in the said Parliament assembled."

† "By the assent of the prelates, earls and barons, and of all the commons of the realm, in the said Parliament assembled."

‡ "These are the things which our lord the king, the prelates, lords, and commons have ordained in this present Parliament."

barons, and royal councillors, with twelve knights of shires and six burgesses, were appointed a commission for the purpose of converting into statutes such petitions as gave rise to measures of general legislation.

But all the petitions of the Commons were not resolved into statutes; they frequently gave occasion merely to ordinances. Many dissertations have been written upon the distinction between the legislative acts designated by these two words. It has been maintained that ordinances were issued by the king alone, by the advice of the Lords, but without the concurrence of the Commons. Originally, this distinction was incorrect, for most ordinances were issued, just as statutes were enacted, upon the request of the Commons. Thus, in 1364, the Parliament having desired the passing of sumptuary laws, the king demanded of both Houses, by the chancellor, "whether they would have such matters as they agreed on to be by way of ordinance or of statute?" And they replied: "By way of ordinance, that they might amend the same at their pleasure."* From this answer it has been inferred, with great appearance of reason, that the nature of statutes was to be perpetual, whereas ordinances were only temporary.

Ordinances were not inscribed, like statutes, upon the rolls of Parliament; they were less solemn in their character, although their object frequently had reference to matters equally legislative and of equally general interest, such as the enactment of jurisdiction or of penalties. It is not more easy to clearly distinguish ordinances from statutes, than great councils from Parliaments properly so called. All that we can say is, that less importance and stability were attributed to this class of legislative measures.

Legislative measures were not always adopted upon the petition of the Commons; the king also exercised the right of initiative, not only in matter of taxation, but in reference to all other subjects of general interest. Thus, in 1333, Sir Jeffrey Scroop of Markham, in the king's presence, and at his command, informed the prelates, earls, barons, and other nobles, of the disorders committed in the country by bands of armed marauders; pointed out the necessity of repressing their outrages; and demanded of them to suggest to the king such measures as they deemed suitable to effect this purpose. The prelates hereupon retired, saying that it did not befit them to deliberate upon such a subject. The other nobles deliberated among themselves, and proposed to the king a series of regulations for the maintenance of the public peace. These regulations were read in presence of the nobles, the knights of the shires, and the "commons— *genz du commun*," who all gave their assent to them, and the necessary measures were adopted in consequence. A result of this deliberation was the restoration of the *Conservators of the Peace*, who had been temporarily appointed by the Earl

* Parliamentary History, vol. i. p. 128.

of Leicester, during the reign of Henry III., and who were the precursors of the justices of the peace.

After all, it is easy to imagine that, in the fourteenth century, confused ideas were entertained as to what was and what was not matter for legislation; since, in our own days, we not only feel, but formally admit, the impossibility of fixing the limit *a priori,* in a philosophic and absolute manner.

LECTURE 23

Continuation of the history of the progress of the Commons House of Parliament during the reign of Edward III. ⁓ Their interference in questions of peace and war, and in the internal administration of the kingdom. ⁓ Their resistance of the influence of the Pope, and of the national clergy, in temporal affairs. ⁓ First efforts of the Commons to repress abuses at elections. ⁓ First traces of the junction of Committees of both Houses to investigate certain questions in common.

IT was not merely in the matter of taxation and of general legislation that the House of Commons, during the reign of Edward III., extended and consolidated its rights. Its interference in the administration of public affairs, in politics properly so called, assumed at this period a development previously unexampled, and an entirely a novel character. It began really to take part in the government of the State. This is proved by a multitude of facts.

First, in the matter of peace and war, its intervention became, at this period, habitual and almost indispensable. Mr. Hallam seems to me to have fallen into error on this subject; he is of opinion that the king alone, in the fourteenth century, desired that the Commons should interfere in questions of this kind, in order that he might cast the responsibility upon them, but that they constantly refused to incur it. I think that this assertion is incorrect. The Commons of the fourteenth century frequently sought and exercised this power, and accepted the attendant responsibility; and they always gained greatly by it. The principal facts are these. In 1328, during the minority of Edward, and while Mortimer reigned in his name, the treaty of peace with Scotland, which fully liberated that kingdom from all feudal subordination to England, was concluded with the consent of the Parliament. The Commons are expressly mentioned; and we may suppose that Mortimer was anxious thereby to cover his own responsibility for a disgraceful treaty. In 1331, Edward consulted the Parliament upon the question of peace or war with France, on account of his continental possessions, and also upon his projected journey to Ireland. The Parliament gave its opinion in favour of peace and of the king's departure for

Ireland. In 1336, it urged the king to declare war against Scotland, saying: "That the king could no longer, with honour, put up with the wrongs and injuries daily done to him and his subjects by the Scots."* In 1341, after Edward's first victories in France, the Parliament pressed him to continue the war, and furnished him with large subsidies; and all classes of society bestirred themselves to support the king in a conflict which had become national. In 1343, the Parliament was convoked to examine and advise what had best be done in the existing state of affairs, especially in regard to the treaty recently concluded by the king with his enemy the king of France. Sir Bartholomew Burghersh told the Parliament that "as the war was begun by the common advice of the prelates, great men, and commons, the king could not treat of, or make peace, without the like assent."† The two houses deliberated separately, and gave their opinion that the king ought to make peace if he could obtain a truce that would be honourable and advantageous to himself and his friends; but if not, the Commons declared that they would aid and maintain his quarrel with all their power. In 1344, when the truce with the king of France had been broken off by him, the Parliament, on being consulted, manifested a desire for peace, but thought it could only be obtained by carrying on the war with energy, and voted large subsidies for the purpose. In 1348, the war had become increasingly burdensome; all the subsidies proved insufficient; and the king again consulted the Parliament "concerning the war undertaken with its consent." The Commons, perceiving that they had gone rather too far in their language, now showed greater reserve and answered "that they were not able to advise anything concerning the war, and therefore desired to be excused as to that point; and that the king will be advised by his nobles and council, and what shall be by them determined, they would consent unto, confirm, and establish.‡ In 1354, the Lord Chamberlain, by the king's command, informed the Parliament: "That there was great hopes of bringing about a peace between England and France, yet the king would not conclude anything without the consent of his Lords and Commons. Wherefore he demanded of them, in the king's name, whether they would assent and agree to a peace, if it might be had by treaty." To this the Commons replied at first, "that what should be agreeable to the king and his council in making of this treaty, would be so to them"; but on being asked again, "If they consented to a perpetual peace, if it might be had," they all unanimously cried out, Yea! Yea! § Finally, on the 25th of January, 1361, peace having been concluded by the treaty of

* Parliamentary History, vol. i. p. 93.

† Ibid. p. 106.

‡ Ibid. p. 115.

§ Ibid. p. 122.

Bretigny, the Parliament was convoked, the treaty was submitted to its inspection and received its approval, and on the 31st a solemn ceremony took place in the cathedral church at Westminster, when all the members of Parliament, both Lords and Commons, individually swore upon the altar to observe the peace.

In 1368, the negotiations with Scotland were submitted to the consideration of the Parliament; the king of Scotland, David Bruce, offered peace on condition of being relieved from all homage of his crown to the king of England. The Lords and Commons replied, "That they could not assent to any such peace, upon any account, without a disherison of the king, his heirs and crown, which they themselves were sworn to preserve, and therefore must advise him not to hearken to any such propositions";* and they voted large subsidies to continue the war.

In 1369, the king consulted the Parliament as to whether he should recommence the war with France, because the conditions of the last treaty had not been observed; the Parliament advised him to do so, and votes subsidies.

These facts prove the most direct and constant intervention of the Commons in matters of peace and war. Nor did they seek to elude this responsibility, so long as the war was successful and national. When the subsidies became excessive, they manifested greater reserve in giving their opinion beforehand. When fortune turned decidedly against Edward III., at the close of his reign, the Commons, as we shall presently see, took advantage of the right of intervention which they had acquired, to possess themselves also of the right of impeaching the ministers to whom they attributed the misfortunes of the time. All this follows in the natural course of things, and clearly demonstrates the continually increasing influence of the Commons in political matters.

In regard to the internal administration of the country, their progress was not less perceptible. Until the reign of Edward III. all attempts to encroach upon the central government had originated with the barons; it was the barons who, under Henry III. and Edward II., had seized upon the right of appointing to great public offices, and of disposing of the revenues of the State. In 1342, the Commons ventured a similar endeavour, less direct and arrogant in its character, but tending towards the same object by more regular and better chosen means. Profiting by the necessities of the king, who was then destitute of funds, and utterly unable to continue the war with France, they presented to him the two following petitions: 1. "That certain by commission may hear the account of those who have received wools, moneys, or other aid for the king, and that the same may be enrolled in the chancery." To this the king consented, upon condition that the treasurer and lord chief baron should be members of the commission. 2. "That the chancellor and other officers of state may be chosen

* Parliamentary History, vol. i. p. 131.

in open Parliament, and at the same time be openly sworn to observe the laws of the land and Magna Charta." To this also the king consented, but with these restrictions: "That if any such office, by the death or other failure of the incumbent, become void, the choice to remain solely in the king, he taking therein the assent of his council; but that every such officer shall be sworn at the next Parliament, according to the petition; and that every Parliament following the king shall resume into his hands all such offices, so as the said officers shall be left liable to answer all objections."* These decisions were immediately converted into statutes. The chancellor and treasurer, with the judges and other officers of the crown, were required to swear to observe them upon the cross of Canterbury. The chancellor, treasurer, and several judges, protested against this act, as being contrary to their first oath and to the laws of the realm; their protest was entered upon the rolls of Parliament, but the statute was nevertheless definitively passed. The Commons had now obtained the most formal recognition of the responsibility of ministers to Parliament. The most pressing necessities alone had extorted consent from the king. Scarcely had the Parliament dissolved, when the king, by his own authority only, formally revoked the statute by writs addressed to all the sheriffs; and it is a most singular circumstance that so illegal an act excited no remonstrance, and that the statute was revoked by the Parliament itself in the year following.

The mere attempt, however, was a great step. It proves that two fundamental ideas had taken possession of the minds of the representatives of the Commons; first, that the Parliament ought to exercise some influence over the choice of the king's ministers; secondly, that these ministers should be responsible to Parliament for their conduct. As to the first point, the Commons of the fourteenth century employed a very bad method of obtaining it, by claiming that their influence over the choice of the agents of the supreme power should be direct, and by interfering directly in the appointment of ministers; they prodigiously weakened, if they did not utterly destroy, ministerial responsibility: and the progress of representative government has proved that indirect influence, exercised in such matters by a majority of the Parliament, is alone admissible and efficacious. But it was a great thing for the Commons to have attained such growth as to dare to entertain such an idea of their rights. They resumed the exercise of these rights, with greater success, at the close of this reign. The king was old and feeble; his arms were everywhere unsuccessful; abuses multiplied at his court; Edward had fallen beneath the sway of favourites; one of his sons, the Duke of Lancaster, alone enjoyed his favour, and abused it; a woman, named Alice Perers or Pierce, possessed a shameful influence over him, which she employed chiefly in supporting the interest of

* Parliamentary History, vol. i. p. 104.

her friends, in the courts of justice. She might often be seen, sitting within the precincts of the judicial tribunals, intimidating by her presence the judges whom she had pestered with her solicitations. A report was spread at the same time that the Duke of Lancaster intended to have himself declared heir to the crown, to the prejudice of the youthful son of the Black Prince, who was then in a dying state, and who possessed the affection of the whole nation. A Parliament was convoked in 1376; and a powerful party in both Houses pronounced against the ministers of the king. In the Upper House, the Black Prince himself led the attack, and in the Lower House, the opposition was headed by Peter de la Mare. The Commons demanded that the king's council should be augmented by ten or twelve members, prelates, lords, or others; that no important matter should be decided without the consent of six or four of them; and finally, that all the officers of the crown should be sworn to receive no present, emolument, or reward beyond their legal salaries and expenses. The king consented to all these demands upon condition that he should himself appoint the new councillors, and that the chancellor, the treasurer, and the keeper of the privy seal should be allowed to discharge the duties of their office without their interference. The Commons next endeavoured to obtain that the justices of peace in each county should be appointed by the lords and knights of that county in Parliament, and should not be removed without their consent; but the king refused to grant this. The Commons continued to complain of the king's evil counsellors, attributing to them the distress into which the king had fallen, the dilapidation of the subsidies, and so forth. Finally, with a view to the immediate application of the principles which they maintained, they formerly impeached the Lords Latimer and Nevil, who occupied posts in the king's household, and four merchants of London, named Lyon, Ellis, Peachey, and Bury, who were farmers of the royal subsidies. This accusation had its effect; the accused persons were declared incapable of all public employment, and banished from the court and council, and their property was confiscated. As for Alice Perers, the Commons attacked her also, and the king was constrained to issue the following ordinance: "Whereas complaint has been brought before the king that some women have pursued causes and actions in the king's court by way of maintenance, and for hire or reward, which thing displeases the king, the king forbids that any woman do it hereafter, and in particular Alice Perers, under the penalty of forfeiting all that the said Alice can forfeit, and of being banished out of the realm."*

Nothing of this kind had previously been attempted by the Commons. This Parliament sat from the end of April to the 6th of July, 1376, that is, for a longer period than any preceding Parliament; the number of its petitions to the

* Rot. Parl. ii. 329.

king was 223, and all its acts were so popular that it received the name of the Good Parliament.

But the Commons were not in a position to maintain unassisted so brilliant a success; their triumph had been due in great measure to the co-operation of the Black Prince and his party in the Upper House; and the Black Prince died before the closing of the Parliament. The king, by settling the crown upon his son Richard, dissipated many fears. A new Parliament was convoked on the 27th of January, 1377, and one of his first acts was to solicit the revocation of the sentence passed in the preceding year against Lord Latimer and Alice Perers; which request was granted. Six or seven only of those knights who had been members of the previous Parliament sat in the new one; and Peter de la Mare was imprisoned. Nevertheless, the new Parliament maintained the rights already acquired in several particulars; it insisted upon the proper appropriation of the subsidies, upon an account being given of the receipts, and so forth. The death of Edward III. which occurred on the 21st of June, 1377, put an end to a struggle which was probably about to arise once more between the Commons and the advisers of the crown.

In addition to this intervention of the House of Commons in the general affairs of the State, some particular facts prove the progress which its influence was making in all respects, and deserve to be remarked in this point of view.

I. The Commons began energetically to resist both the power which the Pope still assumed to exercise in England, and the internal influence of the English clergy themselves. In 1343, they protested against the right which the Pope claimed to have to appoint foreigners to certain vacant ecclesiastical benefices, and against other abuses of the same kind. They called upon his majesty and the lords to aid them in expelling the papal power from the kingdom, and addressed to the Pope himself a letter full of the most indignant remonstrances. Previously, the barons alone had actively interfered in affairs of this kind. In 1366, the king informed the Parliament that the Pope intended to cite him to Avignon to do homage for his crown, according to the terms of the treaty concluded with king John, and also to pay the tribute promised upon that occasion. The Lords on the one hand, and the Commons on the other, replied that king John had no right to contract such engagements without the consent of the Parliament, called upon the king to refuse to comply with the Pope's citation, and promised to support him with all their power. In 1371, the Commons complained that the great offices of the State were occupied by ecclesiastics, to the great detriment of the king and the state, and demanded that in future they should be excluded therefrom, leaving to the king the right of choosing his officers, provided they were laymen. Finally, in 1377, they demanded that no ordinance or statute should be enacted upon petition of the clergy, without the consent of the Commons; and that the Commons should be bound by none of the constitutions which the clergy might make for its own advantage and without their consent, since the clergy would not be bound by the statutes or ordinances of the king to which they had not consented. This conflict between the national representatives and the clergy soon became a permanent habit, which contributed powerfully, in the sixteenth century, to the introduction of the Reformation.

II. In 1337, the Parliament turned its attention to the protection of the national industry. It prohibited the exportation of English wools, and granted great encouragement to those foreign clothworkers who should take up their residence in England. These regulations soon fell into desuetude in consequence of the wars with France; but they prove the disposition of the Parliament to give attention to all matters of public interest.

III. It was also during this reign that, for the first time, we find the Parliament manifesting anxiety about the abuses which were committed at elections, and seeking to prevent their recurrence. In 1372, an ordinance, passed at the suggestion and by the advice of the Commons, prohibited the election of sheriffs during the continuance of their functions, and also of lawyers, because they made use of their authority to procure their own election, and afterwards cared only for their own private interests.*

IV. Finally, it is under this reign that we first find committees of the two Houses uniting to investigate certain questions in common, and afterwards reporting the result of their investigations to their respective Houses. It is remarkable that this usage, so necessary to facilitate the progress of the representative system and to procure good deliberations, should have arisen precisely at that period when the Parliament became divided into two Houses. It was the

---

* The influence of the king upon elections was manifested at this period in a direct manner, or nearly so. Two edicts of Edward III., passed at an interval of more than forty years, prove this. The first, dated on the 3rd of November, 1330, concludes thus: "And because that, before this time, several knights, representatives for counties, were people of ill designs and maintainers of false quarrels, and would not suffer that our good subjects should show the grievances of the common people, nor the matters which ought to be redressed in Parliament, to the great damage of us and our subjects;—we, therefore, charge and command that you cause to be elected, with the common consent of your county, two, the most proper and most sufficient knights, or sergeants of the said county, that are the least suspected of ill designs, or common maintainers of parties, to be of our said Parliament, according to the form of our writ which you have with you. And this we expect you shall do, as you will eschew our anger and indignation." (*Parl. Hist.* vol. i. p. 84.) This writ was issued at the time when the young king had just delivered himself from the yoke of Mortimer and his faction. The second writ, dated in 1373, orders the sheriffs "to cause to be chosen two dubbed knights, or the most worthy, honest, and discreet esquires of that county, the most expert in feats of arms, and no others; and of every city two citizens, of every borough two burgesses, discreet and sufficient, and such who had the greatest skill in shipping and merchandizing."—*Parl. Hist.* vol. i. p. 137.

natural consequence of their former combination in a single assembly. There was no regular or invariable plan with regard to the mode of the formation of these committees. Sometimes the king himself appointed a certain number of lords, and invited the Commons to choose a certain number of their own members to confer with them; sometimes the Commons named the lords with whom they wished to confer; and sometimes each House appointed its own committee.

It is remarkable that most of the parliamentary sessions of this reign begin with a confirmation of Magna Charta and the Charta de Foresta, which were always regarded as the foundation of the public rights and liberties, and also violated with sufficient frequency to render it necessary incessantly to renew their concession.

All these facts prove the immense progress made by representative government in general, and by the House of Commons in particular, during the course of this reign.

LECTURE 24

State of the Parliament under Richard II. ⁓ *Struggle between absolute royalty and parliamentary government.* ⁓ *Origin of the civil list.* ⁓ *Progress of the responsibility of ministers.* ⁓ *Progress of the returns of the employment of the public revenue.* ⁓ *The Commons encroach upon the government.* ⁓ *Reaction against the sway of the Commons.* ⁓ *Violence and fall of Richard II.* ⁓ *Progress of the essential maxims and practices of representative government.*

It is a remarkable fact in the history of England that, during the interval which elapsed between the years of 1216 and 1399, an able monarch always succeeded an incapable king, and *vice versa*. This circumstance proved very favourable to the establishment of free institutions, which never had time either to fall beneath the yoke of an energetic despotism or to dissolve in anarchy.

The reign of Richard II. does not present, like that of Edward III., the spectacle of the struggle of the Commons in defending their rights, and extending them by the very fact that they were defending them against the royal power, which was incessantly striving to evade those rights because they checked its authority, but which was nevertheless sufficiently acute to perceive that it stood in need of the assistance of the people, and could not afford to quarrel with their representatives. During the reign of Richard, the conflict assumes a more general character; it now involves far more than special or occasional acts of resistance. The question at issue now is, whether the king shall govern according to the advice and under the control of his Parliament, or rule alone and in an almost arbitrary manner. A positive conflict arose between parliamentary government and purely royal government; a violent conflict, full of reciprocal iniquities, but in which the question between liberty in general and absolute power was laid down more clearly and completely than it had ever been before.

The vicissitudes of this struggle are broadly outlined in facts. The reign of Richard II. may be divided into two parts. From 1377 to 1389, the government was parliamentary, that is to say, the Parliament exercised the supreme control and really directed all public affairs, notwithstanding the attempts at resistance on the part of the king and his favourites. From 1389 to 1399, this state of things underwent a change, and the king progressively regained the upper hand. Not that the Parliament abandoned or lost all its rights; for that of voting the taxes, in particular, was boldly maintained, and even respected to a certain extent. But generally speaking, the government was arbitrary, the king had the sole disposal of it, and the Parliament, which had lost its preponderating influence, interfered only as an instrument. This state of things was contrary to the desires and instincts of the country, and it was terminated by a tragical event. Richard was deposed by a proscribed exile who landed in England with sixty men, but found both the Parliament and the entire nation disposed to support him, or at all events, not to oppose him. The deposition of Richard and the elevation of the House of Lancaster were the work of force, but of force supported by that powerful adhesion which the silence and immobility of the public afford to enterprises which tend to overthrow an odious or despised government.

Such was the general aspect of this reign. I shall not linger to detail its events, but merely select and bring to light those facts which relate to the condition of the public institutions of the country, and which prove the truth of that which I have just affirmed.

As you have already seen, during the last years of the reign of Edward III., the influence of the Commons in the government had rapidly augmented; and its further progress was favoured by the minority of Richard II. Sixty years before, the nonage of the king would have placed the State under the control of some faction of barons; but during the latter half of the fourteenth century, the Commons take the initiative in all things, and plainly say how they think the government should be administered.

A first Parliament was convoked in the month of September, 1377. Peter de la Mare, formerly the leader of the opposition, was liberated from prison, and chosen speaker of the House of Commons. Three lords selected by the Commons were appointed to confer with them regarding the public necessities. Three propositions were submitted by the Commons to the king and lords: 1. the formation of a council of government; 2. the appointment of "men of virtuous and honest conversation" to guard the person and conduct the education of the king, and to take care "that the charge of the king's household should be borne by the revenues of the crown, so that what was granted to the wars might be expended that way only"; 3. the strict observance of the common law and statutes of the realm, "that they might not be defeated by the singularity of any about the king."* The Lords granted the first proposition, rejected the first part of the second as too harsh and interfering too much with the liberty of the royal person, promised to deliberate upon the second part with the great officers of

* Parliamentary History, vol. i. p. 160.

the king's household, and gave their unhesitating assent to the third proposition.

The second of these propositions contains the germ of the distinction between the civil list and taxes voted for the public expenditure. A subsidy was voted by the Commons, after the establishment of the administration. It was agreed that moneys thus raised should be lodged in the keeping of special treasurers, who should give an account of their receipts and disbursements, in such manner as the king and council should order. Two London merchants, William Walworth and John Philpot, were appointed to this office by the king.

Several other petitions were presented by this Parliament. 1. That the evil councillors of the late king Edward might be removed from the royal councils—which was granted. 2. That, during the king's minority, all the ministers and other great functionaries of State, might be appointed by Parliament; and that if an office fell vacant, while Parliament was not sitting, it should be filled up by the king's council, subject to the approval of the next Parliament—which was granted in the case of the greater officers, but refused in respect to those of less importance. 3. That Parliament should be holden once a year—in reply to which it was promised that "the statutes made for that purpose shall be observed and kept."* It is clear that, in all these matters, the initiative and general direction of the government belonged to the Commons.

On the 25th of April, 1378, a second Parliament met, and voted a poll-tax, as the king had involved himself by loans. The chancellor concluded his speech by saying that, for all past and probable expenditure, the treasurers were prepared to give account.

On the 20th of October, 1378, a third Parliament met, and a fresh subsidy was demanded. The Commons maintained that the king ought not to be in want of one, and that a promise had been made that no further imposts should be levied for a long time. The chancellor, Richard le Scroop, denied that any such promise had been made; and long and violent debates ensued upon this question. The Commons demanded that an account should be given them of the way in which the last subsidy had been spent. The chancellor asserted that they had no right to require this, but finally yielded, under protest that it should not be considered a precedent. The Commons accordingly examined the accounts.

The Commons next requested that five or six lords or prelates should be deputed to confer with them respecting the public charges: thus aspiring to make their own body the centre of deliberation, and affecting to regard the lords only as a part of the king's council. The lords refused their request, and proposed that, according to ancient usage, each house should appoint certain of its mem-

* Parliamentary History, vol. i. pp. 161, 162.

bers to confer together. This suggestion was adopted, and a subsidy voted. The Commons further demanded the appointment of special treasurers to receive and disburse its proceeds; which was granted.

On the 15th of January, 1380, a fourth Parliament was held, for the purpose of demanding fresh subsidies, rendered necessary by the wars with France and Scotland, the revolts in Gascony, and other causes. The chancellor concluded his speech by saying "that the lords of the great council were ready to lay before the Commons the receipts of the last subsidial grants, and the disbursements of the same."

The Commons demanded: 1. That the counsellors given to the king at his accession, should be dismissed (probably because they suspected them of unfaithfulness in the management of the public revenue); 2. That the five chief officers of State should not be changed until the next Parliament; 3. That a commission should be formed to survey and examine, in all his courts and palaces, the state of the king's household, and the expenses and receipts in all the offices—which was granted, and the commission composed of six lords and six members of the House of Commons; 4. That some of the most discreet barons should be placed about the king, in order to give wise answers to foreign ministers. One baron only, the Earl of Warwick, was appointed for this purpose. A subsidy was then voted.

In November, 1380, a fifth Parliament met to vote further subsidies; and a long discussion arose between the Commons and the Lords regarding the amount. A fixed sum of £16,000 was required; to meet which the Commons voted a poll-tax of 15 groats on every individual above 15 years of age, mendicants alone excepted; and annexed to their vote the condition that the rich should help the poor to pay the tax. The Commons moreover voted that "no knight, citizen, or burgess of the present Parliament should be collector of this money"; apparently in order to avoid every suspicion of partiality in its assessment. A violent popular insurrection broke out in consequence of this tax; and in order to quell it, the king was obliged to make promises of general enfranchisement.

On the 14th of September, 1382, a sixth Parliament assembled; but was adjourned on account of a quarrel between the Duke of Lancaster and the Earl of Northumberland, who had both come thither in arms, with a numerous retinue. The importance of these great barons was such that the Parliament could not meet until the king had succeeded in reconciling them. Great agitation was felt in this Parliament, as it did not know how to calm the disturbance in the country. The charter of manumission which had been extorted from the king was revoked. The Commons accused the bad government of the king of having caused the insurrection, and drew a melancholy picture of the deplorable state of the people. A committee of inquiry was appointed in consequence. The

Commons refused to grant a subsidy, basing their refusal upon the disposition of the country to revolt. The king declared that he would not grant his amnesty for all the offences committed during the late insurrection, unless a subsidy were granted; and under the influence of this threat, the Commons yielded.

At the opening of this Parliament, the Commons demanded that the prelates, the lords temporal, the knights, the judges, in a word, the various estates of the realm, should examine, each for their own class, the charges which should be brought; and should report the same to the Commons, who would deliberate upon it. This was an attempt to make themselves a sovereign and undivided assembly; but the king maintained the ancient usage, which required that the Commons should deliberate first of all, and communicate their propositions to the king and lords.

This Parliament was twice prorogued; from the 15th of December to the 15th of January, 1383, and again from the latter date to the 7th of May.

Seven sessions of the Parliament were held from the 7th of May 1383, to the 1st of October 1386. The king endeavoured to free himself from the control of the Parliament. In 1383, he dismissed a very popular chancellor, Richard le Scroop, because he had refused to seal some inconsiderate gifts of property which had become confiscated to the crown. During the same year, the clergy obtained from the king a violent statute against the Lollards or disciples of Wickliffe. The Commons complained of this, saying that the statute was surreptitious; that it had never received their consent, and that "it was not their meaning to bind themselves, or their successors, to the prelates, any more than their ancestors had done before them." They, therefore, demanded and obtained the revocation of the statute; but after their departure, the act of revocation was set aside, and the statute maintained.

In 1383, also, the Commons having demanded to confer with a committee of lords whom they mentioned by name, the king consented to their request, but added that it belonged to him alone to appoint the lords whom he thought fit to send to such conferences. In the same Parliament the Commons prayed the king "to place the most discreet and valuable officers about his person," and to regulate his household in such a way that his revenues might be well administered, and prove sufficient to meet his wants. The king answered that he would summon to him the persons who suited him, and that he would regulate his household by the advice of his council. In 1386, the Commons petitioned that the state of the king's household should be examined every year by the chancellor, the treasurer, and the keeper of the privy seal; and that they should be authorized to reform its abuses. The king replied that he would order such an examination when it pleased him. The Commons next inquired who were the ministers and chief officers of State whom the king intended to place at the head of affairs. The king replied that he had officers sufficient at present, and would change them at his pleasure. All these facts indicate an effort on the part of the king and his council to free themselves from the control of Parliament. In proportion as this desire became apparent, the Commons became, in certain respects, more timid and reserved. In 1383, the king consulted them as to whether he should march in person at the head of his army against France; and they replied that it was not in their province to decide upon such a question, but that it should be referred to the council. In 1385, they were consulted on the question of peace or war with France: and refused to give an opinion. The king insisted upon having an answer, but all that he could obtain from them was that "if they were in the king's place, they would prefer peace." Every circumstance, on both sides, indicates an imminent separation, or at least a progressive estrangement. The king was desirous to escape from the guidance of the Parliament; and the Parliament refused to share the responsibility of the king's council.

Richard was under the sway of two favourites, Robert de Vere, Marquis of Dublin, and Michael de la Pole, Earl of Suffolk. Hence the government was courtly, capricious, destructive, and laid claim to an insolent and frivolous exercise of arbitrary authority. The haughty tone of the chancellor Suffolk was extremely offensive in the speeches with which he opened the Parliaments of 1384 and 1385. The Commons could endure the government (though often tyrannical) of a council of barons with much greater willingness than that of a pack of court favourites. The great feudal aristocracy were deeply rooted in the associations of the country; but the arrogance and frivolity of favourites were unspeakably offensive to the people. The storm broke out in the Parliament which met on the 1st of October, 1386. The Commons, "with one accord," impeached the Earl of Suffolk. The king withdrew to Eltham. The two Houses sent to him to demand the dismissal of the lord treasurer and of the chancellor, relating to whom, they said, they had matters to treat of which could not be safely done whilst he remained in his office. The king sent an evasive answer; and the Parliament declared that it would do nothing so long as the king continued absent, and the Earl of Suffolk remained minister. The king proposed that they should depute forty knights of their number to confer with him. The Parliament refused. After a long and singular correspondence, the king was constrained to yield and to choose new ministers.

Doubt has been cast upon several of these facts, and especially upon the king's correspondence with the Parliament. Knyghton is the only historian who records it, but there is reason to believe it authentic. The Earl of Suffolk was impeached and condemned. The charges brought against him were of little weight as legal crimes, but of great importance as abuses in the government. A committee of eleven lords was appointed by Parliament to regulate all public affairs, and to govern in concert with the king. The Parliament enacted the penalties of high treason against any person who should advise the king not to follow the counsels of this committee, and constrained the king to confirm these resolutions by letters-patent. The king, on his part, made protestation in full Parliament, with his own mouth, "that for any thing which was done in that Parliament he would not any prejudice should come to him or his crown; but that the prerogative and liberties of it should be safe and preserved."

In 1387, the king travelled through the west and north of England; and assembled at Nottingham a council composed of partisans of his favourites. He inquired of the sheriffs of the neighbouring counties what forces they could raise for his assistance, if he should find it necessary to oppose the committee of eleven lords. The sheriffs replied that the people were convinced that the lords were friends to the king, and desired the welfare of the country, and that therefore few persons would be found willing to take up arms against them. The king then commanded the sheriffs to elect to the next Parliament those persons only whom he should nominate. They answered that they could not undertake to secure the election of any persons but those who were to the people's liking. The king then summoned the judges to Nottingham, and proposed to them various questions concerning the rights and prerogatives of the crown. The judges, either intimidated or guided by Sir Robert Tressillian, gave answers tending to establish the arbitrary power of the king and to free his government from the control of the Parliament. This was the evident object of the whole of this struggle.

Dissension now broke out between the king and the lords. A Parliament was convoked. The king inserted in his writs an order to return those persons who were *debatis modernis magis indifferentes;*[1] but he was soon obliged to erase this clause, and to declare it illegal in new writs. The Parliament met on the 3rd of February, 1388, and took precautions to ensure that it should alone decide upon all great public matters, and that it should not be dissolved after having voted a subsidy. An accusation was lodged by five lords, called appellants, against the favourites of the king, and the judges. This accusation really conceals a great party conflict beneath the forms of judicial procedure. The Upper House declared that, on such grave occasions, the Parliament alone could judge, and was bound by none of the laws which regulate the proceedings of other courts. Eighteen persons were condemned, most of them to death, and many by default. The Parliament separated after having sat five months. It was called the *Wonderful Parliament,* and also the *Pitiless Parliament.* It had been careful to declare that the condemnation of the favourite councillors and judges, did not in any way throw discredit upon the king himself.

The authority of the committee of eleven lords over the government was exercised without opposition for a year. In May, 1389, the king assembled his

---

1. Who were in present debates indifferent.

council, and declared that, being now of full age, he was capable of governing his inheritance himself, and that it was not fitting that he should be in a worse condition than every subject in his dominions who could freely dispose of his goods. "It is well known," he said, "that for several years I have lived under your guardianship, and I thank you for the trouble you have taken on my account; but now that I have reached my majority, I am determined to remain no longer under tutelage, but to take in hand the government of my kingdom and to ap-point or revoke my ministers and other officers according to my pleasure." He changed the chancellor and other great officers, and dismissed from his council several of the eleven lords.

Here began the second epoch in this reign—the epoch of reaction against the Parliament. Great obscurity prevails as to the causes which placed Richard II. in a position to effect such a revolution; but he was most probably embold-ened to do so by division in the committee of eleven lords, and by the bad use which some of them had made of their power. The king and his new council governed at first with prudence, and manifested great respect for the Parlia-ment. On the 16th of January, 1390, a Parliament was convoked. The new min-isters resigned their offices, and submitted their conduct to its scrutiny. The Parliament declared that it found no cause for complaint, and the ministers re-sumed their functions. Seven Parliaments were held from 1390 to 1397. They be-came more and more timid and docile, and the king's authority assumed an in-creasingly extended and arbitrary character. These are the principal facts which characterize this reaction:—

In 1391, the Parliament assured the king that the royalty and prerogatives of his crown should ever remain intact and inviolable; that if they had in any way been infringed, it should be reformed; and that the king should enjoy as large liberty as any of his predecessors ever did: "which prayer seemed to our lord the king honest and reasonable," and he consented to it. In 1391 and 1392, the Par-liament admitted the king's power to dispense with the observance of certain statutes in ecclesiastical matters, on condition that these statutes should not be held to be thereby revoked. In 1392, the king, being offended with the city of London, withdrew from it its liberties and imprisoned its magistrates; but shortly afterwards he restored its liberties to the city, and imposed on it a fine of £1000 sterling. In 1394, the judges who had been banished to Ireland by the Parliament of 1388, were recalled. In 1397, a bill was brought forward in the House of Commons, proposing that all extravagant expenditure should be avoided in the royal household; and that those bishops and ladies who had nothing to do at court should not have permission to reside there. The king was incensed at this bill before it was presented to him, and said in the Upper House, "that it was directed against those liberties and royalties which his pro-genitors had enjoyed, and which he was resolved to uphold and maintain." He ordered the Lords to inform the Commons of his resolution, and directed the Duke of Lancaster to command Sir John Bussy, the Speaker of the Commons, to inform him what member had introduced the bill into Parliament. The Commons became alarmed, and humbly besought the king's pardon. At a conference, they placed the bill in the king's hands, and delivered up to him its proposer, Thomas Haxey. The king forgave them, and the Parliament itself declared Haxey guilty of treason. The clergy saved his life by claiming him as a clerk—which proves that at this period ecclesiastics were not excluded from Parliament.

In September, 1397, Richard II. at length judged himself in a position to assume the plenitude of his power, to annul all that had been done in 1388 to limit his authority, and to avenge his injuries.

A Parliament was convoked. Every precaution had been taken to ensure its docility. The sheriffs had been changed; and all sorts of practices had been put in force to influence the elections. Numerous bodies of troops formed the royal guard. The Parliament was opened with great solemnity. The chancellor, the Bishop of Exeter, took as the text of his speech: *Rex unus erit omnibus.*[2] Subsequent events fully corresponded with these preliminaries. All the acts of the Parliament of 1388 were revoked, and their authors accused of treason; five of them were condemned to death. The principal leader of the opposition, the Duke of Gloucester, was assassinated in prison at Calais, after having been constrained to acknowledge his past crimes in a confession in which he formerly accused himself of having "restrained the king of his freedom." After these condemnations the same Parliament held a second session at Shrewsbury, in which the answers of the judges in 1387 were declared good and legitimate, and precisely the same measures were taken to render these new decisions inviolable, which had been employed by the Parliament of 1388 to ensure the observance of its own resolutions. These two sessions lasted sixteen days. In less than two years afterwards, Richard was dethroned.

He thought himself, however, well secured against such a contingency; for he had taken all sorts of precautions firmly to establish the power which he had just regained. The Parliament had granted him, for his lifetime, the duty upon wools and hides, upon condition only that this concession should not be regarded as a precedent by the kings his successors. As several of the petitions and other matters laid before the Parliament during its last session had not been fully terminated, the Parliament at its dissolution appointed a permanent committee of twelve lords and six members of the House of Commons, to whom it transferred its powers to regulate and decide, in concert with the king, all affairs of public business. Richard thus remained surrounded by the men who had just

2. There will be one king among all.

assisted him to regain arbitrary power; and although the mission of this committee was limited to the settlement of those affairs only which the Parliament had not had time to arrange, it did not hesitate to take possession of the entire government. In concert with the king, it issued ordinances, and declared the penalties of high treason against any person who should attempt to resist its authority; and it imposed on all the lords the obligation, under oath, to respect and maintain all that it should enact. All the powers of Parliament were thus usurped by this committee. Private vexations were added to this general usurpation; in spite of the amnesty which had been proclaimed, even by the last Parliament, Richard continued to wreak his vengeance upon the adherents of the Parliament of 1388. He extorted money from seventeen counties under the pretence that they had taken part in the rebellion; and he forced wealthy citizens to sign blank cheques in order to ransom themselves from prosecutions for treason, which blanks he filled up at his pleasure.

Such acts as these could not fail to produce general hatred and indignation; and an accidental cause led to their manifestation. A quarrel existed between the Dukes of Hereford and Norfolk; and the last Parliament had left the dispute to the decision of the king and his committee. A single combat between the two dukes was appointed to take place at Coventry; but the king anticipated the duel, and banished both the dukes, one for ten years, and the other for life. By letters patent, he expressedly authorized the Duke of Hereford to sue, during his banishment, for the livery of any lands that might be bequeathed to him. In 1399, John of Gaunt, Duke of Lancaster and father of Hereford, died. The king and his committee annulled the letters-patent, and confiscated the property of the Duke of Lancaster. Richard then set out for Ireland. On the 4th of July, 1399, the Duke of Hereford, who had become Duke of Lancaster by the death of his father, landed in England. He made rapid progress, and when Richard returned to England, he soon found himself abandoned and taken prisoner. A Parliament was convoked in his name on the 30th of September. Richard abdicated. An accusation in thirty-three articles was drawn up against him; and his deposition was pronounced by the Parliament. Henry of Lancaster claimed the crown in virtue of a pretended right of birth. It was granted to him on the 6th of August, 1399, and new writs were issued for the convocation of a Parliament within six days. This was impossible: so the same Parliament met again, and became the Parliament of Henry IV. Richard, who had been kept prisoner in Pomfret Castle, was put to death on the 23rd of October, 1399.

This royal catastrophe was the work of force, just as the deposition of Edward II. had been; but public opinion and public passion had a much greater share in it. Efforts were made to impart even to these acts of violence an appearance of constitutional regularity, and the progress of parliamentary government may be discerned even in its tragical excitements.

Such were, in a political point of view, the character and progress of this reign. A few particular facts are worthy of notice.

1. The extension of the practice of forced loans. In 1378, a petition was presented that no man should be constrained to lend money to the king; and it was granted. Nevertheless, in 1386, a writ addressed to several inhabitants of Boston enjoins them to make every person possessing property of more than twenty pounds in value contribute to the loan of £200 which the town had promised to grant to the king, and which would be received in deduction from the subsidies of the present Parliament.

2. The principle of the appropriation of subsidies becomes increasingly prevalent.

3. The Commons make efforts to ensure that their petitions should not be altered when passed into statutes. In 1382, they requested the communication of one of the king's ordinances before it was registered: and desired that some of their members should be present during the preparation of the rolls. The affair of Thomas Haxey gives us reason to believe that the practice commenced, during this reign, of proceeding in the form of bills discussed and adopted by both Houses before they were submitted for the sanction of the king. Nevertheless, in 1382, the House of Commons having requested the opinion of the House of Lords on a question which then occupied their attention, the Lords replied that ancient usage required that the Commons should first communicate their opinion to the king and assembled lords. This very fact, however, proves that the present form of initiative was about to introduce itself.

4. In 1384, the town of Shaftesbury addressed a petition to the king, lords and commons, against the sheriff of Dorsetshire, who had made a false return of an election, and left out the name of the person really elected. We are not aware of the result of this petition, but this is the first instance of the official intervention of the Commons in the matter of contested elections. Only three examples of analogous petitions are to be met with in previous times, viz. under Edward II. in 1319, under Edward III. in 1363, and under Richard II. in 1384. Until then, the king alone had examined the petition, and referred its judgment to the ordinary tribunals.

5. In 1382, a statute ordains, under penalty of fine or other punishment, that all the lords and deputies of the Commons shall repair to Parliament when they are summoned; and that all the sheriffs shall cause all due and accustomed elections to be made, without omitting any borough or city.

These particular acts, as well as the general course of events, attest the progress of constitutional maxims and practices.

LECTURE 25

Summary of the history of the Parliament from the death of Richard II. to the accession of the House of Stuart. ⁓ Progress of the forms of procedure, and of the privileges of Parliament. ⁓ Liberty of speech in both Houses. ⁓ Inviolability of members of Parliament. ⁓ Judicial power of the House of Lords. ⁓ Decadence of the Parliament during the wars of the Roses, and under the Tudor dynasty. ⁓ Causes of this decadence of the progress of royal authority, from Henry VII. to Elizabeth. ⁓ Conclusion.

IT is impossible to comprehend the entire scope of the character and influence of great events. Some occurrences, which procure order and liberty for the present, prepare the way for tyranny and confusion in the future; while others, on the contrary, establish absolute power at first, and subsequently give birth to full political freedom. We cannot fail to be struck by this reflection when we consider the prodigious difference which exists between the immediate results and the remote consequences of the deposition of Richard II. It delivered England from an arbitrary, insolent, and disorderly government; but sixty years afterwards it gave rise to the wars of the Red and White Roses, and to all those cruel internal distractions which facilitated the establishment of the Tudor despotism: so that the decay of English liberties, from 1461 to 1640, had its primary source in the event which, in 1399, had consummated their triumph.

In considering the general character of the state of the government from 1399 to 1461, under the first three kings of the House of Lancaster, Henry IV., Henry V., and Henry VI., we must admit that this period was remarkable neither for the unchangeableness nor for the progress of institutions. During this epoch, the Parliament gained none of those signal victories which distinguished the reigns of Edward III. and Richard II.; no really new right, no fundamental and previously unknown guarantee, were added to those already possessed. Neither did arbitrary power again assume the offensive, and obtain the advantage; and the crown and Parliament engaged in no serious conflict calculated to compromise the existence of either party, or notably to change their degree of political importance. In truth, the work of this period was to regularize the results of previous struggles. The Parliament exercised, without much opposition, the right for which it had fought during the fourteenth century, viz., the voting of taxes, the appropriation of the subsidies, the investigation of the public accounts, intervention in the legislature, and the impeachment of the great officers of the crown. The kings, though frequently seeking to elude the application of these rights, never ignored them completely, or braved them openly. The whole of the political machine remained almost unaltered; but though it underwent no great revolutions, it received many important developments in its internal organization. Practical ameliorations were sought after and attained; further consequences were deduced from established principles; and this epoch is more remarkable for various improvements in the springs of parliamentary government, than for the conquest of great rights, or the formation of fundamental institutions.

The internal constitution of the Parliament, especially during the course of this period, made important progress; from this time we may date, with some degree of accuracy, its principal forms of procedure and its most essential privileges.

One of the most essential is, certainly, liberty of speech. During the reign of Henry IV., we find the speaker of the House of Commons demanding it of the king at the opening of every session. One of the first acts of the first Parliament held during this reign, in 1399, was to obtain the revocation of the sentence passed upon Thomas Haxey, in the reign of Richard II. Every circumstance proves that, under Henry IV., the Commons used greater liberty of speech than they had previously enjoyed. It was, indeed, made a subject of special praise to Sir John Tibetot, speaker in the Parliament of 1406. The king soon manifested great distrust of the extension given to this right, which was probably exercised with all the rudeness which characterized the manners of that time. In 1410, he told the Commons that he hoped that they would no longer use unbecoming language, but act with moderation. In 1411, the speaker, Sir Thomas Chaucer, having made the usual demand at the opening of the session, the king replied that he would allow the Commons to speak as others before had done, but that "he would have no novelties introduced, and would enjoy his prerogative." The speaker requested three days to give a written answer to this observation, and then replied "that he desired no other protestation than what other speakers had made; and that if he should speak anything to the king's displeasure, it might be imputed to his own ignorance only, and not to the body of the Commons,"* which the king granted.

We meet with no infringement upon the liberty of speech enjoyed by the

---

* Parliamentary History, vol. i. p. 313.

Commons until the Parliament of 1455, at which time a deputy from Bristol, Thomas Young, complained that he had been arrested and imprisoned in the Tower, six years before, on account of a motion which he had brought forward in the House. The object of this motion had been to declare that, as the king then had no children, the Duke of York was the legitimate heir to the throne. The Commons transmitted this petition to the Lords, and the king commanded his council to do whatever might be judged fitting on behalf of the petitioner.

In all official transactions with the king and the lords, the Speaker was the mouthpiece of the House of Commons, and for him especially liberty of speech was then demanded. He acted in the name, and on the behalf, of the House, on almost all occasions. In 1406, we find him giving his consent, in this capacity, to the act which regulated the succession of the crown.

The inviolability of the members of Parliament was a right of no less importance than liberty of speech. The ancient Saxon laws granted protection and security to the members of the Wittenagemot, in going and returning from the place of meeting, provided they were not notorious robbers and brigands. From the formation of the new Parliament, the same right was claimed by its members, who, as they came to transact the business of the king in his national council, were entitled to exemption from arrest or hindrance. In 1403, Sir Thomas Brooke repaired to Parliament as a representative of Somersetshire; and one of his suite, Richard Cheddre, was maltreated and beaten by John Salage. A statute ordained that Salage should pay double damages to Cheddre, according to the award of the Court of Queen's Bench; and "moreover, it is granted by the said Parliament that the same shall be done in times to come, in similar cases." This circumstance gave rise to a petition of the Commons, who prayed that all lords, knights, citizens, and burgesses, coming to Parliament and residing there, might be, as well as their followers and domestics, under the special protection and defence of the king, until their return home; and that they might be arrested for no debt, contract, or suit, or imprisoned in any manner during that time, under penalty of a fine to be paid to the king, and damages to the person injured. The king replied that provision should be made to this effect. The statute of 1403 was renewed in 1433, during the reign of Henry VI.

In 1430, a complaint was laid before the House of Commons on account of the imprisonment, for debt, of William Lake, the servant of William Mildred, one of the members for London. He was set at liberty by a special act of Parliament.

In 1453, the Commons complained to the king and to the lords of the imprisonment of Thomas Thorpe, their speaker, who had been arrested for debt at the suit of the Duke of York. The Lords referred the matter to the judges, who replied through Sir John Fortescue: "That it was not their part to judge of the Parliament's actions, who were judges and makers of the laws themselves; only they said there were divers *supersedeas* of privilege of Parliament brought into courts; but a general *supersedeas,* to suppress all proceedings, there was not. For, if there should, it would seem as if the High Court of Parliament, that ministered all justice and equity, should hinder the process of the common law, and so put the party complainant without remedy, inasmuch as actions at common law are not determinable in Parliament; but if any member of Parliament be arrested for such cases as are not for treason, felony, or surety of the peace, or for a judgment had before Parliament, it was usual for such person to be quitted of such arrest, and set at liberty to attend his service in Parliament."*

Notwithstanding this answer of the judges, the Lords decided that Thorpe should remain in prison: and ordered the Commons, in the king's name, to elect another speaker, which they did. But this was a party quarrel; Thorpe was attached to the House of Lancaster, and the Duke of York was then in the ascendant. The privilege then existed, but still in a precarious manner, and a special act of Parliament was necessary on every occasion to ensure its being put into practice.

It was also during this period that the right of parliamentary initiative superseded the right of petition. We have already noticed the abuses originated by the initiative which the House of Commons exercised by means of its petitions; and that the petitions were not always faithfully reproduced in the statutes which they had suggested. We have also seen what efforts had already been put forth by the Commons to prevent these trickeries. In 1414, during the reign of Henry V., they complained of them in a special petition, to which the king replied by promising that in future the statutes should correspond exactly to the petitions granted. But this guarantee was very insecure, and the Commons had already begun to obtain more effectual securities by accustoming themselves to draw up in the form of complete bills, the statutes which they had previously suggested by petitions; and sending them to the House of Lords, that they might be discussed and adopted by that House, before they were presented to the king, who then had nothing more to do than to give or refuse his sanction. It is impossible to indicate with precision the period at which this important change took place; for it was accomplished gradually, and was not remarked by the historians of the time. The usage of petitions co-existed for some time with that of bills. The following facts indicate the progress of the change. Under Richard II., in 1382 (and I have already alluded to this fact), the Commons attempted to obtain the opinion of the Lords, upon a certain question, before bringing under the notice of the king. The attempt was repulsed by the Lords, who staked their honour upon not separating from the king, and upon receiv-

* Parliamentary or Constitutional History of England, vol. ii. p. 287.

ing simultaneously and in concert with him, the propositions of the Commons. The complete initiative of the Houses of Parliament arose, naturally and necessarily, from the voting of taxes. Originally, as you have seen, each class of deputies voted alone those taxes which were destined to weigh especially upon themselves; and the knights of the shire deliberated and voted upon this matter with the Lords. When the knights of the shire had fully combined with the deputies of the boroughs—when the House of Commons deliberated and voted, in a body, upon the same taxes—it became necessary that the votes on such matters should receive the consent of the Lords, who would also have to bear the consequences. Bills passed in reference to subsidies were thenceforward discussed and voted by both Houses before they were laid before the king; and the initiative, in its present form, was thus fully established in this particular case. In 1407, a remarkable incident brought this form of proceeding to light, gave it final sanction, and deduced from it at the same time two other parliamentary rights of great importance. In consequence of a debate which arose between the House of Lords and the House of Commons with regard to the initiative of subsidies, three principles were recognised, and have since remained firmly established: 1. Parliamentary initiative in its present form; 2. The exclusive initiative of the Commons in the matter of subsidies; 3. The right of the Houses, that the king should take no cognizance of the subject of their deliberations until they had come to a decision upon it, and were in a position to lay it before him as the desire of the Lords and Commons in Parliament assembled.

It was natural that that which was practised with regard to subsidies should soon extend to all matters; and that the propositions of Parliament, whatever might be their object, should reach the king as emanating from both Houses instead of being merely the petitions of one of them. Mr. Hallam affirms, without giving any particulars, that this practice became general during the reign of Henry VI., and from this period he dates the real division of the legislature into three branches. I am inclined to think that this practice had commenced at an earlier date, although it was rarely carried into effect; and it is certain, from the very constitution of Parliament at this epoch, that it did not become constant and general until a later period.

In 1406, I find the Commons demanding, by the mouth of the speaker, Sir John Tibetot, the right of withdrawing their bills from the House of Lords, at any stage of the deliberation upon them, in order to introduce amendments; which was granted. The Commons were therefore already in the habit of occasionally drawing up their petitions in the form of bills, and of passing them through the House of Lords before presenting them to the king.

At this period, the House of Lords was still regarded as the great council of the king, and as a sort of intermediary between the privy council and the entire Parliament; and a number of propositions on matters of government, and even of legislation, still emanated from the Commons alone, and were presented, in the form of petitions, to the king and lords. The practice of initiative by way of bills adopted by both Houses could not, therefore, have been general. The periods of the king's minority or absence tended increasingly to impart the character of a great council of government to the House of Lords. Accordingly these epochs, and especially the reign of Henry VI., abound in propositions or petitions of the Commons to the Lords. It was at a later period, when the king and his privy council had regained a more independent power than their predecessors had enjoyed—that is to say, under the Tudor dynasty—that the Upper House became entirely disjoined from the government properly so called, and found itself placed, with respect to the king, in almost the same position as the House of Commons. Then alone did the practice of proceeding by bills discussed in both Houses before they were laid before the king, assume a constant and general character, that is to say, the parliamentary initiative was definitively substituted for the ancient right of petition possessed by each House, and especially by the Commons.

With regard to the order of the debates in Parliament, it was an ancient custom that the king should not reply to the petitions of the Commons until the last day of the session; which rendered it impossible to make the concession of subsidies dependent upon the king's answers. They endeavoured to reverse this order, probably during the reign of Richard II.; for the sixth question which he proposed to the judges was whether, when the king had called the attention of Parliament to any subject, the Parliament might attend to other matters before deciding upon the propositions of the king. The judges replied that such a proceeding was an act of treason. The answers of the judges of Richard II. having been declared illegitimate in the Parliament of 1399, the foregoing *dictum* was comprised in the general reprobation. Accordingly, in 1401, the Commons maintained that it was not their custom to grant any subsidy until the king had replied to their petitions, and they demanded that this course should be pursued. The king said that he would confer on the subject with the Lords, and on the last day of the session, he replied "that there was never such use known, but that they should first go through with all other business before their petitions were answered; which ordinance the king intended not to alter." We do not find that the Commons then resisted, or attempted to procure the recognition, in a general manner, of the principle which they asserted. But this principle was frequently put into practice in subsequent Parliaments, and the king was forced not to throw any hindrance in its way. In 1407, Parliament opened on the 20th of October. On the 9th and 14th of November, the Commons presented themselves before the king, explained their numerous grievances, received his answer, and granted no subsidies until the 2nd of December following. In 1410, Parliament met on the 27th of January; and it was not until the 9th of May, after it had obtained satisfaction on several points, among others on the dismissal of two members of the privy council, that it granted a subsidy. This practice became almost constant during the reign of Henry VI. We find an evident proof of this in the Parliament held in November 1455. The Commons sent several times to demand of the Lords the appointment of a Protector for the kingdom, on account of the imbecility of Henry VI.; and the Archbishop of Canterbury urged the Lords to give a definitive answer, "for it is well known that the Commons will not give attention to any affairs of the Parliament until they have obtained an answer, and satisfaction of their request."

The principle had, therefore, become a fact, and was generally admitted as a fact.

It was also during the course of this period that elections to Parliament, and the rights of Parliament in the matter of elections, began to be regulated. I have already observed in treating of the formation of the Parliament, that the electoral system had been definitively established by statutes of Henry IV. in 1405, and of Henry VI. in 1429 and 1432. Many facts prove that at this date the importance of the House of Commons had become so great, that the elections were a subject of frequent frauds. A number of statutes of detail, during the reign of Henry VI., were passed to prevent such frauds, and to regulate the procedure by which they should be investigated and punished. Then also, for the first time, we find conditions imposed on the choice of the electors. The ancient spirit of electoral institutions required that the persons elected should be inhabitants of the county or town which they were chosen to represent. This was converted into an express law by a statute of Henry V. in 1413, which was renewed by a statute of Henry VI., in 1444; but the law has fallen into desuetude by the force of circumstances, without ever having been formally repealed.

The judgment of elections continued to belong, during this period, to the lords and the king's council, who were frequently urged to exercise this prerogative by petitions from the Commons.

It was also at this epoch that the judicial power, which originally resided in the entire Parliament, was declared to belong exclusively to the House of Lords. This declaration was made in 1399, at the suggestion of the Commons themselves, and by the mouth of the Archbishop of Canterbury, who said: "That the Commons were only petitioners, and that all judgment belonged to the king and lords; unless it was in statutes, grants of subsidies, and such like." Since this period the Commons, when they desired to interfere in judgments otherwise than by impeachment, were obliged to employ the means of bills of attainder. They adopted this plan in the case of the Duke of Suffolk in 1450, and very frequently afterwards.

These are the most notable marks of progress made, during this period, by the constitution and forms of Parliament. If we now consider Parliament, no longer in itself and its own internal proceedings, but in its relations to the government properly so called, we shall find that its rights and influence in matters of taxation, legislation, and public administration were the same as it had won under Edward III. and Richard II., and that it merely exercised them with greater assurance and less opposition. Henry IV. tried more than once to resist the power of the House of Commons; but it had set him upon the throne, and felt itself in a position to confine him within the limit of his authority. In 1404, it demanded of him the dismissal of four officers of his household; and he replied with singular humility "that he knew no cause why they should be removed, but as the Lords and Commons judged it for the interest of the kingdom and his own advantage, he would remove them, and would do as much in future to any minister who should incur the hatred of his people." In 1406, the Commons submitted for the approbation of the king thirty articles which, they said, they had drawn up to ensure the better administration of public affairs, and which they demanded that the king's officers should swear to observe. These articles, though of a temporary nature, were intended to repress many existing abuses, and to restrict the royal prerogative in certain respects. The king thought that he could not refuse his assent. Towards the end of his reign, Henry IV. appeared more bold, and less disposed to yield unresistingly to the control of the Parliament; but his death prevented all serious conflict. The glory of Henry V. and the passion for wars with France filled up his somewhat brief reign; the Parliament sustained him in all his measures, and even went so far as to grant him, in 1415, a subsidy for life, with power to use it arbitrarily and at his pleasure. During the minority of Henry VI., or rather during all that part of his reign which was not stained with civil war, and was in fact a long minority, the power of Parliament reached its climax, and absorbed the entire government. All matters were decided between the Lords and Commons; but it was too soon for the nation, thus left to its own guidance, to provide itself with a regular government. Violent factions arose among the aristocracy, which the House of Commons was not in a condition to repress. That great development of public institutions and liberties which had commenced under king John, and continued with such regularity since the reign of Edward III., was suddenly interrupted, and England plunged into the violent anarchy of the wars of the Red and White Roses, to emerge only into the despotism of the House of Tudor.

How came it that institutions, already so strong and active, at least in appearance, decayed so rapidly? How came it that parliamentary government, which seemed in possession of all its essential rights and principles, paused in its progress, and yielded for more than a century to the rule of an almost absolute monarchy? Now that I have reached the conclusion of this course of lectures, I cannot investigate with you the causes of this apparently singular fact;

but they may be discerned in another very remarkable fact—in the analogy which prevails between the history of England and the history of France at this period. In France, also, during the fourteenth and fifteenth centuries, we discern the appearances of attempts at representative government; these incoherent and superficial essays were succeeded by the wars of religion, the League, and the great disorders of the sixteenth century; and order was not restored, France did not regain repose and vigour, until the establishment of absolute power by Cardinal Richelieu and Louis XIV., and by the annihilation, as a political power, of that ancient feudal aristocracy who had been able neither to procure for the country, nor to assume for themselves, in the government of France, their legitimate and lasting position.

In England, as you have just seen, representative government, originating in the thirteenth and fourteenth centuries did not confine itself to incoherent and feeble essays; but established itself upon its essential foundations, and speedily obtained considerable development. The sanguinary conflicts for the succession to the throne, the protracted dissensions of the Red and White Roses, abruptly arrested its progress. Just as in France, from the reign of Louis XI., we hear nothing of attempts at the establishment of free institutions, so in England, during the reigns of Edward IV. and Richard III., the Parliament has no history. In the intervals of the civil war, it appears only as the instrument of the vengeance of the victorious party, and to pass bills of attainder against the leaders of the vanquished faction. It voted a few taxes, but this was the only one of its rights which it still maintained, and even this was eluded by the practice of *Benevolences,* or gifts in appearance voluntary, but in reality compulsory, of which we meet with a few examples in antecedent times, but which received great extension under Edward IV. Finally, more than once several years elapsed without a Parliament being convoked, especially from 1477 to 1482; such a suspension had been unprecedented since 1327.

The civil wars of the fifteenth century, however, are only the superficial, and as it were, external cause of this sudden decadence of representative government in England; in order to discover its true cause, we must penetrate deeper into the state of society.

Until this period, the three great forces in English society—the royal power, the aristocracy, and the Commons—had maintained intimate and continual relations amongst themselves, and had served each other by turns, either as an obstacle or as a means of success. It was by the aid of the great barons that the Commons had been enabled to win their liberties. The royal power, though strong in itself, had nevertheless been obliged to resort sometimes to the barons, and sometimes to the Commons. From the political concurrence of these three great social forces, and from the vicissitudes of their alliances and fortunes, the progress of representative government had resulted. Liberty can be established only where there does not exist in the State any constituted power sufficiently preponderant to usurp absolute authority.[1]

In the latter half of the fifteenth century, the equipoise of these three forces ceased. The royal power disappeared in some sort, in consequence of the imbecility of Henry VI. and afterwards by the uncertainty of the right of succession to the crown. The government fell into the hands of the high aristocracy, who were divided and distracted by their intestine quarrels. The Commons were not in a condition to act the part of mediators between these terrible factions, and to impose upon them respect for public order. The knights of the shire took part in the train of the great barons with whom they were still dependently connected by a multitude of ties: and the towns, thus left alone, could do nothing, but were carried away in the general stream. In this state of disorder and violence, the Commons disappeared, or if they were not materially annihilated, their political power vanished. The high aristocracy worked its own dissolution; many great families were destroyed, and many more were ruined. Henry VII., at his accession, found only the wreck of that nobility which had made his predecessors tremble. The great barons, wearied with their own excesses, and stripped of a great part of their resources, were no longer inclined or able to continue that struggle against the royal power, which had been headed by their ancestors ever since the days of king John. On this side therefore, the royal power no longer had any powerful antagonists. On the other side, the Commons, wasted and enervated by civil war, were not in a condition to take the place of the high aristocracy in the struggle against the royal authority. They had taken part in the government as followers of the nobles; and when they found themselves standing almost alone in presence of the crown, it did not even occur to them that this interference was their right: they, therefore, contented themselves with defending a few special rights, particularly that of consenting to large subsidies; and, in other respects, they allowed themselves to be governed. Hence arose the government of Henry VIII., and at a later period, that of Elizabeth.

More than a century was requisite to enable the English Commons—reinvigorated and strengthened, in a material point of view, by long years of order

---

1. This is yet another illustration of Guizot's emphasis on antagonism and competition in a free society. It will be recalled that for Guizot, it was the equilibrium between various political powers and principles of social organization that had led to the preservation and strengthening of liberty in England. He concludes his historical investigation by arguing that liberty can be established only when there is no single power capable of stifling the development of others to the point of usurping authority and becoming absolute. The same idea can be found in *HCE:* "Nothing but the general freedom of all rights, all interests, and all opinions, the free manifestation and legal coexistence of all these forces, can ever restrain each force and each power within its legitimate limits, prevent it from encroaching on the rest" (*HCE*, p. 244).

and prosperity, and in a moral point of view, by the reformation of religion—to acquire sufficient social importance and intellectual elevation to place themselves, in their turn, at the head of the resistance against despotism, and to draw the ancient aristocracy in their train. This great revolution in the state of society broke out in the reign of Charles I., and determined that political revolution, which, after fifty years of conflict, finally established representative government in England.

THE END

INDEX

abbots, *see* religion and the church

absolute power: acceptance of, 52; Anglo-Norman government, 254–55; division of powers interfering with concept of, 228–29; 372–74, 433–34; English Revolution overthrowing, 435; epoch of pure monarchy, 14–15, 222; imbalance of powers leading to, 433–34; individual will or right, Guizot's criticism of absolutist concept of, xiii, xv, 39–40, 44, 49, 52, 60–65, 112–13, 134–37, 273, 286–95, 297, 360–61; operational, 67; Parliamentary resistance to, 414–24; representative government not admitting of, 226–27, 371; Roman empire, contribution of despotism to fall of, 155–56, 160–66; social state and rise of, 136; sovereignty, theory of, 226; traces found at basis of free governments, 48; Tudor monarchy, 432, 434; universal tempering of, 50–51; Visigoths, not limited amongst, 199–202

Acts of Oxford, 303–8

Adalhard (Abbot of Corbia), 143

Adalides, 211–12

Adela (wife of Stephen, Count of Blois), 234

administrative power, 246–47; centralization, tendency towards, 246–47; nature of, 246; Parliamentary interventions, 406, 408–11, 415–24

aedelis, 171

aerarium, 98

Aetius, Patrician of Gaul, 22, 155

Agila (Visigothic king), 181

Alans, 23, 178, 179

Alaric I (King of Visigoths), 73

Alaric II (King of Visigoths), 73, 180, 185

Albiney, William d', 270

Alboin, 24

aldermen, 37–38

Alemanni, 73

Alexander (Pope), 237

Alexander the Great, 68

Alfaqueque, 211, 213

Alfred (King of England), 26, 31, 35, 38

allodial lands, 91–94; beneficiary lands and, 97, 109, 110; defined, 91–92; etymology of term, 92; feudalism, continuation after, 110; individual independence and isolation, 112–13; male/female inheritance patterns, 92–93; military service as obligation connected with, 94–97; obligations connected to holding of, 93–94; salic land as type of, 92; social class and, 117–19

Almocaden, 211, 213

Alonso the Wise, 210, 211

Amalaric (Visigothic king), 180–81

America, electoral processes in, 344

Anastasius (Emperor), 73

Andely, treaty of, 101, 103, 124

Anglo-Normans, 231–57, 298, 378, 379–80, *see also* Norman Conquest of England

Anglo-Saxons, 24–27, 227–28, 378, 379–80; Briton resistance against, 155; corporations or associations, 36–37; courts, 37; Danish invasions, 25–26; dissolution, tendency towards, 242–43; feudalism and, 30–31; Heptarchy, 24–25, 39; institutions of, 28, 33–34, 35–40, 240–45; invasion of England by, 24, 25; juries, 37–38; male-only inherited (salic) land, 92; monarchy, 42, 43–46; Norman Conquest of, *see* Norman Conquest of England; revolts against Normans, 232, 233; social classes, 29–33; territorial subdivisions, 35–38; towns of, 40, 44; *wehrgeld*, 121; Wittenagemot, 39–44, 69, 196, 202, 228, 242–43, 247, 249, 378, 427

Anianus, refendary of Alaric II, 180

Anselm (Archbishop of Canterbury), 248

antagonism, role of, 129–30, 381, 399–400, 434

antiqua noviter emendata, 186

Antrustions (Leudes), 123–26, 130, 132, 139, 141, 142, 200, 201 apocrisiary, 145

Aquitaine, kingdom of, 73, 76, 85, 86

Arab world: Turkish janissaries, 50; Visigoths and, 184, 201, 216–18

Arcadius (Emperor), 21

Arianism, 181, 182, 183

aristocracy: Anglo-Norman, 252–57; Barons, Council of, see Barons, Council of; barons (English) as special class of vassal, 250–53, 299–300; beneficiary lands granted by, 108–10; dissolution into independent sovereignties, 149–51; Edward the Confessor and, 26; Edward I and, 278–81; etymology of term, 56–57; Franks, 78–79, 83, 84–85, 87; government by, 56–59; Great Charter articles addressing interests of, 267–68, 269; Henry III and, 273–76, 302–5; hereditary status following Charlemagne, 138; House of Lords, see House of Lords; House of Peers (France) and plurality of powers, 53; John King of England's struggles with, 264; 265–66; knights and freeholders versus, 301–5; Leudes as, 124–25, 132; Louis the Débonnair and, 85–86; monarchy versus, 129–30, 381, 400, 434; Norman, 243–44; Roman empire, privileged classes of, 167–68; thanes as, 30; Visigothic *officium palatinum*, 200–202; Wittenagemot, attendance at, 39

Armorica and Armoricans, 21, 22, 73

Arthur (King of Britain), 25

Arthur, Duke of Bretagne, 264

assemblies: Anglo-Saxon territorial divisions by, 35–39; Barons, Council of, see Barons, Council of; Capet, Hugh, dissolution under, 149; Chamber of Deputies (France), plurality of powers in, 53; *Champs de Mars* and *Mai*, 69–70, 142, 143, 149, 196, 197, 199, 202; Charlemagne, held under, 137, 143–48; England, 228, 246–51, 254–55, 256, 269, 299–300, 309, 320–27, 354, 377–81, 427, see also Barons, Council of; Parliament; Wittenagemot; Franks, 80–81, 131–33, 137, 142–50, 196; Germanic tribes, 39, 377–78; monarchy, coexistence with, 380–81; monarchy, convoked by, 43–44; Parlia-

ment, see Parliament; Pavia, assembly of Lombards at, 70, 196; *placitum*, 131, 196; Rome, *comitia* of, 157, 158, 160; Rome, senate of, 167, 168; Toledo, councils of, 182–84, 186, 188, 190–93, 196–99, 205–6, 217; Visigoths, 182, 196–97, 202, see also Toledo, councils of; Wittenagemot, 39–44, 69, 196, 202, 228, 242–43, 247, 249, 378, 427

assessors, 37–38, 204

associations or corporations, 36–37

Ataulphus (Visigothic leader), 179

Athanagild (Visigothic king), 181

Athelstane (King of England), 37, 40, 44

Attila, 179

Augustus (Emperor), 21, 23

Aurelian (Emperor), 71

Austrasia, 75, 76–79, 80, 95, 96

Avitus, *magister militiae*, 179

bachelors, English, 304–5

barbarian epoch, 13, 222

barbarians, see Germanic tribes

Barons, Council of, 228, 229, 246–51, 309; devolution, trend towards, 256; Great Charter, powers granted by, 269, 299; Henry III, charters of, 273, 274, 275; irregularity of, 250; John King of England, under, 264, 265–66, see also Great Charter; members of, 250–51; Oxford, assembly of 1214 meeting at, 264, 300–301; Parliament replacing, 298; powers of, 254–55; Runymead, conference of, 265; Stamford assembly of 1215, 265; Wallingford assembly of 1215, 265

barons (English) as special class of vassal, 250–53, 299–300

Basques, 181, 182

Bavarians, 120, 121, 132

Beaumont, Gustave de, x

Becket, Thomas (Archbishop of Canterbury), 235–38, 249

Belgium, 98, 99

beneficiary lands, 91, 98–110; allodial lands and, 97, 109, 110; arbitrary and absolute will of donor regarding, 101–2; aristocracy, grants made by, 108–10; *census* (fees) as obligation of holding, 106; defined, 98; feudalism and, 97, 98; fidelity and loyalty as obligation of holding, 106–7; hereditary status of, 99–100, 103–4; influential nature of principle of, 114; kings, grants made by, 101–7; legal reasons for revocation of, 101–2; life, conferred for, 99–100, 103; limited time, granted for, 102–3; method of holding, 99–105; military service and, 106; obligations attached to, 105–7; origins of, 98–99; religious institutions' holdings, 125–26; revocability of, 99–102; service as obligation of holding, 106; social class, 118–19

Berry, assassination of Duke of, ix, xviii–xx

Bertrade (wife of Pepin the Short), 80

Bigod, Roger, Earl of Norfolk, Lord Marshal of England, 278, 279, 281, 317

bishops, *see* religion and the church

Black Book of the Exchequer, 321

Black Prince (son of Edward III), 410, 411

Bohun, Humphrey, Earl of Hereford, Constable of England, 278, 279, 317

Bolbech, Guilbon, 321

Bolingbroke, Henry, Duke of Hereford, *See* Henry IV (King of England)

Bonaparte, Napoleon, 246

Boniface, bishop of Mayence, 80

Book of Fiefs, 101

boroughs, *see* towns and boroughs

Bourbon Restoration, ix–xi, xviii–xx

bourgeois, *see* middle class

Bracton, Henry de, 229

Brady, 248

Breviarium Aniani, 180, 185, 206–9

Britain, *see* England

Britons, 231

Brooke, Sir Thomas, 427

Bruce, David (King of Scots), 408

Brunehaut/Brunhault (Queen), 78, 181

Burckhardt, bishop of Wurtzburg, 80

burgage-tenure, 326

Burghersh, Sir Bartholomew, 407

Burgundians/kingdom of Burgundy, 23, 73, 75, 76, 87, 89, 92, 120, 121, 132, 180, 181

Burnet, Bishop, 223

Bury, merchant of London, 410

Bussy, Sir John, 422

Cambridge University deputies to Parliament, 317

Canute (King of England), 26

capacity: children, limitations on liberty of, 293–94, 362; concept of, 175; election, right of, 333–38, 342, 346, 348, 350; Guizot's theory of, 175, 338, 351; incapacitated, limitations on liberty of, 294; social class and, 333–35; variability of conditions of, 336–38

Capet, Hugh, 83, 87, 91, 139, 149, 242

Carloman of Haspengau (patriarch of Pepin family), 76, 78–81

Carloman (son of Charles Martel), 80, 102

Carlovingians, 76, 78–88, 98, 99, 134, 139, 149, 247

Carte, 248, 353

census (fees): beneficiary lands, as obligation for, 106; tributary lands, 111

centenarius, 38, 203

centgrafen, 131

centralized institutions: Anglo-Saxons, 33–34, 39–40, 242–43; Continent, centralization on, 247; division of central power, importance of, 374; Franks, 82–83, 138; Parliament, 309–10; Roman municipal system, 159, 162, 173–74

ceorls, 29, 31–33

chamberlain, 145

Chamber of Deputies (France), plurality of powers in, 53

Champs de Mars and *Mai,* 69–70, 142, 143, 149, 196, 197, 199, 202

Chancery, 254, 327

Chararich (Frankish leader), 99

Charles Martel, 79–80, 102, 103, 105, 109, 136

Charles the Great/Charlemagne, 84–85, 134–41; assemblies held under, 137, 143–48; beneficiary lands and, 99, 102, 103, 104, 106, 108, 109; centralization, tendency towards, 82; division of estates amongst children, 76; free institutions apparently revived under, 134–37; government of, 134–41; Leudes of, 124, 125, 130; military service, imposition of, 96; monarchy's strength under, 130, 137–41; Normans in reign of, 86; reign of, 84–85; *wehrgeld,* 121

Charles the Bald, 86, 96, 97, 99, 103, 104, 107, 138, 149
Charles the Fat, 87
Charles the Simple, 87
Charles I (King of England), 70, 435
Charles II (King of England), 70, 390–91
charters, English, 239, 257, 258–62; Clement V (Pope) letter declaring Edward I's confirmations null and void, 281, 283–84; confirmation of charters by Edward I, 280, 281–83, 317; confirmation of charters by Henry III, 308; Edward I, charters of, 277–84; forests, charters relating to, 269–70, 274, 413; Henry I, charters of, 259–60, 265–66; Henry II, charters of, 261; Henry III, charters of, 272–76; John, *Magna Charta* and, *see* Great Charter; John, possible forest charter of, 269–70; *Magna Charta* or Great Charter, *see* Great Charter; Parliamentary sessions beginning with confirmation of, 413; Stephen, charters of, 260–61; violations of, 259, 260, 269, 270, 274–75, 278–80; William I, charter of, 259
charters, Frankish, 128
Chaucer, Sir Thomas, 426
Cheddre, Richard, 427
Childebert I (son of Clovis), 75
Childebert II (Merovingian king), 76, 101, 105, 123, 124
Childeric I (Frankish leader), 72
Childeric III (Merovingian king), 80, 139
children, limitations on liberty of, 293–94, 362
Chilperic (Merovingian king), 78, 96, 105
Chindasuinth (Visigothic king), 103, 183, 184, 185, 186, 209, 217
Chintila (Visigothic king), 183
Chlodomir (son of Clovis), 75
Christianity, *see* religion and the church
the church, *see* religion and the church
Cimbri, 23
Cinque ports, early political importance of, 310
cities, *see* towns and boroughs
Civil War, English, *see* English Revolution
civitates faederatae, 158

Cixilone (daughter of Erwig), 184
Clarendon, Council and Constitutions of, 235–38, 249
Clarendon, Lord, 223
clarissimi, 167, 168
Clement V (Pope), 281, 283–84
clergy, *see* religion and the church
Clodion (Frankish leader), 72
Clotaire I (son of Clovis), 75, 76, 77
Clotaire II (Merovingian king), 75, 76, 77, 78
cloth and wool industry, Parliamentary protection of, 412
Clotilda (Merovingian Queen), 103
Clovis I (Frankish leader and Merovingian king), 24, 72–75, 99, 100, 180
Clovis II (Merovingian king), 76, 77, 96
Codex Gregorianus, 180
Codex Hermogenianus, 180
Codex Theodosianus, 180
Coere, 157, 166
coining money, 41–42
Coke, Sir Edward, 210
coloniae, 158
combat, trial by, 210, 213
comitia of Rome, 157, 158, 160
Comitre, 211, 213
Commons, House of, *see* House of Commons
Commune Concilium, 248
communitas bachelariae Angliae, 304–5
competition and antagonism, role of, 129–30, 381, 399–400, 434
compurgation, ordeal by, 210, 213, 214
compurgatores (witnesses), 38
Concilium/Concilium regni, 247, 248
conflict, role of, 129–30, 381, 399–400, 434
conjuratores, 131
Conservators of the Peace, 404
Constant, Benjamin, viii
Constantine (Emperor), 72, 162, 163, 164, 165
Constantius (Emperor), 72
constitutional monarchy, epoch of, 14, 222
Constitutiones Imperiales, 180
copyhold, 336
corporations or associations, 36–37
Cortes, acts of, 210, 222
counties: Anglo-Norman, 253, 254; Anglo-Saxon, 35–38; deputies to Parliament

from county, introduction of, 298–305, 307, 308, 315–19, 354, 355–57; election of Parliamentary representatives, 320–27; Franks, 131–33
counts (Frankish), 131–33, 138
courts: Anglo-Norman, 253–54; Anglo-Saxon, 37, 42, 43; county-courts, English, 320–27, 339–40; Frankish, 131; Visigothic, 203–5; Wittenagemot functioning as, 42, 43
crime: Visigothic legislation on, 194–95; *wehrgeld,* 119–22
Cromwell, Oliver, 7
Crusades, 233, 238, 276, 277
curatores, 171–72
curator reipublicae, 171
curia, 159, 169–71, 178, 207, 209
Curia de more, 247, 248
curials, 167–71, 175–77
Curia regis, 247, 248, 249, 253

Dagobert I (Merovingian king), 75, 76, 77, 182, 183
danegeld, 253, 260, 261
Danish invasions of England, 25–26
David, Prince of Wales, 315
De caede et morte hominum, 194
decanus and *decanus ruralis,* 36, 131, 203
decurions, 159, 161, 169
defensores, 172, 203, 207, 208, 209
democratic governments, 59–65
denariales, 127, 128
De Ordine Palatini (On the Order of the Palace), 143–47
Deputies, Chamber of, *see* Chamber of Deputies (France)
Despencer, Hugh le, elder and younger, 383–84, 387
despotism, *see* absolute power
Diocletian (Emperor), 21, 161, 162
direct election, 344–47, 349
dissolution, tendency towards: Anglo-Saxons, 242–43; Frankish kingdoms, 75–76, 83–88
divine law, 51, 187–88, 295
division of powers: absolute power, interfering with concept of, 228–29, 372–74, 433–34; central power, importance of

division of, 374; effects of early development of, 228–29; England, characteristic of, 228; imbalance of powers, effect of, 433–34; key characteristic of representative government, as, 53, 67–69, 227, 371–76; liberty and, 228–29, 373, 375, 433–34; Parliament's division into two houses, 268, 316–17, 353–76, 401
doctrinaire movement, viii, ix
Doomsday Book, 244, 278
Dublin, Robert de Vere, Marquis of, 419
dukes (Frankish), 132–33
duumvir, 171, 207, 208

Eadmer, 233
ecclesiastical powers, *see* religion and the church
economics: *"Enrichissez-vous,"* xv–xvi; Franks, difficulty of wealth creation under landed property system of, 113–14; taxation, *see* taxation; towns and boroughs, *see* towns and boroughs
Edgar Atheling, 233, 242
Edinburgh Review article on Visigoths, 206, 210–18
Edward the Confessor (King of England), 26, 31, 38, 231–32, 234, 242, 244, 260, 261, 266, 308
Edward I (King of England), 252, 257 258, 276, 277–84, 298, 300, 304, 307, 308, 313–17, 324, 327, 354, 355, 381, 382, 387, 401
Edward II (King of England), 353, 354, 382–88, 408, 412, 423
Edward III (King of England), 232, 323, 325, 327, 353, 354, 355, 384, 392, 399–413, 414, 415, 425, 432
Edward the Black Prince (son of Edward III), 410, 411
Edward IV (King of England), 433
Egbert (King of Wessex), 25
Egica (Visigothic king), 184
Egidius (master of Roman militia at Soissons), 72
Eginhard, 102
Eleanor of Guienne (Queen of England, wife of Henry II), 235

election: abuses, Parliamentary concern over, 412; assembling of electors, 340–42; Barons, Council of, not found in, 251; capacity and right of, 333–38, 342, 346, 348, 350; classes and characteristics of electors, 332–38; counties, Parliamentary representatives for, 320–27; deliberation and, 340; development of system, 328–30; direct election, 344–47, 349; false/incomplete/contested elections, 424, 431; fourteenth century, during, 328–38; Frankish assemblies, 80–81; freeholders, role of, 320–27, 333–34, 335–36; indirect election, 347–50; key characteristic of representative government, 69, 227; landowning status and, 320–27, 333–34, 335–36, 337; majority rule, 59–65, 289, 334, 348–49; minority, respect for, 348–49; monarch's influence over, 412; natural rather than theoretical practice of, 328–30; number of choices required in, 342–43; number of electors, 347; open voting, 350–51; party influence, 343; plurality of powers, importance of, 53–54; procedures and forms, 339–52; purpose and object of, 340; regulation of elections, 431; Richard II's interference with, 420; rights, arising out of, 328–32, 344; secret voting, 351; sessions of Parliament and, 401; thirteenth century, during, 320–27; time required to undertake, 344; towns and boroughs, Parliamentary representatives for, 320, 324–27; universal suffrage, 289, 334, 344, 350; Visigothic kings, 181, 183, 190, 191–93

Elizabeth I (Queen of England), 434

Ellis, merchant of London, 410

Emma (wife of Raoul, King of Franks), 87

enfranchisement, 127–28

England, see also individual rulers: Anglo-Normans, 231–57, 298, 378, 379–80; Anglo-Saxon period, see Anglo-Saxons; assemblies, 228, 246–51, 254–55, 256, 269, 299–300, 309, 320–27, 354, 377–81, 427, see also Barons, Council of; Parliament; Wittenagemot; Barons, Council of, see Barons, Council of; charters of, see charters, English; Cromwellian Revolution/Civil War, see English Revolution; Danish invasions, 25–26; electoral processes in modern Britain, 344; feudalism in, 242–44, 252–57; France contrasted with, 43, 433; historical sketch from Norman Conquest to Richard I, 231–39; Houses of Parliament, see House of Commons; House of Lords; Parliament; local institutions surviving in, 247; Magna Charta, see Great Charter; Norman Conquest, see Norman Conquest of England; Parliament, see House of Commons; House of Lords; Parliament; privy council, 248, 315, 386, 392, 429, 431; representative government, development of, 222, 227–30, 433–35; Roman empire, fall of, 21–22; towns and cities, development of, 239, 251; uninterrupted and successful development of representative government in, 222; Wars of the Roses, 381

English bachelors (communitas bachelariae Angliae), 304–5

English Revolution: historical study and, 223; House of Commons and, 381; representative government, restoration of, 434–35

enquiry, Parliamentary right of, 392, 395, 396–97

"Enrichissez-vous," xv–xvi

epochs of political institutions of Europe, 13–16, 221–23

equality/inequality, 60–65, 152, 366–70, 373

equilibrium of powers, importance of, 433–34

Erwig (Visigothic king), 184

escuages, 261, 267, 268, 273, 274

Etichon (brother-in-law of Louis the Débonnair), 110, 118

Eudes (Duke of Aquitaine), 76

Eudes (King of Franks), 87, 103

Euric (Visigothic king), 109, 180, 181, 185, 186

Exchequer: Black Book of the, 321; Court of, 253–54; Red Book of the, 259

excommunication of kings, 190

executive power, 246–47

Exeter, Bishop of (chancellor of Richard II), 422

fact: historic school on division of Parliament, 360, 365–66; philosophic school on division of Parliament, 363–65, 366; sovereignty of, xiii, xiv, 80, 226

Faguet, Émile, vii

family as origin of society, 49

Favila (Duke of Biscay), 184

favoritism, monarchial: Edward II, 383–84; Edward III in his dotage, 409–11; Richard II, 419–20

fee-farm, 310, 326

fees *(census):* beneficiary lands, 106; tributary lands, 111

Ferdinand the Saint, 186

feudalism, 13–14, 151–52; allodial lands surviving, 110, *see also* allodial lands; Anglo-Saxon thanes and, 30–31; aristocracy's dissolution into independent sovereignties under, 149–51; beneficiary lands and, 97, 98, *see also* beneficiary lands; early rudiments of, 131–32; England, in, 242–44, 252–57; epoch of, 13–14, 222; escuages, 261, 267, 268, 273, 274; Great Charter, 267–68; hierarchy of persons as origin of, 30–31, 35; justice and, 152; landed property conditions leading to, 112–14; loyalty and fidelity, duty of, 106–7, 124; military service as obligation under, *see* military service as obligation; monarchy versus, 150–52; Norman Conquest and, 242–44; recommendation as feature of, 110; rise of, 149–52; royalty, replacing diminishing authority of, 107, 129–30; service, duty of, *see* service, duty of; tributary lands and, 111; vassals, *see* vassals and vassalage

fidei commissus, 161

fidelity and loyalty, duty of: beneficiary lands, 106–7; Leudes, 124

fijo d'algo, 214

fines (freda), 132

fiscus, 98

Fitzwilliam, Godfrey, 321

Flanders, 98

Flavius Egica, 210

Florence of Worcester, 250

Fontenay, battle of, 86

forced loans, 424

forests, charters of, 269–70, 274, 413

Fortescue, Sir John, 229, 427

Forum judicum (fuero juzgo), 184, 186–95, 203–17

France, *see also* Franks; Gaul: Chamber of Deputies, plurality of powers in, 53; England contrasted with, 43, 433; House of Peers, plurality of powers in, 53; institutions of, 33, 34; plurality of powers in, 53; royal domain, control of, 42

Francia Romana, 77

Francia Teutonica, 77

Franks, 23, 24, *see also individual rulers;* allodial lands, *see* allodial lands; aristocracy, 78–79, 83, 84–85, 87; assemblies, 80–81, 131–33, 137, 142–50, 196; Carlovingians, 76, 78–88, 98, 99, 134, 139, 149, 247; centralized institutions, 82–83; *Champs de Mars* and *Mai,* 69–70, 142, 143, 149, 196, 197, 199, 202; Charlemagne, *see* Charles the Great/Charlemagne; Clovis, conquests of, 24, 72–75; division of territory leading to dispersal of royal power, 75–76, 83–88; early Frankish chieftains, 71–74; Gaul, invasion of, 71–72, 89, 92, 110, 150, 155; institutions of, 89–100, 129–33, 149–50; juridic arrangements, 131, 133; landed proprietors, 131, 133; landownership, types of, 91; Mayors of the Palace, 78, 80, 83, 99, 142; Merovingian period, 75–83, 95–96, 132, 133, 134, 136, 139, 142, 149; monarchy, 130, 132–33, 138–41; Normans in Carlovingian kingdoms, 86–87; origins of, 71, 77; Pepin the Short and Pepin family, 76, 78–85, 98, 99, 102, 103, 136, 139, 143; Roman empire and, 71–73, 78, 125; social classes, 115–28; tributary lands, 91, 110–12, 119; Visigoths and, 73, 75, 180, 181, 182, 183; *wehrgeld,* 119–22

freda (fines), 132

Fredegonde, 78

freedom generally, *see* liberty

freedom of speech, 426–27

freeholders: electoral rights and, 320–27, 333–34, 335–36, 337; monarchy and aristocracy, knights and freeholders versus, 301–5 free individual will or right, Guizot's criticism of, xiii, xv, 39–40, 44, 49, 52, 60–65, 112–13, 134–37, 273, 286–95, 297, 360–61

French liberalism, vii–viii, xi–xii, xiv

French Revolution, vii, xii, xiv

Frisons, 121

Fuero juzgo (Forum judicum), 184, 186–95, 203–17

Fueros of Castile and Leon, 210–11, 214

Fulrad (Abbot of St. Denis), 80

Gaius, 207

Gaul: corporations or associations, 36–37; Frankish invasion of, 71–72, 89, 92, 110, 150, 155, *see also* Franks; Jews in, 182; Normans in, 27, 86–87; Roman empire, fall of, 21–24; tributary lands of, 110; Visigoths in, 89, 179–81

Gaunt, John of, Duke of Lancaster, 409–10, 417, 422, 423

Gaveston, Piers, 383, 384

Geoffrey, Duke of Bretagne, 235

Germanic tribes: Alans, 23, 178, 179; Alemanni, 73; Anglo-Saxons, *see* Anglo-Saxons; Armorica and Armoricans, 21, 22, 73; Burgundians/kingdom of Burgundy, 23, 73, 75, 76, 87, 89, 92, 120, 121, 132, 180, 181; Franks, *see* Franks; Huns, 179; Lombards, 24, 70, 80, 83, 92, 101, 109, 110, 127, 196; political institutions of, 13, 20–24, 30, 31, 32, 36, 39, 48, 92, 98, 105–6, 109, 110, 116, 129, 131, 142, 378; Roman empire and, 154–56, 162, 166; Sarmatians, 71; Suevi, 23, 73, 179, 181; Visigoths, *see* Visigoths; *wehrgeld*, 119–22

Gesalic (Visigothic king), 180

Gibbon, Edward, 223

Gifford, Walter, Earl, 321

Gloucester, Humphrey, Duke of, 422

Godwin, Earl, 26, 31, 242

Gontran, 101, 123, 124

Goths generally: incursions of, 23; Middle Ages, survival of Gothic law in Spain during, 210–18; Ostrogoths, 73, 180, 181, 202; Roman maxims and institutions, continuing predominance of, 201–2; Visigoths, *see* Visigoths

governments, 56–59; aristocratic, 56–59; Charlemagne's government, 134–41; democratic, 59–65; form and principle, relationship between, 48, 66–67; functions of, 246–47; goal and purpose of, 135; House of Commons' involvement in government of state, 406–13; mixed nature of most actual governments, 47–48, 58–59; Parliament's relationship to government, 378–81, 391–93, 432; representative, *see* representative government; social and political order, relationship between, *see* social and political order, relationship between; social right, principle of, 50; sovereignty of a government, its theory of, 226; types of, 56, 226

grafen, 131

Great Britain, *see* England

Great Charter, 239, 266–70; annulment by John, attempt at, 270; aristocracy, interests of, 267–68, 269; articles of, 267–69; assembly, powers of, 269; Barons, right of vassals to appear at Council of, 267, 299; clergy, interests of, 267; divisions of, 267; feudal institutions, 267–68; London and other towns and cities, provisions regarding, 268–69; merchants, provisions regarding, 269; Parliamentary sessions beginning with confirmation of, 413; the people generally, interests of, 267–69; Runnymead, conference at, 265; separation of two houses of Parliament, origins of, 268

Great Council *(Magnum Concilium)*, 247, 248, 377–78, 429, *see also* Barons, Council of

Great Schools Law, x

Gregory I the Great (Pope), 182

Gregory IV (Pope), 86

Grisella (wife of Rollo the Norman), 87

Grisons, Switzerland, 36

Guizot, François-Pierre-Guillaume: ambassador to London, x; biographical details, viii–xi; capacity, theory of, 175, 338, 351; historian, career as, ix–x, xv; historical method pioneered by, xii–

xiii, 5; historical topics pioneered by, x, xii–xiii; individual will or right, criticism of concept of, xiii, xv, 39–40, 44, 49, 52, 60–65, 112–13, 134–37, 273, 286–95, 297, 360–61; *juste milieu* theory of good government, 351; lectures given by, x, xviii; middle class, as defender of, xv–xvi; philosophical views of, xii–xiii; political career of, ix–x, xviii–xx; political philosophy of, xii–xiii, xv–xvi, 297; political science, criticism of, 328–30; powers, theory of, 331–32; Protestantism of, viii, xi; Rousseau's ideas, criticism of, xiii, 49, 273, 286–89, 295, 297; social and political order, importance to Guizot's thought of relationship between, 19, 28–29; social contract, criticism of idea of, xiii, 49, 273, 286–89; Soult–Guizot Cabinet, x; "true" principles of representative government according to, xv, 47–55, 61–65, 134–37, 226–27, 285–97, 345, 351; writings of, ix, x, xi, xvii, 297

Gundemar (Visigothic king), 182

Gustavus Vasa, 26

Hadrian (Emperor), 161

haereditas, 92

Hale, 248

Hallam, Henry, 392, 406, 429

Harold (King of England), 26, 232, 242

Haxey, Thomas, 422, 426

Heineccius, 204

Helvidius Priscus, 17

Hengist (Anglo-Saxon leader), 24, 25

Henry (nephew of Louis the Débonnair), 110

Henry I (King of England), 233–34, 255, 256, 259–60, 265–66

Henry II (King of England), 234–38, 248, 249, 250, 253, 255, 268, 274, 310

Henry III (King of England), 228, 229, 272–76, 277, 300, 301, 302, 306–9, 313, 326, 383, 405, 408

Henry IV (King of England), 229, 323, 324, 327, 381, 415, 423, 425, 427, 431, 432

Henry V (King of England), 392, 425, 428, 431, 432

Henry VI (King of England), 323, 392, 425, 427, 430, 431, 432, 434

Henry VII (King of England), 381, 434

Henry IV (King of France), 26

Heptarchy, Anglo-Saxon, 24–25, 39

Heraclius (Emperor), 182

hereditary status: aristocracy following Charlemagne, 138; beneficiary lands, 99–100, 103–4; curials, 168, 169; monarchy, 139, 181, 190, 191–93; Parliament, right to attend, 318, 367; salic land, 92; Visigothic kings, 181

Hereford, Henry Bolinbroke, Duke of, *See* Henry IV (King of England)

Hereford, Humphrey Bohun, Earl of; Constable of England, 278, 279, 317

Heretogs, 45

Hermenegild (son of Leovigild), 181

Herodotus, 222

Heruli, 24

Hincmar (Archbishop of Reims), 137, 143

historic school on division of Parliament, 359–60; 365–366

history, study of: Bourbon Restoration, during, xi–xii; development of, 222–25; disdain for past, 6–8; early societies, in, 222–23; epochs of political institutions of Europe, 13–16; goal and purpose, 16–18; Guizot's historical career, ix–x, xv; Guizot's pioneering methods, xii–xiii, 5; Guizot's pioneering topics, x, xii–xiii; liberty, and search for, 223, 224; philosophical history, 222–24; poetic history, 222–23; politics and, 222–25; practical history, 223–24; present times affecting understanding of past, 3–6, 9–10; public life and, 224–25; veneration for past, 8–9

Homer, 222, 224

homicide: Visigothic legislation on, 194–95; *wehrgeld*, 119–22

homines ecclesiastici, 127

homines regii, 127

honorati, 208

Honorius (Emperor), 21, 162

Honorius III (Pope), 274

Horsa (Anglo-Saxon leader), 24

House of Commons: administration and ministers of King, intervention in questions of, 406, 408–11, 415–24; county deputies, introduction of, 298–305, 307, 308, 315–19, 354, 355–57; division of county and town/borough representatives, 355–57; division of Parliament into two houses, origins of, 268, 316–17, 353–76, 401; division of powers, importance of principle of, 229; Edward II's reign, condition during, 382–88; Edward III's reign, condition during, 399–413; election of Parliamentary representatives, *see* election; English Revolution and, 381; government of state, involvement in, 406–13; importance, increase in, 328, 339, 399; joining of county and town/borough representatives, 356–57; legislation, participation in, 403–5; papacy and clergy, resistance to, 411–12; Perers (Pierce), Alice, attack on, 409–11; petitions by or to, *see* petitions; publicity, institution of, 70; resistance of monarchial power by, 400; right to assent to laws and statutes, 387; social structure leading to institution of, 366; Speaker of, 401, 415, 422, 426, 427; towns and boroughs, representatives of, 298, 308, 310–12, 315–19, 354, 355–57; union of Houses to consider certain questions in common, 412–13; war and peace, intervention in questions of, 406–8; Wittenagemot, origins in, 44

House of Lords: division of Parliament into two houses, origins of, 268, 316–17, 353–76, 401; Edward II's reign, condition during, 382–88; elections, judgment of, 431; fourteenth century interests of barons, 356–57; hereditary right to attend, 318, 367; judicial power of Parliament restricted to, 431; Lancastrians, still regarded as king's great council under, 429–30; origins and characteristics of, 366–76; petitions by or to, *see* petitions; social structure leading to institution of, 366; union of Houses to consider certain questions in common, 412–13; Wittenagemot, origins in, 44

House of Peers (France), plurality of powers in, 53

Hubert de Burgh, 274, 275

Hugh Capet, 83, 87, 91, 139, 149, 242

Hugo the Great (Duke of France), 87

Hullmann, Dr., 90, 98

Hume, David, 223

hundreds: Anglo-Normans, 253; Anglo-Saxons, 35–38; Franks, 131–33

Hungerford, Sir Thomas, 401

Huns, 179

Iliad, 74

imbalance of powers, effect of, 433–34

immunity/inviolability of members of Parliament, 427–28

imposts, *see* taxation

incapacitated, limitations on liberty of, 294

indirect election, 347–50

individual will or right, Guizot's criticism of, xiii, xv, 39–40, 44, 49, 52, 60–65, 112–13, 134–37, 273, 286–95, 297, 360–61

inequality/equality, 60–65, 152, 366–70, 373

initiative, Parliamentary right of, 392, 395, 428–31

inlands, 32, 92

Innocent III (Pope), 265, 270

Innocent IV (Pope), 302

institutions: Anglo-Saxon, 28, 33–34, 35–40, 240–45; centralized, *see* centralized institutions; Charlemagne, free institutions apparently revived under, 134–37; France, 33, 34; Franks, 89–100, 129–33, 149–50; Germanic tribes, political institutions of, 13, 20–24, 30, 31, 32, 36, 39, 48, 92, 98, 105–6, 109, 110, 116, 129, 131, 142, 378; local, *see* local institutions; Visigoths, 196–218

Ireland, English conquest of, 238, 261

irenarchae, 171

Irving, Washington, 184

Isabella (Queen of England, wife of Edward II), 384

Islam: Turkish janissaries, 50; Visigoths and, 184, 201, 216–18

isolation, liberty of, 37, 112–13, 133

Italian resistance to Germanic invasions, lack of, 155

janissaries, 50

Jean (Frankish noble), 103–4

Jews: English massacre of, 238; Visigoths and, 182, 184

John Lackland (King of England), 238–39, 250, 256, 258, 262, 263–71, 272, 273, 274, 281, 300, 301, 302, 432, 434, *see also* Great Charter

judges summoned to English Parliament, 315, 319

judices, 131

judicial processes, *see* justice and judicial processes

Judith (wife of Louis the Débonnair), 110

Julian (Count), 184

Julian (Emperor), 9, 72, 165

July Revolution, x

juries, 37–38, 210–13

Juste milieu theory of good government, 351

justice and judicial processes, *see also* law: Anglo-Norman, 249, 253–54; courts, *see* courts; feudalism and, 152; Franks, 131, 133; Great Charter, 268; House of Lords, Parliamentary judicial power restricted to, 431; power of government, as, 246–47; Roman municipal system, 159, 172; social class and, 29; Visigothic judicial system, 203–5; Visigothic laws, 103, 109, 180, 181, 184, 185–95, 203–18; Wittenagemot and, 42, 43

Justinian (Emperor), 181

kingship, *see* monarchy

knights of the shires introduced into Parliament, 298–305, 307, 308, 315–19

Knyghton, 419

La Cava (daughter of Count Julian), 184

Lake, William, 427

Lancaster, House of, 415, 424–34, *see also individual Lancastrian monarchs*

Lancaster, John of Gaunt, Duke of, 409–10, 417, 422, 423

landowners and landed property, *see also* aristocracy; allodial lands, *see* allodial lands; Anglo-Saxon institutions, role in, 37–38, 40, 41; beneficiary lands, *see* beneficiary lands; copyhold, 336; diversity in conditions of property, 112;

electoral rights and, 333–34, 335–36; feudalism, conditions leading to, 112–14; Franks, 91, 131, 133; freeholders, electoral rights and, 320–27, 333–34, 335–36, 337; freeholders, monarchy and aristocracy versus, 301–5; individual independence and isolation, 112–13; social classes and, 90–91, 115–19; tributary lands, 91, 110–12, 119; Visigoths, 202–3

landwehr, 96

Langton, Stephen (Cardinal Archbishop), 265, 270

Languedoc, allodial lands surviving feudalism in, 110

Lara, Don Molrique de, 215

Latimer, Lord, 410, 411

law: Council of Clarendon, articles of, 235–37; divine, 51, 187–88, 295; Edward the Confessor (King of England), laws of, 260, 261, 266; *Forum judicum (Fuero juzgo)*, 184, 186–95, 203–17; Fueros of Castile and Leon, 210–11, 214; Henry I of England, code ascribed to, 234; *lex antiqua* (Visigoths), 109; *lex talionis*, 191; natural, 51, 187–88; Parliamentary assent to laws and statutes, right of, 387, 403–5; Parliamentary participation in legislation, 387, 403–5; petitions' conversion into statutes and ordinances, 403–4, 424, 428, 429; rule of, 51; salic, 92; supremacy of, 230; Visigothic, 103, 109, 180, 181, 184, 185–95, 203–18

legislative power: centralization and, 246–47; nature of, 246; Parliamentary participation in legislation, 387, 403–5; Visigothic, 193–95

legitimate power, 187–90, 293–97

Leicester, Simon de Montfort, Earl of, 275–76, 302, 306–8, 311–12, 404–5

Leofric (Duke of Mercia), 242

Leo the Philosopher (Emperor), 166

Leovigild (Visigothic king), 179, 181–82, 186

Leudes, 123–26, 130, 132, 139, 141, 142, 200, 201

lex antiqua (Visigoths), 109

lex talionis, 191

liberalism in France, vii–viii, xi–xii, xiv

liberi homines, 250

liberty: charters (in England) regarded as foundation of, 413; children, limitations on, 293–94, 362; common deliberation on common affairs as form of, 378; competition and antagonism, role of, 129–30, 381, 399–400, 434; defined, 296; demands of, 17–19; division of powers and, 228–29, 373, 375, 433–34; electoral process derived from existing liberties, 330; guarantees of, 296; history, study of, 223, 224; imbalance of powers, effect of, 433–34; incapacitated, limitations on, 293–94; incomplete, at most dangerous when, 398; individual will or right, Guizot's criticism of, xiii, xv, 39–40, 44, 49, 52, 60–65, 112–13, 134–37, 273, 286–95, 297, 360–61; infancy of societies, falsely discovered in, 115–17, 134, 135–36; isolation, liberty of, 37, 112–13, 133; Leudes versus free men, 124–25; moral requirements of, 17–19; moral versus natural liberty, 134–37; Norman Conquest's effect on Anglo-Saxon institutions, 242, 245; order and freedom, reconciliation of, 17–19; power necessary to, 331, 373, 375; publicity, importance of, see publicity; representation viewed as contrary to, 286–87; rights and liberties indispensable to each other, 173–77, 258, 331, 350; Roman empire, 161–62; Roman municipal system, 173–77; Rousseau's ideas on, Guizot's criticism of, xiii, 49, 273, 286–89, 295, 297; social freedom versus individual independence, 134–37; speech, freedom of, 426–27; theories of, xii, xiii–xiv, 134–37; "true" principles of representative government and, 47–55; Visigoths, 193–95, 199, 200, 202, 204, 205
limitation of power and sovereignty: English concept of, 229–30, 263; importance of, 296; individual sovereignty, limits on, 293–95; legitimate power, concept of, 187–90, 293–97; Visigoths, absolute power not limited amongst, 199–202
Liuva I (Visigothic king), 181
Liuva II (Visigothic king), 182
Livy, 156

loans, forced, 424
local institutions: Anglo-Saxons, 33, 34, 35–39, 242; England, surviving in, 247; Franks, 131–33, 138; Roman municipal system, 158–59; Visigoths, 202–5
Lollards, 418
Lombards, 24, 70, 80, 83, 92, 101, 109, 110, 127, 196
London: early political importance of, 310; Great Charter provisions regarding, 268–69; Henry I, charter granted by, 260
Long Parliament, 70
Lords, House of, see House of Lords
Lords Ordainers, 383, 384
Louis the Débonnair, 76, 83, 85–86, 97, 102, 104, 106–7, 110, 125, 132, 138, 149
Louis the Germanic, 87, 101
Louis V (King of France), 139
Louis the Dauphin (later Louis VIII), 271, 273
Louis IX (Saint Louis, King of France), 306–7
Louis XI (King of France), 433
Louis XIV (King of France), 88, 246, 306–7
Louis XVIII (King of France), ix
Louis-Philippe (King of France), x
loyalty and fidelity, duty of: beneficiary lands, 106–7; Leudes, 124
Lyon, merchant of London, 410

Mabillon, Jean, 103
Mably, Gabriel Bonnot de, 105, 109
Mad Parliament (parliamentum insanum), 312
Magna Charta, see Great Charter
magnates, 250
Magnum Concilium (Great Council), 247, 248, 377–78, 429, see also Barons, Council of
majority rule, 59–65, 289, 334, 348–49
male-only inherited (salic) land, 92
mallum, 131, 202
Manfred King of Naples, 302
Mannert, Konrad, 125
Marculf, 92, 101, 105, 106, 124, 133
Mare, Peter de la, 410, 411, 415
Mariana, Juan de, 205–6
Marius (Emperor), 23

Martel, Charles, 79–80, 102, 103, 105, 109, 136

Marx, Karl, vii, ix, x

Matilda (Queen of England, wife of Henry I), 233

Matilda (Queen of England, daughter of Henry I), 234

Mauclerc, William de, 266

Maurice (Emperor), 182

Mayors of the Palace, 78, 80, 83, 99, 142

Melun, Count of, 271

merchants, Great Charter provisions regarding, 269

Meroveus (Frankish leader), 72

Merovingian period, 75–83, 95–96, 132, 133, 134, 136, 139, 142, 149

Metz, Merovingian kingdom of, 75, 76

Middle Ages, survival of Gothic law in Spain during, 210–18

middle class: English Parliament, introduction into, 308; Guizot as defender of, xv–xvi; Roman municipal system, annihilation by, 156, 172

might and right, 363–64

Mildred, William, 427

military leaders, appointment of, 210–11

military service as obligation: allodial lands, connected with, 94–97; Anglo-Norman aristocracy, 252; beneficiary lands, holders of, 106; English *barones,* 250; Leudes, 124; Roman empire, position of army members in, 167–68; Wittenagemot, ordered by, 41

milites, 250

millenarius, 203

Mill, John Stuart, vii, ix, x

ministeriales, 145

ministers of king, Parliamentary intervention in choice and control of, 406, 408–11, 415–24

minority opinion, respect for, 348–49

missi dominici, 85, 96, 130, 137

mixed nature of most actual governments, 47–48, 58–59

Molina, charter of, 215

monarchy: Anglo-Norman, 252–57; Anglo-Saxons, 42, 43–46; aristocracy versus, 129–30, 381, 400; assemblies coexistent with, 380–81; assemblies convoked by, 43–44; Charlemagne, strength under, 130, 137–41; Clovis, French monarchy viewed as established by, 74, 75; constitutional monarchy, epoch of, 14, 222; deposition of Edward II, 384; excommunication of kings, 190; favoritism and, *see* favoritism, monarchial; feudalism versus, 150–52; Franks, 130, 132–33, 138–41; hereditary status, 139, 181, 190, 191–93; House of Commons' resistance to, 400; knights and freeholders versus, 301–5; ministers of, Parliamentary attempts to control, 408–11; petitions by House of Commons to king and lords, 429–31; petitions by Parliament to king, 386–87, 389–91, 429–31; petitions to king become petitions to Parliament, 385–86, 389–92; pure monarchy, epoch of, 14–15, 222; religious backing for authority of, 140–41; royal domain, public/private control of, 42, 98–99; Visigoths, 179–84, 188, 190, 191–93, 196–218

money, coining, 41–42

Montesquieu, Charles Louis de Secondat, Baron de La Brède et de, xiii, 11, 48, 101, 102, 124

Montfort, Simon de, Earl of Leicester, 275–76, 302, 306–8, 311–12, 404–5

Montlosier, Comte de, 124, 128

morality: church's inheritance of moral ascendancy of Roman empire, 80–81; liberty, moral requirements of, 17–19; natural/divine law regulating human conduct, 51, 187–88

Mortimer, Edmund, Earl of March, 406, 412

Mowbray, Thomas, Duke of Norfolk, 423

munera, 171–72

municipal system, Roman: centralization of system, 159, 162, 173–74; curials, 167–71, 175–77; decadence of, 159–66; first epoch of, 156–59; justice in, 159, 172; middle class, annihilation of, 156, 172; modern states, compared to, 173–74; pillaging by Germanic invaders, 155–56; political and civil power, estrangement of municipal power from, 174–77; religion and the church, role of, 164–65; second epoch of, 159–66; Visigothic Spain and, 206–18

municipal systems generally, *see* towns and boroughs
murder: Visigothic legislation on, 194–95; *wehrgeld*, 119–22
Muslims: Turkish janissaries, 50; Visigoths and, 184, 201, 216–18

Napoleon, ix, 246
Narbonnese Gaul, 21–22
national assemblies, *see* assemblies
natural law, 51, 187–88
Nerva (Emperor), 161
Neustria, 76–79, 80, 86
Nevil, Lord, 410
Nibelungen, poem of, 74
nobles, *see* aristocracy
Norfolk, Roger Bigod, Earl of; Lord Marshal of England, 278, 279, 281, 317
Norfolk, Thomas Mowbray, Duke of, 423
Normans: Carlovingian kingdoms, in, 86–87, 138; Gaul, in, 27, 86–87
Norman Conquest of England, 26–27, 231–32, 240–45; Anglo-Saxon institutions, effect of, 240–45; aristocracy, effect on, 243–44; assemblies of freemen, effect on, 38; feudalism and, 242–44; hierarchy of persons introduced to England by, 30–31, 35; similarity between Anglo-Saxons and Normans, 240–41; towns and boroughs, 310
Northampton, Council of, 249
Northumberland, Henry Percy, Earl of, 417
numerarius, 203

oath, trial by (compurgation), 210, 213, 214
Odoacer, 24
officium palatinum of Visigoths, 200–202, 217
open voting, 350–51
oppression, right to resist, 230
ordeals, trial by, 210, 213
order and liberty, reconciliation of, 17–19
ordinances, *see also* law: petitions' conversion into, 403–4; statutes versus, 404
Orleans, Merovingian kingdom of, 75, 76
Ostrogoths, 73, 180, 181, 202
outlands, 32
Oxford, Acts of, 303–8
Oxford, assembly of 1214 meeting at, 264, 300–301

Oxford, Parliament of (1258), 303–5, 312
Oxford University deputies to Parliament, 317

paganism and Christianity, 4, 9
palatines, 145
Pandects, 229
papacy, *see* religion and the church; *individual popes*
parental authority compared to legitimate power, 293–94
Paris, Matthew, 269, 301
Paris, Merovingian kingdom of, 75, 76
Parliament, 228, 229, 277, 298–305, *see also* Barons, Council of; House of Commons; House of Lords; absolute monarchy, resistance of, 414–24; administration and ministers of King, intervention in questions of, 406, 408–11, 415–24; assent to laws and statutes, right of, 387, 403–5; attendance upon summons required, 424; Barons, replacing Council of, 298; bodies presaging, 246–51; characteristics of, 377–82; charters, sessions beginning with confirmation of, 413; clergy as part of, 316, 318, 422; complete and regular establishment dated to 1295, 312; complete formation dated to 1264, 312; county deputies introduced into, 298–305, 307, 308, 315–19, 354, 355–57; debates, order of, 430–31; decay of, 432–35; different types under Edward I, 313–19; division into two houses, origins of, 268, 316–17, 353–76, 401; early history of, 309–10, *see also* Barons, Council of; Edward I, progress under, 313–19; Edward I, subsidy granted to, 278, 279; Edward II, during reign of, 382–88; Edward III, during reign of, 399–413; election to, *see* election; enquiry, right of, 392, 395, 396–97; first official designation of assembly as, 301; first regular and complete assembly, 316; first use of term, 301; formation of, 258, 259, 269, 277, 285, 298–305, 312; fourteenth century, characteristics and powers in, 377–81, 382–88, 391; government, relationship to, 378–81, 391–93, 432; Great Charter and, 269,

413; hereditary right to attend, 318, 367; historic school on division of, 359–60; 365–366; immunity/inviolability of members of, 427–28; initiative, right of, 392, 395, 428–31; judges summoned to, 315, 319; judicial power restricted to House of Lords, 431; king, individual barons and ecclesiastical powers summoned by, 318; Lancastrians, under 425–34; legislation, participation in, 387, 403–5; Long Parliament, 70; Mad Parliament (*parliamentum insanum*), 312; members of, 318–19; national council, as, 377–81; Parliament of Oxford (1258), 303–5, 312; philosophic school on division of, 359–66; powers of, 377–82; regular convocation of, 400–401; representative government, development as form of, 382; Richard II, during reign of, 414–24; security precautions taken by, 400; sessions, election requirements for, 401; seventeenth century, characteristics and powers in, 378; social class and structure of, 355–56, 359–76; speech, freedom of, 426–27; taxation, voting on, 402–3, 415–18, 424, 428–29, 430–31; town and borough representatives introduced into, 298, 308, 310–12, 315–19, 354, 355–57; union of Houses to consider certain questions in common, 412–13; Wittenagemot, origins in, 44; wool and cloth industry, 412

parties, political, 343
Pascal, Blaise, 52, 53, 68, 227
Pauli Sententiae, 180
Pavia, assembly of Lombards at, 70, 196
peace and war, intervention of House of Commons in questions of, 406–8
Peachey, merchant of London, 410
peers, houses of: English, *see* House of Lords; French House of Peers and plurality of powers, 53
Pelagius, 217
Pembroke, William, Earl of; Marshal of England, 272
Pepin (son of Charlemagne), 125
Pepin the Short and Pepin family, 76, 78–85, 98, 99, 102, 103, 136, 139, 143

Percy, Henry, Earl of Northumberland, 417
Perers (Pierce), Alice, 409–11
Peter des Roches (Bishop of Winchester), 275
petitions: alteration on conversion into statutes, prohibition of, 424, 428; conversion into statutes and ordinances, 403–4, 424, 428, 429; discussion of, 396–97; enquiry, Parliamentary right of, 392, 395, 396–97; House of Commons petitioning king and lords, 429–31; initiative, Parliamentary right of, 392, 395, 428–31; king, House of Commons petitioning lords and, 429–31; king, Parliament petitioning, 386–87, 389–91, 429–31; king, petitions addressed to, becoming petitions to Parliament, 385–86, 389–92; lords, House of Commons petitioning king and, 429–31; Parliament petitioned directly, 385–86, 389–98; Parliament petitioning king, 386–87, 389–91, 429–31; procedures for introducing, 393–94, 396; right of, 391–96; tax approvals conditioned on resolution of grievances presented in, 386–87, 430–31
Philip Augustus (King of France), 264, 265, 271
philosophical history, 223–25
philosophical views of Guizot, xii–xiii
philosophic school on division of Parliament, 359–66
Picts, 22, 37
Pierce (Perers), Alice, 409–11
placita generalia, Visigothic, 182, 196, 202
placitum, 131, 202
plaids, 131
Plantagenets, *see also specific Plantagenet monarchs:* Geoffrey (Count of Anjou), 234, 235; monarchy, founding of, 234, 235
plurality of powers, 52–54, 227
poetic history, 222–23
Pole, Michael de la, Earl of Suffolk, 419
political and social order, relationship between, *see* social and political order, relationship between
political capacity, *see* capacity

political science, Guizot's criticism of, 328–30

politics: European political institutions, epochs of, 13–16; Guizot, political career of, ix–x, xviii–xx; Guizot, political philosophy of, xii–xiii, xv–xvi, 297; history, study of, 222–25; party politics, 343; Visigothic Spain, political predominance of clergy in, 189–91, 197–99

populi liberi, 158

powers: absolute, *see* absolute power; administrative, *see* administrative power; aristocracy, *see* aristocracy; assembly, *see* assemblies; division of, *see* divisions of powers; ecclesiastical, *see* religion and the church; equilibrium of, 433–34; executive power, 246–47; Guizot's theory of, 331–32; imbalance, effect of, 433–34; judicial, 246–47, *see also* justice and judicial processes; legislative, *see* legislative power; legitimate power, 187–90, 293–97; liberty, necessary to, 331, 373, 375; limitation of, *see* limitation of power and sovereignty; monarchial, *see* monarchy; plurality of, 52–54, 227; sovereignty, *see* sovereignty; types of, 246–47

practical history, 223–24

praefecturae, 158

precaria, 79–80, 102–3

privy council, English, 248, 315, 386, 392, 429, 431

Probus (Emperor), 23, 72

proceres, 200, 201, 250

Protestantism: Guizot and, viii, xi; Lollards, 418; reformation of religion, role of, 435; Wickliffe, John, followers of, 418

provinciae, 158

publicity: aristocratic governments, avoidance by, 58; key characteristic of true representative government, as, xiv–xv, 53–55, 69–70, 227

public law, 187–88

public life and study of history, 224–25

public works: Anglo-Saxons, 37, 41; Roman municipal system, 158–59

pure monarchy, epoch of, 14–15, 222

Ragnachar (Frankish leader), 73, 99

Raoul (King of Franks), 87

reason: legitimate power's conformity to, 296–97; representative government based on, 295–96; sovereignty of, xiv, 64

Recared I (Visigothic king), 182, 186

Recared II (Visigothic king), 182

Recesuinth (Visigothic king), 183, 185, 209

Rechiar (Suevi king), 179–80

Red Book of the Exchequer, 259

reformation of religion, effects of, 435, *see also* Protestantism

reges amici, 158

religion and the church: Anglo-Saxons, 30, 36, 39, 42–43; Barons, Council of, attendance of ecclesiastical powers at, 251; beneficiary lands, 125–26; Carlovingians and, 79–81, 83–86, 102–3; Clarendon, Council of, 235–38; divine law, concept of, 51; Great Charter articles addressing interests of, 267; Guizot's Protestantism, viii, xi; Henry I of England's struggles with clergy, 234; Henry II of England and Thomas Becket, 235–38, 261; House of Common's resistance to papacy and clergy, 411–12; Jews, English massacre of, 238; Jews, Visigothic Spain and, 182, 184; John King of England's struggles with clergy, 264, 265, 266; Leudes, bishops and abbots as, 125–26; Lollards, statute against followers of, 418; Louis the Débonnair and, 85–86; monarchy, authority of, 140–41; municipal system, Roman, 164–65; paganism and Christianity, 4, 9; Parliament, clergy summoned to, 316, 318; political power, clergy as, 189–91, 197–99; political predominance of clergy in Visigothic Spain, 189–91; Protestantism, *see* Protestantism; reformation of, 435; right of papacy to make and unmake kings, 80–81, 84; Roman empire and, 80–81, 154–66, 167–68, 177; Roman municipal system and rights of worship, 158; *tabularii*, 127; Visigothic law and government, control of, 186–88, 189, 190–91, 194, 196–99; Visigoths and, 154, 177, 181, 182, 183, 184, 197–99; Wittenagemot, control of, 42–43; Wickliffe, statute against followers of, 418

Renomer (Frankish leader), 73

representative government: absolute power, not admitting of, 226–27, 371; Barons, Council of, not found in, 251; conditions and characteristics necessary to, 67–70, 227; definition of, assumptions underlying, xiv–xv; democratic government compared, 59–65; division of powers, *see* division of powers; election, *see* election; England, development in, 222, 227–30, 433–35; English Revolution restoring, 434–35; epochs of political institutions of Europe, 13–16; form and principle, relationship between, 48, 66–67; Germanic tribes of 5th to 10th century, not existing amongst, 152–53; goal and purpose of, xiv, xv, 53, 371; individual will or right and, 286–95; liberty and representation viewed as contrary, 286–87; majority rule, 59–65; Parliament's development as form of, 382, *see also* Parliament; plurality of powers, 52–54, 227; publicity as key characteristic of true representative government, xiv–xv, 53–55, 69–70, 227; publicity avoided by aristocratic governments, 58; reason, based on, 295–96; responsibility as key characteristic of, 227; Rousseau's ideas on, Guizot's criticism of, xiii, 49, 273, 286–89, 295, 297; social and political order, relationship between, *see* social and political order, relationship between; social right, principle of, 50; source of sovereign power as key to classification of, 48–54, 226–27; theories of, xii, xiii–xv; "true" principles according to Guizot, xv, 47–55, 49–54, 61–65, 134–37, 226–27, 285–97, 345, 351; unity and plurality, 52–53; universality of idea in Europe, 11–12; Wittenagemot not regarded as, 39–40

responsibility as key characteristic of representative government, 227

revolutions: English, *see* English Revolution; French Revolution of 1789, vii, xii, xiv; French Revolution of 1848, x

Rhegino, 138

Richard I Coeur-de-Lion (King of England), 238–39, 249, 256, 262, 263, 268

Richard II (King of England), 324, 410, 411, 414–24, 425, 426, 430, 432

Richard III (King of England), 433

Richelieu, Armand-Jean de Plessis, Cardinal and Duc de, 246, 433

rights: assent to laws and statutes, parliamentary right of, 387; changing nature of, 362–63; electoral rights arising out of other rights, 328–32, 344; enquiry, Parliamentary right of, 392, 395, 396–97; full, direct, and efficacious, worth nothing unless, 350; individual will or right, Guizot's criticism of, xiii, xv, 39–40, 44, 49, 52, 60–65, 112–13, 134–37, 273, 286–95, 297, 360–61; initiative, Parliamentary right of, 392, 395, 428–31; liberties and rights indispensable to each other, 173–77, 258, 331, 350; might and right, 363–64; petition, right of, 391–93; philosophic school on division of Parliament and concept of right, 360–65; relation, implying, 360–62; sovereignty of right, xiii, xiv, 50–52, 80, 225; speech, freedom of, 426–27; Visigothic legislation and, 193–95

Ripuarian Franks, 72, 73, 92, 105, 120, 121, 127

Robert, Duke of Normandy, 232–33, 260

Robert of Winchelsea, Archbishop of Canterbury, 314

Robertson, William, 223

Robert the Strong, 87

Roches, Peter des (Bishop of Winchester), 275

Roderic/Rodrigo (Visigothic king), 184

Rollo (Norman leader), 87

Roman empire, *see also individual emperors*: citizenship in, 157–58; despotism's contribution to fall of, 155–56, 160–66; fall of, 20–24, 155, 177; Franks and, 71–73, 78, 125; Germanic tribes, incursions of, 154–56, 162, 166; liberty and, 161–62; municipal system of, *see* municipal system, Roman; nations conquered by, treatment of, 156–57; public wealth of, 98; religion and the church, 80–81, 154–66, 167–68, 177; Senate, members of, 167, 168; social classes, 167–73; Visigoths, 23, 24, 182, 183

Roman maxims and institutions in Visigothic Spain, continuing predominance of, 199, 201–2, 206–18
Roses, Wars of the, 381, 427, 432–33
Rousseau, Jean-Jacques, xiii, 49, 273, 286–89, 295, 297
Roussel, Jean, 273
Royer-Collard, Pierre-Paul, viii
Runymead, conference at, 265
Russia, Tartar tribes in, 72

Saint Louis (Louis IX, King of France), 306–7
Saint, Remy, 73
Salage, John, 427
Salian Franks, 72, 120, 121
salic land, 92
Saracens: Turkish janissaries, 50; Visigoths and, 184, 201, 216–18
Sarmatians, 71
Savigny, M. de (Friedrich Karl von Savigny), 127, 206–10
Saxon Chronicle, 248
Saxons, *see* Anglo-Saxons
scabini, 149
Scots and Scotland, 22, 25, 37, 278, 316, 406–8
scribae, 171–72
Scroop, Richard le, 416, 418
Scroop, Sir Jeffrey, of Markham, 404
secret voting, 350–51
Senate of Rome, members of, 167, 168
Septimus Severus (Emperor), 162
service, duty of: beneficiary lands, as obligation for, 106; escuage for personal service, 261, 267, 268, 273, 274; Leudes, 124
servientes, 250
shires, *see* counties
Siagrius (King of Romans at Soissons), 72, 73
Sidonius Apollinarius, 180
Sigebert (King of Cologne), 73, 99
Sigebert (Merovingian king), 75
Siggo (Frankish noble), 105
Sirmond, Père, 180
Sisebut (Visigothic king), 182
Sisenand (Visigothic king), 183
Sismondi, Jean Charles Léonard, 74
Siward, Duke of Northumbria, 242

slavery, 29, 33, 112, 119, 121, 194–95
socage, 310, 321, 326
social and political order, relationship between: historical methodology and, 28–29; important theme in Guizot's thought, as, 19, 28–29; infancy of societies, liberty falsely discovered in, 115–17, 134, 136; isolation, liberty of, 37, 112–13, 133; landed property conditions and, 112–14; liberties and rights indispensable to each other, 173–77; moral versus natural liberty (social freedom versus individual independence), 134–37; Parliament's structure and social class, 355–56, 359–76; Roman municipal system, 173–77; true principles of representative government, discerning, 49–54, 134–37; Visigothic legislation, 193–95
social classes, 28–29; allodial lands, 117–19; Anglo-Saxons, 29–33; beneficiary lands, 118–19; capacity and, 333–35; enfranchisement, practice of, 127–28; equality/inequality and natural conditions of social state, 369–70; Franks, 115–28; free men in Frankish period, 126–28; hierarchy of persons as origin of feudalism, 30–31, 35; justice and, 29; landed property, arising from conditions of, 90–91, 115–19; Leudes (Antrustions), 123–26, 130, 132, 139, 141, 142, 200, 201; origin of, 90–91; Parliamentary representation and, 355–56, 359–76; Roman empire, 167–73; tributary lands, 119; *wehrgeld* as guide to, 119–22
social contract, Guizot's criticism of idea of, xiii, 49, 273, 286–89
social right, principle of, 50
soc-men, 32
Soissons: early Frankish power base, as, 72–73; Merovingian kingdom of, 75, 76; national assembly convoked at, 80
Soult-Guizot Cabinet, x
sovereigns, *see* monarchy
sovereignty: absolute power's theory of, 226; aristocracy's dissolution into independent sovereignties under feudalism, 149–51; aristocratic government as

sovereignty of the people assigned to minority, 57–58; division of powers, 53, 67–69; fact, of, xiii, xiv, 80, 226; individual will or right, Guizot's criticism of, xiii, xv, 39–40, 44, 49, 52, 60–65, 112–13, 134–37, 273, 286–95, 297, 360–61; limitation of, *see* limitation of power and sovereignty; multitude, of, 40, 68; people, of, 59–65; reason, of, xiv, 64; representative government, source of sovereign power as key to classification of, 48–54, 226–27; right, of, xiii, xiv, 50–52, 80, 226; Rousseau's ideas on, Guizot's criticism of, xiii, 49, 273, 286–89, 295, 297; single power, resting in, 68; social right, principle of, 50; theories of, 226

Spain: corporations or associations, 36; Roman empire, fall of, 23, 24, 155, 178–79; Visigoths, *see* Visigoths

Speaker of House of Commons, 401, 415, 422, 426, 427

speech, freedom of, 426–27

Spencer, Hugh, elder and younger, 383–84, 387

Staël, Madame de, xiii

state of persons, *see* social classes

States-General, 222

statutes, *see also* law: ordinances versus, 404; petitions' conversion into, 403–4, 424, 428, 429

Stephen III (Pope), 80, 83

Stephen, Count of Blois, 234

Stephen (King of England), 234, 235, 250, 256, 260–61

sub-enfeofment or sub-infeudination (vassals of vassals), 108, 299–300

subsidies, *see* taxation

Suevi, 23, 73, 179, 181

Suffolk, Michael de la Pole, Earl of, 419

Suinthila (Visigothic king), 182–83

susceptor, 171

Swiss Grisons, 36

tabelliones, 172

tabularii, 127

Tacitus, 39, 72, 98

tallage, 310

Tartar tribes in Russia, 72

taxation: Anglo-Norman, 252–53, 261, 263, 275; consent to, principle of, 309–10, 402; Edward I, under, 278; Edward III, under, 402–3; forced loans, 424; granting of subsidies conditioned on resolution of grievances, 386–87, 430–31; Henry III, by, 302; Parliamentary voting of, 402–3, 415–18, 424, 428–29, 430–31; separate voting on, 354–55; towns and boroughs, 310; Wittenagemot, imposition by, 41

territorial subdivisions: Anglo-Saxons, 35–38; Frankish kingdoms, effect on, 75–76, 83–88

Teutfred (Frankish noble), 104

Teutones, 23

thanes, 29–31, 32–33

Theodebert (Merovingian king), 96

Theodoric (King of Ostrogoths), 73, 202

Theodoric I (son of Clovis), 75, 77, 95

Theodoric II (Visigothic king), 179–80, 181

Theodoricianae leges, 180

Theodosius the Great (Emperor), 21

Theudegisil (Visigothic king), 181

Theudes (Visigothic king), 181

Theutfred, Duke of Cordova, 184

thingrafen, 131

Thorismund (Visigothic king), 179

Thorpe, Thomas, 427–28

Thrasea, 17

Thucydides, 223

Tibetot, Sir John, 426, 429

tithings: Anglo-Saxons, 35–38; Franks, 131–33

Tocqueville, Alexis de, vii, ix, x, 28

Toledo, councils of, 182–84, 186, 188, 190–93, 196–99, 205–6, 217

Tories, 241, 248, 315, 320, 324, 387

towns and boroughs: Anglo-Saxon, 40, 44; election of representatives, 320, 324–27; England, development of towns in, 239, 251; Great Charter provisions regarding, 268–69; London, *see* London; multiple forms of, 326; Norman Conquest and, 310; Parliament, representatives introduced into, 298, 308, 310–12, 315–19, 354, 355–57; Roman, *see* municipal system, Roman; taxation, 310

Trajan (Emperor), 161

Tressilian, Sir Robert, 420

tribal Germanic societies, *see* Germanic tribes

tribunals, 248

tributary lands, 91, 110–12, 119

Tudors, House of, 430, 432, 434

Tulga (Visigothic king), 183

tungini, 131

Turks, janissaries of, 50

Turner, Sharon, 22, 25

tyranny, *see* absolute power

United States of America, electoral processes of, 344

unity: European civilization, 221; plurality and, 52–53, 227

universal suffrage, 289, 334, 344, 350

University deputies to Parliament, 317

Vandals, 23, 178, 179

Vascons, 181

vassals and vassalage, 299–300; barons as special class of vassal, 252–53, 299–300; election of representatives to Parliament and, 299–300, 320–27; English national assembly, immediate or direct vassals as constituents of, 299–300, 320–27, 354; escuage for personal service of, 261, 267, 268, 273, 274; Germanic tribes, amongst, 105–6; Great Charter articles relevant to, 267, 268; king's status affected by number and wealth of vassals, 250; Norman Conquest of England, prior to, 31; Parliament, immediate or direct vassals' right to attend, 299–300, 320–27, 354; relationship between superiors and inferiors, 152; sub-enfeofment or sub-infeudination (vassals of vassals), 108, 299–300

Venetian republic, 59, 69

Vere, Robert de, Marquis of Dublin, 419

Vesci, Eustace de, 266

villeins, 32

Villèle government, ix

Visigoths, 178–218; absolute power not limited amongst, 199–202; allodial lands, 92; Arianism, 181, 182, 183; assemblies, 182, 196–97, 202, *see also* Toledo, councils of; beneficiary lands, 103; election of kings of, 181, 183, 190, 191–93; Franks and, 73, 75, 180, 181, 182, 183; Gaul, in, 89, 179–81; institutions, 196–218; Islam and, 184, 201, 216–18; judicial system, 203–5; landowners and landed property, 202–3; laws of, 103, 109, 180, 181, 184, 185–95, 203–18; *lex antiqua,* 109; liberty amongst, 193–95, 199, 200, 202, 204, 205; Middle Ages, survival of Gothic law in Spain during, 210–18; monarchy of, 179–84, 188, 190, 191–93, 196–218; municipal system, Roman, 206–18; *officium palatinum,* 200–202; political predominance of clergy, 189–91, 197–99; religion and the church, 154, 177, 181, 182, 183, 184, 197–99; religious control of Visigothic law and government, 186–88, 189, 190–91, 194, 196–99; Roman empire and, 23, 24, 182, 183; Roman maxims and institutions, continuing predominance of, 199, 201–2, 206–18; Toledo, councils of, 182–84, 186, 188, 190–93, 196–99, 205–6, 217; transfer of monarchy from Gaul to Spain, 181

voting, *see* election

Wales, English conquest of, 278, 315

Wallia (Visigothic king), 179

Wamba (Visigothic king), 183–84, 191

Wapentakes, 36

war and peace, intervention of House of Commons in questions of, 406–8

Wars of the Red and White Roses, 381, 427, 432–33

Washington, George, xi

wehrgeld, 119–22

Whigs, 241, 248, 250, 320, 388

Wickliffe, John, followers of, 418

William I of Normandy (King of England), 26–27, 30, 35, 232, 234, 244, 249, 253, 255, 257, 259, 298, 300, *see also* Norman Conquest

William II Rufus (King of England), 232–33, 239, 249, 256, 259, 260

William, Count of Poitou and Duke of Guienne, 233

William, Earl of Pembroke, Marshal of England, 272

William of Malmesbury, 248

Witiza (Visigothic king), 184

witnesses *(compurgatores)*, 38

Wittenagemot, 39–44, 69, 196, 202, 228, 242–43, 247, 249, 378, 427

women: allodial lands, inheritance of (salic law), 92–93; compurgation allowed for, 214; election, exclusion from, 289

wool and cloth industry, Parliamentary protection of, 412

yeomanry, 32

York, Duke of, 427, 428

Young, Thomas, 426

Zachary (Pope), 80, 83

This book is set in 11 on 13 Adobe Caslon.
Caslon, designed by William Caslon in the early
eighteenth century, was modeled after
Dutch faces of the late seventeenth century.

Printed on paper that is acid-free and meets the requirements of the
American National Standard for Permanence of Paper for Printed Library
Materials, Z39.48-1992. ∞

Book design by Martin Lubin Graphic Design,
Jackson Heights, New York

Typography by Graphic Composition, Inc.,
Athens, Georgia

Printed and bound by Worzalla Publishing Company,
Stevens Point, Wisconsin